Women, Class,
and the
Feminist Imagination
A Socialist-Feminist Reader

In the series
Women in the Political Economy,
edited by Ronnie J. Steinberg

Women, Class, and the Feminist Imagination

A Socialist-Feminist Reader

Edited by
Karen V. Hansen and Ilene J. Philipson

TEMPLE UNIVERSITY PRESS
Philadelphia

Temple University Press, Philadelphia 19122
Copyright © 1990 by Karen V. Hansen and
Ilene J. Philipson

Published 1990
Printed in the United States of America

The paper used in this publication meets the minimum
requirements of American National Standard for
Information Sciences—Permanence of Paper for Printed
Library Materials, ANSI Z39.48-1984 ∞

Library of Congress Cataloging-in-Publication Data
Women, class, and the feminist imagination.
(Women in the political economy)
Bibliography: p.
1. Feminism—United States.   2. Socialism—United
States.   I. Hansen, Karen V.   II. Philipson, Ilene J.
III. Series.
HQ1426.W6365   1990   305.4′2′0973
88-36258
ISBN 0-87722-630-X (cloth)
ISBN 0-87722-654-7 (pbk.)

The Socialist and the Suffragist
—C. P. Gilman, 1912

Said the Socialist to the Suffragist:
"My Cause is greater than yours!
You only work for a Special Class
We for the gain of the General Mass,
Which every good ensures!"

Said the Suffragist to the Socialist:
"You underrate my cause!
While women remain a Subject Class,
You never can move the General Mass,
With your economic laws!"

Said the Socialist to the Suffragist:
"You misinterpret facts,
There is no room for doubt or schism
in Economic determinism—
It governs all our acts!"

Said the Suffragist to the Socialist:
"You men will always find
That this old world will never move
More swiftly in its ancient groove
While women stay behind!"

"A lifted world lifts women up"
The Socialist explained
"You cannot lift the world at all
While half of it is kept so small,"
The Suffragist maintained.

The world awoke and tartly spoke:
"Your work is all the same;
Work together or work apart,
Work, each of you, will all your heart
Just get into the game."

Preface

We began working together on a project to reevaluate socialist feminism in 1982 as editors of *Socialist Review*. Working with another editor, Vicki Smith, we solicited articles addressing the question of what had happened to socialist feminism as a political movement and theoretical perspective. Why had socialist feminism seemingly receded from public visibility in the early 1980s?

We received dozens of replies: from former leaders of the movement who felt that socialist feminism had no currency in the political environment of the 1980s; from others who considered themselves present-day socialist-feminist activists; from those who saw themselves as socialists and feminists but not "socialist-feminists," and from women who were no longer politically active but whose identities still very much included the ill-defined and elusive appellation socialist feminist.

For almost a year and a half, we printed some of the best contributions we received in a series called "Socialist Feminism Today" in the pages of *Socialist Review*. The series generated a fair amount of controversy and a number of important replies, yet after it ended we felt somewhat dissatisfied. With the articles scattered over many issues of the journal, there was a certain lack of coherence. For readers unfamiliar with socialist feminism's history, many authors' remarks were difficult to decipher. And we believed there was something incomplete about presenting analyses of socialist feminism without also presenting examples of writing and research from a socialist-feminist perspective.

This volume is a response to those problems. In a single anthology we try to present a brief history of socialist feminism and provide some of its most pathbreaking articles, evaluate its theory and practice, offer some of the latest thinking on family life, sexuality, and work from a socialist-feminist perspective, and introduce ways of looking at that perspective's relevance for the future. Undoubtedly there are still gaps, failings, important authors whose work is unrepresented here. Yet we hope this collection can serve as a beginning more than an end, a spark for the socialist-feminist movement rather than a requiem.

The process of selecting and editing the articles and writing the introduction awakened us to new forces in the socialist-feminist community, broadly defined, and gave us a wonderful opportunity to work together on a common political and intellectual project. Had either of us taken on this task as an individual, it never would have come to fruition. In consort, however, we developed an efficient and workable division of labor, contributed to each other's intellectual growth, and simply had a good time.

We thank the following people who supported this project in various ways: Vicki Smith, for being there from beginning to end, soliciting articles, editing, critiquing, and laughing with us; Michael Bader, Andrew Bundy, Jeffrey Escoffier, Ruth Fallenbaum, Anita Garey, Kathy Johnson, Jennifer Pierce, Judy Stacey, and Terry Strathman; and *Socialist Review*, for providing the fertile ground upon which the idea for the book was conceived, for being a stimulating intellectual and political community for years and years, and for agreeing to let us reprint thirteen articles in this anthology.

Contents

Women, Class, and the Feminist Imagination

A Socialist-Feminist Reader

1   Women, Class, and the Feminist Imagination

An Introduction

Ilene J. Philipson and Karen V. Hansen

In the 1970s socialist feminism emerged as a major paradigm in feminist thought and strategy. Its exponents criticized both feminism (for its shortsightedness, its failure to challenge capitalism, its reluctance to examine issues of class and race) and socialism (for its inattention to gender, domestic work, and sexuality). Out of this critique grew a flurry of theory building, strategy, and practical attempts to struggle against both capitalist exploitation and male dominance.

Socialist feminists set forth new ways to conceptualize the labor force, the bases for gender inequality, housework, the social origins of male/female psychological differences, women's history, sex, and the effects of ideology. They also founded dozens of socialist-feminist women's unions, reproductive rights organizations, caucuses in mixed (including both men and women) left groups, and organizations that worked with displaced homemakers, rape victims, and trade unionists.

The 1970s and the feminist ferment they symbolized are over, and we have entered an age that many describe as "postfeminist." The political right has dominated national political life for the last decade, defining feminist goals either as mere "special interests" or as radical challenges to American tradition. Where does the nascent socialist-feminist tradition stand in this political environment? Can its unbridled radicalism offer a fresh and challenging perspective on life in the 1990s? Or is it doomed to irrelevance in a country with little history of socialism and a current distaste for left-wing ideas?

In order to assess socialist feminism's future, we believe it is necessary to understand its past—its contributions and its difficulties. What follows is a brief history of socialist feminism as a movement and as a theoretical paradigm. While we make no claim that this is either a fully comprehensive or an unbiased account, we have tried to pinpoint what we believe to be the most crucial developments in socialist feminism's brief but rich history.

The Roots: Civil Rights and the New Left

Women's liberation emerged from the civil rights, student, and antiwar movements of the 1960s. Imbued with an increased sense of political efficacy from their involvement in civil rights and anti–Vietnam War struggles, women activists came to view themselves as important political actors, working to make a new social order. At the same time, unlike their male peers, they were denied political power and leadership positions. Relative deprivation in a time of rising expectations and maturing collective experience gave rise to a new social movement: women's liberation.

Demographic changes in the 1960s affected women's expectations for themselves but did not correspondingly alter the structural obstacles to political empowerment and economic mobility. The birth rate began to decline after its post–World War II peak; birth control pills became available and were widely distributed. Young women remained single for longer periods of time. More women than ever before attended institutions of higher education. Following its postwar decline, women's labor-force participation grew dramatically, primarily in the expanding service sector. Yet a dramatic wage inequality continued to exist, despite women's increased education.

These demographic shifts set a context for change but were not by themselves the immediate cause of political and social turmoil. The spark for "new left" (the term generally used to encompass the student and antiwar movements) and feminist political change was rooted in the South in the 1950s and 1960s. The civil rights movement initiated 1960s activism by drawing attention to and inspiring moral indignation at the racism and systematic inequality of American society and its system of justice. Within the civil rights movement many strong black women leaders set courageous examples and served as movement role models for young white women who lived in the South or went south to work for civil rights. Women confronted the limitations placed on them because of their gender. In November 1965, Casey Hayden and Mary King, two white organizers working in the South, wrote the first widely circulated document raising the issue of sexism within the civil rights movement. Their "memo" was read within SDS (Students for a Democratic Society) as well and presaged later critiques of the new left.[1]

In the movement against U.S. involvement in the war in Vietnam, male dominance was similar to that in the civil rights movement, but the inequalities were even more striking. Most women were relegated to auxiliary roles —doing clerical work and making sandwiches—as opposed to planning strategy and giving speeches, activities with much more authority and public presence. In her contribution to this volume, Barbara Haber, a founder of SDS, recounts:

> For five years in SDS I never so much as chaired a workshop, much less made a speech. I was always being asked to stuff envelopes, and my husband was always being asked to make speeches, so I figured he must be good at speeches and I must be good at envelopes.

The style of the new left reflected its heady, youthful arrogance and made it difficult for women to act as leaders; there was no shortage of young men who were brash, outspoken, and competitive. The revocation of student deferments for the draft in 1967 heightened the marginality of women's role in antiwar organizing; the ultimate heroic act in this period became resisting the draft, an experience unavailable to women. They could counsel draft resisters and organize demonstrations, but women were not in visible leadership positions.

When women within the student and antiwar movements raised issues of this disparity in power and acknowledgment, they were typically ridiculed as petty, oversensitive, and self-serving. At first some women had difficulty accepting the parallel that Casey Hayden and Mary King asserted between female and black oppression. After repeatedly failing in their attempts to enlighten male comrades about sexism, however, many women, seething with anger and frustration, overrode their earlier conviction that the civil rights movement and the importance of opposing the U.S. war effort took precedence over all else, and they abandoned the idea of trying to work with men. In "The Grand Coolie Damn," Marge Piercy communicates the impatience thousands felt at the time:

> We must have the strength of our anger to know what we know.
> No more arguments about shutting up for the greater good should
> make us ashamed of fighting for our freedom. Ever since private
> property was invented, we have been waiting for freedom. That
> passive waiting is supposed to characterize our sex, and if we wait for

the males we know to give up control, our great-granddaughters will get plenty of practice in waiting, too. We are the fastest growing part of the Movement, and for the next few years it would be healthiest for us to work as if we were essentially all the Movement there is, until we can make alliances based on our politics. Any attempts to persuade men that we are serious are a waste of precious time and energy; they are not our constituency.

There is much anger here at Movement men, but I know they have been warped and programmed by the same society that has damn near crippled us. My anger is because they have created in the Movement a microcosm of that oppression and are proud of it. Manipulation and careerism and competition will not evaporate of themselves. Sisters, what we do, we have to do together, and we will see about them.[2]

In 1967 and 1968 huge numbers of movement women left antiwar and civil rights activities to channel their energy, enthusiasm, experience, and wisdom into newly formed women-only consciousness-raising (CR) groups. These autonomous women's groups were modeled after black power and revolutionary Chinese peasant organizations that asserted the need for oppressed people to work independently of their oppressors. They proved to be a supportive forum for discussing the liberation of women, personal and political experiences, frustration with movements for social change that were supposed to be different from the rest of the world, and insights about domination and oppression that had fallen on deaf ears in the new left.

Women in CR groups believed that hierarchy should be eliminated, that leadership and structure were oppressive to women. This belief was a critique of and an attempt to combat the blatant sexism and subordination they had experienced as women in new left and civil rights organizations. The groups allowed women to talk to each other and to discover that their experiences were not unique; their problems were systemic and caused by structural inequalities as opposed to individual idiosyncrasy or neurosis. The revolutionary battle cry of the women's liberation movement became "The personal is political." As women realized their shared oppression, contagious rage was unleashed at male comrades. In essence, this process of "speaking bitterness" transformed what had once been belittled as "women's problems" into legitimate political discourse.

The vented anger went hand in hand with a sense of enthusiasm, awe, and inspiration at women's newfound sisterhood. Emergent feminist theorists asserted that regardless of gender or race, everyone had the same potential as everyone else; women needed only the opportunity to exercise and develop it. In an effort to transcend the disappointment resulting from the false promise of the "participatory democracy" widely espoused in new left writing, women's liberationists ardently supported leaderless groups, felt an antipathy to hierarchy, and developed an acute sensitivity to the potential abuses of power of a "star system." Joanne Cooke expressed her amazement at seeing these principles in operation at the first national women's liberation conference in Lake Villa, Illinois, in 1969:

> For the first time, I heard women discussing alternative ways of solving their problems. Not one woman said, "Well, that's how it is; what're you going to do?" Not one "Dear Abby" platitude. Not one woman apologized for complaints about her lot. Not only were they going to do something about it, they were supporting each other, committing themselves to helping each other in the process. Every woman was a sister and no sister's problem, idea or question was too trivial to be dealt with sympathetically.
>
> No one was in charge. No one was an expert. Women took turns chairing the larger discussions. We took turns driving to pick up late arrivals, we volunteered to take shifts with the children, and we shared responsibility for the phone. Anyone with an idea or an interest to discuss was free to speak up or to set up a workshop.[3]

In hindsight, this practice was simultaneously liberating and undermining. On the one hand, these principles of group process transformed woman's experience of working in social change organizations from that of silent lackey to empowered participant; on the other, the women were idealistic and politically naive insofar as they assumed the absolute good will and endless potential of all in the sisterhood. Internally, this made them vulnerable to the "tyranny of structurelessness," whereby the ideological emphasis on equality and lack of hierarchy masked the exercise of excessive influence and power by some. It also left feminist groups and organizations open to disruption and takeover by hostile, more hierarchical groups.

The Emergence of Political Difference

After the initial euphoria of discovering sisterhood and the exhilaration of acquiring a raised consciousness, internal political divisions emerged within women's liberation and individual consciousness-raising groups. Within "radical feminism"—the term used by women's liberationists to distinguish themselves from liberal feminists in organizations such as the National Organization for Women (NOW)—two hotly debated issues divided women along a political continuum: whether or not to work with men, and whether to create alternative institutions or work within existing ones. At one end of the continuum were the women, those dubbed the "feminists," who focused mostly on the personal dimension of women's oppression and the active role of men and male-dominated institutions and values in maintaining that oppression. At the opposite end of the spectrum were the "politicos," who believed in women's liberation but thought that feminists generally did not pay enough attention to the structural forces of oppression—capitalism and imperialism—that would remain, even with the success of a feminist revolution. The "politicos" embraced the political analysis of the new left but felt they had been betrayed and undermined by male radicals. Yet they often continued to organize with men, particularly in efforts against the Vietnam war, because of their shared political perspective.

In practice, feminists on both ends of the spectrum engaged in similar projects, sometimes distinguishable only by their analysis of the forces leading to the need for the project. Both supported abortion on demand, women-centered health care, twenty-four-hour free, quality day care, rape crisis centers and shelters for battered women. Those at the "feminist" end of the continuum, however, were more likely to look to personal and cultural avenues of social change as opposed to methods that required organizing collectivities. A critical distinguishing feature was the insistence of the "politicos" on the importance of class and workplace issues such as unionizing clerical workers.

Politicos were the women who eventually found their voice in socialist feminism. Increasingly, many began to think of themselves as both socialists and feminists, and wanted to merge the two ideologies in a meaningful, homogeneous manner. In her contribution to this volume, Judy MacLean discusses the importance of putting together these two perspectives:

> I think the main reason we wanted the term [socialist feminist] was that it suggested trying to lead our personal lives in a new way and simultaneously transforming the world. In a way the term meant that as feminists we wouldn't forget about issues like the Vietnam War, which was still raging. . . . I also think that those of us who called ourselves socialists then were scared by the kind of feminism that focused only on our personal lives. We thought you should always keep the rest of the world—what was happening to poor women

and what was happening to Third World women—in mind. Calling ourselves socialist feminists was a way of always remembering that.

Solidifying the Movement

Gradually, feminist organizations began to grow out of the CR groups and women's continuing discontent with the male-dominated new left—from Redstockings in New York to Cell 16 in Boston to Sudsafloppen in San Francisco. In 1969 two organizations central to the development of emerging socialist-feminist ideology and practice were founded: Bread and Roses in Boston, and the Chicago Women's Liberation Union (CWLU). Though both were local organizations, each had an impact on the incipient nationwide movement as they captured media attention and published literature for a national audience. Both attempted to be umbrella structures embracing and sheltering a variety of activities that included consciousness-raising groups, abortion referrals (before abortion was legal), a rape crisis hotline, demonstrations against sexist institutions and against the war, and, in Chicago, a women's liberation rock band. These organizations and others initiated campaigns to organize working women, resurrected the celebration of International Women's Day, challenged sexist advertising, and attempted to revolutionize everyday life by promoting feminist principles in the execution of housework (that is, getting men to do their share) and in the mode of talking and relating to one another.

Bread and Roses lasted only two years, but it inspired many other groups. CWLU purposely established a more accountable and, some would claim, hierarchical leadership structure and rode a more stable course, acting as a model broad-based organization until its demise in 1977. Groups of socialist feminists in twenty cities established their own women's unions, beginning with Pittsburgh in 1970 and continuing through 1975 when the Santa Cruz Women's Union was founded. The unions varied in structure, practice, and the degree to which they embraced Marxism. They all agreed, however, on the goal of striving toward a socialist and feminist future, even if they differed as to how democratic the socialism and how radical the feminism should be.

The New American Movement (NAM), founded as a national organization in 1971, was primarily a new left organization of both men and women, but it was fundamentally committed to socialist feminism. Through the work of such socialist feminists as Kathy Johnson and Peggy Somers, NAM began to issue its own socialist-feminist working papers and published articles about socialism feminism in its nationally distributed newspaper.

What connected these disparate groups was a pervasive and irrepressible interest in ideas—new ideas that connected socialism and feminism, capitalism and patriarchy, rape and imperialism, clitoral orgasms and liberation. Ideas mattered, for everything that had come before seemed up for grabs, open to criticism and fundamental revision. As Deirdre English points out in her contribution to this volume: "These were the days when a small group of women could come up with some good phrases, and a couple of months later these phrases would be rippling across the whole country. . . . It seemed then as though feminism had a limitless potential to be socially transforming and intellectually entertaining." What allowed socialist-feminist ideas to spread across the country as they did was an underground circulation of papers, articles, and pamphlets that were mimeographed or printed at the authors' expense or as a project of a socialist-feminist group or organization. With the significant exception of Juliet Mitchell's *Woman's Estate*, published by Pantheon Books in 1971, there were no socialist-feminist texts for women to turn to. There were the "classics" of course—Marx and Engels, particularly the latter's *Origin of the Family, Private Property, and the State*; the work of women who were socialists or radicals, such as Clara Zetkin, Rosa Luxemburg, Emma Goldman, and Charlotte Perkins Gilman; and the influential *Second Sex* by Simone de Beauvoir, published in the United States in 1953. But none of these spoke to the unique circumstances of American socialist feminists working to bring about a revolution in the early 1970s. Thus, as soon as an article that did discuss socialist feminism appeared in a traditional Marxist periodical, such as the American *Monthly Review* or the British *New Left Review*, it was quickly reprinted as a pamphlet, sold in a growing number of new left or feminist bookstores, and circulated among intellectually hungry socialist feminists. Similarly, socialist feminist articles began to appear in the feminist journals and magazines that had sprouted up in the late 1960s and early 1970s, such as *Women: A Journal of Liberation* and *Quest*; these too were reprinted as pamphlets.

At this time, the Feminist Press began to publish quality socialist-feminist pamphlets with elaborate graphics, cartoons, and photographs. Two new left journals, *Radical America* and *Socialist Revolution*, began publishing in 1968 and 1970 respectively, and each committed itself to printing articles from the burgeoning socialist-feminist movement. Many of these articles too were made into pamphlets by the journals themselves or simply photocopied and sold at nominal prices.

On Thanksgiving weekend in 1972 the first national socialist-feminist conference took place, hosted by the Charlotte Perkins Gilman Chapter of the New American Movement, a women's group based in Durham, North Carolina. About two-hundred women attended, and they avidly discussed a new paper written by members of the Chicago Women's Liberation Union entitled "Socialist Feminism: A Strategy for the Women's Movement." They attended workshops on organizing in social service agencies, women in factories, gay liberation, women as clerical workers, women and the media, and international liberation struggles. In her keynote address to the assembly, Kathy Johnson stressed the need to recognize the problems of working in either the women's liberation movement *or* the socialist left, and asserted that a convergence of the two movements was necessary to fight sexism:

> Women are coming together out of a need to resolve ideological and practical tensions that, to date, have separated women in the autonomous women's movement from those women who have worked in mixed socialist organizations. The convergence of both groups comes from a gut level awareness, on the one hand on the part of socialist women, that our demands will not be tacked on last on a long list, that we will not be just a caucus, that there is no such thing as an "isolated women's issue," and on the other hand, on the part of women in the autonomous movement, that consciousness of oppression alone does not suffice, that such consciousness must be grounded in a social and historical understanding.

The Durham conference ended in a "spirit of sisterhood," according to one participant reporting for the *NAM Newspaper*. It "seemed to signal a new direction, in strategy and spirit, for feminism . . . an important first step in the process of creating a movement that can meet women's real needs in the struggle that challenges capitalism and its hegemony over all the spheres of our lives."[4]

In 1973 a group of socialist-feminist academics and intellectuals formed the Marxist-Feminist Group I, which held weekend retreats in various east coast cities to discuss the rapidly growing body of socialist-feminist scholarship.[5] This group proved so popular that three other east coast groups were formed to accommodate the numbers of women who wished to participate in the discussions, and eventually two similar groups were established in the San Francisco bay area. Each one quickly became a forum for debating the profusion of ideas, theories, and positions that marked these early years of the socialist-feminist movement.

The Marxist-Feminist Groups played a critical role in circulating a large number of papers-in-progress, helping pass them from one woman to another across the country. In this fashion, many papers that became "classics" in the socialist-feminist tradition, such as Gayle Rubin's "The Traffic in Women" and Heidi Hartmann's "The Unhappy Marriage of Marxism and Feminism," were read and critiqued by literally hundreds of women before they were ever formally published.

In this sense, then, socialist feminism represented a truly grassroots movement. The ideas that connected people, provided a sense of identity and purpose, and informed practice were formulated by a multitude of women and men from all over the United States and England and circulated through an extensive and informal network of alternative publishers, organizations, and bookstores. There was no vanguard party, group of leaders, or single book or periodical that defined the course socialist feminism should take. While liberal feminists could look to the National Organization for Women and *Ms.* magazine for direction, socialist feminists had only their scattered articles and pamphlets, their local organizations, and a few recently formed institutions such as *Socialist Revolution* and the New American Movement to nourish and sustain their new movement.

Theoretical Considerations

Out of this welter of activity, socialist feminists began to elucidate general theoretical approaches to understanding women's oppression under capitalism. Among the variety of perspectives offered, two eventually became paradigmatic, providing the vocabulary, variables, and focus that would dominate socialist-feminist discourse for the next decade. By highlighting "dual systems theory" and the "sex/gender system," we do a certain disservice to authors whose work may not fit neatly into either; nonetheless, these two perspectives did set the terms of debate and become the points of departure for almost all future intellectual work within socialist feminism. Before considering them, however, it is necessary to identify the theoretical antecedents from which they both evolved.

Marxist Origins

The women who first began to write from the point of view of both Marxism and feminism found their intellectual roots in Marxist categories of thought and initially attempted to fit women's experience and oppression into those categories. For them, Marxism systematically explained people's oppression, provided a "scientific" understanding of historical change, and offered a vision of a truly just society in which equality, realization of human potential, and the true fulfillment of people's needs were ingredient. That Marxism neither considered gender nor viewed women's oppression as anything other than a derivation of capitalist exploitation was seen as an oversight that could be corrected through attention to women's unique position under capitalism—the position of domestic laborer.

In one of the earliest and most influential pamphlets of the nascent socialist-feminist movement, "The Political Economy of Women's Liberation" (1969), Margaret Benston explained that this oversight occurred because "classes are generally defined by their relation to the means of production and . . . women are not supposed to have any unique relation to the means of production." Such a view was incorrect, Benston argued, because of Marxism's failure to understand women's work in the home. This work provides society with its most basic "use values," that form of production that is crucial to capitalism's functioning but that is not regarded as "real work" since it exists outside the market economy. Benston argued:

> We will tentatively define women, then, as that group of people who are responsible for the production of simple use-values in those activities associated with the home and family.
>
> Since men carry no responsibility for such production, the difference between the two groups lies here. . . . The material basis for the inferior status of women is to be found in just this definition of women. In a society in which money determines value, women are a group who work outside the money economy.

In suggesting a remedy to this situation, Benston found a parallel in Marx's analysis of the proletariat. Just as industrialization provided the working class with a necessary means of organizing as a class (through bringing workers together in factories), the industrialization of housework would overcome women's isolation in the home and introduce them into the market economy. In the tradition of Charlotte Perkins Gilman, Benston called for nothing less than communal eating places and laundries, the socialization of child-rearing tasks, and cooperative living arrangements to demonstrate that "psychic needs for community and warmth can in fact be better satisfied if other structures are substituted for the nuclear family."[6]

Following Benston, many theorists embellished this line of argument. Wally Secombe's "Housewife and Her Labour under Capitalism" (1973) was characteristic. Secombe's work was founded on the assumption that "regardless of their precapitalist origins . . . sex relations and family relations have become capitalist relations in the bourgeois epoch, and must be studied as such." Thus, Secombe defined the family as a unit that "consumes the means of subsistence, purchased in the commodity market, and reproduces labour power to sell to capital in the labour market." The housewife is a "labourer," albeit an "unproductive" one since she doesn't produce surplus value. Yet when "the housewife acts directly upon wage-purchased goods and necessarily alters their form, her labour becomes part of the congealed mass of past labour embodied in labour power." Therefore, every act in which a housewife engages can be conceptualized as reproductive labor: washing dishes, buying and preparing food, emotionally tending to her husband, even caring for her children, who, according to Secombe, are "future worker-commodities."[7]

This line of thought introduced women into the heart of the Marxist schema and demonstrated that they not only played an important role in capitalism's functioning but were necessary for the reproduction of labor power. Although this was an advance over traditional Marxist analyses, which failed to value women's work within the home, it saw the struggle for women's liberation as subsidiary to class struggle, and it failed to speak to the vast array of issues that feminists were discovering and discussing throughout this period: vaginal orgasms, body images, health care, lesbianism, rape, sexist advertising, spirituality, birth control, monogamy, self-defense, and on and on.

Other writers attempted to speak to these sorts of issues by suggesting that women were oppressed not only by capitalism nor exclusively through their role as domestic workers. Juliet Mitchell demonstrated in her widely read article and then pamphlet "Women: The Longest Revolution" (1966) that four "structures" constituted women's second-sex status: production, reproduction, sexuality, and the socialization of children. All four had to be fundamentally transformed for women to be liberated, for there to be a *unité de rupture*. Yet Mitchell continued to give precedence to women's role in production and to the primary role of the economic sphere. In her 1971 book *Woman's Estate*, she asserted:

> The contemporary family can be seen as a triptych of sexual, reproductive and socializing functions (the woman's world) embraced by production (the man's world)—precisely a structure which in the final instance is determined by the economy. . . . Any emancipation movement must still concentrate on the economic element—the entry of women fully into public industry and *the right to earn a living wage*.[8]

In response to this sort of thinking, Mariarosa Dalla Costa wrote an extremely influential article that circulated widely in pamphlet form and dominated discussions in many women's unions and among socialist feminists in the New American Movement and a number of local organizations during the early 1970s. "Women and the Subversion of the Community" (1972) argued forcefully that "the role of the working class housewife . . . is the determinant for the position of all other women." But Dalla Costa adamantly rejected both the traditional Marxist call for housewives to enter industry and the Marxist-feminist demand for the industrialization of housework through such innovations as communal kitchens. She claimed that feminists "who advocate that the liberation of the working class woman lies in their [*sic*] getting jobs outside the home are part of the problem, not the solution. Slavery to an assembly line is not a liberation from slavery to a kitchen sink." Instead, she argued, women must simultaneously liberate themselves from the isolation of the home *and* the exploitation of the capitalist workplace. While this radical reinterpretation of Marxist assumptions had enormous appeal for many socialist feminists, Dalla Costa offered few suggestions of how to "struggle against all situations which presume that women will stay at home" while refusing "the myth of liberation through work" outside the home.[9]

The "wages for housework" movement, originated by Dalla Costa's English translator, Selma James, was an attempt to respond to Dalla Costa's analysis strategically: if housewives would demand just compensation for the real work they perform at home, the capitalist system would eventually collapse because of its dependence on women's unpaid domestic labor. By demanding wages for housework, women would of necessity join together, breaking down their isolation from one another and challenging the foundations of capitalism, while avoiding the exploitation of working in the labor force. To James and her adherents this seemed a truly radical and novel strategy that combined the best of Marxist and feminist analyses.

To most socialist feminists operating in the United States, the idea of wages for housework was a tantalizing proposition worthy of debate but ultimately impractical. James interpreted every activity women perform in the home as part of the reproduction of labor power and thus deserving of compensation: cooking, cleaning, child rearing—even intercourse and pregnancy. Would most women be convinced that the care of their homes, husbands, and children was in essence indistinguishable from factory work? While wages for housework seemed to make sense theoretically, given the emphasis that domestic work was then being given by socialist feminists, no practical activity came out of it.

Sheila Rowbotham attempted to expand the way of looking at women's subordination through two books she wrote in the early 1970s: *Women, Resistance, and Revolution* (1972) and *Woman's Consciousness, Man's World* (1973). While continuing to acknowledge capitalism's salience in exploiting and oppressing women, she pointed to the effect that "patriarchy" plays in structuring women's and men's lives. Although capitalism had "tended to whittle away at the economic and ideological basis of patriarchy," Rowbotham claimed that patriarchy was still exerting a tremendous effect on women's consciousness and daily experience. Rather than having merely died off in the face of the capitalist mode of production, as other authors had suggested, patriarchy had "continued in capitalism as an ever present prop in time of need." [10]

Yet even for Rowbotham, "patriarchy"—defined as the system of male domination that predates capitalism and continues to oppress women into the current period—was of secondary importance in analyzing why women are dominated, abused, belittled, underpaid, harassed, and despised. While socialist feminists in CR groups, socialist feminist unions, and Marxist feminist discussion groups were discovering sexism in every corner of their lives, the theory they were reading continued to focus on their role, or lack thereof, in the economy and the primacy of domestic labor in explaining women's second-sex status. Many socialist feminists, however, did not experience the world primarily through roles as housewives; most were students, academics, professionals, or white-collar workers whose identity did not revolve around cleaning, cooking, and child rearing. A majority were single or divorced, lesbians, and/or members of collective living arrangements in which responsibility for household chores may have been a continuing struggle but was hardly the primary focus of their discontent over their lot as women. Since the personal had to be political, experience or practice had to inform theory, socialist-feminist writers began to break loose from the rigidity of Marxist categories that failed to speak fully to their own lives and those of the women they wished to organize. They began to construct a system of thinking that was both truly socialist *and* truly feminist in content.

Dual Systems Theory

At the 1975 National Conference on Socialist Feminism, Barbara Ehrenreich delivered a keynote address in which she both called for viewing women *qua* women as crucial to any revolutionary struggle—rather than solely through their role as domestic workers—and denounced the prevailing view that deemed women revolutionary subjects only insofar as they were able to participate in the waged market economy. She announced that any

work that brings women together in solidarity and sisterhood to
fight their common oppression is not something peripheral to the
class struggle—it is central to class struggle at this time. That is
to say, socialist feminism does not become socialist only when it
deals with women as workers (paid or unpaid). Socialist feminism is
socialist whenever it deals with women's problems in such a way as to
build solidarity, point the way to collective solutions, and strengthen
a culture of resistance—regardless of whether the actual arena of
struggle is health care, or abortion, or workplace issues, or whatever.

Almost as soon as she uttered it, however, Ehrenreich quickly retreated
from this unorthodox position and contradicted herself:

This is not to say that sisterhood equals class consciousness or
is some kind of mystical substitute for it. It is not. But it is—for
objective kinds of reasons—a principal ingredient, an essential
stepping-stone. . . .
   As a socialist I am convinced that the agent of revolution is not
a group defined by race, or sex, or sexual preference, but a group
defined ultimately by its relation to the system of production—that
is, a class.[11]

This tension between fully recognizing what was then igniting the women's
movement—issues surrounding abortion, sexuality, and health care—and
simultaneously remaining true to a class analysis increasingly haunted
socialist-feminist theory building. How could one account for rape or the
denial of clitoral orgasms or the attempt to outlaw the recently legalized
right to abortion—to mention but a few problems—while continuing to
employ Marxist categories of thought and strategy to bring about a socialist
revolution? The answer emerged through the articulation of "dual systems
theory."
   In 1975 Linda Phelps outlined what would soon become axiomatic for
the socialist-feminist movement in her article "Patriarchy and Capitalism":

If sexism is a social relationship in which males have authority over
females, *patriarchy* is a term which describes the whole system of
interaction which arises from that basic relationship, just as capitalism is a system built on the relationship between capitalist and
worker. Patriarchal and capitalist social relationships are two markedly different ways that human beings have interacted with each
other and have built social, political and economic institutions.[12]

Here at last was a way of thinking that seemed to resolve the tension between feminism and Marxism. It suggested that the mode of production was not sufficient to explain women's oppression under capitalism. It was no longer enough to say that women's experience could be accounted for through acknowledging their role in the reproduction of labor power. Similarly, it could not be assumed that women needed to join the ranks of the labor force in order to participate in revolutionary struggle, nor that women necessarily would be liberated with the advent of socialism.

Patriarchy was a system that had its own history, its own forms of oppression analytically independent of capitalism. According to Zillah Eisenstein, who became the foremost proponent of dual systems theory, "capitalism and patriarchy are neither autonomous systems nor identical: they are, in their present form, mutually dependent."

> This statement of the mutual dependence of patriarchy and capital-
> ism assumes not only the malleability of patriarchy to the needs of
> capital but also the malleability of capital to the needs of patriarchy.
> . . . When one states that capitalism needs patriarchy in order to
> operate efficiently, one is really noting that male supremacy, as a sys-
> tem of sexual hierarchy, supplies capitalism (and systems previous
> to it) with the necessary order and control; this patriarchal system
> of control is necessary to the smooth functioning of the society and
> the economic system and hence should not be undermined.

Socialist feminists gravitated to this perspective. It allowed them to transcend both radical feminism and socialism and to proclaim a unique theory that could combine the best insights of both traditions. As Eisenstein explained, "My discussion uses Marxist class analysis as the thesis, radical feminist patriarchal analysis as the antithesis, and from the two evolves the synthesis of socialist feminism."[13] If capitalism-and-patriarchy or, in Eisenstein's terms, capitalist patriarchy was the system of oppression, socialist feminism was the response.

As Barbara Ehrenreich suggests in her contribution to this volume, dual systems theory represented a "brave idea," a "vast theoretical synthesis," but at the same time remained peculiarly resistant to specification. It was difficult to describe, in an empirical fashion, *how* both capitalism and patriarchy affected every aspect of our lives and reinforced each other. Instead of inspiring new intellectual work that demonstrated the actual links between capitalism and patriarchy in our everyday lives, the dual systems perspective with only a few exceptions did not move much beyond the *as-*

sertion that the interface of capitalism and patriarchy was the source of women's oppression.

The one empirical manifestation of capitalist patriarchy continued to be domestic labor; it was the linchpin that held the two systems together. The sexual division of labor that assigned women to the "private sphere" was the legacy of patriarchy. The character of work that men performed outside the home and that women had to reproduce within it was created by capitalism. Zillah Eisenstein explained:

> Although the sexual division of labor and society antedates capitalism, it has been increasingly institutionalized and specifically defined in terms of the nuclear family because of the needs of advanced capitalism. . . .
>
> The conditions of production in society then, define and shape production, reproduction, and consumption in the family. So, too, the family mode of production, reproduction, and consumption affects commodity production. They work together to define the political economy.[14]

On a basic level, then, if one is to study women, one must focus on the legacy of patriarchy, the private sphere, and reproduction. Conversely, men's lives are located far more in the history of capitalism, the public sphere, and production. Although each sphere affects and reinforces the other, women and men primarily inhabit distinctly separate spheres. As Juliet Mitchell claimed in 1974:

> Men enter into the class-dominated structures of history while women (as women, whatever their actual work in production) remain defined by the kinship patterns of organization. In our society the kinship system is harnessed into the family—where a woman is formed in such a way that that is where she will stay. Differences of class, historical epoch, specific social situations alter the expression of femininity; but in relation to the law of the father, women's position across the board is a comparable one.[15]

What is curious about this claim is that it was speaking to an increasingly outmoded reality, one in which a male breadwinner supported a wife whose sole responsibility was domestic labor. By the mid-1970s, however, 47 percent of all women aged eighteen to sixty-four worked outside the home, and that proportion would rise to 63 percent by the mid-1980s. At a time when more women than ever before were fashioning their identities in the world of production, dual systems theory continued to focus on women as domestic laborers.

In similar fashion, just as dual systems theory failed to accurately assess the direction women's lives were taking in the last quarter of the twentieth century, it misread the historical record. While capitalism was seen as having a historical dynamic, patriarchy was a transhistoric truth. In "relation to the law of the father"—that is, patriarchy—"women's position . . . is a comparable one" Mitchell declared.[16] Eisenstein bluntly stated that a "patriarchal culture is carried over from one historical period to another to protect the sexual hierarchy of society."[17] Thus the division of labor embodied in women's identification with the private sphere and men's with the public was a theoretical construct having as much applicability to the present as to the past. Yet in truth, such division arose historically with capitalist industrialization, when work was transferred from the household to the factory. Prior to this eighteenth-century transformation, life was governed by a single sphere, what historian Philippe Ariès has called the sphere of "sociability."[18] Thus, to project as transhistorical a separation of spheres that is characteristic only of the capitalist period is to deny historical change and hypostatize a peculiar form of gender relations.

The Sex/Gender System

While most socialist-feminist theorists were searching for ways of specifying the workings of capitalist patriarchy, anthropologist Gayle Rubin published an article that transcended the somewhat simplistic coupling of Marxism and feminism represented by dual systems theory. In "The Traffic in Women," Rubin proposed a system of "social life which is the locus of the oppression of women, of sexual minorities, and of certain aspects of human personality within individuals." She named this the "sex/gender system" and defined it as "the set of arrangements by which a society transforms biological sexuality into products of human activity and in which these transformed sexual needs are satisfied."[19]

The sex/gender system is a productive system analogous to the economic system. Its raw materials are biological human beings. Its most fundamental products are kinship and marriage systems, gender identity and personality, sexual fantasy and objects, concepts of childhood, and sex roles. There is an " 'economics' of sex and gender, and what we need is a political economy of sexual systems," Rubin offered. "We need to study each society to determine the exact mechanisms by which particular conventions of sexuality are produced and maintained." For Rubin, patriarchy is simply a moment in the history of sex/gender systems. Its particular use by dual system theorists

> is analogous to using "capitalism" to refer to all modes of production, whereas the usefulness of the term "capitalism" lies precisely in that it distinguishes between the different systems by which societies are provisioned and organized. . . . Any society will have some systematic ways to deal with sex, gender and babies. . . . Patriarchy is a specific form of male dominance, and the use of the term ought to be confined to the Old Testament–style pastoral nomads from whom the term comes, or groups like them.[20]

The sex/gender system, conversely, "is a neutral term which refers to the domain and indicates that oppression is not inevitable in that domain, but is the product of the specific social relations which organize it." Thus sex/ gender systems are defined both historically and cross-culturally, just as are systems of economic production. In the same way that human beings act upon the world to form different modes of production, they create different forms of kinship and gender hierarchy in particular societies and specific historical periods. Patriarchy is one form of organization that the sex/gender system can assume.

By positing the sex/gender system, Rubin offered a way of understanding women's oppression that was analogous to, rather than isomorphic with, a Marxist analysis of the exploitation of the proletariat under capitalism. The sex/gender system neither automatically positions women in the sphere of reproduction where they are oppressed in a historically uniform manner, nor naturally places men in an arena of production that changes according to the dialectical movement of history. Instead, both the economic system and the sex/gender system have modes of production and reproduction. Each contains the potential for defining and deforming human beings to achieve their respective ends. Likewise, each contains the possibility for true human expression and liberation. Yet they are not equally responsible for women's oppression:

> To explain women's usefulness to capitalism is one thing. To argue that this usefulness explains the genesis of the oppression of women is quite another. It is precisely at this point that the analysis of capitalism ceases to explain very much about women and the oppression of women. . . .
> The subordination of women can be seen as a product of the

relationships by which sex and gender are organized and produced. The *economic oppression of women is derivative and secondary* [emphasis added].[21]

What Rubin calls for then, is a "revolution in kinship." Such a revolution would not only liberate women, however; it "would liberate forms of sexual expression, and it would liberate human personality from the straitjacket of gender."[22]

Here then was a new approach to constructing socialist-feminist theory. Rather than attempting to fit women into a Marxist world view or postulating an ahistoric patriarchy operating in perfect, although fairly indistinct, functional unity with capitalism, Gayle Rubin "pointed the way to a mode of analysis which we could call our own, a genuine Marxist-feminist methodology . . . a kind of watermark for Marxist-feminists' theoretical growth," as Rosalind Petchesky claimed in 1977.[23] Rubin's work suggested a truly materialist means of understanding how sex and gender are produced but transcended the specific content of Marxist categories. From her point of view, economic subordination founded on women's domestic work and unequal access to wages and jobs in the labor market was derivative from and secondary to oppression emanating from the sex/gender system. Instead of discovering the ways capitalism and patriarchy equally and simultaneously act to subordinate women, Rubin suggested that socialist feminists focus their intellectual energies on examining the mechanisms by which any given society produces gendered people who in turn reproduce their society's particular sex/gender system.

Theoretical Outcomes

Although many socialist-feminist scholars began to use the sex/gender system as a means of guiding and framing their thinking and research, it was dual systems theory that inspired activists and provided the focus for two American anthologies on socialist-feminist theory: Zillah Eisenstein's *Capitalist Patriarchy and the Case for Socialist Feminism* (1979), and Lydia Sargent's *Women and Revolution: A Discussion of the Unhappy Marriage of Marxism and Feminism* (1981). In both these works the interpenetration of capitalism and patriarchy remains largely at the abstract level, asserted rather than demonstrated.

The exception appears primarily in the work of socialist feminists who, like Heidi Hartmann, examine the relationship between women's exploitation in the labor force and their oppression within the family. As Hartmann points out in "Capitalism, Patriarchy, and Job Segregation by Sex":

> Job segregation by sex . . . is the primary mechanism in capitalist society that maintains the superiority of men over women, because it enforces lower wages for women in the labor market. Low wages keep women dependent on men because they encourage women to marry. Married women must perform domestic chores for their husbands. . . . This process is the present outcome of the continuing interaction of two interlocking systems, capitalism and patriarchy.[24]

But as woman's primary identity as domestic worker continues to decline along with man's role as breadwinner and provider, as the "reproduction of labor power" is increasingly performed by institutions and services outside the family, and as feminists have come to recognize that women's desire to marry and raise children cannot be explained in exclusively economic terms, socialist feminism defined as dual systems theory appears to be at an impasse, even though—as Hartmann's work demonstrates—it is useful in understanding women's role in the labor market.

Yet socialist feminists within the academy are continuing to explore new terrain, develop new insights, expand on and move beyond the framework that Gayle Rubin set forth in her work on the sex/gender system. In the fields of history, psychoanalytic theory, and philosophy and political theory, socialist feminists are in the vanguard of innovative and groundbreaking work.

Spurred to search for strong role models to combat popular conceptions of women's historical invisibility and unrelenting victimization, in the late 1960s and early 1970s feminists turned to history to reinterpret their lives and better understand the contours and dynamics of historical change as well as their current political struggles. Socialist feminists advanced this project by creatively using new sources to study poor and working-class women and insisting that history had to be written from the bottom up. Women's history has since generated great enthusiasm and a large following as it has rediscovered and popularized stories of brave foremothers such as Sojourner Truth, Emma Goldman, Susan B. Anthony, Margaret Sanger, Mother Jones, and Elizabeth Gurley Flynn. In addition, it has rewritten histories of social movements, reconceptualized periodization, and invented new methodologies.

Socialist-feminist women's history typically utilizes insights from the paradigm of the sex/gender system and exercises an acute sensitivity to class and race variation in women's experience over time. A central theme running throughout socialist-feminist history texts is the active participation of women in shaping their own destinies. Mary Ryan, in *Cradle of the Middle Class* (1981), explored the impact of contradictory ideological and economic forces on women and their shifting involvements in voluntary associations. Alice Kessler-Harris in various studies has documented the history of women's labor force participation. In *Heroes of Their Own Lives* (1988) Linda Gordon studied family violence in poor and immigrant families at the turn of the twentieth century, finding that rather than being simply trounced by the homogenizing forces of social control agencies, victims of violence acted with courage, selectively utilized resources, and shaped their lives in ways that heretofore have gone unnoticed. Barbara Ehrenreich in *The Hearts of Men* (1983) has argued persuasively that it is not the women's movement that has seriously damaged the family in the United States, as many have claimed, so much as men's flight from commitment, which antedated the movement's appearance in the 1960s.

A growing number of socialist feminists have been at the forefront of the effort to use psychoanalytic theory to understand both the roots of women's oppression and the etiology of gender. In keeping with Gayle Rubin's call for understanding how gender identity and sexual desire are produced within the sex/gender system, Nancy Chodorow in *The Reproduction of Mothering* (1978) has provided a pathbreaking, psychoanalytically based theory of how women's primary responsibility for mothering gives rise to masculine and feminine personality. Jessica Benjamin has built on this framework to show how sexual desire is produced in her book *The Bonds of Love* (1988).

In the fields of philosophy and political theory, socialist feminists have begun to push against the limitations of a Marxist outlook in an even more radical way than Gayle Rubin did in "The Traffic in Women." Seyla Benhabib and Drucilla Cornell argue in *Feminism as Critique* (1987) that what is needed now is a "displacement of the paradigm of production," in which production, whether in the market economy *or* in the sex/gender system, defines reality. They ask:

> Is the concept of production, which is based on the model of an active subject transforming, making and shaping an object given to it, at all adequate for comprehending activities like childbearing and rearing, care of the sick and elderly? Can nurture, care and the socialization of children be understood in the light of a subject-object model when they are activities which are so thoroughly *intersubjective?* [25]

If socialist feminists are to be truly sensitive to historical change and cross-cultural difference, as Linda Nicholson argues in *Gender and History* (1986), then it should be clear that while the categories of production and reproduction "might be necessary for understanding gender relations in industrial society, neither category is necessarily useful for analyzing earlier [and we may presume, future] societies."[26]

While many of these and other socialist-feminist contributions have enormously enriched our understanding of the world and women's place within it, none provides the all-encompassing theoretical framework that both dual systems theory and the sex/gender system attempted to elicit. In fact, as the political movement out of which socialist-feminist theory initially flowered has waned, much socialist-feminist writing has become more abstract and removed from the realities of present-day life in the United States. It is not accidental that the fields of history and philosophy and the emphasis on unconscious mental life have flourished within socialist feminism, as socialist-feminist activism has declined.

The Decline of Activism and the Rise of the Academy
Demise of the Socialist-Feminist Movement

While it is difficult to pinpoint that exact moment when activists stopped talking about socialist feminism as a movement and began referring to it as "the structural expression of a political and personal tendency,"[27] a clear turning-point was the national conference on socialist feminism held at Antioch College in Yellow Springs, Ohio, in 1975. Numerically, the conference was a tremendous success: 1,600 women attended, and others were turned away for lack of space. Yet despite the promising congregation of experienced organizers, high energy, and stimulating workshops, in one weekend the participants were forced to confront the problems that plagued the movement as a whole. Even though the conference had published principles of unity to screen out women of fundamentally different theoretical persuasions, ideological debates raged ad nauseam. A constellation of caucuses—Marxist-Leninist, Third World, older women, lesbian, antiimperialist—which in other contexts could prove to be constructive, criticized the organization and planning of the conference, several times calling it to a halt.

Such battles were not unique to the conference; they were rife within the women's unions that were the principal organizational expression of socialist feminism. Indeed, by 1975 divisive debates had become endemic to the left as a whole. In part the battles were a result of the resurgence of

Marxism-Leninism on the American left, with its tendency toward sectarianism and its incompatibility with feminism. Because the conference was attended largely by white and middle-class women, rather than working-class women and women of color, the caucuses criticized it and its constituent organizations for the very basic failure to reach underprivileged women. Such criticism brought confusion and disunity rather than allowing the Yellow Springs conference to launch a national organization, as planners had hoped.

Upon returning to their respective cities, conference participants were sobered by the obstacles they faced nationally and were forced to reengage in some of the continuing ideological battles. A few sectarian left organizations such as the Communist Workers Party and the Socialist Workers Party waged vitriolic campaigns to seek out and destroy bastions of democratic socialism, particularly in the women's movement, because they saw feminism as bourgeois, divisive, and ultimately counterrevolutionary. Thus, in the mid-1970s there was a concerted effort to disrupt and otherwise destroy the women's unions, a mission that was more successful in some cities than others. In Chicago, attempts to take over the CWLU eventually wearied the membership, and in the spring of 1977 members voted to disband the organization. In Berkeley, crippling ideological debates resulted from an infusion of new members with more orthodox left politics rather than from a concerted effort to destroy the organization, but the result was the same.

Another precipitating factor in the demise of the women's unions was the inability of activists and theorists alike to identify a unique socialist-feminist practice. Members of women's unions felt they had to distinguish themselves from other feminist organizations in order to justify their separate existence. Women's health centers or rape crisis hotlines were solid feminist projects, but in the eyes of their creators such projects, even though organized by socialist feminists, lacked an explicit *socialist* dimension. So, reasoned organizers, why not simply join NOW and its effort to organize a day-care center instead of mobilizing an independent campaign whose outcome would not be noticeably different? With the exception of reproductive rights groups, with their emphasis on choice and attention to the effects of sterilization abuse on poor and Third World women (in essence combining issues of sex, class, and race oppression), socialist-feminist activism was unable to satisfy the requirements of dual systems theory, which was in ascendance during the mid-1970s. However, while most explicitly socialist-feminist organizations did not succeed, socialist-feminist theory and strategy have made substantive contributions to the understanding of the oppression of women, and individual socialist feminists have had a discernible impact on groups working for social change. They have tirelessly

raised the salience of class and race in understanding women's experience and successfully impressed the importance of understanding diversity
upon their respective organizations and the rest of the women's movement.

The strong intellectual orientation of socialist feminism also has mili-
tated against extensive cultural expression. Linked to Marxism and the
university, socialist feminists have always seemed driven to read, understand, and educate themselves. While this is true in other left movements
as well, it means that the core of people drawn to socialist feminism have
had a predisposition to theoretical work (although they may have been activists and artists as well). Therefore, unlike radical feminists, key theorists
in the movement have tended to be academics rather than poets or cultural intellectuals. Also, the socialist-feminist requirements for a politically
correct culture have often limited spontaneity and creativity. Every activity
has had to meet race, class, and gender criteria, a process that is very
self-conscious, often inflexible, and certainly stilted. While radical feminists have also placed a premium on political "correctness," they have not
seemed to suffer the same stifling effects. Perhaps this is because radical or
cultural feminists' requirements have been easier to fulfill; every activity
simultaneously does not have to meet rigid requirements regarding the
racial, gender, and class composition of the actors or material in order to
be considered worthwhile.

There have been (and are) socialist-feminist cultural expressions. Annie
Popkin discusses in this volume the excitement of creating a shared culture in the heady days of women's liberation. Singer Holly Near is one very
good example of a contemporary socialist-feminist artist who has brought
activists together with the apolitical; her work has raised diverse political
issues and served to bridge communities. But one person does not a culture make. Undeniably, there was a feminist counterculture and a new left
culture, but both have contracted since their heyday in the late 1960s and
early 1970s. Socialist feminists occasionally have attempted to make their
homes in both left and feminist cultures, but as with political strategy, there
has been none uniquely their own.

The Ascendance of the University

Many blame the decline of the socialist-feminist movement, and
other movements of the 1960s and 1970s as well, on an increased interest
in personal and professional life that correspondingly detracted from activists' political involvement and commitment. There is no question that a
generation of activists decided in the 1970s and 1980s to have their long-

postponed families, seek stable employment, and earn enough money to establish an IRA; however, attrition from movement activities cannot be attributed simply to the coming of age of a rebellious youthful generation, obsessed with careers and offspring. At a certain point, both the left and socialist-feminist movements stopped providing a supportive and stimulating community that made risks worth taking. The political climate of the socialist-feminist left in the mid-1970s drove away many activists with its righteous moralism, its internecine battles over theory, personal attacks disguised as political rhetoric, and a feminist belief in the "personal is political" position that many interpreted as an unrestricted license to condemn others. It is critical to point out, however, that the community disintegration occurred within a larger political and economic context in which the potential limits for social change contracted so greatly that organizing, no matter how well-intentioned and strategically directed, was increasingly less effectual and to many seemed futile.

Another issue relevant to the decline of the socialist-feminist movement has been the decline of public forums for intellectual debate outside the university. Russell Jacoby has characterized this process as the absorption and co-optation of left intellectuals by academia. He argues that the university has grown enormously over the past five decades and has become one of the few refuges for left intellectuals. Jacoby laments this process and the absence of what he terms "public intellectuals" from the generation of 1960s and 1970s activists. He defines "public intellectuals" as those who seek and engage a "public world" in vernacular language, those who care about the world at large and speak to an audience beyond narrow university confines.[28] Although Jacoby inconsistently applies his standards to individual scholars, he is persuasive in asserting that the imperatives of university employment make left intellectuals vulnerable to the requirements of narrow specialization and too often end up communicating in academic jargon inaccessible to a lay audience.

Socialist feminists have been among the activists of the sixties and seventies who found a home in the universities. As undergraduates, graduate students, and junior faculty members, many have joined and led the political battles on campuses nationwide to establish women's studies programs. The original objective of women's studies, like that of black studies, was to bring together the academic and the activist, the university and the community. The existence of a multitude of women's studies programs suggests that these struggles have been quite successful, yet many such programs are fledgling, and others continue to receive only marginal funding and limited academic status.

Many young intellectuals who found academic jobs have engaged in scholarship informed by socialist feminism. While socialist feminists are members of labor unions, child-care activists, journalists, community organizers, therapists, writers, social workers, health-care workers, and lawyers, they are most visible in the university. Still, a large number of the authors in this collection are not university affiliated, and those who are attempt to address a wider audience in their writing.

For all its faults, academia is important in preserving radical traditions, particularly in the absence of a vital movement. In a time of political retrenchment, university intellectuals have major responsibility for nurturing the flame of socialist feminism and passing on its history, with the goal of ensuring its future. The university is an ideal (although it should not be the exclusive) place for educating the younger generation about the need for collective social change. Ultimately, this careful banking of ideas is insufficient, but in the short term it is critical.

While some of their scholarship has tended toward the abstract, socialist feminists both inside and outside the academy have produced important ideas and made significant contributions to political movements and to the ways that people live their lives. The need for co-parenting—an insight developed by socialist feminists—has had considerable influence on how women's and men's roles in the family are conceptualized and on many people's child-rearing practices. Demonstrating that men's and women's occupational skills and job categories are of comparable worth is another major contribution made by socialist feminists. Women workers throughout the country are now insisting that "equal pay for equal work" is insufficient to remedy pay inequalities between men and women. They are demanding that jobs be evaluated on the basis of comparable function and difficulty, paid accordingly, and thus used to stem wage inequality caused by the gender segmentation of the labor market. Socialist feminists were also the first to conceive broadly and popularize the issue of the feminization of poverty. Beyond these ideas, feminists working in various organizations—from Jobs with Peace, to the Committee in Solidarity with the People of El Salvador, to local housing groups—and for such publications as *Feminist Studies*, the *Nation, Socialist Review, Mother Jones, Radical America, In These Times*, informed by a socialist understanding of class inequality, have instigated and continue to lead numerous efforts for social and economic change.

It is important to emphasize, however, that the future of socialist feminism is intrinsically tied to the presence of a left oppositional movement in the United States. Its success cannot be discussed independently. Long-term gains rest in collectively building a progressive movement, and history has shown that separate socialist-feminist organizations may not be the most effective means of doing so and occasionally are counterproductive. Therefore, the focus of activism for socialist feminists should be on working within the broad-based women's movement and the left, tirelessly raising issues of class, gender, and race, never forgetting that our project is a collective one.

The Organization of This Book

This collection of essays represents an attempt to assess socialist feminism's past, present, and future. We believe that one must critically evaluate both the contributions and failures of socialist feminism in order to understand fully how it can move forward in the last decade of this century. Most of the authors presented here participated in the socialist-feminist movement of the 1970s. With the exception of those articles presented in the "classics" section, their contributions to this volume were written over the past ten years. They bring to their work a well-honed sensitivity to the issues that have both propelled and stymied socialist-feminist thinking and activism. Their contributions are alternately provocative, revealing, critical, laudatory, informative, visionary. Their disparate backgrounds and familiarity with various disciplines—economics, political theory, psychoanalysis, anthropology, history, literature—give a richness and vibrance to their work. And their experience as both political actors and intellectuals exemplifies the integration of theory and practice that remains an ideal of the socialist-feminist paradigm.

The Past: Socialist-Feminist Classics

Under the heading of "classics" we offer four of the most influential texts in the development of socialist-feminist theory. Juliet Mitchell's "Women: The Longest Revolution" was the first attempt during the second wave of feminism to combine socialist and feminist theory. In "The Traffic in Women" Gayle Rubin proposed the use of the sex/gender system as an analytic concept, adaptable to different modes of production and historical moments; she convincingly argued that the oppression of women is socially constructed and historically changing. Zillah Eisenstein, the most well-known proponent of dual systems theory, attempted to synthesize the critical understandings of patriarchy and capitalism in "Constructing a Theory of Capitalist Patriarchy and Socialist Feminism." And Heidi Hartmann's groundbreaking piece on women and work, "Capitalism, Patriarchy, and Job Segregation by Sex," exemplified the most effective application of dual systems theory, in examining the relationship of power to the division of labor by sex.

The Past: Socialist-Feminist Organizations

During the late 1960s and the 1970s the ferment of women's liberation prompted the founding of a multitude of groups and organizations. Among these were socialist-feminist organizations founded by women who were outraged by the sexism of the new left and dissatisfied with the inattention to capitalist exploitation and imperialism of the autonomous women's movement. In 1969 Bread and Roses and the first socialist-feminist women's union, the Chicago Women's Liberation Union (CWLU), were established, and others followed suit in the next six years. Though virtually all seventeen explicitly socialist-feminist women's unions collapsed in 1976 and 1977, other socialist-feminist, single-issue groups sprang up and have continued to thrive well into the 1980s.

Combining her experience as a member of Bread and Roses with extensive research, Annie Popkin has documented the rich history of the early socialist component of the women's liberation movement in "The Social Experience of Bread and Roses." At the forefront of consciousness raising within their community and in Boston as a whole, members of Bread and Roses challenged sexism in alternative institutions and heterosexism within their own ranks, discovered the power of friendships with other women, and analyzed the political dimension of private life.

In "Women's Unions and the Search for a Political Identity," Karen V. Hansen picks up where Popkin's history ends in order to explore the political involvements of women who adopted the principal politics of Bread and Roses but formed different kinds of organizations to implement them. Hansen finds that the tension between socialism and feminism—and allegiances split between the left and the women's movement—had disruptive as well as creative consequences throughout the life of the women's unions. With their white middle-class membership, isolation from the racial and class constituency they wished to reach, and an inability to translate abstract theory into concrete activism, the unions found themselves vulnerable to sectarian takeover and self-destruction.

Judith Sealander and Dorothy Smith approach the feminist activism of the 1970s by comparing three local institutions of differing political orientations and contrasting their successes and failures in "The Rise and Fall of Feminist Organizations in the 1970s." By 1980 none of these Dayton organizations existed any longer. They shared with the women's unions an inability to find a strategic focus and difficulty in building a multiclass and multiracial base. They were further frustrated by the limitations of scant resources and only a small core of committed activists.

Adele Clarke and Alice Wolfson examine the more successful story of a movement whose effectiveness they credit to socialist-feminist initiative, vision, and leadership. In "Class, Race and Reproductive Rights," Clarke and Wolfson insist that reproductive rights efforts "must address *both* social and individual levels of action," which means demanding a full range of reproductive services and access to them for all women. In outlining the contradictions involved in organizing around the issue, the authors assert the need for a national socialist-feminist movement and remind us: "Whatever work we undertake, we must ground it in the concrete conditions of our lives."

The Past: Reevaluating Socialist Feminism

As we have already suggested, socialist feminism has been in a period of retrenchment during the 1980s. While some argue that it is alive in the work of individual political actors who maintain a socialist-feminist outlook, others suggest that it is hibernating within the confines of academia, awaiting the reemergence of a left movement in the United States; still others assert that socialist feminism is "dead." This section offers a variety of viewpoints on the question.

In "Life without Father," Barbara Ehrenreich trenchantly argues that socialist feminists have been too deferential to Marxism. While dual systems theory was a partial attempt to rectify this error, it was fundamentally premised on a world that is now receding from sight, one in which both individual men and the ruling class were dependent upon women's work in the home (the reproduction of labor power) to survive. In order to be relevant in the current period, socialist feminists now must be able to account for the enormous changes that have occurred in the past quarter-century —transformations in the international structure of capital as well as in the psyches of individual men who no longer opt for long-term relationships with women.

Conversely, in "Conceptualizing and Changing Consciousness," Sandra Morgen argues that socialist feminists must engage critical Marxist theory. She locates much of socialist feminism's vitality in its ability to direct Marxist theorizing toward questions of feeling, consciousness, and an appreciation of emotional life. For Morgen, socialist feminism has "the potential to give the Marxist human subject a historically and socially constituted consciousness that can ensure a place for agency in theories of social change."

Judith Van Allen continues this critique in "Capitalism without Patriarchy." She challenges the functionalist assumptions inherent in the view that capitalism and patriarchy form a seamless web of oppression that only revolution or "smashing the family" can alter. As Van Allen's discussion of the right to abortion aptly illustrates, even within the ruling class there are competing needs and interests regarding women's roles in the home and in the paid labor force. It is in feminists' interests to be able to identify these cleavages and locate arenas in which to agitate effectively for feminist demands.

Finally, Deirdre English, Barbara Epstein, Barbara Haber, and Judy MacLean, all long-time activists and writers in the socialist-feminist movement, offer their personal experiences, feelings, and beliefs about the viability of the socialist-feminist project. Deeply divided in the positions they espouse, they reveal in the course of this roundtable discussion, "The Impasse of Socialist Feminism," how profoundly the personal and the political are intertwined.

The Present: Family Life in Postindustrial America

For over a decade the media, politicians, religious leaders, government officials, and the new right have bemoaned the "crisis" in the family. Everything from inner-city crime to an inability to compete successfully with the Japanese in the world economy has been explained by the breakdown of the family. When causes are sought for this breakdown or crisis, sexual liberation, feminism, government interference, the decline of religion, and drugs are often summoned forth for blame. The authors presented here, however, offer more subtle and complex views of the changes that have transformed contemporary family life.

In "The Fading Dream," Elliott Currie, Robert Dunn, and David Fogarty show how economic developments in the 1970s and 1980s have sorted Americans into "winners" and "losers." Where one falls in this restratification depends not only on one's sex, color, and age but also on what kind of family arrangement one lives in. For those lucky enough to be in households where there is more than one wage earner, family "speedup" has become the norm, and women have had to bear the overwhelming burden of this speedup.

Judith Stacey examines the more personal side of this restratification process in "Sexism by a Subtler Name?" In the best socialist-feminist tradition, she focuses on the complex, reciprocal effects of family, work, and gender consciousness in the heart of postindustrial society—California's Silicon Valley. She demonstrates that for large numbers of women feminism eased the transition out of oppressive relationships into the world of school, work, and raising children on their own. Yet she also shows that feminism has not been very successful in helping women survive in a society that offers them dead-end jobs and brittle, transitory relationships with men. In order to become a relevant, dynamic force in women's lives once again, feminism must speak to the new realities of a post-industrial, postfeminist society.

In a direct critique of Stacey's article, Rayna Rapp argues in "Is the Legacy of Second-Wave Feminism Postfeminism?" that the very term "postfeminist" hinders attempts to move forward, to find *social* rather than *individual* solutions to women's problems. By looking at black women and women in labor unions, Rapp forcefully asserts that "movements that may feel 'dead' to second-wave feminists are actually just beginning or continuing for other groups."[29]

Maxine Baca Zinn takes up Rapp's focus on the connections among gender, race, and class in "Minority Families in Crisis," demonstrating that family structure is the consequence, not the cause, of poverty. By concentrating on the "losers" in the restratification process, Baca Zinn shows that blacks' overrepresentation in the secondary labor market, the decline of agricultural and industrial manufacturing jobs, and the shift from urban to suburban job sites are causes of black family crisis rather than results of a breakdown in family life.

Ilene J. Philipson provides an alternative means of looking at changes in the contemporary family in "Heterosexual Antagonisms and the Politics of Mothering." She argues that to understand the current "crisis," it is necessary to recognize the complex interplay between a historically determined social structure and the molding of gendered personalities in the family. By taking a psychoanalytic approach to recent shifts in family structure, Philipson demonstrates that mothers' isolated and exclusive responsibility for rearing children gives rise to sons and daughters who find heterosexual relations difficult and the formation of families precarious.

In "When Women and Men Mother," Diane Ehrensaft continues to focus on the interface of female/male and parent/child relationships to account for change within the family. Ehrensaft offers shared parenting by mother and father as an important social and psychological corrective to female-dominated child rearing. Far beyond simply arguing for its necessity, she demonstrates the subtle and often challenging effects that co-parenting has on male-female relations and on the children of parents who are attempting to transcend traditional gender arrangements.

The Present: Sexuality and Pornography

Throughout the 1970s sexuality was not a primary focus of socialist-feminist theory or formal discussion. Although reproductive rights and parenting were, and are, focal points, sexual practices and identities did not enter into socialist-feminist discourse. Perhaps this is part of a Marxist legacy that eschews such discussion; perhaps sexuality did not seem to be a potential linchpin between capitalism and patriarchy and thus could be overlooked. Whatever the reason, it was not until the 1980s, when cultural feminists throughout the country began forming organizations to protest violent pornography, that socialist feminists began to examine sexuality as a serious political topic.

The issue of pornography has deeply divided feminists, perhaps because it encapsulates so many and such complicated moral, intellectual, and political issues: the tolerance of difference, free speech, the applicability of universal standards of morality, the question of whether there is a correct sexuality, the relationships between psychopathology and sex, fantasy and reality, cultural symbols and sexual play, the primacy of the sexual drive, male violence, social construction versus essentialism. In "I'm Black and Blue from the Rolling Stones and I'm Not Sure How I Feel about It," Kate Ellis views pornography, sado-masochism, and even the "insignia of war, repression, or torture" as potentially contributing both to women's sexual danger and restriction *and* to their empowerment and pleasure. Ellis identifies herself as a "sex radical" who seeks greater sexual freedom for women rather than greater protection from pornography and the dangers that may lie in exploring sexual pleasure.

Ilene J. Philipson takes issue with Ellis in "Beyond the Virgin and the Whore," arguing that the way many socialist feminists have criticized the antipornography movement serves to revitalize the dichotomous categories of good girl and bad girl, antipornography feminist and sex radical. She suggests that socialist feminists need to move beyond mere critique of other feminists and develop a theory of sexuality that transcends anachronistic notions of sexual repression and liberation in order to argue for women's sexual freedom.

Lorna Weir and Leo Casey expand on Philipson's position by defining pornography as a "tactic by means of which power incorporates and intensifies sexuality, rather than a war in which sexuality resists power." In "Subverting Power in Sexuality," Weir and Casey contend that neither a moralistic naturalism nor a superficial "anything goes" view of sexual liberation can speak to the complexities of sexual behavior. Following on the work of Michel Foucault, Weir and Casey argue that control of sexuality is manifested no longer through repression but through constant stimulation.

The Present: Women, Work, and the Labor Movement

Issues of women and work, central to the socialist-feminist political project, have proved to be among the most fruitful areas of research and organizing. The past decade has seen the issue of pay equity effectively raised in local as well as national organizing efforts as unions have come to terms with the importance of the issue in organizing and maintaining women members. Many legal cases concerning discrimination against women workers have yielded significant changes. Organizers and academics have also grappled with the consequences of the technological advances of the postindustrial information age in the workplace.

Alice Kessler-Harris, in addressing the relationship of history to public policy, speaks to the challenge faced by progressive academics when she says we have a "responsibility as scholars to speak to public issues." Her global overview of the emerging marketplace, "The Just Price, the Free Market, and the Value of Women," offers a "picture of wage relations that are not systemic but constructed and processual. . . . Like the labor market itself, the wage relation is constructed out of subjective experience and rests ultimately on the legitimacy of historically specific notions of gender 'difference.'" Kessler-Harris heralds comparable worth as the first step toward the latest "revaluation of women" and articulates the need for women's historians to provide examples, the "balm of experience," for unraveling the current debate and understanding the perceptions and contributions of women's work over time.

Johanna Brenner is more cautious about the potential of legislating a solution to women's economic disenfranchisement. In "Feminist Political Discourses," she reviews the liberal assumptions behind political philosophies and how they influence political organizing. According to Brenner, legislative responses to the feminization of poverty basically attempt to make up for what husbands do not provide their wives, counterproductively play on notions of women as victims, accentuate wives' dependence on husbands, and separate "good" women from "bad" as well as white from black. Brenner cautions that comparable worth potentially institutionalizes divisions within society—between men and women, blue collar and white collar—thereby making these dichotomies more difficult to overcome in the future.

Ronnie Steinberg responds to Brenner by portraying the struggle for pay equity as a strategy to keep larger economic and political agendas alive. In "Radical Challenges in a Liberal World," Steinberg points to the fundamental power imbalance that has kept comparable worth from being fully implemented. Yet despite its limitations, comparable worth has improved wages (for people of color more than for women), has "broadened public thinking on what discrimination is and redefined standards of fairness," sparked a debate on the very meaning of the market and how it determines wages, and challenged basic assumptions of meritocracy in the marketplace.

In "The New Economy," Barbara Baran returns to the issue raised by Kessler-Harris regarding the value of women's work. She finds that the feminization of white-collar work has accompanied technological innovation in the office. Although the structure of the office work force has changed, skill has actually increased, while jobs at the bottom of the clerical hierarchy have been eliminated. Baran concludes that even though female labor in the insurance industry is *skilled*, it is *cheap* and lacks "the social rewards that neoclassical economic theory would have us believe are associated with skill."

The Future

As we near the beginning of the twenty-first century, we confront a host of problems no single book can address. We have chosen to present a few key issues of concern to feminists of all persuasions: the family, women and work, and our visions for the future. The articles in this section build on the foundation constructed by second-wave feminism, challenge apolitical scholarship in the face of racism and adversity, suggest that we reclaim science and technology as feminist terrain, and dare to ask overarching, difficult questions about the future of society.

In "The Future of Motherhood," Elayne Rapping laments the feminist capitulation of reproductive issues and egalitarian visions to male institutions and power. In controversial cases such as that of Baby M, Rapping claims that feminists have retreated to a single-minded focus on "maternal rights," clinging to the romantic ideal of motherhood and to two of the few things women can "own and control, our bodies and our biological offspring." In searching for a vision to pass on to the postfeminist generation of young women and men, she discusses the child-rearing experiences of black women as a progressive example of flexibility and compassion. "It is a model that is accepting of difference, accepting of the fragility of the biological 'maternal bond,' accepting of the need for radical alternatives in these nasty times."

In "Second Thoughts on the Second Wave," Deborah Rosenfelt and Judith Stacey examine three controversial texts in trying to comprehend the "postfeminist retreat from sexual politics to a more conservative pro-family vision, one that simply assumes the inevitability or superiority of heterosexual marriage and motherhood." Postfeminism as they character-ize it is not anti-feminist but socially conservative, depoliticized, and much more pessimistic than feminism about the potential for changing male be-havior. At the same time it accepts the modern condition of women—the need to manage both career and family—as a fact of life, however unfair. According to Rosenfelt and Stacey, recognizing and attempting to address problems of women's contemporary situation—the incompatibility between having a good education, earning a decent salary, and finding an acceptable husband; the tension between erotic and maternal feelings; and the strenu-ous demands of combining full-time employment and motherhood—have the potential to revitalize feminism, with "its capacity for self-criticism" and its "liberating vision."

In "The Race for Theory," Barbara Christian raises fundamental ques-tions about the politics and usefulness of academically fashionable decon-structionism. In achieving academic preeminence, the new literary theory has displaced the writer with the critic, politics with "neutrality," and cul-tural diversity in writing with standard, male, Western classics. Christian criticizes all theories that devalue material reality and politics, particularly those that become monolithic and eventually prescriptive. She cites ex-amples from the Black Arts Movement of the 1960s and from feminist lit-erary criticism today to show how these abstract approaches to learning can stifle creativity, rob literature of its sensuality and meaning, and gloss over differences in their inability to deconstruct the complexity of life. Christian encourages us to be historically sensitive to the full meaning of literature, to root theory in practice, to understand a work's political dimensions and intent, and to recognize the vision and inspiration that writing can provide its readers.

Finally, Donna Haraway sets an ambitious agenda for socialist femi-nism when she recommends that we abandon the dualities of "hierarchi-cal domination"—public/private, male/female—and transcend outmoded theories that no longer have the capacity to explain our late twentieth-century condition, let alone that of the twenty-first century. Like Christian, Haraway rejects totalizing theory. In using the metaphor of the cyborg—an organism part human, part machine—she also rejects radical feminism and other attempts to create a universal identity of woman. Her vision in

"A Manifesto for Cyborgs" challenges us to imagine a kind of politics that will "embrace partial, contradictory, permanently unclosed constructions of personal and collective selves and still be faithful, effective—and ironically, socialist feminist." Like Rapping, she urges us to accept, to analyze, and indeed to embrace science and technology because they "provide fresh sources of power, [and] we need fresh sources of analysis and political action." Her portrait of the future is unsettling to many socialist feminists, but the postmodern order requires a new conceptual framework and a transformed vocabulary. In breaking through the paradigm used to analyze the industrial order, Haraway reformulates old categories and provides some tools for beginning.

Notes

1. E.g., Marge Piercy, "The Grand Coolie Damn," in Robin Morgan, ed., *Sisterhood Is Powerful* (New York: Vintage Books, 1970); Robin Morgan, "Goodbye to All That," in *Going Too Far: The Personal Chronicle of a Feminist* (New York: Vintage Books, 1978); *Notes from the First Year* (New York: New York Radical Women, 1968); *Notes from the Second Year* (New York: Notes, 1970).
2. Piercy, "Grand Coolie Damn," 491–92.
3. Joanne Cooke, "Here's to You, Mrs. Robinson," *Motive* nos. 6–7 (1969): 4.
4. Torie Osborn, *NAM Newspaper* 2, no. 4 (1972).
5. During the 1970s the terms "Marxist feminist" and "socialist feminist" in most cases were used interchangeably, and this certainly was the case for the Marxist-Feminist Groups. Increasingly, however, "Marxist feminism" has come to denote a perspective in which Marxism, or traditional class analysis, is primary. The term "socialist feminism" does not privilege class over gender or Marxism over feminism, and continues to imply a dual perspective.
6. Margaret Benston, "The Political Economy of Women's Liberation" (originally published in *Monthly Review*, September 1969; reprinted as a pamphlet by Bay Area Radical Education Project, which is the source cited here), 1, 4, 12.
7. Wally Secombe, "The Housewife and Her Labour under Capitalism," *New Left Review* No. 83 (1973): 5n., 7, 9, 19.
8. Juliet Mitchell, *Woman's Estate* (1971; New York: Vintage Books, 1973), 148–49.
9. Mariarosa Dalla Costa, "Women and the Subversion of the Community," *Radical America* 6 (July 1972): 68, 81, 96.
10. Sheila Rowbotham, *Woman's Consciousness, Man's World* (1973; Baltimore, Md.: Penguin Books, 1975), 119, 120.
11. Barbara Ehrenreich, "Speech," *Socialist Revolution* 26 (October–December 1975): 91, 92, 89.
12. Linda Phelps, "Patriarchy and Capitalism," *Quest* 2, no. 2 (1975): 39.
13. Zillah Eisenstein, "Constructing a Theory of Capitalist Patriarchy and Socialist Feminism," in Eisenstein, ed., *Capitalist Patriarchy and the Case for Socialist Feminism* (New York: Monthly Review Press, 1979), 22, 27–28, 6; see also Chapter 4 in this book.

14. Ibid., 29–30.

15. Juliet Mitchell, *Psychoanalysis and Feminism* (New York: Pantheon Books, 1974), p. 406.

16. Ibid.

17. Eisenstein, "Constructing a Theory," 25.

18. Philippe Ariès, *Centuries of Childhood* (New York: Vintage Books, 1962), 407.

19. Gayle Rubin, "The Traffic in Women: Notes on the 'Political Economy' of Sex," in Rayna Rapp Reiter, ed., *Toward an Anthropology of Women* (New York: Monthly Review Press, 1975), 159; see also Chapter 3 in this book.

20. Ibid., 177, 167–68.

21. Ibid., 168, 163, 177.

22. Ibid., 199, 200.

23. Rosalind Petchesky, "Dissolving the Hyphen: A Report on Marxist-Feminist Groups 1–5," in Eisenstein, *Capitalist Patriarchy*, 376.

24. Heidi I. Hartmann, "Capitalism, Patriarchy, and Job Segregation by Sex," *Signs* 1, no. 3, pt. 2 (1976): 137–69; see also Chapter 5 in this book.

25. Seyla Benhabib and Drucilla Cornell, "Introduction: Beyond the Politics of Gender," in Seyla Benhabib and Drucilla Cornell, eds., *Feminism as Critique* (Minneapolis: University of Minnesota Press, 1987), 2.

26. Linda J. Nicholson, *Gender and History* (New York: Columbia University Press, 1986), 199.

27. Petchesky, "Dissolving the Hyphen," 373.

28. Russell Jacoby, *The Last Intellectuals: American Culture in the Age of Academe* (New York: Basic Books, 1987).

29. Throughout this volume the term "second-wave feminists" refers to the feminists of the 1960s and 1970s, as opposed to those who formed the first American feminist movement in the late nineteenth and early twentieth centuries.

I.   The Past

Socialist-Feminist Classics

2   **Women**

The Longest Revolution

Juliet Mitchell

The situation of women is different from that of any other social group. This is because they are not one of a number of isolable units but half a totality: the human species. Women are essential and irreplaceable; they cannot therefore be exploited in the same way as other social groups can. They are fundamental to the human condition, yet in their economic, social, and political roles they are marginal. It is precisely this combination—fundamental and marginal at one and the same time—that has been fatal to them. Within the world of men their position is comparable to that of an oppressed minority, but they also exist outside the world of men. The one state justifies the other and precludes protest. In advanced industrial society, women's work is only marginal to the total economy. Yet it is through work that man changes natural conditions and thereby produces society. Until there is a revolution in production, the labor situation will prescribe women's situation within the world of men. But women are offered a universe of their own: the family. Like woman herself the family appears as a natural object, but it is actually a cultural creation. There is

Source: This article is reprinted from the *New Left Review* 40 (November–December 1966), by permission of the publisher, *New Left Review*, London W1E 6QZ, England.

nothing inevitable about the form or role of the family any more than there is about the character or role of women. It is the function of ideology to present these given social types as aspects of nature itself. Both can be exalted, paradoxically, as ideals. The "true" woman and the "true" family are images of peace and plenty; in actuality they may both be sites of violence and despair. The apparently natural condition can be made to appear more attractive than the arduous advance of human beings toward culture. But what Marx wrote about the bourgeois myths of the Golden Ancient World describes precisely women's realm: "in one way the child-like world of the ancients appears to be superior, and this is so, insofar as we seek for closed shape, form and established limitation. The ancients provide a narrow satisfaction, whereas the modern world leaves us unsatisfied or where it appears to be satisfied with itself is vulgar and mean."

Women in Socialist Theory

The problem of the subordination of women and the need for their liberation was recognized by all the great socialist thinkers in the nineteenth century. It is part of the classical heritage of the revolutionary movement. Yet today, in the West, the problem has become a subsidiary if not an invisible element in the preoccupations of socialists. Perhaps no other major issue has been so forgotten. In England the cultural heritage of Puritanism, always strong on the left, contributed to a widespread diffusion of essentially conservative beliefs among many who would otherwise count themselves as "progressive." A *locus classicus* of these attitudes is Peter Townsend's remarkable statement: "Traditionally Socialists have ignored the family or they have openly tried to weaken it—alleging nepotism and the restrictions placed upon individual fulfilment by family ties. Extreme attempts to create societies on a basis other than the family have failed dismally. It is significant that a Socialist usually addresses a colleague as 'brother' and a Communist uses the term 'comrade.' The chief means of fulfilment in life is to be a member of, and reproduce a family. There is nothing to be gained by concealing this truth."[1]

How has this counterrevolution come about? Why has the problem of woman's condition become an area of silence within contemporary socialism? August Bebel, whose book *Woman in the Past, Present, and Future* was one of the standard texts of the German Social-Democratic Party in the early years of this century, wrote: "Every Socialist recognises the dependence of the workman on the capitalist, and cannot understand that others, and especially the capitalists themselves, should fail to recognise it also; but the same Socialist often does not recognise the dependence of women on men because the question touches his own dear self more or less nearly."[2] But this genre of explanation—psychologistic and moralistic—is clearly inadequate. Much deeper and more structural causes have clearly been at work. To consider these would require a major historical study, impossible here. But it can be said with some certainty that part of the explanation for the decline in socialist debate on the subject lies not only in the real historical processes but in the original weaknesses in the traditional discussion of the subject in the classics. For while the great studies of the last century all stressed the importance of the problem, they did not *solve* it theoretically. The limitations of their approach have never been subsequently transcended.

Charles Fourier was the most ardent and voluminous advocate of women's liberation and of sexual freedom among the early socialists. In a well-known passage he wrote: "The change in a historical epoch can always be determined by the progress of women towards freedom, because in the relation of woman to man, of the weak to the strong, the victory of human nature over brutality is most evident. The degree of emancipation of women is the natural measure of general emancipation."[3] Marx quoted this formulation with approval in *The Holy Family*. But characteristically, in his early writings he gave it a more universal and philosophical meaning. The emancipation of women would be not only as Fourier, with his greater preoccupation with sexual liberation, saw it—an index of humanization in the civic sense of the victory of humaneness over brutality—but in the more fundamental sense of the progress of the human over the animal, the cultural over the natural: "The relation of man to woman is the *most natural* relation of human being to human being. It indicates, therefore, how far man's *natural* behaviour has become human, and how far his *human* essence has become a *natural* essence for him, how far his *human nature* has become *nature* for him."[4] This theme is typical of the early Marx.

Marx and Engels

Fourier's ideas remained at the level of utopian moral injunction. Marx used and transformed them, integrating them into a philosophical critique of human history. But he retained the abstraction of Fourier's conception of the position of women as an index of general social advance. This in effect makes it merely a symbol—it accords the problem a universal importance at the cost of depriving it of its specific substance. Symbols are allusions to or derivations of something else. In Marx's early writings woman becomes an anthropological entity, an ontological category, of a highly abstract kind. Contrarily, in his later work, where he is concerned with describing the family, Marx differentiates it as a phenomenon according to time and place: "Marriage, property, the family remain unattacked, in theory, because they are the practical basis on which the bourgeoisie has erected its domination, and because in their bourgeois form they are the conditions which make the bourgeois a bourgeois. . . . This attitude of the bourgeois to the conditions of his existence acquires one of its universal forms in bourgeois morality. One cannot, in general, speak of the family *as such*. Historically, the bourgeois gives the family the character of the bourgeois family, in which boredom and money are the binding link, and which also includes the bourgeois dissolution of the family, which does not prevent the family itself from always continuing to exist. Its dirty existence has its counterpart in the holy concept of it in official phraseology and universal hypocrisy. . . . [Among the proletariat] the concept of the family does not exist at all. . . . In the eighteenth century the concept of the family was abolished by the philosophers, because the actual family was already in process of dissolution at the highest pinnacles of civilisation. The internal family bond was dissolved, the separate components constituting the concept of the family were dissolved, for example, obedience, piety, fidelity in marriage, etc.; but the real body of the family, the property relation, the exclusive attitude in relation to other families, forced cohabitation—relations produced by the existence of children, the structure of modern towns, the formation of capital, etc.—all these were preserved, although with numerous violations because the existence of the family has been made necessary by its connection with the mode of production that exists independently of the will of bourgeois society."[5] Or, later still, in *Capital*: "It is, of course, just as absurd to hold the Teutonic-Christian form of the family to be absolute and final as it would be to apply that character to the ancient Roman, the ancient Greek, or the eastern forms which, moreover, taken together form a series in historic development."[6] What is striking is that here the problem of women has been submerged in an analysis of the family. The difficulties of this approach can be seen in the somewhat apocalyptic note of Marx's comments on the fate of the bourgeois family here and elsewhere (for example, in the *Communist Manifesto*). There was little historical warrant for the idea that it was in effective dissolution, and indeed could no longer be seen in the working class. Marx thus moves from general philosophical formulations about women in the early writings to specific historical comments on the family in the later texts. There is a serious disjunction between the two. The common framework of both, of course, was his analysis of the economy, and of the evolution of property.

It was left to Engles to systematize these theses in *The Origin of the Family, Private Property, and the State*, after Marx's death. Engels declared that the inequality of the sexes was one of the first antagonisms within the human species. The first class antagonism "coincides with the development of the antagonism between man and woman in the monogamous marriage, and the first class oppression with that of the female sex by the male."[7] Basing much of his theory on Morgan's inaccurate anthropological investigations, Engels nevertheless had some valuable insights. Inheritance, which is the key to his economist account, was first matrilineal, but with the increase of wealth became patrilineal. This was woman's greatest single setback. The wife's fidelity becomes essential, and monogamy is irrevocably established. The wife in the communistic, patriarchal family is a public servant, with monogamy she becomes a private one. Engles effectively reduces the problem of woman to her capacity to work. He therefore gives her physiological weakness as a primary cause of her oppression. He locates the moment of her exploitation at the point of the transition from communal to private property. If inability to work is the cause of her inferior status, ability to work will bring her liberation: "The emancipation of women and their equality with men are impossible and must remain so as long as women are excluded from socially productive work and restricted to housework, which is private. The emancipation of women becomes possible only when women are enabled to take part in production on a large, social, scale, and when domestic duties require their attention only to a minor degree."[8] Or: "The first premise for the emancipation of women is the reintroduction of the entire female sex into public industry. . . . This . . . demands that the quality possessed by the individual family of being the economic unit of society be abolished."[9] Engels thus finds a solution schematically appropriate to his analysis of the origin of feminine oppression. The position of women, then, in the work of Marx and Engels remains dissociated from, or subsidiary to, a discussion of the family, which is in its turn subordinated as merely a precondition of private property. Their solutions retain this overly economist stress, or enter the realm of dislocated speculation.

Bebel, Engels's disciple, attempted to provide a programmatic account of woman's oppression as such, not simply as a by-product of the evolution of the family and of private property: "From the beginning of time oppression was the common lot of woman and the labourer. . . . *Woman was the first human being that tasted bondage,* woman was a slave *before the slave existed.*"[10] He acknowledged, with Marx and Engels, the importance of physical inferiority in accounting for woman's subordination but, while stressing inheritance, added that a biological element—her maternal function—was one of the fundamental conditions that made her economically dependent on the man. But Bebel, too, was unable to do more than state that sexual equality was impossible without socialism. His vision of the future was a vague reverie, quite disconnected from his description of the past. The absence of a strategic concern forced him into voluntarist optimism divorced from reality. Lenin himself, although he made a number of specific suggestions, inherited a tradition of thought that simply pointed to the a priori equation of socialism with feminine liberation without showing concretely how it would transform woman's condition: "Unless women are brought to take an independent part not only in political life generally, but also in daily and universal public service, it is no use talking about full and stable democracy, let alone socialism." [11]

The liberation of women remains a normative ideal, an adjunct to socialist theory, not structurally integrated into it.

The Second Sex

The contrary is true of Beauvoir's massive work *The Second Sex*—to this day the greatest single contribution on the subject. Here the focus is the status of women through the ages. But socialism as such emerges as a curiously contingent solution at the end of the work, in a muffled epilogue. Beauvoir's main theoretical innovation was to fuse the "economic" and "reproductive" explanations of women's subordination by a psychological interpretation of both. Man asserts himself as subject and free being by opposing other consciousnesses. He is distinct from animals precisely in that he creates and invents (not in that he reproduces himself), but he tries to escape the burden of his freedom by giving himself a spurious "immortality" in his children. He dominates woman both to imprison another consciousness that reflects his own and to provide him with children that are securely his (his fear of illegitimacy). The notions obviously have a considerable force. But they are very atemporal: it is not easy to see why socialism should modify the basic "ontological" desire for a thinglike freedom which Beauvoir sees as the motor behind the fixation with inheritance in the property system, or the enslavement of women that derived from it. In fact she has since criticized this aspect of her book for idealism: "I should take a more materialist position today in the first volume. I should base the notion of woman as *other* and the Manichean argument it entails not on an idealistic and a priori struggle of consciences, but on the facts of supply and demand. This modification would not necessitate any changes in the subsequent development of my argument." [12] Concurrent, however, with the idealist psychological explanation, Beauvoir uses an orthodox economist approach. This leads to a definite evolutionism in her treatment in Volume 1, which becomes a retrospective narrative of the different forms of the feminine condition in different societies through time —mainly in terms of the property system and its effects on women. To this she adds various suprahistorical themes—myths of the eternal feminine, types of women through the ages, literary treatments of women—which do not modify the fundamental structure of her argument. The prospect for women's liberation at the end is quite divorced from any historical development.

Thus, the classical literature on the problem of woman's condition is predominantly economist in emphasis, stressing her simple subordination to the institutions of private property. Her biological status underpins both her weakness as a producer, in work relations, and her importance as a possession, in reproductive relations. The fullest and most recent interpretation gives both factors a psychological cast. The framework of discussion is an evolutionist one that nevertheless fails noticeably to project a convincing image of the future, beyond asserting that socialism will involve the liberation of women as one of its constituent "moments."

What is the solution to this impasse? It must lie in differentiating woman's condition, much more radically than in the past, into its separate structures; which together form a complex—not a simple—unity. This will mean rejecting the idea that woman's condition can be deduced derivatively from the economy or equated symbolically with society. Rather, it must be seen as a *specific* structure, which is a unity of different elements. The variations of woman's condition throughout history will be the result of different combinations of these elements—much as Marx's analysis of the economy in *Precapitalist Economic Formations* is an account of the different combinations of the factors of production, not a linear narrative of economic development. Because the unity of woman's condition at any one time is the product of several structures, it is always "overdetermined."[13] The key structures can be listed as follows: Production, Reproduction, Sex, and Socialization of Children. The concrete combination of these produces the "complex unity" of her position, but each separate structure may have reached a different "moment" at any given historical time. Each then must be examined separately to see what the present unity is and how it might be changed. The discussion that follows does not pretend to give a historical account of each sector. It is only concerned with some general reflections on the different roles of women and some of their interconnections.

Production

The biological differentiation of the sexes and the division of labor have, throughout history, seemed an interlocked necessity. Anatomically smaller and weaker, woman's physiology and her psychobiological metabolism appear to render her a less useful member of a work force. It is always stressed how, particularly in the early stages of social development, man's physical superiority gave him the means of conquest over nature, which was denied to women. Once woman was accorded the menial tasks involved in maintenance while man undertook conquest and creation, she became an aspect of the things preserved: private property and children. All the socialist writers on the subject mentioned earlier—Marx, Engels, Bebel, Beauvoir—link the confirmation and continuation of woman's oppression after the establishment of her physical inferiority for hard manual work with the advent of private property.

But woman's physical weakness has never prevented her from performing work as such (quite apart from bringing up children)—only specific types of work, in specific societies. In primitive, ancient, oriental, medieval, and capitalist societies the *volume* of work performed by women has always been considerable; it is only its form that is in question. Domestic labor, even today is enormous if quantified in terms of productive labor.[14] In any case, women's physique has never permanently or even predominantly relegated them to menial domestic chores. In many peasant societies, women have worked in the fields as much as or more than men.

The assumption behind most classical discussion—that the crucial factor starting the whole development of feminine subordination was women's lesser capacity for demanding physical work—is in fact a major oversimplification. Even within these terms, in history it has been woman's lesser capacity for violence as well as for work that has determined her subordination. In most societies woman has not only been less able than man to perform arduous kinds of work; she has also been less able to fight. Man has the strength to assert himself not only against nature but also against his fellows. *Social coercion* has interplayed with the straightforward division of labor, based on biological capacity, to a much greater extent than is generally admitted. Of course, it may not be actualized as direct aggression. In primitive societies women's physical unsuitability for the hunt is evident. In agricultural societies where women's inferiority is socially instituted, they are given the arduous task of tilling and cultivation. For this, coercion is necessary. In developed civilizations and more complex societies women's physical deficiencies again become relevant. Women are no use either for war or in the construction of cities. But with early industrialization coercion once more becomes important. As Marx wrote: "Insofar as machinery dispenses with muscular power, it becomes a means of employing labourers of slight muscular strength, and those whose bodily development is incomplete, but whose limbs are all the more supple. The labour of women and children was, therefore, the first thing sought for by capitalists who used machinery."[15]

René Dumont points out that in many zones of tropical Africa today men are often idle, while women are forced to work all day.[16] This exploitation has no "natural" source whatever. Women may perform their "heavy" duties in contemporary African peasant societies not for fear of physical reprisal by their men but because these duties are "customary" and built into the role structures of the society. A further point is that coercion implies a different relationship from coercer to coerced than exploitation does. It is political rather than economic. In describing coercion, Marx said that the master treated the slave or serf as the "inorganic and natural condition of its own reproduction." That is to say, labor itself becomes like other natural things—cattle or soil: "The original conditions of production appear as natural prerequisites, *natural conditions of the existence of the producer,* just as his living body, however reproduced and developed by him, is not originally established by himself, but appears as his *prerequisite.*"[17] This is preeminently woman's condition. For far from woman's physical weakness removing her from productive work, her social weakness has in these cases evidently made her the major slave of it.

This truth, elementary though it may seem, has nevertheless been constantly ignored by writers on the subject, with the result that an illegitimate optimism creeps into their predictions of the future. For if it is just the biological incapacity for the hardest physical work that has determined the subordination of women, then the prospect of an advanced machine technology, abolishing the need for strenuous physical exertion, would seem to promise the liberation of women. For a moment industrialization itself thus seems to herald women's liberation. Engels, for instance, wrote: "The first premise for the emancipation of women is the reintroduction of the entire female sex into public industry. . . . And this has become possible only as a result of modern large-scale industry, which not only permits of the participation of women in production in large numbers, but actually calls for it and, moreover, strives to convert private domestic work also into a public industry."[18] What Marx said of early industrialism is no less, but also *no more* true of an automated society: "It is obvious that the fact of the collective working group being composed of individuals of both sexes and all ages, must necessarily, *under suitable conditions,* become a source of human development; although in its spontaneously developed, brutal, capitalistic form, where the labourer exists for the process of production, and not the process of production for the labourer that fact is a pestiferous source of corruption and slavery."[19] Industrial labor and automated technology both promise the preconditions for woman's liberation alongside man's—but no more than the preconditions. It is only too obvious that the advent of industrialization has not so far freed women in this sense, either in the West or in the East. In the West it is true that there was a great influx of women into jobs in the expanding industrial economy, but this soon leveled out, and there has been relatively little increase in recent decades. Beauvoir hoped that automation would make a decisive, qualitative difference by abolishing altogether the physical differential between the sexes. But any reliance on this in itself accords an independent role to technique which history does not justify. Under capitalism, automation could possibly lead to an ever growing structural unemployment that would expel women— the latest and least integrated recruits to the labor force and ideologically the most expendable for a bourgeois society—from production after only a brief interlude in it. Technology is mediated by the total social structure, and it is this that will determine woman's future in work relations.

Physical deficiency is not now, any more than in the past, a sufficient explanation of woman's relegation to inferior status. Coercion has been ameliorated to an ideology shared by both sexes. Commenting on the results of her questionnaire of working women, Viola Klein notes: "There is no trace of feminist egalitarianism—militant or otherwise—in any of the women's answers to our questionnaire; nor is it even implicitly assumed that women have a 'Right to Work.' "[20] Denied, or refusing, a role in *production*, woman does not even create the *pre*conditions of her liberation.

Reproduction

Women's absence from the critical sector of production historically, of course, has been caused not just by their physical weakness in a context of coercion but also by their role in reproduction. Maternity necessitates periodic withdrawals from work, but this is not a decisive phenomenon. It is rather women's role in reproduction that has become, in capitalist society at least, the spiritual "complement" of men's role in production.[21] Bearing children, bringing them up, and maintaining the home —these form the core of woman's natural vocation, in this ideology. This belief has attained great force because of the seeming universality of the family as a human institution. There is little doubt that Marxist analyses have underplayed the fundamental problems posed here. The complete failure to give any operative content to the slogan of "abolition" of the family is striking evidence of this (as well as of the vacuity of the notion). The void thus created has been quickly occupied by traditional beliefs such as Townsend's, quoted above.

The biological function of maternity is a universal, atemporal fact and as such has seemed to escape the categories of Marxist historical analysis. From it follows—apparently—the stability and omnipresence of the family, if in very different forms.[22] Once this is accepted, women's social subordination—however emphasized as an honorable but different role (compare the "separate but equal" ideologies of southern racists)—can be seen to follow inevitably as an *insurmountable* biohistorical fact. The causal chain then becomes Maternity, Family, Absence from Production and Public Life, Sexual Inequality.

The linchpin in this line of argument is the idea of the family. The notion that "family" and "society" are virtually coextensive terms, or that an advanced society not founded on the nuclear family is now inconceivable, is widespread. It can be seriously discussed only by asking just what the family is—or, rather, what women's role in the family is. Once this is done, the problem appears in quite a new light. For it is obvious that woman's role in the family—primitive, feudal, or bourgeois—partakes of three quite different structures: reproduction, sexuality, and the socialization of children. These are historically, not intrinsically, related to each other in the present modern family. Biological parentage is not necessarily identical with social parentage (adoption). It is thus essential to discuss not the family as an unanalyzed entity but the separate *structures* that today compose it but may tomorrow be decomposed into a new pattern.

Reproduction, it has been stressed, is a seemingly constant atemporal phenomenon—part of biology rather than history. In fact, this is an illusion. What is true is that the "mode of reproduction" does not vary with the "mode of production"; it can remain effectively the same through a number of different modes of production. For it has been defined till now by its uncontrollable, natural character. To this extent, it has been an unmodified biological fact. As long as reproduction remained a natural phenomenon, of course, women were effectively doomed to social exploitation. In any sense, they were not masters of a large part of their lives. They had no choice as to whether or how often they gave birth to children (apart from repeated abortion); their existence was essentially subject to biological processes outside their control.

Contraception

Contraception, which was invented as a rational technique only in the nineteenth century, was thus an innovation of world-historic importance. It is only now, in the form of "the pill," just beginning to show what immense consequences it could have. For what it means is that at last the mode of reproduction could potentially be transformed. Once childbearing becomes totally voluntary (how much so is it in the West, even today?), its significance is fundamentally different. It need no longer be the sole or ultimate vocation of woman; it becomes one option among others.

Marx sees history as the development of man's transformation of nature and thereby of himself—of human nature—in different modes of production. Today there are the technical possibilities for the humanization of the most natural part of human culture. This is what a change in the mode of reproduction could mean.

We are far from this state of affairs as yet. In France and Italy the sale of any form of contraception remains illegal. The oral contraceptive is the privilege of a moneyed minority in a few Western countries. Even here the progress has been realized in a typically conservative and exploitative form. It is made only for women, who are thus guinea pigs in a venture that involves both sexes.

The fact of overwhelming importance is that easily available contraception threatens to dissociate sexual from reproductive experience—which all contemporary bourgeois ideology tries to make inseparable, as the *raison d'être* of the family.

Reproduction and Production

At present, reproduction in our society is often a kind of sad mimicry of production. Work in a capitalist society is an alienation of labor in the making of a social product that is confiscated by capital. But it can still sometimes be a real act of creation, purposive and responsible, even in conditions of the worst exploitation. Maternity is often a caricature of this. The biological product—the child—is treated as if it were a solid product. Parenthood becomes a kind of substitute for work, an activity in which the child is seen as an object created by the mother, in the same way as a commodity is created by a worker. Naturally, the child does not literally escape, but the mother's alienation can be much worse than that of the worker whose product is appropriated by the boss. No human being can create another human being. A person's biological origin is an abstraction. The child as an autonomous person inevitably threatens the activity that claims to create it continually merely as a *possession* of the parent. Possessions are felt as extensions of the self. The child as a possession is supremely this. Anything the child does is therefore a threat to the mother herself, who has renounced her autonomy through this misconception of her reproductive role. There are few more precarious ventures on which to base a life.

Furthermore, even if the woman has emotional control over her child, legally and economically both she and it are subject to the father. The social cult of maternity is matched by the real socioeconomic powerlessness of the mother. The psychological and practical benefits men receive from this are obvious. The converse of women's quest for creation in the child is man's retreat from his work into the family: "When we come home, we lay aside our mask and drop our tools, and are no longer lawyers, sailors, soldiers, statesmen, clergymen, but only men. We fall again into our most human relations, which, after all, are the whole of what belongs to us as we are in ourselves."[23]

Unlike her nonproductive status, her capacity for maternity *is* a definition of woman. But it is only a physiological definition. So long as it is allowed to remain a substitute for action and creativity, and the home an area of relaxation for the man, woman will remain confined to the species, to her universal and natural condition.

Sexuality

Sexuality has traditionally been the most tabooed dimension of women's situation. The meaning of sexual freedom and its connexion with women's freedom is a particularly difficult subject which few socialist writers have cared to broach. Fourier alone identified the two totally, in lyrical strophes describing a sexual paradise of permutations—the famous phalansteries. "Socialist morality" in the Soviet Union for a long time debarred serious discussion of the subject within the world Communist movement. Marx himself—in this respect somewhat less liberal than Engels—early in his life expressed traditional views on the matter: "The sanctification of the sexual instinct through exclusivity, the checking of instinct by laws, the moral beauty which makes nature's commandment ideal in the form of an emotional bond—[this is] the spiritual essence of marriage."[24]

Yet it is obvious that throughout history women have been appropriated as sexual objects, as much as progenitors or producers. Indeed, the sexual relation can be assimilated to the statute of possession much more easily and completely than the productive or reproductive relationship. Contemporary sexual vocabulary bears eloquent witness to this—it is a comprehensive lexicon of reification. Later, Marx was well aware of it: "Marriage . . . is incontestably a form of exclusive private property."[25] But neither he nor his successors ever tried seriously to envisage the implications for socialism, or even for a structural analysis of women's condition. Communism, Marx stressed in the same passage, would not mean mere "communalisation" of women as common property. Beyond this, he never ventured.

Some historical considerations are in order here. For if socialists have said nothing, the gap has been filled by liberal ideologues. Wayland Young argues in a recent book, *Eros Denied*, that Western civilization has been uniquely repressive sexually, and in a plea for greater sexual freedom today, he compares it at some length with oriental and ancient societies. It is striking, however, that his book makes no reference whatever to women's status in these different societies, or to the different forms of marriage contract prevalent in them. This makes the whole argument a purely formal exercise—an obverse of socialist discussions of women's position that ignore the problem of sexual freedom and its meanings. For while it is true that certain oriental or ancient (and indeed primitive) cultures were much less puritan than Western societies, it is absurd to regard sexual freedom as a kind of "transposable value" that can be abstracted from its social structure. In effect, in many of these societies sexual openness was accompanied by a form of polygamous exploitation that made it in practice an expression simply of masculine domination. Since art was the province of man, too, this freedom found a natural and often powerful expression in art—which is often quoted as if it were evidence of the total quality of human relationships in the society. Nothing could be more misleading. What is necessary, rather than this naive, hortatory core of historical example, is some account of the covariation between the degrees of sexual liberty and openness and the position and dignity of women in different societies.

Some points are immediately obvious. The actual history is much more dialectical than any liberal account presents it. Unlimited juridical polygamy—whatever the sexualization of the culture that accompanies it—is clearly a total derogation of woman's autonomy and constitutes an extreme form of oppression. Ancient China is a perfect illustration. Wittfogel describes the extraordinary despotism of the Chinese *paterfamilias*—"a liturgical (semi-official) policeman of his kin group."[26] In the West, however, the advent of monogamy was in no sense an *absolute* improvement. It certainly did not create a one-to-one equality—far from it. Engels commented accurately: "Monogamy does not by any means make its appearance in history as the reconciliation of man and woman, still less as the highest form of such a reconciliation. On the contrary, it appears as the subjugation of one sex by the other, as the proclamation of a conflict between the sexes entirely unknown hitherto in prehistoric times."[27] But in the Christian era monogamy took on a very specific form in the West. It was allied with an unprecedented regime of general sexual repression which, in its Pauline version, had a markedly antifeminine bias, inherited from Judaism. With time, this became diluted—feudal society, despite its subsequent reputation for asceticism, practiced formal monogamy with considerable actual acceptance of polygamous behavior, at least within the ruling class. But here again the extent of sexual freedom was only an index of masculine domination. In England, the truly major change occurred in the sixteenth century with the rise of militant puritanism and the increase of market relations in the economy. Lawrence Stone observes: "In practice, if not in theory, the early sixteenth-century nobility was a polygamous society, and some contrived to live with a succession of women despite the official prohibition on divorce. . . . But impressed by Calvinist criticisms of the double standard, in the late sixteenth century public opinion began to object to the open maintenance of a mistress."[28] Capitalism and the attendant demands of the newly emergent bourgeoisie accorded woman a new status as wife and mother. Her legal rights improved; there was vigorous controversy over her social position; wife-beating was condemned. "In a woman the bourgeois man is looking for a counterpart, not an equal."[29] At the social periphery woman did occasionally achieve an equality that was more than her feminine function in a market society. In the extreme sects women often had completely equal rights: Fox argued that the Redemption restored prelapsarian equality, and Quaker women thereby gained a real autonomy. But once most of the sects were institutionalized, the need for family discipline was reemphasized and women's obedience with it. As Keith Thomas says, the Puritans "had done something to raise women's status, but not really very much."[30] The patriarchal system was retained and maintained by the economic mode of production. The transition to complete effective monogamy accompanied the transition to modern bourgeois society as we know it today. Like the market system itself it represented a historic advance, at great historic cost. The formal, juridical equality of capitalist society and capitalist rationality now applied as much to the marital as to the labor contract. In both cases, nominal parity masks real exploitation and inequality. But in both cases, the formal equality is itself a certain progress, which can help to make possible a further advance.

For the situation today is defined by a new contradiction. Once formal conjugal equality (monogamy) is established, sexual freedom as such— which under polygamous conditions was usually a form of exploitation— becomes, conversely, a possible force for liberation. It then means, simply, the freedom for both sexes to transcend the limits of present sexual institutions.

Historically, then, there has been a dialectical movement in which sexual expression was "sacrificed" in an epoch of more or less puritan repression, which nevertheless produced a greater parity of sexual roles, which in turn creates the precondition for a genuine sexual liberation in the dual sense of equality *and* freedom—whose unity defines socialism.

This movement can be verified within the history of the "sentiments." The cult of *love* emerged only in the twelfth century in opposition to legal marital forms and with a heightened valorization of women (courtly love). Gradually thereafter it became diffused and assimilated to marriage as such, which in its bourgeois form (romantic love) became a *free* choice for *life*. What is striking here is that monogamy, as an institution in the West, anticipated the idea of love by many centuries. The two have subsequently been officially harmonized, but the tension between them has never been abolished. There is a formal contradiction between the voluntary contractual character of "marriage" and the spontaneous uncontrollable character of "love"—the passion that is celebrated precisely for its involuntary force. The notion that it occurs only once in every life and can therefore be integrated into a voluntary contract becomes decreasingly plausible in the light of everyday experience—once sexual repression as a psycho-ideological system becomes at all relaxed.

Obviously, the main breach in the traditional value pattern has so far been the increase in premarital sexual experience. This is now virtually legitimized in contemporary bourgeois society. But its implications are explosive for the ideological conception of marriage that dominates this society: that of an exclusive and permanent bond. A recent American anthology, *The Family and the Sexual Revolution*, reveals this very clearly: "As far as extramarital relations are concerned, the anti-sexualists are still fighting a strong, if losing, battle. The very heart of the Judeo-Christian sex ethic is that men and women shall remain virginal until marriage and that they shall be completely faithful after marriage. In regard to premarital chastity, this ethic seems clearly on the way out, and in many segments of the populace is more and more becoming a dead letter." [31]

The current wave of sexual liberalization, in the present context, could become conducive to the greater general freedom of women. Equally, it could presage new forms of oppression. The puritan-bourgeois creation of woman as "counterpart" produced the *precondition* for emancipation. But it gave statutory legal equality to the sexes at the cost of greatly intensified repression. Subsequently—like private property itself—it has become a brake on the further development of a free sexuality. Capitalist market relations have historically been a precondition of socialism; bourgeois marital relations (contrary to the denunciation of the *Communist Manifesto*) may equally be a precondition of women's liberation.

Socialization

Woman's biological destiny as mother becomes a cultural vocation in her role as socializer of children. In bringing up children, woman achieves her main social definition. Her suitability for socialization springs from her physiological condition: her ability to lactate and occasionally relative inability to undertake strenuous work loads. It should be said at the outset that suitability is not inevitability. Lévi-Strauss writes: "In every human group, women give birth to children and take care of them, and men rather have as their speciality hunting and warlike activities. Even there, though, we have ambiguous cases: of course, men never give birth to babies, but in many societies . . . they are made to act as if they did."[32] Evans-Pritchard's description of the Nuer tribe depicts just such a situation. And another anthropologist, Margaret Mead, comments on the element of wish fulfillment in the assumption of a *natural* correlation of femininity and nurturance: "We have assumed that because it is convenient for a mother to wish to care for her child, this is a trait with which women have been more generously endowed by a careful teleological process of evolution. We have assumed that because men have hunted, an activity requiring enterprise, bravery, and initiative, they have been endowed with these useful aptitudes as part of their sex-temperament."[33] However, the cultural allocation of roles in bringing up children—and the limits of its variability—is not the essential problem for consideration. What is much more important is to analyze the nature of the socialization process itself and its requirements.

Talcott Parsons in his detailed analysis claims that it is essential for the child to have two "parents": one who plays an "expressive" role, and one who plays an "instrumental" role.[34] The nuclear family revolves around the two axes of generational hierarchy and of these two roles. In typically Parsonian idiom, he claims that "at least one fundamental feature of the external situation of social systems—here a feature of the physiological organism—is a crucial reference point for differentiation in the family. This lies in the division of organisms into lactating and non-lactating classes." In all groups, he and his colleagues assert, even in those primitive tribes discussed by Pritchard and Mead, the male plays the instrumental role *in relation* to the wife-mother. At one stage the mother plays an instrumental and expressive role vis-à-vis her infant: this is pre-Oedipally when she is the source of approval and disapproval as well as of love and care. However, after this, the father or male substitute (in matrilineal societies, the mother's brother) takes over. In a modern industrial society two types of role are clearly important: the adult familial roles in the family of procreation, and the adult occupational role. The function of the family as such reflects the function of the women within it; it is primarily expressive. The persons playing the integrative-adaptive-expressive role cannot be off all the time on instrumental-occupational errands—hence there is a built-in inhibition of the woman's work outside the home. Parson's analysis makes clear the exact role of the maternal socializer in contemporary American society.[35] It fails to go on to state that other aspects and modes of socialization are conceivable. What is valuable in Parsons' work is simply his insistence on the central importance of socialization as a process which is constitutive of any society (no Marxist has so far provided a comparable analysis). His general conclusion is that "it seems to be without serious qualification the opinion of competent personality psychologists that, though personalities differ greatly in their degrees of rigidity, certain broad fundamental patterns of 'character' are laid down in childhood (so far as they are not genetically inherited) and are not radically changed by adult experience. The exact degree to which this is the case or the exact age levels at which plasticity becomes greatly diminished, are not at issue here. The important thing is the fact of childhood character formation and its relative stability after that.[36]

Infancy

This seems indisputable. One of the great revolutions of modern psychology has been the discovery of the decisive specific weight of infancy in the course of an individual life—a psychic time disproportionately greater than the chronological time. Freud began the revolution with his work on infantile sexuality; Klein radicalized it with her work on the first year of the infant's life. The result is that today we know far more than ever before how delicate and precarious a process the passage from birth to childhood is for everyone. The fate of the adult personality can be largely decided in the initial months of life. The preconditions for the later stability and integration demand an extraordinary degree of care and intelligence on the part of the adult who is socializing the child, as well as a persistence through time of the same person.

These undoubted advances in the scientific understanding of childhood have been widely used as an argument to reassert women's quintessential maternal function, at a time when the traditional family has seemed increasingly eroded. John Bowlby, studying evacuee children in World War II, declared: "Essential for mental health is that the infant and young child should experience a warm, intimate and continuous relationship with his mother,"[37] setting a trend that has become cumulative since. The emphasis of familial ideology has shifted away from a cult of the biological ordeal of maternity (the pain that makes the child precious, and so on) to a celebration of mother care as a social act. This can reach ludicrous extremes: "For the mother, breast-feeding becomes a complement to the act of creation. It gives her a heightened sense of fulfilment and allows her to participate in a relationship as close to perfection as any that a woman can hope to achieve. . . . The simple fact of giving birth, however, does not of itself fulfil this need and longing. . . . Motherliness is a way of life. It enables a woman to express her total self with the tender feelings, the protective attitude the encompassing love of the motherly woman."[38] The tautologies, the mystifications (an *act* of creation; a *process* surely?) the sheer absurdities —"as close to perfection as any woman can hope to achieve"—point to the gap between reality and ideology.

Familial Patterns

This ideology corresponds in dislocated form to a real change in the pattern of the family. As the family has become smaller, each child has become more important; the actual *act* of reproduction occupies less and less time, and the socializing and nurturance processes increase commensurately in significance. Bourgeois society is obsessed by the physical, moral, and sexual problems of childhood and adolescence.[39] Ultimate responsibility for these is placed on the mother. Thus the mother's "maternal" role has retreated as her socializing role has increased. In the 1890s in England a mother spent fifteen years in a state of pregnancy and lactation; in the 1960s she spends an average of four years. Compulsory schooling from the age of five, of course, reduces the maternal function very greatly after the initial vulnerable years.

The present situation is then one in which the qualitative importance of socialization during the early years of the child's life has acquired a much greater significance than in the past—while the quantitative amount of a mother's life spent in either gestation or child rearing has greatly diminished. It follows that socialization cannot simply be elevated to the woman's new maternal vocation. Used as a mystique, it becomes an instrument of oppression. Moreover, there is no inherent reason why the biological and social mother should coincide. The process of socialization is, in the Kleinian sense, invariable—but the person of the socializer can vary.

Bruno Bettelheim, observing kibbutz methods, notes that the child who is reared by a trained nurse (though normally maternally breastfed) does not suffer the backwash of typical parental anxieties and thus may positively gain by the system.[40] This possibility should not be fetishized in its turn (Jean Baby, speaking of the post-four-year-old child, goes so far as to say that "complete separation appears indispensable to guarantee the liberty of the child as well as of the mother.")[41] But what it does reveal is the viability of plural forms of socialization—not necessarily tied to the nuclear family or to the biological parent.

Conclusion

The lesson of these reflections is that the liberation of women can be achieved only if *all four* structures in which they are integrated are transformed. A modification of any one of them can be offset by a reinforcement of another, so that mere permutation of the form of exploitation is achieved. The history of the last sixty years provides ample evidence of this. In the early twentieth century, militant feminism in England or the United States surpassed the labor movement in the violence of its assault on bourgeois society, in pursuit of suffrage. This political right was eventually won. Nonetheless, though a simple completion of the formal legal equality of bourgeois society, it left the socioeconomic situation of women virtually unchanged. The wider legacy of the suffrage was nil: the suffragettes proved quite unable to move beyond their own initial demands, and many of their leading figures later became extreme reactionaries.

The Russian Revolution produced a quite different experience. In the Soviet Union in the 1920s, advanced social legislation aimed at liberating women, above all, in the field of sexuality: divorce was made free and automatic for either partner, thus effectively liquidating marriage; illegitimacy was abolished, abortion was free, and so on. The social and demographic effects of these laws in a backward, semiliterate society bent on rapid industrialization (needing, therefore, a high birth rate) were—predictably —catastrophic. Stalinism soon produced a restoration of iron traditional norms. Inheritance was reinstated, divorce became inaccessible, abortion illegal. "The State cannot exist without the family. Marriage is a positive value for the Socialist Soviet State only if the partners see in it a lifelong union. So-called free love is a bourgeois invention and has nothing in common with the principles of conduct of a Soviet citizen. Moreover, marriage receives its full value for the State only if there is progeny, and the consorts experience the highest happiness of parenthood," wrote the official journal of the Commissariat of Justice in 1939.[42] Women still retained the right and obligation to work, but because these gains had not been integrated into the earlier attempts to abolish the family and free sexuality, no general liberation occurred.

In China, still another experience is being played out today. At a comparable stage of the revolution, all the emphasis is being placed on liberating women in *production*. This has produced an impressive social promotion of women. But it has been accompanied by a tremendous repression of sexuality and a rigorous puritanism (currently rampant in civic life). This corresponds not only to the need to mobilize women massively in economic life but to a deep cultural reaction against the corruption and prostitution prevalent in Imperial and Kuo Ming Tang China (a phenomenon unlike anything in Czarist Russia). Because the exploitation of women was so great in the *ancien régime*, women's participation at village level in the Chinese Revolution was uniquely high. As for reproduction, for demographic reasons, the Russian cult of maternity in the 1930s and 1940s has not been repeated; indeed, China may be one of the first countries in the world to provide free, state-authorized contraception to the population on a universal scale. Again, however, given the low level of industrialization and fear produced by imperialist encirclement, no all-round advance could be expected.

It is only in the highly developed societies of the West that an authentic liberation of women can be envisaged today. But for this to occur, there must be a transformation of all the structures into which they are integrated, and an *unité de rupture*.[43] A revolutionary movement must base its analysis on the uneven development of each and attack the weakest link in the combination. This may then become the point of departure for a general transformation. What is the situation of the different structures today?

Status of the Structures

1. PRODUCTION. The long-term development of the forces of production must command any socialist perspective. The hopes that the advent of machine technology raised as early as the nineteenth century have already been discussed. They proved illusory. Today, automation promises the *technical* possibility of abolishing completely the physical differential between man and woman in production, but under capitalist relations of production the *social* possibility of this abolition is permanently threatened and can easily be turned into its opposite: the actual diminution of woman's role in production as the labor force contracts.

This concerns the future. For the present, the main fact to register is that woman's role in production is virtually stationary and has been so for a long time now. In England in 1911, women made up 30 percent of the work force; in the 1960s, 34 percent. The composition of these jobs has not changed decisively either. The jobs are very rarely "careers." When they are not in the lowest positions on the factory floor, they are normally in white-collar auxiliary positions such as secretarial work—supportive to masculine roles. They are often jobs with a high "expressive" content, such as "service" tasks. Parsons says bluntly: "Within the occupational organisation they are analogous to the wife-mother role in the family."[44] The educational system underpins this role structure: 75 percent of eighteen-year-old girls in England are receiving neither training nor education today. The pattern of "instrumental" father and "expressive" mother is not substantially changed when the woman is gainfully employed, as her job tends to be inferior to that of the man's, to which the family then adapts.

Thus, in all essentials, work as such—of the amount and type effectively available today—has not proved a salvation for women.

2. REPRODUCTION. Scientific advance in contraception could, as we have seen, make involuntary reproduction—which accounts for the vast majority of births in the world today, and for a major proportion even in the West—a phenomenon of the past. But oral contraception, which has so far been developed in a form that exactly repeats the sexual inequality of Western society, is only at its beginnings. It is inadequately distributed across classes and countries and awaits further technical improvements. Its main initial impact is, in the advanced countries, likely to be psychological—it will certainly free women's sexual experience from many of the anxieties and inhibitions that have always afflicted it.[45] It will definitely divorce sexuality from procreation as necessary complements.

The demographic pattern of reproduction in the West may or may not be widely affected by oral contraception. One of the most striking phenomena of very recent years in the United States has been the sudden increase in the birth rate. In the last decade it has been higher than that of under-developed countries such as India, Pakistan, and Burma. In fact, this reflects simply the lesser economic burden of a large family in conditions of economic boom in the richest country in the world. But it also reflects the magnification of familial ideology as a social force. This leads to the next structure.

3. SOCIALIZATION. The changes in the composition of the work force, the size of the family, the structure of education, and so on—however limited from an ideal standpoint—have undoubtedly diminished the societal function and importance of the family. As an organization it is not

a significant unit in the political power system; it plays little part in economic production; and it is rarely the sole agency of integration into the larger society. Thus at the macroscopic level it serves very little purpose.

The result has been a major displacement of emphasis on to the family's psychosocial function, for the infant and for the couple.[46] Parsons writes: "The trend of the evidence points to the beginning of the relative stabilisation of a *new* type of family structure in a new relation to a general social structure, one in which the family is more specialised than before, but not in any general sense less important, because the society is dependent *more* exclusively on it for the performance of *certain* of its vital functions.[47] The vital nucleus of truth in the emphasis on socialization of the child has been discussed. It is essential that socialists should acknowledge it and integrate it entirely into any program for the liberation of women. It is noticeable that recent "vanguard" work by French Marxists—Baby, Sullerot, Texier —accords the problem its real importance. However, there is no doubt that the need for permanent, intelligent care of children in the initial three or four years of their lives can be (and has been) exploited ideologically to perpetuate the family as a total unit, when its other functions have been visibly declining. Indeed, the attempt to focus women's existence exclusively on bringing up children is manifestly harmful to children. Socialization as an exceptionally delicate process requires a serene and mature socializer— a type that the frustrations of a *purely* familial role are not likely to produce. Exclusive maternity is often in this sense counterproductive. The mother discharges her own frustrations and anxieties in a fixation on the child. An increased awareness of the critical importance of socialization, far from leading to a restitution of classical maternal roles, should lead to a reconsideration of them—of what makes a good socializing agent, who can genuinely provide security and stability for the child.

The same arguments apply, a fortiori, to the psychosocial role of the family for the couple. The belief that the family provides an impregnable enclave of intimacy and security in an atomized and chaotic cosmos assumes the absurd—that the family can be isolated from the community and that its internal relationships will not reproduce in their own terms the external relationships that dominate the society. The family as refuge in a bourgeois society inevitably becomes a reflection of it.

4. SEXUALITY. It is difficult not to conclude that the major structure which at present is in rapid evolution is sexuality. Production, reproduction, and socialization are all more or less stationary in the West today, in the sense that they have not changed for three or more decades. There is, moreover, no widespread *demand* for changes in them on the part of women themselves—the governing ideology has effectively prevented criti-

cal consciousness. By contrast, the dominant sexual ideology is proving less and less successful in regulating spontaneous behavior. Marriage in its classical form is increasingly threatened by the liberalization of relationships before and after it, which affects all classes today. In this sense, it is evidently the weak link in the chain—the particular structure that is the site of the most contradictions. The progressive potential of these contradictions has already been emphasized. In a context of juridical equality, the liberation of sexual experience from relations that are extraneous to it—whether procreation or property—could lead to true inter-sexual freedom. But it could also lead simply to new forms of neocapitalist ideology and practice. For one of the forces behind the current acceleration of sexual freedom has undoubtedly been the conversion of contemporary capitalism from a production-and-work ethos to a consumption-and-fun ethos.

Riesman commented on this development early in the 1950s: "There is not only a growth of leisure, but work itself becomes both less interesting and less demanding for many . . . more than before, as job-mindedness declines, sex permeates the daytime as well as the playtime consciousness. It is viewed as a consumption good not only by the old leisure classes, but by the modern leisure masses."[48] The gist of Riesman's argument is that in a society bored by work, sex is the only activity, the only reminder of one's energies, the only competitive act; the last defense against *vis inertiae*. This same insight can be found, with greater theoretical depth, in Marcuse's notion of "repressive de-sublimation"—the freeing of sexuality for its own frustration in the service of a totally coordinated and drugged social machine.[49] Bourgeois society at present can well afford a play area of premarital *non*procreative sexuality. Even marriage can save itself by increasing divorce and remarriage rates, signifying the importance of the institution itself.

These considerations make it clear that sexuality, while it may at present contain the greatest potential for liberation, can equally well be organized against any increase of its human possibilities. New forms of reification are emerging that may void sexual freedom of any meaning. This is a reminder that while one structure may be the *weak link* in a unity like that of woman's condition, there can never be a solution through it alone. The utopianism of Fourier or Wilhelm Reich was precisely to think that sexuality could inaugurate such a general solution. Lenin's remark to Clara Zetkin is a salutary if overstated corrective: "However wild and revolutionary [sexual freedom] may be, it is still really quite bourgeois. It is, mainly, a hobby of the intellectuals and of the sections nearest them. There is no place for it in the Party, in the class-conscious, fighting, proletariat."[50] For a general solution can be found only in a strategy that affects *all* the structures of women's exploitation. This means a rejection of two beliefs prevalent on the left:

The first, *reformism*, now takes the form of limited ameliorative demands: equal pay for women, more nursery schools, better retraining facilities, and so on. In its contemporary version it is wholly divorced from any fundamental critique of women's condition or any vision of their real liberation (it was not always so). Insofar as it represents a tepid embellishment of the status quo, it has very little progressive content.

The second, *voluntarism*, takes the form of maximalist demands—the abolition of the family, abrogation of all sexual restrictions, forceful separation of parents from children—which have no chance of winning any wide support at present, and which merely serve as a substitute for the job of theoretical analysis or practical persuasion. By pitching the whole subject in totally intransigent terms, voluntarism objectively helps to maintain it outside the framework of normal political discussion.

What, then, is the responsible revolutionary attitude? It must include both immediate and fundamental demands in a single critique of the *whole* of women's situation, that does not fetishize any dimension of it. Modern industrial development, as has been seen, tends toward the separating out of the originally unified function of the family—procreation, socialization, sexuality, economic subsistence, and so on—even if this "structural differentiation" (to use Parsons' term) has been checked and disguised by the maintenance of a powerful family ideology. This differentiation provides the real historical basis for the ideal demands that should be posed; structural differentiation is precisely what distinguishes an advanced from a primitive society (in which all social functions are fused *en bloc*).[51]

In practical terms this means a coherent system of demands. The four elements of women's condition cannot merely be considered each in isolation; they form a structure of specific interrelations. The contemporary bourgeois family can be seen as a triptych of sexual, reproductive, and socializatory functions (the woman's world) embraced by production (the man's world)—precisely a structure that in the final instance is determined by the economy. The exclusion of women from production—social human activity—and their confinement to a monolithic condensation of functions in a unity, the family, which is precisely unified in the *natural part* of each function is the root cause of the contemporary *social* definition of women as *natural* beings. Hence the main thrust of any emancipation movement must still concentrate on the economic element—the entry of women fully into public industry. The error of the old socialists was to see the other elements as reducible to the economic; hence, the call for the entry of women into production was accompanied by the purely abstract slogan of the abolition of the family. Economic demands are still primary but must be accompanied by coherent policies for the other three elements, policies that may at particular junctures take over the primary role in immediate action.

Economically, the most elementary demand is not the right to work or to receive equal pay for work—the two traditional reformist demands—but *the right to equal work itself*. At present, women perform unskilled, uncreative service jobs that can be regarded as "extensions" of their expressive familial role. They are overwhelmingly waitresses, office cleaners, hairdressers, clerks, typists. In the working class, occupational mobility is thus sometimes easier for girls than boys—they can enter the white-collar sector at a lower level. But only two in a hundred women are in administrative or managerial jobs, and less than five in a thousand are in the professions. Women are poorly unionized (25 percent) and receive less money than men for the manual work they do perform: in 1961 the average industrial wage for women was less than half that for men, which, even setting off part-time work, represents a massive increment of exploitation for the employer.

Education

The whole pyramid of discrimination rests on a solid extra-economic foundation—education. The demand for equal work, in Britain, should above all take the form of a demand for an *equal educational system*, since this is at present the main single filter selecting women for inferior work roles. Currently, there is something like equal education for both sexes up to age fifteen. Thereafter, three times more boys than girls continue their education. Only one in four university students is a girl. There is no evidence whatever of progress: the proportion of girl university students is the same as it was in the 1920s. Until these injustices are ended, there is no chance of equal work for women. It goes without saying that the content of the educational system, which actually instills limitation of aspiration in girls, needs to be changed as much as methods of selection. Education is probably the key area for immediate economic advance at present.

Only if it is founded on equality can production be truly differentiated from reproduction and the family. But this in turn requires a whole set of noneconomic demands as a complement. Reproduction, sexuality, and socialization also need to be free from coercive forms of unification. Traditionally, the socialist movement has called for the "abolition of the bourgeois family." This slogan must be rejected as incorrect today. It is maximalist in the bad sense, posing a demand that is merely a negation without any coherent construction subsequent to it. Its weakness can be seen by comparing it to the call for the abolition of the private ownership of the means of production, whose solution—social ownership—is contained in the negation itself. Marx himself allied the two demands and pointed out their equal futility: "This tendency to oppose general private property to private property is expressed in animal form; *marriage* . . . is contrasted with the community of women, in which women become communal and common property."[52] The reason for the historic weakness of the notion is that the family was never analyzed structurally—in terms of its different functions. It was a hypostasized entity; the abstraction of its abolition corresponds to the abstraction of its conception.

The strategic concern for socialists should be for the equality of the sexes, not the abolition of the family. The consequences of this demand are no less radical, but they are concrete and positive and can be integrated into the real course of history. The family as it exists at present is, in fact, incompatible with the equality of the sexes. But this equality will come not from its administrative abolition but from the historical differentiation of its functions. The revolutionary demand should be for the liberation of these functions from a monolithic fusion that oppresses each. Dissociation of reproduction from sexuality frees sexuality from alienation in unwanted reproduction (and fear of it), and reproduction from subjugation to chance and uncontrollable causality. It is thus an elementary demand to press for free state provision of oral contraception. The legalization of homosexuality—which is one of the forms of nonreproductive sexuality—should be supported for just the same reason, and regressive campaigns against it in Cuba or elsewhere should be unhesitatingly criticized. The straightforward abolition of illegitimacy as a legal notion, as in Sweden and Russia, has a similar implication: it would separate marriage civically from parenthood.

From Nature to Culture

The problem of socialization poses more difficult questions, as has been seen. But the need for intensive maternal care in the early years of a child's life does not mean that the present single sanctioned form of socialization—marriage and family—is inevitable. Far from it. The fundamental characteristic of the present system of marriage and family is in our society its *monolithism:* there is only one institutionalized form of intersexual or intergenerational relationship possible. It is that or nothing. This is why it is essentially a denial of life. For all human experience shows that intersexual and intergenerational relationships are infinitely various—indeed, much of our creative literature is a celebration of the fact—while the institutionalized expression of them in our capitalist society is utterly simple and rigid. It is the poverty and simplicity of the institutions in this area of life that are such an oppression. Any society will require some institutionalized and social recognition of personal relationships. But there is absolutely no reason why there should be only one legitimized form— and a multitude of unlegitimized experiences. Socialism should properly mean not the abolition of the family but the diversification of the socially acknowledged relationships that are today forcibly and rigidly compressed into it. This would mean a plural range of institutions—whereas the family is only one, and its abolition implies none. Couples living together or not living together, long-term unions with children, single parents bringing up children, children socialized by conventional rather than biological parents, extended kin groups—all these could be encompassed in a range of institutions matching the free invention and variety of men and women.

It would be illusory to try to specify these institutions. Circumstantial accounts of the future are idealist and, worse, static. Socialism will be a process of change, of becoming. A fixed image of the future is in the worst sense ahistorical; the form that socialism takes will depend on the prior type of capitalism and the nature of its collapse. As Marx wrote: "What [is progress] if not the absolute elaboration of [man's] creative dispositions, without any preconditions other than antecedent historical evolution which makes the totality of this evolution—i.e., the evolution of all human powers as such, unmeasured by any *previously established* yardstick—an end in itself? What is this, if not a situation where man does not reproduce himself in any determined form, but produces his totality? Where he does not seek to remain something formed by the past, but is the absolute movement of becoming?"[53] The liberation of women under socialism will not be "rational" but a human achievement, in the long passage from Nature to Culture that is the definition of history and society.

Notes

1. Peter Townsend, *A Society for People*, in *Conviction*, ed. Norman Mackenzie (1958), 119–20.

2. August Bebel, *Die Frau und der Sozialismus* (1883), trans. H. B. Adams Walther, *Woman in the Past, Present, and Future* (1885), p. 113.

3. Charles Fourier, *Théorie des quatre mouvements*, in *Oeuvres complètes* (1841), 1:195; cited in Karl Marx, *The Holy Family* (1845, trans. 1956), 259.

4. Karl Marx, *Private Property and Communism* (1844), in *Early Writings*, trans. T. B. Bottomore (1963), 154.

5. Karl Marx, *The German Ideology* (1845–46, trans. 1965), 192–93.

6. Karl Marx, *Capital* (1867), ed. 1961, 1:490.

7. Friedrich Engels, *The Origin of the Family, Private Property, and the State* (1884), in Marx-Engels, *Selected Works* (1962), 11:225.

8. Ibid., 311.

9. Ibid., 233.

10. Bebel, *Die Frau*, 7.

11. V. I. Lenin, *The Tasks of the Proletariat*, in *Our Revolution* (1917), in *Collected Works*, 24:70.

12. Simone de Beauvoir, *Force of Circumstance* (1965), 192.

13. See Louis Althusser, *Contradiction et surdétermination*, in *Pour Marx* (1965). Althusser advances the notion of a complex totality in which each independent sector has its own autonomous reality but each of which is ultimately, but only ultimately, determined by the economic. This complex totality means that no contradiction in society is ever simple. As each sector can move at a different pace, the synthesis of the different time scales in the total social structure means that contradictions sometimes cancel each other out and sometimes reinforce one another. To describe this complexity, Althusser uses the Freudian term "overdetermination." The phrase "*unité de rupture*" (mentioned below) refers to the moment when the contradictions so reinforce one another as to coalesce into the conditions for a revolutionary change.

14. Apologists who make out that housework, though time-consuming, is light and relatively enjoyable are refusing to acknowledge the null and degrading routine it entails. Lenin commented crisply, "You all know that even when women have full rights, they still remain factually down-trodden because all housework is left to them. In most cases housework is the most unproductive, the most barbarous and the most arduous work a woman can do. It is exceptionally petty and does not include anything that would in any way promote the development of the woman" (*Collected Works*, 30:43). It has been calculated in Sweden that 2,340 million hours a year are spent by women in housework, compared with 1,290 million hours in industry. The Chase Manhattan Bank estimated a woman's overall working hours as averaging 99.6 per week.

15. Marx, *Capital*, 394.

16. "The African woman experiences a threefold servitude: through forced marriage; through her dowry and polygamy, which increases the leisure time of men and simultaneously their social prestige; and finally through the very unequal division of labour": René Dumont, *L'Afrique noire est mal partie* (1962), 210.

17. Marx, *Precapitalist Economic Formations*, 87.

18. Engels, *Origin of the Family*, 2:233, 311.

19. Marx, *Capital*, 1:394.

20. Viola Klein, *Working Wives*, Institute of Personnel Management Occasional Papers No. 15 (1960), 13.

21. Maternity is *the* distinctive feature on which both sexes base their hopes: for oppression or liberation. The notion of woman's potential superiority on account of her procreative function reaches the absurd in Margherita Repetto, *Maternità e famiglia: Condizioni per la libertà della donna, rivista trimestrale* 11–12 (1964), but is found even in Evelyne Sullerot, *Demain les femmes* (1965).

22. Philippe Ariès in *Centuries of Childhood* (1962) shows that though the family may in some form always have existed, it was often submerged under more forceful structures. In fact, according to Ariès it has only acquired its present significance with the advent of industrialization.

23. J.A. Froude, *Nemesis of Faith* (1849), 103.

24. Karl Marx, *Chapitre de marriage*, in *Oeuvres complètes* (ed. Molitor), *Oeuvres philosophiques*, 1:25.

25. Marx, *Private Property and Communism*, 153.

26. Karl Wittfogel, *Oriental Despotism* (1957), 116.

27. Engels, *Origin of the Family*, 2:224.

28. Lawrence Stone, *The Crisis of the Aristocracy* (1965), 663–64.

29. Simone de Beauvoir, *La marche longue* (1957), trans. *The Long March* (1958), 141.

30. Keith Thomas, "Women and the Civil War Sects," *Past and Present* No. 13 (1958): 43.

31. Albert Ellis, *The Folklore of Sex*, in *The Family and the Sexual Revolution*, ed. E. M. Schur (1964), 35.

32. Claude Lévi-Strauss, *The Family*, in *Man, Culture, and Society*, ed. H. L. Shapiro (1956), 274.

33. Margaret Mead, *Sex and Temperament*, in Schur, *The Family and the Sexual Revolution*, 207–8.

34. Talcott Parsons and Robert F. Bales, *Family, Socialization, and Interaction Process* (1956), 313. "The instrumental-expressive distinction we interpret as essentially the differentiation of function, and hence of relative influence, in terms of 'external' vs. 'internal' functions of the system. The area of instrumental function concerns relations of the system to its situation outside the system, to meeting the adaptive conditions of its maintenance of equilibrium, and 'instrumentally' establishing the desired relations to *external* goal-objects. The expressive area concerns the 'internal' affairs of the system, the maintenance of integrative relations between the members, and regulation of the patterns and tension levels of its component units" (ibid., 47).

35. One of Parsons's main theoretical innovations is his contention that what the child strives to internalize will vary with the content of the reciprocal role relationships in which he is a participant. R. D. Laing, in *Family and Individual Structure* (1966), contends that a child may internalize an entire system—i.e. "the family."

36. Talcott Parsons, *The Social System* (1952), 227.

37. John Bowlby, cited in Bruno Bettelheim, *Does Communal Education Work? The Case of the Kibbutz*, in Schur, *The Family and the Sexual Revolution*, 295.

38. Betty Ann Countrywoman, in *Redbook*, June 1960, cited in Betty Friedan, *The Feminine Mystique* (1963), 58.

39. David Riesman, while correctly observing this, makes a rather vain criticism of it. "There has been a tendency in current social research, influenced as it is by psychoanalysis, to over-emphasize and over-generalize the importance of very early childhood in character formation. . . . It is increasingly recognized, however, that character may change greatly after this early period. . . . Cultures differ widely not only in their timing of the various steps in character formation but also in the agents they rely on at each step": *The Lonely Crowd* (1950), 38–39.

40. Bettelheim, *Does Communal Education Work?* 303.

41. Jean Baby: *Un monde meilleur* (1964), 99.

42. *Sotsialisticheskaya Zakonnost* (1939. No. 2), cited in N. Timasheff, *The Attempt to Abolish the Family in Russia*, in *The Family*, ed. N. W. Bell and E. F. Vogel (1960), 59.

43. See Louis Althusser, *Contradiction*.

44. Parsons and Bales, *Family*, 15n.

45. Jean Baby records the results of an inquiry carried out into attitudes to marriage, contraception, and abortion of 3,191 women in Czechoslovakia in 1959: 80

percent of the women had limited sexual satisfaction because of fear of conception. (*Un monde meilleur*, 82n).

46. See Berger and Kellner, Marriage and the Construction of Reality, *Diogenes*, Summer 1964, for analyses of marriage and parenthood "nomic-building" structure.

47. Parsons and Bales, *Family*, 9–10.

48. Riesman, *Lonely Crowd*, 154.

49. Marcuse offers the prospect of a leisure society produced by automation and the consequent shift from a Promethean to an Orphic ethos (eroticism over work effort); he sees in this the true liberation of sexual energy for its own aesthetic end. Though he illustrates the difference (*Eros and Civilization*, 1955), this notion is too close to images of primitive societies dominated by the aura of maternal relaxation: "Satisfaction . . . would be *without toil*—that is, without the rule of alienated labour over the human existence. Under primitive conditions, alienation has *not yet* arisen because of the primitive character of the needs themselves, the rudimentary (personal or sexual) character of the division of labour, and the absence of an institutionalised hierarchical specialisation of functions. Under the 'ideal' conditions of mature industrial civilisation, alienation would be completed by general automatisation of labour, reduction of labour time to a minimum, and exchangeability of functions, . . . the reduction of the working day to a point where the mere quantum of labour time no longer arrests human development is the first prerequisite for freedom" (p. 138). Against the consumer use of sex illustrated by Riesman, Marcuse poses the necessity for equal distribution of leisure, and hence the "regression to a lower standard of life"; a new set of values ("gratification of the basic human needs, the freedom from guilt and fear") against an automated-TV culture. This is premature.

50. Clara Zetkin, *Reminiscences of Lenin* (1925, trans. 1929), 52–53.

51. See Ben Brewster, Introduction to Lukács on Bukharin, *New Left Review* No. 39, p. 25.) The capitalist mode of production separates the family from its earlier immediate association with the economy, and this marginality is unaffected directly by the transformation of the relations of production from private to public ownership in the transition to a socialist society. As the essence of woman's contemporary problem derives from this marginality, for this problem, *but for this problem only*, the distinction between industrial and preindustrial societies is the significant one. Categories meaningful for one element of the social totality may well be irrelevant or even pernicious if extended to the whole of historical development. Similar arguments, but principally lack of space in a short article, must excuse the total neglect of problems arising from class distinctions in the functions and status of women.

52. Marx, *Private Property and Communism*, 153.

53. Karl Marx, *Precapitalist Economic Formations*, 85.

3 The Traffic in Women

Notes on the "Political Economy" of Sex

Gayle Rubin

The literature on women—both feminist and antifeminist—is a long rumination on the question of the nature and genesis of women's oppression and social subordination. The question is not a trivial one, since the answers given determine our visions of the future, and our evaluation of whether or not it is realistic to hope for a sexually egalitarian society. More important, the analysis of the causes of women's oppression forms the basis for any assessment of just what would have to be changed in order to achieve a society without gender hierarchy. Thus, if innate male aggression and dominance are at the root of female oppression, then the feminist program would logically require either the extermination of the offending sex or else a eugenics project to modify its character. If sexism is a by-product of capitalism's relentless appetite for profit, then sexism would wither away in the advent of a successful socialist revolution. If the world-historical defeat of women occurred at the hands of an armed patriarchal revolt, then it is time for Amazon guerrillas to start training in the Adirondacks.

It lies outside the scope of this paper to conduct a sustained critique of some of the currently popular explanations of the genesis of sexual inequality—theories such as the popular evolution exemplified by *The Imperial Animal*, the alleged overthrow of prehistoric matriarchies, or the attempt to extract all the phenomena of social subordination from the first

Source: This article is reprinted from *Toward an Anthology of Women*, ed. Rayna Rapp Reiter (New York: Monthly Review Press, 1976), pp. 157–210, by permission of the publisher. Copyright © 1976, Monthly Review Press, 122 West 27th Street, New York, NY 10001.

volume of *Capital.* Instead, I want to sketch some elements of an alternative explanation of the problem.

Marx once asked: "What is a Negro slave? A man of the black race. The one explanation is as good as the other. A Negro is a Negro. He only becomes a slave in certain relations. A cotton spinning jenny is a machine for spinning cotton. It becomes *capital* only in certain relations. Torn from these relationships it is no more capital than gold in itself is money or sugar is the price of sugar."[1] One might paraphrase: What is a domesticated woman? A female of the species. The one explanation is as good as the other. A woman is a woman. She becomes a domestic, a wife, a chattel, a playboy bunny, a prostitute, or a human dictaphone only in certain relations. Torn from these relationships, she is no more the helpmate of man than gold in itself is money . . . and so on. What then are these relationships by which a female becomes an oppressed woman?

The place to begin to unravel the system of relationships by which women become the prey of men is in the overlapping works of Claude Lévi-Strauss and Sigmund Freud. The domestication of women, under other names, is discussed at length in both of their *oeuvres.* In reading through these works, one begins to have a sense of a systematic social apparatus that takes up females as raw materials and fashions domesticated women as products. Neither Freud nor Lévi-Strauss sees his work in this light, and certainly neither turns a critical glance upon the processes he describes. Their analyses and descriptions must be read, therefore, in something like the way Marx read the classical political economists who preceded him.[2] Freud and Lévi-Strauss are in some sense analogous to Ricardo and Smith: They see neither the implications of what they are saying nor the implicit critique that their work can generate when subjected to a feminist eye. Nevertheless, they provide conceptual tools with which one can build descriptions of the part of social life that is the locus of the oppression of women, of sexual minorities, and of certain aspects of human personality within individuals. I call that part of social life the "sex/gender system," for lack of a more elegant term. As a preliminary definition, a "sex/gender system" is the set of arrangements by which a society transforms biological sexuality into products of human activity and in which these transformed sexual needs are satisfied.

The purpose of this essay is to arrive at a more fully developed definition of the sex/gender system by way of a somewhat idiosyncratic and exegetical reading of Lévi-Strauss and Freud. I use the word "exegetical" deliberately. The dictionary defines "exegesis" as a "critical explanation or analysis; especially, interpretation of the Scriptures." At times, my reading of Lévi-Strauss and Freud is freely interpretive, moving from the explicit content of a text to its presuppositions and implications. My reading of certain psychoanalytic texts is filtered through a lens provided by Jacques Lacan, whose own interpretation of the Freudian scripture has been heavily influenced by Lévi-Strauss.[3]

I will return later to a refinement of the definition of a sex/gender system. First, however, I will try to demonstrate the need for such a concept by discussing the failure of classical Marxism to fully express or conceptualize sex oppression. This failure results from the fact that Marxism, as a theory of social life, is relatively unconcerned with sex. In Marx's map of the social world, human beings are workers, peasants, or capitalists; that they are also men and women is not seen as very significant. By contrast, in the maps of social reality drawn by Freud and Lévi-Strauss, there is a deep recognition of the place of sexuality in society and of the profound differences between the social experience of men and women.

Marx

No other theory accounts for the oppression of women—in its endless variety and monotonous similarity, cross-culturally and throughout history—with anything like the explanatory power of the Marxist theory of class oppression. Therefore, it is not surprising that there have been numerous attempts to apply Marxist analysis to the question of women. There are many ways of doing this. It has been argued that women are a reserve labor force for capitalism, that women's generally lower wages provide extra surplus to a capitalist employer, that women serve the ends of capitalist consumerism in their roles as administrators of family consumption, and so forth.

However, a number of articles have tried to do something much more ambitious—to locate the oppression of women in the heart of the capitalist dynamic by pointing to the relationship between housework and the reproduction of labor.[4] To do this is to place women squarely in the definition of capitalism, the process in which capital is produced by the extraction of surplus value from labor by capital.

Briefly, Marx argued that capitalism is distinguished from all other modes of production by its unique aim: the creation and expansion of capital. Whereas other modes of production might find their purpose in making useful things to satisfy human needs, or in producing a surplus for a ruling nobility, or in producing to ensure sufficient sacrifice for the edification of the gods, capitalism produces capital. Capitalism is a set of social relations—forms of property, and so forth—in which production takes the form of turning money, things, and people into capital. And capital is a quantity of goods or money which, when exchanged for labor, reproduces and augments itself by extracting unpaid labor, or surplus value, from labor and into itself. "The result of the capitalist production process is neither a mere product (use-value) nor a *commodity*, that is, a use-value which has exchange value. Its result, its product, is the creation of *surplus-value* for capital, and consequently the actual *transformation* of money or commodity into capital."[5]

The exchange between capital and labor which produces surplus value, and hence capital, is highly specific. The worker gets a wage; the capitalist gets the things the worker has made during his or her time of employment. If the total value of the things the worker has made exceeds the value of his or her wage, the aim of capitalism has been achieved. The capitalist gets back the cost of the wage, plus an increment—surplus value. This can occur because the wage is determined not by the value of what the laborer makes but by the value of what it takes to keep him or her going—to reproduce him or her from day to day, and to reproduce the entire work force from one generation to the next. Thus, surplus value is the difference between what the laboring class produces as a whole and the amount of that total which is recycled into maintaining the laboring class.

> The capital given in exchange for labour power is converted into necessaries, by the consumption of which the muscles, nerves, bones, and brains of existing labourers are reproduced, and new labourers are begotten. . . . The individual consumption of the labourer, whether it proceed within the workshop or outside it, whether it be part of the process of production or not, forms therefore a factor of the production and reproduction of capital; just as cleaning machinery does.[6]

> Given the individual, the production of labour-power consists in his reproduction of himself or his maintenance. For his maintenance he requires a given quantity of the means of subsistence. . . . Labour-power sets itself in action only by working. But thereby a definite quantity of human muscle, brain, nerve, etc., is wasted, and these require to be restored.[7]

The amount of the difference between the reproduction of labor power and its products depends, therefore, on the determination of what it takes to reproduce that labor power. Marx tends to make that determination on the basis of the quantity of commodities—food, clothing, housing, fuel —that would be necessary to maintain the health, life, and strength of a worker. But these commodities must be consumed before they can be sustenance, and they are not immediately in consumable form when they are purchased by the wage. Additional labor must be performed upon these things before they can be turned into people. Food must be cooked, clothes cleaned, beds made, wood chopped. Housework is therefore a key element in the process of the reproduction of the laborer from whom surplus value is taken. Since it is usually women who do housework, it has been observed that it is through the reproduction of labor power that women are articulated into the surplus value nexus that is the sine qua non of capitalism.[8] It can be further argued that since no wage is paid for housework, the labor of women in the home contributes to the ultimate quantity of surplus value realized by the capitalist. But to explain women's usefulness to capitalism is one thing. To argue that this usefulness explains the genesis of the oppression of women is quite another. It is precisely at this point that the analysis of capitalism ceases to explain very much about women and the oppression of women.

Women are oppressed in societies that can by no stretch of the imagination be described as capitalist. In the Amazon valley and the New Guinea highlands, women are frequently kept in their place by gang rape when the ordinary mechanisms of masculine intimation prove insufficient. "We tame our women with the banana," said one Mundurucu man.[9] The ethnographic record is littered with practices whose effect is to keep women "in their place"—men's cults, secret initiations, arcane male knowledge, and so on. And precapitalist, feudal Europe was hardly a society in which there was no sexism. Capitalism has taken over, and rewired, notions of male and female that predate it by centuries. No analysis of the reproduction of labor power under capitalism can explain foot-binding, chastity belts, or any of the incredible array of Byzantine, fetishized indignities—let alone the more ordinary ones—that have been inflicted upon women in various times and places. The analysis of the reproduction of labor power does not even explain why it is usually women rather than men who do domestic work in the home.

In this light it is interesting to return to Marx's discussion of the reproduction of labor. What is necessary to reproduce the worker is determined in part by the biological needs of the human organism, in part by the physical conditions of the place in which it lives, and in part by cultural tradition. Marx observed that beer is necessary for the reproduction of the English working class, and wine for the French.

The number and extent of his [the worker's] so-called necessary wants, as also the modes of satisfying them, are themselves the product of historical development, and depend therefore to a great extent on the degree of civilization of a country, more particularly on the conditions under which, and consequently on the habits and degree of comfort in which, the class of free labourers has been formed. *In contradistinction therefore to the case of other commodities, there enters into the determination of the value of labour-power a historical and moral element.*[10]

It is precisely this "historical and moral element" which determines that a "wife" is among the necessities of a worker, that women rather than men do housework, and that capitalism is heir to a long tradition in which women do not inherit, in which women do not lead, and in which women do not talk to God. It is this "historical and moral element" that presented capitalism with a cultural heritage of forms of masculinity and femininity. It is within this "historical and moral element" that the entire domain of sex, sexuality, and sex oppression is subsumed. And the briefness of Marx's comment only serves to emphasize the vast area of social life that it covers and leaves unexamined. Only by subjecting this "historical and moral element" to analysis can the structure of sex oppression be delineated.

Engels

In *The Origin of the Family, Private Property, and the State,* Engels sees sex oppression as part of capitalism's heritage from prior social forms. Moreover, Engels integrates sex and sexuality into his theory of society. *Origin* is a frustrating book. Like the nineteenth-century tomes on the history of marriage and the family which it echoes, the state of the evidence in *Origin* renders it quaint to a reader familiar with more recent developments in anthropology. Nevertheless, it is a book whose considerable insight should not be overshadowed by its limitations. The idea that the "relations of sexuality" can and should be distinguished from the "relations of production" is not the least of Engels's intuitions:

According to the materialistic conception, the determining factor in history is, in the final instance, the production and reproduction of immediate life. *This again, is of a twofold character: on the one hand, the production of the means of existence, of food, clothing, and shelter and the tools necessary for that production; on the other side, the production of human beings themselves,* the propagation of the species. The social organization under which the people of a particular historical epoch and a particular country live is determined by both kinds of production: by the stage of development of labor on the one hand, and of the family on the other.[11]

This passage indicates an important recognition—that a human group must do more than apply its activity to reshaping the natural world in order to clothe, feed, and warm itself. We usually call the system by which elements of the natural world are transformed into objects of human consumption the "economy." But the needs that are satisfied by economic activity even in the richest Marxian sense do not exhaust fundamental human requirements. A human group must also reproduce itself from generation to generation. The needs of sexuality and procreation must be satisfied as much as the need to eat, and one of the most obvious deductions to be made from the data of anthropology is that these needs are hardly ever satisfied in any "natural" form, any more than are the needs for food. Hunger is hunger, but what counts as food is culturally determined and obtained. Every society has some form of organized economic activity. Sex is sex, but what counts as sex is equally culturally determined and obtained. Every society also has a sex/gender system—a set of arrangements by which the biological raw material of human sex and procreation is shaped by human, social intervention and satisfied in a conventional manner, no matter how bizarre some of the conventions may be.[12]

The realm of human sex, gender, and procreation has been subjected to, and changed by, relentless social activity for millennia. Sex as we know it—gender identity, sexual desire and fantasy, concepts of childhood—is itself a social product. We need to understand the relations of its production and forget, for a while, about food, clothing, automobiles, and transistor radios. In most Marxist tradition, and even in Engels's book, the concept of the "second aspect of material life" has tended to fade into the background or to be incorporated into the usual notions of "material life." Engels's suggestion has never been followed up and subjected to the refinement it needs. But he does indicate the existence and importance of the domain of social life that I want to call the sex/gender system.

Other names have been proposed for the sex/gender system. The most common alternatives are "mode of reproduction" and "patriarchy." It may be foolish to quibble about terms, but both of these can lead to confusion. All three proposals have been made in order to introduce a distinction between "economic" systems and "sexual" systems and to indicate that sexual systems have a certain autonomy and cannot always be explained in terms of economic forces. "Mode of reproduction," for instance, has been proposed in opposition to the more familiar "mode of production." But this terminology links the economy to production, and the sexual system to reproduction. It reduces the richness of either system, since "productions" and "reproductions" take place in both. Every mode of production involves reproduction—of tools, labor, and social relations. We cannot relegate all the multifaceted aspects of social reproduction to the sex system. Replacement of machinery is an example of reproduction in the economy. On the other hand, we cannot limit the sex system to "reproduction" in either the social or biological sense of the term. A sex/gender system is not simply the reproductive moment of a "mode of production." The formation of gender identity is an example of production in the realm of the sexual system. And a sex/gender system involves more than the "relations of pro-creation," reproduction in the biological sense.

The term "patriarchy" was introduced to distinguish the forces maintaining sexism from other social forces, such as capitalism. But the use of "patriarchy" obscures other distinctions. Its use is analogous to using "capitalism" to refer to all modes of production, whereas the usefulness of the term "capitalism" lies precisely in that it distinguishes between the different systems by which societies are provisioned and organized. Any society will have some system of political economy. Such a system may be egalitarian or socialist. It may be class-stratified, in which case the oppressed class may consist of serfs, peasants, or slaves. The oppressed class may consist of wage laborers, in which case the system is properly labeled "capitalist." The power of the term lies in its implication that, in fact, there are alternatives to capitalism.

Similarly, any society will have some systematic ways to deal with sex, gender, and babies. Such a system may be sexually egalitarian, at least in theory, or it may be "gender-stratified," as seems to be the case for most or all of the known examples. But it is important—even in the face of a depressing history—to maintain a distinction between the human capacity and necessity to create a sexual world, and the empirically oppressive ways in which sexual worlds have been organized. "Patriarchy" subsumes both meanings into the same term. "Sex/gender system," on the other hand, is a neutral term that refers to the domain and indicates that oppression is not inevitable in that domain but is the product of the specific social relations that organize it.

Finally, there are gender-stratified systems that are not adequately described as patriarchal. Many New Guinea societies (Enga, Maring, Bena Bena, Huli, Melpa, Kuma, Gahuku-Gama, Fore, Marind Anim, ad nauseam) are viciously oppressive to women.[13] But the power of males in these groups is founded not on their roles as fathers or patriarchs but on their collective adult maleness, embodied in secret cults, men's houses, warfare, exchange networks, ritual knowledge, and various initiation procedures.

Patriarchy is a specific form of male dominance, and the use of the term ought to be confined to the Old Testament–style pastoral nomads from whom the term comes, or groups like them. Abraham was a patriarch— one old man whose absolute power over wives, children, herds, and dependents was an aspect of the institution of fatherhood, as defined in the social group in which he lived.

Whichever term we use, what is important is to develop concepts that adequately describe the social organization of sexuality and the reproduction of the conventions of sex and gender. We need to pursue the project Engels abandoned when he located the subordination of women in a development within the mode of production.[14] To do this, we can imitate Engels in his method rather than in his results. Engels approached the task of analyzing the "second aspect of material life" by way of an examination of a theory of kinship systems. Kinship systems are and do many things. But they are made up of and reproduce concrete forms of socially organized sexuality. Kinship systems are observable and empirical forms of sex/gender systems.

Kinship
(On the part played by sexuality in the
transition from ape to "man")

To an anthropologist, a kinship system is not a list of biological relatives. It is a system of categories and statuses which often contradict actual genetic relationships. There are dozens of examples in which socially defined kinship status takes precedence over biology. The Nuer custom of "woman marriage" is a case in point. The Nuer define the status of fatherhood as belonging to the person in whose name cattle bridewealth is given for the mother. Thus, a woman can be married to another woman, and be husband to the wife and father of her children, despite the fact that she is not the inseminator.

In pre-state societies, kinship is the idiom of social interaction, organizing economic, political, and ceremonial as well as sexual activity. One's duties, responsibilities, and privileges vis-à-vis others are defined in terms of mutual kinship or lack thereof. The exchange of goods and services, production and distribution, hostility and solidarity, ritual and ceremony all take place within the organizational structure of kinship. The ubiquity and adaptive effectiveness of kinship has led many anthropologists to consider its invention and the invention of language the two developments that decisively marked the discontinuity between semihuman hominids and human beings.[15]

While the idea of the importance of kinship enjoys the status of a first principle in anthropology, the internal workings of kinship systems have long been a focus of intense controversy. Kinship systems vary wildly from one culture to the next. They contain all sorts of bewildering rules that govern whom one may or may not marry. Their internal complexity is dazzling. Kinship systems have for decades provoked the anthropological imagination into trying to explain incest taboos, cross-cousin marriage, terms of descent, relationships of avoidance or forced intimacy, clans and sections, taboos on names—the diverse array of items found in descriptions of actual kinship systems. In the nineteenth century several thinkers attempted to write comprehensive accounts of the nature and history of human sexual systems.[16] One of these was *Ancient Society*, by Lewis Henry Morgan. It was this book that inspired Engels to write *The Origin of the Family, Private Property, and the State*. Engels's theory is based upon Morgan's account of kinship and marriage.

In taking up Engels's project of extracting a theory of sex oppression from the study of kinship, we have the advantage of the maturation of ethnology since the nineteenth century. We also have the advantage of a peculiar and particularly appropriate book, Lévi-Strauss's *Elementary Structures of Kinship*. This is the boldest twentieth-century version of the nineteenth-century attempt to understand human marriage. It is a book in which kinship is explicitly conceived of as an imposition of cultural organization upon the facts of biological procreation. It is permeated with an awareness of the importance of sexuality in human society. It is a description of society that does not assume an abstract, genderless human subject. On the contrary, the human subject in Lévi-Strauss's work is always either male or female, and the divergent social destinies of the two sexes can therefore be traced. Since Lévi-Strauss sees the essence of kinship systems in an exchange of women between men, he constructs an implicit theory of sex oppression. Aptly, the book is dedicated to the memory of Lewis Henry Morgan.

"Vile and precious merchandise" (Monique Wittig)

The Elementary Structures of Kinship is a grand statement on the origin and nature of human society. It is a treatise on the kinship systems of approximately one-third of the ethnographic globe. Most fundamentally, it is an attempt to discern the structural principles of kinship. Lévi-Strauss argues that the application of these principles (summarized in the last chapter of *Elementary Structures*) to kinship data reveals an intelligible logic in the taboos and marriage rules that have perplexed and mystified Western anthropologists. He constructs a chess game of such complexity that it cannot be recapitulated here. But two of his chess pieces are particularly relevant to women—the "gift" and the incest taboo, whose dual articulation adds up to his concept of the exchange of women.

Elementary Structures is in part a radical gloss on another famous theory of primitive social organization, Marcel Mauss's *Essay on the Gift*.[17] It was Mauss who first theorized as to the significance of one of the most striking features of primitive societies: the extent to which giving, receiving, and reciprocating gifts dominates social intercourse. In such societies all sorts of things circulate in exchange—food, spells, rituals, words, names, ornaments, tools, and powers: "Your own mother, your own sister, your own pigs, your own yams that you have piled up, you may not eat. Other people's mothers, other people's sisters, other people's pigs, other people's yams that they have piled up, you may eat."[18]

In a typical gift transaction, neither party gains anything. In the Trobriand Islands each household maintains a garden of yams, and each household eats yams. But the yams a household grows and the yams it eats are not the same. At harvest time a man sends the yams he has cultivated to the household of his sister; the household in which he lives is provisioned by his wife's brother.[19] Since such a procedure appears to be a useless one from the point of view of accumulation or trade, its logic has been sought elsewhere. Mauss proposed that the significance of gift-giving is that it expresses, affirms, or creates a social link between the partners of an exchange. Gift-giving confers upon its participants a special relationship of trust, solidarity, and mutual aid. One can solicit a friendly relationship in the offer of a gift; acceptance implies a willingness to return a gift and a confirmation of the relationship. Gift exchange may also be the idiom of competition and rivalry. There are many examples in which one person humiliates another by giving more than can be reciprocated. Some political systems, such as the Big Man systems of highland New Guinea, are based on exchange that is unequal on the material plane. An aspiring Big Man wants to give away more goods than can be reciprocated. He gets his return in political prestige.

Although both Mauss and Lévi-Strauss emphasize the solidary aspects of gift exchange, the other purposes served by gift-giving only strengthen the point that it is a ubiquitous means of social commerce. Mauss proposed that gifts were the threads of social discourse, the means by which such societies were held together in the absence of specialized governmental institutions. "The gift is the primitive way of achieving the peace that in civil society is secured by the state. . . . Composing society, the gift was the liberation of culture."[20]

Lévi-Strauss adds to the theory of primitive reciprocity the idea that marriages are a most basic form of gift exchange, in which it is women who are the most precious of gifts. He argues that the incest taboo should best be understood as a mechanism to ensure that such exchanges take place between families and between groups. Since the existence of incest taboos is universal but the content of their prohibitions variable, they cannot be explained as having the aim of preventing the occurrence of genetically close matings. Rather, the incest taboo imposes the social aim of exogamy and alliance upon the biological events of sex and procreation. The incest taboo divides the universe of sexual choice into categories of permitted and prohibited sexual partners. Specifically, by forbidding unions within a group, it enjoins marital exchange between groups.

> The prohibition on the sexual use of a daughter or a sister compels
> them to be given in marriage to another man, and at the same time
> it establishes a right to the daughter or sister of this other man. . . .
> The woman whom one does not take is, for that very reason, offered
> up. . . . The prohibition of incest is less a rule prohibiting marriage
> with the mother, sister, or daughter, than a rule obliging the mother,
> sister, or daughter to be given to others. It is the supreme rule of the
> gift.[21]

The result of a gift of women is more profound than the result of other gift transactions, because the relationship thus established is not just one of reciprocity, but one of kinship. The exchange partners have become affines, and their descendants will be related by blood: "Two people may meet in friendship and exchange gifts and yet quarrel and fight in later times, but intermarriage connects them in a permanent manner."[22] As is the case with other gift-giving, marriages are not always so simply activities to make peace. Marriages may be highly competitive, and there are plenty of affines who fight each other. Nevertheless, in a general sense the argument is that the taboo on incest results in a wide network of relations, a set of people whose connections with one another are a kinship structure. All other levels, amounts, and directions of exchange—including hostile ones—are ordered by this structure. The marriage ceremonies recorded in the ethnographic literature are moments in a ceaseless and ordered procession in which women, children, shells, words, cattle names, fish, ancestors, whale's teeth, pigs, yams, spells, dances, mats, and so on, pass from hand to hand, leaving as their tracks the ties that bind. Kinship is organization, and organization gives power.

But who is organized? If it is women who are being transacted, then it is the men who give and take them who are linked, the woman being a conduit of a relationship rather than a partner to it.[23] The exchange of women does not necessarily imply that women are objectified, in the modern sense, since objects in the primitive world are imbued with highly personal qualities. But it does imply a distinction between gift and giver. If women are the gifts, then it is men who are the exchange partners. And it is the partners, not the presents, upon whom reciprocal exchange confers its quasi-mystical power of social linkage. The relations of this system are such that women are in no position to realize the benefits of their own circulation. As long as the relations specify that men exchange women, it is men who are the beneficiaries of the product of such exchanges—social organization.

> The total relationship of exchange which constitutes marriage is not established between a man and a woman, but between two groups of men, and the woman figures only as one of the objects in the exchange, not as one of the partners. . . . This remains true even when the girl's feelings are taken into consideration, as, moreover, is usually the case. In acquiescing to the proposed union, she precipitates or allows the exchange to take place, she cannot alter its nature.[24]

To enter into a gift exchange as a partner, one must have something to give. If women are for men to dispose of, they are in no position to give themselves away.

> "What woman," mused a young Northern Melpa man, "is ever strong enough to get up and say, 'Let us make *moka*, let us find wives and pigs, let us give our daughters to men, let us wage war, let us kill our enemies!' No indeed not! . . . they are little rubbish things who stay at home simply, don't you see?"[25]

What woman indeed! The Melpa women of whom the young man spoke can't get wives; they *are* wives, and what they get are husbands, an entirely different matter. The Melpa women can't give their daughters to men, because they do not have the same rights in their daughters that their male kin have, rights of bestowal (although *not* of ownership).

The "exchange of women" is a seductive and powerful concept. It is attractive in that it places the oppression of women within social systems rather than in biology. Moreover, it suggests that we look for the ultimate locus of women's oppression within the traffic in women rather than within the traffic in merchandise. It is certainly not difficult to find ethnographic and historical examples of trafficking in women. Women are given in marriage, taken in battle, exchanged for favors, sent as tribute, traded, bought, and sold. Far from being confined to the "primitive" world, these practices seem only to become more pronounced and commercialized in more "civilized" societies. Men are of course also trafficked—but as slaves, hustlers, athletic stars, serfs, or in some other catastrophic social status, rather than as men. Women are transacted as slaves, serfs, and prostitutes but also simply as women. And if men have been sexual subjects—exchangers—and women sexual semi-objects—gifts—for much of human history, then many customs, clichés, and personality traits seem to make a great deal of sense (among others, the curious custom by which a father gives away the bride).

The "exchange of women" is also a problematic concept. Since Lévi-Strauss argues that the incest taboo and the results of its application constitute the origin of culture, it can be deduced that the world-historical defeat of women occurred with the origin of culture and is a prerequisite of culture. If his analysis is adopted in its pure form, the feminist program must include a task even more onerous than the extermination of men; it must attempt to get rid of culture and substitute some entirely new phenomenon on the face of the earth. However, it would be a dubious proposition at best to argue that if there were no exchange of women there would be no culture, if for no other reason than that culture is, by definition, inventive. It is even debatable that "exchange of women" adequately describes all the empirical evidence of kinship systems. Some cultures, such as the Lele and the Kuma, exchange women explicitly and overtly. In other cultures the exchange of women can be inferred. In some—particularly those hunters and gatherers excluded from Lévi-Strauss's sample—the efficacy of the concept becomes altogether questionable. What are we to make of a concept that seems so useful and yet so difficult?

The "exchange of women" is neither a definition of culture nor a system in and of itself. The concept is an acute but condensed apprehension of certain aspects of the social relations of sex and gender. A kinship system is an imposition of social ends upon a part of the natural world. It is therefore "production" in the most general sense of the term: a molding, a transformation of objects (in this case, people) to and by a subjective purpose.[26] It has its own relations of production, distribution, and exchange, which include certain "property" forms in people. These forms are not exclusive, private property rights but rather different sorts of rights that various people have in other people. Marriage transactions—the gifts and material that circulate in the ceremonies marking a marriage—are a rich source of data for determining exactly who has which rights in whom. It is not difficult to deduce from such transactions that in most cases women's rights are considerably more residual than men's.

Kinship systems do not merely exchange women. They exchange sexual access, genealogical status, lineage names and ancestors, rights and people —men, women, and children—in concrete systems of social relationships. These relationships always include certain rights for men, others for women. "Exchange of women" is a shorthand expression for the social relations of a kinship system specifying that men have certain rights in their female kin and that women do not have the same rights either to themselves or to their male kin. In this sense the exchange of women is a profound perception of a system in which women do not have full rights to themselves. The exchange of women becomes an obfuscation if it is seen as a cultural necessity and when it is used as the single tool with which an analysis of a particular kinship system is approached.

If Lévi-Strauss is correct in seeing the exchange of women as a fundamental principle of kinship, the subordination of women can be seen as a product of the relationships by which sex and gender are organized and produced. The economic oppression of women is derivative and secondary. But there is an "economics" of sex and gender, and what we need is a political economy of sexual systems. We need to study each society to determine the exact mechanisms by which particular conventions of sexuality are produced and maintained. The "exchange of women" is an initial step toward building an arsenal of concepts with which sexual systems can be described.

Psychoanalysis and Its Discontents

The battle between psychoanalysis and the women's and gay movements has become legendary. In part, this confrontation between sexual revolutionaries and the clinical establishment has been due to the evolution of psychoanalysis in the United States, where clinical tradition has fetishized anatomy. The child is thought to travel through its organismic stages until it reaches its anatomical destiny and the missionary position. Clinical practice has often seen its mission as the repair of individuals who somehow have become derailed en route to their "biological" aim. Transforming moral law into scientific law, clinical practice has acted to enforce sexual convention upon unruly participants. In this sense psychoanalysis has often become more than a theory of the mechanisms of the reproduction of sexual arrangements; it has been one of those mechanisms. Since the aim of the feminist and gay revolts is to dismantle the apparatus of sexual enforcement, a critique of psychoanalysis has been in order.

But the rejection of Freud by the women's and gay movements has deeper roots in the rejection by psychoanalysis of its own insights. Nowhere are the effects on women of male-dominated social systems better documented than within the clinical literature. According to Freudian orthodoxy, the attainment of "normal" femininity extracts severe costs from women. The theory of gender acquisition could have been the basis of a critique of sex roles. Instead, the radical implications of Freud's theory have been radically repressed. This tendency is evident even in the original formulations of the theory, but it has been exacerbated over time until the potential for a critical psychoanalytic theory of gender is visible only in the symptomatology of its denial—an intricate rationalization of sex roles as they are. It is not the purpose of this paper to conduct a psychoanalysis of the psychoanalytic unconscious, but I do hope to demonstrate that it exists. Moreover, the salvage of psychoanalysis from its own motivated repression is not for the sake of Freud's good name. Psychoanalysis contains a unique set of concepts for understanding men, women, and sexuality. It is a theory of sexuality in human society. Most important, psychoanalysis provides a description of the mechanisms by which the sexes are divided and deformed, of how bisexual, androgynous infants are transformed into boys and girls.[27] Psychoanalysis is a feminist theory *manqué*.

The Oedipus Hex

Until the late 1920s the psychoanalytic movement did not have a distinctive theory of feminine development. Instead, variants of an "Electra complex" in women had been proposed, in which female experience was thought to be a mirror image of the Oedipal complex described for males. The boy loved his mother but gave her up out of fear of the father's threat of castration. The girl, it was thought, loved her father and gave him up out of fear of maternal vengeance. This formulation assumed that both children were subject to a biological imperative toward heterosexuality. It also assumed that the children were already, before the Oedipal phase, "little" men and women.

Freud had voiced reservations about jumping to conclusions about women on the basis of data gathered from men. But his objections remained general until the discovery of the pre-Oedipal phase in women. The concept of the pre-Oedipal phase enabled both Freud and Jeanne

Lampl de Groot to articulate the classic psychoanalytic theory of femininity.[28] The idea of the pre-Oedipal phase in women produced a dislocation of the biologically derived presuppositions which underlay notions of an Electra complex. In the pre-Oedipal phase, children of both sexes were psychically indistinguishable, which meant that their differentiation into masculine and feminine children had to be explained rather than assumed. Pre-Oedipal children were described as bisexual. Both sexes exhibited the full range of libidinal attitudes, active and passive. And for children of both sexes, the mother was the object of desire.

In particular, the characteristics of the pre-Oedipal female challenged the ideas of a primordial heterosexuality and gender identity. Since the girl's libidinal activity was directed toward the mother, her adult heterosexuality had to be explained:

> It would be a solution of ideal simplicity if we could suppose that
> from a particular age onwards the elementary influence of the
> mutual attraction between the sexes makes itself felt and impels the
> small woman towards men. . . . But we are not going to find things
> so easy; we scarcely know whether we are to believe seriously in the
> power of which poets talk so much and with such enthusiasm but
> which cannot be further dissected analytically.[29]

Moreover, the girl did not manifest a "feminine" libidinal attitude. Since her desire for the mother was active and aggressive, her ultimate accession to "femininity" had also to be explained: "In conformity with its peculiar nature, psychoanalysis does not try to describe what a woman is . . . but sets about enquiring how she comes into being, how a woman develops out of a child with a bisexual disposition."[30]

In short, feminine development could no longer be taken for granted as a reflex of biology. Rather, it had become immensely problematic. It is in explaining the acquisition of "femininity" that Freud employs the concepts of penis envy and castration, which have infuriated feminists since he first introduced them. The girl turns from the mother and represses the "masculine" elements of her libido as a result of her recognition that she is castrated. She compares her tiny clitoris to the larger penis and, in the face of its evident superior ability to satisfy the mother, falls prey to penis envy and a sense of inferiority. She gives up her struggle for the mother and assumes a passive feminine position vis-à-vis the father. Freud's account can be read as claiming that femininity is a consequence of the anatomical differences between the sexes. He has therefore been accused of biological determinism. Nevertheless, even in his most anatomically stated versions

of the female castration complex, the "inferiority" of the woman's genitals
is a product of the situational context: the girl feels less "equipped" to possess and satisfy the mother. If the pre-Oedipal lesbian were not confronted
by the heterosexuality of the mother, she might draw different conclusions
about the relative status of her genitals.

Freud was never as much of a biological determinist as some would
have him. He repeatedly stressed that all adult sexuality resulted from psychic, not biologic, development. But his writing is often ambiguous, and
his wording leaves plenty of room for the biological interpretations that
have been so popular in American psychoanalysis. In France, on the other
hand, the trend in psychoanalytic theory has been to debiologize Freud
and to conceive of psychoanalysis as a theory of information rather than
of organs. Jacques Lacan, the instigator of this line of thinking, insists that
Freud never meant to say anything about anatomy, that Freud's theory was
instead about language and the cultural meanings imposed upon anatomy.
The debate over the "real" Freud is extremely interesting, but it is not
my purpose here to contribute to it. Rather, I want to rephrase the classic
theory of femininity in Lacan's terminology, after introducing some of the
pieces on Lacan's conceptual chessboard.

Kinship, Lacan, and the Phallus

Lacan suggests that psychoanalysis is the study of the traces left
in the psyches of individuals as a result of their conscription into systems
of kinship.

> Isn't it striking that Lévi-Strauss, in suggesting that implication of
> the structures of language with that part of the social laws which
> regulate marriage ties and kinship, is already conquering the very
> terrain in which Freud situates the unconscious?

> For where on earth would one situate the determinations of the
> unconsciousness if it is not in those nominal cadres in which mar-
> riage ties and kinship are always grounded. . . . And how would one
> apprehend the analytical conflicts and their Oedipean prototype
> outside the engagements which have fixed, long before the subject
> came into the world, not only his destiny, but his identity itself?

> This is precisely where the Oedipus complex . . . may be said, in this
> connection, to mark the limits which our discipline assigns to sub-
> jectivity: that is to say, what the subject can know of his unconscious

participation in the movement of the complex structures of marriage ties, by verifying the symbolic effects in his individual existence of the tangential movement towards incest.[31]

Kinship is the culturalization of biological sexuality on the societal level; psychoanalysis describes the transformation of the biological sexuality of individuals as they are enculturated.

Kinship terminology contains information about the system. Kin terms demarcate statuses and indicate some of the attributes of those statuses. For instance, in the Trobriand Islands a man calls the women of his clan by the term for "sister." He calls the women of clans into which he can marry by a term indicating their marriageability. When the young Trobriand male learns these terms, he learns which women he can safely desire. In Lacan's scheme the Oedipal crisis occurs when a child learns of the sexual rules embedded in the terms for family and relatives. The crisis begins when the child comprehends the system and his or her place in it; the crisis is resolved when the child accepts that place and accedes to it. Even if the child refuses that place, he or she cannot escape knowledge of it. Before the Oedipal phase the sexuality of the child is labile and relatively unstructured. Each child contains all the sexual possibilities available to human expression. But in any given society only some of these possibilities will be expressed, while others will be constrained. When the child leaves the Oedipal phase, its libido and gender identity have been organized in conformity with the rules of the culture that is domesticating it.

The Oedipal complex is an apparatus for the production of sexual personality. It is a truism to say that societies will inculcate in their young the character traits appropriate to carrying on the business of society. For instance, E. P. Thompson speaks of the transformation of the personality structure of the English working class as artisans were changed into good industrial workers.[32] Just as the social forms of labor demand certain kinds of personality, the social forms of sex and gender demand certain kinds of people. In the most general terms, the Oedipal complex is a machine that fashions the appropriate forms of sexual individuals.[33]

In the Lacanian theory of psychoanalysis, it is the kin terms that indicate a structure of relationships that will determine the role of any individual or object within the Oedipal drama. For instance, Lacan makes a distinction between the "function of the father" and a particular father who embodies this function. In the same way, he makes a radical distinction between the penis and the "phallus," between organ and information. The phallus is a set of meanings conferred upon the penis. The differentiation between phallus and penis in contemporary French psychoanalytic terminology emphasizes the idea that the penis could not and does not play the role attributed to it in the classical terminology of the castration complex.[34]

In Freud's terminology, the Oedipal complex presents two alternatives to a child: to have a penis or to be castrated. In contrast, the Lacanian theory of the castration complex leaves behind all reference to anatomical reality:

> The theory of the castration complex amounts to having the male organ play a dominant role—this time as a symbol—*to the extent that its absence or presence transforms an anatomical difference into a major classification of humans, and to the extent that, for each subject, this presence or absence is not taken for granted, is not reduced purely and simply to a given, but is the problematical result of an intra- and intersubjective process* (the subject's assumption of his own sex).[35]

The alternative presented to the child may be rephrased as an alternative between having and not having the phallus. Castration is the not having of the (symbolic) phallus. Castration is not a real "lack" but a meaning conferred upon the genitals of a woman:

> Castration may derive support from . . . the apprehension in the Real of the absence of the penis in women—but even this supposes a symbolization of the object, since the Real is full, and "lacks" nothing. Insofar as one finds castration in the genesis of neurosis, it is never real but symbolic.[36]

The phallus is, as it were, a distinctive feature differentiating "castrated" and "noncastrated." The presence or absence of the phallus carries the differences between two sexual statuses, "man" and "woman."[37] Since these are not equal, the phallus also carries a meaning of the dominance of men over women, and it may be inferred that "penis envy" is a recognition thereof. Moreover, as long as men have rights in women that women do not have in themselves, the phallus also carries the meaning of the difference between "exchanger" and "exchanged," gift and giver. Ultimately, neither the classical Freudian nor the rephrased Lacanian theories of the Oedipal process make sense unless at least this much of the paleolithic relations of sexuality are still with us. We still live in a "phallic" culture.

Lacan also speaks of the phallus as a symbolic object that is exchanged within and between families.[38] It is interesting to think about this observation in terms of primitive marriage transactions and exchange networks. In those transactions the exchange of women is usually one of many cycles of exchange. Usually, there are other objects circulating as well as women. Women move in one direction, cattle, shells, or mats in the other. In one sense, the Oedipal complex is an expression of the circulation of the phallus in intrafamily exchange, an inversion of the circulation of women in interfamily exchange. In the cycle of exchange manifested by the Oedipal complex, the phallus passes through the medium of women from one man to another—from father to son, from mother's brother to sister's son, and so forth. In this family *Kula* ring, women go one way, the phallus the other. It is where we aren't. In this sense, the phallus is more than a feature that distinguishes the sexes; it is the embodiment of the male status, to which men accede and in which certain rights inhere—among them, the right to a woman. It is an expression of the transmission of male dominance. It passes through women and settles upon men.[39] The tracks it leaves include gender identity, the division of the sexes. But it leaves more than this. It leaves "penis envy," which acquires a rich meaning of the disquietude of women in a phallic culture.

Oedipus Revisited

We return now to the two pre-Oedipal androgynes, sitting on the border between biology and culture. Lévi-Strauss places the incest taboo on that border, arguing that its initiation of the exchange of women constitutes the origin of society. In this sense, the incest taboo and the exchange of women are the content of the original social contract.[40] For individuals the Oedipal crisis occurs at the same divide, when the incest taboo initiates the exchange of the phallus.

The Oedipal crisis is precipitated by certain items of information. The children discover the differences between the sexes and that each child must become one or the other gender. They also discover the incest taboo and that some sexuality is prohibited—in this case, the mother is unavailable to either child because she "belongs" to the father. Last, they discover that the two genders do not have the same sexual "rights" or futures.

In the normal course of events, the boy renounces his mother for fear that otherwise his father will castrate him (refuse to give him the phallus, make him a girl). But by this act of renunciation the boy affirms the relationships that have given mother to father and will give him, if he becomes a man, a woman of his own. In exchange for the boy's affirmation of his father's right to his mother, the father affirms the phallus in his son (does not castrate him). The boy exchanges his mother for the phallus, the symbolic token that can later be exchanged for a woman. The only thing required of him is a little patience. He retains his initial libidinal organization and the sex of his original love object. The social contract to which he has agreed will eventually recognize his own rights and provide him with a woman of his own.

What happens to the girl is more complex. She, like the boy, discovers the taboo against incest and the division of the sexes. She also discovers some unpleasant information about the gender to which she is being assigned. For the boy, the taboo on incest is a taboo on certain women. For the girl, it is a taboo on all women. Since she is in a homosexual position vis-à-vis the mother, the rule of heterosexuality that dominates the scenario makes her position excruciatingly untenable. The mother, and all women by extension, can be properly beloved only by someone "with a penis" (phallus). Since the girl has no "phallus," she has no "right" to love her mother or another woman, since she is herself destined to some man. She does not have the symbolic token that can be exchanged for a woman.

If Freud's wording of this moment of the female Oedipal crisis is ambiguous, Lampl de Groot's formulation makes the context that confers meaning upon the genitals explicit: "*If the little girl comes to the conclusion that such an organ is really indispensable to the possession of the mother, she experiences* in addition to the narcissistic insults common to both sexes still another blow, namely *a feeling of inferiority about her genitals.*"[41] The girl concludes that the "penis" is indispensable for the possession of the mother because only those who possess the phallus have a "right" to a woman and the token of exchange. She does not come to her conclusion because of the natural superiority of the penis either in and of itself, or as an instrument for making love. The hierarchical arrangement of the male and female genitals is a result of the definitions of the situation—the rule of obligatory heterosexuality and the relegation of women (those without the phallus, castrated) to men (those with the phallus).

The girl then begins to turn away from the mother, and toward the father. "To the girl, it [castration] is an accomplished fact, which is irrevocable, but the recognition of which compels her finally to renounce her first love object and to taste to the full the bitterness of its loss . . . the father is chosen as a love-object, the enemy becomes the beloved."[42] This recognition of "castration" forces the girl to redefine her relationship to herself, her mother, and her father.

She turns from the mother because she does not have the phallus to give her. She turns from the mother also in anger and disappointment, because the mother did not give her a "penis" (phallus). But the mother, a woman in a phallic culture, does not have the phallus to give away (having gone through the Oedipal crisis herself a generation earlier). The girl then turns to the father because only he can "give her the phallus," and it is only through him that she can enter into the symbolic exchange system in which the phallus circulates. But the father does not give her the phallus in the same way that he gives it to the boy. The phallus is affirmed in the boy, who then has it to give away. The girl never gets the phallus. It passes through her and in its passage is transformed into a child. When she "recognizes her castration," she accedes to the place of a woman in a phallic exchange network. She can "get" the phallus—in intercourse, or as a child—but only as a gift from a man. She never gets to give it away.

When she turns to the father, she also represses the "active" portions of her libido:

> The turning away from her mother is an extremely important step
> in the course of a little girl's development. It is more than a mere
> change of object . . . hand in hand with it there is to be observed
> a marked lowering of the active sexual impulses and a rise of the
> passive ones. . . . The transition to the father object is accomplished
> with the help of the passive trends in so far as they have escaped
> the catastrophe. The path to the development of femininity now lies
> open to the girl.[43]

The ascendance of passivity in the girl is due to her recognition of the futility of realizing her active desire, and of the unequal terms of the struggle. Freud locates active desire in the clitoris and passive desire in the vagina, and thus describes the repression of active desire as the repression of clitoral eroticism in favor of passive vaginal eroticism. In this scheme, cultural stereotypes have been mapped onto the genitals. Since the work of Masters and Johnson, it is evident that this genital division is a false one. Any organ —penis, clitoris, vagina—can be the locus of either active or passive eroticism. What is important in Freud's scheme, however. is not the geography of desire but its self-confidence. It is not an organ that is repressed but a segment of erotic possibility. Freud notes that "more constraint has been applied to the libido when it is pressed into the service of the feminine function."[44] The girl has been robbed.

If the Oedipal phase proceeds normally and the girl "accepts her castration," her libidinal structure and object choice are now congruent with the female gender role. She has become a little woman—feminine, passive, heterosexual. Actually, Freud suggests that there are three alternate routes out of the Oedipal catastrophe. The girl may simply freak out, repress sexuality altogether, and become asexual. She may protest, cling to her narcissism and desire, and become either "masculine" or homosexual. Or she may accept the situation, sign the social contract, and attain "normality."

Karen Horney is critical of the entire Freud/Lampl de Groot scheme. But in the course of her critique she articulates its implications:

> When she [the girl] first turns to a man (the father), it is in the main only by way of the narrow bridge of resentment. . . . We should feel it a contradiction if the relation of woman to man did not retain throughout life some tinge of this enforced substitute for that which was really desired. . . . The same character of something remote from instinct, secondary and substitutive, would, even in normal women, adhere to the wish for motherhood. . . . The special point about Freud's viewpoint is rather that it sees the wish for motherhood not as an innate formation, but as something that can be reduced psychologically to its ontogenetic elements and draws its energy originally from homosexual or phallic instinctual elements. . . . It would follow, finally, that women's whole reaction to life would be based on a strong subterranean resentment.[45]

Horney considers these implications to be so farfetched that they challenge the validity of Freud's entire scheme. But it is certainly plausible to argue instead that the creation of "femininity" in women in the course of socialization is an act of psychic brutality, and that it leaves in women an immense resentment of the suppression to which they were subjected. It is also possible to argue that women have few means for realizing and expressing their residual anger. One can read Freud's essays on femininity as descriptions of how a group is prepared psychologically, at a tender age, to live with its oppression.

There is an additional element in the classic discussions of the attainment of womanhood. The girl first turns to the father because she must, because she is "castrated" (a helpless woman). She then discovers that "castration" is a prerequisite to the father's love, that she must be a woman for him to love her. She therefore begins to desire "castration," and what had previously been a disaster becomes a wish. "Analytic experience leaves no room for doubt that the little girl's first libidinal relation to her father is masochistic, and the masochistic wish in its earliest distinctively feminine phase is: 'I want to be castrated by my father.'"[46] Deutsch argues that such masochism may conflict with the ego, causing some women to flee the entire situation in defense of their self-regard. Those women to whom the choice is "between finding bliss in suffering or peace in renunciation" will have difficulty in attaining a healthy attitude to intercourse and motherhood.[47] Why Deutsch appears to consider such women to be special cases, rather than the norm, is not clear from her discussion.

The psychoanalytic theory of femininity is one that sees female development based largely on pain and humiliation, and it takes some fancy footwork to explain why anyone ought to enjoy being a woman. At this point in the classic discussions, biology makes a triumphant return. The fancy footwork consists in arguing that finding joy in pain is adaptive to the role of women in reproduction, since childbirth and defloration are "painful." Would it not make more sense to question the entire procedure? If women, in finding their place in a sexual system, are robbed of libido and forced into a masochistic eroticism, why did the analysts not argue for novel arrangements instead of rationalizing the old ones?

Freud's theory of femininity has been subjected to feminist critique since it was first published. To the extent that the theory is a rationalization of female subordination, this critique has been justified. To the extent that the theory is a description of a process that subordinates women, the critique is a mistake. As a description of how phallic culture domesticates women, and the effects in women of their domestication, psychoanalytic theory has no parallel.[48] And since psychoanalysis is a theory of gender, dismissing it would be suicidal for a political movement dedicated to eradicating gender hierarchy (or gender itself). We cannot dismantle something that we underestimate or do not understand. The oppression of women is deep; equal pay, equal work, and all the female politicians in the world will not extirpate the roots of sexism. Lévi-Strauss and Freud elucidate what would otherwise be poorly perceived parts of the deep structures of sex oppression. They serve as reminders of the intractability and magnitude of what we fight, and their analyses provide preliminary charts of the social machinery we must rearrange.

Women Unite to Off the Oedipal Residue of Culture

The precision of the fit between Freud and Lévi-Strauss is striking. Kinship systems require a division of the sexes. The Oedipal phase divides the sexes. Kinship systems include sets of rules governing sexuality. The Oedipal crisis is the assimilation of these rules and taboos. Compulsory heterosexuality is the product of kinship. The Oedipal phase constitutes heterosexual desire. Kinship rests on a radical difference between the rights of men and women. The Oedipal complex confers male rights upon the boy and forces the girl to accommodate herself to her lesser rights.

This fit between Lévi-Strauss and Freud is by implication an argument that our sex/gender system is still organized by the principles outlined by Lévi-Strauss, despite the entirely nonmodern character of his data base. The more recent data on which Freud bases his theories testifies to the endurance of these sexual structures. If my reading of Freud and Lévi-Strauss is accurate, it suggests that the feminist movement must attempt to resolve the Oedipal crisis of culture by reorganizing the domain of sex and gender in such a way that each individual's Oedipal experience would be less destructive. The dimensions of such a task are difficult to imagine, but at least, certain conditions would have to be met.

Several elements of the Oedipal crisis would have to be altered in order for the phase not to have such disastrous effects on the young female ego. The Oedipal phase institutes a contradiction in the girl by placing irreconcilable demands upon her. On the one hand, the girl's love for the mother is induced by the mother's job of child care. The girl is then forced to abandon this love because of the female sex role—to belong to a man. If the sexual division of labor were such that adults of both sexes cared for children equally, primary object choice would be bisexual. If heterosexuality were not obligatory, this early love would not have to be suppressed, and the penis would not be overvalued. If the sexual property system were reorganized in such a way that men did not have overriding rights in women (if there were no exchange of women) and if there were no gender, the entire Oedipal drama would be a relic. In short, feminism must call for a revolution in kinship.

The organization of sex and gender once had functions other than itself —it organized society. Now, it only organizes and reproduces itself. The kinds of relationships of sexuality established in the dim human past still dominate our sexual lives, our ideas about men and women, and the ways we raise our children. But they lack the functional load they once carried. One of the most conspicuous features of kinship is that it has been systematically stripped of its functions—political, economic, educational, and organizational. It has been reduced to its barest bones—*sex and gender*.

Human sexual life will always be subject to convention and human intervention. It will never be completely "natural," if only because our species is social, cultural, and articulate. The wild profusion of infantile sexuality will always be tamed. The confrontation between immature and helpless infants and the developed social life of their elders will probably always leave some residue of disturbance. But the mechanisms and aims of this process need not be largely independent of conscious choice. Cultural evolution provides us with the opportunity to seize control of the means of sexuality, reproduction, and socialization and to make conscious decisions to liberate human sexual life from the archaic relationships that deform it. Ultimately, a thoroughgoing feminist revolution would liberate more than women. It would liberate forms of sexual expression, and it would liberate human personality from the straitjacket of gender.

"Daddy, daddy, you bastard, I'm through" (Sylvia Plath)

In the course of this essay I have tried to construct a theory of women's oppression by borrowing concepts from anthropology and psychoanalysis. But Lévi-Strauss and Freud write within an intellectual tradition produced by a culture in which women are oppressed. The danger in my enterprise is that the sexism in the tradition of which both authors are a part tends to be dragged in with each borrowing. "We cannot utter a single destructive proposition which has not already slipped into the form, the logic, and the implicit postulations of precisely what it seeks to contest."[49] And what slips in is formidable. Both psychoanalysis and structural anthropology are, in one sense, the most sophisticated ideologies of sexism around.[50]

For instance, Lévi-Strauss sees women as being like words, which are misused when they are not "communicated" and exchanged. On the last page of a very long book he observes that this creates something of a contradiction in women, since women are at the same time "speakers" and "spoken." His only comment on this contradiction is this:

> But woman could never become just a sign and nothing more, since
> even in a man's world she is still a person, and since insofar as she
> is defined as a sign she must be recognized as a generator of signs.
> In the matrimonial dialogue of men, woman is never purely what is
> spoken about; for if women in general represent a certain category
> of signs, destined to a certain kind of communication, each woman
> preserves a particular value arising from her talent, before and after
> marriage, for taking her part in a duet. In contrast to words, which
> have wholly become signs, woman has remained at once a sign and a
> value. *This explains why the relations between the sexes have preserved that*
> *affective richness, ardour and mystery which doubtless originally permeated*
> *the entire universe of human communications.*[51]

This is an extraordinary statement. Why is he not, at this point, denouncing what kinship systems do to women, instead of presenting one of the greatest rip-offs of all time as the root of romance?

A similar insensitivity is revealed within psychoanalysis by the inconsistency with which it assimilates the critical implications of its own theory. For instance, Freud did not hesitate to recognize that his findings posed a challenge to conventional morality:

We cannot avoid observing with critical eyes, and we have found that it is impossible to give our support to conventional sexual morality or to approve highly of the means by which society attempts to arrange the practical problems of sexuality in life. *We can demonstrate with ease that what the world calls its code of morals demands more sacrifices than it is worth,* and that its behavior is neither dictated by honesty nor instituted with wisdom.[52]

Nevertheless, when psychoanalysis demonstrates with equal facility that the ordinary components of feminine personality are masochism, self-hatred, and passivity,[53] a similar judgment is *not* made. Instead, a double standard of interpretation is employed. Masochism is bad for men, essential to women. Adequate narcissism is necessary for men, impossible for women. Passivity is tragic in a man; lack of passivity is tragic in a woman.

It is this double standard that enables clinicians to try to accommodate women to a role whose destructiveness is so lucidly detailed in their own theories. It is the same inconsistent attitude that permits therapists to consider lesbianism as a problem to be cured, rather than as the resistance to a bad situation that their own theory suggests.[54]

There are points within the analytic discussions of femininity where one might say, "This is oppression of women," or "We can demonstrate with ease that what the world calls femininity demands more sacrifices than it is worth." It is precisely at such points that the implications of the theory are ignored and replaced with formulations whose purpose is to keep those implications firmly lodged in the theoretical unconscious. It is at these points that all sorts of mysterious chemical substances, joys in pain, and biological aims are substituted for a critical assessment of the costs of femininity. These substitutions are the symptoms of theoretical repression in that they are not consistent with the usual canons of psychoanalytic argument. The extent to which these rationalizations of femininity go against the grain of psychoanalytic logic is strong evidence for the extent of the need to suppress the radical and feminist implications of the theory of femininity (Deutsch's discussions are excellent examples of this process of substitution and repression).

The argument that must be woven in order to assimilate Lévi-Strauss and Freud into feminist theory is somewhat tortuous. I have engaged it for several reasons. First, while neither Lévi-Strauss nor Freud questions the undoubted sexism endemic to the systems they describe, the questions that ought to be posed are blindingly obvious. Second, their work enables us to isolate sex and gender from "mode of production" and to counter a certain tendency to explain sex oppression as a reflex of economic forces. Their work provides a framework in which the full weight of sexuality and marriage can be incorporated into an analysis of sex oppression. It suggests a conception of the women's movement as analogous to, rather than isomorphic with, the working-class movement, each addressing a different source of human discontent. In Marx's vision the working-class movement would do more than throw off the burden of its own exploitation. It also had the potential to change society, to liberate humanity, to create a classless society. Perhaps the women's movement has the task of effecting the same kind of social change for a system of which Marx had only an imperfect apperception. Something of this sort is implicit in Wittig—the dictatorship of the Amazon *guérillères* is a temporary means for achieving a genderless society.

The sex/gender system is not immutably oppressive and has lost much of its traditional function. Nevertheless, it will not wither away in the absence of opposition. It still carries the social burden of sex and gender, of socializing the young, and of providing ultimate propositions about the nature of human beings themselves. And it serves economic and political ends other than those it was originally designed to further.[55] The sex/gender system must be reorganized through political action.

Finally, the exegesis of Lévi-Strauss and Freud suggests a certain vision of feminist politics and the feminist utopia. It suggests that we should aim not for the elimination of men but for the elimination of the social system that creates sexism and gender. I personally find a vision of an Amazon matriarchate, in which men are reduced to servitude or oblivion (depending on the possibilities for parthenogenetic reproduction), distasteful and inadequate. Such a vision maintains gender and the division of the sexes. It is a vision that simply inverts the arguments of those who base their case for inevitable male dominance on ineradicable and *significant* biological differences between the sexes. But we are not only oppressed *as* women; we are oppressed by having to *be* women—or men, as the case may be. I personally feel that the feminist movement must dream of even more than the elimination of the oppression of women. It must dream of the elimination of obligatory sexualities and sex roles. The dream I find most compelling is one of an androgynous and genderless (though not sexless) society, in which one's sexual anatomy is irrelevant to who one is, what one does, and with whom one makes love.

The Political Economy of Sex

It would be nice to be able to conclude here with the implications for feminism and gay liberation of the overlap between Freud and Lévi-Strauss. But I must suggest, tentatively, a next step on the agenda: a Marxian analysis of sex/gender systems. Sex/gender systems are not ahistorical emanations of the human mind; they are products of historical human activity.

We need, for instance, an analysis of the evolution of sexual exchange along the lines of Marx's discussion in *Capital* of the evolution of money and commodities. There is an economics and a politics to sex/gender systems that are obscured by the concept of "exchange of women." For instance, a system in which women are exchangeable only for one another has different effects on women than one in which there is a commodity equivalent for women.

> That marriage in simple societies involves an "exchange" is a somewhat vague notion that has often confused the analysis of social systems. The extreme case is the exchange of "sisters," formerly practiced in parts of Australia and Africa. Here the term has the precise dictionary meaning of "to be received as an equivalent for," "to give and receive reciprocally." From quite a different standpoint the virtually universal incest prohibition means that marriage systems necessarily involve "exchanging" siblings for spouses, giving rise to a reciprocity that is purely notational. But in most societies marriage is mediated by a set of intermediary transactions. If we see these transactions as simply implying immediate or long-term reciprocity, then the analysis is likely to be blurred. . . . The analysis is further limited if one regards the passage of property simply as a symbol of the transfer of rights, for then the nature of the objects handed over . . . is of little importance. . . . Neither of these approaches is wrong; both are inadequate.[56]

There are systems in which there is no equivalent for a woman. To get a wife, a man must have a daughter, a sister, or other female kinswoman in whom he has a right of bestowal. He must have control over some female flesh. The Lele and Kuma are cases in point. Lele men scheme constantly in order to stake claims in some as yet unborn girl, and scheme further to make good their claims.[57] A Kuma girl's marriage is determined by an intricate web of debts, and she has little say in choosing her husband. A girl is usually married against her will, and her groom shoots an arrow into her thigh to symbolically prevent her from running away. The young wives almost always do run away, only to be returned to their new husbands by an elaborate conspiracy enacted by their kin and affines.[58]

In other societies there is an equivalent for women. A woman can be converted into bridewealth, and bridewealth can be in turn converted into a woman. The dynamics of such systems vary accordingly, as does the specific kind of pressure exerted upon women. The marriage of a Melpa woman is not a return for a previous debt. Each transaction is self-contained, in that the payment of bridewealth in pigs and shells will cancel the debt. The Melpa woman therefore has more latitude in choosing her husband than does her Kuma counterpart; still, her destiny is linked to bridewealth. If her husband's kin are slow to pay, her kin may encourage her to leave him; on the other hand, if her consanguineal kin are satisfied with the balance of payments, they may refuse to back her in the event that she wants to leave her husband. Moreover, her male kinsmen use the bridewealth for their own purposes, in *moka* exchange and for their own marriages. If a woman leaves her husband, some or all of the bridewealth will have to be returned. If, as is usually the case, the pigs and shells have been distributed or promised, her kin will be reluctant to back her in the event of marital discord. And each time a woman divorces and remarries, her value in bridewealth tends to depreciate. On the whole, her male consanguines will lose in the event of a divorce, unless the groom has been delinquent in his payments. While the Melpa woman is freer as a new bride than a Kuma woman, the bridewealth system makes divorce difficult or impossible.[59]

In some societies, like the Nuer, bridewealth can only be converted into brides. In others, bridewealth can be converted into something else, like political prestige. In this case, a woman's marriage is implicated in a political system. In the Big Man systems of Highland New Guinea, the material that circulates for women also circulates in the exchanges on which political power is based. Within the political system men are in constant need of valuables to disburse, and they are dependent upon input. They depend not only on their immediate partners but on the partners of their partners, to several degrees of remove. If a man has to return some bridewealth, he may not be able to give it to someone who planned to give it to someone else who intended to use it to give a feast upon which his status depends. Big Men are therefore concerned with the domestic affairs of others, whose relationship with them may be extremely indirect. There are cases in which headmen intervene in marital disputes involving indirect trading partners in order that *moka* exchanges not be disrupted.[60] The weight of this entire system may come to rest upon one woman kept in a miserable marriage.

In short, there are other questions to ask of a marriage system than whether or not it exchanges women. Is the woman traded for a woman, or is there an equivalent? Is this equivalent only for women, or can it be turned into something else? If it can be turned into something else, is it turned into political power or wealth? On the other hand, can bridewealth be obtained only in marital exchange, or can it be obtained from elsewhere? Can women be accumulated through amassing wealth? Can wealth be accumulated by disposing of women? Is a marriage system part of a system of stratification?[61]

These last questions point to another task for a political economy of sex. Kinship and marriage are always parts of total social systems and are always tied into economic and political arrangements.

> Lévi-Strauss . . . rightly argues that the structural implications of a marriage can only be understood if we think of it as one item in a whole series of transactions between kin groups. So far, so good. But in none of the examples which he provides in his book does he carry this principle far enough. The reciprocities of kinship obligation are not merely symbols of alliance, they are also economic transactions, political transactions, charters to rights of domicile and land use. No useful picture of "how a kinship system works" can be provided unless these several aspects or implications of the kinship organization are considered simultaneously.[62]

Among the Kachin, the relationship of a tenant to a landlord is also a relationship between a son-in-law and a father-in-law. "The procedure for acquiring land rights of any kind is in almost all cases tantamount to marrying a woman from the lineage of the lord." In the Kachin system, bridewealth moves from commoners to aristocrats, women moving in the opposite direction.

> From an economic aspect the effect of matrilateral cross-cousin marriage is that, on balance, the headman's lineage constantly pays wealth to the chief's lineage in the form of bridewealth. The payment can also, from an analytical point of view, be regarded as a rent paid to the senior landlord by the tenant. The most important part of this payment is in the form of consumer goods—namely cattle. The chief converts this perishable wealth into imperishable prestige through the medium of spectacular feasting. The ultimate consumers of the goods are in this way the original producers, namely, the commoners who attend the feast.[63]

In another example, it is traditional in the Trobriands for a man to send a harvest gift—*urigubu*—of yams to his sister's household. For the commoners, this amounts to a simple circulation of yams. But the chief is polygamous and marries a woman from each subdistrict within his domain. Each of these subdistricts therefore sends *urigubu* to the chief, providing him with a bulging storehouse out of which he finances feasts, craft production, and *kula* expeditions. This "fund of power" underwrites the political system and forms the basis for chiefly power.[64]

In some systems, position in a political hierarchy and position in a marriage system are intimately linked. In traditional Tonga women married up in rank. Thus, low-ranking lineages would send women to higher-ranking lineages. Women of the highest lineage were married into the "house of Fiji," a lineage defined as outside the political system. If the highest-ranking chief gave his sister to a lineage other than one that had no part in the ranking system, he would no longer be the highest-ranking chief. Rather, the lineage of his sister's son would outrank his own. In times of political rearrangement, the demotion of the previous high-ranking lineage was formalized when it gave a wife to a lineage that it had formerly outranked. In traditional Hawaii the situation was the reverse. Women married down, and the dominant lineage gave wives to junior lines. A paramount would either marry a sister or obtain a wife from a distant island. When a junior lineage usurped rank, it formalized its position by giving a wife to its former senior line.

There is even some tantalizing data suggesting that marriage systems may be implicated in the evolution of social strata and perhaps in the development of early states. The first round of the political consolidation that resulted in the formation of a state in Madagascar occurred when one chief obtained title to several autonomous districts through the vagaries of marriage and inheritance.[65] In Samoa legends place the origin of the paramount title—the *Tafa'ifa*—as a result of intermarriage between ranking members of four major lineages. My thoughts are too speculative, my data too sketchy, to say much on this subject. But a search ought to be undertaken for data that might demonstrate how marriage systems intersect with large-scale political processes such as state-making. Marriage systems may be implicated in a number of ways: in the accumulation of wealth and the maintenance of differential access to political and economic resources; in the building of alliances; in the consolidation of high-ranking persons into a single closed stratum of endogamous kin.

These examples—like the Kachin and the Trobriand ones—indicate that sexual systems cannot, in the final analysis, be understood in complete isolation. A full-bodied analysis of women in a single society, or throughout history, must take *everything* into account: the evolution of commodity forms in women, systems of land tenure, political arrangements, subsistence technology, and so on. Equally important, economic and political analyses are incomplete if they do not consider women, marriage, and sexuality. The traditional concerns of anthropology and social science—such as the evolution of social stratification and the origin of the state—must be reworked to include the implications of matrilateral cross-cousin marriage, surplus extracted in the form of daughters, the conversion of female labor into male wealth, the conversion of female lives into marriage alliances, the contribution of marriage to political power, and the transformations that all these varied aspects of society have undergone in the course of time.

This sort of endeavor is, in the final analysis, exactly what Engels tried to do in his effort to make coherent so many diverse aspects of social life. He tried to relate men and women, town and country, kinship and state, forms of property, systems of land tenure, convertibility of wealth, forms of exchange, the technology of food production, and forms of trade—to name a few—in a systematic historical account. Eventually, someone will have to write a new version of *The Origin of the Family, Private Property, and the State*, recognizing the mutual interdependence of sexuality, economics, and politics without underestimating the full significance of each in human society.

Notes

Acknowledgments: Acknowledgments are an inadequate expression of how much this paper, like most, is the product of many minds. They are also necessary to free others of the responsibility for what is ultimately a personal vision of a collective conversation. I want to free and thank the following persons: Tom Anderson and Arlene Gorelick, with whom I coauthored the paper from which this one evolved; Rayna Reiter, Larry Shields, Ray Kelly, Peggy White, Norma Diamond, Randy Reiter, Frederick Wyatt, Anne Locksley, Juliet Mitchell, and Susan Harding for countless conversations and ideas; Marshall Sahlins for the revelation of anthropology; Rod Aya for elucidating Marx; Lynn Eden for merciless editing; the members of Women's Studies 340/004 for my initiation into teaching; Sally Brenner for heroic typing; Susan Lowes for incredible patience; and Emma Goldman for the title.

1. Karl Marx, *Wage-Labor and Capital* (New York: International Publishers, 1971), 28.

2. On this, see Louis Althusser and Etienne Balibar, *Reading "Capital"* (London: New Left Books, 1970), 69.

3. Moving between Marxism, structuralism, and psychoanalysis produces a certain clash of epistemologies. In particular, structuralism is a can from which worms crawl out all over the epistemological map. Rather than trying to cope with this problem, I have more or less ignored the fact that Lacan and Lévi-Strauss are among the

foremost living ancestors of the contemporary French intellectual revolution (see Michel Foucault, *The Order of Things* [New York: Pantheon, 1970]). It would be fun, interesting, and, if this were France, essential to start my argument from the center of the structuralist maze and work my way out from there, along the lines of a "dialectical theory of signifying practices" (see Robert Hefner, "The *Tel Quel* Ideology: Material Practice upon Material Practice," *Substance* 8 [1974]: 127–38).

4. See Margaret Benston, "The Political Economy of Women's Liberation," *Monthly Review* 21, no. 4 (1969): 13–27; Mariarosa Dalla Costa, *The Power of Women and the Subversion of the Community* (Bristol: Falling Wall Press, 1972); Isabel Larguia and John Dumoulin, "Towards a Science of Women's Liberation," *NACLA Newsletter* 6, no. 10 (1972): 3–20; Ira Gerstein, "Domestic Work and Capitalism," *Radical America* 7, nos. 4–5 (1973): 101–28.; Lise Vogel, "The Earthly Family," *Radical America* 7, nos. 4–5 (1973): 9–50; Wally Secombe, "Housework under Capitalism," *New Left Review* 83 (1974): 3–24; Jean Gardiner, "Political Economy of Female Labor in Capitalist Society," 1974 (unpublished manuscript); M. and J. Rowntree, "More on the Political Economy of Women's Liberation," *Monthly Review* 21, no. 8 (1970): 26–32.

5. Karl Marx, *Theories of Surplus Value*, pt. 1 (Moscow: Progress Publishers, 1969), 399 (original emphasis).

6. Karl Marx, *Capital* (New York: International Publishers, 1972), 1: 572.

7. Ibid., 171.

8. A lot of the debate on women and housework has centered on the question of whether or not housework is "productive" labor. Strictly speaking, housework is not ordinarily "productive" in the technical sense of the term: Ian Gough, "Marx and Productive Labour," *New Left Review* 76 (1972): 47–72; Marx, *Theories of Surplus Value*, 387–413. But this distinction is irrelevant to the main line of the argument. Housework may not be "productive" in the sense of directly producing surplus value and capital yet be a crucial element in the production of surplus value and capital.

9. Robert Murphy, "Social Structure and Sex Antagonism," *Southwestern Journal of Anthropology* 15, no. 1 (1959): 81–96.

10. Marx, *Capital*, 1:171 (my emphasis).

11. Frederick Engels, *The Origin of the Family, Private Property, and the State*, ed. Eleanor Leacock (New York: International Publishers, 1972), 71–72 (my emphasis).

12. That some of them are pretty bizarre, from our point of view, only demonstrates the point that sexuality is expressed through the intervention of culture (see Clellan Ford and Frank Beach, *Patterns of Sexual Behavior* [New York: Harper & Row, 1972]). Some examples may be chosen from among the exotica in which anthropologists delight. Among the Banaro, marriage involves several socially sanctioned sexual partnerships. When a woman is married, she is initiated into intercourse by the sib-friend of her groom's father. After bearing a child by this man, she begins to have intercourse with her husband. She also has an institutionalized partnership with the sib-friend of her husband. A man's partners include his wife, the wife of his sib-friend, and the wife of his sib-friend's son (Richard Thurnwald, "Banaro Society," *Memoirs of the American Anthropological Association* 3, no. 4 [1916]: 251–391). Multiple intercourse is a more pronounced custom among the Marind Anim. At the time of marriage, the bride has intercourse with all of the members of the groom's clan, the groom coming last. Every major festival is accompanied by a practice known as *otiv-bombari*, in which semen is collected for ritual purposes. A few women have intercourse with many men, and the resulting semen is collected in coconut-shell buckets. A Marind male is subjected to multiple homosexual intercourse during initiation

(J. Van Baal, *Dema* [The Hague: Nijhoff, 1966]). Among the Etoro, heterosexual intercourse is taboo for between 205 and 260 days a year (Raymond Kelly, "Witchcraft and Sexual Relations: An Exploration of the Social and Semantic Implications of the Structure of Belief," paper read at 73rd annual meeting of the American Anthropological Association, Mexico City, 1974). In much of New Guinea, men fear copulation and think that it will kill them if they engage in it without magical precautions (R. M. Glasse, "The Mask of Venery," paper read at 70th annual meeting of the American Anthropological Association, New York City, 1971; M. J. Meggitt, "Male-Female Relationships in the Highlands of Australian New Guinea," *American Anthropologist* 66, no. 4, pt. 2 [1970]: 204–24). Usually, such ideas of feminine pollution express the subordination of women. But symbolic systems contain internal contradictions, whose logical extensions sometimes lead to inversions of the propositions on which a system is based. In New Britain, men's fear of sex is so extreme that rape appears to be feared by men rather than women. Women run after the men, who flee from them, women are the sexual aggressors, and it is bridegrooms who are reluctant (Jane Goodale and Ann Chowning, "The Contaminating Woman," paper read at the 70th annual meeting of the American Anthropological Association, New York City, 1971). Other interesting variations can be found in Nur Yalman, "On the Purity of Women in the Castes of Ceylon and Malabar," *Journal of the Royal Anthropological Institute* 93, no. 1 (1963): 25–58; and Kathleen Gough, "The Nayars and the Definition of Marriage," *Journal of the Royal Anthropological Institute* 89 (1959): 23–24.

13. See Ronald Berndt, *Excess and Restraint* (Chicago: University of Chicago Press, 1962); L. L. Langness, "Sexual Antagonism in the New Guinea Highlands: A Bena Bena Example," *Oceania* 37, no. 3 (1967); Kenneth Read, "The Nama Cult of the Central Highlands, New Guinea," *Oceania* 23, no. 1 (1952); Meggitt, "Male-Female Relationships"; Glasse, "Mask of Venery"; Marilyn Strathern, *Women in Between* (New York: Seminar, 1972); Marie Reay, *The Kuma* (London: Cambridge University Press, 1959); Van Baal, *Dema*; Shirley Lindenbaum, "A Wife Is the Hand of Man," paper read at 72d annual meeting of the American Anthropological Association, Mexico City, 1973.

14. Engels (*Origin of the Family*, 120–21) thought that men acquired wealth in the form of herds and, wanting to pass this wealth to their own children, overthrew "mother right" in favor of patrilineal inheritance. "The overthrow of mother right was the *world historical defeat of the female sex*. The man took command in the home also; the woman was degraded and reduced to servitude; she became the slave of his lust and a mere instrument for the production of children" original emphasis. As has been often pointed out, women do not necessarily have significant social authority in societies practicing matrilineal inheritance.

15. Frank Livingstone, "Genetics, Ecology, and the Origins of Incest and Exogamy," *Current Anthropology* 10, no. 1 (1969); Claude Lévi-Strauss, *The Elementary Structures of Kinship* (Boston: Beacon Press, 1969).

16. See Elizabeth Fee, "The Sexual Politics of Victorian Social Anthropology," *Feminist Studies* 1 (Winter–Spring 1973): 23–29.

17. See also Marshall Sahlins, *Stone Age Economics* (Chicago: Aldine-Atherton, 1972), chap. 4.

18. Arapesh, cited in Lévi-Strauss, *Elementary Structures*, 27.

19. Bronislaw Malinowski, *The Sexual Life of Savages* (London: Routledge & Kegan Paul, 1929).

20. Sahlins, *Stone Age Economics*, 169, 175.

21. Lévi-Strauss, *Elementary Structures*, 51, 481.

22. Best, cited in ibid., 481.

23. "What, would you like to marry your sister? What is the matter with you? Don't you want a brother-in-law? Don't you realize that if you marry another man's sister and another man marries your sister, you will have at least two brothers-in-law, while if you marry your own sister you will have none? With whom will you hunt, with whom will you garden, whom will you go visit?" (Arapesh, cited in ibid., 485).

24. Ibid., 115. This analysis of society as based on bonds between men by means of women makes the separatist responses of the women's movement thoroughly intelligible. Separatism can be seen as a mutation in social structure, as an attempt to form social groups based on unmediated bonds between women. It can also be seen as a radical denial of men's "rights" in women and as a claim by women of rights in themselves.

25. Strathern, *Women in Between*, 161.

26. For this sense of production, see Karl Marx, *Pre-capitalist Economic Formations* (New York: International Publishers, 1971), 80–99.

27. "In studying women we cannot neglect the methods of a science of the mind, a theory that attempts to explain how women become women and men, men. The borderline between the biological and the social which finds expression in the family is the land psychoanalysis sets out to chart, the land where sexual distinction originates" (Juliet Mitchell, *Woman's Estate* [New York: Vintage, 1971], 167). "What is the *object* of psychoanalysis? . . . but the *'effects,'* prolonged into the surviving adult, of the extraordinary adventure which from birth the liquidation of the Oedipal phase transforms a small animal conceived by a man and a woman into a small human child . . . the 'effects' still present in the survivors of the forced 'humanization' of the small human animal into a *man* or a *woman*" (Louis Althusser, "Freud and Lacan," *New Left Review* 55 [1969]: 57, 59; original emphasis).

28. The psychoanalytic theories of feminity were articulated in the context of a debate that took place largely in the *International Journal of Psychoanalysis* and *Psychoanalytic Quarterly* in the late 1920s and early 1930s. Articles representing the range of discussion include Sigmund Freud, "Some Psychical Consequences of the Anatomical Distinction between the Sexes," in *The Complete Works of Sigmund Freud*, ed. J. Strachey (London: Hogarth, 1961), Freud, "Female Sexuality," in ibid., vol. 21; Freud, "Femininity," in *New Introductory Lecture in Psychoanalysis*, ed. J. Strachey (New York: Norton, 1965); Jeanne Lampl de Groot, "Problems of Femininity," *Psychoanalytic Quarterly* 2 (1933): 489–518, and "The Evolution of the Oedipus Complex in Women," in *The Psychoanalytic Reader*, ed. R. Fleiss (New York: International Universities Press, 1948); Helene Deutsch, "The Significance of Masochism in the Mental Life of Women," and "On Female Homosexuality," both in Fliess, *Psychoanalytic Reader*; Karen Horney, "The Denial of the Vagina," in Horney, *Feminine Psychology*, ed. Harold Kelman (New York: Norton, 1973); Ernest Jones, "The Phallic Phase," *International Journal of Psychoanalysis* 14 (1933): 1–33 (some of these cited sources are reprints; for the original chronology, see J. Chasseguet-Smirgel, *Female Sexuality* [Ann Arbor: University of Michigan Press, 1970]).

The debate was complex, and I have simplified it. Freud, Lampl de Groot, and Deutsch argued that femininity developed out of a bisexual, "phallic" girl-child; Horney and Jones argued for an innate femininity. The debate was not without its ironies. Horney defended women against penis envy by postulating that women are born and not made; Deutsch, who considered women to be made and not born,

developed a theory of feminine masochism whose best rival is *Story of O.* I have attributed the core of the "Freudian" version of female development equally to Freud and
to Lampl de Groot. In reading through the articles, it has seemed to me that the
theory is at least as much hers as it is his.

29. Freud, "Femininity," 119.

30. Ibid., 116.

31. Jacques Lacan, "The Function of Language in Psychoanalysis," in Anthony
Wilden, *The Language of Self* (Baltimore, Md.: Johns Hopkins University Press,
1968), 48, 126, 40.

32. E. P. Thompson, *The Making of the English Working Class* (New York: Vintage
Books, 1963).

33. See also the discussion of different forms of "historical individuality" in
Althusser and Balibar, *Reading "Capital,"* 112, 251–53.

34. I have taken my position on Freud somewhere between the French structuralist interpretations and American biologistic ones, because I think that Freud's
wording is similarly somewhere in the middle. He does talk about penises, about the
"inferiority" of the clitoris, about the psychic consequences of anatomy. The Lacani-
ans, on the other hand, argue from Freud's text that he is unintelligible if his words
are taken literally, and that a thoroughly nonanatomical theory can be deduced as
Freud's intention (see Althusser, "Freud and Lacan"). I think that they are right; the
penis is walking around too much for its role to be taken literally. The detachability
of the penis and its transformation in fantasy (e.g., penis = feces = child = gift)
argue strongly for a symbolic interpretation. Nevertheless, I think that Freud was
less consistent than either I or Lacan would like, and some gesture must be made to
what he said, even as we play with what he must have meant. See Althusser, "Freud
and Lacan."

35. Jeffrey Mehlman, *French Freud: Structural Studies in Psychoanalysis*, No. 48
(New Haven, Conn.: Yale French Studies, 1972), 198–99 (my emphasis).

36. Lacan, "Function of Language," 271.

37. See Roman Jakobson and Morris Halle, *Fundamentals of Language* (The
Hague: Mouton, 1971), on distinctive features.

38. See also Wilden, *Language of the Self*, 303–5.

39. The pre-Oedipal mother is the "phallic mother"; she is believed to possess
the phallus. The Oedipal-inducing information is that the mother does not possess the phallus. In other words, the crisis is precipitated by the "castration" of the
mother, by the recognition that the phallus only passes through her but does not
settle on her. The "phallus" must pass through her, since the relationship of a male
to every other male is defined through a woman. A man is linked to a son by a
mother, to his nephew by virtue of a sister, and so on. Every relationship between
male kin is defined by the woman between them. If power is a male prerogative, and
must be passed on, it must go through the woman-in-between. Marshall Sahlins (personal communication) once suggested that the reason women are so often defined
as stupid, polluting, disorderly, silly, profane, or whatever, is that such categoriza-
tions define women as "incapable" of possessing the power that must be transferred
through them.

40. See Sahlins, *Stone Age Economics*, chap. 4.

41. Lampl de Groot, "Problems of Femininity," 497 (my emphasis).

42. Lampl de Groot, "Evolution of the Oedipus Complex," 213.

43. Freud, "Female Sexuality," 239.

44. Freud, "Femininity," 131.

45. Horney, "Denial of the Vagina," 148–49.

46. Deutsch, "Significance of Masochism," 228.

47. Ibid., 231.

48. See also Mitchell, *Woman's Estate*; and Christopher Lasch, "Freud and Women," *New York Review of Books* 21, no. 15 (1974).

49. Jacques Derrida, "Structure, Sign, and Play in the Discourse of the Human Sciences," in *The Structuralist Controversy*, edited by R. Macksey and E. Donato (Baltimore: Johns Hopkins Press, 1972) p. 250.

50. Parts of Wittig's *Les Guérillères* appear to be tirades against Lévi-Strauss and Lacan. For instance: "Has he not indeed written, power and the possession of women, leisure and the enjoyment of women? He writes that you are currency, an item of exchange. He writes, barter, barter, possession and acquisition of women and merchandise. Better for you to see your guts in the sun and utter the death rattle than to live a life that anyone can appropriate. What belongs to you on this earth? Only death. No power on earth can take that away from you. And—consider explain tell yourself—if happiness consists in the possession of something, then hold fast to this sovereign happiness—to die." (Monique Wittig, *Les Guérillères* [New York: Avon, 1973] 115–16; see also 106–7, 113–14, 134). The awareness of French feminists of Lévi-Strauss and Lacan is most clearly evident in a group called "Psychoanalyse et Politique" which defined its task as a feminist use and critique of Lacanian psychoanalysis.

51. Lévi-Strauss, *Elementary Structures*, 496 (my emphasis).

52. Sigmund Freud, *A General Introduction to Psychoanalysis* (Garden City, N.Y.: Garden City Publishing, 1943), 376–77 (my emphasis).

53. "Every woman adores a fascist," said Sylvia Plath.

54. One clinician, Charlotte Wolff (*Love between Women* [London: Duckworth, 1971]), has taken the psychoanalytic theory of womanhood to its logical extreme and proposed that lesbianism is a healthy response to female socialization: "Women who do not rebel against the status of object have declared themselves defeated as persons in their own right (p. 65). "The lesbian girl is the one who, by all means at her disposal, will try to find a place of safety inside and outside the family, through her fight for equality with the male. She will not, like other women, play up to him: indeed, she despises the very idea of it" (p. 59). "The lesbian was and is unquestionably in the avant-garde of the fight for equality of the sexes, and for the psychical liberation of women" (p. 66). It is revealing to compare Wolff's discussion with the articles on lesbianism in Judd Marmor, *Sexual Inversion* (London: Basic Books, 1965).

55. John Finley Scott, "The Role of Collegiate Sororities in Maintaining Class and Ethnic Endogamy," *American Sociological Review* 30, no. 4 (1965).

56. Jack Goody and S. J. Tambiah, *Bridewealth and Dowry* (Cambridge: Cambridge University Press, 1973), 2.

57. Mary Douglas, *The Lele of Kasai* (London: Oxford University Press, 1963).

58. Reay, *The Kuma*.

59. Strathern, *Women in Between*.

60. Ralph Bulmer, "Political Aspects of the Moka Ceremonial Exchange System among the Kyaka People of the Western Highlands of New Guinea," *Oceania* 31, no. 1 (1969): 11.

61. Another line of inquiry would compare bridewealth systems to dowry systems. Many of these questions are treated in Goody and Tambiah, *Bridewealth*.

62. Edmund Leach, *Rethinking Anthropology* (New York: Humanities Press, 1971), 90.

63. Ibid., 88–89.

64. Bronislaw Malinowski, "The Primitive Economics of the Trobriand Islanders," in *Cultures of the Pacific*, ed. T. Harding and B. Wallace (New York: Free Press, 1970).

65. Henry Wright, personal communication.

4 # Constructing a Theory of Capitalist Patriarchy and Socialist Feminism

Zillah Eisenstein

Radical feminists and male leftists, in confusing socialist women and socialist feminists, fail to recognize the political distinction between being a woman and being a feminist. But the difference between socialist women and socialist feminists needs to be articulated if the ties between radical feminism and socialist feminists are to be understood. The commitment of this paper is to make these important distinctions by articulating the growing efforts of socialist feminists to understand the mutual dependence of patriarchy and capitalism, an effort they are alone in making.

Although there are socialist women who are committed to understanding and changing the system of capitalism, socialist feminists are committed to understanding the system of power deriving from capitalist patriarchy. I choose this phrase, capitalist patriarchy, to emphasize the existing mutual dependence of the capitalist class structure and male supremacy. Understanding the interdependence of patriarchy and capitalism is essential to the political analysis of socialist feminism. It becomes necessary to understand that patriarchy (as male supremacy) existed before capitalism and continues in postcapitalist societies. And yet to say that, within the present system of power, either patriarchy or capitalism causes the other is to fail to understand their present mutually reinforcing system and dialectical relationship, a relationship that must be understood if the structure of oppression is to be changed. Socialist feminism in this sense moves beyond

Source: This article is reprinted from the *Insurgent Sociologist* 7, no. 3 (Spring 1977), pp. 3–17, by permission of the publisher, *Critical Sociology*, Sociology Department, University of Oregon, Eugene, OR 97403.

singular Marxist analysis and isolated radical feminist theory. The capitalist class structure and the hierarchical sexual structuring of society are the problem.

Power is dealt with in a dichotomous way by socialist women and radical feminists. In these analyses, they see power as deriving from either one's sex or one's economic class position. The critique of power as it is rooted in the male/female distinction focuses most often on patriarchy. The critique of power as it is rooted in the bourgeoisie/proletariat distinction focuses on capitalism. One studies *either* the social relations of production *or* the social relations of reproduction,[1] domestic *or* wage labor, the private *or* the public realms, the family *or* the economy, ideology *or* material conditions, the sexual division of labor *or* capitalist class relations, as oppressive. Even though almost all women are implicated in both sides of these activities, "woman" is dealt with as though she were not. Such a conceptual picture of woman hampers one's understanding of the complexity of her oppression. Dichotomy wins out over reality. I will attempt here to replace this dichotomous thinking with a dialectical approach.[2]

The synthesis of radical feminism and Marxist analysis is a necessary first step in formulating a cohesive feminist political theory. This new formulation, socialist feminism, is not a mere adding together of these two theories of power. It is rather a real mix of the interrelationships between capitalism and patriarchy as expressed through the sexual division of labor. To define capitalist patriarchy as the source of the problem is at the same time to suggest that socialist feminism is the answer. My discussion uses Marxist class analysis as the thesis, radical feminist patriarchal analysis as the antithesis, and from the two evolves the synthesis of socialist feminism. I will argue that the recognition of class analysis, patriarchal theory, and the dialectical method are supremely important in constructing socialist feminist theory.

Thesis: Woman as Class
Marx: Revolutionary Ontology and Women's Liberation

The importance of Marxist analysis to the study of women's oppression is twofold. First, it provides a necessary class analysis for the study of power. Second, it provides a method of analysis that is historical and dialectical. Although the dialectic (as method) is most often connected to the study of class and class conflict, it can also be used to articulate the patriarchal relations of women's existence and hence their revolutionary potential.

One can use the dialectic to clarify this potential because Marxist analysis provides one with the tools for understanding all power relations, and there is nothing about the dialectical and historical method that limits it only to understanding class relations. What I want to do here is to utilize Marx's analysis (class conflict) but also to extract his method and apply it to dimensions of power relations to which he was not sensitive. In this sense, I am using Marx's method to expand our present understanding of material relations in capitalism to include material relations in capitalist patriarchy.

These relations are illuminated by Marx's theories of exploitation and alienation. There has already been much discussion among socialist women and socialist feminists about the importance of the theory of exploitation in understanding woman's oppression,[3] so I will examine this only briefly. I focus more particularly on the importance of Marx's dialectical revolutionary ontology as it is presented in his theory of alienation. Although the substantive discussion of alienation applies to women workers in the labor force and in qualified ways to nonpaid domestic workers as housewives, I am particularly interested here in the method of analysis rather than in the content of Marx's discussion of alienation. By not reducing the analysis to class and class conflict as expressed in the theory of exploitation, we can extend the dialectical method present in the theory of alienation to the particular revolutionary potential of women. Essentially this means that although the theory of alienation includes exploitation, it should not be reduced to it.[4]

The theory of alienation and its commitment to "species life" in Communist society is necessary to understand the revolutionary capacity of human beings.[5] The theory of alienation specifies the relationship between essence and existence. Without this, human beings would be exploited in capitalist relations, but they would not necessarily be potentially revolutionary. Exploitation—without the presence of these relations specified in the theory of alienation and without the construction of the individual and the society that this entails—would leave us with an exploited person. But because of the potential for species life in the individual, the exploited worker is also the potential revolutionary. Without the potential of species life we would have Aristotle's happy slave, not Marx's revolutionary proletariat. And this potential exists in men and women, regardless of their position in the class structure or their relation to exploitation. The actualizing of this potential, however, is differentiated according to one's class.

With his theory of alienation, Marx is critically probing the nature of capitalism. By capitalism, Marx and Engels meant the entire process of commodity production. In examining the exploitation inherent in this process, Marx developed his theory of power. Power or powerlessness derives from one's class position; hence, oppression is a result of capitalist organization and is based in a lack of power and control. Through productive labor capitalist society exploits the worker who creates surplus value for the bourgeoisie. The surplus labor, which is inherent in profit, is derived from the difference between the actual and necessary labor time of the worker.

> Productive labor, in its meaning for capitalist production, is wage-labor which, exchanged against the valuable part of capital (the part of the capital that is spent on wages), reproduces not only this part of the capital (or the value of its own labor-power), but in addition produces surplus-value for the capitalist. . . . Only that wage labor is production which produces capital.[6]

The class structure, which manifests itself in social, political, and cultural forms as well, is economic at its base. Society is divided into the bourgeoisie and the proletariat. The basis of separation and conflict between the two is the relation each one has to the modes of production; hence, the proletariat's exploitation in which surplus value is extracted from its productive labor is its oppression.

This Marxist indictment of capitalist relations is subsumed into its revolutionary ontology of social and human existence. It posits within each individual a dialectic between essence and existence which is manifested as revolutionary consciousness in society. Both the criticism of class existence as alienating and exploitative and the revolutionary ontology of the theory make Marxist analysis critical to developing a feminist theory that incorporates but moves beyond a theory of class consciousness.

What is crucial for the application of Marx to the "woman question" is this way of thinking, which does not limit people's capacities to what society may force them to be. In his theory of alienation, expressed through his conception of "species being," Marx poses a revolutionary method of analysis. "Species beings" are those beings who ultimately reach their human potential for creative labor, social consciousness, and social living through the struggle against capitalist society, and who fully internalize these capacities in Communist society. This basic ontological structure defines one's existence alongside one's essence. Reality for Marx is thus more than mere existence. It embodies within it a movement toward human essence. This is not a totally abstract human essence but rather an essence we can understand in historical contexts. "Species being" is the conception of what is possible for people in the unalienated society but exists only as essence in capitalist society.

When extended to women, this revolutionary ontology suggests that the possibility of their freedom exists alongside their exploitation and oppression. This conflict between existence and essence lays the basis for revolutionary consciousness and activity. It allows an internally critical appraisal of any particular moment. Women's existence and essence have not merged in this society. Woman is potentially more than what she is. She is definitely structured by what she is—and this *defines* real possibilities for tomorrow by what she is today. But what she is today does not *determine* the outer limits of her capacities or potentialities. This analysis is of course the same for the alienated worker. The worker cut off from his or her creative abilities is still a creative being in terms of potential. What you can be is not necessarily what you are.

The contradiction of existence and essence lies, therefore, at the base of the revolutionary proletariat as well as the revolutionary woman. One's class position defines consciousness for Marx, but if we utilize the revolutionary ontological method, it need not be limited to this. If we wish to say that women are defined in terms of their sex as well, patriarchal relations define their consciousness and have implications for their revolutionary potential as a result. The method—of posing revolutionary potential as it reflects conflicts between people's real conditions (existence) and their possibilities (essence)—can be extended to understand the patriarchal relations inhibiting the development of human essence. The reality of social relations involves both capitalist class *and* patriarchal relations. In this sense, the conception of species life points to the revolutionary potential of men and women for Marx.

However, the social relations defining the potential for woman's revolutionary consciousness are more complex than Marx understood them to be. He did not see that a more complex set of relations made species life unavailable to women and that hence its actualization could not come through dismantling the class system alone. As a result, Marx's statements on women are limited in depth; he never questioned patriarchy as the hierarchical sexual ordering of society, as we shall see. But his writings on women are important because of his commitment to uncover the tensions between species life and capitalist alienated forms of social experience for all human beings.

There are partial statements on the family and women's exploitation in the Paris *Manuscripts, The Communist Manifesto, The German Ideology,* and *Capital.* Marx clarifies his position on the bourgeois family in *The Communist Manifesto.* The family relation has been reduced to a mere money relation.

The bourgeois sees in his wife a mere instrument of production. On what foundation is the present family, the bourgeois family, based?

On capital, on private gain. . . . The bourgeois claptrap about the family and education, about hallowed co-relation of parent and child, becomes all the more disgusting the more, by the action of modern industry, all family ties among the proletarians are torn asunder, and then children transformed into simple articles of commerce and instruments of labour.[7]

The relations of private property become the mode of exchange. The development of these bourgeois priorities transforms the social relations in the family; and, as is apparent in *The German Ideology*, the family—which Marx sees as the only social relationship—becomes a subordinate need.[8]

The concerns of private property and possession pervade man-woman relations. In "On the Jewish Question" Marx writes: "The species relation itself, the relation between man and woman, etc., becomes an object of commerce. The woman is bought and sold."[9] The mentality of "having" twists species relationships into those of ownership and domination, and marriage into prostitution. And so in the 1844 *Manuscripts* Marx writes:

Finally, this movement of opposing universal private property to private property finds expression in the animal form of opposing to *marriage* (certainly a *form of exclusive private property*) the *community of women* in which a woman becomes a piece of *communal* and *common* property. . . . Just as woman passes from marriage to general prostitution, so the entire world of wealth (that is, of man's subjective substance) passes from the relationship of exclusive marriage with the owner of private property to a state of universal prostitution with the community.[10]

Marx sees the problem of women as arising from their status as mere instruments of production, and thus he sees the solution in the socialist revolution. In the *Manifesto* he writes that "the abolition of the present system of production must bring with it the abolition of the community of women springing from that system, i.e., of prostitution, both public and private."[11] Given his analysis of woman's existence as reflective of class relations that define society for her both within and outside of marriage, the destruction of capitalism would transform her condition.

The bourgeois family is seen by Marx as an *instrument* of capitalist society, with no dimensions particular unto itself. Woman's oppression is her exploitation in a class society through bourgeois marriage and the family. Her powerlessness reflects capitalist arrangements.

The sexual division of labor as the sexual definition of roles, purposes, activities, and so on, has no specific existence for Marx. Woman is perceived as just another victim, undistinguished from the proletariat in general, of the pernicious class division of labor. Marx saw no sexual distinctions and functions unique to this one group of producers as ultimately definitive of the power structure. He had little or no sense of woman's biological-reproduction or maternal functions as critical in creating different varieties of a division of labor within the family. As a result, Marx perceived the exploitation of men and women as deriving from the same source and assumed that their oppression could be understood in the same structural terms. Revolutionary consciousness is limited to understanding the class relation of exploitation. We shall see later that it is only with the conceptual differentiation of the hierarchical sexual ordering of society, as a phenomenon of patriarchy, that women's oppression can be understood as connected to although distinct from the "general" oppression of the proletariat.

There is no reason to doubt that in Communist society (where *all* are to achieve species existence), life would still be structured by a sexual division of labor that would entail different life options for men and women. Sex roles would involve preassigned tasks for women, which would necessitate continued alienation and isolation. Essence and existence would still not be one. Marx did not understand that the sexual division of labor and society organizes noncreative and isolating work particularly for women. The destruction of capitalism and capitalist exploitation does not ensure species existence—that is, creative work, social community, and critical consciousness—for women.

Women's Exploitation in History

In *The German Ideology*, Marx and Engels discuss the division of labor in early precapitalist society in familial terms. It is "a further extension of the natural division of labour imposed by the family. The social structure is therefore limited to an extension of the family; patriarchal family chieftains; below them the members of the tribe; finally slaves. The slavery latent in the family only develops gradually." [12] The division of labor "imposed by the family" is spoken of as natural, and whether this means "necessary" or "good," it is a division accepted by Marx and Engels. The division of labor in the family is not reflective of the economic society that defines and surrounds it—as in *The Communist Manifesto*—but rather at this early historical stage it structures the society and its division of labor.

Marx and Engels's analysis of the family continues: "With these, there develops the division of labour in the sexual act, then that division of labour which develops spontaneously or 'naturally' by virtue of natural predisposition (e.g., physical strength), needs, accidents, etc."[13] The first division of labor is the "natural" division of labor in the family through the sex act. The act of child breeding begins the division of labor.[14] The activity of procreation develops a division of labor, although the full dimensions of this division are never explored. It is through this act that the first appearance of property arises within the family. For Marx and Engels, this is when wife and child become the slaves of the husband.

> This latent slavery in the family, though still very crude, is the first property, but even at this early stage it corresponds perfectly to the definition of modern economists who call it the power of disposing of the labor power of others. Division of labor and private property are moreover identical expressions.[15]

There are here seeds of an early, albeit crude, insight into the sexual division of labor, although there is no discussion of it as such. What weakens and finally limits the insight is that for Marx and Engels this division of labor deriving from the sex act is coincidental and *identical* with the birth of private property: "division of labor and private property are moreover identical expressions."[16] The division of labor has no specific quality of its own. Property arising from a division of labor arising from the act of procreation is not differentiated from property arising from the relations of capital. There is no notion here that inequalities might arise from the sex act itself. The family is seen as the locus of the division of labor in society; but it has no existence outside the series of property relations. *The German Ideology* presents, then, a skeletal analysis of women's condition as it changes through material conditions. Although reproduction is acknowledged as the first source of the division of labor, it never receives any specific examination in terms of its relationship to the capitalist division of labor. Reproduction and production are seen as one, as they come to be analyzed in relation to the capitalist division of labor in society.

According to Engels in *The Origin of the Family, Private Property, and the State*, the social organization of society is determined by production and the family.[17] He repeats here the theme developed in *The German Ideology*: the "first division of labor is that between man and woman for child breeding," and the first social antagonism arises with the antagonism between man and woman in monogamous marriage.[18] The latter point is apparently obvious to Engels, but what this antagonism is based on is never made clear. His claim is that the first class antagonism *accompanies* (arises with) the antagonism between man and woman. One would not think that the antagonism referred to was one of class. Yet he ultimately speaks of the conflict between man and woman as class conflict: the man is the bourgeoisie within the family, the wife the proletariat.[19] But "bourgeoisie" and "proletariat" are positions of power deriving from one's relation to the economic means of production, not the sex act of reproduction. Categorizing them as such subsumes the relations of reproduction under the relations of production. It appears contradictory that Engels acknowledges male/female relations within the family as defining the division of labor in society and yet completely subsumes them under categories of analysis related to production. He offers no explanation that could resolve this dilemma because it stands outside the terms of his analysis.

We have seen that Engels acknowledges the family's primal role historically in structuring society and that the division of labor emanates from it to the society. Yet the categories of analysis explaining the slavery of the woman in the family derive entirely from the relations of production. The family comes to be defined by the historical economic modes rather than itself taking part in defining the economy as well as society. The flow has been reversed. The family is no longer spoken of as a source of the division of labor coincident with economic relations. Economic existence comes to determine the family.[20] Hence, Engels assumes that the family will disintegrate with the elimination of capitalism instead of analyzing how the family itself comes to support an economic mode. He forgets his own analysis of the "first division of labor" and instead analyzes the family as merely a reflective mirror of society with no particular political existence to comprehend. Although he acknowledges the problem of woman's existence within the private domestic sphere—outside and opposed to social production—he sees this as reflecting the relations of production rooted in private property. Woman's activity in reproduction (which limits her activity in production) is not seen as problematic at this point.

The family has become a microcosm of the political economy for Engels. "It contains in miniature all the contradictions which later extend throughout society and its state."[21] The man is the bourgeoisie, the woman the proletariat. What is most interesting here is that Engels does not use the categories of male as bourgeoisie and female as proletariat outside the family. People are assigned class positions in the larger society according to their relations to the means of production, not their sex. He is using different criteria inside and outside the family to define membership within a class. If these categories were built upon like bases of power, one could move in and out of the family with the same units of analysis being applicable. And if one wants to say that *ultimately* the usage of proletariat/bourgeoisie by Engels within the family is economic, there are evidently still other considerations involved. If this were not so, then he would not have (1) class divisions in the family as bourgeoisie/male, proletariat/female and (2) class divisions in society in terms of ownership/nonownership of the means of production. Even though, for him, these *ultimately* mean the same thing, what do they reflect *initially* about the relations of the family and capitalism? It would seem that these considerations have to do with power emanating from the sexual differences between men and women in their relations to reproduction. This was not grasped by Engels, however.

Most of the time Engels works from his simple equation: oppression equals exploitation. Class existence defines powerlessness for Engels, although he has the core for understanding that woman's oppression is more complex than the system of exploitation. Even though he recognizes that the family conceals domestic slavery, he believes at the same time that there are no differences (in kind) between domestic slavery and the wage slavery of the husband. They both derive from capitalism. "The emancipation of woman will only be possible when woman can take part in production of a large-social scale and domestic work no longer claims anything but an insignificant amount of her time."[22] The real equality of women will come for Engels with the end of exploitation by capital and the transference of private housework to public industry. Given the lack of understanding of the sexual division of labor, however, even if domestic work were made public, it most probably would remain, for Engels, woman's work.

In conclusion, then, we can see that the analysis sketched by Marx and Engels in *The German Ideology* and then further developed by Engels in *The Origin of the Family, Private Property, and the State* reveals their belief that the family, at least historically, structured the division of labor in society and that in some sense this reflects the division of labor in the sex act. Initially, the family structure defined in some sense the structure of society.

> According to the materialistic conception, the determining factor
> in history is, in the final instance, the production and reproduction
> of immediate life. This, again, is of a twofold character: on the one
> side, the production of the means of existence, of food, clothing and
> shelter and the tools necessary for that production; on the other
> side, the production of human beings themselves, the propagation
> of the species. The social organization under which the people of
> a particular historical epoch and a particular country live is deter-
> mined by both kinds of production; by the stage of development of
> labor on the one hand and of the family on the other.[23]

This analysis is lost, however, through the discussion of the family in capitalist society, where the family comes to be viewed as just another part of the superstructure, totally reflective of class society. The relations of reproduction become subsumed under the relations of production. The point to be made is not that the family does not reflect society but that through both its patriarchal structure and its patriarchal ideology the family and the need for reproduction structure society as well. This reciprocal relationship, between family and society, production and reproduction, defines the life of women. The study of women's oppression, then, must deal with both sexual and economic material conditions if one is to understand oppression rather than merely understand economic exploitation.

While these criticisms are important in assessing the particular contribution of Marx and Engels, they should by no means prompt one to reject either their class analysis or their ontological and historical method. The point rather is that the historical materialist method must be extended to incorporate women's relations to the sexual division of labor and society as producer and reproducer, as well as to incorporate the ideological formulation of this relationship.[24] Only then will her existence be understood in its true complexity and species life become available to her too.

Antithesis: Woman as Sex
Patriarchy and the Radical Feminists

Although radical feminism is conventionally dated with the recent Women's Liberation Movement, around 1969–70, it has important historical ties to the liberal feminism of Mary Wollstonecraft, Elizabeth Cady Stanton, and Harriet Taylor Mill, women who spoke of sexual politics long before Kate Millett did.[25] These women understood in their own fragmented way that men have power as men in a society organized into "sexual spheres." But while they spoke of power in caste terms, they were only beginning to understand the *structure of power* enforced upon them through the sexual division of labor and society. The claims of these feminists remained reformist because the necessary connections between sexual oppression, the sexual division of labor and society, and the economic class structure were not made.

Radical feminism today has a much more sophisticated understanding of sexual power than had these feminist forebears. With this new understanding, radical feminism has replaced the struggle for the vote and legal reforms with the revolutionary demand for the destruction of patriarchy. It is the biological family, the hierarchical sexual division of society, and sex roles themselves that must be fundamentally reorganized. The sexual division of labor and society expresses the most basic hierarchical division in our society between masculine and feminine roles. It is the basic mechanism of control for patriarchal culture. It designates the fact that roles, purposes, activity, one's labor are *determined* sexually. It expresses the very notion that the biological distinction male/female is used to distinguish social functions and individual power.[26]

In much the same way that radical feminists have found the analysis of Wollstonecraft, Stanton, and Taylor incomplete, they have found the politics and theories of the left insufficient. The existing radical analyses of society failed, in their view, to relate the structure of the economic class system to its origins in the sexual class system. Out of a desire to remedy this theoretical shortcoming, radical feminism has developed. These women were not satisfied with the Marxist definition of power and the equation between women's oppression and exploitation. Economic class did not seem to be at the center of their lives.[27] Rather than economic power, sexual power seemed to be central to any larger and meaningful revolutionary analysis. They perceived history as patriarchal and its struggles deriving from sex conflict; the dividing reality not economic class but sexual class; the battle lines drawn between men and women rather than between bourgeoisie and proletariat; the determining relation to reproduction, not to production.

Radical feminism offers a criticism of patriarchy through the analysis of sex roles themselves. Patriarchy is defined as a sexual system of power in which the male role is superior in possession of power and economic privilege. Patriarchy is the male hierarchical ordering of society. Although the legal institutional base of patriarchy used to be more explicit, the basic relations of power have remained intact. The patriarchal system is preserved, via marriage and the family, through the sexual division of labor and society. Sex roles themselves are understood to be units of power and oppression. Woman's position in this power structure is defined as derived not from the economic class structure but from the autonomous patriarchal organization of society. As a power structure, patriarchy is rooted in biological reality rather than in an economic or historical one. Manifested through male force and control, the roots of patriarchy are located in women's reproductive selves.

Through this analysis, radical feminists bridge the dichotomy of the personal/public. Sex, as the personal, is the political as well. Women share their position of oppression because of the very politics of the society. And this is a sexual politics that gives privileges to men and oppresses women. The structuring of society through the sexual division limits the realm of activity, work, desires, and aspirations of women. "Sex is a status category with political implications."[28]

Shulamith Firestone: Sexual Dialectics

In her book *The Dialectic of Sex*, Shulamith Firestone offers what is perhaps a paradigmatic expression of radical feminism. The specific oppression that women experience, argues Firestone, is directly related to their unique biology. Woman's reproductive function is *inherently* central to her oppression, and thus so too is the biological family. *Oppression in society is sexual: power is divided along sex lines.* In other words, a sex class evolves directly from biological reality. According to Firestone, "The sexual imbalance of power is biologically based."[29] Men and women are anatomically different and hence not equally privileged. From this male/female distinction the domination of one group by another is derived.[30]

As Firestone presents this novel idea of a sex class, she obviously departs from the classical Marxist meaning of class. It no longer means an economic category denoting ownership of private property or the relation to the means of production. Woman, as a sex, is a class. Man is the other and opposing class.

What are the limitations of Firestone's analysis? In trying to answer and reject the economic theory of power, she artificially separates the sexual and economic spheres (a separation most blatantly problematic in her analysis of the family). Instead of showing their interconnection, Firestone replaces capitalism with patriarchy as the oppressive system. She fails to move further through an additive or synthesizing perspective because she chooses to deal with sexuality as the key oppression of modern times, rather than to view oppression as a more *complex reality*. It is not that she does not see economic oppression as problematic for women, but rather that she does not view it as the key source of oppression. The either/or formulations about woman's situation stunt the analysis. Even though Firestone is aware of the economic dimensions of power, her insistence on seeing women as *either* sexual beings *or* economic beings moves her away from dealing with the complex mix of woman's existence. So divided, woman becomes a predominantly sexual being, and existence becomes one-dimensional. Dichotomy wins out over woman's complexity. In the same way that Marxist analysis is not extended to the specificity of women's oppression, radical feminism cannot understand the full reality of our economic existence and, therefore, is incapable of understanding the specificity of women's existence. Patriarchy remains a generalized ahistorical power structure.

We can locate a problem in Firestone's analysis in her discussion of biology and equality. Firestone has negated the social and historical framework of Marx and instead treats woman's biology as an atemporal static condition. She sees a woman's biology as *inherently* oppressive rather than defined as such by social and cultural power relationships. The problem is, however, that inequality is a concept that connotes a *social context*, while Firestone speaks of it only in terms of nature. It is true that women's and men's bodies differ biologically, but to speak of this as inequality is to impose a social assessment on a biological difference.[31] Firestone unselfconsciously accepts part of patriarchal ideology by collapsing the distinction between biological difference and biological inequality. She acknowledges that one cannot justify a discriminatory sex class system in terms of its origin in nature[32]—but one cannot *explain* it in such terms either. What is needed here is to show how woman's sexuality has been interpreted differently throughout history. The implication of Firestone's analysis is that no dialectic is set up between woman and society; she operates as a biological determinist. In other words, there is nothing social or historical about the power relationship between man and woman as she discusses it. It is innately defined by biological "inequalities." Biology is important in defining power relations because of its cultural and political definition and use. In this sense, patriarchy is not a biological system but a political one with a specific history.

To know there are universal elements to women's oppression is important. But women's existence has limited meaning when the specificity of our existence is relegated to the universal. All history may be patriarchal, but this does not mean that the differences between historical periods are not important. The specifics elucidate the general meaning of patriarchal existence.

To understand the specificity of women's lives, we must take account of two processes: (1) history defined in terms of class struggle—feudal, capitalist, socialist; (2) patriarchal history as it is structured in these periods. Although patriarchy takes on specific qualities at specific moments, it cannot be fully understood divorced from its universal existence. For instance, the conceptualizing of motherhood, the fact of the sexual hierarchical division of labor, and that of the family need to be understood as expressions of patriarchy at various particular historical moments. These historical moments, also, are a part of a historically and culturally continuous reality. This generalization does not become concrete and real, however, until it is understood in its particular form. It is important, therefore, living in a capitalist society, to understand both the likenesses and differences between feudal patriarchy and capitalist patriarchy. It is the likenesses that have particular meaning for us if we are to try to make sure that they do not continue their life in the new society. Capitalist relations of patriarchy are connected to precapitalist forms. We need to challenge the precapitalist elements that are *maintained* in capitalist society. They have been maintained in capitalism while not deriving from capitalist needs, although they have been defined, now, in a capitalist context. It is the maintenance of these precapitalist forms that constructs patriarchal history for us.

Firestone's asocial, ahistorical framework becomes most limiting in relation to her discussion of technology. In her view, it is ultimately technology that will free woman from her body through contraception and eventually extra-uterine reproduction. Feminism is the natural outcome of this new technology. Technology is therefore at the base of woman's liberation. Although in response to these arguments we can acknowledge that contraception has freed women in important ways, still the question remains whether birth control, abortion rights, and so on will ever be allowed to develop to the degree that would permit woman to (politically) control reproduction. Witness statements of Laos and Cambodia declaring birth control illegal until their countries are repopulated. Women's control of reproduction would be necessary for Firestone's feminist revolution, and it seems implausible that such a revolution will be "made" for women by technology itself.

Firestone's end analysis loses its plausibility when we understand that technology is an intrinsic dimension of a society's power structure. Male ruling-class needs define technological developments; therefore, without a change of those in power (and hence those who define the purposes of technology), technology is an unlikely liberator. One must remain critical of technology and ever aware of the motivations behind technological change.[33]

The question of the control of technology, however, does point to the very question of needed power, to questions that arise from the various dimensions of my argument thus far. How do women organize for this revolutionary action? How is technology connected to the sexual-economic power structure? On what basis do women have revolutionary potential? If the feminist revolution is not made for women by the technicians, then we need to formulate more specifically the answers to these questions.

The thrust of Firestone's analysis is to isolate sex oppression from the economic class organization of society, although she realizes herself that economic suffering contributes to woman's oppression at least as much as any female ills.[34] She does note that a woman, even when well educated, will not earn as much money as a man. A woman also suffers from the lack of money when she decides to care for children. This in itself should invalidate a totally biological argument for the basis of a revolution needed in the family. Firestone speaks of wanting to relate the structure of the economic class system to its origins in the sexual class system, but she fails to do this. Even if we accept the idea that economic oppression was a basic defense of sexual oppression historically, today the two systems support each other. They are mutually dependent now. This relationship only gets distorted when one tries to define it in causal and dichotomized terms.

The connections and relationships between the two systems remain undefined in the writings of radical feminism. Hence, power is dealt with in terms of half the dichotomy. Power is sexually based and not economic in its initial structuring. Capitalism does not appear within the theoretical analysis to define woman's web of power. And ties between patriarchy as a system of power and woman's biology are also usually kept separate. Instead of seeing a historical formulation of woman's oppression, we are presented with biological determinism. A final outcome of this dichotomizing of material reality is to sever the relationship between these conditions and their supporting ideologies. Neither Marxists nor radical feminists deal with the interrelationships between ideas and real conditions sufficiently as a result. If reality becomes segmented, it is not surprising that ideological representations of that reality become severed as well.

Synthesis: Socialist Feminism
Exploitation and Oppression

Marxist analysis seeks a historical explanation of existing power relationships in terms of economic class relations, and radical feminism deals with the biological reality of power. Socialist feminism, on the other hand, analyzes power in terms of its class origins as well as its patriarchal roots. In such an analysis capitalism and patriarchy are not simply autonomous systems, but neither are they one and the same thing. They are, in present form, mutually dependent.

As a socialist feminist, I argue that oppression and exploitation are not equivalent concepts, as they were for Marx and Engels. Exploitation speaks to the economic reality of capitalist class relations, whereas oppression refers to power as it is defined within patriarchal and capitalist relations. Exploitation is a descriptive assessment of men and women workers in the labor force in capitalist society; woman's oppression reflects her exploitation if she is a wage laborer within capitalism but at the same time reflects the relations that define her existence in the patriarchal sexual hierarchy, which defines her as mother, domestic laborer, consumer. Power, or the converse—oppression—derives from both sex and class, and this is manifested through both the material and the ideological dimensions of patriarchy and capitalism. Oppression includes exploitation but reflects a more complex reality. It reflects the hierarchical relations of the sexual division of labor and society.

This system of oppression, which connotes the *mutual dependence* of capitalism and patriarchy as they are currently practiced, is what I have chosen to call capitalist patriarchy. It is the contemporary expression of the relationship between these two systems, although the historical development of capitalist patriarchy can be dated from the mid-eighteenth century in England and the mid-nineteenth century in America. Both periods reflect the developing relationship between patriarchy and the new industrial capitalism. Capitalist patriarchy, by definition, breaks through the dichotomies of class and sex, private and public, domestic and wage labor, family and economy, personal and political, ideology and material conditions.

As we have seen, Marx and Engels believed man's oppression to exist in his exploited position as worker in capitalist society. They assumed that woman's existence was parallel to his. They equated the two when they suggested that domestic slavery was the same, in nature and essence, as wage slavery. Because Marx and Engels did not study the *particular* existence of women in domestic slavery, by default they conceived it in parallel terms with wage labor. They acknowledged woman as exploited in the proletariat if she worked within the labor force; if she was relegated to domestic slavery, they saw her as a nonwage slave. Her existence was perceived in terms of the categories of wage labor. Domestic slavery was not seen as a sexual category as well. Capitalism "exploited" women; there was no conception of how patriarchy and capitalism defined women's "oppression" in coordination with each other. Marx and Engels adopted Feuerbach's stance that the general (class) condition defined the specific case (women).

Today, especially with the insights of radical feminism, we see not only that the equation of exploitation and oppression is problematic but also that if one uses Marx's own categories of productive labor as wage labor, domestic slaves are not "exploited" in the same way as wage slaves. They would have to be paid a wage for this to be true. Women as domestic laborers have no direct relation to wages even if the basic stealing of one's labor (though this takes different forms) is parallel between the two.

The reduction of oppression to exploitation within Marxist analysis rests upon the equation between the economic class structure and the structure of power in society. I differ with this assessment in that I believe that women's oppression is rooted in more than her class position (her exploitation) and that one must address as well her position within patriarchy—both structurally and ideologically—to fully understand woman's oppression. It is the particular relation and operation of the hierarchical sexual ordering of society within the class structure, or the understanding of the class structure within the sexual ordering of society, that focuses upon human activity in capitalist patriarchy. They exist together and cannot be understood when falsely isolated. It is important to note here that in dealing with these questions, one breaks down the division between material existence (economic or sexual) and ideology. This is because the sexual division of labor and society, which lays the basis for patriarchy as we know it, has both material form (sex roles themselves) and ideological reality (the stereotypes, myths, and ideas that define these roles). They exist in an internal web.

If women's existence is defined by capitalism and patriarchy through their ruling ideologies and institutions, then an understanding of either capitalism alone or patriarchy in isolation will not deal with the problem of women's oppression. As Juliet Mitchell has written: "The overthrow of the capitalist economy and the political challenge that effects this do not in themselves mean a transformation of patriarchal ideology."[35] The overthrow does not necessitate the destruction of patriarchal institutions, either. Although practiced differently in each place, the sexual division of labor exists in the Soviet Union, in Cuba, in China. It is true that the histories of these societies have been different, and limitations in the struggle against patriarchy have been defined in terms of the particularities of their cultures. There has been real progress in women's lives, particularly in China and Cuba, but it would be inaccurate to say that a sexual division of labor and society does not exist in these societies. It is only recently in Cuba that the sexual division of labor has been tackled as a particular problem for the revolution. As we can see, patriarchy is cross-cultural by definition, though it is actualized differently in different societies via the institutionalizing of sexual hierarchy. The contours of sex roles may differ societally, but power has resided and does reside with the male.

Today patriarchy, the power of the male through these sexual roles in capitalism, is institutionalized in the nuclear family.[36] Juliet Mitchell ties this to the "law of the prehistoric murdered father."[37] In finding the certain root of patriarchy in this mythic crime among men at the dawn of our life as a social group, Mitchell risks discussing patriarchy more in terms of the ideology it produces than in terms of its connection to its material formulation in the confrontation between man and woman. She roots the Oedipus complex in the universal patriarchal culture. But culture is defined for her in terms of an exchange system that exists today primarily in ideological form. For Mitchell, patriarchy precedes capitalism through the universal existence of the Oedipus complex.

I contend, however, that patriarchy precedes capitalism through the existence of the sexual ordering of society, which derives from ideological and political interpretations of biological difference. In other words, men have chosen to interpret and politically use the fact that women are the reproducers of humanity. And given both this fact of reproduction and the political control of it, we have the relations of reproduction arising in a particular formulation of woman's oppression. Although there is a patriarchal culture carried over from one historical period to another to protect the sexual hierarchy of society, I question whether the Oedipus complex is really the tool by which to understand this culture. Today the sexual division of society is based on real differences that accrue from years of ideological pressure. Material conditions define necessary ideologies, and ideologies in their turn have impact on reality and alter reality. There is a two-way flow here. Women are products of their social history, yet women can shape their own lives as well.

In socialist feminism, historical materialism is not defined in terms of the relations of production without understanding its connection to the series of relations that arise from woman's sexuality, which are tied to the relations of reproduction.[38] And the ideological formulations of these relations are key here. An understanding of feminist materialism must direct us to an understanding of the particular existence of women in capitalist patriarchy. The general approaches of both Marxists in terms of class, and radical feminists in terms of sex obfuscate the reality of power relations in women's lives.

Pioneers in Feminist Materialism: de Beauvoir and Mitchell

Simone de Beauvoir confronts the interrelationship between sexuality and history in *The Second Sex*. She states that "the division of the sexes is a biological fact, not an event in human history." And yet she goes on to say that "we must view the facts of biology in the light of an ontological, economic, social, and psychological context. She understands that women are defined by men and as such cast in the role of the "other," but she also realizes that the sexual monism of Freud and the economic monism of Engles are inappropriate for the full analysis of women's oppression.[39]

Beauvoir's initial insights were further developed by Juliet Mitchell in her *Woman's Estate*. In this important book Mitchell offers a rigorous criticism of classical socialist theory, criticizing it for locating woman's oppression too narrowly in the family and in an undifferentiated manner. She rejects the reduction of woman's problem to her incapacity to work, which stresses her simple subordination to the institutions of private property.[40]

What Mitchell does instead is to define four basic structures in which woman's powerlessness is rooted. These "structures" of (a) production, (b) reproduction, (c) sexuality, and (d) socialization of children define the four-dimensional existence of women in capitalist society. To be able to cope with the series of oppressions women experience, Mitchell thinks it first necessary to differentiate among them. Reproduction is the "natural" role in producing children. The biological function of maternity is a universal, atemporal fact that has come to define woman's existence. Woman is socializer in that "woman's biological destiny as mother becomes a cultural vocation in her role as a socializer of children."[41] The causal flow that Mitchell constructs of woman's oppressive existence derives from woman's capacity as reproducer and its connected consequences for her social and economic activity. Woman's biological capacity defines her social and economic purpose. Maternity has set up the family as a historical necessity, and the family has become woman's world. Hence, woman is excluded from production and public life, an exclusion that results in sexual inequality and in woman's resulting powerlessness.

The four structures are meant to be inclusive of women's activity. Production or work is activity that exists both inside and outside the family. Reproduction most often takes place within the family structure, whereas the structure of sexuality affects women in all areas of life. The socialization of children that is done by mothers is located within the family, although socialization takes place at all times. Mitchell locates woman's oppression in structures which, though not limited to the family, do not exclude it. Both the family and society in general are implicated in woman's oppression. Thus Mitchell is led to conclude that by focusing on the destruction of the family (as does Firestone at one extreme and Engels at another), one does not necessarily substantially alter woman's situation. For Mitchell, "socialism would properly mean not the abolition of the family but the diversification of the socially acknowledged relationships which are forcibly and rigidly compressed into it."[42]

Mitchell analyzes the family in capitalism as a supportive pillar to woman's oppressive condition because it supports both capitalism and the sexual division of labor and society. According to her, capitalism sees conflict and disruption as very much a part of people's lives. The family provides the affection bonds and a medium of calm for life to be maintained amid the disruption. The family supports capitalism economically in that it provides a productive labor force at the same time that it supplies the market with an arena for massive consumption. The family also performs an ideological role in that it cultivates the notions of individualism, freedom, and equality basic to the belief structure of society, albeit they are at odds with social and economic reality.[43]

The importance of Mitchell's analysis consists in her picturing of the different dimensions of woman's activity without denying her sexuality or her class oppression. She focuses on the very powerlessness that women experience because they are reproductive beings, sexual beings, working individuals, and socializers of children. She makes it clear that woman's oppression is based in part on the support the family gives the capitalist system in trapping woman in sexual and class oppression via these different structures. Her analysis sees power in its more complex reality. We are still left, however, with the basic problem of clarifying the relationship of the family and the political economy in capitalist patriarchal society.

The Sexual Division of Labor and Society in Capitalist Patriarchy: Toward a New Feminist Theory

One of the critical problems in trying to construct a persuasive argument about the interconnections of patriarchy and capitalism is that the language at hand (the family versus the economy) treats them as separate systems. In order to avoid this false separation I will discuss how patriarchy and capitalism operate within the sexual division of labor and society, rather than within the family. The sexual hierarchical division of labor cuts through this splitting of the family and the economy. As the most basic definition of people's activity, purposes, goals, desires, and dreams, according to their biological sex, the sexual division of labor and society is at the structural and ideological base of patriarchy and capitalism. It divides men and women into their respective hierarchical sex roles, and it structures their related duties in the family domain and within the economy.

This statement of the mutual dependence of patriarchy and capitalism assumes not only the malleability of patriarchy to the needs of capital but also the malleability of capital to the needs of patriarchy. In other words, when one states that capitalism needs patriarchy in order to operate efficiently, one is really noting that male supremacy, as a system of sexual hierarchy, supplies capitalism (and systems previous to it) with the necessary order and control; this patriarchal system of control is necessary to the smooth functioning of society and of the economic system and hence should not be undermined. This argument is to underscore the importance of the system of cultural, social, economic, and political control that emanates from the system of male supremacy. To the extent that the concern with profit and the concern with societal control are inextricably connected (but cannot be reduced to each other), patriarchy and capitalism become an *integral process,* with specific elements of each system necessitated by the other.

Capitalism uses patriarchy—and patriarchy is defined by the needs of capital. This statement does not undermine the foregoing claim that at the same time that one system uses the other, it must organize around the needs of the other in order to protect the specific quality of the other, lest the other system lose its specific character and with it its unique value. If I were to state this as simply as possible, I could say that patriarchy (as male supremacy) provides the sexual hierarchical ordering of society for political control and, as a political system, cannot be reduced to its economic structure; while capitalism, as an economic class system driven by the pursuit of profit, feeds off the patriarchal ordering. Together they form the political economy of the society; not merely one or another but a particular blend of the two.

There are real problems with this oversimplified statement. Mainly it severs relations that exist within both spheres. For instance, capitalism has a set of controls that emanate directly from the economic class relations of society and their organization in the workplace. And, of course, the biggest problem with this example is that it seems to assume a harmony between the two systems at all points, whereas in fact an uneasy relation between the two systems seems to be appearing as we move further into advanced capitalism. This conflict appears in some sense in the competing pulls on women between their employers and their husbands. The role of women in the labor force seems to undermine some of the control of patriarchal relations, as the double day becomes more obvious. The ghettoization of women in the labor force, however, does maintain a system of hierarchical control of women, both sexually and economically, which leaves the sexual hierarchy of society intact. And deference to patriarchal hierarchy and control is shown in the very fact that the search for cheap labor has not led to a full integration of women into all parts of the labor force. Although women's labor is cheaper, the system of control that maintains both the necessary order of the society and, with it, the cheapness of women's labor must be protected by segregating women in the labor force. The *justification*, however, for women's double day and unequal wages is less well protected today.

Although the sexual division of labor and society antedates capitalism, it has come to be further institutionalized and specifically defined through the nuclear family in terms of the needs of advanced capitalism. It now has much more form and structure than it did in precapitalist societies.[44] In precapitalist society the home was defined as the producing economic unit. Men, women, and children worked together in the home or on the farm to produce the goods necessary for their lives. Women still were procreators and child raisers, but the necessities and organization of work *limited the impact* of the sexual role distinction. This is not to say that sexual equality existed but rather to point to the importance of understanding the specific structure and use of the sexual division of labor today.

With the rise of industrial capitalism, men were brought out of the home into the wage-labor economy, disrupting the earlier organization of labor. Women became relegated to the home, considered nonproductive, and viewed *solely* in terms of the previous loosely defined sex roles. Although women were "mothers" before industrial capitalism, this was not an exclusive role, whereas with industrial capitalism women became "housewives." "The housewife emerged, alongside the proletariat—the two characteristic laborers of developed capitalist society."[45] The work that women continued to perform in the home was not conceived of as work. Productive labor was now defined as wage labor, labor that produces surplus profit—capital. "In sheer quantity, household labor, including child care, constitutes a huge amount of socially necessary production. Nevertheless, in a society based on commodity production, it is not usually considered 'real work' since it is outside of trade and the market place."[46]

The conditions of production in society, then, define and shape production, reproduction, and consumption in the family. So, too, the family mode of production, reproduction, and consumption affects commodity production. They work together to define the political economy. Within a capitalist patriarchal economy—where profit, which necessitates a system of political order and control, is the basic priority of the ruling class—the sexual division of labor and society serves a specific purpose. It stabilizes the society through the family while it organizes a realm of work, as domestic labor, for which there is either no pay (for housewives) or limited pay (for paid houseworkers) or unequal pay (in the paid labor force). This last category shows the ultimate connection of women as affected by the sexual division of labor within the class structure. Her position as a paid worker is defined in terms of being a "woman," which is a direct reflection of the hierarchical sexual divisions in a society organized around the profit motive.

All the processes involved in domestic work help in the perpetuation of the existing society. (1) Women stabilize patriarchal structures (the family, housewife, mother) by fulfilling these very roles. (2) Simultaneously, women are reproducing new workers, for both the paid and the unpaid labor force; they "care for" the men and children of the society. (3) They work in the labor force as well, for lesser wages. (4) They stabilize the economy through their role as consumers. And this role is perpetuated very specifically through patriarchal institutions and ideology. If the other side of production is consumption, the other side of capitalism is patriarchy.

It is important to note the discrepancy between patriarchal ideology and the material reality of women's lives. Although all women are defined as mothers (and nonworkers) as a group, close to 45 percent of the women in the United States work in the paid labor force, and almost all labor in the home. Today 38.6 million women hold jobs in the labor force. "Nearly a quarter of all working women are single, while 19% are either widowed, divorced or separated, and another 26% are married to men who earn less than $10,000 a year."[47] Because women are not defined as workers within the ruling ideology, however, they are not paid for their labor, or are paid less than men. The sexual definition of woman as mother keeps her in the home doing unpaid labor and/or enables her to be hired at a lower wage because of her sexual definition of inferiority. During periods of high unemployment women either do not find jobs or are paid at even lower rate. The sexual division of labor and society remains intact even with women in the paid economy. Ideology adjusts to this by defining women as working mothers. And the two jobs get done for less than the price of one.

The bourgeoisie profits from the basic arrangement of women's work, as do all individual men who benefit from labor done for them in the home. All men, regardless of class, benefit, although differentially, from the system of privileges they acquire within patriarchal society. This system could not be organized as such if the ideology and structures of sex roles were not basic to the society. It is this ideology that largely protects the sexual division of labor and society along with the artificial needs that have been created through the class system.

When the ruling class desires the preservation of the family, this reflects its commitment to a division of labor that not only secures the greatest profit but also hierarchically orders the society culturally and politically. Once the sexual division of labor is challenged, particularly in terms of its connection to the capitalist order, one of the basic forms of the organization of work—especially affecting the home but with wide ramifications for the entire society—will be challenged. This challenge endangers a free labor pool (which infiltrates almost all aspects of living) and a cheap labor pool, and also endangers the fundamental social and political organization of the society, which is sexual hierarchy itself. The very order and control that derive from the arrangements of power implied in the sexual organization of society will be destroyed.

If we realize that there are basically two kinds of work in capitalist society, wage labor and domestic labor, we realize that we must alter the way we think about workers. What is really needed at this point is further work on what class analysis specifically means for women. The assignment of class for a woman is often done in terms of her husband's class standing.[48] That is, class categories are primarily male-defined categories; woman is not viewed as an autonomous being; the categories become confused. According to what criteria is a woman termed middle class?

> A secretary who makes a low salary but is a college graduate and the daughter of a doctor is considered "middle class" or even "upper middle," while a (male) truck driver with a high school education who makes twice as much money is probably "working class," or maybe "lower middle."[49]

What does it mean to say that a middle-class woman's life is different and easier than a working-class woman's life when her status as such is significantly different from that of her middle-class male "equivalent"? What of the woman who earns no money at all (as houseworker) and is termed middle class because her husband is? Does she have the same freedom, autonomy, or control over her life as the middle-class man who earns his own way? How does her position compare to that of a single woman with a poorly paid job?

> Clearly a man who is labeled upper or middle class (whatever, precisely, that may mean) has more money, power, security and freedom of choice than his female counterpart. Most women are wives and mothers, dependent wholly or in part on a man's support, and what the Man Giveth, he can take away.[50]

I do not mean by these questions to imply that class labels are meaningless, or that class privilege does not exist among women, or that housewives (houseworkers) are a class by themselves. What I am suggesting is that we must develop a vocabulary and conceptual tools that deal with the question of differential power among women in terms of their relation to men *and* the class structure. Only then will we see the effect on our understanding of organizing women.

A feminist class analysis must begin with distinctions drawn among women in terms of the work they do within the political economy as a whole (the family and the paid labor force). This would involve making distinctions among (1) working women outside the home, distinguishing professional from nonprofessional; (2) houseworkers, distinguishing housewives from wealthy women who do not work; (3) women who are houseworkers (housewives) and also work outside the home; (4) welfare women; and (5) unemployed women. Whether a woman is (a) married, (b) single, or (c) divorced is also important in analyzing how her work defines her class position. These class distinctions need to be further defined in terms of the issue of race.[51]

We then need to study how women within these categories relate to the major activities of women in terms of the shared experience of women (rather than in terms of the class differentiations among them)—reproduction, child rearing, sexuality, consumption, maintenance of home. What we will discover in this exploratory feminist class analysis, then, is a complicated and varied pattern whose multigridded conceptualization mirrors the complexity of sex and class differentials in the reality of women's life and experience.

The model with which we would be working would direct attention to class differences within the context of the basic relationship between the sexual hierarchy of society and capitalism. Such an analysis of socialist feminism could continue to explore the relationships between these systems, which in essence are not separate systems and hence need to be dealt with in their internal web. Also, such an examination should serve one overriding objective of the liberation of woman. It should seek to realize her potential for living in social community rather than in isolated homes; her potential for creative work rather than alienating or mindless work; her potential for critical consciousness as opposed to false consciousness; and her potential for uninhibited sexuality arising from new conceptions of sexuality.

Some Notes on Strategy

What does all the preceding imply about a strategy for revolution? It implies that the existing conceptions of revolutionary strategy are inadequate and need rethinking. First, the existing conceptions of a potentially revolutionary proletariat are inadequate for the goals of socialist feminism. Second, there are real doubts whether this potential, as defined in classical Marxist terms, will ever become reality in the United States. And although I think the development of theory and strategy should be interrelated, I see them as somewhat separate activities. Theory allows one to think about new possibilities. Strategy grows out of the possibilities.

This discussion has been devoted to developing socialist feminist theory, and I am hesitant to develop statements of strategy from it. Strategy will rather have to be fully articulated from political attempts to use the theory. When one tries abstractly to define strategy from new and developing statements of theory, the tendency to impose existing revolutionary strategies on reality is too great. Existing formulations of strategy tend to limit and distort new possibilities for organizing for revolutionary change.

The importance of socialist feminist strategy, to the extent that it exists, is that it grows out of women's struggle with their daily existence—production, reproduction, children, consumption, jobs. The potential for revolutionary consciousness derives from the fact that women's lives under capitalist patriarchy are being squeezed, from the most intimate levels—such as how they feed their children—to the more public levels of their monotonous, tiring, low-skill, sex-defined, low-wage jobs. Women are working in the labor force, and for less, and they are maintaining the family system, having less to make do with. This is the base from which consciousness can develop. We need to try organizing political action and developing political consciousness about our oppression within the hierarchical sexual division of society and from an understanding of how this connects to the capitalist division of labor. Or consciousness will develop then from our everyday lives. I agree with Nancy Hartsock that "the power of feminism grows out of contact with everyday life. The significance of contemporary feminism is in the reinvention of a mode of analysis which has the power to comprehend and thereby transform everyday life."[52]

One has to ask whose everyday life we are speaking about. Although there are real and severing differences among women's everyday lives, there are also points of contact that lay a basis for cross-class organizing. The differences must be acknowledged and struggled with for a sense of political *priority*. The commonality derives from the particular roles women share in patriarchy. From this commonality begins the feminist struggle.

Many of the socialist feminists I have worked with in the women's movement were radical feminists first. They first felt their oppression as women and then, as they came to understand that capitalism was fully implicated in this system of oppression, became committed to socialism as well. Similarly, there are more and more women as housewives who are coming to understand their daily lives as part of a much larger system. Women working outside the home, both professional and nonprofessional, who bear the pressures and anxieties about being competent mothers and caretakers of the home, are becoming conscious of their "double day" of work.

Male leftists and socialist women often say that women, as women, cannot be organized because of their isolation in the home, the privatization of their lives, their commitments to their husbands' class. But a strategy to reach all women, regardless of class, has never been tried in a self-conscious manner. That its implementation will be difficult goes without saying. But a beginning is already in process as women try to take some control over their lives.

Notes

Acknowledgments: This paper was first delivered in the spring of 1975 at Cornell University's Women's Studies Weekly Seminar. I wish to thank Beau Brosscup, Sarah Eisenstein, Ellen Wade, Jackie Fralley, Isaac Kramnick, Miriam Brody Kramnick, Carol Stevenson, and Judy Humble for working on several of the earlier versions.

1. Sheila Rowbotham, in *Women, Resistance, and Revolution* (New York: Pantheon, 1972), makes clear that the social relations of production as well as reproduction need to be dealt with in any revolutionary theory.

2. For our purposes here, dialectics helps us focus on the *processes* of power. Hence, in order to understand power, one needs to analyze the *relations* that define power rather than treating it as a thing abstracted from the real conditions of society. Any "moment" embodies the relations of power that define it. The only way to understand what the "moment" is, is to understand it as a reflection of the processes involved in it. By definition, this requires one to see "moments" as parts of other "moments" rather than as cut off from each other. Seeing things in separation from each other, as part of either/or options, reflects the dichotomous thinking of positivism. By trying to understand the elements defining the synthesis of power embodied in any moment, one is forced to come to terms with the conflict embodied within it, and hence the dialectical processes of power. See Karl Marx, *Grundrisse*, ed. Martin Nicolaus (New York: Vintage, 1973); and Bertell Ollman, *Alienation: Marx's Conception of Man in Capitalist Society* (New York: Oxford University Press, 1971).

3. For this discussion one can see: Mariarosa Dalla Costa, "Women and the Subversion of the Community," and Selma James, "A Woman's Place," in *The Power of Women and the Subversion of the Community* (Bristol: Falling Wall Press, 1972); Ira Gerstein, "Domestic Work and Capitalism," and Lise Vogel, "The Earthly Family," in *Radical America* 7 (July–October 1973): 4–5; Wally Secombe, "The Housewife and Her Labour under Capitalism," *New Left Review* No. 83 (January–February 1973); B. Magas, Margaret Coulson, and H. Wainwright, "The Housewife and Her Labour under Capitalism—A Critique," and Jean Gardiner, "Women's Domestic Labour," *New Left Review* No. 89 (January–February 1975).

4. I do not think the Althusserian dichotomized view of the "early Hegelian Marx" and the later "materialist Marx" is a helpful distinction. Rather, I think the theories of alienation and exploitation are integrated throughout Marx's work, though they are given different priority in specific writings. The *Grundrisse* stands as persuasive proof of this position. See Marx, *Grundrisse*, and David McLellan's discussion of the importance of the *Grundrisse* in his *Karl Marx: His Life and Thought* (New York: Harper & Row, 1973).

5. For a discussion of species being, see Karl Marx, *The Economic and Philosophic Manuscripts of 1844* (New York: International Publishers, 1964); *The German Ideology* (New York: International Publishers, 1947); "On the Jewish Question," in Kurt H. Guddat and Lloyd D. Easton, eds., *Writings of the Young Marx on Philosophy and Society* (New York: Anchor Books, 1967). Also see Shlomo Avineri, *The Social and Political*

Thought of Karl Marx (New York: Cambridge University Press, 1968); Richard Bernstein, *Praxis and Action* (Philadelphia: University of Pennsylvania Press, 1971); and Ollman, *Alienation.*

6. Karl Marx, *Theories of Surplus Value* (Moscow: Progress Publishers, 1963), 1:152. Also see Karl Marx, *Capital* (New York: International Publishers, 1967), vol. 1.

7. Karl Marx, *The Communist Manifesto* (Chicago: Gateway Press, 1954), 48–49.

8. Marx, *German Ideology*, 17.

9. Marx, "On the Jewish Question," 246.

10. Marx, *Manuscripts*, 50.

11. Marx, *Communist Manifesto*, 50.

12. Marx, *German Ideology*, 9.

13. Ibid., 20.

14. Frederick Engels, "The Early Development of the Family," Free Press pamphlet reprint of first two chapters of *Origin of the Family* (see n. 17), 65.

15. Marx, *German Ideology*, 21, 22.

16. Ibid.

17. Frederick Engels, *The Origin of the Family, Private Property, and the State* (New York: International Publishers, 1942). Engels's analysis differentiates three historical periods—savagery, barbarism, and civilization—within which he traces the evolution of the family. The form of marriage coincident with savagery is group marriage. The family here is a group, and the only limitation on it is the prohibition of sexual activity between parents and children, and between children. With such an arrangement one can be certain only who the mother is, and hence the line of inheritance is through the mother. This is termed the era of mother right. In the second period of barbarism the pairing marriage develops. The male line becomes more important, and the defeat of mother right is imminent. With civilization comes monogamy; marriage and the family are based on private property.

The transition through these stages involved, according to Engels, catastrophic transformation in the lives of women. It saw the "overthrow of mother right which was the world historic defeat of the female sex" ("Early Development," 75). Woman was relegated to the private household and the breeding of children. Parallel to this was the increase of wealth in society, which "made the man's position in the family more important than the woman's and on the other hand created an impulse to exploit this strengthened position in order to overthrow in favor of his children, the traditional order of inheritance," *Origins of the Family*, 14. For Engels, history has been the retrogression of women's power from mother right in primitive communism to her subordination in the second stage of barbarism. However, for all that Engels explains *how* and *why* the switch from group sex to monogamous sex happens, it could be the structuring element of history as much as the relations of private property are. He really asserts rather than argues his position that private property relations necessitate monogamy.

18. Ibid., 65, 66.

19. Marx, *Communist Manifesto*.

20. See Eli Zaretsky, "Capitalism, the Family, and Personal Life," pts. 1–2, *Socialist Revolution* Nos. 13–14 (January–April 1973): 69–125, and 15 (May–June 1973): 19–70, for a discussion of the historical and economic changes in the family.

21. Engels, *Origin of the Family*, 57.

22. Frederick Engels, *The Woman Question* (New York: International Publishers, 1951), 11.

23. Frederick Engels, *The Origin of the Family, Private Property, and the State*, ed. Eleanor Leacock (New York: International Publishers, 1972), 71–72.

24. "Ideology" is used here to refer to the ruling ideas of the society (see Marx, *German Ideology*). In this sense it is seen as a distortion of reality and as protective of existing power arrangements. More specifically, ideology means the ideas that protect both male and capitalist power arrangements. It is important to note that although material conditions often do create the conditions for certain ideologies, I also see ideology and material conditions in a dialectical relationship. Each is involved in *partially* defining the other. For instance, the "idea" that women are weak and passive is both a distortion of women's capacities and a partial description of reality—a reality *defined* by the ruling ideology.

25. The definition of liberal feminism applies to the reformist understanding of the sexual division of labor. It is a theory that reflects a criticism of the limitations of sex roles but does not comprehend the connection between sex roles and the sexual division of labor and capitalism. Limited by the historical boundaries of the time, early liberal feminists were unable to decipher the capitalist male power structure and instead applauded values that implicated them further within it. They were bound not only by the material conditions of the time (lack of birth control, etc.) but also by the liberal ideology of the time, which presented segmented, individualistic conceptions of power.

26. For classical versions of the sexual division of labor, see J. S. Mill, *On the Subjection of Women* (New York: Fawcett, 1971), and J. J. Rousseau, *Emile* (London: J. J. Dent, 1911).

27. Although radical feminism is often labeled as bourgeois by male leftists and socialist women, I think this conception is simplistic and hence problematic for several reasons. Radical feminist analysis cuts across class lines in its caste analysis and in this sense is meant to relate to the reality of all women. Hence, in terms of priorities, the theory does not distinguish between working-class and bourgeois women, recognizing the inadequacy of such distinctions. At the same time, the origins of the theory have been developed by many women who would be termed working class. It is inaccurate to say that radical feminists are bourgeois women, mainly because the "bourgeois" woman has not really been identified yet in terms of a class analysis specifically pertaining to women.

28. Kate Millett, *Sexual Politics* (New York: Doubleday, 1970), 24.

29. Shulamith Firestone, *The Dialectic of Sex* (New York: Bantam, 1970).

30. Ibid., p. 8.

31. Some people may say that to be stronger is to be more equal, or that inequality exists biologically because men are stronger than women. But this is not Firestone's argument. She argues that it is woman as a reproductive being that is at the root of our inequality. Historically, pregnancy made women physically vulnerable, but less so today. Firestone does not restrict her thesis as true only historically; she offers it as contemporary analysis.

32. Firestone, *Dialectic of Sex*, 10.

33. It is important to know if technological changes and innovations around birth control are tied only to concerns with population control in an era of overpopulation, or if they reflect fundamental changes in the way women are viewed in this society. It matters whether women are still viewed as baby machines or not, because these views could come to define technological progress in birth control as nonprogressive.

34. Firestone, *Dialectic of Sex*, 8.

35. Juliet Mitchell, *Psychoanalysis and Feminism* (New York: Pantheon, 1974), 414. Within the women's movement there is a varied dialogue on the dimensions and meaning of socialist feminism. In some sense, the appropriate questions are still being formulated. Juliet Mitchell spoke to this issue in *Woman's Estate* (New York: Pantheon, 1971), 99, when she said, "We should ask the feminist questions, but try to come up with some Marxist answers." In *Psychoanalysis and Feminism*, 364–65, she is still trying to define the "important" questions. "It seems to me that 'why did it happen' and 'historically when?' are both false questions. The questions that should, I think, be asked in place of these are: how does it happen and when does it take place in our society?" In other words, we can start by asking, how does it happen now?

36. Sheila Rowbotham, in *Woman's Consciousness, Man's World* (Baltimore, Md., Penguin, 1973), defines patriarchal authority as "based on control over the woman's productive capacity and over her person" (p. 17). Juliet Mitchell sees patriarchy as defining women as exchange objects based on the exploitation of their role as propagators; hence, she states, "it is not a question of changing (or ending) who has or how one has babies. It is a question of overthrowing patriarchy" (*Psychoanalysis and Feminism*, 407–8, 416).

37. See Mitchell, *Psychoanalysis and Feminism*.

38. See Rowbotham, *Women, Resistance, and Revolution*, for the use of this model of historical materialism in the study of history.

39. Simone de Beauvoir, *The Second Sex* (New York: Bantam, 1952), xix, 33, 54.

40. Juliet Mitchell, "Women: The Longest Revolution" (Free Press pamphlet), 4, 6 (see also Chapter 2 in this book); and *Woman's Estate*. It has been pointed out that Mitchell herself did not fully understand women's essential role in society as workers. She termed them a marginal or reserve labor force rather than viewing them as necessary to the economy, both as domestic laborers and as wage laborers.

41. Mitchell, "Longest Revolution," 10, 16.

42. Ibid., p. 28. It is interesting to note that in *Psychoanalysis and Feminism*, Mitchell focuses on the relationship *between* families as key to understanding women in patriarchal culture: it is the relationship between families that distinguishes human society from other primate groups (p. 374); "The legally controlled exchange of women is the primary factor that distinguishes mankind from all other primates, from a cultural standpoint" (p. 372). It is hence socially necessary for the kinship structure to have exogamous exchange. The psychology of patriarchy that Mitchell constructs is based on the relations of the kinship structure.

43. Mitchell, *Woman's Estate*, 155.

44. Ibid., p. 156. See Linda Gordon, "Families," Free Press pamphlet; A. Gordon, M. J. Buhle, and N. Schrom, "Women in American Society," *Radical America* 5 (July–August 1971): 4; Mitchell, *Psychoanalysis and Feminism*; Mary Ryan, *Womanhood in America* (New York: Viewpoints, 1975); R. Baxandall, L. Gordon, and S. Reverby, *America's Working Women* (New York: Vintage Books, 1976); and Zaretsky, "Capitalism."

45. Zaretsky, "Capitalism," 114.

46. Margaret Benston, "The Political Economy of Women's Liberation," Free Press pamphlet, p. 15.

47. *Newsweek*, December 6, 1976, p. 69.

48. The concept of "class" is a problematic category today whether it is being used to analyze men or women. The difficulty, however, is furthered when one is

dealing with women because of the concept's "classical" exclusion of women as autonomous beings.

49. Ellen Willis, "Economic Reality and the Limits of Feminism" *Ms.* No. 1 (June 1973): 110.

50. Ibid.

51. Although I have not dealt specifically with the issue of race in this paper, it is an integral part of the analysis of socialist feminism. The question of race has fallen outside the scope of this particular paper, in its examination of the relationship between sex and class, but I think that the question of race is absolutely fundamental to an understanding of women's class and sexual identity. To the extent that this paper does not include the discussion of race, it is an incomplete study of the specificity of women's oppression.

52. Nancy Hartsock, "Feminist Theory and the Development of Revolutionary Strategy" (unpublished manuscript, Johns Hopkins University, 1976), 19; portions of this paper appeared as "Fundamental Feminism, Process and Perspective," *Quest* 2 (Fall 1975): 67–79.

5 Capitalism, Patriarchy, and Job Segregation by Sex

Heidi I. Hartmann

The division of labor by sex appears to have been universal throughout human history. In our society the sexual division of labor is hierarchical, with men on top and women on the bottom. Anthropology and history suggest, however, that the division was not always hierarchical. The development and importance of a sex-ordered division of labor is my subject here. I contend that the roots of women's present social status lie in this sex-ordered division of labor. I believe that not only must the hierarchical nature of the division of labor between the sexes be eliminated, but the very division of labor between the sexes itself must be eliminated if women are to attain equal social status with men and if women and men are to attain the full development of their human potential.

The primary questions for investigation, then, would seem to be, first, how a more sexually egalitarian division became a less egalitarian one; and second, how this hierarchical division of labor became extended to wage labor in the modern period. Many anthropological studies suggest that the first process, sexual stratification, occurred together with the increasing productiveness, specialization, and complexity of society: for example, through the establishment of settled agriculture, private property, or the state. It occurred as human society emerged from the primitive and became "civilized." In this perspective capitalism is a relative latecomer, whereas

Source: This article is reprinted from *Signs: Journal of Women in Culture and Society* 1, no. 3, pt. 2 (1976), pp. 137–69, by permission of the publisher, The University of Chicago Press, 5801 Ellis Avenue, Chicago, IL 60637. © 1976 by The University of Chicago. All rights reserved.

patriarchy, the hierarchical relation between men and women in which men are dominant and women are subordinate, was an early arrival.[1]

I want to argue that before capitalism a patriarchal system was established in which men controlled the labor of women and children in the family, and that in so doing men learned the techniques of hierarchical organization and control. With the advent of public-private separations' such as those created by the emergence of state apparatus and economic systems based on wider exchange and larger production units, the problem for men became one of maintaining their control over the labor power of women. In other words, a direct personal system of control was translated into an indirect, impersonal system of control, mediated by society-wide institutions. The mechanisms available to men were (1) the traditional division of labor between the sexes, and (2) techniques of hierarchical organization and control. These mechanisms were crucial in the second process, the extension of a sex-ordered division of labor to the wage-labor system, during the period of the emergence of capitalism in western Europe and the United States.

The emergence of capitalism in the fifteenth to eighteenth centuries threatened patriarchal control based on institutional authority as it destroyed many old institutions and created new ones, such as a "free" market in labor. It threatened to bring all women and children into the labor force and hence to destroy the family and the basis of the power of men over women (that is, the control over their labor power within the family).[2] If it was the theoretical tendency of pure capitalism to eradicate all arbitrary differences of status among laborers, to make all laborers equal in the marketplace, why are women still in an inferior position to men in the labor market? The possible answers are legion; they range from neoclassical views that the process is not complete or is hampered by market imperfections to the radical view that production requires hierarchy even if the market nominally requires "equality."[3] All these explanations, it seems to me, ignore the role of men—ordinary men, men as men, men as workers—in maintaining women's inferiority in the labor market. The radical view, in particular, emphasizes the role of men as capitalists in creating hierarchies in the production process in order to maintain their power. Capitalists do this by segmenting the labor market (along race, sex, and ethnic lines, among others) and playing workers off against each other. I argue that male workers have played and continue to play a crucial role in maintaining sexual divisions in the labor process.

Job segregation by sex, in my view, is the primary mechanism in capitalist society that maintains the superiority of men over women, because it enforces lower wages for women in the labor market. Low wages keep women dependent on men because they encourage women to marry. Married women must perform domestic chores for their husbands. Men benefit, then, from both higher wages and the domestic division of labor. This domestic division of labor, in turn, acts to weaken women's position in the labor market. Thus, the hierarchical domestic division of labor is perpetuated by the labor market, and vice versa. This process is the present outcome of the continuing interaction of two interlocking systems, capitalism and patriarchy. Patriarchy, far from being vanquished by capitalism, is still very virile; it shapes the form that modern capitalism takes, just as the development of capitalism has transformed patriarchal institutions. The resulting mutual accommodation between patriarchy and capitalism has created a vicious circle for women.

My argument contrasts with the traditional views of both neoclassical and Marxist economists. Both ignore patriarchy, a social system with a material base. The neoclassical economists tend to exonerate the capitalist system, attributing job segregation to exogenous *ideological* factors, such as sexist attitudes. Marxist economists tend to attribute job segregation to capitalists, ignoring the part played by male workers and the effect of centuries of patriarchal social relations. I hope to redress the balance.

The line of argument I have outlined here and develop further below is perhaps incapable of proof. This discussion, I hope, will establish its plausibility rather than its incontrovertibility. The first part briefly reviews evidence and explanations offered in the anthropological literature for the creation of dominance-dependence relations between men and women. The second part reviews the historical literature on the division of labor by sex during the emergence of capitalism and the Industrial Revolution in England and the United States. This part focuses on the extension of male-female dominance-dependence relations to the wage-labor market and the key role played by men in maintaining job segregation by sex and hence male superiority.

Anthropological Perspectives on the Division of Labor by Sex

Some anthropologists explain male dominance by arguing that it has existed since the very beginning of human society. Sherry Ortner suggests that indeed "female is to male as nature is to culture." According to Ortner, culture devalues nature; females are associated with nature, are considered closer to nature in all cultures,[4] and are thus devalued. Her view is compatible with that of Michelle Rosaldo, who emphasizes the public-private split,[5] and that of Claude Lévi-Strauss, who assumes the subordination of women during the process of the creation of society.

According to Lévi-Strauss, culture began with the exchange of women by men to cement bonds between families—thereby creating *society*. In fact, he sees a fundamental tension between the family (that is, the domestic realm in which women reside closer to nature) and society, which requires that families break down their autonomy to exchange with one another. The exchange of women is a mechanism that enforces the interdependence of families and creates society. By analogy, Lévi-Strauss suggests that the division of labor between the sexes is the mechanism that enforces "a reciprocal state of dependency between the sexes." It also assures heterosexual marriage. "When it is stated that one sex must perform certain tasks, this also means that the other sex is forbidden to do them."[6] Thus the existence of a sexual division of labor is a universal of human society, though the exact division of the tasks by sex varies enormously.[7] Moreover, because it is men who exchange women and women who are exchanged in creating social bonds, men benefit more than women from these social bonds, and the division of labor between the sexes is a hierarchical one.[8]

While this first school of anthropological thought, comprising the "universalists," is based primarily on Lévi-Strauss and the exchange of women, Nancy Chodorow, following Rosaldo and Ortner, emphasizes women's confinement to the domestic sphere. Chodorow locates this confinement in the mothering role. She constructs the universality of patriarchy on the universal fact that women mother. Female mothering reproduces itself via the creation of gender-specific personality structures.[9]

Two other major schools of thought on the origins of the sexual division of labor merit attention. Both reject the universality, at least in theory if not in practice, of the sex-ordered division of labor. One is the "feminist-revisionist" school, which argues that we cannot be certain that the division of labor is male supremacist; it may be separate but equal (as Lévi-Strauss occasionally seems to indicate), but we will never know because the bias of the observers makes comparisons impossible. This school is culturally relativist in the extreme, but it nevertheless contributes to our knowledge of women's work and status by stressing the accomplishments of females in their part of the division of labor.[10]

The second school also rejects the universality of sex-ordered division of labor but, unlike the relativists, seeks to compare societies in order to isolate the variables that coincide with greater or lesser autonomy of women. This "variationist" school is subdivided according to the characteristics its members emphasize: the contribution of women to subsistence and their control over their contribution, the organization of tribal versus state soci-

eties, the requirements of the mode of production, the emergence of wealth
and private property, the boundaries of the private and public spheres.[11] A
complete review of these approaches is impossible here, but I will cite a few
examples from this literature to illustrate the relevance of these variables
for the creation of a sex-ordered division of labor.

Among the !Kung, a hunting and gathering people in South-West Africa
(Namibia), the women have a great deal of autonomy and influence. Draper
argues that this is the result of (1) the contribution of 60–80 percent of the
community's food by the women and their retention of control over its distribution; (2) equal absence from the camp and equal range and mobility
of the male hunters and the female gatherers (the women are not dependent on the men for protection in their gathering range); (3) the flexibility
of sex roles and the willingness of adults to do the work of the opposite sex
(with the exceptions that women do not hunt and men do not remove nasal
mucus or feces from children!); (4) the absence of physical expression of
aggression; (5) the small size (seventeen to sixty-five) of and flexible membership in living groups; (6) a close, public settlement arrangement with
huts situated in a circle around the campfire.[12]

In the late 1960s when Patricia Draper did her fieldwork, some of the
!Kung were beginning to settle in small villages, where the men took up
herding and the women agriculture like other groups (such as the Bantu),
who were already settled. There, agriculture and food preparation were
more time consuming for the women than gathering had been, and though
they continued to gather from time to time, the new agricultural pursuits
kept the women closer to home. The men's herding, in contrast, kept them
mobile and offered greater contact with aspects of the world outside the
!Kung: the Bantus, politics, wage work, and advanced knowledge (for example, about domesticated animals). These new sex roles were maintained
with more rigidity. Boys and girls came to be socialized differently. Men
began to feel their work superior to the women's and to consider property
theirs (rather than jointly owned with the women). The "ranking of individuals in terms of prestige and differential worth ha[d] begun."[13] Houses,
made more permanent and private, were no longer arranged in a circle.
The women in particular felt that the group as a whole had less ability to
observe, and perhaps to sanction, the behavior of married couples. Doubtless these changes occurred partly because of the influence of the male-
dominated Western culture on the !Kung. The overall result, according to
Draper, was a decrease in the status and influence of women, the denigration of their work, and an increase, for women, in the importance of
the family unit at the expense of the influence of the group as a whole.
The delineation of public and private spheres placed men in the public

and women in the private sphere, and the public sphere came to be valued more.

Ester Boserup, in *Woman's Role in Economic Development*, writes extensively of the particular problems created for women when Third World tribal groups came into contact with Western colonial administrations.[14] The usual result was the creation or strengthening of male dominance: for example, when administrations taught men advanced agricultural techniques where women were farmers, or schooled men in trading where women were traders. The Europeans encouraged men to head and support their families, superseding women's traditional responsibilities. Previous to colonization, according to Rwoy Leavitt: "In regions like Africa and Southeast Asia, where shifting agriculture and the female farmer predominate, the women work very hard and receive limited support from their husbands, but they also have some economic independence, considerable freedom of movement, and an important place in the community. . . . In traditional African marriages the woman is expected to support herself and her children and to feed the family, including her husband, with the food she grows." [15] Boserup supports this view of the economic role of women before the influence of Europeans began to be felt.

Europeans also entrusted local governance to male leaders and ignored the women's traditional participation in tribal society. That the women had highly organized and yet nonhierarchical governmental structures, which were unknown to and ignored by the colonists, is illustrated by the case of the Igbo in Nigeria. Judith Van Allen reports that Igbo women held *mikiri*, or meetings, which were democratic discussions with no official leaders and "which articulated women's interests *as opposed to* those of men." The women needed these meetings because they lived in patrilocal villages and had few kinship ties with each other, and because they had their own separate economic activities, their own crops, and their own trading, which they needed to protect from men. When a man offended the women, by violating the women's market rules or letting his cows into the women's yam fields, the women often retaliated as a group by "sitting on a man"—carrying on loudly at his home late at night and "perhaps demolishing his hut or plastering it with mud and roughing him up a bit." Women also sometimes executed collective strikes and boycotts. With the advent of the British administrators and their inevitably unfavorable policies toward women, the Igbo women adapted their tactics and used them against the British. For example, in response to an attempt to tax the women farmers, tens of thousands of women were involved in riots at administrative centers over an area of 6,000 square miles containing a population of two million people. The "Women's War," as it was called, was coordinated through the market *mikiri* network.[16] Van Allen goes on to detail the disintegration of the *mikiri* in the face of British colonial and missionary policies.

In a study of a somewhat different process of state formation, Muller looks at the decline of Anglo-Saxon and Welsh tribal society and the formation of the English nation-state, a process that occurred from the eighth to the fifteenth century. Muller writes:

> The transition from tribe to state is historically probably the greatest watershed in the decline in the status of women. . . . This is not to deny that in what we call "tribal," that is, pre-state, society there is not a wide variation in the status of women and even that in certain pre-state societies, women may be in what we would consider an abject position *vis à vis* the men in that society. . . . We believe that the causes for these variations in status can be found, as in the case of State Societies, in the material conditions which give rise to the social and economic positions therein.[17]

Viana Muller stresses that in the Welsh and Anglo-Saxon tribes "the right of individual maintenance was so well entrenched that these rights were not entrusted to a patriarchal head of a nuclear family, but were, rather, vested in the larger social group of the *gwely* [four-generation kinship group]."[18] Both men and women upon adulthood received a share of cattle from the *gwely*. The cattle provided their personal maintenance and prevented an individual from becoming dependent upon another. Thus, although in the tribal system land inheritance was patrilineal and residence patrilocal, a married woman had her own means of economic subsistence. Women were political participants both in their husbands' and in their own natal lineages. Like a man, a woman was responsible for her children's crimes, and she and her natal lineages (*not* her spouse's) were responsible for her crimes.

Tribal customs were, however, undermined by the emergence of the state: "We can observe the development of public—as opposed to social—male authority, through the political structure imposed by the emerging state. Since the state is interested in the alienation of the tribal resource base —its land and its labor power—it finds it convenient to use the traditional gender division of labor and resources in tribal society and places them in a hierarchical relationship both internally (husband over wife and children) and externally (lords over peasants and serfs)."[19] The king established regional administrative units without regard to tribal jurisdictions, appointed his own administrators, bypassed the authority of the tribal chiefs, and levied obligations on the males as "heads" of individual households. Tribal groups lost collective responsibility for their members, and women and children lost their group rights and came under the authority of their husbands. Woman's work became private for the benefit of her husband, rather than public for the benefit of the kin group. As Muller points out, there must have been tendencies evident in tribal society that created the preconditions for a hierarchical, male-dominated state, for it was not equally likely that the emerging state would be female. Among these tendencies, for example, were male ownership of land and greater male participation in military expeditions, probably especially those farther away.[20]

This summary of several studies from the third school of anthropology, the variationist school, points to a number of variables that help to explain a decrease in woman's social status. They suggest that increased sexual stratification occurs along with a general process of social stratification (which at least in some versions seems to depend on and foster an increase in social surplus—to support the higher groups in the hierarchy). As a result, a decrease in the social status of woman occurs when (1) she loses control of subsistence through a change in production methods and devaluation of her share of the division of labor; (2) her work becomes private and family centered rather than social and kin focused; and/or (3) some men assert their power over other men through the state mechanism by elevating these subordinate men in their families, using the nuclear family against the kin group.[21] In this way the division of labor between men and women becomes a more hierarchical one. Control over women is maintained directly in the family by the man, but it is sustained by social institutions, such as the state and religion.

The work in this school of anthropology suggests that patriarchy did not always exist but rather that it emerged as social conditions changed. Moreover, men participated in this transformation. Because it benefited men relative to women, men have had a stake in reproducing patriarchy. Although there is a great deal of controversy among anthropologists about the origins of patriarchy, and more work needs to be done to establish the validity of this interpretation, I believe the weight of the evidence supports it. In any case, most anthropologists agree that patriarchy emerged long before capitalism, even if they disagree about its origins.

In England, as we have seen, the formation of the state marks the end of Anglo-Saxon tribal society and the beginning of feudal society. Throughout feudal society the tendencies toward the privatization of family life and the increase of male power within the family appear to strengthen, as does their institutional support from church and state. By the time of the emergence of capitalism in the fifteenth through eighteenth centuries, the nuclear, patriarchal peasant family had become the basic production unit in society.[22]

The Emergence of Capitalism and the Industrial Revolution

The key process in the emergence of capitalism in England and the United States was primitive accumulation, the prior accumulation that was necessary for capitalism to establish itself.[23] Primitive accumulation was a twofold process that set the preconditions for the expansion of the scale of production: first, free laborers had to be accumulated; second, large amounts of capital had to be accumulated. The first was achieved through enclosures and the removal of people from the land, their subsistence base, so that they were forced to work for wages. The second was achieved through both the growth of smaller farms and shop capital amassed through banking facilities, and vast increases in merchant capital, the profits from the slave trade, and colonial exploitation.

The creation of a wage-labor force and the increase in the scale of production that occurred with the emergence of capitalism had in some ways a more severe impact on women than on men. To understand this impact, let us look at the work of women before this transition occurred and the changes that took place as it occurred.[24] In the 1500s and 1600s, agriculture, woolen textiles (carried on as a by-industry of agriculture), and the various crafts and trades in the towns were the major sources of livelihood for the English population. In the rural areas men worked in the fields on small farms that they owned or rented. Women tended the household plots, small gardens and orchards, animals, and dairies; they also spun and wove. A portion of what they produced was sold in small markets to supply the villages, towns, and cities, and in this way women supplied a considerable proportion of their families' cash income, as well as their subsistence in kind. In addition to the tenants and farmers, there was a small wage-earning class of men and women who worked on the larger farms. Occasionally, tenants and their wives worked for wages as well, the men more often than the women.[25] As small farmers and cottagers were displaced by larger farmers in the seventeenth and eighteenth centuries, their wives lost their main sources of support, while the men were able to continue as wage laborers to some extent. Thus women, deprived of these essential household plots, suffered relatively greater unemployment, and the families as a whole were deprived of a large part of their subsistence.[26]

In the 1700s the demand for cotton textiles grew, and English merchants found they could utilize the labor of the English agricultural population, who were already familiar with the arts of spinning and weaving. The merchants distributed materials to be spun and woven, creating a domestic industrial system that occupied many displaced farm families. This putting-out system, however, proved inadequate. The complexities of distribution and collection and, perhaps more important, the control the workers had over the production process (they could take time off, work intermittently, steal materials) prevented an increase in the supply of textiles sufficient to meet the merchants' needs. To solve these problems, first spinning, in the late 1700s, and then weaving, in the early 1800s, were organized in factories. The textile factories were located in the rural areas at first, in order both to take advantage of the labor of children and women by escaping the restrictions of the guilds in the cities, and to utilize waterpower. When spinning was industrialized, women spinners at home suffered greater unemployment, while the demand for male handloom weavers increased. When weaving was mechanized, the need for handloom weavers fell off as well.[27]

In this way domestic industry, created by emerging capitalism, was later superseded and destroyed by the progress of capitalist industrialization. In the process women, children, and men in the rural areas all suffered dislocation and disruption but experienced them in different ways. Women, forced into unemployment more frequently than men by the capitalization of agriculture, were more available to labor, both in the domestic putting-out system and in the early factories. It is often argued both that men resisted going into the factories because they did not want to lose their independence and that women and children were more docile and malleable. If this was in fact the case, it would appear that these "character traits" of women and men were already established before the advent of the capitalistic organization of industry and that they had grown out of the authority structure prevailing in the previous period of small-scale, family agriculture. Many historians suggest that within the family, men were the heads of households and that women, even though they contributed a large part of their families' subsistence, were subordinate.[28]

We may never know the facts of the authority structure within the preindustrial family, since much of what we do know is from prescriptive literature or otherwise class biased, and little is known about the point of view of the people themselves. Nevertheless, the evidence on family life and on relative wages and levels of living suggests that women were subordinate within the family. This conclusion is consonant with the anthropological literature reviewed above, which describes the emergence of patriarchal social relations along with early societal stratification. Moreover, the history of the early factories suggests that capitalists took advantage of this authority structure, finding women and children more vulnerable, both because of familial relations and because they were simply more desperate economically following changes in agriculture that left them unemployed.[29]

The transition to capitalism in the cities and towns was experienced somewhat differently than in the rural areas, but it tends to substantiate the line of argument just set out: men and women had different places in the familial authority structure, and capitalism proceeded in a way that built on that authority structure. In the towns and cities before the transition to capitalism, a system of family industry prevailed: a family of artisans worked together at home to produce goods for exchange. Adults were organized in guilds, which had social and religious functions as well as industrial ones. Within trades carried on as family industries, women and men generally performed different tasks: in general, the men worked at what were considered more skilled tasks, the women at processing the raw materials or finishing the end product. Men, usually the heads of the production units, had the status of master artisans. For though women usually belonged to their husbands' guilds, they did so as appendages; girls were rarely apprenticed to a trade and thus rarely become journeymen or masters. Married women participated in the production process and probably acquired important skills, but they usually controlled the production process only if they were widowed, when guilds often gave them the right to hire apprentices and journeymen. Young men may have married within their guilds (the daughters of artisans in the same trade). In fact, young women and girls had a unique and very important role as extra or casual laborers in a system where the guilds prohibited hiring additional workers from outside the family, and undoubtedly they learned skills that were useful when they married.[30] Nevertheless, girls appear not to have been trained as carefully as boys were and, as adults, not to have attained the same status in the guilds.

Although in most trades men were the central workers and women the assistants, other trades were so identified by sex that family industry did not prevail.[31] Carpentry and millinery were two such trades. Male carpenters and female milliners both hired apprentices and assistants and attained the status of master craftspersons. According to Clark, although some women's trades, such as millinery, were highly skilled and organized in guilds, many women's trades were apparently difficult to organize in strong guilds because most women's skills could not be easily monopolized. All women, as part of their home duties, knew the arts of textile manufacturing, sewing, food processing, and, to some extent, trading.

In the seventeenth and eighteenth centuries the family industry system and the guilds began to break down in the face of the demand for larger output. Capitalists began to organize production on a larger scale, and production became separated from the home as the size of establishments grew. Women were excluded from participation in the industries in which they had assisted men, once these no longer took place at home, where married women apparently tended to remain to carry on their domestic work. Yet many women out of necessity sought work in capitalistically organized industry as wage laborers. When women entered wage labor they appear to have been at a disadvantage relative to men. First, as in agriculture, there was already a tradition of lower wages for women (in the previously limited area of wage work). Second, women appear to have been less well trained than men and to have obtained less desirable jobs. And third, they appear to have been less well organized than men.

Because I think the ability of men to organize themselves played a crucial role in limiting women's participation in the wage-labor market, I want to offer, first, some evidence to support the assertion that men were better organized and, second, some plausible reasons for their superiority in this area. I am not arguing that men had greater organizational abilities at all times and all places, or in all areas or types of organization, but it is plausible that they did in England during this period, particularly in the area of economic production. As evidence of their superiority we have first the guilds themselves, which were better organized among men's trades than women's and in which, in joint trades, men had superior positions—women were seldom admitted to the hierarchical ladder of progression. Second, we have the evidence of the rise of male professions and the elimination of female ones during the sixteenth and seventeenth centuries. The medical profession, male from its inception, established itself through hierarchical organization, the monopolization of new "scientific" skills, and the assistance of the state. Midwifery was virtually wiped out by the men. Brewing provides another example. Male brewers organized a fellowship, petitioned the king for monopoly rights (in exchange for a tax on every quart they brewed), and succeeded in forcing the numerous small-scale brewsters to buy from them.[32] Third, throughout the formative period of industrial capitalism, men appear to have been better able to organize themselves as wage workers. And as we shall see below, as factory production became established, men used their labor organizations to limit women's place in the labor market.

As to why men might have had superior organizational ability during this transitional period, I think we must consider the development of patriarchal social relations in the nuclear family, as reinforced by the state and religion, a process briefly described above for Anglo-Saxon England. Since men's superior position was reinforced by the state, and men acted in the political arena as heads of households and in the households as heads of production units, it seems likely that men would develop more organizational structures beyond their households. Women, in an inferior position at home and without the support of the state, would be less likely to be able to do so. Men's organizational knowledge, then, grew out of their position in the family and in the division of labor. Clearly, further investigation of organizations before and during the transition period is necessary to establish the mechanisms by which men came to control this public sphere.

Thus, the capitalistic organization of industry, in removing work from the home, served to increase the subordination of women, since it served to increase the relative importance of the area of men's domination. But it is important to remember that men's domination was already established and that it clearly influenced the direction and shape that capitalist development took. As Alice Clark has argued, with the separation of work from the home men became less dependent on women for industrial production, while women became more dependent on men economically. Much like the African women discussed above, English married women who had once supported themselves and their children became the domestic servants of their husbands. Men increased their control over technology, production, and marketing as they excluded women from industry, education, and political organization.[33]

When women participated in the wage-labor market, they did so in a position as clearly limited by patriarchy as it was by capitalism. Men's control over women's labor was altered by the wage-labor system, but it was not eliminated. In the labor market the dominant position of men was maintained by sex-ordered job segregation. Women's jobs were lower paid, considered less skilled, and often involved less exercise of authority or control.[34] Men acted to enforce job segregation in the labor market; they utilized trade-union associations and strengthened the domestic division of labor, which required women to do housework, child care, and related chores. Women's subordinate position in the labor market reinforced their subordinate position in the family, and that in turn reinforced their labor-market position.

The process of industrialization and the establishment of the factory system, particularly in the textile industry, illustrate the role played by men's trade-union associations. Textile factories employed children at first, but as they expanded, they began to utilize the labor of adult women and of whole families. While the number of married women working has been greatly exaggerated, apparently enough of them had followed their work into the factories to cause both their husbands and the upper classes concern about home life and the care of children.[35] Smelser has argued that in the early factories the family industry system and male control could often be maintained. For example, adult male spinners often hired their own or related children as helpers, and whole families were often employed by the same factory for the same length of working day.[36] Technological change, however, increasingly made this difficult, and factory legislation that limited the hours of children but not of adults further exacerbated the difficulties of the "family factory system."

The demands of the factory laborers in the 1820s and 1830s had been designed to maintain the family factory system,[37] but by 1840 male factory operatives were calling for an eight-hour-a-day limit on the work of children between nine and thirteen and for forbidding the employment of younger children. According to Smelser, this caused parents difficulty in training and supervising their children; to remedy it, male workers and the middle and upper classes began to recommend that women, too, be removed from the factories.[38]

The upper classes of the Victorian Age, the age that elevated women to their pedestals, seem to have been motivated by moral outrage and concern for the future of the English race (and for the reproduction of the working class): "In the male," said Lord Shaftesbury, "the moral effects of the system are very sad, but in the female they are infinitely worse, not alone upon themselves, but upon their families, upon society, and, I may add, upon the country itself. It is bad enough if you corrupt the man, but if you corrupt the woman, you poison the waters of life at the very fountain."[39] Engels appears to have been outraged for similar reasons: "We find here precisely the same features reappearing which the Factories' Report presented,—the work of women up to the hour of confinement, incapacity as housekeepers, neglect of home and children, indifference, actual dislike to family life, and demoralization; further the crowding out of men from employment, the constant improvement of machinery, early emancipation of children, husbands supported by their wives and children, etc., etc."[40] Here, Engels has touched upon the reasons for the opposition of the male workers to the situation. Engels was apparently ambivalent about whose side he was on, for while he often seems to share the attitudes of the men and of the upper classes, he also refers to the trade unions as elite organizations of grown-up men who achieve benefits for themselves but not for the unskilled, women, or children.[41]

That male workers viewed the employment of women as a threat to their jobs is not surprising, given an economic system in which competition among workers was characteristic. That women were paid lower wages exacerbated the threat. But why their response was to attempt to exclude women rather than to organize them is explained not by capitalism but by patriarchal relations between men and women: men wanted to assure that women would continue to perform the appropriate tasks at home.

Engels reports an incident that probably occurred in the 1830s. Male Glasgow spinners had formed a secret union: "The Committee put a price on the heads of all blacklegs [strikebreakers] . . . and deliberately organized arson in factories. One factory to be set on fire had women blacklegs on the premises who had taken the places of men at the spinning machines. A certain Mrs. MacPherson, the mother of one of these girls, was murdered and those responsible were shipped off to America at the expense of the union."[42] Hostility to the competition of young females, almost certainly less well trained and lower paid, was common enough. But if anything, the wage work of married women was thought even less excusable.

In 1846 the *Ten Hours' Advocate* stated clearly that it hoped for the day when such threats would be removed altogether: "It is needless for us to say, that all attempts to improve the morals and physical condition of female factory workers will be abortive, unless their hours are materially reduced. Indeed we may go so far as to say, that married females would be much better occupied in performing the domestic duties of the household, than following the never-tiring motion of machinery. We therefore hope the day is not distant, when the husband will be able to provide for his wife and family, without sending the former to endure the drudgery of a cotton mill."[43] Eventually, male trade unionists realized that women could not be removed altogether, but their attitude was still ambivalent. One local wrote to the Women's Trade Union League, organized in 1889 to encourage unionization among women workers: "Please send an organizer to this town as we have decided that if the women here cannot be organized they must be exterminated."[44]

The deplorable situation of women in the labor market was explained in a variety of ways by British historians and economists writing in the late nineteenth and early twentieth centuries. Some accepted the logic of the male unions that women belonged at home if possible and that men's wages should be increased. Ivy Pinchbeck, for example, stated: "The industrial revolution marked a real advance, since it led to the assumption that men's wages should be paid on a family basis, and prepared the way for the more modern conception that in the rearing of children and in homemaking, the married woman makes an adequate economic contribution."[45] Others argued that this system would only perpetuate women's low economic status. Examining the literature from this period, especially the Webb-Rathbone-Fawcett-Edgeworth series in the *Economic Journal*, is important because it sets the framework for nearly all the explanations of women's position in the labor market that have been used since. In addition, this literature tends to support my argument that job segregation was detrimental to women and that male unions tended to enforce it.

Several writers who focused on job segregation and noncompeting groups as the central mechanism discussed the actions of male unionists as well. Sidney Webb offered as a justification for the lower wages women received the explanation that they rarely did the same grade of work, even when engaged in the same occupation or industry. He cited cigarmaking: men made fancy cigars; women made cheap ones requiring less skill. Yet he also acknowledged the role male unions played in preventing women from gaining skills and admitted the possibility that, even for equal work, women received lower wages.[46]

Millicent Fawcett argued that equal pay for equal work was a fraud for women: because they had been kept from obtaining equal skills, their work (at the same jobs) was, in fact, not equal. The essence of trade-union policy, she felt, was to exclude women if they were less efficient and, furthermore, to keep them less efficient.[47] As Eleanor Rathbone put it in 1917, male union leaders will support equal pay as "an effective way of maintaining the exclusion of women while appearing as the champions of equality between the sexes." Many of the followers, she thought, "are obviously rather shocked in their hearts at the idea of a woman earning a man's pay."[48]

Rathbone also considered seriously the different family responsibilities of women. They are a reality, she insisted; men do support their families more often than women do, and men want sufficient money to do this. But she did not necessarily agree with this arrangement; she simply acknowledged that most people considered it "a fundamental part of the social structure":

> The line of argument I have been following usually either irritates
> or depresses all women who have the interests of their own sex at
> heart, because it seems to point to an impasse. If the wages of men
> and women are really based upon fundamentally different condi-
> tions, and if these conditions cannot be changed, then it would seem
> . . . that women are the eternal blacklegs, doomed despite them-
> selves to injure the prospects of men whenever they are brought into
> competition with them. . . . If that were really so, then it would seem
> as if men were justified in treating women, as in practice they have
> treated them—as a kind of industrial lepers, segregated in trades
> which men have agreed to abandon to them, permitted to occupy
> themselves in making clothes or in doing domestic services for each

other, and in performing those subsidiary processes in the big staple trades, which are so monotonous or unskilled that men do not care to claim them.[49]

World War I, however, had raised women's expectations, and women were not likely to go back to their place willingly—even though the male unions had been promised that the women's jobs were only temporary—especially since, in addition to their wages, married women whose husbands were at war received government allowances according to family size. Rathbone wrote: "The future solution of the problem is doubtful and difficult, and . . . it opens up unpleasant possibilities of class antagonism and sex antagonism; . . . for women especially it seems to offer a choice between being exploited by capitalists or dragooned and oppressed by trade unionists. It is a dismal alternative."[50] She recommended the continuation of allowances after the war because they would ensure that families would not have to rely on men's wages, that women who stayed at home would be paid for their work, and that women in the labor market could compete equally with men, since their "required" wages would not be different. By 1918 Fawcett also thought equal pay for equal work a realizable goal. Advancement in the labor market required equal pay in order not to undercut the men's wages. The main obstacles, she argued, were the male unions and social customs. Both led to overcrowding in the women's jobs.[51]

In 1922, F. Y. Edgeworth formalized Fawcett's job segregation and overcrowding model: job segregation by sex caused overcrowding in female sectors, which allowed men's wages to be higher and forced women's wages to be lower than they would be otherwise. Edgeworth agreed that male unions were the main cause of overcrowding.[52] He argued that men *should* have an advantage because of their family responsibilities, and the corollary: that since women do not have the same family responsibilities as men and may even be subsidized by men, their participation will tend to pull wages down. And he seemed to suggest that equal competition in the job market would result in lower wages even for single women vis-à-vis single men, because women required 20 percent less food for top efficiency. In this last, Edgeworth was simply taking seriously what many had remarked upon—that women have a lower standard of living than men and are willing to work for less.[53] Edgeworth concluded that restrictions on women's work should be removed, but that because unfettered competition would probably drag down the wages of men for the reasons noted above, men and families should be compensated for losses due to the increased participation of women.[54]

The main explanation the English literature offers for lower wages is job segregation by sex, and for both lower wages and the existence of job segregation it offers several interdependent explanations: (1) the exclusionary policies of male unions, (2) the financial responsibility of men for their families, (3) the willingness of women to work for less (and their inability to get more) because of subsidies or a lower standard of living, and (4) women's lack of training and skills. The English historical literature strongly suggests that job segregation by sex is patriarchal in origin, of rather long standing, and difficult to eradicate. Men's ability to organize in labor unions—stemming perhaps from a greater knowledge of the technique of hierarchical organization—appears to be key in their ability to maintain job segregation and the domestic division of labor.

Turning to the United States experience provides an opportunity, first, to explore shifts in the sex composition of jobs, and second, to consider further the role of unions, particularly in establishing protective legislation. The American literature, especially the works of Edith Abbott and Elizabeth Baker, emphasizes sex shifts in jobs and, in contrast to the English literature, relies more heavily on technology as an explanatory phenomenon.[55]

Conditions in the United States differed from those in England. First, the division of labor within colonial farm families was probably more rigid, with men in the fields and women producing manufactured articles at home. Second, the early textile factories employed young single women from the farms of New England; a conscious effort was made, probably out of necessity, to avoid the creation of a family labor system and to preserve the labor of men for agriculture.[56] This changed, however, with the eventual dominance of manufacture over agriculture as the leading sector in the economy, and with immigration. Third, the shortage of labor plus dire necessity in colonial and frontier America perhaps created more opportunities for women in nontraditional pursuits outside the family; colonial women were engaged in a wide variety of occupations.[57] Fourth, shortages of labor continued to operate in women's favor at various points throughout the nineteenth and twentieth centuries. Fifth, the constant arrival of new groups of immigrants created an extremely heterogeneous labor force, with varying skill levels and organizational development—and rampant antagonisms.[58]

Major shifts in the sex composition of employment occurred in boot and shoe manufacture, textile manufacture, teaching, cigarmaking, and clerical work.[59] In all of these except textiles, the shift was toward more women. New occupations opened up for both men and women, but men seemed to dominate in most of them—though there were exceptions: telephone operating and typing, for example, became women's jobs.

In all cases of increase in female employment, the women were partially stimulated by a sharp rise in the demand for the service or product. During the late 1700s and early 1800s, domestic demand for ready-made boots went up because of the War of 1812, a greater number of slaves, general population expansion, and the settling of the frontier. Demand for teachers increased rapidly before, during, and after the Civil War as public education spread. The demand for cheap, machine-made cigars grew rapidly at the end of the nineteenth century. The upward shift in the numbers of clerical workers came between 1890 and 1930, when businesses grew larger and became more centralized, requ ring more administration, distribution, transportation, marketing, and communication.

In several cases the shift to women was accompanied by technical innovations that increased output and sometimes reduced the skill required of the worker. By 1800 boot- and shoemakers had devised a division of labor that allowed women to work on sewing the uppers at home. In the 1850s sewing machines were applied to boots and shoes in factories. In the 1870s the use of wooden molds, rather than hand bunching, simplified cigarmaking, and in the 1880s machinery was brought in. And in clerical work the typewriter, of course, greatly increased the productivity of clerical labor. The mule spinner, machinery introduced in the textile industry, was traditionally operated by males. In printing, where male unions were successful in excluding women, the unions insisted on staffing the new linotypes.[60]

The central purposes of subdividing the labor process, simplifying tasks, and introducing machines were to raise production, to cheapen it, and to increase management's control over the labor process. Subdivision of the labor process ordinarily allowed the use of less skilled labor in one or more subportions of the task. Cheapening of labor power and more control over labor were the motive forces behind scientific management and earlier efforts to reorganize labor.[61] Machinery was an aid in the process, not a motive force. Machinery, unskilled labor, and women workers often went together.

In addition to greater demand and technical change, often a shortage of the usual supply of labor contributed to a change in the labor force. In textiles, for example, when in the 1840s the young New England farm women were attracted to new job opportunities for middle-class women, such as teaching, their places in the mills were taken by immigrants. In boots and shoes the increased demand could not be met by the available trained shoemakers, nor in clerical work was the supply of high-school-educated males equal to the demand. Moreover, the changes that occurred in the job structure of clerical work in particular reduced its attractiveness to men

—with expansion, the jobs became dead-end ones—while for women the opportunities compared favorably with their opportunities elsewhere.[62]

Cigarmaking amply illustrates both the opposition of male unionists to impending sex changes in labor-force composition in their industries and the form that opposition took: protective legislation.[63] Cigarmaking was a home industry before 1800, when women on farms in Connecticut and elsewhere made rather rough cigars and traded them at village stores. Early factories employed women, but they were soon replaced by skilled male immigrants whose products could compete with fancy European cigars. By 1860 women were only 9 percent of those employed in cigarmaking. This switch to men was followed by one to women, but not without opposition from the men. In 1869 the wooden mold was introduced, and so were Bohemian immigrant women (who had been skilled workers in cigar factories in Austria-Hungary).[64] The Bohemian women, established by tobacco companies in tenements, perfected a division of labor in which young girls (and later their husbands)[65] could use the molds. Beginning in 1873 the Cigarmakers International Union agitated vociferously against home work, which was eventually restricted (for example, in New York in 1894). In the late 1880s machinery was introduced into the factories, and women were used as strikebreakers. The union turned to protective legislation.

The attitude of the Cigarmakers International Union toward women was ambivalent at best. The union excluded women in 1864 but admitted them in 1867. In 1875 it prohibited locals from excluding women but apparently never imposed sanctions on offending locals.[66] In 1878 a Baltimore local wrote Adolph Strasser, the union president: "We have combatted from its incipiency the movement of the introduction of female labor in any capacity whatever, be it bunch maker, roller, or what not."[67] Lest these ambiguities be interpreted as national-local conflicts, let Strasser speak for himself (1879): "We cannot drive the females out of the trade, but we can restrict their daily quota of labor through factory laws. No girl under 18 should be employed more than eight hours per day; all overwork should be prohibited."[68]

Because the women were unskilled workers, it may be erroneous to interpret this as animosity to *women* per se. Rather it was the fear of the skilled for the unskilled. Yet male unions denied women skills, while they offered them to young boys. This is quite clear in the case of printing.[69]

Women had been engaged as typesetters in printing from colonial times. It was a skilled trade, but required no heavy work. Abbott attributed the jealousy of the men in the trade to the fact that it was a trade "suited" to women. In any case, male unions seem to have been hostile to the employment of women from the beginning. In 1854 the National Typographical Union resolved not to "encourage by its act the employment of female compositors."[70] Baker suggests that the unions discouraged girls from learning the trade, and so women learned what they could in non-union shops or as strikebreakers.[71] In 1869 at the annual convention of the National Labor Union, of which the National Typographical Union was a member, a struggle occurred over the seating of Susan B. Anthony, because she had allegedly used women compositors as strikebreakers. She had, she admitted, because they could learn the trade no other way.[72] In 1870 the Typographical Union did charter a women's local in New York City. Its president, Augusta Lewis, who was also corresponding secretary of the National Typographical Union, did not think it could hold out for very long because, although the union women supported the union men, the union men did not support the union women: "It is the general opinion of female compositors that they are more justly treated by what is termed 'rat' foremen, printers, and employers than they are by union men."[73] The women's local eventually folded in 1878.

Apparently, the general lack of support was successful from the men's point of view, for in 1910 Abbott claimed that "officers of other trade unions frequently refer to the policy of the printers as an example of the way in which trade union control may be successful in checking or preventing the employment of women."[74] The Typographical Union strongly backed equal pay for equal work as a way to protect the men's wage scale, not to encourage women; women, who had fewer skills, could not demand and expect to receive equal wages.[75]

Unions excluded women in many ways, not the least among them protective legislation.[76] In this the unions were aided by the prevailing social sentiment about work for women, especially married women, which was seen as a social evil that ideally should be wiped out,[77] and by a strong concern on the part of "social feminists" and others that women workers were severely exploited because they were unorganized.[78] The social feminists did not intend to exclude women from desirable occupations, but their strategy paved the way for this exclusion because, to get protection for working women—which they felt was so desperately needed—they argued that women as a sex were weaker than men and more in need of protection.[79] Their strategy was successful in 1908 when, in *Muller v. Oregon*, the Supreme Court upheld maximum-hours laws for women, saying: "The two sexes differ in structure of body, in the capacity for long-continued labor particularly when done standing, the influence of vigorous health upon the future well-being of the race, the self-reliance which enables one to assert full rights, and in the capacity to maintain the struggle for subsistence. This difference justifies a difference in legislation and upholds that which is designed to compensate for some of the burdens which rest upon her."[80]

In 1916, in *Bunting v. Oregon,* Louis Brandeis used virtually the same data on the ill effects of long hours of work to argue successfully for maximum-hours laws for men as well as women. *Bunting* was not, however, followed by a spate of maximum-hours law for men, as *Muller* had been by laws for women. In general, unions did not support protective legislation for men, although they continued to do so for women. Protective legislation, rather than organization, was the preferred strategy only for women.[81]

The effect of the laws was limited by their narrow coverage and inadequate enforcement; nevertheless, in those few occupations such as printing where night work or long hours were essential, women were effectively excluded.[82] While the laws may have protected women in the "sweated" trades, women who were beginning to get established in "men's jobs" were turned back. Some of these women fought back successfully, but the struggle is still being waged today along many of the same battle lines. As Ann C. Hill argued, the effect of these laws, psychically and socially, has been devastating. They confirmed woman's "alien" status as a worker.[83]

Throughout this discussion of the development of the wage-labor force in England and the United States, I have emphasized the role of male workers in restricting women's sphere in the labor market, but I do not think the role of employers was unimportant. Recent work on labor-market segmentation theory provides a framework for looking at the part played by employers.[84] According to this model, one mechanism that creates segmentation is the conscious though not necessarily conspiratorial action of capitalists; they act to exacerbate existing divisions among workers in order to divide them further, thus weakening their class unity and reducing their bargaining power.[85] The creation of complex internal job structures is itself part of this attempt. In fact, the whole range of different levels of jobs serves to obfuscate the basic two-class nature of capitalist society.[86] This model suggests, first, that sex segregation is one aspect of the labor-market segmentation inherent in advanced capitalism, and second, that capitalists have consciously attempted to exacerbate sex divisions. Thus, if the foregoing analysis has emphasized the continuous nature of job segregation by sex (present in all stages of capitalism and before)[87] and the conscious actions of male workers, it is important to note that the actions of capitalists may have been crucial in calling forth those responses from male workers.

Historically, male workers have been instrumental in limiting the participation of women in the labor market. Male unions have carried out the policies and attitudes of the earlier guilds, and they have continued to reap benefits for male workers. Capitalists inherited job segregation by sex, but they have quite often been able to use it to their own advantage. If they can supersede experienced men with cheaper women, so much the better;

if they can weaken labor by threatening to do so, that's good, too; or if, failing that, they can use those status differences to reward men and buy their allegiance to capitalism with patriarchal benefits, that's okay too.[88]

But even though capitalists' actions are important in explaining the current virility of sex segregation, labor-market segmentation theory overemphasizes the role of capitalists and ignores the actions of workers themselves in perpetuating segmentation. Those workers in the more desirable jobs act to hang on to the jobs, their material rewards, and their subjective benefits.[89] Workers, through unions, have been party to the creation and maintenance of hierarchical and parallel (that is, separate but unequal) job structures. Perhaps the relative importance of capitalists and male workers in instituting and maintaining job segregation by sex has varied in different periods. Capitalists during the transition to capitalism, for example, seemed quite able to change the sex composition of jobs: when weaving was shifted to factories equipped with power looms, women wove, even though most handloom weavers had been men; and mule spinning was introduced with male operators, even though women had used the earlier spinning jennies and water frames. As industrialization progressed and conditions stabilized somewhat, male unions gained in strength and were often able to preserve or extend male arenas. Nevertheless, in times of overwhelming social or economic necessity, occasioned by vast increases in the demand for labor in, for example, teaching or clerical work, male capitalists were capable of overpowering male workers. Thus, in periods of economic change capitalists' actions may be more instrumental in instituting or changing a sex-segregated labor force—while workers fight a defensive battle. In other periods male workers may be more important in maintaining sex-segregated jobs; they may be able to prevent the encroachment of or even to drive out cheaper female labor, thus increasing the benefits to their own sex.[90]

Conclusion

The present status of women in the labor market and the current arrangement of sex-segregated jobs is the result of a long process of interaction between patriarchy and capitalism. I have emphasized the actions of male workers throughout this process because I believe that emphasis to be correct. Men will have to be forced to give up their favored positions in the division of labor—in the labor market and at home—if women's subordination is to end and if men are to begin to escape class oppression and exploitation.[91] Capitalists have indeed used women as unskilled, underpaid labor to undercut male workers, yet this is only a case of the chickens coming home to roost—a case of men's co-optation by and support for patriarchal society, with its hierarchy among men, being turned back on the men themselves with a vengeance. Capitalism grew on top of patriarchy; patriarchal capitalism is stratified society par excellence. If non-ruling-class men are to be free, they will have to recognize their co-optation by patriarchal capitalism and relinquish their patriarchal benefits. If women are to be free, they must fight against both patriarchal power and capitalist organization of society.

Because both the sexual division of labor and male domination are of such long standing, it will be very difficult to eradicate them and impossible to eradicate the latter while the former exists. The two are now so inextricably intertwined that it is necessary to eradicate the sexual division of labor itself in order to end male domination.[92] Very basic changes at all levels of society and culture are required to liberate women. I have argued here that the maintenance of job segregation by sex is a key root of women's status, and I have relied on the operation of society-wide institutions to explain the maintenance of job segregation by sex. But the consequences of that division of labor go very deep, down to the level of the subconscious. The subconscious influences behavior patterns, which form the micro underpinnings (or complements) of social institutions and are in turn reinforced by those social institutions.

I believe we need to investigate these micro phenomena as well as the macro ones I have discussed. For example, it appears to be a very deeply ingrained behavioral rule that men cannot be subordinate to women of a similar social class. Manifestations of this rule have been noted in restaurants, where waitresses experience difficulty in giving orders to bartenders unless the bartender can reorganize the situation to allow himself autonomy; among executives, where women executives are seen to be most successful if they have little contact with others at their level and manage only small staffs; and among industrial workers, where female factory inspectors cannot successfully correct the work of male production workers.[93] There is also a deeply ingrained fear of being identified with the other sex. As a general rule, men and women must never do anything that is not masculine or feminine, respectively. Male executives, for example, often exchange handshakes with male secretaries, a show of respect that probably works to help preserve their masculinity.[94]

At the next deeper level, we must study the subconscious—both how these behavioral rules are internalized and how they grow out of personality structure.[95] At this level, the formation of personality, there have been several attempts to study the production of gender, the *socially* imposed differentiation of humans based on biological sex differences.[96] A materialist interpretation of reality, of course, suggests that gender production grows out of the extant division of labor between the sexes and in a dialectical process, reinforces that very division of labor itself.[97] In my view, because of these deep ramifications of the sexual division of labor, we will not eradicate sex-ordered task division until we eradicate the socially imposed gender differences between us and, therefore, the very sexual division of labor itself.

In attacking both patriarchy and capitalism we will have to find ways to change both society-wide institutions and our most deeply ingrained habits. It will be a long, hard struggle.

Notes

Acknowledgments: I would like to thank many women at the New School for sharing their knowledge with me and offering encouragement and debate, in particular, Amy Hirsch, Christine Gailey, Nadine Felton, Penny Ciancanelli, Rayna Reiter, and Viana Muller. I would also like to thank Amy Bridges, Carl Degler, David Gordon, Fran Blau, Grace Horowitz, Linda Gordon, Suad Joseph, Susan Strasser, and Tom Vietorisz for helpful comments.

1. I define patriarchy as a set of social relations that has a material base and in which there are hierarchical relations between men, and solidarity among them, which enable them to control women. Patriarchy is thus the system of male oppression of women. Rubin argues that we should use the term "sex/gender system" to refer to that realm outside the economic system (and not always coordinate with it) where gender stratification based on sex differences is produced and reproduced. Patriarchy is thus only one form, a male-dominant one, of a sex/gender system. Rubin argues further that "patriarchy" should be reserved for pastoral nomadic societies as described in the Old Testament where male power was synonomous with fatherhood. (see Gayle Rubin, "The Traffic in Women," in *Toward an Anthropology of Women*, ed. Rayna Rapp Reiter [New York: Monthly Review Press, 1975]; see also Chapter 3 in this book. While I agree with Rubin's first point, I think her second point makes the usage of "patriarchy" too restrictive. It is a good label for most male-dominant societies. Viana Muller ("The Formation of the State and the Oppression of Women: A Case Study in England and Wales," mimeographed [New York: New School for Social Research, 1975], 4 n.2) offers a broader definition of patriarchy "as a social system in which the status of women is defined primarily as wards of their husbands, fathers, and brothers," where wardship has economic and political dimensions. Muller relies on Karen Sacks, "Engels Revisited: Women, the Organization of Production, and Private Property," in *Woman, Culture, and Society*, ed. Michelle Z. Rosaldo and Louise Lamphere (Stanford, Calif.: Stanford University Press, 1974). Patriarchy as a system between and among men as well as between men and women is further explained in a draft paper, "The Unhappy Marriage of Marxism and Feminism: Towards a New Union," by Amy Bridges and Heidi Hartmann.

2. Marx and Engels perceived the progress of capitalism in this way, that it would bring women and children into the labor market and thus erode the family. Yet despite Engels's acknowledgment, in *The Origin of the Family, Private Property, and the State* (New York: International Publishers, 1972), that men oppress women in the family, he does not see that oppression as based on the control of women's labor; if anything, he seems to lament the passing of the male-controlled family (see his *Condition of the Working Class in England in 1844* [Stanford, Calif.: Stanford University Press, 1968], esp. 161–64).

3. See Richard C. Edwards, Michael Reich, and David M. Gordon, "Labor Market Segmentation in American Capitalism," draft essay, and the book they edited, *Labor Market Segmentation* (Lexington, Ky.: Heath, 1975), for an explication of this view.

4. Sherry B. Ortner, "Is Female to Male as Nature Is to Culture?" *Feminist Studies* 1, no. 2 (1972): 5–6: "The universality of female subordination, the fact that it exists within every type of social and economic arrangement, and in societies of every degree of complexity, indicates to me that we are up against something very profound, very stubborn, something that cannot be remedied merely by rearranging a few tasks and roles in the social system, nor even by rearranging the whole economic structure."

Ortner specifically rejects a biological basis for this association of women with nature and the concomitant devaluation of both. Biological differences "only take on significance of superior/inferior within the framework of culturally defined value systems" (p. 9). The biological explanation is, of course, the other major explanation for the universality of female subordination. I, too, deny the validity of this explanation and will not discuss it here. Female physiology does, however, play a role in supporting a cultural view of women as closer to nature, as Ortner argues persuasively (pp. 12–14), following Simone de Beauvoir. Ortner's article was reprinted in Rosaldo and Lamphere, *Woman, Culture, and Society*, in slightly revised form.

5. Michelle Z. Rosaldo, "Woman, Culture, and Society: A Theoretical Overview," in Rosaldo and Lamphere, *Woman, Culture, and Society.*

6. Claude Lévi-Strauss, "The Family," in *Man, Culture and Society*, ed. Harry L. Shapiro (New York: Oxford University Press, 1971), pp. 347–48. "One of the strongest field recollections of this writer was his meeting, among the Bororo of central Brazil, of a man about thirty years old: unclean, ill-fed, sad, and lonesome. When asked if the man was seriously ill, the natives' answer came as a shock: what was wrong with him?—nothing at all, he was just a bachelor. And true enough, in a society where labor is systematically shared between men and women and where only the married status permits the man to benefit from the fruits of woman's work, including delousing, body painting, and hair-plucking as well as vegetable food and cooked food (since the Bororo woman tills the soil and makes pots), a bachelor is really only half a human being" (p. 341).

7. For further discussion of both the universality and variety of the division of labor by sex, see Melville J. Herskovits, *Economic Anthropology* (New York: Norton, 1965), esp. chap. 7; Theodore Caplow, *The Sociology of Work* (New York: McGraw-Hill, 1964), esp. chap. 1.

8. For more on the exchange of women and its significance for women, see Rubin, "The Traffic in Women."

9. Nancy Chodorow, *The Reproduction of Mothering* (Berkeley: University of Cali-

fornia Press, 1978). Chodorow offers an important alternative interpretation of the Oedipus complex (see her "Family Structure and Feminine Personality" in Rosaldo and Lamphere, *Woman, Culture, and Society*).

10. Several of the articles in the Rosaldo and Lamphere collection are of this variety (see particularly Collier and Stack). Also see Ernestine Friedl, "The Position of Women: Appearance and Reality," *Anthropological Quarterly* 40, no. 3 (1967): 97–108.

11. For an example of one particular emphasis, Ruby B. Leavitt states: "The most important clue to woman's status anywhere is her degree of participation in economic life and her control over property and the products she produces, both of which factors appear to be related to the kinship system of a society" ("Women in Other Cultures," in *Woman and Sexist Society*, ed. Vivian Gornick and Barbara K. Moran [New York: New American Library, 1972], p. 396). In a historical study that also seeks to address the questions of women's status, Joanne McNamara and Suzanne Wemple ("The Power of Woman through the Family in Medieval Europe: 500–1100," *Feminist Studies* 1, nos. 3–4 [1973]: 126–41) emphasize the private-public split in their discussion of women's loss of status during this period.

12. Patricia Draper, "!Kung Women: Contrasts in Sexual Egalitarianism in Foraging and Sedentary Contexts," in Reiter, *Toward an Anthropology of Women*.

13. Ibid., 108.

14. Ester Boserup, *Woman's Role in Economic Development* (London: Allen & Unwin, 1970).

15. Leavitt, "Women in Other Cultures," 412, 413.

16. Judith Van Allen, "'Sitting on a Man': Colonialism and the Lost Political Institutions of Igbo Women," *Canadian Journal of African Studies* 6, no. 2 (1972): 169, 170, 174–75. The British naturally thought the women were directed in their struggle by the men, though very few men participated in the riots.

17. Muller, "Formation of the State," 1. I am very grateful to Viana Muller for allowing me to summarize parts of her unpublished paper.

18. Ibid., 14.

19. Ibid., 25.

20. The examples of the !Kung, the Igbo, the Anglo-Saxons, and the groups discussed in Boserup, *Woman's Role*, all suggest that the process of expansion of state or emerging-state societies and the conquest of other peoples was an extremely important mechanism for spreading hierarchy and male domination. In fact, the role of warfare and imperialism raises the question of whether the state, to establish itself, creates the patriarchal family, or the patriarchal family creates the state (Thomas Vietorisz, personal communication). Surely emerging patriarchal social relations in pre-state societies paved the way for both male public power (i.e., male control of the state apparatus) and the privatization of patriarchal power in the family. Surely also this privatization—and the concomitant decline of tribal power—strengthened, and was strengthened by, the state.

21. This point is stressed especially by Muller but is also illustrated by the !Kung. Muller states: "The men, although lowered from clansmen to peasants, were elevated to heads of nuclear families, with a modicum of both public power [through the state and religion] and a measure of private power through the decree of the Church-State that they were to be lords over their wives" ("Formation of the State," 35).

22. Both Hill and Stone describe England during this period as a patriarchal

society in which the institutions of the nuclear family, the state, and religion were being strengthened: see Christopher Hill, *Society and Puritanism* (New York: Schocken Books, 1964), esp. chap. 13; Lawrence Stone, *The Crisis of the Aristocracy, 1558– 1641*, abridged ed. (New York: Oxford University Press, 1967), esp. chap. 11. Recent demographic research verifies the establishment of the nuclear family prior to the industrial revolution; see Peter Laslett, ed., *Household and Family in Past Time* (Cambridge: Cambridge University Press, 1972). Because of limitations of my knowledge and space, and because I sought to discuss, first, the concept and establishment of patriarchy, and second, its transformation in a wage-labor society, I am skipping over the rise and fall of feudal society and the emergence of family-centered petty commodity production and focusing in the next section on the disintegration of this family-centered production, creation of the wage-labor force, and the maintenance of job segregation in a capitalist context.

23. See Karl Marx, "The So-called Primitive Accumulation," in *Capital* (New York: International Publishers, 1967), vol. 1, pt. 8; Stephen Hymer, "Robinson Crusoe and the Secret of Primitive Accumulation," *Monthly Review* 23, no. 4 (1971): 11–36.

24. This account relies primarily on that of Alice Clark, *The Working Life of Women in the Seventeenth Century* (New York: Harcourt, Brace & Howe, 1920). Her account is supported by many others, such as B. L. Hutchins, *Women in Modern Industry* (London: G. Bell, 1915); Georgiana Hill, *Women in English Life from Medieval to Modern Times*, 2 vols. (London: Richard Bentley, 1896); F. W. Tickner, *Women in English Economic History* (New York: Dutton, 1923); Ivy Pinchbeck, *Women Workers and the Industrial Revolution, 1750–1850* (London: Frank Cass, 1930; rpt. 1969).

25. Women and men in England had been employed as agricultural laborers for several centuries. Clark found that by the seventeenth century the wages of men were higher than women's and the tasks done were different, though similar in skill and strength requirements (*Working Life of Women*, 60). Wages for agricultural (and other work) were often set by local authorities. These wage differentials reflected the relative social status of men and women and the social norms of the time. Women were considered to require lower wages because they ate less, for example, and were expected to have fewer luxuries, such as tobacco (see Clark and Pinchbeck *Women Workers*, throughout for substantiation of women's lower standard of living). Laura Oren has substantiated this for English women during the period 1860–1950 (see n. 53 below).

26. The problem of female unemployment in the countryside was a generally recognized one that figured prominently in the debate about poor-law reform, for example. As a remedy, it was suggested that rural families be allowed to retain small household plots, that women be used more in agricultural wage labor and also in the putting-out system, and that men's wages be adjusted upward (see Pinchbeck, *Women Workers*, 69–84).

27. See Stephen Marglin, "What Do Bosses Do? The Origins and Functions of Hierarchy in Capitalist Production," *Review of Radical Political Economics* 6, no. 2 (1974): 60–112, for a discussion of the transition from putting out to factories. The sexual division of labor changed several times in the textile industry. Hutchins writes that the further back one goes in history, the more was the industry controlled by women. By the seventeenth century, though, men had become professional handloom weavers, and it was often claimed that men had superior strength or skill— which was required for certain types of weaves or fabrics. Thus, the increase in

demand for handloom weavers in the late 1700s brought increased employment for men. When weaving was mechanized in the factories, women operated the power looms, and male handloom weavers became unemployed. When jenny and waterframe spinning were replaced by mule spinning, supposedly requiring more strength, men took that over and displaced women spinners. A similar transition occurred in the United States. It is important to keep in mind that both men and women engaged in various processes of textile manufacture as a by-industry, and this was intensified under putting out (see Pinchbeck, *Women Workers*, chaps. 6–9).

28. See Clark, *Working Life of Women*; Pinchbeck, *Women Workers*; E. P. Thompson, *The Making of the English Working Class* (New York: Vintage Books, 1963).

29. In fact, the earliest factories utilized the labor of poor children, already separated from their families, who were apprenticed to factory owners by parish authorities. They were perhaps the most desperate and vulnerable of all.

30. Hutchins, *Women in Modern Industry*, 16. See also Olive J. Jocelyn, *English Apprenticeship and Child Labor* (London: T. Fisher Unwin, 1912), 149–50, on the labor of girls; and Clark, *Working Life of Women*, chap. 5, on the organization of family industry in towns.

31. The seventeenth century already found the crafts and trades divided by sex. Much work needs to be done on the development of guilds to shed light on the sexual division of labor and on the nature of women's organizations. Such work would enable us to trace more accurately the decline in women's status from the tribal period, through feudalism, to the emergence of capitalism.

32. See Clark, *Working Life of Women*, 221–31 for the brewers, and 242–84 for the medical profession.

33. Ibid., chap. 7. Eli Zaretsky, in "Capitalism, the Family, and Personal Life," *Socialist Revolution* nos. 13–14 (1973), follows a similar interpretation of history and offers different conclusions. Capitalism exacerbated the sexual division of labor and created the *appearance* that women work for their husbands; in reality, women who did domestic work at home were working for capital. Thus, according to Zaretsky, the present situation has its roots more in capitalism than in patriarchy. Although capitalism may have increased the consequence for women of the domestic division of labor, surely patriarchy tells us more about why men didn't stay home. That women worked for men in the home, as well as for capital, is also a reality.

34. William Lazonick argues in "Marxian Theory and the Development of the Labor Force in England" (Ph.D. diss., Harvard University, 1975) that the degree of authority required of the worker was often decisive in determining the sex of the worker. Thus, handloom weavers in cottage industry were men because this allowed them to control the production process and the labor of the female spinners. In the spinning factories, mule spinners were men because mule spinners were required to supervise the labor of piecers, usually young boys. Men's position as heads of families established their position as heads of production units, and vice versa. While this is certainly plausible, I think it requires further investigation. Lazonick's work in this area (see chap. 4, "Segments of the Labour Force: Women, Children, and Irish") is very valuable.

35. Perhaps 25 percent of female textile factory workers were married women: see Pinchbeck, *Women Workers*, 198; Margaret Hewitt, *Wives and Mothers in Victorian Industry* (London: Rockliff, 1958), 14ff. It is important to remember also that factory employment was far from the dominant employment of women. Most women worked as domestic servants.

36. Neil Smelser, *Social Change and the Industrial Revolution* (Chicago: University of Chicago Press, 1959), chaps. 9–11. Other researchers have also established that in some cases there was a considerable degree of familial control over some aspects of the work process. See Tamara Hareven's research on mills in New Hampshire; e.g., "Family Time and Industrial Time: The Interaction between Family and Work in a Planned Corporation Town, 1900–1924," *Journal of Urban History* 1, no. 3 (1975): 365–89. Michael Anderson, *Family Structure in Nineteenth Century Lancashire* (Cambridge: Cambridge University Press, 1971), argues, on the basis of demographic data, that the "practice of allowing operatives to employ assistants, though widespread, can at no period have resulted in a predominantly parent-child pattern of employment" (p. 116). Also see Amy Hirsch's treatment of this question in "Capitalism and the Working Class Family in British Textile Industries during the Industrial Revolution," mimeographed (New York: New School for Social Research, 1975).

37. "[The factory operatives'] agitation in the 1820's and 1830's was one avenue taken to protect the traditional relationship between adult and child, to perpetuate the structure of wages, to limit the recruitment of labourers into industry, and to maintain the father's economic authority" (Smelser, *Social Change*, 265). Lazonick argues that the workers' main interests were not in maintaining their familial dominance in industry but in maintaining their family life outside industry. According to Smelser, agitation before 1840 sought to establish equal-length days for all workers, which would tend to maintain the family in the factory, whereas after 1840 male workers came to accept the notion that married women and children should stay at home.

38. The question of the motives of the various groups involved in passing the factory acts is indeed a thorny one. Women workers themselves may have favored the legislation as an improvement in their working conditions, but some undoubtedly needed the income that longer hours enabled. Most women working in the mills were young, single women who perhaps benefited from the protection. Single women, though "liberated" by the mills from direct domination in their families (about which there was much discussion in the 1800s), were nevertheless kept in their place by the conditions facing them in the labor market. Because of their age and sex, job segregation and lower wages assured their inability to be completely self-sufficient. Ruling-class men, especially those associated with the larger firms, may have had an interest in factory legislation in order to eliminate unfair competition. Working-class and ruling-class men may have cooperated to maintain men's dominant position in the labor market and in the family.

39. From Mary Merryweather, *Factory Life*, cited in Hill, *Women in English Life*, 2: 200. The original is recorded in *Hansard Parliamentary Debates*, 3d ser., House of Commons, 7 June 1842.

40. Frederick Engels, *The Condition of the Working Class in England in 1844* (London: Allen & Unwin, 1892), 199.

41. Ibid., xv.

42. Engels, *The Condition of the Working Class in England in 1844* (Stanford, Calif.: Stanford University Press, 1968), 251.

43. Smelser, *Social Change* 301. Similarly, Pinchbeck quotes from a deputation of the West Riding Short-Time Committee which demanded "the gradual withdrawal of all females from the factories" because "home, its cares, its employments, is woman's true sphere." Gladstone thought this a good suggestion, easily implemented by appropriate laws: e.g., "forbidding a female to work in a factory after her marriage

and during the life-time of her husband" (Pinchbeck, *Women Workers*, 200 n.3, from the *Manchester and Salford Advertiser*, 8, 15 January 1842).

44. Quoted in G. D. H. Cole and Raymond Postgate, *The Common People, 1746–1946*, 4th ed. (London: Methuen, 1949), 432.

45. Pinchbeck, *Women Workers*, 312–13. The history of the emergence of capitalism and the Industrial Revolution clearly shows that the "family wage" is a recent phenomenon. Before the late 1800s it was expected that working-class (and earlier, middle- and upper-class) married women would support themselves. Andrew Ure, a manufacturer, wrote in 1835: "Factory females have also in general much lower wages than males, and they have been pitied on this account with perhaps an injudicious sympathy, since the low price of their labour here tends to make household duties their most profitable as well as agreeable occupation, and prevents them from being tempted by the mill to abandon the care of their offspring at home. Thus Providence effects its purposes with a wisdom and efficacy which should repress the short-sighted presumption of human devices" (*The Philosophy of Manufacturers* [London: C. Knight, 1835], 475). The development of the family wage is discussed in somewhat greater detail in Heidi Hartmann, "Capitalism and Women's Work in the Home, 1900–1930" (Ph.D. diss., Yale University, 1974). More work needs to be done on this concept.

46. Sidney Webb, "The Alleged Differences in the Wages Paid to Men and Women for Similar Work," *Economic Journal* 1, no. 4 (1891): 639. The competition between men and women in industry is, indeed, not so much a direct underselling in wages as a struggle to secure the better paid kinds of work (p. 658).

47. Millicent G. Fawcett, "Mr. Sidney Webb's Article on Women's Wages." *Economic Journal* 2, no. 1 (1892): 173–76. In her review of *Women in the Printing Trades*, ed. J. Ramsay Mac Donald (*Economic Journal* 14, no. 2 [1904]: 295–99). Fawcett wrote that a trade union in Scotland "decided that women must either be paid the same rates as men or got rid of altogether" (p. 296). She cites "the constant and vigilant opposition of Trades Unions to the employment and the technical training of women in the better paid and more skilled branches of trade" (p. 297); for example, the London Society of Journeymen Bookbinders tried to get the highly skilled job of laying gold leaf—a women's job—assigned to the male union members.

48. Eleanor F. Rathbone. "The Remuneration of Women's Services," *Economic Journal* 27, no. 1 (1917): 58.

49. Ibid., 62, 63.

50. Ibid., 64.

51. Millicent G. Fawcett, "Equal Pay for Equal Work," *Economic Journal* 28, no. 1 (1918): 1–6.

52. "The pressure of male trade unions appears to be largely responsible for that crowding of women into comparatively few occupations, which is universally recognized as a main factor in the depression of their wages" (F. Y. Edgeworth, "Equal Pay to Men and Women for Equal Work," *Economic Journal* 32, no. 4 [1922]: 439).

53. While this reasoning may sound circular, I believe it is quite valid. As Marx said, wages are determined by the value of the socially necessary commodities required to maintain the worker, and what is necessary is the product of historical development, of customs of comfort, of trade union activity, etc. (*Capital*, 1:171). Laura Oren has examined the literature on the level of living of working-class families and found that, indeed, within the family, women have less food, less leisure, and less pocket money ("The Welfare of Women in Laboring Families: England, 1860–

1950," *Feminist Studies* 1, nos. 3–4 [1973]: 107–25). That women, like immigrant groups, can reproduce themselves on less, and have for centuries, is a contributing factor in their lower wages.

54. Edgeworth's conclusions are typical of those of neoclassical economists. In furthering Fawcett's analysis he further abstracted from reality. Whereas Fawcett had realized that women were not less efficient than men, and Rathbone had argued similarly, Edgeworth clung to the notion that men deserved more and sought to justify it theoretically. He opposed family allowances, also with neoclassical reasoning, because they would raise taxes, discourage investment, encourage the reproduction of the poorer classes, and remove the incentive for men to work. Edgeworth reports the comment of a lady inspector: "I almost agree with the social worker who said that if the husband got out of work the only thing that the wife should do is to sit down and cry, because if she did anything else he would remain out of work" ("Equal Pay," 453).

55. See Edith Abbott, *Women in Industry* (New York: Arno Press, 1969); Elizabeth F. Baker, *Technology and Woman's Work* (New York: Columbia University Press, 1964).

56. Abbott, *Women in Industry*, esp. chap. 4.

57. Ibid., chap. 2.

58. These antagonisms were often increased by employers. During a cigarmakers' strike in New York City in 1877 employers brought in unskilled Native American girls. By printing on the boxes "These cigars were made by American girls, " they sold many more boxes of the imperfect cigars than they had expected to (Abbott, *Women in Industry*, p. 207).

59. This summary is based on Abbott and is substantiated by both Baker, *Technology*, and Helen L. Sumner, *History of Women in Industry in the United States, 1910*, in United States Bureau of Labor, *Report on Condition of Women and Child Wage-Earners in the United States* (Washington, D.C.: Government Printing Office, 1911), vol. 9.

60. Baker and Abbott rely heavily on technological factors coupled with biological sex differences as explanations of shifts in the sex composition of jobs. The increased speed of machines and sometimes increased weight are cited as favoring men, who are stronger and have longer endurance, etc. Yet often each cites statistics which indicate that the same types of machines are used by both sexes: e.g., mule spinning machines. I would argue that these perceived differences are merely rationalizations used to justify the current sex assignment of tasks. Social pressures were powerful mechanisms of enforcement. Abbott gives several examples of this. A woman had apparently learned the mule in Lawrence and went to Waltham when mules were introduced there. She had to leave, however, because according to a male operative, "The men made unpleasant remarks and it was too hard for her, being the only woman." And: "Some of the oldest employees in the New England mills to-day [1910] say they can remember when weaving was so universally considered women's work that a 'man weaver' was held up to public ridicule for holding a 'woman's job'" (*Women in Industry*, 92, 95).

61. See Harry Braverman, *Labor and Monopoly Capital* (New York: Monthly Review Press, 1974), esp. chaps. 3–5.

62. Elyce J. Rotella, "Occupational Segregation and the Supply of Women to the American Clerical Labor Force, 1870–1930" (paper presented at the Berkshire Conference on the History of Women, Radcliffe College, 25–27 October 1974). Despite the long-standing recognition of job segregation and shifts in sex composition,

there are surprisingly few studies of the process of shifting. In addition to Rotella for clerical workers there is Margery Davies, "Woman's Place Is at the Typewriter," *Radical America* 8, no. 4 (1974): 1–28. Valerie K. Oppenheimer discusses the shift in elementary teaching in *The Female Labor Force in the United States* (Berkeley: Institute of International Studies, University of California, 1970). And Abbott and Baker discuss several shifts.

63. This account is based primarily on Abbott, *Women in Industry*, chap. 9, and Baker, *Technology*, 31–36.

64. According to Abbott, Samuel Gompers claimed the Bohemian women were brought in for the express purpose of strikebreaking (*Women in Industry*, 197n.).

65. These Bohemian women came to America first, leaving their husbands behind to work in the fields. Their husbands, who were unskilled at the cigar trade, came over later (ibid., 199).

66. In 1877 a Cincinnati local struck to exclude women and was apparently successful. The *Cincinnati Inquirer* said: "The men say the women are killing the industry. It would seem that they hope to retaliate by killing the women" (ibid., 207).

67. Baker, *Technology*, 34.

68. John B. Andrews and W. D. P. Bliss, *History of Women in Trade Unions*, in Bureau of Labor, *Woman and Child Wage-Earners*, vol. 10. Although the proportion of women in cigarmaking did increase eventually, in many other manufacturing industries the proportion of women decreased over time. Textiles and clothing are the outstanding examples (see Abbott, *Women in Industry*, 320, and her "History of Industrial Employment of Women in the United States," *Journal of Political Economy* 14 [October 1906]: 461–501). Helen Sumner, cited in U.S. Bureau of Labor Statistics, Bulletin 175, p. 25, concluded that men had taken over the skilled jobs in women's traditional fields, and women had to take unskilled work wherever they could find it (p. 28).

69. This account is based primarily on Abbott and Baker. The hostility to training women seems generalizable. The International Molders Union resolved: "Any member, honorary or active, who devotes his time in whole or in part to the instruction of female help in the foundry, or in any branch of the trade shall be expelled from the Union" (Gail Falk, "Women and Unions: A Historical View," mimeographed [New Haven, Conn.: Yale Law School, 1970]; published in somewhat shortened form in *Women's Rights Law Reporter* 1 [Spring 1973]: 54–65).

70. Abbott, *Women in Industry*, 252–53.

71. Baker, *Technology*, 39–40.

72. See Falk, "Women and Unions."

73. Eleanor Flexner, *Century of Struggle* (New York: Atheneum, 1970), 136.

74. Abbott, *Women in Industry*, 260.

75. Baker observed that the testimony on the Equal Pay Act in 1963 was about evenly divided between those emphasizing women's needs and those emphasizing the protection of men (*Technology*, 419).

76. Falk, *Women and Unions*, noted that unions used constitutional exclusion, exclusion from apprenticeship, limitation of women to helper categories or nonladder apprenticeships, limitation of proportion of union members who could be women (quotas) and excessively high fees. Moreover, the craft unions of this period, pre-1930, had a general hostility toward organizing the unskilled, even those attached to their crafts.

77. Such a diverse group as Caroll Wright, first U.S. Labor Commissioner, and

Samuel Gompers and Mother Mary Jones—traditional and radical labor organizers; respectively (Falk), James L. Davis, U.S. Secretary of Labor, 1922; and Florence Kelley, head of the National Consumers League, all held views that were variations of this theme. See Baker, *Technology*, 84, 400; Falk, "Women and Unions"; and Ann C. Hill, "Protective Labor Legislation for Women: Its Origin and Effect," mimeographed (New Haven, Conn.: Yale Law School, 1970), parts of which have been published in Barbara A. Babcock, Ann E. Freedman, Eleanor H. Norton, and Susan C. Ross, *Sex Discrimination and the Law: Causes and Remedies* (Boston: Little, Brown, 1975), a law text that provides an excellent analysis of protective legislation, discrimination against women, etc.

78. William O'Neill characterized as "social feminists" those women who participated in various reform movements in the late nineteenth and early twentieth centuries to distinguish them from earlier feminists such as Stanton and Anthony. The social feminists came to support women's rights because they thought it would help advance the cause of their reforms; they were not primarily interested in advancing the cause of women's rights (*Everyone Was Brave* [Chicago: Quadrangle Books, 1969], esp. chap. 3). William H. Chafe, *The American Woman* (New York: Oxford University Press, 1972), also provides an excellent discussion of the debate around protective laws.

79. What was achievable, from the legislatures and the courts, was what the social feminists aimed for. Because in Ritchie v. People (155 Ill 98 [1895]), the court had held that sex alone was not a valid basis for a legislature to abridge the right of an adult to contract for work and thus struck down a maximum-hours law for women, and because a maximum-hours law for baking employees had been struck down by the U.S. Supreme Court (Lockner), advocates of protective labor legislation believed their task would be difficult. The famous "Brandeis Brief" compiled hundreds of pages on the harmful effects of long hours of work and argued that women needed "especial protection" (see Babcock et al., *Sex Discrimination*).

80. Babcock et al., *Sex Discrimination*, 32.

81. In 1914 the AFL voted to abandon the legislative road to reform (see Hill, "Protective Labor Legislation").

82. Some states excluded women entirely from certain occupations: mining, meter reading, taxicab driving, core making, streetcar conducting, elevator operating, etc. (ibid.).

83. These conclusions are based on Ann C. Hill and are also supported by Baker. At the same time that women were being excluded from certain skilled jobs in the labor force and otherwise protected, the home duties of women were emphasized in popular literature, through the home economics movement, in colleges and high schools, etc. A movement toward the stabilization of the nuclear family with one breadwinner, the male, is discernible (see Hartmann, "Capitalism and Women's Work").

84. Edwards, Reich, and Gordon use "labor-market segmentation" to refer to a process in which the labor market becomes divided into different submarkets, each with its own characteristic behaviors: these segments can be different layers of a hierarchy or different groups within one layer (*Labor Market Segmentation*).

85. Michael Reich, "Racial Discrimination and the White Income Distribution" (Ph.D. diss., Harvard University, 1973), sets forth this divide-and-rule model more thoroughly. In the labor-market segmentation model there is another tendency toward segmentation in addition to the divide-and-rule mechanism. It arises out of

the uneven development of advanced capitalism: i.e., the process of creation of a core and a peripheral economy. In fact, in the Edwards, Reich, and Gordon view, labor-market segmentation comes to the fore only under monopoly capitalism, as large corporations seek to extend control over their labor markets.

86. Thomas Vietorisz, "From Class to Hierarchy: Some Non-Price Aspects on the Transformation Problem" (paper presented at the Conference on Urban Political Economy, New School for Social Research, New York, 15–16 February 1975).

87. The strong divisions of the labor market by sex and race that existed even in the competitive phase of capitalism call into question the dominance of labor homogenization during that phase—as presented by Edwards, Reich, and Gordon, *Labor Market Segmentation*.

88. Capitalists are not always able to use patriarchy to their advantage. Men's ability to retain as much of women's labor in the home as they have done may hamper capitalist development during expansive phases. Men's resistance to female workers whom capitalists want to utilize also undoubtedly slows down capitalist advance.

89. Engels, Marx, and Lenin all recognized the *material* rewards the labor aristocracy reaps. It is important not to reduce these to *subjective* benefits, for then the problems arising out of intraclass divisions will be minimized. Castles and Kosack appear to make this error; see their "Function of Labour Immigration in Western European Capitalism," *New Left Review*, no. 73 (1972): 3–12, where references to Marx et al. can be found.

90. David Gordon suggested to me this "cyclical model" of the relative strengths of employer and workers.

91. Most Marxist-feminist attempts to deal with the problems raised in Marxist analysis by the social position of women seem to ignore the basic conflicts between the sexes, apparently in the interest of stressing the underlying class solidarity that should obtain among women and men workers. Bridges and Hartmann's draft paper (n. 1 above) reviews this literature. When a friend (female) said, "We are much more likely to be able to get Thieu out of Vietnam than we are to get men to do the dishes," she was right.

92. In our society, women's jobs are synonymous with low-status, low-paying jobs: "We may replace the familiar statement that women earn less because they are in low paying occupations with the statement that women earn less because they are in *women's jobs*. . . . As long as the labor market is divided on the basis of sex, it is likely that the tasks allocated to women will be ranked as less prestigious or important, reflecting women's lower social status in the society at large" (Francine Blau [Weisskoff], "Women's Place in the Labor Market," *American Economic Review* 62, no. 4 [1972]: 161).

93. Caplow, *Sociology of Work*, 237ff., discusses several behavioral rules and their impact. Harold Willensky, "Women's Work: Economic Growth, Ideology, Structure," *Industrial Relations* 7, no. 3 (1968): 235–48, also discusses the implication for labor-market phenomena of several behavioral rules.

94. "The use of tabooed words, the fostering of sports and other interests which women do not share, and participation in activities which women are intended to disapprove of—hard drinking, gambling, practical jokes, and sexual essays of various kinds—all suggest that the adult male group is to a large extent engaged in a reaction *against* feminine influence, and therefore cannot tolerate the presence of women without changing its character entirely" (Caplow, *Sociology of Work*, 239). Of course, the lines of division between masculine and feminine are constantly shift-

ing. At various times in the nineteenth century, teaching, selling in retail stores, and office work were each thought to be totally unsuitable for women. This variability of the boundaries between men's jobs and women's jobs is one reason why an effort to locate basic behavioral principles would seem to make sense—though, ultimately, of course, these rules are shaped by the division of labor itself.

95. Caplow based his rules on the Freudian view that men identify freedom from female dominance with maturity: i.e., they seek to escape their mothers.

96. See Rubin, "The Traffic in Women," and Juliet Mitchell, *Feminism and Psychoanalysis* (New York: Pantheon Books, 1974), who seek to re-create Freud from a feminist perspective. So does Shulamith Firestone, *The Dialectic of Sex* (New York: Bantam Books, 1971).

97. E.g., the current domestic division of labor in which women nurture children profoundly affects (differentially) the personality structures of girls and boys. For a non-Freudian interpretation of this phenomenon, see Chodorow, *Reproduction of Mothering*.

Socialist-Feminist Organizations

6   The Social Experience of Bread and Roses
Building a Community and Creating a Culture

Annie Popkin

Boston area women created Bread and Roses, a women's liberation organization, in the summer of 1969. Like other new women's liberation groups forming throughout the United States, Bread and Roses differed from the National Organization for Women (NOW) and other liberal reform women's groups in that its members were for the most part younger, their experiences and consciousness shaped by the social movements of the 1960s, especially the civil rights and new left movements.[1] These women sought to radically transform the class, race, and gender power relationships of American society.

Although Bread and Roses was one of the first and most influential women's liberation groups, its organizational existence was brief; it disbanded in 1971. But during those few years some five hundred women either came to a Bread and Roses meeting or passed through the office. At any one time about 150 women formed the activist core. They were

Source: This article was adapted by the author (1988) from Annie Popkin, "Bread and Roses: An Early Moment in the Development of Socialist Feminism" (Ph.D. diss., Brandeis University, 1978).

mostly white, college-educated women in their mid-twenties, generally from middle-class backgrounds. Some were married, more were single; some were lesbians, more were heterosexual. The basic structure of Bread and Roses, although fluid, consisted of the consciousness-raising group (referred to as a collective), the mass meeting, and the work or project group. Each member was to be a part of at least a collective and the mass meeting. It was in the collectives that Bread and Roses women worked out what the perspective "the personal is political and the political is personal"—a major contribution to subsequent politics—would mean in their daily lives.

What follows is a case study of the culture and community of this one organization. The story of its formation, growth, and demise is told elsewhere.[2]

A major goal of Bread and Roses was to transform social relations not only within the organization but beyond, in the lives of its members. The starting point was an insistence on the political nature and the political significance of personal life. The meaning of the slogan "the personal is political and the political is personal" had strategic implications. First, personal life was seen as a fundamental element of the political reality of society. Personal life did not merely reflect politics; it *was* politics. This idea and its practice in the collectives and everyday life led to many new insights. The most basic was the insight that the oppression of women was rooted in a system of male supremacy; it was not merely the result of wrong attitudes held by some men. A corollary was that even the most seemingly egalitarian relationships between men and women were mediated by sexual politics —the fact that men as a group had more power than women. Another important insight was that psychological oppression was as important to understand and to change as was material oppression.

Personal life was seen, then, as a critical arena for social change; individual change prefigured social change. In Bread and Roses this idea meant two things. One was the emphasis on the role of individual and small-group consciousness raising in bringing about social change. The second was the belief, to be carried out in practice, that the forms of the present-day social struggle contained in embryo the forms of the future revolutionary society.

Drawing on the excitement and energy they had experienced in caucusing as women in various mixed left organizations, founding members of Bread and Roses came to stress the importance of consciousness raising as a new strategy for change. Their assumption was that women (and other people) would have to understand their own oppression first as part of the larger strategy for change. They thought that by looking at, sharing, and analyzing their experiences together, they would be able to generalize to the condition of all women. Later feminists would see, in the context of challenges from the women of doubly and triply oppressed groups, that a more diverse membership would be necessary before valid speculations about "all women" could be made. In fact, such generalizations have given way to very specific descriptions and analyses of and by such groups as working-class women, women of color, lesbians, physically challenged women, and others.[3] At the time, however, Bread and Roses women thought that the nature of the process of consciousness raising—the actual emotional and intellectual sharing and growth—would heighten the commitment of the women to the group, to other women, and to the fight against oppression.

The collective was the basic organizational manifestation of these ideas in Bread and Roses. Groups of women met together to examine the concrete ways in which they were oppressed and to develop their thinking; they reinterpreted their past in the light of their new feminist perspective. Two of the most common feelings shared initially were anger at men and excitement at finding other women with whom they had unknowingly shared so much. This was the period of building trust and forging solidarity. In many collectives women supplemented meeting time with other group activities, both social (dinners, retreats, dances, trips, parties) and more organizationally political: staging small "zap actions,"[4] learning self-defense together, attending demonstrations as a group.

Bread and Roses represented both a continuation of the new left and an ideological break with it.[5] At first, many members tried to understand what the fact that they were socialist women—they called themselves women revolutionaries—meant in terms of political strategy and daily life. By the end, many were attempting to weave socialism and feminism together. The recognition of the identity of the personal and political was the starting point of this new synthesis. Bread and Roses embodied the idea organizationally yet harbored tensions that led to the building of a community rather than a lasting organization. Although many members made serious attempts at innovations in the structure and process of creating an organization and a movement, the particular ways in which these women worked out the personal-is-political theme evolved on the one hand into the politicization of private life and on the other hand into an emphasis on culture and community—at the unintended cost of diminished political and organizational activism.

Women's Community

As Bread and Roses women made changes in their lives, one traditional form of support, the heterosexual couple, proved less and less adequate to meet their new needs. Women had to form new networks. They sought, with various levels of self-consciousness, to build a community and a culture.[6] The community they created outlasted the formal organization. It is paradoxical that while being in Bread and Roses gave women the support they needed in order to change, these personal changes fed back into Bread and Roses, creating tensions that ultimately, within the larger sociopolitical context, contributed to the decline of the organization. In addition, women's sense of community was powerful at the time, perhaps bringing about the unintentional loss of an inclusiveness that could have helped diversify the group.

From the perspective that the personal is political, almost everything in women's lives was a potential target of struggle. Women were changing in many contexts: in friendships, in self-image, in sexual relations and the experience of sexuality, in work and new forms of competence, in the imagining and creating of new alternatives.

The time was an exciting one. One woman remembers experiencing "euphoria, discovery, and growth at the same time as conflict, struggle, and pain." For many women there was great personal upheaval and turmoil; for others the experience was a source of equilibrium and evolution. Looking back, many women saw their new relationships with and appreciation of other women as the most important and lasting change that Bread and Roses and the women's movement brought them.

For many, friendships with other women had always been important, and Bread and Roses legitimated this importance. One woman wrote about her experience: "I always took my female friendships seriously, but used to regard it as regressive on my part. Now I value the importance and intensity of my friendships with women." Another said: "I had always had close women friends, but during Bread and Roses the bonds were more intense and affirmed; women became—and remain—a cherished resource."

For other women, fewer in number, the new friendships and interest in women were radical departures from their past. "I don't feel contemptuous of other women, as I often did before," said one, and another wrote that "during Bread and Roses . . . my intense hostility toward other women disappeared." Some may have wanted closer relationships with other women before Bread and Roses but had not known how to make them happen. This socialized isolation and competition between women would be named and analyzed by later feminists as internalized oppression or, more specifically, internalized sexism.

Almost all the women reported a deepening of feelings of trust, respect, and warmth for other women. The experience of struggle together in the collectives brought the exciting sense of finally being taken seriously, being held in high regard, and being put first by other women. Many women found their primary emotional relationships at the time with other women. Even those in heterosexual couples directed most of their energies, emotions, work, and politics into building a women's movement, organization, and community.

For many women, as their feelings for one another intensified and expanded, the relative importance of men diminished. Women began to look to other women for the kinds of support and emotional sustenance they had theretofore sought in men. They began creating networks of support to help lessen traditional dependence on men and on the couple relationship. In addition, as women turned to other women for the affection they had previously sought from men, some discovered that many sensual feelings were liberated. Many felt freer to be expressive and affectionate; even in such public settings as mass meetings, women held each other, caressed each other, gave each other back rubs and hugs. These physical expressions of affection were shared by both lesbians and heterosexual women, though each group experienced the changes differently.

Of course, not everyone shared the euphoria of the women's community. Some women wanted to be with men and found the social pressure not to be with men burdensome. One woman, in talking about the effects of Bread and Roses on her expectations of couples, wrote: "It had a lot to do with the breakup of my marriage because it encouraged me to treat my husband as MAN (read—horror) instead of a person; i.e., [it] encouraged perpetuation of stereotypes about sex differences and encouraged seeing him as very powerful and as defining my life." Her experience resonated with that of others (women at the time had not yet developed an analysis that men were not "the enemy").

Sisterhood

Underlying the efforts at building a new community and new relationships with other women were explicit ideological formulations. Women talked of coming together as "sisters," or in "sisterhood." Thinking of other women as sisters in the family sense carried with it the desire for an unbreakable bond. Women wanted the intensity, the closeness, the permanence and reliability of a "family" in its ideal form. The family metaphor was borrowed from the language of the black movement, in which people called each other "sister" and "brother" to indicate solidarity and the fact that they wanted to create a separate community, distinct from "the Man."

There were two discernible stages in the development of the concepts of sisterhood and solidarity among women. At first, Bread and Roses women saw themselves bound together by virtue of their common oppression in sexist society. In the collectives, women explored painful experiences more deeply and with support for each other arising from mutual understanding. This was a stage of self-knowledge and comaraderie based on shared suffering—"victims' commiserating." It was not necessarily expressed in action. However, many women did engage in a form of "public testimony" at mass meetings, speaking out about their anger, their hurt, their mistreatment by men and by the institutions of America; and this public testimony was often acrimonious, mutually reinforcing, and energizing. Fiery speeches about the personal experience of sexism led women not only to feel bonds with one another but also to take action against institutions perceived as oppressive: hence the spray-painting of the Playboy Club in Boston and the "zap action" at local counterculture radio station WBCN, which commonly used demeaning language about women.

In this period, differences were minimized in the interest of building a cohesive group. One Bread and Roses member wrote about this stage in her collective: "A lot of what we had considered our individuality now appeared to be nothing but various styles of defense; burdensome, inflexible, and no longer necessary within the context of the group. We abandoned these defenses happily in exchange for a sense of interchangeability and group identity."[7] The sense of solidarity was an important stage of sisterhood in which women could come to feel closer, to trust and identify with one another.

This approach to sisterhood, however, did generate certain tensions. Some women felt excluded because their past experiences or present lifestyle veered from the norm. Some experienced other women's euphoric sisterhood as a form of judgment or cliquishness. These women bucked against the constraints they felt in the "we're all the same" ideology, but the organization as a whole was not yet able to recognize and appreciate different qualities and skills. One example was the debate over whether the articles that women wrote and circulated were to be signed or to remain anonymous. Those who preferred anonymity felt that name signing would lead to inequalities. A later author, reviewing this stage of sisterhood in the larger women's liberation movement, stated: "Sisterhood was a mobilizing idea and there was power in great numbers of women bonding together. But also it was used sometimes as a method of control: to challenge another woman's ideas was labelled 'unsisterly.'"[8]

The second stage began after the initial exploration of the past was over and the continuing examination of present oppression well underway. At this point many women wanted to move beyond experiencing themselves primarily as victims; they wanted to take positive action to make themselves strong, competent agents in control of their lives. The ways in which they set about accomplishing the task included emulating strong women by taking risks and learning skills. In the context of the late 1960s, many looked to Vietnamese and Black Panther women as concrete symbols of strength and resistance amid the most oppressive of conditions. The posters that embellished the walls of women's houses and were carried as placards in demonstrations showed Vietnamese women, arms rippling with muscles, working the crops or standing alone with a child in one arm and a rifle in the other; Angela Davis with clenched fist and expansive Afro; pregnant Panther women in jail. In recognition of a Black Panther activist jailed at the time, women chanted in International Women's Day marches and other demonstrations: "Erica Huggins, Live Like Her!" Bread and Roses women wanted to be as strong as their Third World sisters and sisters of color in the United States; hence, the concept of sisterhood was expanded to include group power.[9] The progression from sisterhood as shared suffering to sisterhood as shared strength was necessary to make Bread and Roses and the women's liberation movement instruments of change rather than of support for existing conditions.

Concepts of Activism: Living Up to the Group and Risk-Taking

Most women reported experiencing a life-giving energy from the kinds of talks they were having in their collectives, among friends, in twos and threes, in work projects. The vision that women painted of how relationships could be, how work could be, how society could be was a grand one, and people wanted to move toward it. The mutual support within small groups was often strong enough to carry over into the outside world. A woman in a "second generation" consciousness-raising group started by a Bread and Roses member[10] wrote about this kind of energy and support:

> Even outside the group meetings I think all of us found ourselves acting in a way we called "living up to the group," but which often did not arise out of any group discussion. The simple presence of the group in one's imagination, and the public commitment to our sex which joining the group implied, were incentive enough.[11]

"Living up to the group," whether to the collective or to the larger organization and its stated ideals, was a widespread phenomenon. The internalization of the strength and support of the group, combined with the continuity that weekly meetings and a visible organization provided, made possible many of the changes that women were making in "real life."

The concept and practice of "risk-taking" were also very important during the time of Bread and Roses. The concept had historical origins in the civil rights movement: for example, in the exhortation to "put one's life on the line." The use of the concept by Bread and Roses women was both an incorporation of the civil rights movement's idea and a response to the contemporary challenges contained in the increasingly militant rhetoric and tactics of Weatherman [12] (in turn, a response to the *fact* of risks taken by Black Panthers and the Vietnamese).

Risk traditionally implied physical or economic loss or injury. Bread and Roses women expanded this concept, as with so many other concepts in their analysis, to include the psychological and the emotional. Danger in these arenas was seen to be as real as, although different from, physical danger,[13] and it became the focus of risk-taking in Bread and Roses.

The risks that members recounted most often were those they took *within* the organization, especially in the collectives. They talked about "self-exposure in the group" and "opening up in the collective as I hadn't in any previous context." Many women felt exposed and scared. One was "scared to speak my feelings in a group, scared I'd come out ugly, empty (still fear the ugly, true, hollow, miserable, inherited-from-my-mother core of me)."[14] Another woman wrote that she was "talking with others about parts of myself I had previously been ashamed of."

For some women, merely "speaking up in groups" was new and frightening. Others spoke of taking leadership roles as risky, not only because of the possibility that any group of leaders might become objects of public scrutiny and censure but because, in the context of the Bread and Roses antileadership ideology, anyone who assumed such a role seemed doomed to criticism from the start. Still other women found it difficult to take a political position at all. One talked of the risks of "taking political stands and developing political convictions" and another of "speaking out in groups and learning political analysis." Some risked taking unpopular positions within the organization itself. Women were struggling to take their ideas seriously.

Some women perceived risks in their relations with other women in the movement. Often that meant asking for a kind of love, support, and openness that had traditionally been reserved for the heterosexual couple. For some it meant "having sexual relationships with women" or "coming out" as lesbians—very risky in the contemporary context of homophobia both in the larger society and in the women's movement.

Others felt that past relationships—with women *and* men—had been threatened. "When I first went into the women's movement," wrote one, "I basically lost practically every friend that I had at that time. It was quite horrible." And another suffered "ridicule from 'non-converted' friends— the males I expected it (and got it) from, but the women I knew often were *very* defensive and critical—'I' don't need the movement." To lose women friends for something that seemed so obviously to benefit all women was an especially painful blow. Yet when the costs of one's actions were so high, expectations became equally high; these were conditions in which great change was both possible and necessary.

Some women saw their risks as internal ones: changing self-definitions, or insecurities about the new and as yet undefined shape of their future lives. They were calling into question basic givens and values, basic ways of experiencing the world, leaving themselves with little certainty and much confusion and fear. One woman told how she thought that merely belonging to Bread and Roses would be a risk:

> I remember being afraid of Bread and Roses at first—fear that I would lose my femininity, hate men (which I did for a while), be tossed into a role-less life with no new "me" to fill it. So, for me, it all felt like a risk. Also, I had a fear of women, especially groups of women—so this too was real learning.

Many choices about risk-taking were carried out individually but with the knowledge that other Bread and Roses women (and, in fact, women throughout the country) were taking the same kinds of risks. Using the concept of risk-taking implied kinship with other radical groups and their activities, such as the larger left movement and the struggles of people of color in this country and the Third World.

Relationships with Women: Sensuality and Sexuality

There may be no clear line separating women's love for friends and women's love for lovers. Affection, sensuality, and sexuality are feelings that frequently merge in women's experience. Conscious of this fusion, I would nevertheless distinguish two elements: the liberation of sensuality and expression of affection for women, and the emergence of a lesbian women's movement culture that made making love with women an "accepted" social possibility for more women.[15]

Feeling freer and more comfortable about sexuality was an important bond among many Bread and Roses women. Many discussions started with women's recognition of their own estrangement from their bodies and their sexuality. Women had been brought up to accept sexuality as defined by men—to worry, for instance, about their shapes or their attractiveness. Basic to the emerging analysis of sexuality was an examination of the power relations implicit in heterosexual couples in a sexist society. "When women feel powerless and inferior in a relationship, it is not surprising to feel humiliated and unsatisfied in bed. Similarly, a man must feel some contempt for a woman he believes to be not his equal."[16] Women launched an attack on three fronts—to change the power relations in their personal lives *and* in society, and at the same time to create a supportive atmosphere in which to explore their own sexual feelings.

Learning about sexuality meant unlearning many traditional attitudes, such as the notion of value in being passive, ignorant, or uninitiated. The depth of the internalization of many stereotypes made dismantling them painful, exciting, and energizing. An important aspect of the learning process was perceived to be "understanding orgasm"[17] and learning how to masturbate. Women saw a reflection of their sexual oppression in the fact that so many did not know how to masturbate or, if they did, had such deep-seated inhibitions and prohibitions against it that they felt guilty. Therefore, some women began to write articles and give talks encouraging other women to try to masturbate, to have sexual fantasies, to learn what made their bodies feel good. In Saturday morning sessions on sexuality at the Bread and Roses office, women shared their experiences and feelings. Classes were set up on "Women and Their Bodies."[18]

The orgasm orientation helped many women who had been considered or considered themselves "frigid." Many reported that Anne Koedt's "Myth of the Vaginal Orgasm," had more influence on their lives than any other single article.[19] One such woman (a member of the Health Book Collective), in an open letter to her "dear sisters," recalled her reaction in 1969:

> One night I came home late from work and found my husband asleep; I had lots on my mind, couldn't get to sleep and picked up one of the many articles that always sit on my dresser waiting to be read. Only this time it happened to be "The Myth of the Vaginal Orgasm." I was stunned; I really couldn't believe what I was reading. If what Anne Koedt was saying was really true . . . could it really be so . . . after all those years of just thinking that it was *my* problem that I didn't like sex as much as he did . . . all the pretending and putting myself down. I shook him awake, made him sit up while I read him the whole bloody paper. He knew about my clitoris and had tried to stimulate it, but I had stopped him! If he knew about my clitoris,

why hadn't he told me about it when it was clear that I didn't know?
Well, he thought I didn't like it. I went to sleep in turmoil, but the
next morning I put my newfound information somewhere in the
back of my brain. I was not ready to face the implications. . . . It
took time before I could admit even to my closest women friends
that maybe I never had an orgasm, that maybe my marriage was not
a model one, that maybe *my* husband oppressed me. (Shortly after
I read the myth paper I was driving several friends home from a
meeting. One friend in the back seat started talking about Anne
Koedt's paper and admitted that she had never had an orgasm and
felt very angry and deprived. My experience was the same, but I
couldn't admit it yet.)[20]

Her response was an example of a common process: the experience of a
sudden insight, followed by the hard work necessary to integrate it into
one's self-understanding. The alternation of new insight and the struggle
needed for real change was a process shared by many women at this time.

There were some differences of opinion as to whether orgasms, masturbation, and sexual relationships should be matters of central concern.
Some women criticized the emphasis, maintaining that to make orgasms a
separate focus followed the lead of American society, which, by separating
sex from other kinds of physical sensations and social relationships, mystified sexuality and alienated people from it. Some women criticized the
actual concept of sexual liberation. An extreme version of this critique was
published by Female Liberation, a Boston radical-feminist organization. In
No More Fun and Games, Roxanne Dunbar wrote:

"Sexual liberation" for women is about as liberating as the free
drug use demanded by white radicals would be to urban ghetto
blacks, who are oppressed and, in fact, destroyed by the "freedom"
to take drugs. Those demanding the freedoms of sex and drugs
are mostly young, white men and in this they are supported by the
system. . . . For most women, right now, sex means brutalization,
rape, submission, someone having power over them, another baby
to care for and support. . . . Sex still means power. Women find this
hard to believe, because to women it means oppression and at best,
maintenance (being kept) and a little affection. But because the new
myth of sexual liberation is so prevailing, sex itself has become a
defense for many young women.[21]

One logical extension of this analysis was celibacy, which was in fact coun-
seled by members of Female Liberation. Many women in Bread and Roses

found Female Liberation's positions threatening and often discounted them by calling its members "crazies." Others found the articles provocative, often crystallizing nascent feelings they themselves had had but could not articulate.

Talking about sex, defusing romantic ideas about men, and loving women created a sexually charged atmosphere. This sexual energy accounted for much of the excitement that women felt with each other and about Bread and Roses. As one woman said, the exploration of sexuality "affected me individually, in my relationship with my husband. But more important, feeling better about my own body freed me and other people to explore relationships with women."

Although the energy did not always manifest itself in overt sexuality, it did in part lead to the cessation of relations with men for many women. One lesbian who "came out" during the Bread and Roses period asserted:

> I think that a lot of women in Bread and Roses had sort of stopped
> relating to men, had become celibate, and I think that the "smash
> monogamy" thing was an important thing in keeping that together.
> It was like, you know, all for one and one for all. You'd give up your
> relationship with boys because you were having this wonderful thing
> with lots of women. In lots of ways, the gay thing was what brought
> sensuality back into the women's movement. And it was important
> because you can't live all your life in this, you know, platonic level.

Much of the energy that had previously gone into sexual, and especially couple relationships, was now being directed toward women friends and the women's community in general. This accounted for much of the strength and intensity of these new ties. Even women who remained in traditional heterosexual couples reported "getting high" from the energy level among women.

Lesbianism

This generalized sexual energy also found expression in making love with women. The excitement of the possibility touched most women, even those who felt threatened by it. Several processes were going on simultaneously. Women were "coming out"—both those who had had inklings of their lesbianism but no channel for expressing these feelings and women who had never before had such feelings. At the same time some primarily heterosexual women were experimenting with their sexual feelings for women—which created confusion and ultimately hostility.

The confused feelings about lesbianism were highlighted by a woman who had sexual relationships with other women during Bread and Roses but did not consider herself gay. She describes the climate for lesbians as "volatile, hostile, difficult. We all supported lesbianism, but within the organization, lesbians had difficulties."

"We all supported lesbians" was shorthand for a kind of liberalism that covered up many underlying tensions and fears. The right of women to love women seemed to be at the heart of feminism. Yet women had grown up in a society that devalued homosexuality. No politically correct feminist could be "against lesbianism," yet the very moralism of that imperative support, in the context of everyone's socialized homophobia, led to confused thinking. Some lesbians claimed the right to leadership and moral authority: hence the widely quoted slogan "Feminism is the theory; lesbianism is the practice." But it was difficult for lesbians to feel safe and for straight women to examine their own feelings, much less to formulate a well-though-out "position."

Soon after the formation of Bread and Roses, women within the group went together to gay bars, to meetings of Daughters of Bilitis and Gay Liberation. The first organization-wide public confrontation happened at a Bread and Roses retreat in the spring of 1970. In an "Open Letter to My Sisters," one woman chronicled how she had been driven away from men and had been led to loving women through her experiences in the women's movement. She saw loving women as a route toward loving herself better. Working so closely with women had made all this possible; nevertheless, despite whisperings of "loving women" in the air, the subject was still taboo. The "Open Letter" took a hard line on this taboo:

> You may "love" your sister—you may not make love with her. If it really can't be helped we won't totally shut you out, but of course you understand we can't have you speaking for women's liberation any more. . . . In short, you are the second-class citizens we need to keep us from hitting bottom, to keep us from completely losing men's approval—you are our women, every movement needs some so that it can be political. . . . The irony of it all is that I probably never would have discovered my homosexuality without women's liberation. You have helped to create what you now despise and fear.[22]

The bitterness she felt at the time was to become more generalized among lesbians in Bread and Roses. However, their relief once the issue surfaced openly was immense.

That was the beginning of women's "coming out in waves," in the words of one Bread and Roses member who numbered herself among them. In reality, the proportion that actually "came out" was small. Although almost one-fourth of the women I questioned reported having had sexual relationships with women during Bread and Roses, only 6 percent felt that they "came out" at the time.[23] However, the possibility affected nearly everyone; it arose within and helped create a climate in which women were getting stronger and taking care of each other.

The mixed immediate emotional effects in the women's community were exhilaration, excitement, and fear. Some women felt that their sexuality and lifestyle were being challenged. For a while, as one lesbian noted: "It was a *weird* scene; for a long time you were out of it if you weren't with a man, then all of a sudden you were *in* this weird way—you were 'cool.' [I] didn't trust a lot of women who came out then." Difficulties also arose as women came to have different expectations of each other, some wanting experimentation—to "try things out"; others wanting commitment. When some women formed couples, others began to feel excluded. And as lesbian couples fell apart or as lesbians had short, sometimes unhappy affairs, tensions and pain grew.

Yet however much pain was caused, important new options were opening for women. The possibility of being in an equal, respectful relationship was enhanced, since it was not quite as easy to fall into socially prescribed sex roles in a same-sex couple. Some women felt that they were able to experience a level of intimacy and trust that they had never known before, with either men or women. They were also able to experience a new form of solidarity, which came from getting all their needs met from one source; the gay liberation movement made popular the slogan "An army of lovers cannot fail." There were also costs and dangers—an army of ex-lovers might not be so strong! The sexual tension between women that was at one level creative and exciting could in another instance become inhibiting or obsessive.

Relations with Men and Seeking Alternatives

Many Bread and Roses women recalled the decreased importance of men in their day-to-day lives, especially during the first year of the organization. Doing things with other women—politically and socially—simply became the priority; the heterosexual couple relationship receded for many into the emotional background. This was particularly true for women who had been married or coupled for some time prior to the formation of the organization. One woman was representative of this group: "I had the typical married woman's setup—with a husband in the background, a generalized hatred for men, a few other husbands in a limited dose, and very little contact with men during Bread and Roses." In effect, many mates were "holding the fort and keeping the home fires burning" while very active women were going to meetings, study groups, demonstrations and women's celebrations. Unmarried women report "feeling cut off from men," "seeing less of men than ever," and "withdrawing from intense relationships with men at the time."

An important backdrop for the decreased presence of men in the lives of Bread and Roses women was the deterioration and factionalization of the mixed left movement. Activities connected with Students for a Democratic Society (SDS), the antiwar movement, and mixed left underground journals were dying out at this time; the political and social context in which women could relate to men was considerably diminished. And as the mixed movement was getting weaker, the women's movement was growing, getting stronger and making more emotional and time demands on women.

Some women were not part of any mixed-sex social network. Their political choices meant that men were not in their social lives in any way for most of the time that they were active in Bread and Roses. For some women this was a relief:

> The whole period I was in the women's movement, I mean from the moment I got into the women's movement, I stopped thinking about guys. . . . I mostly went out with them before that because I had to, and as soon as it stopped being a status thing, that you had to go out with a guy, I stopped going out with them.

Other women wanted to go out with men but did not know how to meet them; one previous avenue of social interaction—politics—was now sex segregated.

In order to think and act differently with regard to women's traditional sexual roles in couples and families, there had to be real alternatives. Those informally sanctioned by Bread and Roses members were celibacy, the single life, women's households, and lesbian relationships. Although these options had existed in various forms before, women's evaluation of them changed during this time.

Celibacy could be viewed in several ways. At a practical level, celibacy was a response to the separation of women's social and political life from men's. One woman who was celibate for much of the time that she was in Bread and Roses commented: "A lot of things came together for me personally at that time that made me withdraw from sexual relationships and also . . . it wasn't so much sex, it was that I really just wasn't relating to men." Many women saw celibacy not as an end but as a moratorium in which to think about whether or not to have a sexual relationship.

At an ideological level, celibacy was not only a reaction against having to define oneself as part of a couple but also against having to define oneself sexually to the world at large. Celibacy was part of an analysis made popular by Dana Densmore in her article "On Celibacy," in *No More Fun and Games*:

> Sex is not essential to life, as eating is. . . . The guerillas don't screw.
> . . . They have important things to do, things that require all their
> energy. . . . We must come to realize that we don't need sex, that
> celibacy is not a dragon but even a state that could be desirable, in
> many cases preferable to sex. How repugnant it really is, after all, to
> make love to a man who despises you, who fears you and wants to
> hold you down.[24]

Her arguments were most appealing to those women who were angriest at men and most threatening to those who felt that their identity and security were bound up in their heterosexual relationships.

The social acceptance of celibacy was important to single women in Bread and Roses. One woman wrote that it gave her "the support to not get in a couple for a long time—whatever time I needed till I felt ready to be in one." Many single women had made a conscious and deliberate choice not to be defined as some male's girlfriend or wife. They felt that an important part of their identity was vested in their self-definition as single women— in a growing, supportive subcommunity of single women.[25]

Some single women were quite adamant that their status was a statement about women in society. Such militance often masked more ambiguous feelings, as illustrated by one women's reminiscence:

> I think I was very self-righteous about being single and being totally
> true and uncompromising about my feelings about men. But now
> that seems to me like it was pretty much a defensive stance, that was
> pretty destructive and unsympathetic toward other people. And
> destructive toward myself in a lot of ways. But really didn't have that
> much to do with sex, as sex. It was more about relationships, and
> *where your commitments were*. [Emphasis added]

The ties between single women were very strong. Many felt that they were giving their whole life to Bread and Roses and were afraid that women who went home to men at night were not. Those single women who wanted to relate to men personally sometimes had difficulty balancing lovers and the community. Some felt that each new male lover called into question their commitment to women and was too reminiscent of the history of women's friendships being broken up or interrupted by new boyfriends.

Were men the enemy? Many women were unclear. They knew sexism was a system of oppression. But how responsible were individual men for their power and for imposing the system on women? Anger fed separatist feelings. Women didn't yet know how to live with men or work politically with men and still be primarily committed to women and women's liberation.[26]

For women who remained in heterosexual couples, the move toward political autonomy was paralleled by one toward emotional autonomy; they struggled for independence and self-respect while maintaining their ties with men. Some were fighting against the "man in their head" as well as the Man, and sometimes had to start with the "man in their bed."[27] The difficult problems of how to survive in a couple *or* as a single woman were no longer to be discussed only between best friends or in therapy; they became the open province of the collective, the mass meeting, or the women who just happened to be in the same place at the same time. No social encounter, social relationship, or mode of personal interaction was too insignificant or too personal for scrutiny.

Women's Culture

The self-conscious explorations into changing relationships among women laid the basis for a new community and represented the beginnings of a new type of women's culture. Bread and Roses women were actively confronting dominant culture—which they labeled white, male, and middle class—on many levels. Individually and collectively, they rejected old values and expressed new values imaginatively.[28]

Direct Action: Challenging Cultural Hegemony

Bread and Roses women challenged the norms of the dominant culture in innovative ways, including dressing up in meetings, guerrilla theater, "zap actions," and other forms of celebration. Zap actions were usually events that had some theatrical quality about them (a quality reminiscent of the Yippies, and perhaps the form was borrowed from them). A Redstockings[29] woman contrasted zap actions with one-on-one confrontations:

the former, she said, use "our presence as a group and/or the media to make women's oppression into social issues."[30] The point of zap actions was not to organize women into the movement but rather to set ideas in their minds, ideas for later rumination. Different "targets" were chosen for various reasons by different groups within Bread and Roses. Most often the decisions about zaps and their execution were decentralized, carried out on the collective or informal friendship group level. Targets for large actions included the Playboy Club, the *Boston Globe*, and the Massachusetts legislature's abortion hearings.

The zap action staged by a large group of women (cross-cutting the collectives) at WBCN, a Boston countercultural radio station, in response to an advertisement which proclaimed "if you're a chick, they need typists." Thirty angry Bread and Roses women stormed the station to protest its "male chauvinism." The statement they presented explained:

> The male supremist [*sic*] assumption was that "chicks" by their very nature type; we do fifteen words a minute at birth and work our way up. Many phone calls later, they modified it to, "If you're a chick and can type, they need typists." No men need apply. It's beneath male dignity. . . . Could a radio station get away with an ad that ran, "And if you're black, we need janitors"?

The women were especially insulted that such an advertisement had been written by WBCN staff, because they had hoped for more from the alternative media than from the establishment stations. They were continually disappointed. The statement continued:

> And it's not just that ad, which only represents one of the many oppressive stereotypes and assumptions that comprise the currency of rock culture—the so-called "cultural revolution" we hear so much about on WBCN. Hip culture and values are supposed to be more real and honest than centerfolds or Doris Day, but it's not so. The old dream images dressed up slicker or funkier are no more liberating than their American midcult originals.

The written protest was accompanied by eight baby chicks, to point out that "*women* are *not* chicks," and demanded "in partial reparation" an hour of prime evening time on International Women's Day for a women's liberation program:

> This will require use of recording facilities adequate to our needs and free advertising the week preceding, with publicity spots writ-

ten and recorded by us. No station can claim to be a "community
station" when, for one thing, it puts down or ignores 51% of the
people.[31]

The station manager agreed to their demands. The action was also covered
the next day by the *Boston Globe*, bringing the issue to the attention of an
even wider audience.[32]

Any demonstration, gathering, or casual stroll in the city could take on
the dimensions of a small zap action, as many women carried with them
stickers made up by the New England Free Press (the labor was donated:
some of the printers were Bread and Roses members). Posted in locations ranging from neutral (a utility pole) to offensive targets (the Playboy
Club), the stickers carried such messages as "This Woman Is Not for Sale,"
"Women are not cars; Women are not cigarettes; Women are not servants,"
"It's not your *Heart* he's after" (for use on Valentine's Day), and "Not with
My Body You Don't!"

Zap actions were important for both the organization and the individual
members of Bread and Roses. Each action reinfused the participants and
the group as a whole with energy and spirit, heightening the sense of creative activism as well as identification with the organization. The actions
helped to focus public attention on women's issues, making Bread and
Roses more visible as a women's liberation organization. The leaflets that
were usually distributed to accompany the actions gave other women the
chance to think further. Zaps encouraged creativity and spontaneity, qualities often structured out of other political organizations. They democratized the organization in that any group of individuals could plan and carry
out an action of their own creation. They also had the advantage of being
activities in the "outside" world that provided on-the-spot feedback. Participants could assess the results of a zap, learn immediately what "worked"
and what didn't, and soon thereafter apply their learning to a new situation
—the next action.[33]

Other forms of direct action included doing "guerrilla theater" skits (in
a Harvard Square boutique, for example), dressing up in bright colors (and
sometime strange outfits that were purposely not stylish), and bringing a
generally festive spirit to activities. One occasion that became a tradition
was the celebration of International Women's Day. The day was first observed in 1908 but had been lost in the intervening years; Bread and Roses
(and other women's liberation groups) reclaimed it. In 1970, the first time
that Bread and Roses commemorated the day as a group, many plans were
made for a procession that would pass by the Charles Street Jail (to greet
the women prisoners), among other stops. A subgroup of women sewed

banners and flags made in the configuration of the Vietnamese NFL flag but with the colors changed: a black band for anarchism, a red band for Communism, and the star in the middle made of any one of a variety of brightly colored flowered materials to symbolize joyfulness and creativity of women. Another group crocheted hats; still others set women's liberation lyrics to old melodies and passed out song sheets to the marchers. Women marched with arms around each other or holding hands or singly, enjoying one another's company and the visible presence of Bread and Roses in Boston city streets. Clenched fists were raised to women working in buildings along the route of the march; a return salute was cheered. Many participants remembered such demonstrations as highlights of the expression of the spirit of the organization, the movement, and the time.

Artistic and Creative Manifestations

The creative process allowed people to express and share with others their feelings and ways of seeing. At their best, cultural products presented a vision of how society could be. There were many dimensions to this process. On one level women were reclaiming a history that had been kept from them. On another level participants were finding their own means of artistic creation. On a third level they were creating culture in a self-conscious way to cement relations among women, and to draw them into a collectivity in opposition to the prevailing culture.[34]

Words and ideas in the form of poems, manifestos, open letters, leaflets, essays, chants, and spray-painting poured out. A one-liner in a Bread and Roses newsletter suggested "Re media: sayitwriteitsingitplayitliveit."[35] Women showed their writing to friends and published it in journals, newsletters, and the underground press; they gave and attended poetry readings. Women wrote about the condition of their lives, about false consciousness, and about their dreams.

Many Bread and Roses women were part of a vast network of women around the country who were writing for themselves and others, publishing such journals as *Off Our Backs* and *Women: A Journal of Liberation*. Locally, an underground newspaper called *The Old Mole* became increasingly feminist as more Bread and Roses women joined the staff (or women on the staff joined Bread and Roses) and wrote articles on the situation of women. Some Bread and Roses members and other feminists started the women's journal *Hysteria*. These two publications, plus the *Second Wave*, created a developing feminist view of the phenomenology of women's everyday life.

Music was integral to the new culture. Some women wrote songs, some wrote new lyrics to old songs. Songs used over the years include "The Battle Hymn of Women," "Bella Ciao" (from the Italian Communist song of the same name), "When the Women Come Marching In," "Bread and Roses," and the chant "Power: Power to Our Sisters."[36] The choruses and chants especially were rendered with great enthusiasm at demonstrations, rallies, and sometimes meetings. Often, writing new lyrics was a collaborative process: a collective or a work group or several friends would produce the song together. In addition, Bread and Roses women began to have all-women parties and dances, with some of the music provided by newly formed women's bands and female vocalists.

Learning Skills

In building a women's culture, many Bread and Roses women revived reclaimed traditionally "feminine" crafts—expressions of creativity that had been the province of women historically but now flourished in new ways in the supportive atmosphere of the new community. Women knitted, crocheted, beaded, and embroidered everywhere—in meetings, while visiting, on subways, watching television—in bright colors celebrating womanhood and community. Other artforms that became important to smaller groups of women were batik, postermaking, weaving, and photography. Women were reclaiming a history they had not known. Many were learning new skills. The environment that Bread and Roses women were creating with one another made many women feel safe and supported, freer to experiment with their creativity and bring to fruition ideas that they had previously kept in the realm of fantasy.

Some women focused on skills that had been traditionally masculine, sometimes calling them survival skills: self-defense, auto mechanics, carpentry, electrical wiring, plumbing, "fixing things, bikes, cars, everything." Women questioned ceding those skills to men. Moving toward greater self-reliance, they wanted to become "handy" around the house, to learn to do "manual things, to learn about how machines work and how to work them." Some women pursued these skills to the extent of becoming full-time carpenters, machinists, and printers. Others basically wanted to feel competent by being able to fix things, to demystify the processes. Still others felt that the effort, and the *idea* that such work was within their grasp, was more important than the actual learning of a particular new skill. One such woman noted that in her "few efforts at mechanical self-help (e.g., fixing stereo wires)", what was most important was "a less helpless *attitude* about such things."

A basic and emotionally loaded skill that many women learned was the art of self-defense. For some women this came out of an analysis that stated, in short, that sexism would be perpetuated as long as women remained victims of men's physical violence on the street and in the home. These women thought the only way to stop rape and male violence was to fight power with power. Various forms of martial arts were introduced, the most popular of which, in Bread and Roses, was tae kwon do, a form of Korean karate. Some women who signed up for trial-period classes could not make it through the rigorous training for physical or psychological reasons. Others became quite strong and confident, if not competent. A few went on to get black belts and become karate teachers for women. One group of women formed the "Stick-it-in-the-Wall, Mother-fucker" collective and went to the various women's karate classes teaching women how to run together in groups, how to stay close, how to follow an appointed, experienced leader. Although most Bread and Roses women did not gain a new "skill" as karate experts, most who went to even a few classes found this minimal exposure enough to change their self-concept and boost their morale.

The variety of new skills was an expression of imagination taking hold in politics, of women trying things that they had never done before, both to reach new people in new ways and to express parts of themselves that they had never before given free rein to or thought appropriate to political activity. These kinds of activities strengthened the solidarity among Bread and Roses women as well as widening the constituency to women who had not been "political" before.

A Way of Life and a Moral Context

The efforts by Bread and Roses women to create a community and a culture had models in earlier movements, notably the new left and black civil rights. In all three cases the movement became moral and social context within which people could make important decisions about their lives—what to do in the future; how to evaluate actions, work relationships. The movement was also a source of friends. One woman who had come from the new left said:

My whole lifestyle was completely determined by the movement. And so then Bread and Roses (or the women's movement) became the newer form and it was a better form for me. . . . All my emotional needs were tied in with politics, because it was how I was living. . . .

It certainly gave me a sense of security and importance about what
I was doing and being part of something that seemed important
to me.

Especially with the disintegration of the left into various sects and factions,
many "movement" women looked to Bread and Roses as a new source of
support both politically and socially.

Women who had not been part of the new left were excited to find that
they could take part in making collective decisions, "For me," said one,
"Bread and Roses was a new kind of *collective* experience. . . . It was my
first collective experience which was *conscious, intelligent, willed*—with other
people attempting to coordinate their behavior with their sense of Right, of
social responsibility which went beyond philanthropy and ideological pap."
For many new people who were not already socialists, the experience was
a radicalizing one.

Whether they had been politically active or not, Bread and Roses made
a qualitative change in women's lives. Many described it as the first time
their lives had meaning, the first time they had found a cause they wanted
to fight for. Energy and emotion previously directed toward men and relationships with men was freed up for new things—selves, sisters, the movement. Because it was the first time many had taken themselves seriously,
they began to be confident that others took them seriously as well. One
woman wrote that had she not been in Bread and Roses, "I would not have
had the sense of what it felt like to be an active participant in history, in my
life, Cambridge, whatever." Women firmly believed that they were acting
both for themselves and for other women, that they could serve as models
for others and also learn from them.

The Importance of Process

The Bread and Roses analysis of social relationships led many
members to stress the importance of *process* in social change. Essentially, this
started with the traditional problem of the relationship between means and
ends, then went beyond the usual formulations. To many Bread and Roses
women, a *non*feminist socialist movement struggling for power could not
become a feminist socialism once it was in power. Put even more strongly,
they saw present-day social relationships as both shaping and containing
future relationships and, in fact, future visions and possibilities. One member wrote about this in an open letter.

As Mao says, we must try to be socialist men and women while building the socialist country. The failing of so many movements is that their practice has not been consistent with their vision: while preaching socialism, people have fallen prey to privatistic, individualistic, anti-collective behavior and styles. We must constantly be aware of these contradictions in our personal and political struggles. At least two things we must continue to develop within the women's movement are collective efforts (work projects, etc.) and self-criticism.[37]

Bread and Roses can be seen as an attempt to realize these principles organizationally: to politicize personal relationships and to personalize political relationships within the organization. The latter part of the dynamic proved problematic: the lack of formal structures led to such problems as cliquism, personalized leadership, and a situation in which such a statement as "This freaks me out" could become a point of order during a meeting. The problem of priorities, both at meetings and within the organization as a whole, remained unsolved. The former process, however, was more successful—the very method of consciousness raising attested to the belief in the impossibility of personal solutions. Bread and Roses women's experience in the collectives, following their experience in the new left, led to defining the problem of male supremacy in such a way that it could not be solved personally. The concept of cultural oppression pointed one way toward change: fighting cultural oppression collectively became a necessity.

In the collectives women challenged the bourgeois ideology of individual inadequacy, powerlessness, and "personal problems" that required "personal solutions." In addition to the ideological attack, the practice of the collectives was a challenge to the hegemony of American individualism: the process of sharing feelings and experience broke through isolation toward feelings of solidarity and support, and from there, toward strength for change. The positive feelings engendered in the process of mutual recognition and analysis reinforced the ideological commitment to collective social change.[38]

Organization versus Community

Implicit, then, in the principle of "the personal is political" was a cultural emphasis: hegemony—the sway of the dominant culture as the only legitimate culture—became a major target of Bread and Roses as nascent socialist-feminism.[39] Given this target, developing a community and a culture became as important as developing a lasting formal organization. As members attempted to make Bread and Roses into an enduring community, those women who also sought to make it an "organization" were more ambivalent about the merits of formal organizations.

One must also consider "external" factors in accounting for the atrophy of the organization relative to the community. One was the general fragmentation of the new left and the dissolution of its organizations. A second was the organizational challenge posed by new generations of women participating in Bread and Roses. The first generation had shared many experiences in the new left of the 1960s and had raised their consciousness together. Newer members came into the organization toward the end of the first year (the summer and fall of 1970) with a consciousness that was "raised" but different from that of the founders. Some of these women had not been politically active previously, and their interpretations of women's liberation had been mediated by television, newspapers, and other liberal nonmovement sources. They had gone through very different processes of consciousness raising and therefore had a very different relationship to the ideas of basic social change. A second group joined Bread and Roses in the fall of 1970 from the left, particularly though not exclusively from Weatherman. They had not experienced [firsthand] the steps toward women's liberation that earlier members had taken but came to the organization in part because, in the words of one founding member, they thought "it was the only thing happening on the left." These particular women were more interested in women's actions with an antiimperialist focus and in building a women's community than in trying to work out the tensions involved in putting socialism and feminism together in theory and practice within an organization.

Internally, the logic of the "personal is political" ideology was that everything was a potential focus of political struggle and that nothing lay outside the realm of politics and of socialist and feminist concerns. This view represented a theoretical strength of Bread and Roses; however, it had problematic organizational implications: for example, the difficulty in defining political priorities. Everything mattered, and seemed to matter equally—goals and process, changing class society, and changing women's lives. The question of setting priorities often got phrased in terms of the tensions between "political" and "personal" (or "women's issues") and later between socialism and feminism.

Another problematic implication was the politicization of issues that became divisive within the organization, such as lifestyle politics and sexual orientation. Some women interpreted "the personal is political" to mean that one tried to change one's life as thoroughly and continuously as possible. Challenging all facets of one's life and oneself came to be considered by some as political activities and ends in themselves; these women tried to live their lives as models or examples of their vision. The practice was called "lifestyle politics" by those not engaged in it. The concept was not peculiar to Bread and Roses; it was both a form of new left politics and a nonpolitical aspect of the counterculture, the content of which at any particular time was contextually determined.[40]

Many of the women who were trying to live as models (though they were not a majority in Bread and Roses) asked themselves the question "How can we be liberated in a nonliberated society?"[41] A number of members perceived this as a tension, setting up these polarizations: hard politics versus lifestyle politics; socialism versus (implicit) "hippie" lifestyle; political action organizing versus lifestyle issues; outreach versus counterculture; and politics versus individualistically defined lifestyle (at the time often defined as politics versus lesbianism). As in many such dichotomies perceived by members at the time, hindsight suggests that they need not have been so polarized. And indeed, specific alternative lifestyles changed over time. At the start of Bread and Roses the main alternative was a variation on beadmaking, counterculture anarchism; by the end the main alternative was lesbianism, a "lifestyle" that was also for some people a theoretical and programmatic political issue. What started out for many women as new feelings of permission, exploration, and experimentation got transformed into a conflict that many members later saw as the reason for the demise of the organization.

The task that Bread and Roses set out to accomplish was an extremely difficult one. Members sought to create a growing political organization and at the same time to change themselves and their lives in accordance with their developing analysis of male supremacy. The tensions created by the politicization of private life could not, at that time, be contained in an organization. However, the community that Bread and Roses women created was able to incorporate these tensions, to resolve some of them, and create parallel projects and organizations for others.

What women experienced as an overarching community and social context in Bread and Roses, has, in the late 1980s, broken down into smaller communities (among lesbians, older women, differently abled women, and women of color, for example), networks for issues such as child care, and friendship and work groups. Shared values, experiences, and perspectives of socialist feminism inform the practice of women working in such diverse organizations, projects, and institutions as rape crisis centers, battered women's shelters, city human relations councils, groups to unlearn racism,

YWCA, women's studies in universities, the peace movement, and support work against the wars in Central America. These become isolated support systems in the absence of a vital political movement to connect them and to challenge the basic power relations of society. Yet still-evolving communities continue to provide support and challenge for women changing themselves and society. As women from more diverse populations strategize together, there is hope for more inclusive communities and a radical social movement.

Notes

Acknowledgments: I wish to thank Judy Smith, Jennie Bricker, Diane Balser, and Leslie Cagan for their helpful comments on an earlier draft of this article, and Deborah Gerson and Hola Hadley for our conversations and thinking together.

1. For an excellent account of the origins of the women's liberation movement in the movements of the 1960s, see Sara Evans, *Personal Politics: The Roots of Women's Liberation in the Civil Rights Movement and the New Left* (New York: Vintage Books, 1980).

2. This article comes from a chapter in my dissertation, "Bread and Roses: An Early Moment in the Development of Socialist Feminism" (Brandeis University, 1978), in which I analyzed the sociopolitical background of the women who formed Bread and Roses, the organization and community they created, and the development of the content of the perspective that the "personal is political and the political is personal." As a participant-observer I had access to contemporary documents written by members of Bread and Roses and other women's liberation groups. In addition, several years later I sent twenty-page open-ended questionnaires to 100 Bread and Roses members, and I interviewed many singly and in groups; these respondents constituted my "sample." At that time I also obtained journals, correspondence, unpublished articles, and one doctoral thesis about the Bread and Roses experience and era. All this material forms the basis of the thoughts to follow. Unless otherwise noted, quotations are from the dissertation.

3. See, e.g., Cherie Moraga and Gloria Anzaldua, eds., *This Bridge Called My Back: Writings by Radical Women of Color* (Watertown, Mass.: Persephone Press, 1981); Audre Lorde, *Sister Outsider* (Trumansburg, NY: Crossing Press, 1984); Susan E. Browne, Debra Connors and Nanci Stern (eds.) *With the Power of Each Breath: A Disabled Women's Anthology* (Pittsburgh, P.A.: Cleis Press, 1985).

4. "Zap actions" were usually single events, activism oriented toward the outside public.

5. The newly formed group had ambitious goals. The first draft of "The Purpose of Bread and Roses" illustrated its initial high expectations: "Bread and Roses is an organization of Socialist women. We believe that a socialist revolution is a necessary precondition to the liberation of women, although we know that we will not be liberated unless we continually fight against the oppression of women. For this reason we believe that a women's movement must be autonomous in order to fight against male supremacy as it exists in all institutions, and in its structural basis, the bourgeois family. We believe that capitalism has to be overthrown to create a socialist

society, which means one free of all forms of exploitation, racism, imperialism, and male supremacy, in which the means of production are owned by the people and the distribution of services is controlled by them. Bread and Roses is composed of women who believe in and work for these principles."

6. A new left community and culture already existed. What began as a small number of folk music enthusiasts and leftover beatniks flowered in the late 1960s into a counterculture that professed values of community, cooperation, gentleness, and love. Many women held high hopes for counterculture communities, hopes that were dashed as they became more conscious that sex roles and power relations continued to diminish and demean them.

7. Judith Herman, "Dear Kathie," photocopied letter, December 1972, p. 4.

8. Carol Hanisch, "The Liberal Takeover of Women's Liberation," in *Feminist Revolution* (New Paltz, N.Y.: Redstockings, 1975), 130.

9. Unlike the tendency toward Third Worldism among many factions of the new left at the time, which romanticized Third World liberation struggles and glorified violence and warfare, women's liberationists valued the strength and power of women in these struggles. Yet even among women who thought themselves conscious, without solid grounding in intimate knowledge of the lives of the women involved, the attraction would at times be romanticization.

10. Many consciousness-raising groups formed either by members of existing collectives or by participants in orientation meetings had lives very separate from Bread and Roses; such collectives I call "second generation."

11. Unsigned, "Our Collective: One Member's Views," photocopied handout, p. 2.

12. Weatherman was a small, militant offshoot of SDS. The group's members thought the function of U.S. leftists living in the "belly of the beast" was to assist the antiimperialist struggles of third world nations. They believed in armed confrontation and soon went underground.

13. The women's liberation movement also articulated the realistic fear of male violence that women did (and do) have to live with in daily life.

14. Her statement revealed both her self-hatred and the "daughter" orientation of the period that sometimes resulted in blaming mothers.

15. To separate these two elements is to do harm to the intimate connection between them. As women met more of one another's emotional needs, they became increasingly affectionate among themselves. In this context some women could more easily discover their lesbian feelings, but also, lesbians were by their existence and their rhetoric helping other women to be more affectionate and to explore their sexual feelings for women.

16. Boston Women's Health Care Collective, *Women and Their Bodies* (Boston: New England Free Press, 1970), 17.

17. The phrase comes from an article by Susan Lydon, variously titled "Understanding Orgasm" and "The Politics of Orgasm." Under the latter it appeared in the popular anthology edited by Robin Morgan, *Sisterhood Is Powerful* (New York: Vintage Books, 1970).

18. The "doctor's project," an early work group formed to compile a list of "good" gynecologists, expanded its goals. Members started teaching a course and compiling the book *Women and Their Bodies*, first published by the New England Free Press. The early editions, used in classes for high school and older women, were thoroughly revised for a commercial press edition: Boston Women's Health Col-

lective, *Our Bodies, Ourselves* (New York: Simon & Schuster, 1971, 1973). The most recent edition, again revised and greatly expanded, is *The New Our Bodies, Ourselves* (New York: Simon & Schuster, 1984). The book has been translated into thirteen languages.

19. Anne Koedt, *The Myth of the Vaginal Orgasm* (Boston: New England Free Press, n.d.), has been reprinted, among other places in Leslie B. Tanner, ed., *Voices from Women's Liberation* (New York: New American Library, 1970).

20. Nancy Hawley, "Dear Sisters," photocopied handout, 8 October 1970, pp. 5–6.

21. Roxanne Dunbar, "'Sexual Liberation': More of the Same Thing," *No More Fun and Games* No. 3 (November 1969): 50, 54. Several issues of this journal from Female Liberation/Cell 16 contain articles that are variants on this theme. Many Bread and Roses women read these journals, with a wide variation in response.

22. Mary, "Open Letter to My Sisters," photocopied letter, subsequently re-printed in *Women: A Journal of Liberation* and *Hysteria*, among other places.

23. In addition, one woman "knew [she] was gay but was afraid to come out." At the time of the study, 11.3 percent considered themselves gay. One woman who came out during Bread and Roses had been very active in gay politics but was living with a man at the time of the study; to the question "Do you consider yourself gay?" she responded, "Good question and one that I can't answer."

24. Dana Densmore, "On Celibacy," *No More Fun and Games* No. 1.

25. This community was new at the level of consciousness and ideology, not prac-tice, because there have always been women without men and women valorizing other women. Feminist historians have been shedding new light on past communities of women and on friendships between single and married women. See, e.g., Lillian Faderman's *Surpassing the Love of Man: Female Friendships in the Nineteenth Century* (New York: William Morrow, 1981).

26. Some men tried to be supportive but did not know how, and women did not really know how to tell them. There was no support vehicle for women with men; in some collectives women felt that talking about such problems took up "too much time." Women of color, because of the clear effects of racism on their communities, very early on saw the importance of working with men, and many felt alienated by what they saw as the "anti-men" stance of the wider women's movement.

27. Jenny Thierman, "Feminism: Bringing It All Back Home," *Countrywomen* No. 17 (October 1975): 20–23.

28. During my writing of the original study, conversations on culture with Phyllis Ewen, Linda Dittmar, and Donna Huse were provocative.

29. Redstockings was an early women's liberation organization in New York City.

30. Carol Hanisch, "A Critique of the Miss America Protest," in Shulamith Fire-stone and Anne Koedt, eds., *Notes from the Second Year: Women's Liberation* (New York: Notes, 1970), 88. She continues, "In such actions we speak to men as a group as well as to women. It is a rare opportunity to talk to men in a situation where they can't talk back. (Men must begin to learn to listen.) Our power of solidarity, not our individual intellectual exchanges, will change men." Bread and Roses women were in general less interested in this aspect of zapping, because the primary audience they wanted to reach was women.

31. "On WBCN—'The American Revolution Stereo Rock Radio Station,'" mimeographed leaflet. The last line invited women to join women's liberation by calling Bread and Roses, and gave the office phone number. The reverse side of the

leaflet was a "press release" recounting the storming of the radio station, and gave the names of three Bread and Roses women for "more information."

32. *Boston Globe*, 14 February 1970, p. 3.

33. Not everyone participated equally in zap actions, nor did everyone agree on their merit. Some women were uncomfortable making "a spectacle" of themselves; others felt that the actions often alienated more women than they "turned on." Although no one was pressured into participating, at least one respondent criticized the false consensus that held zaps up as a model.

34. A self-conscious women's movement culture was just beginning. Some later thinking on the place of culture in a movement was provided by the Chicago Women's Liberation Rock Band: "It has long been assumed that the extent to which a revolutionary movement survives, or even flourishes, is the extent to which people perceive that their needs are not being met in the current society. . . . We maintain that at least in a society like ours, defining an alternative feminist, socialist vision is the Queen pin in the achievement of social change. Without this vision, people in America will not work for change. In addition, the vision must be so powerful, so urgent, so compelling, so immediate, so utterly convincing that women can no longer stand living the way they do. The vision must be explicit and concrete enough so that not only are needs for overturning the patriarchy defined, but also *needs for getting that better society are generated.* . . . We want to build a culture which defines and makes clear needs that are very different from the needs of this culture" ("Developing a Revolutionary Culture," *Women: A Journal of Liberation* 3, no. 2 (1972): 2, 3.

35. *Bread and Roses Newsletter*, n.d. (postmarked 4 December 1970).

36. A sample from "The Battle Hymn of Women"—words by Meredith Tax; tune, "John Brown's Body" (© Meredith Tax and the chorus is from an earlier song by Len Chandler—a civil rights song).

Mine eyes have seen the glory of the flame of women's rage,
Kept smoldering for centuries, now burning in this age.
We no longer will be pris'ners in that same old gilded cage,
For we are marching on

CHORUS

Move on over or we'll move on over you;
Move on over or we'll move on over you;
Move on over or we'll move on over you,
For women's time has come.

It is we who've done your cooking, done your cleaning, kept your rules,
We gave birth to your children and we taught them in your schools,
We've kept this system running but we're laying down our tools,
For we are marching on.

CHORUS

We have broken through our shackles; now we sing a battle song.
We march for liberation and we're many thousands strong.
We'll build a new society; we waited much too long,
But we are marching on.

37. Carol McEldowney, open letter (ca. 1969–70), p. 2.

38. Most of the women in my sample retained some form of this political commitment at the time of the study.

39. This contrasts sharply with the narrow definition of the political, focusing on the seizure of state power, that was characteristic of the growing number of Marxist-Leninist sects at the time this study was done. It is not surprising that these groups tended to be hostile to socialist-feminist concerns (while often borrowing feminist ideas to enhance their recruitment efforts).

40. Examples on the left at this time included the Weatherman style of living at subsistence level and of smashing monogamy. The basic idea was that people could, by their very way of living, embody visions to show other people that the established ways of living one's life were not the only ways.

41. Most women in Bread and Roses did not think it possible to be liberated in a nonliberated society. They talked of the ongoing process toward liberation, of a future reality that would serve as a model for alternative ways to live.

7   Women's Unions and the Search for a Political Identity

Karen V. Hansen

Socialist feminism developed as the attempt to merge two movements and two theoretical perspectives. It held great promise to those repelled by the sexism of the left and frustrated by the political limitations of feminism. As part of the nascent development of this combined perspective, women's unions were formed, autonomous organizations for women only, which in theory allowed women to address women's concerns, unhindered by men. They were independent community organizations, not tied to one particular labor union or political party. Seventeen such unions were founded between 1969 and 1975.

Using union documents and material from interviews with those who participated in the women's unions across the country, I would like to advance the dialogue on the past and future of socialist feminism. In particular I want to address the question, how can we account for the demise of one of the most significant attempts to combine socialist-feminist theory with political practice? In addition to a much-needed historical picture of the rise and fall of these groups, I want to explore the political issue, so relevant to a socialist-feminist politics today, of the effort to define and live out a unique socialist-feminist political identity. What have been some of the difficulties in this project historically? More than ten years after the last published evaluation of the women's unions,[1] and with the wisdom gained

Source: This article is reprinted from *Socialist Review* No. 86 (March–April, 1986), pp. 67–95, by permission of the publisher, *Socialist Review*, 3202 Adeline, Berkeley, CA 94703.

by hindsight, a new assessment of that brief history of the movement can help us learn about ongoing and future attempts at social change.

One must examine several factors in order to understand the bases of strength *and* decline of the women's unions. First, the unions were closely tied to the left—not to a specific organization but to the movement as a whole. This close association undermined the cohesiveness of the women's unions because of the divisive internal disputes it caused and because of the decline of the left's size and vitality between 1970 and 1980.[2]

Second, forging a socialist-feminist theoretical perspective that attempted to address and remedy all sources of domination and exploitation —simultaneously—made it hard for the women's unions to achieve concrete change. In particular, women struggled with the challenge of incorporating a personal dimension, historically unique to the women's liberation movement, into the agenda for fundamental structural change.[3] While absolutely essential to the perspective, the integration of the personal and the political posed a host of problems with which even veteran political activists had had little experience. Because of this ultimately global agenda for change, the unions were largely unsuccessful in reaching a broad community.

Although it was initially ill defined, the promise of socialist feminism was great. It embodied a meta-theory of liberation. The unions provided a forum for refining the theory and for defining the politics of those who found the theory so appealing. Yet, I argue, the existence of such a forum simultaneously proved to be a major source of tension and conflict for the unions. Because it was a relatively unformulated perspective, those who called themselves socialist feminists covered a broad political spectrum (broad within the terrain of the left). Women entering the unions had differing ideas of what it should mean—some heavily emphasized antiimperialism, others child rearing. Meanwhile, there were those, most notably in left sectarian groups, who recognized socialist feminism as an important political tendency on the left and struggled to usurp the label and redefine it in their own image. Thus, the history of these socialist-feminist organizations is the history of the struggle to solidify a socialist-feminist identity. And it was, in part, the process of formulating this identity that contributed to the eventual demise of the majority of the women's unions.

Defining Socialist Feminism

The unions were autonomous—emerging from yet independent of the new left. Angry and fed up with rampant sexism on the left, women

TABLE 7-1. SOCIALIST-FEMINIST WOMEN'S UNIONS

Organization	Founded	Dissolved	Longevity
Chicago Women's Liberation Union	Fall 1969	Spring 1977	7.5 yr.
Pittsburgh Radical Women's Union	April 1970	January 1971	0.75
Half of Brooklyn	1971	n.a.	—
Baltimore Women's Union	1972	1982	10.0
Berkeley-Oakland Women's Union	January 1973	October 1976	3.75
Los Angeles Women's Liberation Union	March 1973	April 1975	2.0
Boston Women's Union	Winter 1974	May 1976	2.5
San Diego Women's Union	March 1974	n.a.	—
San Francisco Women's Union	April 1974	February 1976	1.8
Eugene Women's Union	October 1974	n.a.	—
Valley Women's Union	1974	1977	3.0
San Jose Women's Union	February 1975	n.a.	—
Santa Cruz Women's Union	February 1975	n.a.	—
Lexington Women's Union	n.a.	1976	—
Springfield Women's Union	n.a.	1976	—
New York Women's Union	n.a.	1976	—
Twin Cities Women's Union	n.a.	1976	—

had organized the women's liberation movement, which, many gradually concluded, lacked sufficient structure to support a broad movement. The unions were founded to fill that gap. Their primary purpose was to provide a forum for theoretical development and a structure for activism.

Seventeen women's unions were founded between 1969 and 1975 (see Table 7-1) with activist cores ranging from seven women to two hundred and mailing lists as large as nine hundred. The average organizational life of those unions was almost four years.[4] They were geographically concentrated on the west coast, in the industrial Midwest, and on the northeastern seaboard. Typically, these areas were also centers of other progressive political activity.[5]

The union participants were largely white, middle-class, college-educated women in their mid- to late twenties.[6] Most were between college and professional careers. A significant proportion were lesbian (in some unions, over half the membership). The vast majority of women were not married. Some were divorced, and many were involved in "primary relationships." Because they were living in an unprecedented historical circumstance in which women were both able to delay childbirth and enjoy a reduced set of societal pressures to have families, very few women had children. A majority had been politicized during the 1960s through their involvement in civil rights struggles, antiwar organizing, and Students for a Democratic Society (SDS).

The struggle to define socialist feminism was a key issue in the women's unions. Socialist feminists and union activists in particular devoted much time and energy to theoretical development. They acted on the assumption, strongly held by the left at the time, that articulating a precise and correct theory would inform strategic activism and ultimately bring about the revolution. Socialist feminists were building theory that identified both capitalism and patriarchy as sources of oppression. One early proponent of socialist feminism points to the motivation for linking critiques of capitalism and patriarchy:

> Socialist feminism was an attempt to understand feminism in a real unselfish way. I think that had both its strengths and weaknesses. We weren't just thinking about our own lives. We were trying to look at the whole world—women in Third World countries or women who were poor. I think it was a good impulse that led us to do that—not wanting to be selfish and wanting to make the world better.

Socialist-feminist theory asserted a need for the transformation of relations between women and men as well as economic and political structures. As Barbara Ehrenreich put it, socialist feminism asked "the hard questions."[7] How do capitalism and patriarchy intermesh in their tangle of oppression? In what ways are the private lives of women connected to exploitation of the Third World and the oppression of women? Socialist feminism promised to contextualize feminism by holding fast to a class analysis without abandoning the personal dimension of politics.

The result of the emphasis on social structures meant that individual action, though necessary, was insufficient. In a keynote speech at the Antioch National Conference on Socialist Feminism in 1975, Ehrenreich emphasized the importance of collective action:

> Whatever the issue, we do not seek individual solutions for individual women. We seek collective solutions and forms of struggle that heighten *collective* confidence. . . . Actually there is a material reason for this distinction between us and the bourgeois feminists. Socialist-feminist organizing focuses on working-class women who do not have the option of individual solutions (promotions, tenure, etc.) of the kind that are available to women in the professional-managerial stratum.[8]

The emphasis on the Big Picture gave socialist feminism great appeal: working on a socialist-feminist project would simultaneously address all society's ills. At the same time it provided an intensely moral framework for socialist feminists: they were not concerned *just* about class issues or *just* about sexism; they were putting everything together to form a *"totalistic* understanding of the revolutionary transformation" of society.[9] Yet the Big Picture, while giving socialist feminists a moral grounding, rarely emerged from a fully agreed-upon theoretical grounding. Important theoretical divisions within the socialist-feminist framework became evident in the unions' process of defining themselves vis-à-vis the new left and the women's movement.

The Importance of the Left

Socialist feminism had two competing audiences: the new left—comprising the antiwar movement, the student movement, SDS—and the women's movement. I argue that the new left was the primary audience for the socialist-feminist women's unions, personally and theoretically; indeed, the unions were fundamentally shaped by it. The socialist-feminist movement arose from the new left with the intent of building on its strengths and correcting its weaknesses. In its political work the movement did not abandon the philosophy of the new left so much as the men of the new left.

The women's movement was also important but secondarily so. Although individually, socialist feminists felt themselves to be personally accountable to a feminist philosophy, as a movement the women's unions were more closely allied with the left. Feminist concern about issues of meeting process, egalitarian and participatory structures, and sexism permeated the unions at every level, yet a new left sensibility was deeply ingrained, and direct-action organizing was more likely to be undertaken with the left than with the women's movement. A tension between socialism and feminism— alliances with the left versus the women's movement—existed throughout the life of the women's unions, practically and theoretically.

This duality was inherited from a political division within the women's liberation movement: women were labeled "feminists" and "politicos." The "feminists" focused primarily on the way in which the oppression of women was manifested in personal life and on the active role of men and male- dominated institutions and values. They regarded patriarchal structures as the paramount obstacle to women's liberation (in the parlance of the left, the "primary contradiction" in the debate over which was historically prior and fundamentally more important: class, race, or gender). The "feminist" tendency was one that we would label "radical feminist" today. It should be noted that these titles have been used differently over several decades; their precise meaning continues to be debated. Radical feminism is a label that in the late 1960s and early 1970s referred to women's lib- erationists. They were women to the left of or more *radical* than NOW feminists. Most of the older generation of socialist-feminists once called themselves radical feminists. Today the term has come to mean something quite different.

The "politicos" were those women who argued that capitalism (and secondarily imperialism) was the key social structure causing women's op- pression. They accepted the political and economic analysis of the new left but felt they had been betrayed and undermined as women by male radi- cals. They believed in the need for an autonomous women's movement but thought that feminists who lacked a class analysis could contribute little to substantive, lasting social change. The "politico" tendency is one we would label socialist feminist today. Most women did not unambiguously fall into either typification; within the "politico" tendency some women leaned more toward feminism and others toward socialism.

The left deeply influenced the theory of socialist feminism. As sectors of the new left had turned toward Marxism for a wide-ranging analysis of capitalism and imperialism, new left women began to study Marx. Femi- nism, however, was not to be circumscribed by "the Woman Question" as delineated in the works of Marx and Engels. In the search for the primary contradiction, the socialist-feminist analysis did not subordinate gender to class. The tension between the two primary analyses was absolutely central to the search for a unique identity.

Much of the history of socialist feminism reflects the ongoing debate between feminists and men on the left. The men hurled both overt and hidden accusations at socialist feminists about the need for a *real* theory. New left women felt accountable to these criticisms and defensively tried to justify their theoretical and strategic perspectives. They were unwilling, however, to repress their newly expressed rage and emerging solidarity with sisters, as many on the left demanded. Their search for a merging of the two perspectives resulted in the hybrid of socialist-feminism.

Because of the left's emphasis on theory during the 1970s and because of the need to define their world view more clearly, the women's unions identified theoretical development as a primary activity. This led to ideological debates ad infinitum and also to an unprecedented situation in movement-building. In a search for praxis, theoretical development became the work of unions as a whole. The ultrademocratic ethos of the 1970s dictated that activists share in intellectual activities, formerly reserved for an elite core. Not all members had skills conducive to theoretical work, and many found it incomprehensible or boring. Never before, to the best of my knowledge, had there been a broad-based movement whose agenda was to do theoretical work.

The Elusive Agenda

A corollary of the problem posed by the ongoing efforts to define socialist feminism was that of outlining an activist agenda. If it was not clear what socialist feminism was, neither was it clear what constituted a socialist-feminist project. Jo Freeman, a historian of the women's movement, refers to one aspect of this situation as the "radical paradox":

> Many politicos, viewing themselves as radicals, found repugnant the possibility of pursuing the "reformist" issues which might be solved without altering the basic structure of the system and thus, they felt, only strengthen the system. However, their search for a sufficiently radical action and/or issue came to naught, and they found themselves unable to do anything out of a fear that it might be counterrevolutionary. The structure of available opportunities for action did not provide any that were permitted by their value structure.[10]

There were certain issues that socialist feminists designated as central: reproductive rights, twenty-four-hour free quality day care, equal pay for equal work.[11] However, many of these issues were also adopted by mainstream feminists. Union activists spent many lengthy meetings searching for the specifically and uniquely socialist-feminist project. One woman who personally confronted this issue as a national officeholder for the New American Movement said:

> The hardest thing was trying to figure out what a feminist project would be. And the women always wanted it to be the *perfect* showcase for socialist feminism. . . . We always had this attitude, which I am now so critical of, which is that socialist feminism is so much better than everything in regular feminism. So any time we came up with something ordinary it didn't sound good enough. It didn't have a socialist component to it. How is that different from what the liberals are doing? And so we didn't do it. And we ended up trying to figure out what it was going to be for years.

For example, how would a socialist-feminist day-care center be different from a "bourgeois" feminist one? From the beginning, socialist feminists faced an identity crisis: If a socialist feminist could not be distinguished from a liberal feminist on the basis of her activism, what then did it mean to be a socialist feminist? This paradox was one that women's union activists never resolved.

The underside of this discussion of activism was the issue of constituency. In its major documents the socialist-feminist analysis defined working-class women as its primary constituency. Yet socialist feminism advocated the liberation of all oppressed people, not just the working class and not just women. In effect, the constituency became ambiguous. Working-class women were identified as privileged actors and hence the primary target for organizing. But while they were seen as the desirable constituency, the demographic composition of the women's unions was primarily middle class and white. In other words, union members were generally not members of the constituency they hoped to organize—Third World women, working-class women, and so on. Liberal guilt raged ashamedly while the "socially required rhetoric" of the 1970s demanded attention to the working class.[12] The contest over the appropriate degree of working-class membership rose and fell in relation to sieges on the unions by workerist and Marxist-Leninist perspectives.

Regardless of the guilt evoked in discussions, the task of defining "working class" remained a major obstacle. Were working-class women those whose fathers had working-class jobs while the women were growing up? Or were they women who currently worked in pink- or blue-collar jobs, regardless of their family background? The thought that a woman's categorization in a feminist organization would be based on her relationship to

male family members seemed ludicrous to most women. This all contributed to the volatility of discussion about the issue, with exchanges taking
the form of attack and defense rather than comradely debate. The mostly
middle-class union members had a theoretical understanding of the oppression of working-class women but generally little real-life experience
of their problems. As a result, their time was spent second-guessing the
primary issues for working-class women. The working-class constituency
remained elusive to the women's unions, never being clearly defined or
understood and forever posing the contradiction between the privileged
target group and reality.

Structure and Political Activism

Early in their history the unions had to confront the issue of
structure: should a union form an umbrella or a membership organization?
The umbrella philosophy provided a pluralistic structure in an attempt to
maximize and coordinate the impact of feminist organizing while allowing
for a diversity of projects and people. It flexibly incorporated work projects
that operated autonomously of the larger organization but simultaneously
united the groups by connecting them within a citywide socialist-feminist
community. In contrast, a membership organization required members to
agree with the *"Principles of Unity"* and to pay dues. This *theoretically* resulted
in an organization of like-minded people, working on common projects
with a minimum of ideological differences.[13]

Both structures proved to have problems. Umbrella unions found that
autonomous groups frequently were so disconnected from the centralized
structure that they saw no point in maintaining their affiliation with the
larger organization. An anonymous author discussed the problem in the
Chicago Women's Liberation Union (CWLU), originally founded as a federation of individuals and community-organizing projects:

> The variety, diversity and autonomy was such that groups often left
> the Union (Emma Goldman Health Center, Rape Crisis Hotline,
> Women's Graphics Collective) rather than add to the strength of
> the organization as a whole. The "umbrella" could only embrace so
> much. Beyond a certain point, it could not grow.[14]

In some cases, the absence of clear political allegiances left the organizations vulnerable to external threats of takeover. The CWLU, for example,
was threatened with takeover several times in its eight-year history by such

groups as the Socialist Workers' Party, the Revolutionary Union, the Communist Workers' Party, and the October League.[15] Work-group members who went to citywide membership meetings tired of arguing with destructive sectarians and questioned why they were spending so much energy on ideological battles rather than on their organizing projects. When a left sectarian group organized as a chapter in 1975, a group of thirty independent women within the union lobbied to expel them. Despite the efforts of a self-appointed group within CWLU to mediate, arguing that "the tactic of purging the sectarians was itself antifeminist," the steering committee voted to expel them. Shortly thereafter CWLU disbanded.

Interestingly, membership unions also faced sectarian takeover attempts, though none was successful. The major problem of the membership structure was insularity. Although the unions had project groups, members committed their primary allegiance to the union. The projects grew out of the union and had greater difficulty rooting in the community than maintaining union ties. There was no mechanism for building a mass base, and so the organization appealed to and recruited from the already converted left.

In practice, the decision about which structure to implement reflected the continuum of political differences outlined earlier. Although all identified themselves as socialist feminist, some unions leaned more toward feminism and others more toward socialist politics. At the socialist end of the spectrum were the membership organizations such as the San Francisco Women's Union (SFWU). It was the most orthodox left union and modeled its structure on democratic-centralist organizations of the left. The focus of this type of union was on organizing (direct action) more than on service provision; for example, SFWU had a Clerical Workers Group that attempted to organize clerical workers in the financial district, as well as a Health Workers Group and a Prison Study Group. At the other end of the spectrum were the umbrella organizations whose projects, like Chicago's were diverse (including a women's rock band, a Liberation School, and Direct Action for Rights in Employment) and included more "women's projects": an abortion counseling service (before abortion was legal), a women's graphics collective, and a rape crisis hotline. Most unions fell somewhere in between. Several unions had antiimperialist committees that focused on antiwar work and often cosponsored demonstrations with other left organizations.[16]

Organizations of both types wrote statements of their political principles, which most unions called "Principles of Unity." The first union, Chicago, wrote seven paragraphs describing its political principles; four years later San Francisco's Principles of Unity required sixteen pages. Unions took the task very seriously and often spent months of tortuous political debate carefully working out their perspective in every detail. Given the confusions about what socialist feminism really was and what the unions were to do, this project seemed critical, but the ideological battles encountered in the tedious writing process foreshadowed later obsessions in which union members would mire themselves.

Most unions had a central decision-making organ to coordinate information and activities and occasionally to provide political leadership. In most of the women's unions there were supposedly no leaders; singling out leaders was considered antithetical to feminism. "Every woman a leader" was the philosophy.[17] Steering committees often rotated members in an effort to provide skills to many women and to prevent some individuals from monopolizing power within the organization. Inevitably, some women proved more influential than others, either formally or informally. On a national level, writers and theorists of the movement were especially influential, even when their work was credited only to the organization—a common practice at the time. On a local level, a combination of commitment to the work, intelligence, personality, "charisma," friendship networks, and time available to do union work produced de facto leadership.[18] Because of the feminist critique of hierarchy and aggressiveness, even those women whose organizations chose to elect them to leadership roles received contradictory messages about their exercise of authority. For example, in Half of Brooklyn (the Brooklyn women's union), several original organizers took the initiative to explore political directions. According to one of them, the membership was extremely angry and critical because

(1) rational analysis is a male trip always being laid on women by macho type people;
(2) we were elitists by virtue of our excessive activity and proposals;
(3) we were manipulative because planning strategies and arguing for them is manipulative.

Ironically, the membership simultaneously criticized the "leaders" for

(1) not having provided channels for rational analysis all along;
(2) not being active enough in Half of Brooklyn and for being in too many other projects;
(3) not having been more assertive about goals and strategy.[19]

In the San Francisco Women's Union—the exception that proved the rule —the women elected a triumvirate, which was expected to provide political direction and strategic leadership and to advise union members accordingly. But even in this situation ambivalence about leadership and distrust of authority worked as a double-edged sword for leaders and others who were outspoken or tried to exercise the authority delegated to them.

Lesbian-straight relationships were as central to the women's unions as they had been to the rest of the women's movement. The unions had a large lesbian membership and prided themselves on their members' ability to fuse lesbian and straight concerns and transcend the divisions that had earlier bisected the women's movement. Lesbians were represented in most union work groups, including child care, which was identified as a straight women's issue in the early 1970s. Many women found women's union activity to be a satisfying way to build a multidimensional, nonheterosexist feminist and socialist movement.

This was a welcome departure from the infamous 1971 "gay-straight split" when, in a burst of self-righteousness, some lesbians within the women's movement broke with existing women's organizations to form their own. They were infuriated with the bias against homosexuality and decided to work independently. True to the ideological shifts of the time, they proclaimed that the only feminist was a "woman identified woman." Socially and politically this meant being a separatist; sexually it meant being a lesbian. Many lingering angry feelings on both sides of this virulent split remain today.

In spite of the women's unions' attempts to transcend such divisions, there was a tension about the moral imperative implied in the notion of lesbianism as a pure form of feminist practice. One member of the Berkeley-Oakland Women's Union (BOWU) described the tension at a mass meeting:

> There was one very large women's union meeting that was about relationships. And when we got into small groups, one of the lesbian women said, "I'm not particularly interested in hearing about women's relationships with men. If women want to do that, it's fine, but I don't want to hear about it." Nobody said, "You're full of shit. If you're going to talk about your lover I'm going to talk about my lover." That was a rule. If those women didn't want to talk about men, you shouldn't talk about men. They chose to be in women's communities where they didn't have to deal with men; they didn't come to a women's union meeting to hear about men.

The union veteran acknowledged the role of straight women in giving up power and accommodating the tyranny of "political correctness":

> The heterosexual women have got to take responsibility for being so spineless. . . . We bent under the pressure and did not push back and say, "This is absurd. . . ." Out of my own guilt, and not wanting to be oppressive, I allowed myself to get pushed around. It's part of being a woman.

Obviously, tensions surrounding the issue of homosexuality did not altogether evaporate; nevertheless, individual positions on debates within the unions were not predictable on the basis of someone's sexual orientation. This was an important step forward from the earlier days of the women's movement when political positions were more directly derived from sexual preferences.

The tone of union meetings was generally hard edged and critical. The new left and the civil rights movement, in their various incarnations, were built out of righteous indignation at the country's callous injustices. One person I interviewed situated the climate within American traditions:

> In this country the idea of politics and personal purity is sort of a religious notion of politics. And the critique that politics suck— because politicians are crooks, because they don't mean what they say—is the web and warp of the movement, of the culture. And so if you're going to be radical, and you're going to be different, then of course you have to be none of those hypocritical, anti-democratic, impure, opportunistic, self-interested things.

The feminist movement unleashed a rage all its own but within the context of the widespread moral absolutism and political purism of the time. It extended moral authority into the realm of personal life. Every personal act became a political act, a public act, and therefore open to public scrutiny and judgment.

The founding conference of the San Diego Women's Union in March 1974 offers an example of the level of tension that was not unfamiliar to the left at that time:

> Breaking down into small groups to discuss socialist-feminism had been planned, but this never really happened because heavy criticism of the conference so far was raised from the floor. Major discussion took place around the heterosexual bias and racism of the P[lanning] C[ommittee], who were attacked as straight, white and bourgeois. The PC was easily guilt-tripped into silence, they totally abnegated their power and women from the audience took the chair. The third world women felt they had no input, that their input should have been actively sought by the PC during the planning stages of the conference. Some lesbians felt they had been patronized. Why women felt so hostile we could not totally understand, but we have a few ideas. . . . The "confrontation politics" of some of the most vocal women did not allow for dialogue. There was little effort to really understand what other women were saying.

We felt that this part of the conference was conducted in a non-feminist and non-socialist way, and that the trashing of women was unnecessary. One of the members of the ad hoc PC later said that although the process and dynamics were bad, the conference did accomplish the goal of bringing women together and many women felt it was an important and necessary step for women to voice their anger and bitterness. There seemed to be a general consensus that the criticisms presented were valid, but the women who took over the conference did so in an undemocratic way; there were no votes. If there were women who disagreed with this process, nothing was heard from them, probably because of the intimidating guilt-tripped atmosphere.[20]

Guilt was liberally exploited in union meetings. Middle-class white women who were attempting to rectify the endless wrongs of the white middle-class world were extremely susceptible to criticisms of political incorrectness.

Intimidation was also a part of the mass meeting atmosphere, which, when combined with guilt, produced much acrimony. The "Feminist" caucus that withdrew from BOWU within six months of its founding identified a central problem in the union: "The use of tradition as a legitimating tool, the invocation of a bogus unity, the top-down nature of discussions, and the prevention of debate—combine to produce an atmosphere of intimidation."[21] Undoubtedly, the battle they inspired over the feminist (or nonfeminist) nature of the organization contributed to this political atmosphere. One member of the "Feminist" caucus described what happened:

We went in very purist, very hostile, very antagonistic. Given who showed up to the women's union, if we had been intent on being influential we probably could have been, if we had really been trying to share ideas and build the women's union. I think we really went in to attack it. It's hard to impute motives; I don't know what anybody's motives were. . . . It's not that the criticisms were inappropriate; it's just that it wasn't an organization-building style at all.

Some veteran union members thought the intensity of dissension was inevitable. The early feminist movement emerged on the shaky ground of a shared oppression. At that time, most energy was focused on developing sisterhood and discovering common experiences through discussions of class, race, and sexual preference. The shift to political activity elicited ideological and stylistic differences that had been dormant:

At a conscious intellectual level, there was a different politics, different visions; at a more primitive level, there were issues of competition, anger, aggression, hostility, assertion, all of which were not okay for women to do because they were "male" traits. Well, you can't negate a whole part of everybody's personality and expect that to not come out the back door somehow.

The result, for mass meetings, was an environment where only the brave, the politically correct, or the thick-skinned would speak. Many women described the mass meetings as almost unbearable. But not all union members experienced them as hopeless. For example, one woman, a "red diaper baby," said that although the meetings were somewhat tedious, the project at hand—building a socialist-feminist movement—outweighed any minor obstacles or discomfort. The women's unions were a political dream to her and therefore she was willing to make sacrifices in order to ensure their long-term viability.

The acrimony, while not unique to mass meetings, did not pervade the union at every level. Many union veterans regarded their involvement in work groups or union projects as their most satisfying political activity ever. The successful groups were small, eight to ten people, and tended to be more politically homogeneous than the unions as a whole. One woman in the Clerical Work Group in the San Francisco Women's Union described the sisterhood that developed out of a common project: "In our work groups . . . we did try to take care of each other. We became wonderful friends. We hung in there with each other. . . . We always did our work in twos or threes so no one would be alone—always very collective, very supportive, very loving." The most stable and longest-lived groups had a clear sense of purpose (whether a study group or a project), were more politically and socially homogeneous, and were able to develop trust within the group. Some work groups continued long after the union folded; for example, Blazing Star, once a chapter of CWLU, continued to publish a newspaper targeted to the lesbian and gay community in Chicago.

The insularity of the women's unions—a key to their collective lack of effectiveness and longevity—was evident in the character of their outreach programs and efforts to integrate new members. The unions attempted to be accountable to their elusive constituency. A vague conception of their constituency shaped the politics of the unions:

For example, these kinds of discussions in the Valley Women's Union became focused on lesbian/straight tensions within the organization. Some women feared that our strong organizational stand affirming

lesbianism as a political and personal choice and our opposition
to heterosexual privilege would drive away working-class women.
Others saw internal political development and the need to raise
consciousness on lesbian politics among *all* socialist feminists as a priority. Still others argued that there were many working-class lesbians
in our community—why weren't we trying to organize them?[22]

Many unions established outreach committees to grapple with this issue.
Some advocated joining Third World and working-class women in coalition
work as a way to overcome cultural barriers. Others asserted that working-
class women should be approached directly through projects that would
appeal to them and serve their needs. Alternatively, one sector of the SFWU
argued for making the union a "mass" organization by eliminating membership criteria. This was proposed on the assumption (with no evidence
one way or the other) that it was specifically the membership criteria (dues
and agreement with the Principles of Unity) that kept working-class and
Third World women from joining.

Fundamentally, the unions did not recruit outside the left. The membership had a core group of committed activists that was relatively constant and a periphery that was constantly changing. Typically, the character of the periphery changed little, although individuals shuffled through
some unions as though they were revolving doors. The closed quality of
the groups resulted from a minimal success in outreach, the absence of
organizing skills, a lack of knowledge about the constituency, and, for the
membership unions, a desire (however unsuccessful) to keep the unions
ideologically pure.

One example of the frustrated outreach efforts was the attempt of the
Children's Group in BOWU to produce a broadside. The group advertised
a meeting for working-class mothers who were dissatisfied with available
day-care options. One member described the broadside and the elephan-
tine process that produced it:

> It had a big title across the top. . . . And the print was smaller than in
> *Socialist Review*, and would take somebody two hours to stand up and
> read, going into our politics. It was very well done, and thorough.
> We were the most obsessive group you'll ever want to meet. So until
> you could possibly get something out, you'd have to study it, you'd
> have to have a study group about it, read thoroughly, make sure
> you had the politics correct, then by consensus, in a group of eight,
> there was no division of labor where you allocated responsibility
> to a subgroup—the whole group had to agree on everything. So it

took months to put up the broadside. We had a great time. Very nice graphic art. And two people showed up to the meeting, which is a lot, given the broadside. . . . We didn't know how to organize groups other than ourselves.

Many women found it difficult to reach out to communities and people of whom they had little understanding. Recruitment and outreach were problems for most unions throughout the duration of their existence.

When outreach was successful, integrating new members was problematic—whether into the hostile environment of a mass meeting or the close-knit amicable work group. Many unions established a committee to teach new members the organization's history and familiarize them with its political perspective. However, few unions ever dealt effectively with the continuous problem they faced: young women needed a way to gain theoretical sophistication and to become oriented to the unions. Women politicized outside the new left did not easily comprehend the vehemence of the political debates, and those who became socialist feminists without ever having been in a consciousness-raising group sometimes failed to understand the power of the idea that "the personal is political." One woman from the Children's Group and Planning Committee in BOWU identified a critical ideological gap that led to a fundamental disunity within the union:

I remember at one point I thought, "The problem with the union is that we never provided the basis of feminism for people who joined later in the organization's history." I remember thinking, "My God, these people have probably never read the eight great articles from 1968 and 1969 from Women's Liberation." I felt that they really did not understand on some level the systematic way sexism functions.

The difficulty in educating new generations of activists who did not share an older generation's political history was not easily overcome.

The Demise of the Women's Unions
The Decline of the Left

The collapse of virtually all the women's unions in 1976 cannot be separated from the decline of the left in the 1970s. Out of the ashes of SDS arose many organizations—democratic-socialist, Marxist-Leninist, and Maoist. In the search for answers during the 1970s the discourse of Marxism-Leninism went beyond the confines of the new Communist movement and permeated debate in all sectors of the left. As I have argued, the women's unions similarly were not exempt from the debates or immune to the seductive appeal of a more "definitive" analysis.

This diversification of the left posed severe problems for feminism within the unions, for three reasons. First, some members had multiple commitments, and their energy was absorbed by extra-union activities: for example, union members in many cities simultaneously belonged to a women's union and to the October League, a Marxist-Leninist organization.

Second, and more important, within Marxism-Leninism there was little room for feminist thought. Issues of feminism within a Marxist-Leninist framework were reduced to "the Woman Question" and defined solely in terms of women's condition as workers under capitalism. In addition, many Marxist-Leninist organizations objected to homosexuality—which, ironically, did not prevent lesbians from joining their ranks but kept key feminist issues of sexuality at bay. The self-doubt and liberal guilt of women activists transcended the gay-straight divisions. Feminism within the unions was attacked and theoretically on the defensive. Women's issues were accused of subverting the "true" revolution, which could come only from working-class militancy. The attack was made explicit in a leaflet distributed by Worker's Viewpoint, some of whose members infiltrated the Chicago Women's Liberation Union:

> Feminism, the reactionary ideology of the women's "liberation" movement, is a hodgepodge of liberalism, illusions of bourgeois democracy, individualism, pragmatism, and hedonism. It reflects the degenerate and parasitic character of the moribund capitalism and has nothing in common with the rising revolutionary spirit and vitality of the working class and oppressed people.[23]

They also issued calls to "Defeat Feminism," "Oppose Homosexuality," and "Defeat the ERA." While only a fraction of the union membership believed the leaflet's charges, unions as a whole typically felt obliged to schedule meeting time to discuss the issue. The women who adopted the Marxist-Leninist perspective, in their insistence on the theoretical centrality of class, lost sight of what was revolutionary about feminism. And those who had to battle with Marxism-Leninism were robbed of the energy to attend to other work.

Third, the democratic left faced an identity crisis in the mid-1970s. When the war in Vietnam ended and it became evident that a U.S. revolution was not around the corner, many radicals were no longer certain what it meant to be a socialist in America. One NAM activist and member of the Pittsburgh Radical Women's Union described the effect of the identity crisis on the left in general:

> Our snobbery about other activists in the world seems misplaced.
> I feel like we spent so much time having debates among ourselves
> when other people were taking political action, even if it was not the
> "most correct" thing in the world to do. It was okay to have those
> debates but to feel that what we were doing was so much better than
> everybody else seems a little grandiose to me now. We really felt
> that building a socialist movement was the most important thing
> that could be done in the world because if the United States became
> socialist it would get rid of imperialism, plus it would eliminate all
> the problems of the people within the United States. Therefore, why
> shouldn't we spend a few years trying to figure out how to do it? I
> think I lost my faith that what we were doing would ever get into the
> real world, and then it just seemed that we were doing something
> to amuse ourselves. That's when I started wondering if it would
> have made any difference if I'd sat around and smoked dope instead
> during those years.

This identity crisis similarly affected the women's unions. On the one hand, socialist feminists witnessed the progressive erosion of the mass base of the left, as well as its driving spirit and clarity. On the other hand, they saw the women's movement thriving. What did this mean for those who attempted to synthesize the best of these two movements? Several women claimed that the diminished strength of the left in this country limited the future for the women's movement because the two, in a larger sense, were symbiotic and needed each other to create and sustain a viable progressive movement.

Internal Strife

One major source of strain within the unions lay in the basic analytic precepts of socialist-feminism—the critique of society was overarching and lacked a clear strategic direction. How was a movement to fight capitalism, sexism, racism, and imperialism and achieve concrete results? How would a movement expunge private property short of a revolution? The analysis, however, did assign responsibility for oppression to more concrete institutions; for example, the socialist-feminist analysis identified the nuclear family as a center of women's oppression. A popular slogan of the time was "Smash the Family." But in the case of a smashed family, who suffered? The ruling class? Who benefited? The working class? The movement? All women? The woman raising her three children on the salary of a clerical worker? The point is, victories were not definitive, in part because when targets were concrete, they were not very far reaching, and when the targets were overarching societal forces, they were difficult to combat. These issues were identical to those historically faced by the left, but for socialist feminists they were further complicated by the attempt to incorporate personal life into the political domain.

The complexity of purpose heightened the tension between theory and practice which already existed within the women's unions. At an extreme, the search for the correct theoretical target precluded activism. The result was immobility and eventual demoralization.

Another source of strain within the unions was the absence of a clear political identity, which in turn contributed to the lack of political cohesion. Socialist feminism was created through the tedious process of debate and exploration. Because the Principles of Unity were ineffective in screening members who had ideological differences, women with widely divergent politics were free to enter the unions.[24] This included infiltrators from the sectarian left whose objective was to take over or destroy the unions. As women within the unions in major metropolitan areas such as Baltimore, Boston, and Berkeley adopted a Marxist-Leninist perspective, their ideological shift created even greater political disunity. Further, the internal dissension drained and wearied even the most ardent union members and made them eager to *do* something productive. While Chicago was the only union to disband because of sectarian invasion, many experienced a midstream takeover attempt and were familiar with the destructiveness of virulent and divisive sectarian tactics.

In many ways the shift to the Marxist-Leninist perspective was part of women's search for answers, with many turning from the ambiguity of a socialist-feminist perspective to the illusion of certainty provided by the Marxist-Leninist line. Yet acting by the firmer guidelines of Marxism-Leninism served to intensify the contradictions between theory and practice. A perfect example was the final debate in BOWU before it dissolved. A working-class caucus formed in 1975, composed primarily of new, younger members. In 1976, in response to the union's demographic profile, they proposed that the union limit new membership solely to working-class and Third World women. Many long-standing members, believing that this went one step too far in a long journey into fantasy, left the union. One week later it folded.

In contrast, middle-class feminist organizations such as NOW accepted, even idealized, their middle-class status. NOW strove to guarantee the associated privileges of upward mobility and middle-class status to its membership. It is no accident that such an organization remained a viable political force in the 1970s, a time of recession and economic insecurity. While in part NOW was successful because it did not challenge the basic precepts and inequalities inherent in the American economic system, it also built a movement on the solid basis of the identity of a majority of its members. This does not imply that the women's unions should have adopted the NOW position on class, or that NOW's basic acceptance of the capitalist system was tenable. Nor does it imply that activists should not try to transcend their racial and class boundaries in organizing. It does imply that an organization must, without illusion, acknowledge what it is and who its members are. The unions could have accepted the realities of their membership and from there attempted to expand their base.

Precipitating Factors

The sources of strain affecting the women's unions do not altogether explain why virtually all of them collapsed in 1976 and 1977.[25] To understand this we must look at the National Conference on Socialist Feminism at Yellow Springs, Ohio, in 1975. The conference, though not causing the death of the unions, did crystallize the futility that many women were feeling about the union project.

The National Conference held the promise of catapulting the movement forward and forming a national organization. It was a rave success in terms of attendance: 1,600 women were registered, and more were turned away because of limited facilities. The event initially seemed like a dream come true—a national gathering of socialist feminists full of energy and ideas, the promise of a burgeoning movement with socialism on the horizon. All plenaries had to be held twice so everyone could attend. In many "excellent" workshops women generated and discussed ideas, in essence validating each other's perspectives, organizing efforts, and commitment to future work.

Despite the excitement of women gathered from all over the nation, the conference ultimately proved disappointing. It dispelled any illusions of demographic diversity: the participants represented the white middle-class base of the movement. Yet under its appearance of homogeneity, it became a forum for the ideological debates that had been raging within the whole of the progressive movement and had paralyzed the women's unions in particular. One long-time socialist feminist from Pittsburgh described the breakdown: "Soon into the conference we had to scrap a lot of the agendas and gather on the commons to hear mostly white women denounce the planners as a bunch of racists and then have open mike about that for hours."

Barbara Dudley, keynote speaker and a BOWU activist, analyzed the conference dynamics:

> Because the conference was supposedly a socialist-feminist conference, the irony and disrespect of calling a "socialist-feminist caucus" prevented what was probably the majority political position from being presented in a coherent manner in opposition to other caucus views. The anti-imperialist caucus, the Marxist-Leninist caucus, the third-world women's caucus, the lesbian caucus, the older women's caucus, etc. presented statements that were not always consistent with socialist feminism and were sometimes openly contradictory even to the basic principles of unity of the conference, and yet neither the planning committee nor any other groups systematically responded to these statements. The result was a growing confusion rather than clarity and unity about what socialist feminism is.[26]

The Yellow Springs conference confirmed that theoretical unity did not exist and in turn called the strength of the movement into question.

The battles at the conference were symptomatic of the tensions and fissures on the left. Within a year of the conference the unions began to fold. Most unions suffered the ideological divisions present at the conference. When several buckled under, others quickly followed in domino fashion. By this time a national network had been established, and it disseminated news of each union's collapse, demoralizing those still intact. One core activist in Berkeley-Oakland related the common feeling of despair:

> We were watching women's unions falling all over. . . . I remember feeling like all our cousins had cancer and died, and we were trying to hold on tenaciously and keep going. History was a larger force than us. . . . I remember watching and thinking "There's no way we're going to be able to sustain this. We're a victim of the same forces that all the other women's unions were, and we don't even have the alliance with women of the other women's unions to hold onto so we could rebuild again."

In sum, the search for the perfect political project as well as the attempt to diversify the women's unions and make them representative of their theoretical constituency immobilized the unions and called into question their reason for existence. The unions precariously balanced their uncertain identity—the tension between socialism and feminism—with their internal instability. Once the process of disintegration began after the Yellow Springs conference, it accelerated and proved impossible to reverse.

Conclusion

Socialist feminism has proved strategically difficult to implement —the women's unions provide the classic historical example. One major reason was the lack of a clear definition of political perspective and purpose. Bereft of a strategy, in the context of deep divisions about the very meaning of socialist feminism, the women's unions floundered, eventually tearing themselves asunder.

It was not working-class and Third World women who found the socialist-feminist perspective appealing but white, middle-class, educated women. This contradiction between the membership and the theoretical constituency was never successfully resolved by the unions and in fact proved to be key in undermining some of them. In order for an organization to survive, it must deal with what it is, who its members are, why it is not something else; and it must accept these circumstances, embracing the opportunities they represent rather than wallowing in self-blame, denial, and guilt—all paralyzing emotions. Otherwise, as happened so often, the members will continue to chastise themselves and leave the group vulnerable to takeover when someone shows up claiming to be a member of the dispossessed group and manipulates them through their paralysis. There has to be middle ground between recognizing the race and class biases of a perspective or an organization and flagellating a membership to the point that it is nonfunctional.

As an ideal, socialist feminism inspired many. The women's unions raised significant issues—twenty-four-hour quality day care, reproductive rights, unionization of women workers, and equal pay for equal work. Translated into the organizational form of unions, however, it proved disappointing and inadequate. The women's unions tried to bridge two separate movements but remained critics of both, never managing to transform either. In the union environment many women experienced acrimony and distrust, which undermined their feelings of satisfaction and political efficacy.

Even so, many union veterans described their women's union experience as the most important one in their political development. The unions were a place where political left-feminist women could work with generally like-minded women. They provided a forum for "defining the body politic" for thousands of women. They offered an environment where women could work independently of men, developing, through their participation in work groups, a variety of skills essential to political organizing.

Despite the lack of an organizational framework, socialist-feminist principles still inform the current political work of many women who were once women's union members. Many union veterans continue to be politically active in reproductive rights organizing, union struggles, the peace movement, NOW, National Lawyers Guild, and other progressive organizations and movements. In short, many women remain activists in various spheres, but they have not found an organized politics that replaces the constructive aspects of the unions.

Most of the women I interviewed continue to think of themselves as socialists and feminists, although few find occasion to identify themselves as such. Most women think the hyphenated term "socialist-feminist" a time-bound description and inappropriate in a conservative climate where any political identification to the left of "Democrat" is considered terrorist. The perspective they helped to create, however, continues to inform their professional and political work.

To return to a central question: is socialist feminism dead? It cannot be while so many women continue to think of themselves as both socialist and feminist, while journals like *Feminist Studies* publish vital research into socialist-feminist questions, and while innumerable organizations and movement activities are informed by a socialist-feminist politics.

Nevertheless the attempt of the women's unions to implement socialist-feminist theory sadly failed. In my opinion, one cannot simply dismiss their collapse as historical circumstance; riddled with the same internal contradictions, I doubt they would have made much more impact at some other moment.

There are lessons to be learned that apply to other movements today. The union veterans I spoke with emphasized over and over several lessons from their own history that are important for contemporary socialist-feminist politics. First, theory development alone is not a sufficient basis for political activity; at the same time, strategy needs to be specific and tactics concrete. Second, the political base of an organization must be acknowledged. Ties to a theoretical constituency cannot be superficially imposed; to be effective, a political body must be directly connected to and involved in the community it is trying to organize.

The most striking lesson to me is the need to record history and educate those who did not share it. We must continue to inform others about our mistakes as well as our successes, about the exploitative nature of capitalism, the horrors of American foreign policy, and our own role in oppressing other people. Treating newcomers uninformed about politics and/or history with disdain and mistrust is simply self-indulgent and counterproductive. It is important not to dismiss someone who does not know the significance of 1956, has never heard of SDS (let alone the Hungarian revolution), or cannot say for certain on which side America fought in Vietnam. Without compassion, humility, and effective outreach, organizations become insular, living in a world their members create, remote from the reality they are trying to influence. Although activists tire of repeatedly trying to enlighten comrades and potential allies, the struggle does not end —education is the very essence of social change.

Notes

Acknowledgments: Many thanks to the women's union veterans who generously shared their personal and political wisdom with me. Unreferenced quotations throughout this paper are from interviews with them. Thanks also to the following people who read earlier drafts of this article and pushed me to clarify my argument as well as my political perspective: Barbara Baran, Andrew Bundy, McGeorge Bundy, Becky Cannon, Barbara Epstein, Barbara Haber, Arlie Hochschild, Andy Kivel, Judy MacLean, Ilene Philipson, Neil Smelser, Vicki Smith, Judy Stacey, Susan Staggenborg, Ron Zboray, and of course the Socialist Review collective.

1. Red Apple Collective, "Socialist-Feminist Women's Unions: Past and Present," *Socialist Review* No. 38 (March–April 1978): 37–58.

2. Without the left, the unions would not have existed, and the left continues to be a critical force in making room for progressive activism of all kinds today. What I am trying to describe is the way in which the unions related to the left.

3. I use the term "women's liberation movement" to identify a certain tendency within the women's movement as a whole. The WLM grew more directly out of the antiwar and student movements and was more radical than the primary existing feminist institutions of the time (e.g., NOW). It was absorbed by the larger movement and no longer distinct, except as a tendency, by about 1973.

4. These data are not representative—they are biased toward the more stable, visible, longer-lived unions, about which information is available.

5. At roughly the same time, other socialist-feminist organizations that were not unions were founded, such as the New American Movement (NAM), which included men, and Bread and Roses (see Chapter 6).

6. The average age in 1975 of women I interviewed was twenty-nine.

7. Barbara Ehrenreich, "Life without Father: Reconsidering Socialist-Feminist Theory," *Socialist Review* No. 73 (January–February 1984): 49; also Chapter 10 in this book.

8. Barbara Ehrenreich, "Speech," *Socialist Revolution* No. 26 (October–December 1975): 92 (original emphasis).

9. Ibid., p. 86.

10. Jo Freeman, *The Politics of Women's Liberation* (New York: David McKay, 1975), 242.

11. For good discussion of this perspective, see Adele Clark and Alice Wolfson, "Socialist Feminism and Reproductive Rights," *Socialist Review* No. 78 (November–December 1984): 110–20.

12. Barbara Epstein coined the quoted phrase.

13. Unions to adopt the umbrella structure included the Chicago Women's Liberation Union, Santa Cruz Women's Union, and Los Angeles Women's Liberation Union. Membership organizations included the Baltimore Women's Union, San Francisco Women's Union, and Berkeley-Oakland Women's Union.

14. "A Critical History of the CWLU," n.d.

15. This information on the struggles in the CWLU is from Suzanne Staggenborg, "Patterns of Collective Action in the Abortion Conflict: An Organizational Analysis of the Pro-Choice Movement" (Ph.D. diss., Northwestern University, 1985), 94.

16. Many of the women's unions then in existence sent delegations to the conference with Vietnamese women sponsored by the Women's Strike for Peace, in Canada in 1973. This connection with the Vietnamese women had lasting effects on the conference participants, encouraging them to continue their antiimperialist work.

17. Ann Hunter Popkin, "Bread and Roses: An Early Moment in the Development of Socialist Feminism" (Ph.D. diss., Brandeis University, 1978); see also Chapter 6 in this book.

18. For a careful, extensive discussion of this issue, see Joreen's "Tyranny of Structurelessness," in A. Koedt, E. Levine, and A. Rapone, eds., *Radical Feminism* (New York: Quadrangle Books, 1973), 285–99.

19. Inex Martinez, "So You Want Sisters to Unite," *Woman: A Journal of Liberation*, 1972, p. 50.

20. "Socialist-Feminist Conference—San Diego, 3/24," *Berkeley/Oakland Women's Union Newsletter* 2, no. 3 (1974): 9.

21. Dair L. Gellespie, Barbara Gruen, Carol Hatch, Carrie Joy, Ann Leffler, Elinor Lerner Ratner, Laura McKinley, Stacey Oliker, Margaret Polatnick, Barbara Schemel, and Nancy Walker, "Toward a Feminist Perspective: A Preliminary Analysis," n.d., p. S5.

22. Red Apple Collective, "Socialist-Feminist Women's Unions."

23. Discussion paper within CWLU, p. 3, n.d.

24. For example, in Half of Brooklyn members ranged from steadfast socialists to women who "wanted to be convinced that 'being political' was worthwhile."

25. Baltimore Women's Union was the real exception; it continued to meet until 1982. It experienced the same divisions as other unions in 1975; however, although the group size diminished, it continued to work relatively harmoniously on projects ranging from political education ("Feminist Fridays") to organizing against street violence aimed at women.

26. Barbara Dudley, "Report on the Conference," *Socialist Revolution* No. 26 (October–December 1975), p. 109.

8   The Rise and Fall of Feminist Organizations in the 1970s
Dayton as a Case Study

Judith Sealander and Dorothy Smith

In 1972 the United States Congress passed the Equal Rights Amendment (ERA), *Ms.* magazine published its first issue, and women ran in the Boston marathon for the first time. A decade of federal congressional and executive decision-making had created a new legal structure that seemed to nourish feminism. Who could doubt that the movement would continue to make gains when in less than a decade it had achieved the Equal Pay Act, affirmative action programs, Title VII and Title IX, the Equal Employment Opportunity Commission, and other programs? Who could doubt given the overwhelming majority favoring the amendment in the Washington vote, that state ratification of the ERA would take place quickly and easily? Who could doubt, given the continued flood of women into the work force, that wage disparities would soon begin to disappear? Who could doubt that by the 1980s the prospects for feminism would seem even brighter?

What feminist would have thought that instead, in 1981, even such a staunch supporter of the women's movement as Barbara Ehrenreich would write that feminism had "peaked" and that the forces of antifeminism were becoming ever more powerful?[1] What feminist in 1972 would have predicted a decade's bitter battle and final defeat for the ERA? What feminist

Source: This article is reprinted from *Feminist Studies* 12, no. 2 (Summer 1986), pp. 321–41, by permission of the authors. Copyright © 1986, Judith Sealander and Dorothy Smith.

would have predicted the overwhelming reelection in 1984 of a president who headed an administration that openly derided the need for affirmative action programs and lobbied for a constitutional amendment banning abortion?

Feminists, then, do not enjoy the luxury to wax proud over victories or to be nostalgic over past battles lost or won. Instead, we need the kind of clear insight into the history of the movement that derives from careful analysis and documented research. Yet such research is not readily available. In 1968 feminist protest at the annual Miss America contest got front-page coverage with stories of man-hating bra burners. More than twenty years later, much of the analysis of contemporary feminism has remained on that condescending and inaccurate level. Although a few scholars have attempted to study the gains and failures of contemporary feminism, their articles remain tentative and speculative, more concerned with the origins than the nature of the movement, and in need of the concrete detail a case study can provide.[2]

Why choose Dayton, Ohio, for such a case study? First, a wealth of evidence exists there. Due to the aggressive collecting policies of a Wright State University archivist, the complete organizational files of three important feminist groups have been saved and inventoried. Membership lists in the files provide the names of many people to contact for interviews. The extensive written and oral evidence about the history of feminist organizations in Dayton may, in fact, be unparalleled. So far as we know, the records of contemporary feminist organizations in most other cities are still held in private hands or have been lost or destroyed.

Second, the fact that the records of Dayton Women's Liberation, the Dayton Women's Center, and Dayton Women Working sit in cardboard boxes at a university archive rather than in cabinets in organizational offices suggests a second reason to choose Dayton, Ohio, for a historical case study. The decade 1970–80 exists as a meaningful and completed period in the history of contemporary Dayton feminism, for three major organizations began and ended within that period. A look at their rise and fall raises questions and suggests answers about the nature of contemporary feminism that would be more difficult to derive from an examination of existing organizations.[3]

Third, since the early twentieth century Dayton has shared with Muncie, Indiana, a reputation as a typical small American city. With decidedly unrandom regularity, pollsters in the 1970s continued to choose this city of roughly 200,000 citizens for random sampling. It was a frequent test market, and its population was given sneak previews of new movies, soaps, and underarm deodorants. Pollster Richard Scammon claimed in 1980 that the average American voter was "a forty-seven-year-old housewife from the outskirts of Dayton, Ohio, whose husband is a machinist."[4]

Moreover, Dayton typifies the problems of many American towns and communities trying to make the often painful shift from an industrial to a service economy. Although manufacturing in Dayton declined by over 20 percent during the 1970s, and one company alone laid off more than 14,000 workers, Dayton achieved a net gain for the decade of 17,000 new jobs. Most of these, however, were, "women's jobs"—jobs in the lower-paying service sectors. In 1950, Dayton possessed the highest number of color television sets per capita in the country. It was a city filled with people whose healthy paychecks, earned in the area's auto, tire, and printing factories, made the purchase of such luxuries possible. By 1970, however, Dayton no longer enjoyed that enviable image of a city of highly paid, skilled union workers. Service sector work had filled the gaps caused by the closing of plants but had not fattened wallets. The new "typical" Dayton worker was a female bank teller, not a unionized autoworker.

For all these reasons, a history of feminism in Dayton can provide an examination of organizational success and failure in a city widely viewed as far more typical than New York, Chicago, San Francisco, or Boston—the four "movement" cities which, to date, remain the focus of most journalistic comment about feminism. Such a history can also provide an examination of feminist organizations in a city that typified, sometimes even prophesied, the changes in the national economy that had the most direct and important implications for female roles and status.

The Early Women's Movement

The women's movement arrived in Dayton in September 1969 via Ann Arbor, Michigan—not, as might have been expected, via nearby Antioch College in Yellow Springs, Ohio. Cheryl Radican, a University of Cincinnati student, had herself newly arrived in Dayton, accompanying her divinity school student husband. While commuting back and forth to Cincinnati to finish her degree, Radican also began to write for Dayton's recently established underground newspaper, the *Minority Report*, a left-liberal newsletter staffed by volunteers who wrote the stories and then sold the issues on street corners and area college campuses. At a national underground newspaper conference in Ann Arbor in the summer of 1969, Radican met other women angry about their subordinate staff roles. As had happened at earlier meetings of student radicals, the women at the newspaper conference formed a separate caucus and told the men to stay away.

Radican, "filled with the power of sisterhood," enthusiastically returned home and formed Dayton's first consciousness-raising (CR) group.[5]

This first group grew rapidly by word of mouth. By January 1970 a new CR group was forming every month, first in Dayton neighborhoods and then on nearby college campuses such as Antioch and Wright State University in Dayton. The typical woman in these groups was not a radical, even though Radican and many of her friends saw themselves as social activists, committed especially to protesting the war in Vietnam. A member of a CR group was likely to be a white "liberal Democrat," college educated, married, and middle class. In 1969 she was far more likely to be in school or at home than at work full time, though she was not necessarily at home with small children.[6] At least one-quarter of the women in the first CR groups were middle-aged, self-described *"Better Homes and Gardens* housewives . . . casualties of the 1950s."[7] Radican first organized her friends; not surprisingly, these friends were often students, wives of ministers or divinity students, wives of teachers or college professors, and women active in the League of Women Voters and church children's education groups.[8]

The experience of joining CR groups, however, often proved radicalizing to these nonradical women. In the mid-1960s hundreds of similarly earnest middle-class white women had gone south demanding civil rights for blacks. They had expected opposition; they had not expected to be treated as inferiors and maids by their own co-workers and as "loose" women by the press. Similarly, in 1970 members of three CR groups in Dayton traveled to Columbus, Ohio, to take part in a large pro-abortion rally. They returned to find themselves described by the local media as "fourteen braless, makeup-less women." In fact, as one participant exclaimed, "We were all carefully dressed. One of us was in a mink coat and open-toed shoes. . . . They [reporters] just kept asking if the women were wearing bras."[9]

By mid-1970 these kinds of patronizing experiences had convinced women in several CR groups that they had to unite, take their case to the public, and work with more than the ten to twelve women in their own groups. Dayton Women's Liberation (DWL) emerged from these discussions. It quickly established a phone bank, staffed by members, to answer questions about feminism. It set up a speakers' bureau; members traveled to high schools, police stations, and—on a regular basis—the television studio where Phil Donahue, still a local Dayton talk show host, filmed his programs. Although the organization issued a pamphlet denouncing the Vietnam War, Dayton Women's Liberation generally continued to emphasize CR participation rather than political activism. And most CR groups continued to explore personal issues, such as relationships with mothers, children, and husbands. By 1975, however, two other feminist organizations that were more concerned with programs to change politics and society—the Dayton Women's Center and Dayton Women Working—had joined DWL.

In 1973 the City Commission granted Dayton Women's Liberation funds to establish a "neighborhood Women's Center, focusing on the needs of women in the surrounding area . . . establishing a place for women to explore common concerns, to share and expand their knowledge." The proposal outlined several programs: self-help classes, a walk-in center and meeting place for women, an advocacy and referral service for women in need, political and personal counseling, a lending library, child care for women using the center, and educational programs.[10]

Dayton Women Working initially was a product of one Women's Center member's efforts to engage in "political counseling and action."[11] In 1975, frustrated that her male colleagues in the Dayton chapter of the socialist New American Movement (NAM) did not take women's employment issues seriously, Sherrie Holmes organized the first Dayton chapter of the National Organization for Women (NOW) and drew up plans for a Women in the Work Force Task Force. Within months the NOW task force decided to establish itself as a separate organization, choosing in April 1975 the name Dayton Women Working (DWW).

Dayton Women Working, begun—to protest her male colleagues' inattention—by a woman who saw herself as a socialist and radical, linked the women's movement in Dayton to the new left and linked Dayton to a national network of feminist groups interested in workplace problems. In fact, DWW helped to create that network. In 1977 it was a founding member of the National Women's Employment Project (NWEP), a consortium of six working women's organizations. The NWEP, launched with a $25,000 grant from the Rockefeller Family Fund, chose to emphasize the problems of office workers and to focus first on an employer notorious for discrimination against women clerical workers: the banking industry.[12] Dayton Women Working joined with the older and better-established consortium members, especially Boston's 9 to 5, and adopted this emphasis.

The Feminist Organizations

What did these three groups accomplish? How did they fail? In what ways did their troubles illustrate problems faced by other feminist groups in other cities? What is their legacy? Examination of programs, finances, and membership can provide partial answers to these questions.

Organized feminism in Dayton in the 1970s achieved community-wide visibility with well-planned campaigns and successful projects. Because it did not succeed in anchoring itself to a stable base of committed dues-paying members, however, it suffered continual money and membership problems.

The Women's Center rented a two-story frame house on North Main Street near downtown Dayton in October 1973. Cleaning, painting, and floor-waxing parties generated enthusiasm and prepared the building for occupancy. More than a hundred women attended a grand opening party in January 1974.[13] Within months the center had a full program of activities, including classes in self-defense, women's legal rights, careers, health, sexuality, auto mechanics, pottery, and yoga. Two therapy groups met weekly. There were regular community forums on topics of interest to women, such as day-care options and married women's property rights. Building on the Dayton Women's Liberation tradition, the staff compiled information for a referral service for women in need of community services.

Several women's groups met at the center, including a parent support group, a socialist-feminist discussion group, the Women on Rape Task Force, and a large lesbian organization called Sappho's Army. The center's four paid staff members, as well as members of its collective, accepted invitations to speak at local universities, church groups, Parent Teacher Association meetings, social workers' associations, and women's clubs. The Women's Center began to issue a newsletter, and stories about the center appeared in eight local newspapers and on two radio and two television stations. After the center had been open for two months, the collective reported that over three hundred women had used the center's facilities.[14]

By 1975 the Women's Center programs had expanded significantly. Hundreds of women used its facilities for classes, counseling and feminist therapy, and activities and discussion groups. The center's referral service thrived, passing along the names of feminist doctors, lawyers, and welfare workers. It also provided advice to women about employment and legal rights, and maintained regularly updated files on educational opportunities, job listings, and financial aid.[15] In 1975 the center opened its extremely popular Daycare Parents' Cooperative.[16] The Women's Center's many programs thus made feminism quite visible in Dayton. It "was a smorgasbord of services," and during its seven-year history approximately two thousand Dayton women a year helped themselves.[17]

Dayton Women Working also spread the feminist message with initially successful, attention-getting projects. Member organizations of the NWEP —Women Employed in Chicago, 9 to 5 in Boston, Dayton Women Working, Cleveland Women Working, Women Organized for Employment in

San Francisco, and Women Office Workers in New York—agreed to monitor and investigate the effectiveness of post-1964 federal antidiscrimination laws and executive orders.[18] NWEP's own effectiveness suffered from serious internal disputes about equitable distribution of grant monies, which led to the departure by October 1977 of Women Employed in Chicago. Nevertheless, the five remaining organizations set to work on a national investigation of conditions for female clerical workers in banks.[19]

Dayton Women Working plunged enthusiastically into the project, which was designed to provide both a case study of employment discrimination against women and a study of the degree of employer compliance with antidiscrimination laws. The group's analysis of the banking industry of Dayton was to be its most important project and most significant success. It soon learned that three-quarters of the employees of the three major banks in Dayton were women, and more than 89 percent of these women worked in poorly paid office and clerical jobs. Using bank affirmative action reports, surveys and interviews with female bank employees, annual reports, banking directories, and other documents in the public record, Dayton Women Working printed a pamphlet that charged, among other things, that major Dayton banks were not seriously committed to equal employment opportunity. As one letter to a bank stated, banks were limiting their affirmative action efforts to plans that were "inadequate" and out of date.[20] Banks, as holders of federal deposits, had the status of federal contractors and as such had to fulfill federal guidelines regarding affirmative action in employment. The Labor Department, as the agency responsible for enforcement of contract compliance, agreed in 1978 to investigate Dayton Women Working's charges that the Third National Bank, First National Bank, and Winters National Bank of Dayton practiced employment discrimination against women.[21]

The banking study generated much local publicity, and open meetings attracted large crowds.[22] Women employed in banks began to mail in anonymous testimonials. Citing fear of job reprisal, one woman (who, like most bank employees, asked that her name not be used) wrote: "I used to be a person who was hurt that I was paid so little. I thought there was something wrong with me, that I was being singled out. However, I recently learned that this is not the case, that many of the women in my department that have been with the bank a long time, make even less than I do."[23]

Barred from distributing materials within banking offices, members of Dayton Women Working stood on downtown street corners handing out some two thousand questionnaires to women office workers headed toward banks. Women who filled out the twenty-six-item questionnaires used a point system to rate their jobs: a "yes" equaled two points, a "not sure" one point, and a "no" zero points. Questions included "Are you permitted to discuss salaries with co-workers?" "Are there training programs available within your bank?" "Are women promoted at the same rate as men?" "Is there an effective grievance procedure to deal with discrimination?" Banks rating fewer than twenty points were "not good places to work. Watch out or call D.W.W."[24] In May of 1980, U.S. Department of Labor investigators charged Third National Bank with a "pattern of discrimination against its minority and women employees" and in initial review documents assessed nearly one million dollars in back pay for 110 employees who had "suffered the effects of past discrimination."[25]

However, by 1980 Dayton Women Working, on the verge of disbanding, was unable to capitalize on this victory. Despite its many programs and its contact with thousands of Dayton women who used its services, the Dayton Women's Center was equally unable to use the visibility and success of many of its projects to enter the next decade as a strong and growing feminist organization. Most Dayton Women's Liberation CR groups had ceased to meet as early as 1975. Personal and ideological conflicts, declining activism, small membership, and recurrent financial crises were all problems that plagued organized feminism in Dayton.

A staff of four paid workers ran the Women's Center and oversaw its programs. A Women's Center collective, with a rotating leadership, provided that staff with program and policy direction. Almost from the beginning, conflicts marred relationships between collective and staff. Even more important, the collective itself often divided into two warring camps. One group identified itself as socialist and saw women as an oppressed class to be organized as part of a larger movement to transform society. The other group defined itself as feminist, wanted an independent women's movement, saw women's issues as most important, and feared a close association with male-led politics. The conflict became bitter and open early in 1977 when some NAM members, including men, used the printing facilities at the Women's Center. Angry memos flew between the two factions, and collective meetings became battlegrounds.[26]

In retrospect, Kathy Ellison, who judged herself to be a neutral collective member, felt that the fights were more personal than political: "From time to time these great political struggles would happen. I never thought the conflict was real; I felt it was more personality and power struggles. For whatever reasons, these strong-minded women didn't get along, and they had to imbue their interpersonal fights with issue overtones."[27] But Robin Suits, a longtime member of both the collective and the staff, perceived that in the women's movement the personal *was* political: "As your consciousness got raised, and you began to see things in more political ways, you got a sense that there was only one right way. Everybody had a slightly different way, and the groups became smaller and more splintered over the most ridiculous things."[28]

Group Process and Leadership

Both the Women's Center and Dayton Women's Liberation, each with at least some connections to student activism or the new left, adopted the antihierarchical, antileader stances of these other movements. Members of SDS, for instance, proclaimed: "Let the people decide." A rhetoric of shared decision-making, however, did not prevent many new left groups from following a strong leader. An emphasis on democracy, in fact, contributed to split many groups into competing factions. And Dayton feminist groups were not unique. With so many women's problems demanding attention, disagreement readily surfaced about which problems were most important. By 1970 feminists across the country were debating priority lists for problems and challenging each other's analyses of the causes of sexism. Radical feminist groups such as the New York Radical Feminists, the Feminists, and the Redstockings emphasized the universality of male oppression. Socialist-feminist groups such as Bread and Roses considered class structure important too. Male domination could not be explained or countered in universalist terms. More moderate groups like NOW called for neither drastic changes in traditional marriage and child-rearing patterns nor for an economic revolution. Instead, they urged legal, educational, and employment opportunity reforms; changes in states' property rights laws; the passage of the ERA; and equal access for women to schools and jobs.[29]

The emphasis on equality and democracy itself caused tension. In Dayton Women's Liberation, for instance, women selected CR groups by lot. The random choice procedure obviously emphasized common sisterhood and equality, but it also meant that groups were formed of women who sometimes had little in common. An early member, Carrie LaBriola, recalled: "I actively disliked some of the people [in my group]." It meant, for some, that discussions of controversial topics, such as abortion, were "too painful" and ceased. Here too the Dayton experiences echoed those in other cities. In New York one disgruntled member called the Feminists' emphasis on egalitarianism "an anti-individual mania." By 1970, the Feminists' lot system for division of tasks had become more elaborate; new rules sought to prevent the formation of cliques or the emergence of "stars." But instead of bringing egalitarian harmony, the system contributed to conflicts that caused many members to resign.[30]

Painful discussions and memberships splintered into factions were not problems for Dayton Women Working, but apathy was. Noreen Willhelm and Sherrie Holmes, the two driving forces behind Dayton Women Working, were white political activists in their twenties. The average member of Dayton Women Working was also a young white woman.[31] Nevertheless, neither Willhelm nor Holmes led lives similar to those of their members. Neither had ever married; both had borne babies out of wedlock. Both lived in communal houses, had come of age in the late 1960s as anti–Vietnam War protesters, and had ties with leftist politics. In fact, to blur the differences between them and the more traditional members, Wilhelm and Holmes once discussed wearing phony wedding rings to meetings.[32] Kathy Ellison, a friend of Holmes and a member of Dayton Women Working while a law student, remembered that Holmes and Willhelm made decisions to avoid certain feminist issues that might "alienate your average secretary or clerk." She recalled that abortion, socialism, and lesbianism, for instance, were not to be debated.

The leaders of Dayton Women Working staged many imaginative events that grabbed newspaper headlines. For instance, the group's Pettiest Boss awards earned the organization plenty of free local publicity. Contenders for one Petty Boss contest included the head of a jewelry firm who used clear nail polish on his fingernails and had his secretary paint the right-hand nails, a boss who required an employee to go to his home to feed his dog, a physician who sent his bookkeeper downtown to buy a plunger to fix a clogged toilet, and a businessman who required his secretary to check him over carefully each day to see that he was properly dressed and that his socks matched. Charles Moody, the physician, received his award when several Dayton Women Working members showed up at his offices unannounced to deliver a toilet plunger with a rose attached.[33]

Still, despite the efforts of Holmes and other spokespersons who generated publicity and avoided controversial topics such as lesbianism, Dayton Women Working leaders failed to recruit an active membership. A memo Holmes sent to the national NAM program coordinating board illustrated a major problem. Rather than viewing her members as friends and compatriots, she seemed to see them as "the clerical sector." Unsuccessfully urging the national NAM leadership to support her efforts, she argued that "this [Dayton] project is important because (1) it is an important part of a nation-wide test of the organizing potential of clericals, (2) it is important for N.A.M. to build ties with this sector, (3) it is important to build ties with other clerical organizers."[34]

Of course, historical examples abound of successful movements in which leaders were not friends with their followers. Holmes did not have to be "your average secretary or clerk"; she did not have to marry and share her members' personal lives or moral values. But she did have to build ties. She did have to persuade members that Dayton Women Working deserved their loyalty, support, and dedication; that the organization could be a vehicle for change in their lives.

In fact, DWW leaders did build some ties with other clerical organizers, government officials, and private philanthropists. But ties with their own members, who became accustomed to having programs delivered to them ready-made, were the crucial and neglected ones. Phrases in Holmes's letter echoed those used to justify projects such as the 1965 Economic Research and Action Projects (ERAP) of SDS, meant to build ties with the "urban poverty sector." The northern college student radicals who decamped to urban poverty in 1965 and 1966 were often genuinely committed to helping; they worked hard, received no salary, and lived on peanut butter. And some ERAP projects, such as those in Boston and Cleveland, succeeded in organizing welfare mothers, sowing the seeds for a national welfare rights movement. But many ERAP projects failed at least partially because their leaders were unable to communicate a sense of shared interest and mission with the often confused, sometimes hostile, residents of urban ghettoes.[35]

Holmes's rhetoric echoed that of some early twentieth-century American feminists. Alice Paul, for instance, had tried during the 1920s to make the Woman's Party a "vanguard" party, promoting absolute equality for women, including "industrial equality" for women workers. But few workers joined the Woman's Party; it remained a small organization of well-educated women, run in an authoritarian fashion by Paul and her coterie.[36] Sherrie Holmes was not another feminist generation's version of Alice Paul, however. She was no blue blood sporting graduate degrees. She defined herself as a leftist but had no master plan for Dayton Women Working to emerge as a vanguard party. Still, her attempts to forge links between leftist activists and women workers echoed Paul's. And like Paul, she seemed to possess greater skill in constructing phrases strategically calculated to appeal to leftists than in attracting politically moderate women workers.

Of course, Dayton Women Working was part of a larger network and linked its efforts to those of the NWEP. In each of the NWEP chapters, Noreen Willhelm argued, one woman *was* the organization. If Sherrie Holmes "was" Dayton Women Working, Helen Williams "was" Cleveland Women Working, and Karen Nussbaum "was" Boston 9 to 5. In that respect, at least, the entire NWEP resembled the Woman's Party, in which "[Alice Paul] is the party."[37] These strong, intelligent women took on big challenges. But in many cases, not just that of Dayton Women Working, the romance of battles against American banking czars or federal power brokers wooed them away from the tedium of membership drives, and they, with feminist leaders from past decades, reproduced organizations without sufficient grassroots strength. And women office workers, socialized already by job and family to be deferential and quiet, were often silent when they confronted their own organizations' authority figures. Unlike meetings at the Dayton Women's Center, which often boiled with charges, countercharges, and both good and bad feelings, Dayton Women Working held its meetings punctually at the end of workdays and followed Robert's Rules.

The Feminist Legacy

Thousands of women utilized the services of the Women's Center; only a small percentage joined the collective and worked hard to keep the center a vital force in the community. Over two hundred women filled out membership cards and joined Dayton Women Working, but far fewer came regularly to meetings. Many did not even pay the nominal three-dollar yearly dues. If these groups had focused on grassroots organization, would they have enjoyed greater success? A great influx of new members would not automatically have assured strength and stability. New left organizing provides a cautionary example. In 1965, spurred by the escalation of the war in Vietnam, thousands of new members flooded into SDS, but such quick growth, Todd Gitlin has argued did not really help the organization. All the new members and concomitant attention changed SDS into a mass movement too quickly, with leaders who increasingly became media stars, their speeches were shaped by television rather than constituency demands.[38]

Hundreds, even thousands, of active, committed members would not have ensured the longevity of Dayton Women Working, the Women's Center, or Dayton Women's Liberation. But such a membership could have provided a potential for strength, and through dues and donations it certainly could have provided funds. Lack of money became, along with membership recruitment and involvement, a serious problem for Dayton feminist groups as well as their national umbrellas. On both a national and a local level, leaders depended heavily on monies granted by the federal government or private philanthropies. When those funding sources disappeared, so too did the organizations they fostered. In that sense, feminist organizations in Dayton were not just outgrowths of 1960s activism or products of the women's movement. They were also legacies of the national programs that had made federal monies available for local community action projects.

During the mid- and late 1960s Dayton received large amounts of federal money under one of Lyndon Johnson's Great Society programs, Model Cities. Healthy Model Cities grants continued under the Nixon administration. Locally elected Priority Boards made recommendations to the City Commission about projects in their neighborhoods to be funded by Model Cities and in November 1973 the Dayton City Commission, using federal Model City monies, awarded the Women's Center $15,000.[39] Comprehensive Employment and Training Act (CETA) and Volunteers in Service to America (VISTA) money provided part-time staff and interns. Between 1976 and 1980 the great bulk of monies available to Dayton Women Working were federal funds. CETA paid the salaries of its full-time director-organizer, its full-time program-organizer, and its part-time office manager.[40]

Between 1978 and 1979 the VISTA program provided funds for a VISTA worker who was, ironically, installed at Dayton Women Working offices with federal money in order to "allow constituents to develop their leadership skills and make decisions" affecting Dayton Women Working. The paid VISTA worker was to "encourage members to volunteer their time."[41]

Dayton churches and church districts, such as the United Church of Christ and the Miami Presbytery, provided a few thousand dollars to Dayton Women Working and the Women's Center. By 1980, however, both organizations found that they "had worn out their welcome" at these private charities, which were inclined to give only one or two years' seed money.[42] In both organizations, membership dues provided only token support.

By the end of 1980, Dayton Women's Liberation, Dayton Women Working, and Dayton Women's Center had died. A preliminary autopsy would suggest that the causes of death included excessive dependence on federal funding and ambitious programs that eclipsed grassroots organizing. Such an autopsy would also note changes in political and economic climates; Dayton organizations were certainly not the only feminist groups in the country to find funding sources less sympathetic and to experience a backlash against feminism. Finally, an autopsy would indicate that these three organizations died when subjected to the great stresses inherent in any social movement as it ages and moves from initial dreams and optimism to long-range realistic assessment. As Noreen Willhelm realized in retrospect, Dayton Women Working leaders "did get caught up in our myth before we had even created it."[43] Sherrie Holmes had "this initial fantasy about the Women's Center, that all we had to do was provide this place and women who wanted to change society would all come there and continue to build the movement."[44] Clearly, the slow building of a movement proved to be a harder task.

The task was complicated by the fact that organized feminism in Dayton, in common with organized feminism in other cities, failed to embrace working-class or minority women in any significant numbers, even though the Women's Center house was located in one of Dayton's few truly mixed-race neighborhoods. The leaders of the groups were white and overwhelmingly middle-class women who sometimes seemed unaware of their own patronizing attitude when they tried to organize even white working-class women. Not surprisingly, meaningful contacts with the black community proved difficult. Moreover, as Cheryl Radican explained, "We [in feminist organizations] felt a lot of hesitation" about recruiting blacks. Radican and others who sympathized with the civil rights movement "did not want to drive a wedge into their black unity."[45] These white women, who had little direct contact with the black community and few friendships with blacks, seemed to feel that for black women, issues of race superseded those of sex. The fact that many black women might have agreed with such an assessment did not negate the fact that few were consulted.

Also complicating the task of building a movement was the fact that neither Dayton Women Working nor the Women's Center achieved a clear focus and sense of purpose. Dayton Women Working did not see itself as a union for clerical workers; in fact, its leaders made little attempt to contact leaders of Dayton unions. The union leadership in Dayton, a town where traditional heavy-industry unions like the Steel Workers and the United Auto Workers still dominated, returned the disdain. But Dayton Women Working did not really see itself functioning as a women's center for women clerical workers, providing a place for women office workers to come together to talk about home lives, social relationships, and struggles at work.

Interestingly, the NWEP, which Dayton Women Working had helped create, did solve the dilemma of focus by forming a firm alliance with the union movement. Although it too ceased to exist formally in 1979, NWEP became, under the new name Working Women, a project of the National Association of Office Workers. In 1981 Working Women and the Service Employees International Union formed District 925, specifically to organize office workers.[46]

The Women's Center, by 1977 torn by dissension, had its own problems setting an agenda. Frequent and bitter controversies erupted. Some collective members thought the center should be more openly socialist; others sought to downplay leftist politics. Some wanted a more visible role for lesbians; some did not. Even the wildly successful day-care co-op caused conflict as babies and children crowded into space formerly devoted to other programs. This disunity led to angry resignations, and statements of "exhaustion" were commonplace.[47] Many of the young, middle-class women who had given their energies to Dayton Women Working and the Women's Center began to direct their energies elsewhere. Many took full-time jobs; some went to graduate or law school; others started families.

Conclusion

This analysis chronicles the rise and fall of feminist organizations in Dayton. It does not, however, chronicle the rise and fall of feminism itself. Although none of the three organizations here examined survived, not all their ideas and programs disappeared. In that sense, their deaths were not a failure for feminism. Dayton Women Working played a central role in stirring interest among national unions in organizing office workers, and District 925 exists partly as Dayton Women Working's legacy. Although disillusioned with infighting or specific projects, no members of these Dayton feminist groups contacted for interviews were disillusioned with feminism itself. In fact, they have continued to live independent, self-confident lives centered by feminism. Some entered traditional male-only occupations: one, for instance, became a forester; another, an engineer. Others continued to work long hours for feminist causes, staffing rape hotlines and battered women's shelters. Moreover, in important ways, feminism in Dayton itself had become, as one Women's Center member put it, "mainstreamed" by the late 1970s.[48] Other groups with fewer radical connections began to offer some of the services first provided by the three feminist groups. For instance, the Dayton YWCA opened its Career Development Center, offering seminars and workshops for women workers, and a city-funded Victim-Witness Project offered advocacy and counseling for rape victims.[49]

But mainstreaming always imposes a price. In the late 1980s many of the objectives of organized feminism in Dayton during the 1970s remain goals and dreams. Most Dayton women clerical workers remain unorganized and poorly paid. Women still have problems with child care, health care, and the host of other issues that concerned the Women's Center. And many federally funded programs meant to help women cope with those problems have disappeared. An organization called the Dayton Women's Center is still listed in the Dayton phone book, but those calling its number hear the voices of members of a local "Right to Life" group. In 1980 the center's collective sent a letter to the women on its mailing list, announcing its "difficult decision" to close. "We need new strategies, new weapons, and new blood," the letter writers concluded.[50] In the 1980s, many Dayton feminists were still seeking those visions, tools, and energies.

The Principal Informants

KATIE EGART, active in antiwar student politics in the 1960s and a 1972 graduate of the University of Dayton, worked for the Community Schools Project of the Dayton Model Cities Program during the time she was involved with Dayton Women's Liberation. She is now an engineer.

KATHY ELLISON, a Smith College graduate, was a law student in her twenties when she became a member of the Women's Center collective. She is now a Dayton attorney who started Dayton's first all-woman law firm.

JAN GRIESINGER, a graduate of the United Theological Seminary, became a civil rights activist in Dayton in the 1960s and was a self-described leftist. In her thirties she became involved in the women's movement and is still involved through her work in the peace movement and the United Church of Christ.

SHERRIE HOLMES, a self-described social activist, was in her early twenties when she became a central figure in the Dayton women's movement. She has since moved to California, where she has worked as a grant administrator.

CARRIE LABRIOLA, was a full-time mother with two infants when she attended Dayton Women's Liberation meetings. She is now a newspaper reporter in Dayton.

MARY MORGAN, had been active in Democratic party politics and was in her mid-forties when she began attending CR groups. A schoolteacher, she was married and living in a Dayton suburb. She is now working to develop a rural women's community near Athens, Ohio.

CHERYL RADICAN, a college student in her twenties when she became a key organizer of Dayton Women's Liberation, has since moved to Washington state, where she works as a forester.

JOAN RUTH ROSE was in her forties and the divorced mother of two teenage daughters at the time of her involvement in early Dayton Women's Liberation activities. She belonged to antiwar and civil rights organizations in Dayton, still considers herself a political activist, and now works as a counselor in a battered women's shelter in Springfield, Ohio.

ROBIN SUITS, a member of the Women's Center, had moved to Dayton from New York in 1968 to coordinate a church-funded project called Summer in the City, which sponsored street theater, workshops, and door-to-door canvassing, all meant to improve black-white relations and attack racism. She is now a public relations specialist.

NOREEN WILLHELM, in her early twenties when she became a leader of Dayton Women Working, had come from Toledo, Ohio, to help organize protests against the municipal utilities corporation. She is now a newspaper reporter in Dayton.

Susan Zurcher, a sculptor, was working for Dayton's City Beautiful Project at the time of her involvement in the women's movement in Dayton. Zurcher's work has since gained national recognition; she shows in major galleries and is now an artist in New York City.

Notes

1. Barbara Ehrenreich, "The Women's Movements: Feminist and Antifeminist," *Radical America* 15 (Spring 1981): 101.

2. See, e.g., William Chafe, "Feminism of the 1970s," *Dissent* 21 (Fall 1974): 508–17.

3. See Judith Ezekiel, "Contribution à l'histoire du mouvement féministe américaine: L'étude de cas de Dayton, Ohio, 1969–1980" (Ph.D. diss., University of Paris VIII, 1986).

4. Richard Scammon, quoted in *Dayton Daily News*, 20 July 1980. For a popularized summary of Dayton's history see Bruce Ronald, *Dayton, the Gem City* (Tulsa, Okla.: Continental Heritage Press, 1981).

5. Cheryl Radican, telephone interview from Richland, Washington, with Judith Sealander, 4 January 1985. For discussion of women in Students for a Democratic Society, see Sara Evans, *Personal Politics: The Roots of Women's Liberation in the Civil Rights Movement and the New Left* (New York: Vintage Books, 1979), esp. chaps. 6–7.

6. Carrie LaBriola, interview with Judith Sealander, Dayton, Ohio, 17 October 1984.

7. Tape-recorded group discussion with Jan Griesinger, Joan Ruth Rose, Mary Morgan, Katie Egart, Yellow Springs, Ohio, 17 October 1983.

8. *Dayton Women's Liberation Newsletter*, September 1970, records of Dayton Women's Liberation (hereafter cited as DWL), Department of Archives and Special Collections, Wright State University, Dayton, Ohio.

9. LaBriola interview.

10. Model Cities grant proposal submitted by Dayton Women's Liberation, 15 October 1973, box 1, #1, records of Dayton Women's Center (hereafter cited as DWC), Department of Archives and Special Collections, Wright State University, Dayton, Ohio.

11. Sherrie Holmes, interview with Dorothy Smith, San Rafael, California, 30 June 1983.

12. Minutes of National Women's Employment Project meeting, 8 October 1977, Chicago, "N.W.E.P. Memos and Correspondence," box 4, #1, records of Dayton Women Working (hereafter cited as DWW), Department of Archives and Special Collections, Wright State University Library, Dayton, Ohio.

13. Susan Zurcher, interview with Dorothy Smith, Dayton, Ohio, 17 February 1984; Robin Suits, interview with Dorothy Smith, Yellow Springs, Ohio, 25 February 1984; Minutes, Women's Center collective, 23 January 1974 (box 1, #4, DWC).

14. Letter from Women's Center collective to Fair River Oaks Council Priority Board, 12 March 1974 (box 1, #2, DWC).

15. Suits interview. See also "What's Happening at the Women's Center," printed newsletter (box 4, #3, DWC).

16. Holmes and Suits interviews.

17. Holmes interview.

18. Memo to National Women's Employment Project Board from Heleny Cook, 13 April 1977, "N.W.E.P. Memos and Correspondence" (box 4, #2, DWW); also Noreen Willhelm, interview with Judith Sealander, Dayton, Ohio, 18 July 1983.

19. Memo to National Women's Employment Project Board from Heleny Cook, 31 October 1977, "N.W.E.P. Memos and Correspondence" (box 4, #2, DWW); also Willhelm interview.

20. Noreen Willhelm to Mr. Marvin Michel, Vice-President, Personnel, First National Bank, Dayton, 13 February 1978, "Correspondence, Banking Study" (box 3, #14, DWW).

21. Introduction, "Banks: Discrimination in Employment, a Dayton Working Women Study: Employment Discrimination in Dayton's Three Largest Commercial Banks," 10 July 1978 (DWW).

22. Ibid.

23. Notes on Banking Industry Research, evidence compiled by Dayton Women Working and Cleveland Women Working, 1979 (box 3, #15, DWW), 15.

24. Dayton Women Working, "Progress Report," January–July 1978, box 1, #8, DWW.

25. Banking Industry Research, 3.

26. Minutes of Women's Center collective, 26 January, 2, 9, and 23 February 1977 (box 1, #4, DWC). See also letter from Roberta Fischer to Women's Caucus of New American Movement, 17 January 1977; letter from Women's Caucus of New American Movement to Women's Center collective, 27 January 1977 (both in box 1, #3, DWC).

27. Kathy Ellison, interview with Judith Sealander, Dayton, Ohio, 10 August 1983.

28. Suits interview.

29. See, e.g., Evans, *Personal Politics*, chap. 9; Chafe, "Feminism of the 1970s"; Wini Breines, *Community and Organization in the New Left, 1962–1968: The Great Refusal* (South Hadley, Mass.: Bergin & Garvey, 1982); Todd Gitlin, "The Dynamics of the New Left," *Motive*, (November 1970), p. 45; Kirkpatrick Sale, S.D.S. (New York: Vintage Books, 1973); and Judith Hole and Ellen Levine, *Rebirth of Feminism* (New York: Quadrangle Books, 1971).

30. Hole and Levine, *Rebirth*, 145–49.

31. Dayton Women Working was made up primarily of white women. Membership cards do not list race, and although recollections about percentages differ, all agree that there were few black members. A rise in black members occurred after Deborah Walker, a black hospital worker, joined in 1979 and began to recruit actively.

32. Holmes and Willhelm interviews.

33. See *Dayton Daily News* and *Dayton Journal Herald*, both for 5 May 1978.

34. Sherrie Holmes, typewritten memo [early 1977?] (DWW).

35. See Evans, *Personal Politics*, chap. 6; Sale, *S.D.S.*, chaps. 2–4; and Mitchell Goodman, ed., *The Movement toward a New America* (Philadelphia: Pilgrim Press, Knopf, 1970).

36. Nancy Cott, "Feminist Politics in the 1920s: The National Woman's Party," *Journal of American History* 71 (June 1984): 43–61.

37. Inez Haynes Irwin, quoted in ibid., 45.

38. Todd Gitlin, *The Whole World Is Watching: Mass Media in the Making and Unmaking of the New Left* (Berkeley: University of California Press, 1980).

39. Dayton City Manager's Office Special Projects Files: Model Cities Program, Department of Archives and Special Collections, Wright State University, *Dayton Women's Liberation Newsletter*, November 1973 (DWI).

40. See Financial Statements of Dayton Women Working, "Financial Records" (box 1, #3, DWW).

41. Volunteers in Service to America Study, "Project Report," HQ02-390-3 (interviewer, Charles Hefner), 8 September 1978; "Fundraising—V.I.S.T.A." (both in box 1, #19, DWW).

42. Financial Statements of Dayton Women Working. See also letters to women on Women's Center mailing list, June 1974, October 1975, 8 November 1976, 25 July 1977 (box 4, #3, DWC); Minutes, Women's Center collective, 9 March 1977 (box 1, #4, DWC).

43. Willhelm interview.

44. Holmes interview.

45. Radican interview.

46. Memo, Ellen Cassedy to National Women's Employment Project Board, "Future of N.W.E.P.," 10 May 1979 (box 4, #2, DWW); Steve Askin, "Female Rights Spell Trouble for Bosses," *In These Times*, July 27–August 9, 1983, p. 11.

47. Morgan interview.

48. Ellison interview.

49. Letter to women on Women's Center mailing list, 31 December 1980 (box 4, #3, DWC).

50. Ibid.

9   **Class, Race, and**
Reproductive Rights

Adele Clarke and Alice Wolfson

Is socialist feminism a theory without practice, or are there
groups of activists attempting to embody that theory in substantive work?
Despite the absence of a nationally cohesive socialist-feminist movement,
we argue here that the reproductive rights movement that emerged in the
1970s was largely initiated and now is often led by socialist feminists.

In what follows we first examine the historical intersection of socialist
feminism and reproductive rights, then discuss five major contradictions
confronted by socialist feminists in the reproductive rights movement and
some directions taken toward their resolution. We both have worked with
the Committee to Defend Reproductive Rights (CDRR) in San Francisco.

From Abortion Rights to Reproductive Rights

Within the women's liberation movement of the late 1960s, the
right to abortion quickly became a major issue because of its fundamental
relation to women's liberation and because so many of us shared the personal horrors of illegal abortions. Today, younger women often have no
memory of the shame, the injuries, and the deaths that illegal, back-alley
abortions caused. The very act of saying to another person "Yes, I had an
abortion" has in itself been an act of resistance and liberation. Through-

Source: This article is reprinted from *Socialist Review* No. 78 (November–December
1984), pp. 110–20, by permission of the publisher, *Socialist Review*, 3202 Adeline,
Berkeley, CA 94703.

out the country, in every place where feminists considered women's issues, abortion counseling and underground referrals usually were the first feminist services organized. Many women in the reproductive rights movement today trace their commitment back to this early work.

The step from counseling for illegal abortions to organizing the fight for legality was a short one, and many feminists put a great deal of energy into the abortion rights movement. Even at its inception, this movement included a panoply of political perspectives and organizations. These ranged from liberal "individual right to choose" groups to the highly organized population control lobby (for example, Planned Parenthood International and Zero Population Growth, Inc.) for whom legal abortion in the United States was an advantageous strategy for promoting the not-always-voluntary international limitation of populations.

One group of early feminist participants (often called "bourgeois" feminists) forged a feminist version of the individual rights/individual choice perspective. They formed the National Abortion Rights Action League (NARAL), a single-issue organization with state and local affiliates focused primarily on legislative and electoral work.

In contrast, "women's liberation" or "radical feminists" organized mostly at the grassroots level. When these women did local work in racially mixed, poor, urban areas, they quickly raised other issues around health and reproduction. They included race and class analyses that previously had too often been ignored within emerging feminist perspectives.

Many activist women entered into direct confrontation with the larger health-care system through the campaign to legalize abortion. Socialist-leaning feminists were often further radicalized by increasingly apparent contradictions within this movement. For example, they found arguments in support of abortion as cost-effective for limiting numbers of welfare and AFDC (Aid to Families with Dependent Children) recipients to be classist, racist, and opportunist. Socialist feminists began to articulate politics that better reflected broader issues of reproductive health and freedom.

Despite such efforts, however, the pre-1973 abortion rights movement ultimately failed to build a multi-issue movement around reproduction. Many groups balked at making connections to other issues affecting both men and women. Some feared the abortion cause would be hurt if they introduced other issues; others, limited by class bias, simply did not see the connections between these issues. After the legalization of abortion in 1973, most abortion rights groups disintegrated or disbanded. Those that had made explicit connections to other women's health issues often provided bases for forming new groups.

Socialist feminists were often the founders and most active participants in new groups focused on political advocacy work. In contrast, groups that provided services focused on forging independent feminist health institutions and/or hoped to change the nature of the health-care system through feminist example and competition.[1] After abortion rights were won, these competing strategies were hotly debated in the feminist community.

Organizations providing direct clinical medical services included the network of Feminist Women's Health Centers and other women's clinics across the country. Political advocacy groups included the Coalition for the Medical Rights of Women, the Committee to End Sterilization Abuse, Women's Health Concerns, the Philadelphia Women's Health Collective, the Boston Women's Health Collective, and the National Women's Health Network.

The names of these advocacy groups indicate some of the concerns they addressed. All recognized both access to abortion services and sterilization abuse with its connections to population control as important issues. Other early issues included a national health service, DES (diethylstilbestrol), the Dalkon Shield IUD (intrauterine device), occupational health, reproductive health hazards, and the right to informed consent through patient package inserts with drugs (for example, with the "pill" and in estrogen replacement therapy). Some of the issues, such as occupational health, sterilization, and reproductive health hazards, have been jointly addressed with the "male" left. Other issues, minimized or negated by that left, were then and have remained confined to the women's health movement.

Between 1973 and 1977 the old "Right to Life" movement, early opponent of legalized abortion, gained new strength and power through association with the new right. The first major fruit of this alliance was the passage of the Hyde Amendment in 1977, the first federal legislation to eliminate federal funding for abortions for women on Medicaid.

During this period, the only groups maintaining any apparatus to deal with abortion rights were NARAL, Planned Parenthood, the Religious Coalition for Abortion Rights, and other mainstream liberal groups. The National Organization for Women (founded in 1966) supported abortion rights in 1968, despite a serious split in the organization over this issue.[2] By 1977, however, abortion and other reproductive issues were on NOW's back burner, subordinated to its fight for the Equal Rights Amendment. The splitting of these issues was, in our view, shortsighted and disadvantageous for both movements.

Socialist feminists were among the first to recognize that the attack launched by the new right on a woman's right to abortion was not the isolated issue portrayed by the Right-to-Lifers. Rather, this attack represented the forefront of a broader right-wing social movement and ideology designed to push back the democratic gains made by the civil rights, women's, and gay movements since the 1960s.

Many socialist feminists understood the urgent need to fight the abortion fight once again. They began to place *this* abortion rights struggle within the broader context of the fight for reproductive rights. The women's health movement had developed analyses of a broad range of salient reproductive issues that should not be ignored this time around. No traditional abortion rights organizations, however, were receptive to what has come to be known as a reproductive rights analysis and multi-issue agenda.

Socialist feminists argued that an explicit reproductive rights movement should be organized to assert that abortion rights are linked to a wide array of other reproductive rights, and that *all* are crucial to reproductive freedom and autonomy. Then, even if forced by the historical moment to work primarily on abortion, the wider analyses would broaden the scope of the work and serve to implicate the entire system. To this end, socialist and other feminists founded in 1977 a number of new, mostly local, grassroots organizations, including the Committee for Abortion Rights and Against Sterilization Abuse, the Committee to Defend Reproductive Rights, and Twin Cities Reproductive Rights, plus a national organization, the Reproductive Rights National Network.

The Reproductive Rights Perspective

The socialist-feminist analysis of reproductive rights essentially *is* the reproductive rights analysis. Within the reproductive rights movement, different socialist and other feminists may emphasize varying issues, but we are all committed to reproductive issues as a whole rather than abortion as a single-issue politics.[3]

Reproductive freedom is prerequisite for any kind of liberation for women. The right to decide whether and when to bear a child is fundamental to a woman's control of her own body, her sexuality, her work and life choices. Reproduction is a fundamental human right; neither the state nor the actions of others should deny any person reproductive autonomy. Mandatory motherhood precludes self-determination. This is why abortion, the final line of defense against an unwanted pregnancy, is the bottom line within a reproductive rights perspective.

The central assumption of the socialist-feminist/reproductive rights perspective is that reproductive rights issues must be viewed in their specific social, historical, and institutional contexts. Reproductive freedom, as Rosalind Petchesky has noted, is irreducibly social *and* individual at the same time—as is the very nature of reproduction itself: "It operates 'at the core of social life' as well as within and upon women's bodies."[4] Reproductive rights work, therefore, must address *both* social and individual levels of action.

As socialist feminists, we see the concrete ability to exercise these rights as dependent upon *access* to the full array of reproductive services. The bulk of reproductive rights work to date has been focused on keeping abortion legal and accessible on national, state, and local levels. Despite this necessary emphasis, the reproductive rights movement has also effectively maintained the struggle against sterilization abuse,[5] fought for access to birth control (especially for teens, through opposition to the law that would require informing parents); and, in concert with the broader women's health movement, mounted multiple battles around the hazards of specific birth control methods (the pill, the IUD, and Depo-Provera). Issues of disability and reproductive rights have recently been raised as well.[6]

The reproductive rights movement has also begun to confront the complex and challenging issues engendered by the proliferation of reproductive technologies.[7] There are difficult and painful debates in the women's movement around these issues, for which there are no easy answers or positions to be taken.[8]

These technologies promote a vivid *commodification of children*. Children become "luxury items" in the marketplace of individual or familial consumption, something to be afforded—in terms of money, time, and energy. In this commodified vision the few children a woman has should be "perfect"—the "right" sex, the "right" race, and "right" intelligence, well timed and certainly not disabled. This ideology advocates both quality control and quantity control over reproduction. The elaboration of reproductive technologies makes such controls increasingly feasible. The potential neo-eugenic applications of these technologies are considerable; due to their high and usually uninsured costs, their use has been almost exclusively toward the production of "healthy, white, high-class babies."[9]

Thus, while contraceptive and reproductive technologies have enhanced *control* over reproduction, they do *not* intrinsically or necessarily bring about a social world that supports genuine reproductive freedom. The fight for that support is at the heart of reproductive rights work.

Contradictions in Reproductive Rights Work

As socialist feminists, we have identified five major contradictions in reproductive rights work today.

"Free Abortion on Demand" versus Roe *v.* Wade

Socialist feminists working on abortion in the early 1970s argued for "Free Abortion on Demand." Abortion was seen as a fundamental and autonomous health right for women; moreover, within a broader socialist framework, the state should provide funding for all. When in 1973 the *Roe* v. *Wade* decision finally legalized abortion, it was shorn of socialist and feminist supports. Specifically, the Supreme Court did not see fit to allow a woman to decide on her own—the decision was to be made in consultation with her physician. Further, the decision was based on the constitutional "right to privacy" rather than the right to bodily autonomy and integrity. This left the right to abortion vulnerable to an array of legal assaults. Last, the court made no mention of state funding. It has since (*McRae* v. *Harris*, 1980) found the denial of federal and state funding constitutional within the "right to privacy" framework. Subsequent Supreme Court decisions have similarly reaffirmed and even strengthened physicians' roles in abortion decisions and politics. Moreover, as this volume goes to press, the Supreme Court is reviewing the *Roe* v. *Wade* decision itself.

Thus, although abortion remains legal, we have obviously not achieved our goal of "Free Abortion on Demand;" and even its legality is highly tenuous. The challenge for socialist feminists in the reproductive rights movement is to reintroduce this more progressive agenda in the midst of state fiscal austerity and in the face of increasingly violent groups' opposing the right to choose.

Legislative/Regulatory Work versus Movement-Building

Much of the actual daily work of reproductive rights activists has focused on legislative and bureaucratic actions. Attacks on abortion have been largely legislative, and attacks on informed consent to sterilization have been regulatory. The contradiction for socialist feminists here lies in being forced into the uneasy position of appealing to an unsympathetic government to create and protect our "legal" rights. Although the democratic and progressive aspects of liberalized abortion laws and protective regulations are clear, the reproductive rights movement fights such struggles on an alien and inherently suspect turf.

The actual work on regulations and legislation is often narrow in scope. Lobbying, testifying, critiquing legislation and regulations, and monitoring can be tedious, intimidating, alienating, and difficult. Such work risks narrowing the movement because it does not appeal to many people. The challenge for socialist feminists in the reproductive rights movement is to develop creative and radicalizing ways to involve many people in a sustained struggle.

Holding Ground versus Moving Ahead on Our Own Agenda

The constant need to defend abortion rights makes it difficult to work on the broader spectrum of reproductive rights. Except for sterilization abuse, the reproductive rights movement has not adequately addressed such issues as birth control, sexuality, perinatal care, workplace hazards to reproduction, and the childbearing or custody rights of lesbians, gay men, single people, the disabled, and the poor.

Moreover, we have not addressed child care from a socialist-feminist perspective, despite our clear understanding of its importance to women's day-to-day autonomy. Due to the immediacy of their needs, child-care advocates have emphasized service provision rather than political activism. Given a broader and more cohesive socialist-feminist movement, or a more feminist socialist movement, we believe the full panoply of reproductive rights issues, including child care, could be addressed.

Do We Lose If We Win on Abortion?

A fourth contradiction is that the reproductive rights movement, unlike movements addressing more global issues (such as the anti-nuclear movement), faces the imminent possibility of success. As socialist feminists we confront the problem of building a protest movement of mass organizations with the capability of surviving and redirecting themselves when limited or even fundamental gains are won. Generating monies to support a broader agenda is difficult because progressive funding sources— our only sources—seem much less willing to support programs not dealing with abortion.

For example, a majority of participants joined the reproductive rights movement to work explicitly against the Right to Life attack on abortion. After some limited but important victories on abortion rights (such as *Akron Center for Reproductive Health* v. *City of Akron*, 1983), some groups could not sustain earlier participation. They died.

Other groups attempted to rechannel participation. In one such effort, CDRR in San Francisco began to focus more attention on issues of *access* to abortion. A focus on access—which speaks to federal and state funding—offers the opportunity for more grassroots organizing and coalition-building. Yet it has its own contradictions. Access has been limited for specific groups of women (teens, older women, low-income women, federally employed workers, and women beyond the first trimester of pregnancy) rather than for *all* women, and the issue thus holds less mass appeal than issues of legality. To address this contradiction, CDRR is now trying to develop an analysis and material to enable women to grasp clearly how all our reproductive interests and fates are linked together.

Any woman's loss of reproductive rights is a blow to women's liberation. Because of this, as socialist feminists we have come to see the issue of *access* to abortion as the only form of reproductive rights work possibly leading to reclaiming "Free Abortion on Demand" as one of our movement's most progressive goals. However, this goal is all too easily displaced by the need to fight yet again to keep abortion legal.

Who Fights for Reproductive Rights?

Although we are basically a white, middle-class, heterosexual women's movement, recent changes are encouraging. One major development has been the emergence of a nationwide, autonomous black women's health movement. In 1983 the First National Black Women's Health Conference met in Atlanta, sponsored by the Black Women's Health Project of the National Women's Health Network. This national movement with local chapters broadens the reproductive rights constituency.

The reproductive rights movement has been most effectively antiracist in work against sterilization abuse. Long-standing coalitions have been established with Hispanic and black organizations, and some local grassroots organizations such as the San Francisco–based Action Committee for Abortion Rights have directly addressed racism from their inception. But racism in the reproductive rights movement remains problematic. The 1983 meetings of the Reproductive Rights National Network, a coalition of local groups, focused on "Combatting Racism: Building an Antiracist Multiracial Movement" and formed a Third World Women's Caucus. Sadly, this caucus ended with the demise of the Reproductive Rights National Network, a casualty of the Reagan era.

Disabled women have also been missing from the ranks of reproductive rights groups, but this is slowly changing. The 1983 Reproductive Rights National Network Conference had sessions on disability and reproductive rights, and analyses and resources were developed.[10] Last, many reproductive rights organizations lack a lesbian presence affecting the articulation of and struggles for lesbian reproductive rights. Lesbian rights to child custody, alternative insemination, and nonheterosexist health care need to be addressed seriously by the reproductive rights movement in concert with lesbian community organizations.

The contradiction of being a white, middle-class, heterosexual movement arguing on behalf of all women remains with us, though we have begun to address it more directly. Addressing *all* these contradictions is, in fact, helping us to broaden our own political analysis.

The Future of Socialist Feminism and Reproductive Rights

We have argued that socialist feminism is alive and active in the reproductive rights movement. Despite the contradictions outlined above, it is clear to us that the reproductive rights analysis and movement have been comfortable and productive for many socialist feminists. They allow us to work on basic feminist issues, often within autonomous women's groups, and to develop an analysis that leads to progressive social change.

Yet the larger problem of the absence of a cohesive national socialist-feminist movement leaves us isolated. As socialists, we often feel the constraints inherent in reproductive rights work. We may seek a more immediate confrontation with imperialism, such as that offered by working on Latin American, antimilitarist, or antinuclear issues. As feminists, however, we have almost no other activist organizations to turn to. No broader movement exists from which we can directly draw members and to which members might return for renewal, political redirection, and personal connection with a larger whole.

We confront this dilemma routinely in our work as socialist feminists in the reproductive rights movement. Whether and how to attempt to generate a national socialist-feminist organization is a question before all women who identify themselves as such. The reproductive rights movement's success in creating numerous local organizations and a national presence, however transitory, gives us hope that such an organization could exist. One lesson from addressing the contradictions of the reproductive rights movement is that whatever work we undertake, we must ground it in the concrete conditions of our lives. The personal remains profoundly political.

Notes

1. For an excellent historical analysis, see Sheryl Ruzek, *The Women's Health Movement: Feminist Alternatives to Medical Care* (New York: Praeger, 1978).

2. Many conservative feminists opposed this position and left NOW to form the Women's Equity Action League, focusing on legal and economic issues. "Radicals," including socialist feminists, left NOW at about the same time but chiefly because of elitist structural issues.

3. For a fuller discussion of the reproductive rights perspective, see Committee for Abortion Rights and Against Sterilization Abuse, *Women under Attack: Abortion, Sterilization, and Reproductive Freedom* (New York: CARASA, 1979); National Lawyers Guild, *Reproductive Freedom: Speakers Handbook on Abortion Rights and Sterilization Abuse* (New York: NLG, 1979); Rosalind Petchesky, "Reproductive Freedom: Beyond a Woman's Right to Choose," *Signs* 5, no. 4 (1980): 661–85; Rosalind Petchesky, *Abortion and Woman's Choice: The State, Sexuality, and Reproductive Freedom* (New York: Longman, 1984); Thomas M. Shapiro, *Population Control Politics: Women, Sterilization, and Reproductive Choice* (Philadelphia: Temple University Press, 1985).

4. Petchesky, "Reproductive Freedom," 665.

5. See Adele Clarke, "Subtle Sterilization Abuse: A Reproductive Rights Perspective," in Rita Arditti et al., eds., *Test Tube Women: What Future for Motherhood?* (Boston: Pandora/Routledge & Kegan Paul, 1984).

6. See Michelle Fine and Adrienne Asch, "The Question of Disability: No Easy Answers for the Women's Movement," *Reproductive Rights Newsletter*, Fall 1982; and Anne Finger, "Claiming All of Our Bodies: Reproductive Rights and Disabilities," in Arditti et al., *Test Tube Women*.

7. See Arditti et al., *Test Tube Women*; Helen B. Holmes et al., eds., *The Custom-Made Child? Women-Centered Perspectives* (Clifton, N.J.: Humana, 1981); Ruth Hubbard, "Some Legal and Policy Implications of Recent Advances in Prenatal Diagnosis and Fetal Therapy," *Women's Rights Law Reporter* 7, no. 3 (1982): 201–28; Suzanne Lyon, "Technology and Reproductive Rights: How Advances in Technology Can Be Used to Limit Women's Reproductive Rights," *Women's Rights Law Reporter* 7, no. 3 (1982): 223–27; and Betsy Hartmann, *Reproductive Rights and Wrongs: The Global Politics of Population Control and Contraceptive Choice* (New York: Harper and Row, 1987).

8. See "Genetic Screening" in *Off Our Backs*, May 1983, and letters on the topic in the July issue.

9. Thanks to Kay Kaufman for this point.

10. See Finger, "Claiming All of Our Bodies"; and Fine and Asch, "Question of Disability."

Reevaluating Socialist Feminism

10   Life without Father
Reconsidering Socialist-Feminist Theory

Barbara Ehrenreich

By the late 1970s, most socialist feminists accepted as "theory" a certain description of the world: "the system" we confronted was actually composed of two systems or structures, capitalism and patriarchy. These two systems or structures were of roughly equal weight (never mind that capitalism was a mere infant compared to patriarchy or, on the other hand, that patriarchy had no visible corporate headquarters). And capitalism and patriarchy were remarkably congenial and reinforced each other in thousands of ways (which it was the task of socialist feminists to enumerate). As Zillah Eisenstein wrote in her 1979 anthology *Capitalist Patriarchy and the Case for Socialist Feminism*, patriarchy and capitalism meshed so neatly that they had become "an *integral process:* specific elements of each system are necessitated by the other." Capitalism plus patriarchy described the whole world—or nearly: racism usually required extensive addenda—and that world was as orderly and smoothly functioning as the Newtonian universe.

It was a brave idea. Today, few people venture vast theoretical syntheses. In the course of time, many of the socialist-feminist system-builders

Source: This article is reprinted from *Socialist Review* No. 73 (January–February 1984), pp. 48–57, by permission of the publisher, *Socialist Review*, 3202 Adeline, Berkeley, CA 94703.

of the 1970s have become struggling academics, constrained to publish in respectable journals and keep their noses to the empirical grindstone. No longer do people meet, as many of us did, intensely and repeatedly, with an agenda of discovering the connections between *everything*—sex and class, housework and factory work, the family and the state, race and gender, sexuality and profits. If "capitalism plus patriarchy" was too easy an answer, at least we (the socialist feminists of the 1970s) asked the hard questions.

In a practical sense, too, it was a good theory, because it served to validate the existence of socialist feminism. And I do not say this to trivialize the theory as self-serving. In the mid-1970s in particular, socialist feminists were an embattled species. On the one hand there was cultural and/or separatist feminism, drifting off toward spirituality, Great Goddess worship, and sociobiological theories of eternal male perfidy; to these "radical" feminists, socialist feminists were male-identified dupes of the left, which they always described as the "male left." On the other hand there was the left, which featured at the time a flourishing Marxist-Leninist tendency, bent on self-proletarianization and the "rectification" of everyone else; to it, socialist feminists were agents of the petite bourgeoisie on assignment to distract working-class women from the main event, the class struggle.[1] The Marxist-Leninists and separatist feminists were extremes in a much wider radical context, but they helped define a political atmosphere in which socialist feminism was hard put to establish that it was neither an oxymoron nor a form of treason.

The capitalism-plus-patriarchy paradigm was an ingenious defensive stance. If the world was really made up of two systems that were distinct and could not be reduced to each other, it was never enough to be just a socialist or just a feminist. If patriarchy was not only distinct but truly a "system" and not an attitude (like sexism) or a structure of the unconscious (as Juliet Mitchell saw it), those who opposed patriarchy were not just jousting with superstructural windmills; they were doing something real and "material." Finally, if patriarchy and capitalism were mutually reinforcing, it didn't make any sense to take on one without the other. If "the system" was capitalist-patriarchy, the only thoroughgoing oppositional politics was its mirror image, socialist feminism.

Not all socialist feminists were perfectly comfortable with the capitalism-plus-patriarchy formulation, however. For one thing, there always seemed to be something a little static and structuralist about it. Deirdre English and I argued, in our book *For Her Own Good*, that "patriarchy" ought to be left where Marx last saw it—in preindustrial European society—and that modern feminists should get on with the task of describing our own "sex/

gender system," to use Gayle Rubin's phrase, in all its historic specificity. In addition, we were not convinced that capitalism and patriarchy were on as good terms as socialist-feminist theory demanded. If the theory couldn't account for the clashes as well as the reinforcements, it couldn't account for change—such as the emergence of feminism itself in the late eighteenth-century ferment of bourgeois and *antipatriarchal* liberalism. The world of capitalism plus patriarchy, endlessly abetting each other to form a closed system with just one seam, was a world without change, a world without a subject.

There is another problem. Things *have* changed, and in ways that make capitalist-patriarchy (or, better, "patriarchal capitalism") almost seem like a good deal. Socialist feminists—not to mention many plain feminists and socialists—went wrong in assuming that "the system," whatever it was called, would, left to itself, reproduce itself.

Woman as Domestic Worker

The linchpin of socialist-feminist theory, the factor that put women, so to speak, on the Marxist map, was domestic work. In theory this work included everything women do in the home, from cooking and cleaning to reading bedtime stories and having sex. Radical feminists were quick to point out how women's efforts, whether serving coffee in a move-ment office or polishing the coffee table in a suburban home, served the interests of individual men. Socialist feminists, coming along a few years later, asserted that women's domestic work served not only men but capital. As Zillah Eisenstein put it:

> All the processes involved in domestic work help in the perpetua-tion of the existing society: (1) Women stabilize patriarchal struc-tures (the family, housewife, mother, etc.) by fulfilling these roles. (2) Simultaneously, women are reproducing new workers, for both the paid and unpaid labor force. . . . (3) They work as well in the labor force for lesser wages. (4) They stabilize the economy through their role as consumers. . . . If the other side of production is consumption, the other side of capitalism is patriarchy.[2]

The discovery of the importance of women's domestic work put some flesh on the abstract union of capitalism and patriarchy. First, it gave patri-archy, which had otherwise had a somewhat ghostly quality (stretched as it was to include everything from rape to domestic slovenliness), a "material base" in "men's control over women's labor power." Second, it revealed a vivid parallel between "the private sphere," where patriarchy was still ensconced, and the "public sphere," where capital called the shots. In the public sphere men labored at production, and in the private sphere women labored at "reproduction" (not only physical reproduction but the reproduction of attitudes and capabilities required for all types of work). Finally it showed how essential patriarchy was to capitalism: most capitalist institutions produced only things, but the quintessential patriarchal institution, the family, produced the men who produced things—thanks to the labor of women.

It was not altogether clear where one went with this insight into the centrality of women's domestic work. If what women did in the home was so critical to the reproduction of both capitalism and patriarchy, shouldn't women be advised to stop doing it? Perhaps to sabotage it? The "wages for housework" position, which surfaced in this country in 1974, provided a strategic answer and an unintended caricature of American socialist-feminist theory. American socialist feminists had argued that women's work was "necessary" to capitalism; the Italian feminists who launched wages-for-housework insisted, with considerable eloquence, that domestic work actually produced surplus value for the capitalists, just as what we ordinarily thought of as "productive" work in the public sphere did. If you were going to say that women's domestic work reproduced the labor power needed by capital, you might as well go all the way and say it was as much a part of the productive process as the extraction and preparation of raw materials for manufacturing. Thus the home was an adjunct to the factory; in fact it was part of the great "social factory" (schools and all other sites of social reproduction) that kept the literal factories running. Women's domestic activities were no longer a shadowy contribution but a potentially quantifiable productive factor with the distinguished Marxist status of "producing surplus value." The only difference between the man laboring for Fiat or Ford and the woman laboring in her kitchen was that she was unpaid—a patriarchal oversight that wages-for-housework would correct.

This proposal and the accompanying theory sent shock waves through American and British socialist-feminist networks. There were debates over the practicality of the demand: who would pay the wages for housework, which would, after all, constitute an enormous redistribution of wealth? There were even more debates at the level of high theory: was it scientifically accurate to say that housework produced surplus value? (A debate which, in my opinion, produced almost nothing of value.) Unfortunately, there was much less attention to the bizarre but utterly logical extreme to which wages-for-housework theory took homegrown socialist-feminist theory. Everything women did in the home was in the service of capital and indispensable to capital. When a mother kissed her children goodnight, she was "reproducing labor power." When a childless working woman brushed her teeth, she too was reproducing labor power (her own, in this case), as an American wages-for-housework advocate argued in an exchange I participated in. This was commodity fetishism with a vengeance, and even with the modification that kissing, for example, serves the miniature patriarchy of the family more directly than corporate capital, it all boiled down to the same thing, since patriarchy was firmly in league with capital.

The Obsolescence of Capitalism-plus-Patriarchy

From the vantage point of 1984, the debates of 1975 have an almost wistful quality. They (men, capitalists) needed us (women) to do all our traditional "womanly" things, and, if theory were to be trusted, they would apparently go to great lengths to keep us at it. Well, they don't seem to need us anymore—at least not that way—and if this was not completely evident in 1975, it is inescapable today.

No matter how valuable the services of a full-time homemaker may be, fewer and fewer men earn enough to support one. The reasons for the disappearance of the male "family wage" and the associated influx of married women into the work force have been discussed at length. The relevant point here is that for all we say about the "double day," employed women do far less housework than those who are full-time homemakers, twenty-six hours per week as compared with fifty-five hours per week.[3] Other family members may be compensating in part (though most studies I have seen show little increase in husbands' contributions), but it is hard not to conclude that the net amount of housework done has decreased dramatically. (By as much as 29 million hours per week per year during the peak years of women's influx into the labor market. Of course a certain amount of this work has been taken up by the commercial sector, especially by restaurants and fast food places.) If women's work were as essential to the status quo as socialist-feminist theory argued, capitalism would have been seriously weakened by this withdrawal of women's labor. Yet no one is arguing, for example, that the decline of American productivity is due to unironed shirts and cold breakfasts. Nor has any sector of capital come forth and offered to restore the male family wage so that women can get back to their housework.

If capital does not seem to need women's domestic work as much as theory predicted, what about individual men? Mid-1970s feminist theory tended to portray men as enthusiastic claimants of women's services and labor, eagerly enlisting us to provide them with clean laundry, homecooked meals, and heirs. If we have learned anything in the years since then, it is that men have an unexpected ability to survive on fast food and the emotional solace of short-term relationships. There are, as Marxists say, "material" reasons for this. First, it is physically possible, thanks to laundromats, frozen food, and other conveniences, for even a poor man to live alone and without servants. Second, there have always been alternatives to spending a "family wage" on an actual family, but in the last few decades these alternatives have become more numerous and alluring. Not only are there the classic temptations of drink, gambling, and "loose women" to choose from but stereos, well-appointed bachelor apartments, Club Med, sports cars, and so forth. For these and other reasons, American men have been abdicating their traditional roles as husbands, breadwinners, and the petty patriarchs of the capitalism-plus-patriarchy paradigm.[4]

In a larger sense, events and some belated realizations of the last few years should have undermined any faith we had in capital's willingness to promote the "reproduction of labor power." Capital, as well as labor, is internationally mobile, making U.S. corporations relatively independent of a working class born and bred in this or any one country. Furthermore, capitalists are not required to be industrial capitalists; they can disinvest in production and reinvest in real estate, financial speculation, or, if it suits their fancy, antiques; and they have done so despite any number of exhortations and supply-side incentives. In their actual practices and policies, capitalists and their representatives display remarkable indifference to the "reproduction of labor power," or, in less commoditized terms, the perpetuation of human life.

This is not to say that individual companies or industries do not maintain a detailed interest in our lives as consumers. They do, especially if we are lucky enough to be above "the buying point" in personal resources. But it is no longer possible to discern a uniform patriarchal or even pronatalist bias to this concern. Capitalists have figured out that two-paycheck couples buy more than husband-plus-housewife units, and that a society of singles potentially buys more than a society in which households are shared by three or more people. In times of labor insurgency, far-seeing representatives of the capitalist class have taken a minute interest in how ordinary people organize their lives, raise their children, and so on. But this is not such a time, and it seems plain to me that the manufacturers of components for missile heads (a mile from where I sit) do not care whether my children are docile or cranky, and that the people who laced our drinking water with toxins (a mile the other way) could not much care whether I scrub the floors.

With hindsight, I am struck by what a *benevolent* system the capitalism-plus-patriarchy paradigm implied. In order to put women's hidden and private interests on the economic map, we had to assume that they reflected some much larger, systemic need. Since these efforts of women are in fact efforts to care and nurture, we had to project the functions of caring and nurturing onto the large, impersonal "structures" governing our all-too-functional construct of the world. Capitalism, inscribed with the will to "reproduce," became "patriarchal capitalism." This suggested that in a sense our theory was a family metaphor for the world: capitalists were "fathers," male workers were "sons," and all women were wives/daughters, both mediating the relations between fathers and sons[5] and producing more sons (and daughters) to keep the whole system going. The daughters had the worst deal, but at least they were members of the family, and this family, like actual ones, intended to keep on going—a motivation that is no longer so easy to attribute to the men who command our resources and our labor.

I think now that the capitalism-plus-patriarchy paradigm overpersonalized (and humanized) capitalism precisely because it depersonalized women. The paradigm granted "the system" an undue benevolence because it had no room for motive or caring on the part of women. Once all the interactions and efforts of child raising have been reduced to "reproducing labor power" (and children have been reduced to units of future labor power), there is no place for human aspiration or resistance. Once it has been determined that "all the processes involved in domestic work help in the perpetuation of the existing society," the women who perform these "processes" have lost all potential autonomy and human subjectivity. And once it is declared that all acts other than production are really "reproduction" (of labor power and the same old system of domination), only one kind of resistance *is* possible. Suicide, or the willful destruction of labor power.

Ironically, the intent of the capitalism-plus-patriarchy paradigm was to validate feminism and insert women, as actors, into the Marxist political calculus. The problem was that we were too deferential to Marxism. Socialist feminists tried to account for large areas of women's experience—actually everyone's experience—in the language of commodities and exchange, as if that were the "scientific" way to proceed. It would have been better perhaps to turn the tables: for example, instead of asking, "How can we account for women's work in the home in Marxist terms?" we should have asked, "How can we account for what *men* do *outside* the home in feminist terms, in women's terms?" Trying to fit all of women's experience into the terms of the market didn't work, and adding on patriarchy as an additional "structure" didn't help.

So where do we go from here? Is it possible to be a socialist feminist without a "socialist-feminist theory"? Yes, of course it is. After all, those who are plain socialists or feminists get along—with no evident embarrassment—on just half a theory at best. The socialist-feminist project has always been larger and more daring than that of either of our progenitors, so if we have fumbled, it is in part because we attempted more.

But we do need a better way to understand the world we seek to act in. I hesitate to say we need a new "theory," because that word suggests a new set of structures and laws of mechanics to connect them. If not capitalism-plus-patriarchy, you are probably thinking, what is it? The point is that "it" is changing, and in a more violent and cataclysmic fashion than we had any reason to expect. The statics of capitalism-plus-patriarchy help explain a world that is already receding from view—a world of relative affluence and apparent stability—where categories like "the family," "the state," and "the economy" were fixed and solid anchor points for theory. Today, there is little we can take as fixed. "The family," so long reified in theory, looks more like an improvisation than an institution. A new technological revolution, on the scale of the one that swept in industrial capitalism (and state socialism), is transforming not only production but perception. Whole industries collapse into obsolescence; entire classes face ruthless dislocation. At the same time, the gap between the races domestically, between the north and the south internationally, widens to obscene proportions. Everywhere, women are being proletarianized and impoverished, becoming migrants, refugees, and inevitably "cheap labor." Meanwhile, the great and lesser powers race to omnicide, making a mockery of all our diverse aspirations, struggles, and movements. Truly, "all that is solid melts into air"—that is, if it is not vaporized instantaneously.

I still believe that if there is a vantage point from which to comprehend and change the world, our world today, it will be socialist and feminist. Socialist—or perhaps here I should say Marxist—because a Marxist way of thinking, at its best, helps us understand the cutting edge of change, the blind driving force of capital, the dislocations, innovations, and global reshufflings. Feminist because feminism offers our best insight into that which is most ancient and intractable about our common situation: the gulf that divides the species by gender and, tragically, divides us all from nature and that which is most human in our nature. This is our intellectual heritage, and I do not think we have yet seen its full power—or our own.

Notes

1. Here I am passing over the story of the destruction of organized socialist feminism by various Marxist-Leninist and Maoist groups in 1975–77. In that period, sectarian groups joined and harassed or merely attacked from outside more than twenty socialist-feminist women's unions around the country, dragging almost all of

them down to their deaths in arcane squabbles over the "correct line." I have never seen an adequate—or even inadequate—account of this nasty phase of left feminist history that addresses why the sects decided to go after socialist-feminist organizations at this time, and why socialist-feminist organizations, including the successful and level-headed Chicago Women's Liberation Union, crumbled in the face of so much bullshit. I would appreciate hearing from anyone with insights or relevant anecdotes to offer.

2. I don't mean to pick on Zillah Eisenstein; many other writers could be quoted, especially if I were doing a thorough review of socialist-feminist theory and its nuances (which I clearly am not). Eisenstein is singled out here because her introduction to and chapter in *Capitalist Patriarchy and the Case for Socialist Feminism* (New York: Monthly Review Press, 1979) seem to me to provide an excellent state-of-the-art summary of mid-1970s socialist-feminist theory. The passage cited is on page 29.

3. Joann Vanek, "Time Spent in Housework," *Scientific American*, November 1974, p. 116.

4. One poignant indication of this shift in male values and expectations: when I was in my early twenties (in the early 1960s), it seemed to require a certain daring and resourcefulness to dodge the traditional female fate of becoming a full-time housewife and mother. Today, I hear over and over from young women that they would like to have a family or at least a child but do not expect ever to be in a stable enough relationship to carry this off.

5. Insofar as the capitalists paid their workers enough to support a wife, thus buying off the workers with patriarchal privilege and ensuring labor peace—a crude summary of Heidi Hartmann's much more complex and interesting argument. The family metaphor was developed extensively by Batya Weinbaum in *The Curious Courtship of Women's Liberation and Socialism* (Boston: South End Press, 1980).

11   # Conceptualizing and Changing Consciousness
Socialist-Feminist Perspectives

Sandra Morgen

The "unhappy marriage" between Marxism and feminism, consummated in the early development of socialist feminism, has been a central image in critical reflections on the current state of socialist-feminist theory.[1] Judging that "the honeymoon is over,"[2] socialist feminists have pondered the possibilities of trial separation, a *ménage à trois*, and divorce as alternatives to settling for a long-term unhappy marriage. At the risk of stretching this image beyond its usefulness, this essay proposes "greater communication"—that favorite of marriage counselors—between socialist feminism and Marxism before we sign those final papers. I begin with a very brief and selective history of the development of socialist-feminist thought, focusing on how its engagement with Marxism has changed over time. This sets the stage for my argument that a new relationship between socialist feminism and Marxism is in order in which socialist feminism is a contributor as well as a borrower.

The Development of Socialist-Feminist Thought

Socialist-feminist critiques of Marxism have centered on the incapacity of orthodox Marxist theory and socialist practice to comprehend

Source: An earlier and longer version of this article appears in Jean O'Barr, ed., *Women and the New Academy: Gender and Cultural Contexts* (Madison: University of Wisconsin Press, 1989), pp. 140–66.

gender and to encompass the experiences and needs of women. Some of the earliest contemporary socialist feminists sought a synthesis of Marxism and feminism that essentially applied the theory and method of historical materialism to women's lives and concerns. Juliet Mitchell claimed in 1966 that socialist feminists ought to "ask the feminist questions, but try to come up with some Marxist answers."[3] And in fact that is what much early socialist-feminist theory did in focusing on the question of the sexual division of labor, particularly the question of women's unpaid labor in the home.

Margaret Benston defined housework as a form of production,[4] stimulating a long debate within socialist feminism and between socialist feminists and Marxists about the nature of domestic labor.[5] The domestic labor debate raised a series of questions regarding the nature of women's work in the home and its relationship to capital accumulation and the reproduction of labor power and relations of production. Marxist categories and frameworks of analysis were stretched and revised in an effort to understand housework, and in the process the family and the sexual division of labor were problematized. But this debate, especially those aspects concerning whether housework was "productive" or "unproductive labor," remained rather firmly on traditional Marxist terrain.

A major change was signaled when socialist feminists turned their attention to issues such as abortion, reproductive rights, sexuality, and the family —issues that did not presume the primacy of class relations or the centrality of the "point of production." The first systematic effort to synthesize Marxist and feminist theory was Mitchell's analysis of the interrelatedness of the four "structures"—production, reproduction, sexuality, and the socialization of children—that determine women's condition in society.[6] Mitchell broke loose from traditional Marxist categories of what constitutes oppression, and of the aspects of social life that shape human experience, to pose questions that came to be conceptualized in socialist-feminist theory as having to do with reproduction.

Trying to be good Marxists and, I would argue, trying to create a theoretical language that paralleled Marxism and thus was more likely to be heard by Marxists, socialist feminists sought to analyze the issues of family, procreation, and sexuality by conceptualizing a "mode of reproduction" that was to be examined historically in relation to the mode of production.[7] These theories highlighted a series of relationships that existed between the social organization of fertility and women's reproduction, the raising of children, women's unpaid work in the home, sex segregation in the labor force, the changing demographics of the labor force, and the organization of production and labor resistance.

It was a body of literature that aimed in several important directions, each posing significant challenges to traditional Marxist theory. First, women became important *as women,* not just as part of a genderless class, and the nature of women's oppression expanded to encompass their gender-specific experiences in reproduction. Second, once a mode of reproduction (or relations of reproduction) was granted theoretical autonomy (that is, not subsumed under relations of production), patriarchy was historicized and given a central role in the analysis of social formations. Moreover, struggles over the broadly defined reproductive capacities and activities of women—whether between men and women within families or between men of different classes[8]—were conceptualized as *political* and viewed as part of the movement of history. Finally, socialist-feminist theory thematized the relationships between patriarchy and capitalism, gender and class, gender consciousness and class consciousness.

For all its important insights and implications, the reproduction debate was mired in conceptual confusion and fell prey to a stagnating theoretical dualism.[9] This dualism postulates two separate systems of oppression, or the "dualist notion of a social totality as a composite of two discrete systems —patriarchy and mode of production."[10] The problem with this dualism was its failure to really explain the relationship between capitalism and patriarchy, or class and gender oppression.[11]

Despite these problems this literature has been invaluable in revealing the interconnections between domains of social relations and in helping to focus what Joan Kelly called a "doubled vision." "Doubled vision," Kelly argued, allows us to

> treat the family in relation to society; treat sexual and reproductive experience in terms of political economy; and treat productive relations of class in connection with class hierarchy. . . . From this perspective, our personal, social, and historical experience is seen to be shaped by the simultaneous operations of work and sex, relations that are systematically bound to each other—and always have been so bound. . . . [We now see] the relation of the sexes as formed by both socioeconomic and sexual-familial structures in their systematic connectedness.[12]

While "doubled vision" has helped to reconceptualize social life, the real move beyond a socialist feminism entrapped by dualist theorizing has been the refocusing of attention on the "intersection" of gender, race, and class in women's lives and in the constitution of social relations of power. While this is a welcome development in socialist feminism, it comes long after strong, black feminist voices have testified that race is at least as significant as gender and class for understanding the oppression of women of color.[13] Moreover, black feminists have argued that "capitalist patriarchy" was too narrow a concept to name the system of power that was founded on white supremacy as well as patriarchy and capitalism.[14]

As early as 1977 the Combahee River Collective declared that it was "actively committed to struggling against racial, sexual, heterosexual, and class oppression" and saw its "particular task as the development of integrated analysis and practice based upon the fact that the major systems of oppression are interlocking."[15] A few years later Angela Davis's *Woman, Race, and Class* (1981) exemplified the power of analysis that explores the interrelatedness of gender, race, and class in shaping the experiences of women. That same year, Gloria Joseph called for a new marriage (to replace the "unhappy" one of socialism and feminism)—that of black revolutionary socialism and socialist feminism.[16]

I believe that the historical shift from "dualist thinking" to "doubled vision" in socialist-feminist theory is indebted in large measure to the still fledgling incorporation of race—and to some extent ethnicity and culture—in theories of women's oppression and experience.[17] Race upset the applecart, so to speak—those neat models that counterposed gender and class, patriarchy and capitalism. Dualist frameworks such as the public-private and "capitalist patriarchy" had to be reexamined, and socialist feminists began to take more seriously not only the gender-specific nature of class experience but the class- and race-specific experiences of gender.[18] Clearly, it was not just socialist feminists who began to appreciate the importance of understanding differences among women; "diversity" had become a watchword (and one often given only lip service) in the larger feminist movement. Nevertheless, this new perspective helped to breathe new life into socialist-feminist theory and political practice.

Toward an Improved Relationship between Socialist Feminism and Marxism

Despite the vitality of socialist-feminist theory, Marxists have generally failed to appreciate how compelling is its critique of the Marxist paradigm or how promising are some of its theoretical insights. Lise Vogel suggests that much socialist-feminist work is ignored or treated as a "specialist literature" and peripheralized; either way, she concludes, "Marxism remains surprisingly untouched by socialist-feminist research." In a similar vein, Judith Stacey and Barrie Thorne assess Marxism as "remarkably un-

transformed," due to both resistance on the part of Marxists, and to socialist feminists' inclinations to develop "autonomous and almost exclusively
female institutions, conferences, and publications." [19]

Nevertheless, I believe that socialist feminism is uniquely situated to
offer Marxism insights that are sorely needed as contemporary Marxism
weathers its own current theoretical problems. [20] Contemporary Marxist
theorists, particularly critical Marxists, are seeking to move beyond the economic reductionism of Marxist orthodoxy. Critical Marxism is embroiled
in a debate about the relationship between, and primacy of, human agency
and structure in history. [21] In the process, the issues of ideology and consciousness have come to the forefront of Marxist theory to an unprecedented extent. This movement provides a strategic opening for socialist
feminists, whose work on ideology and consciousness has the potential to
be a significant force in the current debates and theoretical reformulations.

Both Marxist and feminist theory give consciousness a significant role in
the process of social transformation. Traditionally, Marxists have argued
that since class is the primary contradiction and point of struggle under
capitalism, it is class consciousness that has revolutionary importance. On
the other hand, feminists have regarded gender consciousness and women's
mobilization as fundamental for women's empowerment. Marxists view the
formation of class consciousness as a process that takes place primarily at
the "point of production" in struggles between labor and capital. Feminists
argue that gender consciousness emerges as women recognize their shared
oppression and organize as women.

Feminist and Marxist theorists, however, do share a number of fundamental assumptions about ideology and consciousness, though these areas
of overlap are often overlooked. Both Marxist and feminist theories adopt
what John Thompson calls a "critical conception of ideology . . . in which
ideology is essentially linked to the process of sustaining asymmetrical relations of power, that is, to the process of maintaining domination." [22] For
both, the study of ideology is inextricably linked to relations of domination.
Feminist and Marxist theories focus on the social and historical processes
that generate, sustain, and potentially alter ideology and consciousness.
And these traditions, while recognizing the pervasiveness of dominant ideology, highlight the oppositional ideologies (class, racial-ethnic, or gender
based) that exist in given historical circumstances and assert the power of
such ideologies in political life.

Many feminists, including socialist feminists, have argued that Marxism is not a useful theoretical framework for understanding ideology or
consciousness because of its inattention to and theoretical subordination of
the realm of ideation. Marxist economic reductionism imbues the mode of

production with such deterministic influence that the analysis of ideology has suffered enormously. When traditional Marxist theory has examined ideology, it has been largely to focus on how relations of production shape institutions and processes that inculcate and reinforce bourgeois ideology,[23] or on how the "vanguard" potential of proletarian ideology, rooted in the material conditions of working-class life, can lead a revolutionary movement for the overthrow of capitalism. As accurate as these assessments of the weaknesses of traditional Marxist theory are, the conception of Marxism that led many feminists to reject its value and turn to alternative sources is dated; in fact, a great deal of current Marxist theory takes ideology and consciousness very seriously.[24]

I am not the first to note the convergence between socialist feminism and critical Marxism. British socialist feminists have been influenced by critical Marxist theory, beginning with Juliet Mitchell's indebtedness to Louis Althusser. Michèle Barrett's work rests on a critical Marxist foundation, and many of the authors in the important collection *Feminism and Materialism* demonstrate a sensitivity to these recent developments in Marxist thinking.[25] North American feminists, however—including most socialist feminists—have not shown as much interest in or engagement with critical Marxist theory.[26]

Two major figures in the shift in Marxist theory are Althusser and Antonio Gramsci. Both rejected the reductionist concept of ideology that viewed it as a mechanical reflection of the mode or relations of production.[27] Post-Althusserian Marxism sees ideology as "relatively autonomous" from the relations of production; that is, these relations specify "for a particular historical context, the limits to the autonomous operation of ideology."[28] Althusserian theory views ideology as lived experience, and explores how individuals are constructed and reproduced—"interpellated" —in ideology. Chantal Mouffe credits Gramsci with breaking away from the conception of ideology as "false consciousness" and revealing how reductionism wrongly posits a necessary "class-belonging" to all ideology.[29]

Michèle Barrett has argued that critical Marxism, with its more sophisticated understanding of ideology, can better "accommodate the oppression of women as a relatively autonomous element of the social formation." She sees feminist theory as part of a general challenge to economic reductionism in Marxism and envisions a "fruitful alignment of interests between those who seek to raise the question of gender and its place in Marxist theory, and those who seek to challenge economism in Marxism, insisting on the importance of ideological processes."[30] While I share this vision, I suggest that in fact the debt of socialist-feminist theory to critical Marxism may *not* be as great as Barrett proposes; it seems that much of the analysis of ideology and consciousness by socialist feminists and Marxists has been parallel rather than convergent.

For example, it was not to Marxism but more often to psychoanalytic and poststructuralist theories that many feminists turned as they sought to conceptualize consciousness, particularly the relationship of the body, sexuality, and consciousness.[31] Work incorporating these theories has highlighted the importance of feelings, the unconscious, language, and the roles of childbearer and child rearer in the development of women's consciousness.[32] Armed with these understandings and a deeper appreciation of the ways that gender, race, and class shape and constrain consciousness in concrete historical situations, socialist feminists have broken new ground in understanding the role of human agency in social change and the complex relationship between oppression and resistance. With these new perspectives socialist feminists have a great deal to offer critical Marxism in a mutual endeavor to understand what motivates, fosters, constrains, and undermines struggles for empowerment by subordinate groups.

Socialist-Feminist Perspectives on Ideology and Consciousness

Once feminists and Marxists increasingly turned their attention to the active struggle of human actors to modify, change, and transform oppressive social relations, the need to better understand consciousness became apparent. For somewhere in the complex dialectic of oppression and resistance lies the process through which people become aware of oppression and the possibilities for change. In that process historical, ideological, cultural, and political-economic forces shape experience and the interpretations of experience, visions of alternatives and the routes toward those alternatives.

In my view, socialist-feminist theory offers three main perspectives on ideology and consciousness that have the potential to engage and influence developing Marxist theories: (1) frameworks for analyzing the relationship of ideology, consciousness, and historical conditions which focus on the process of consciousness formation and change; (2) analysis of the specificity of class and gender consciousness; and (3) theories of consciousness that take account of the historical/material and the psychological/unconscious forces shaping consciousness and political action.

Sarah Eisenstein's social-historical case study of the development of working women's consciousness in New York in the early twentieth century is an excellent example of emerging socialist-feminist theory demonstrating these insights. Eisenstein argues that as women were drawn into the labor force, their consciousness regarding the social relations of production was shaped by their work experiences. Unlike most Marxist analyses, however, Eisenstein's discussion is not limited to the development of class consciousness. For these women, she says, "work in factory or store was their first collective experience in a situation where the social position they share *as women* could emerge." In the context of the particular historical conditions of women's overwhelming concentration in "female occupations," their organization into separate union locals, and the ideological milieus available to them, women workers' consciousness entailed a collective identity as *women* as well as members of a *class*. Furthermore, Eisenstein continues, "the awareness of collective identity among women wage-earners was affected in the first instance by variations in their ethnic, regional and occupational milieux."[33]

Eisenstein also explores the process by which ideologies inform action in specific historical circumstances. Extending Frank Parkin's analysis of the relationship of the working class to the dominant cultural ideology as a process of negotiation—rather than as wholesale acceptance or rejection —Eisenstein shows the importance of analyzing both dominant and oppositional ideologies as they are interpreted and transformed in real life experience. She concludes that

> working women in the period under discussion generally accepted the central elements of the prevailing image of womanhood [Victorian, e.g., cult of true womanhood] but they did so in terms which demonstrate the mediation of their own experiences. Where they developed ideas which were explicitly critical of prevailing ideology, these did not represent a simple reflection of the arguments of the labor, feminist, or socialist movements with which they were in contact, but a characteristic "negotiation" of them in light of working women's particular situation.[34]

Eisenstein's work shows how class experience and consciousness are interpreted through the laws of gender and ethnicity, and it demonstrates an approach to the analysis of the complex process by which ideologies, history, and material circumstances are interpreted and actively negotiated by women in their efforts to comprehend, live with, and change the conditions of their lives.

In addition to other excellent historical studies that explore working-class women's consciousness,[35] socialist feminists have examined political consciousness and activism among contemporary working-class women in the United States[36] and among peasant and working-class women in the Third World.[37] These studies build on and extend socialist-feminist understandings of political economy to reveal both the complex roots of women's consciousness and the different avenues groups of women have taken toward political action.

Women's experience and consciousness of class, for example, tend to be different from those of men not only because men and women occupy different positions in the labor force and in the organization of the economy as a whole but also because the multiplicity of women's roles in the workplace, in families, and in communities positions them differently in relation to political processes and to the state. That these differences can have a significant impact on women's political consciousness and the choices women make about political action is demonstrated in a recent book I edited with Ann Bookman on the activism of contemporary working-class women in the United States.[38] The articles in this book show, for example, how working-class women have often turned to community and neighborhood organization not because they *lack* class consciousness but because as women with limited incomes, and sometimes as victims of racial or ethnic oppression, concerns with housing, education, health care, neighborhood safety, and families were the most important political issues in their lives. Moreover, for many women of color and poor women, an awareness of and struggle against their oppression as women has emerged from involvement in neighborhood and community organization or in struggles at the workplace rather than in organizing around the gender-specific issues central to the agenda of feminism.

Socialist-feminist analyses of the historical and contemporary experiences of women involved in political action reveal that because work, family, and community are not usually experienced as discrete entities (that is, separate spheres) in women's lives, women develop political visions that are shaped by their multiple responsibilities in and among these spheres. This helps to explain why women have been at the forefront of campaigns that target issues emerging from the intersection of work, family, and community, issues such as child care, parental leave, community development and housing, and toxic waste.

Race, class, and culture dramatically influence the resources and constraints that condition women's lives. There is no "woman's" consciousness, then, that flows from a gendered position in the social structure; rather, gender consciousness is shaped fundamentally by a woman's class and race position, which structures her work inside and outside the family, her reproductive experiences, and her relationship to the state. Too often, gender consciousness, race consciousness, and class consciousness are examined as discrete "things" that must be seen in relation to each other, usually in different combinations for different groups of women. This belies the fact that these social relations so interpenetrate that they are better understood as constituting (rather than simply modifying—or coloring, if you will) one another.

The task of developing theoretical frameworks within which to address the articulation of gender, race, and class is a crucial one. But as Pratibha Parmar warns, to analyze this articulation "solely at a theoretical level yields very generalized observations which would be undermined by a lack of reference to specific instances. It is crucial that these observations are grounded in concrete and specific material situations."[39] Much of the thrust of current socialist-feminist scholarship does just this: it examines the linkages and interpenetrations of gender, race, and class in specific historical and cultural cases.

Rosalind Petchesky proposes a conceptualization of consciousness that reflects and expresses the multifaceted insights of socialist-feminist theory. She defines consciousness as a

> dynamic process of accommodating the conflicting ideologies and values imposed by the dominant culture and various oppositional cultures on one's own sense of felt need. That sense, in turn, grows out of material and social constraints that may disrupt ideological pre-conceptions rooted in class and life situations and in the unconsciousness and the body. Consciousness is thus a series of negotiations back and forth between ideology, social reality, and desire.[40]

Throughout her definition the dynamism of consciousness is emphasized. The statement allows for complexity and conflict both within and between dominant and oppositional ideologies while retaining the materialist conception of the importance of historical conditions and class. The feminist recognition of the importance of feeling and of the important contribution of psychology to the understanding of mental and emotional life, however, is also incorporated, as is the experience of the body, so essential to recent feminist theories of consciousness. The interaction of consciousness and ideology, particularly the way consciousness can break out of the grip of received ideas, is underlined and embedded in a framework within which consciousness is socially constituted and constituting.

A focus on process and the emphasis on subjectivity and feeling are themes that have enjoyed a central place in contemporary feminist theory. Socialist feminists have harnessed these themes to the analysis of political economy.[41] When the analysis of the process of consciousness development is placed in the context of socialist-feminist understandings of the interconnectedness of "public" and "private" domains (personal and political, work and family) and of the intersection of gender, race, and class, the ensuing explanatory frameworks are very powerful.

It is my contention that the definition of consciousness proposed by Petchesky and the approaches that socialist feminists have developed to analyze consciousness have the potential to give the Marxist human subject a historically and socially constituted consciousness that can ensure a place for agency in theories of social change. Moreover, the work on the gender and race specificity of class experience and consciousness is critical to Marxists as they reassess the meaning and centrality of class in their theory. Of course, socialist feminism can make an impact on Marxism only if there is meaningful dialogue between them. And it is easy to be disheartened about this possibility, given that the Marxist record of taking gender and feminist theory seriously is still weak.

So why do I pose this challenge at a time when many socialist feminists seem ready to give up not only on Marxism but also on socialist feminism, as do some of the authors in this book? While I agree with other contributors that there are weaknesses in socialist-feminist theory and that socialist feminism has failed to develop a distinctive political practice, I do not believe that socialist feminism is dead. The 1980s have been full of premature post-mortems. Socialist feminists still occupy an important structural position between feminists and other progressive and critical theorists and movements. Moreover, much of the vitality of socialist feminism has come and continues to grow from our engagement with theories and movements outside of feminism—those of the working class, of peoples of color, and of revolutionary socialism. I have highlighted here an area of socialist-feminist thought rich in insight and importance for both activists and theorists. While socialist feminism has encountered impasses over the past decade and still faces both theoretical and political hurdles, there are promising paths ahead.

Notes

1. This idea received its first circulation in a working paper by Amy Bridges and Heidi Hartmann, "The Unhappy Marriage of Marxism and Feminism," July 1975. This draft was substantially revised and circulated most widely in the following form: Heidi Hartmann, "The Unhappy Marriage of Marxism and Feminism: Towards a More Progressive Union," in *Women and Revolution: A Discussion of the Unhappy Marriage of Marxism and Feminism*, ed. Lydia Sargent (Boston: South End Press, 1981), 1–41.

2. Lydia Sargent, "New Left Women and Men: The Honeymoon Is Over," in Sargent, *Women and Revolution*, xiii–xxxii.

3. Juliet Mitchell, *Woman's Estate* (New York: Random House, 1971), 99.

4. Margaret Benston, "The Political Economy of Women's Liberation," *Monthly Review* 21, no. 4 (1969): 13–27.

5. See Pat Armstrong and Hugh Armstrong, "Beyond Sexless Class and Classless Sex: Towards Feminist Marxism," *Studies in Political Economy* 10 (Winter 1983); M. Coulson, B. Magas, and H. Wainwright, "The Housewife and Her Labor under Capitalism—A Critique," *New Left Review* 89 (1975): 59–71; M. Dalla Costa and Selma James, *The Power of Women and the Subversion of the Community* (Bristol: Falling Wall Press, 1975); Bonnie Fox, ed., *Hidden in the Household: Women's Domestic Labor under Capitalism* (Toronto: Women's Press, 1980); J. Gardiner, "Women's Domestic Labor," *New Left Review* 89 (1975): 47–72; Annette Kuhn and Annmarie Wolpe, eds., *Feminism and Materialism* (London: Routledge & Kegan Paul, 1978); Pat Mainardi, "The Politics of Housework," in *Sisterhood Is Powerful*, ed. Robin Morgan (New York: Random House, 1970); Maxine Molyneux, "Beyond the Domestic Labor Debate," *New Left Review* 116 (1979): 3–27; Peggy Morton, "A Woman's Work Is Never Done," in *From Feminism to Liberation*, ed. E. H. Altbach (Cambridge, Mass.: Schenkman, 1971); Wally Seccombe, "The Housewife and Her Labor under Capitalism," *New Left Review* 83 (1974): 3–24.

6. Mitchell, *Woman's Estate*.

7. See Lourdes Beneria and Gita Sen, "Accumulation, Reproduction, and Women's Roles in Economic Development," *Signs* 7, no. 3 (1981): 279–98; Renate Bridenthal, "The Dialectics of Production and Reproduction in History," *Radical America* 10, no. 2 (1976): 3–11; Hartmann, "The Unhappy Marriage of Marxism and Feminism"; Heidi Hartmann and Ann Markusen, "Contemporary Marxist Theory and Practice: A Feminist Critique," *Review of Radical Political Economics* 12, no. 2 (Summer 1980); M. Mackintosh, "Reproduction and Patriarchy: A Critique of Meillasoux's *Femmes, Greniers, et Capitaux*," *Capital and Class* 2 (1977); Roisin McDonough and Rachel Harrison, "Patriarchy and Relations of Production," in Kuhn and Wolfe, *Feminism and Materialism*; Bridget O'Laughlin, "Production and Reproduction: Meillasoux's *Femmes, Greniers, et Capitaux*," *Critique of Anthropology* 8 (Spring 1977); Women's Work Study Group, "Loom, Broom, and Womb: Maintenance and Production," *Radical America* 10, no. 2 (1981): 29–45; Mary O'Brien, *The Politics of Reproduction* (London: Routledge & Kegan Paul, 1981).

8. See Claude Meillasoux, "From Reproduction to Production—A Marxist Approach to Economic Anthropology," *Economy and Society* 1, no. 1 (1972): 93–105.

9. See Michèle Barrett, *Women's Oppression Today* (London: Verso Books, 1980); F. Edholm, O. Harris, and K. Young. "Conceptualizing Women," *Critique of Anthropology* 3, nos. 9–10 (1977): 101–30.

10. See Linda Burnham and Miriam Louie, "The Impossible Marriage—A Critique of Socialist Feminism," *Line of March* 17 (1985): 39. The Burnham and Louie critique is part of the more comprehensive question of the assumptions and premises of socialist feminism.

11. Socialist feminists have made the same internal critique of theoretical dualism. See, e.g., Barbara Ehrenreich, "Life without Father: Reconsidering Socialist-Feminist Theory," *Socialist Review* 14, no. 1 (January–February 1984): 48–58, and Chapter 10 in this book; Zillah Eisenstein, ed., *Capitalist Patriarchy and the Case for Socialist Feminism* (New York: Monthly Review Press, 1979); Iris Young, "Socialist

Feminism and the Limits of Dual Systems Theory," in Sargent, *Women and Revolution*; Judith Van Allen, "Capitalism without Patriarchy," *Socialist Review* 14, no. 5 (September–October 1984): 81–91, and Chapter 12 in this volume.

12. Joan Kelly, "The Doubled Vision of Feminist Theory," *Feminist Studies* 5, no. 1 (1979): 216–29.

13. Some of the early black feminist writings from the late 1960s and early 1970s include Frances Beale, "Double Jeopardy: To Be Black and Female," *New Generation* 51 (1969): 23–28; Toni Cade, ed., *The Black Woman: An Anthology* (New York: Signet, 1970); Pauli Murray, "The Liberation of Black Women," in *Voices of the New Feminism*, ed. M. Thompson (Boston: Beacon Press, 1970).

14. See critiques by Angela Davis, *Women, Race, and Class* (New York: Random House, 1981); Bonnie Dill, "The Dialectics of Black Womanhood," *Signs* 4, no. 3 (Spring 1979): 543–55, and "Race, Class and Gender: Prospects for an All-Inclusive Sisterhood," *Feminist Studies* 9, no. 1 (1983): 131–50; June Jordan, "Second Thoughts of a Black Feminist," *Ms.* 5 (1977): 113–15; bell hooks, *Ain't I a Woman? Black Women and Feminism* (Boston: South End Press, 1981); bell hooks, *Feminist Theory: From Margin to Center* (Boston: South End Press, 1984); Gloria Hull, Patricia Bell Scott, and Barbara Smith, *All the Women Are White, All the Blacks Are Men, but Some of Us Are Brave: Black Women's Studies* (Old Westbury, N.Y.: Feminist Press, 1982); Gloria Joseph, "The Incompatible Ménage à Trois: Marxism, Feminism, and Racism," in Sargent, *Women and Revolution*.

15. Combahee River Collective, "A Black Feminist Statement," in Hull, Scott, and Smith, *All the Women Are White*, 13.

16. Joseph, "Incompatible Ménage à Trois."

17. It would be a mistake to overestimate the extent to which the perspectives of women of color or the experience of race has influenced feminist theory in general, or socialist feminism in particular. E.g., in Alison Jaggar, *Feminist Politics and Human Nature* (Totowa, N.J.: Rowman & Allanheld, 1983), the author subsumes black feminism under the different typologies of feminist theory rather than devoting a section to its unique perspectives. While feminists have devoted more attention to diversity among women and the voices of women of color, the analysis of race and racism still lags far behind feminist theoretical work on gender or class.

18. See, e.g., Bettina Aptheker, *Women's Legacy: Essays in Race, Sex, and Class in American History* (Amherst: University of Massachusetts Press, 1982); Amy Swerlow and Hannah Lessinger, eds., *Class, Race, and Sex: The Dynamics of Control* (Boston: C. K. Hall, 1983); Carol Stack, "Different Voices, Different Visions: Race, Gender and Moral Reasoning," and Sandra Morgen, "The Dream of Diversity, the Dilemmas of Difference: Race and Class Contradiction in a Feminist Health Clinic," both in Johnnetta Cole, ed., *Anthropology for the Nineties* (New York: Free Press, 1988).

19. Lise Vogel, "Feminist Scholarship: The Impact of Marxism," in Bertell Ollman and Edward Vernoff, eds., *The Left Academy: Marxist Scholarship on American Campuses* (New York: Praeger, 1986), 1–34. Judith Stacey and Barrie Thorne, "The Missing Feminist Revolution in Sociology," *Social Problems* 32, no. 4 (1985): 301–16.

20. For discussions of current theoretical debates within Marxism today, see Stuart Hall, "Cultural Studies: Two Paradigms," *Media, Culture and Society* 2 (1980): 57–72; Ernesto LaClau, *Politics and Ideology in Marxist Theory* (London: New Left Books, 1977); E. P. Thompson, "Politics of Theory," in *People's History and Socialist Theory*, ed. R. Samuel (London: Routledge & Kegan Paul, 1981); Raymond Williams, "Base and Superstructure in Marxist Cultural Theory," *New Left Review* 82

(1973): 973, and *Marxism and Literature* (New York: Oxford University Press, 1977); L. Althusser and E. Balibar, *Reading "Capital"* (London: New Left Books, 1970).

21. "Critical Marxism" is a term I use to encompass significant twentieth-century Marxist theory that aims to revise Marxism, particularly to counter economic reductionism. Sweeping broadly, I include the Frankfurt school, cultural studies, cultural Marxism, and Marxist "structuralists." The very significant theoretical and political differences within this large grouping are ignored here, as my focus is on the overriding theoretical issues and the potential dialogue socialist feminists must initiate to participate in and influence these debates.

22. John Thompson, *Studies in the Theory of Ideology* (Berkeley: University of California Press, 1984), 4.

23. E.g., Samuel Bowles and Herbert Gintis, *Schooling in Capitalist America* (London: Routledge & Kegan Paul, 1976).

24. For a summary and overview, see Jorge Larrain, *Marxism and Ideology* (London: Macmillan, 1983).

25. Kuhn and Wolpe, *Feminism and Materialism.*

26. This is more than an impression, though its demonstration awaits the socio-intellectual history of socialist feminism that I suggest is needed. Checking the bibliographic references cited in articles in two of the important North American collections of socialist-feminist theory—Eisenstein, *Capitalist Patriarchy*, and Sargent, *Women and Revolution*—I found the primary references to Marxist scholarship to be to the works of Marx and Engels themselves. There is little reference to critical Marxist scholarship with the exception of articles by N. Hartsock, I. Young, C. Riddiough, and A. Furguson and N. Folbre.

27. Louis Althusser, *Lenin and Philosophy and Other Essays* (London: New Left Books, 1971); Antonio Gramsci, *Selections from the Prison Notebooks* (New York: International Publishers, 1971).

28. Barrett, *Women's Oppression Today*, 97.

29. Chantal Mouffe, *Gramsci and Marxist Theory* (Boston: Routledge & Kegan Paul, 1979).

30. Barrett, *Women's Oppression Today*, 31, 85.

31. See work by M. Bakhtin, J. Derrida, M. Foucault, J. Lacan. For feminist incorporation of these theoretical perspectives, see E. Marks and I. de Courtivron, eds., *New French Feminisms: An Anthology* (New York: Schocken, 1981); Gayatri Spivak, "Displacement and the Discourse of Woman," in *Derrida and After*, ed. M. Krupnick (Bloomington: Indiana University Press, 1983); and selected essays by Teresa de Lauretis, *Feminist Studies, Critical Studies* (Bloomington: Indiana University Press, 1986).

32. Juliet Mitchell, *Psychoanalysis and Feminism* (New York: Vintage Books, 1975); Gayle Rubin, "The Traffic in Women," in Rayna Rapp Reiter, ed., *Toward an Anthropology of Women* (New York: Monthly Review Press, 1975), and Chapter 3 in this book; Dorothy Dinnerstein, *The Mermaid and the Minotaur: Sexual Arrangements and Human Malaise* (New York: Harper & Row, 1977); Nancy Chodorow, *The Reproduction of Mothering: Psychoanalysis and the Sociology of Gender* (Berkeley: University of California Press, 1978); Sarah Ruddick, "Maternal Thinking," *Feminist Studies* 6, no. 4 (1980); Hélène Cixous, "The Laughter of the Medusa," *Signs* 1, no. 4 (1976): 875–93.

33. Sarah Eisenstein, *Give Us Bread but Give Us Roses: Working Women's Consciousness in the U.S.–1890 to the First World War* (London: Routledge & Kegan Paul, 1983), 40 (my emphasis), 147.

34. Ibid., 47.

35. See Ruth Milkman, ed., *Women, Work, and Protest: A Century of U.S. Women's Labor History* (Boston: Routledge & Kegan Paul, 1985); Kathy Peiss, *Cheap Amusements: Working Women and Leisure in Turn of the Century New York* (Philadelphia: Temple University Press, 1986); Deborah Gray White, *Ar'n't I a Woman? Female Slaves in the Plantation South* (New York: Norton, 1985).

36. See Ann Bookman and Sandra Morgen, *Women and the Politics of Empowerment* (Philadelphia: Temple University Press, 1988); Karen Sacks and Dorothy Remy, eds., *My Troubles Are Going to Have Trouble with Me: Everyday Trials and Triumphs of Women Workers* (New Brunswick, N.J.: Rutgers University Press, 1982); Kathleen McCourt, *Working Class Women and Grassroots Politics* (Bloomington: Indiana University Press, 1977); Ida Susser, *Norman Street: Poverty and Politics in an Urban Neighborhood* (New York: Oxford University Press, 1982); Karen Sacks, *Caring by the Hour: Women, Work, and Organizing at Duke Medical Center* (Urbana: University of Illinois Press, 1987); Pat Zavella, *Women's Work and Chicano Families: Cannery Workers of the Santa Clara Valley* (Ithaca, N.Y.: Cornell University Press, 1987).

37. See Eleanor Leacock and Helen Safa, eds., *Women's Work: Development and the Division of Labor by Gender* (South Hadley, Mass.: Bergin and Garvey, 1986); June Nash and Maria Patricia Fernandez-Kelly, eds., *Women and Men, and the International Division of Labor* (Albany, N.Y.: Suny Press, 1983); Aihwa Ong, *Spirits of Resistance and Capitalist Discipline* (Albany, N.Y.: Suny Press, 1987); Claire Robertson and Iris Berger, *Women and Class in Africa* (New York: Africana, 1986); Martha Ackelsberg, "Mujeres Libres: Community and Individuality—Organizing Women in the Spanish Civil War," *Radical America* 18, no. 4:7–19; Carol Andreas, *When Women Rebel: The Rise of Popular Feminism in Peru* (Westport, Conn.: Lawrence Hill, 1985).

38. Sandra Morgen and Ann Bookman, "Rethinking Women and Politics: An Introductory Essay," in Morgen and Bookman, *Women and the Politics of Empowerment.*

39. Pratibha Parmar, "Gender, Race, and Class: Asian Women in Resistance," in Centre for Contemporary Cultural Studies, *The Empire Strikes Back: Race and Racism in 1970s Britain* (Birmington, England: Centre for Contemporary Cultural Studies, University of Birmingham, 1982).

40. Rosalind Petchesky, *Abortion and Woman's Choice* (Boston: Northeastern University Press, 1984), 366.

41. See Nancy Hartsock, "Feminist Theory and the Development of Revolutionary Strategy," in Eisenstein, *Capitalist Patriarchy*; Arlie Hochschild, *The Managed Heart: The Commercialization of Feeling* (Berkeley: University of California Press, 1983); Sandra Morgen, "Towards a Politics of Feelings; Beyond the Dialectic of Thought and Action," *Women's Studies* 10, no. 2 (1983): 203–23.

12   Capitalism without Patriarchy

Judith Van Allen

Socialist feminism grew out of a unity of theory and practice in the early women's liberation movement. Because we broke away from new left groups just as they were turning more toward Marxist theory and Third World national liberation movements for intellectual and political guidance, socialist feminism evolved through theoretical confrontations with Marxism intermingled with daily confrontations with socialist men over practice.

Even when we moved into autonomous women's groups, we still thought of ourselves as part of the left, and our theory and practice continued to evolve together. With the demise of socialist-feminist unions, socialist feminism as an organizational form declined and took up residence in the academy. There Marxist-feminist theory has evolved and grown more sophisticated, but it has lost its direct link to political practice.[1]

Socialist feminists doing academic work often take an explicitly political stance in their writing: they write in order to change the world. And academic socialist feminists often support feminist and democratic socialist organizations. But those socialist feminists solidly situated in academia and writing Marxist-feminist analyses are rarely the same women as those trying to work out strategies for organizations or for the left.

The reasons for this frequent divorce of theory from practice are varied and complicated, but some are obvious. Political activism is difficult to combine with a full-time academic job. Many academic socialist feminists are in

Source: This article is reprinted from *Socialist Review* No. 77 (September–October 1984), pp. 81–91, by permission of the publisher, *Socialist Review*, 3202 Adeline, Berkeley, CA 94703.

or connected with women's studies programs that must be constantly defended against political financial assaults. Deeper and perhaps even more serious is the always existing tension on the left between "theorists" and "activists," a tension that often broke into open hostility within women's liberation, given its incipient antiintellectualism and tendency to identify theoretical ideas as "male."

Women's studies programs have offered a partial haven from the destructive effects of feminist antiintellectualism, and since the mid-1970s, Marxist-feminist analyses and theories have in fact blossomed tremendously. But if that theory is to be of direct political use, it must be brought to bear on questions of feminist political strategy. Marxist-feminist scholars have produced valuable historical and theoretical work that can be drawn upon to create strategy, but they have rarely taken the leap into making strategic inferences from their own work.

Therefore, for those of us committed to building a genuinely feminist democratic left, the task is twofold: we must incorporate the best and discard the worst of existing Marxist-feminist theory, and build stronger ties between "strategists" and "theorists" in order to restore some unity to socialist-feminist theory and practice.

Breaking the Functionalist Myth

Socialist feminism for the future must jettison the conceptual baggage of Marxist-feminist functionalism that we acquired in the "high ideology" period of the 1970s. In that functionalist conception, "capitalism" and "patriarchy" were seen as interdependent and abstract systems, each with its own inexorable needs, together forming a seamless web of "capitalist patriarchy." We saw capitalism as functioning to reinforce and support patriarchy, and patriarchy functioning to reinforce and support capitalism, not as the result of historical contingency but by necessity: the logic of capitalism demanded the patriarchal nuclear family and the free labor of the housewife.

The only way out of this functionalist equilibrium seemed to be socialist revolution, and we looked with romantic eyes at women guerrillas in the Third World as models of women's liberation, our admiration for them fueled by our very real rage at our own country's actions in Vietnam. In our small groups we studiously read "Goldflower's Story" and discussed women in China as a guide to how we were going to achieve liberation for women in the United States.

This functionalist fantasy, which pictured patriarchy/capitalism as the problem and socialism/feminism as the solution, left us ill prepared for the political realities of the 1970s and 1980s. We have come to see that adding feminism to bad Marxism does not improve the character of either one: vulgar Marxism cannot be redeemed by the love of a good woman. Uncritical support for liberation struggles left many of us ripe for disillusion when we started to learn more about what was going on in various Third World countries and how those revolutions did not liberate women in our terms. Many of us reacted with surprise and sometimes a sense of betrayal and bitterness. Some socialist feminists rejected any identification with existing socialism and became "radical feminists" or simply "feminists." Those of us who remained "socialist feminists" were left wondering just how we should understand what was happening to women in those Third World societies.

This crisis of belief caused many of us to reevaluate our ideas. We have given up drawing direct analogies between our experience and that of women in Third World countries. But we are still trying to analyze what the links are between their oppression and ours. We are moving beyond uncritical acceptance of laundry lists of "feminist progress" and the ruling revolutionary parties' line that it's "just a matter of time" before bad ideology withers away. Instead, we are developing structural analyses of kinship and the division of labor inside and outside the household in revolutionary societies and examining how various forms of revolutionary socialism and family structure do or do not create new conditions that could foster further struggles over gender relations.[2]

There has always been a threat of this more dialectical perspective running through the fabric of socialist feminism. Since the early 1970s different voices have periodically pointed out that the process of capitalist development has opened possibilities for feminist as well as socialist struggle. The dominant discourse, however, has been functionalist. We marched behind banners proclaiming "Smash the Family," a slogan representing not only a strategy for freeing women at the "primary site of their oppression" (a goal that put us in happy but brief congruence with radical feminists) but also a way to smash capitalism, which "needed" the patriarchal nuclear family to survive.

We were wrong about capitalism's supposed needs, but our slogans were in fact quite functional in meeting *our* needs. In those early years of women's liberation, we needed strong polemics and slogans. They were the dynamite we used to explode Marxist and other male left categories, and we needed their power to strengthen our resolve during those years of vitriolic ridicule from both our "brothers" and what we then called the "pig press." Our mistake was in turning our slogans into theory and producing Marxist-feminist theory that assumed a functionalist fit between the two reified entities "capitalism" and "patriarchy."

This indissoluble linkage of capitalism and patriarchy in opposition to feminism has been Marxist feminism's most alluring, and for a time comforting, error. During the period of the Vietnam War and our intense commitment to national liberation movements, we did not want to see anything good coming out of capitalism. Even when we talked about capitalist development "opening possibilities for struggle," our emphasis tended to be on how such development "heightened the contradictions" in women's lives (whether in the nineteenth-century bourgeoisie or in 1950s suburbia) and so provoked feminist struggle. Therefore, we tended to overlook or underemphasize the ways in which advanced capitalist development—itself proceeding through political struggles between workers and employers, and women and men—was "smashing" the very family we often saw as so necessary for the survival of American capitalism.

By the late 1970s many of us recognized the significance of both the massive incorporation of new categories of women—white women, middle-class women, mothers of young children—into the permanent labor force, and the turmoil in family life that such incorporation was provoking. These changes forced us to rethink the idea that our position as women was determined by a certain system with certain needs. We are now in a better position to understand feminism neither as a response to a functionally unified "capitalist patriarchy" nor as a tool used by "monolithic capitalism" to extract women's labor from the family household. We can see it instead as one of the social forces in a continuous historical process of social restructuring through political struggle, a dialectical process in which change is generated by internal conflicts and contradictions.

Within this process, feminism, as a political movement challenging laws, institutions, and patriarchal ideology, is a source as well as an effect of the social transformations we are experiencing.[3] It is both a response to the suffering entailed in the wrenching apart of old patterns of social responsibility and the anarchic relations that exist while new patterns of responsibility are being (temporarily) established, and an attempt to realize the liberatory possibilities created within that anarchy.

A dialectical perspective can lead us away from the temptation to characterize political conflicts over gender relations in terms of unity *or* contradiction between the abstract categories "patriarchy" and "capitalism," and instead push us to examine the contradictory nature of feminist goals within capitalist society to see, for example, how feminist goals may sometimes conflict with and sometimes overlap the interests of particular sectors of capital or particular sectors of organized labor.[4]

The issue of abortion highlights this contradictory nature. The right to control one's own body has become a core definition of feminism in this society, which indicates feminism's deep connection to the liberal individualist ideology that is part of capitalism. The 1973 Supreme Court decision legalizing abortion responded to a climate of opinion created by feminists, even though the court based its decision on a woman's "right of privacy," not on her "right to control her own body." Since 1973, conservatives have been trying to reverse the decision and have succeeded in denying poor women the right to abortion in many states by cutting off federal funding. But they have not been able to overcome the feminist challenge to patriarchal ideology: abortion is now a public issue, not a shameful backroom secret. Why?

Not because feminism is strong enough to defeat a monolithic "capitalist patriarchy" but because internal divisions and conflicts of interest within the contemporary United States made it easier for us to win some parts of the reproductive freedom we want. Fiscal and moral conservatives in their opposition to abortion should be seen as representing only some of the many contradictory interests within capitalism. A relegation of women to the home and a coerced rise in the fertility rate would make women less available for wage labor in the expanding service sector, which puts the interests of capitalists in that sector at odds with conservatives' expressed goals. Conservative assaults on feminism, however, do fuel the ideological fires that help maintain the sexual division of labor in the household and sex segregation in the labor market. These in turn keep women "in their place" as cheap, relatively docile labor, which benefits those same service-sector capitalists.

Legal abortion, contraception, and sterilization—as distinct from authentic reproductive freedom—are problematic for women in any society as long as they remain only legal rights rather than substantive rights embedded in a structure providing comparable pay, workers' control over their workplaces, and economic accessibility of abortion to all women. As they now exist, contraception, abortion, and sterilization can all too easily serve an employer's interest in women as wage laborers, because their legal availability can make it possible for employers to exert more control over women's reproductive choices. Given current conditions in the economy, that control is more likely to be used to reduce than to enhance women's roles as reproducers. Therefore, in the long run, conservatives fighting abortion rights are probably waging a losing battle against historical change: as more and more women move into wage labor, their demands for autonomy will increase, not decrease. Even "counterprocesses" such as the automation of clerical work are more likely to create new arenas of political struggle than to prompt a mass exodus of women from wage labor.

If a woman is dependent on her job for her support—as more and more women will be—and she can get an abortion if she gets pregnant, what is to prevent an employer from demanding that she get an abortion in order to keep her job? Or get herself sterilized and "solve the problem" permanently? When jobs are hard to find, an employer need not demand anything. Some women workers at American Cyanamide have already had themselves sterilized for fear of losing their jobs because the corporation "had expressed concern that a fertile woman would sue if she gave birth to an abnormal child."[5] How many other women have been sterilized, or have had abortions "before the boss noticed"?

The repressiveness of "population control" in the Third World bears ample warning of the uses to which potentially liberating technology can be put when women themselves do not set the priorities. The right to bear and raise a child without sacrificing one's health, one's sanity, or one's job, and without having to be a man's wife, will be a much more difficult right to gain than was the right not to have a child. Such a demand cuts across the capitalist division between work and family and demands radical changes in both, thereby putting feminists at odds with many more of the social forces within our society than does the demand for legal abortion.

In our early socialist-feminist focus on "smashing the (patriarchal nuclear) family," we spent too much time beating a dead norm and too often spoke as though the rapid movement of women into wage labor, the growth and sudden visibility of the two-job family, and the increasing numbers of women raising children on their own ("outside the patriarchal control of men") were the direct results of feminist campaigns and the diffusion of feminist ideas into the mainstream. Lacking any analysis of structural change, the right and many of the mass media held feminists responsible for all these developments, and sometimes it was tempting for us to believe their assessments of our power.

Toward a Socialist-Feminist Strategy

Now we are in a better position to analyze the transformations of the last decades and their contradictory meaning for women. We can see more clearly the limitations inherent in the liberatory possibilities we have gained. Since the 1960s women have been quietly absorbing many of the contradictions and dislocations of capitalist structural change. As wage workers we are directly and indirectly pressured not to have children, or to handle the needs of those children we already have "on our own time." We work a "double day," continuing to carry most of the responsibility for children and housework even when we work full time. We absorb much of the cost of inflation for the working class by becoming the "second wage earner" in the family: our lower wages in "women's jobs" are enough to offset the inflation that is destroying the family wage—as long as there is a "first" wage earner. As structural unemployment and Reaganomics put more and more men out of work, however, the hidden costs became much more visible. Even *Newsweek* and *Time* have discovered that a wife's wage can't support the family of an unemployed auto worker and that most men, even when unemployed, do not take on a significant share of housework and child care.

For those women who are raising children on their own, managing wage work and motherhood is even worse: for the majority of single mothers the price of independence is poverty, the direct result of their having to support their children on women's wages that average 59 percent of men's wages (54 percent for black women) in a society that is increasingly privatizing the costs of child rearing to parents, which means, in these cases, primarily to mothers. Less than 25 percent of absent fathers pay regular child support, whether because they are unemployed, poorly paid, or incarcerated, or—in the case of higher paid (and predominantly white) absent fathers— because they choose to keep their wages for themselves.[6] Increases in the number of households headed by single mothers and by elderly women have produced what we now call the "feminization of poverty."

The woman raising children alone shows most clearly the contradictory nature of current social restructuring. The increased availability of wage labor to women and the growth of the welfare state, both part of the development of advanced capitalism, make it possible—not easy, but possible— for women with children to choose to leave oppressive marriages and for single women to choose to have children on their own. But with the weakening of patriarchal control goes the weakening of male responsibility. The "patriarchal" message in the decline of child-support payments is fairly clear: "No sex and housework, honey, no money. And if I don't have control over my kids, why should I pay for them?" The "capitalist" message, increasingly, is: "No job, no money. But of course if you're over forty-five (forty? thirty-five?) you're unemployable anyway. And if you're going to be taking time off to take care of sick kids, forget it."

Figuring out feminist strategies to confront such contradictory situations is no simple task, and there are no sure or lasting solutions. In working out strategy, we need to keep in mind a strong sense of our present social relations as a "moment" in a centuries-long process of capitalist-induced but not capitalist-determined social change. We need to remember that neither "defeats" nor "victories" are permanent, and we need to be able to laugh wryly at the ironies and paradoxes of living as feminists in capitalist society.

Struggles among sectors of capital, between different sectors of capital and different categories of workers, and between women and men have been continuously forming and reforming work and family life as long as there have been "capital" and "workers." As socialist feminists we need to engage in this process both organizationally and ideologically, by building stronger personal and organizational ties between socialist-feminist scholars (some of whom are activists) and socialist-feminist activists (some of whom are scholars) in order to produce strategy that flows both from practice and from sophisticated theory. And most important, we need to make that strategy an integral part of left strategy. We know from rueful experience that producing good Marxist-feminist theory is not enough to get that theory incorporated into the male-dominated discourse of the democratic left. This takes considerable political struggle, and in that struggle we need one another.

Feminism as a political force nourishes and sustains feminist scholarship, just as feminist scholarship, in keeping up the fight on the ideological front, nourishes and sustains activist feminists. At this point, however, those of us trying to create a genuinely feminist democratic left could use a bit more direct sustenance: we should apply more of that scholarly intelligence to the task of figuring out socialist-feminist strategy.

We need to push toward Marxist-feminist categories of analysis that make it impossible to "think economics" without thinking gender and racial division of labor, housework, child care, and child support; or to "think the state" without thinking gender and racial hierarchy, reproductive control, secondary welfare system, and the gender gap. Then we need to use whatever clout we can muster to push such analysis to the heart of left discourse. After all, if our male comrades had read, discussed, and internalized half a dozen of the most influential Marxist-feminist writings of the 1970s, we could all engage together in discussion of how to make Marxist-feminist theory more "dialectical" and how to apply it to questions of strategy.

We still have some way to go to get to that point, but feminism has had its effect. We've come a long way from the left in which men could yell, in response to a woman speaker, "Take her off the stage and fuck her!"— and be cheered by other men in the crowd.[7] Socialist feminism has generally succeeded in silencing sexist shouts and laughter; now we need to try to replace tolerant, even respectful, male silence with shared speech in a female and male left discourse that is genuinely socialist feminist.

Notes

Acknowledgments: I would like to thank Wendy Sarvasy, Judy Stacey, Liv Brown, and the Socialist Review collective for their useful comments and encouragement.

1. I use "Marxist feminist" not to name a political category distinct from "socialist feminist" but to refer to the predominantly academy-based work that attempts

to synthesize Marxist and feminist theory. In this usage, all Marxist feminists are socialist feminists, but not vice versa.

2. As a model of this kind of analysis, see Judith Stacey, *Patriarchy and Socialist Revolution in China* (Berkeley: University of California Press, 1983). See also Gay Seidman, "Women in Zimbabwe: Post-Independence Struggles," *Feminist Studies* 10, no. 3 (Fall, 1984). An early example is Norma Diamond's "Collectivization, Kinship, and the Status of Women in Rural China," in Rayna Reiter, ed., *Toward an Anthropology of Women* (New York: Monthly Review Press, 1975). The difference in approach can be seen by comparing Stacey with Elisabeth Croll, "Women in Rural Production and Reproduction in the Soviet Union, China, Cuba and Tanzania," pts. 1–2, *Signs* 7, no. 2 (1981), a special issue on development and the sexual division of labor, which includes a range of generally Marxist-feminist analytical approaches. I include myself in the indictment and am currently revising my own work on African women and revolutionary socialism. Michèle Barrett, *Women's Oppression Today* (London: Verso Editions, 1980), 10–19.

3. I continue to use the term "patriarchal" rather than "gendered" or "male dominant" in order to call attention to the continuing connection between men's domination over women and men's actual and potential domination as fathers. Understanding the patriarchal aspects of male domination allows us to make sense of incest, of demands for control of female teenage sexuality, and of the still virile social category of "illegitimacy" in a way that the concept of gender hierarchy does not. However, having been convinced by Michèle Barrett's arguments, I am using only the adjective "patriarchal," rather than the noun "patriarchy," in order to emphasize that precapitalist gender hierarchy and division of labor are transformed and embedded throughout capitalist society, rather than focused in the family or in other structures that operate as part of a separate "relatively autonomous system" of male domination.

4. See, e.g., Ruth Milkman, "Organizing the Sexual Division of Labor: Historical Perspectives on 'Women's Work' and the American Labor Movement," *Socialist Review* 10, no. 1 (January–February 1980), for an application of this kind of analysis to a particular historical case; Nancy Hartsock, *Money, Sex and Power: Toward a Feminist Historical Materialism* (New York: Longman, 1983), for an extension of Marxian analysis of the "level of reproduction" in order to develop a structural theory of gender domination rooted in women's "daily, sensuous life activity"; and Zillah Eisenstein, *Feminism and the State* (New York: Monthly Review Press, 1984), for historical-structural analysis that uses the concept of patriarchy and analyzes contradictions within the "capitalist patriarchal state" from a strategic perspective.

5. Henry Myers, ed., *Women at Work: How They're Reshaping America* (New York: Dow Jones Books, 1979), cited in a review by June Nash, *Signs* 7, no. 2 (1981): 493.

6. Child support is emerging as another problematic feminist issue. Liberal feminists are joining with conservatives who want to get women off welfare to support legislative attempts to force individual fathers to pay. Such laws could be used punitively against poor and minority men and women, as AFDC policy already is. As socialists, we should be criticizing these proposals and supporting programs that socialize more of the costs of child rearing. See Wendy Sarvasy and Judith Van Allen, "Fighting the Feminization of Poverty: Socialist Feminist Analysis and Strategy," paper presented at the American Economic Association Meeting, URPE (Union of Radical Political Economists) Section, December 1983.

7. This incident, which took place at an antiwar rally in January 1969, is described in Sara Evans, *Personal Politics* (New York: Vintage Books, 1979), 225.

13   The Impasse of Socialist Feminism: A Conversation

Deirdre English, Barbara Epstein,
Barbara Haber, and Judy MacLean

ILENE PHILIPSON: Where is socialist feminism today? Has it died, and if so, why has it died? If it is alive, where is it alive? How did you become socialist feminists? Do you still consider yourselves to be socialist feminists? If not, why not? And what sorts of things are you doing now that bear on your identity as socialist feminists?

BARBARA HABER: I became a feminist out of my experience in the new left, particularly out of my experience in SDS and before that in the civil rights movement. I was a reluctant feminist; I didn't want to join the feminists because I was married to a male "heavy" and I wanted to stay married. I wanted to retain the status of the special woman that I got from the male "heavies" to a point. Yet I was labeled a bitch; I was kept from any real decision-making. For five years in SDS I never so much as chaired a workshop, much less made a speech. I was always being asked to stuff envelopes, and my husband was always being asked to make speeches, so I figured he must be good at speeches and I must be good at envelopes. Yet a lot of my friends were among the very earliest women who formed what weren't yet called consciousness-raising groups but were women breaking off and meeting alone without the men.

I became a feminist one night in Champaign-Urbana in December 1966 at an SDS conference. Many of the women marched out because of sexism and had their own meeting. I didn't attend; instead, I sat in the student

Source: This roundtable discussion, facilitated by Ilene Philipson, is reprinted from *Socialist Review* No. 79 (January–February 1985), pp. 93–110, by permission of the publisher, *Socialist Review*, 3202 Adeline, Berkeley, CA 94703.

union talking with Al Haber and Carl Oglesby, and noticed after a while that there was a group of men sitting at a table discussing what had happened to "their" women. I went to that meeting, and so did a few other women who had not gone to the women's meeting. There were about five women and about thirty men. As I listened to the men talk about their attitudes toward women, I felt my anger rising and I discovered that I was a feminist, and I started talking back. The student union closed at midnight, so we went to sit outside. When we went outside I suggested that we move the chairs into the corner to get out of the wind, and I was ignored. My husband then said why don't we move the chairs into the corner and get out of the wind, and they all moved their chairs. We discussed that and other things too. I particularly remember the men's view of women sexually as passive holes needing to be filled. They couldn't really understand that that wasn't how we experienced ourselves. That's how I became a feminist.

From the beginning we all called ourselves radical feminists; I was not a socialist. I was a new left radical, and I'm still an unreconstructed new left–radical feminist. I was always ambivalent about being a feminist because of the sacrifices that seemed to be involved, such as giving up the idea of getting power in the male hierarchy, and confronting the fear of loss of personal relationships. From the beginning we started raking our personal relationships, including our sex lives, over the coals, and it was hard then to go back to those relationships.

As things heated up and Weatherman got to be a big thing, there were really disgusting confrontations between women focusing on feminism—that is, on the oppression of women and male domination—and the Weatherwomen, who were saying that feminism was a bourgeois indulgence. As an example, at a United Front against Fascism conference sponsored by the Black Panthers in Oakland, my women's group was attacked by Weathermen who turned over our chairs and knocked us around on the lawn because we were feminists.

The tension between being a radical and being a feminist was widespread in the early 1970s. I was in a women's collective in Berkeley where we argued about whether imperialism was the primary contradiction, or whether male supremacy was the primary contradiction, or whether we needed to have a primary contradiction.

For those of us who were heterosexual, there was a second contradiction starting in the early 1970s when many, many women became lesbians. At that time it was definitely seen as the "correct" thing to do. For a while my appetite for men went away totally because it was just impossible to consider wanting a man.

At some point I couldn't tolerate these contradictions anymore; all of it seemed quite horrible to me, so I withdrew from politics and missed the period when all the socialist feminists' unions formed, killed themselves, and disappeared. I missed that on purpose. When I started getting political again, I knew I wanted to be a feminist in a mixed movement. Part of that was because I had remained heterosexual, had divorced, was single, and wanted to work in movements with men; I didn't want to separate myself from men. Part of it was because I felt that the range of issues that I wanted to address, such as war and foreign policy, were in that part of the movement.

When a Marxist-feminist conference group was forming in the San Francisco Bay Area in 1979, I was invited to be part of the planning committee. I was very honored because I was one of the few non-academic women to be part of the committee. I announced at the start that I wasn't a Marxist, and what I meant by that was that I considered Marx a great teacher but that as a feminist I found it ironic to take on the name of the father, since I preferred to be identified with the kind of world I wanted and how I wanted to get there rather than with a great father figure. I knew that Marx didn't have all the answers, that he didn't understand male supremacy, spirituality, or the relationship between people and nature, all of which I felt were important.

I have been part of the Marxist-feminist conference group ever since it began, but I have never honestly felt like either a Marxist feminist or a socialist feminist. I really don't think of myself as a socialist as much as I think of myself as a radical. I don't think socialism and feminism fit together very well. Theoretically, I think the attempt to subsume feminism, which is really what socialist feminism did, under a Marxist method and analysis was a mistake to begin with. It drained feminism of the core of its energy, which emanated from living our lives in new ways and having our theory come from that practice. We yielded all that to the women who now call themselves radical feminists.

One of the things I want us to talk about is how that part of the movement has continued to grow even though it has flaws. Radical feminists working in the peace movement have managed to incorporate an antiimperialist, anticapitalist analysis that is compatible with socialism. They have managed to grow, not because they've had the correct theory but because they've been doing interesting political work and living unusual, risk-taking lives that have forced them to confront new issues.

JUDY MacLEAN: I became a socialist feminist in 1970–71 when I moved to Pittsburgh, Pennsylvania, to go to grad school. I dropped out at the end of that year to become a political activist in the antiwar movement. The people who made the most sense to me in the antiwar movement called themselves socialists. Some of these women were in a group called the Pittsburgh Radical Women's Union, which I joined. There I got my first experiences with consciousness raising and public speaking. The Radical Women's Union folded (it was too disorganized and structureless to last) but in the spring of 1971 many of us worked on a large demonstration against the Vietnam War in Washington, D.C. After that, we started talking about a more permanent organization, and we hooked up with the group organizing New American Movement nationally. From the beginning we were very, very clear that we wanted the organization to be what we called "socialist feminist." A group of women went to those first meetings of NAM and forced everybody else to take that identity on.

I think the main reason we wanted the term was that it suggested trying to lead our personal lives in a new way and simultaneously transforming the world. In a way the term meant that as feminists we wouldn't forget about issues like the Vietnam War, which was still raging. The fact that all these politicians who called themselves liberals had such a bad record on Vietnam made it seem important to go beyond liberalism if you were not going to sell out the Third World. I also think that those of us who called ourselves socialists then were scared by the kind of feminism that focused only on our personal lives. We thought you should always keep the rest of the world—what was happening to poor women and what was happening to Third World women—in mind. Calling ourselves socialist feminists was a way of always remembering that.

I became an organizer for the New American Movement and talked about socialist feminism a lot. One of the things that I always said in introducing socialist feminism was that we were concerned about the liberation of women but also about the liberation of all people, and that we thought socialism was the best way to do that. I would say that on one side of us were the radical feminists and on the other side were the liberal feminists, and I'd always make that distinction, as I think a lot of socialist feminists did. We divided the world of feminism into three parts and suggested we were a third of it, while numerically we were about 2 percent, or something like that.

In looking back, however, I'd say the two groups that contributed the most to social change have been the liberal feminists and the radical feminists. There was something about the way we called ourselves socialist feminists that made us feel superior. It was as though we had something to teach everybody else; we assumed that everybody else didn't understand socialism or didn't understand feminism. Using the term socialist feminism actually separated me from women whose ideas I shared in many cases.

I think a lot of the most exciting ideas about feminism that tie our personal lives to the larger political context come from women who call themselves radical feminists or cultural feminists. I'm thinking here of all the issues around violence against women—rape, battery, sexual harassment, pornography. I've also found that radical feminists have much more meaningful things to say about being a lesbian. After many years of trying intellectually to tie up Marxism and lesbianism, I've concluded there's not much connection.

On the other hand, the women who have organized large numbers of people, which was one of the goals we socialist feminists claimed (although we never actually did it), have been the women we called liberal feminists, women in the National Organization for Women and similar groups. These feminists have also been the ones who've been most successful at translating the insights of the radical feminists into terms that have meant real changes in the daily lives of millions of American women. We socialist feminists didn't do much of that.

So, about 1980 I stopped wanting to give talks where I said I'm a socialist feminist and therefore I'm better than these other women. I felt we hadn't proved ourselves better than those other kinds of feminists, and I feel that our ideas haven't caught fire on an intellectual level in the way that the radical feminists' have. Nor have our ideas gone on to reach a mass level. But if someone were to ask me, are you a socialist, I would still say yes. And if someone would ask, are you feminist, I would still say yes. I've often felt that when people try to combine feminism and socialism, it's the socialism that brings more of the stodginess. I think it might have to do with the state of world socialism, which I don't think has had a new idea in a while.

BARBARA EPSTEIN: There are two reasons why I've always felt awkward calling myself a socialist feminist. One is an intellectual reason, very much like Judy's, that even though I disagree with much of what radical feminists have said, I have also learned more from them, and they have said more new things that have set my thinking going in various directions than socialist feminists. I don't know, then, whether there ever has been such a thing as socialist feminism. I don't really know what it is; it feels like an uncomfortable merging of two traditions that really hasn't been worked out.

There's also an emotional reason why I feel uncomfortable calling myself a socialist feminist. I was very much involved in the peace movement when I was in high school. I joined the Communist Party when I was in my first year in college, and so the left really became my history, my identification, my family. I experienced the women's movement as telling me that I was no longer allowed to belong to the left. I really felt the women's movement tore apart the home that I had made for myself.

I was in the Communist Party when women began organizing around issues of feminism, and initially I had a very distant response to it. The issue that was being raised was why didn't women get listened to in meetings. Women were saying we are the wives and girlfriends; we do the shitwork and we don't play a leadership role. I didn't fit into those categories. I really was taken seriously and was not regarded as an appendage to some man. It wasn't that I thought women were treated equally; it was that the issues being raised simply were not my issues. After I left the Party, I was invited to a very early women's group in Berkeley. The women told me that the issue they were working on was why they were treated as sex objects and not taken seriously within the movement. My frank response was that I wished I had their problems.

Now that was also something that you were not allowed to say in that period. On the left there were plenty of times when I had the feeling that I had things to say that you weren't supposed to say, but it never felt quite as sharp as it did with feminism. Partly because feminism was addressing more personal issues, and partly because there was a kind of transformative zeal to the women's movement, I felt utterly shut out and told to run my own life in a way that I didn't want to run it, told that I was a traitor when I tried to pursue issues that seemed very important to me. So I had a lot of bitterness about the women's movement. Basically, I was told that it was not proper for me to work in the mixed movement and that it was also not proper for me to want to be in a relationship with a man and admit it. I often had the feeling that women who were conventionally attractive and very sure of themselves had a much easier time in the women's movement, because they could move away from relationships with men for a time and know they could go back to them. Lesbians too had their own sorts of relationships, which were valorized in the women's movement at a certain stage.

I now feel much more comfortable with feminism than I used to, because I'm now more sure of myself and I can say these things, and I'm less afraid that people can force me to do things I don't want to do. But I also think there is now more space in feminism than there used to be. There was a period when there really was a correct line, and I think that as bad as a correct line is in any political movement, it's particularly destructive when it's developed around issues of personal life.

Like Barbara Haber, I am now working in the peace movement, and I have found that I am more comfortable with feminism in that context than I have been in any other context. It's not just that it's a mixed movement; it's because it's tied to a goal that is not limited by gender. I feel personally much more comfortable with the feminism that is tied to the peace movement and tied to the goals that the peace movement has.

DEIRDRE ENGLISH: Originally I was a new leftist, but I didn't know how to put my growing awareness of sexist attitudes into a leftist context. By the early 1970s in New York, I became aware of women who called themselves "radical feminists." I remember being excited by the statement "feminism *includes* socialism." It meant that feminism alone projected such sweeping and utopian changes that it could socialize the economy as well as revolutionize private relations, the family, and, of course, the left itself. Unlike liberal, reformist feminists, radical feminists saw that there really was a long road to creating different gender relations, and that that road would have to include fundamental transformations in all external structures and belief systems. At the same time, unlike the elusive socialist project, the feminist revolution could be worked on right away. These were the days when a small group of women could come up with some good phrases, and a couple of months later these phrases would be rippling across the whole country.

The idea of socialist feminism, as it started to be articulated in journals like *Radical America* and *Socialist Revolution*, was resented by many of the radical feminists. They believed that women who called themselves socialist feminists were from the male left and didn't understand how revolutionary feminism itself was. But the term "socialist feminism" prevailed in the 1970s. I don't think many women think of "radical feminism" now in the way they did then.

In 1974 a socialist feminist intellectual network arose in the East, very much through the leadership of Linda Gordon, who deserves real credit. It was called the Marxist-Feminist Group, or M/F Group 1 (later, groups 2, 3, and 4 formed in various east coast cities). We met for frequent weekend retreats, and women came from Cambridge, New York, New Haven, Washington, and all over the east coast. Right from the very first meeting the group was extremely academic—heavy on historians, economists, and sociologists, and low on activists or even members of "lowlier" professions such as journalism, therapy, and the arts.

I think these women, like me, were impressed by the vision of independent, radical, feminist theory. They wanted to put the socialist tradition together not with mainstream or liberal feminist reforms (as many left men seemed quick to suspect) but with the much more intellectually dramatic radical feminism. The power inherent in each world view may be the reason why the synthesis proved to be, as is often said, an unhappy marriage.

This M/F group was the most valuable intellectual forum I've ever been in in my life, despite its ivory tower tendencies. There is an energy that exists when people are discovering new ideas, feeding on each other, breaking ground. I first heard discussions of many topics that later emerged as crucial issues: the dual structure of the labor force, the rise of the single woman and later the single-woman head of household, the neglected importance of reproduction in economic theory, the centrality of the demand for control over our own bodies, the influx of women into service-sector jobs, and the explosive potential of the demand for comparable worth.

I think that this atmosphere of intellectual rigor, and the widespread Marxist influence in women's studies that it was part of, was a helpful background for the research that I was doing together with Barbara Ehrenreich. We hoped to bring together the best of the socialist heritage with the new excitement of feminism. A lot of our work had to do with looking at women in relation to the particulars of their class position and their moment in a changing economic order. Barbara and I had endless discussions in which we connected gender relations with everything from the mechanisms of production and consumption to body language and foreign policy. There was a feeling after every one of those conversations of seeing the world differently.

It seemed then as though feminism had a limitless potential to be socially transforming and intellectually entertaining. It's very sad that in such a short time so much of that energy has drained away, while, in the face of the right, we have to pedal hard to stay in the same place, or fight for demands initiated by mainstream feminists. I still expect a new, reenergizing burst of feminist insight. But when?

Socialist Feminism's Demise

PHILIPSON: Some people say that socialist feminism, as a theory, as a form of self-identification, is dead. Is it? Do you disagree or agree with that, and why?

MACLEAN: As a term and as a means of excluding other women, it is dead. The ideas that we were trying to put across, however, have become very much a part of every aspect of the women's movement. For example, we used to say that we were the only feminists who cared about Third World women. Now it's true that we sat in our little rooms full of white women and *cared* about these women, but we were never able to take that caring out into the world in any way.

Meanwhile, black, Latina, and other minority women have formed their own feminist organizations, and frequently they are the kind we scorned as "liberal." Minority women have also done significant writing on themes we used to deride as "radical feminist." The women's movement as a whole is more concerned about racism, I believe, than any other American social movement that was organized for some purpose besides directly opposing racism. So, something we socialist feminists believed in has spread throughout the women's movement. The tragedy, though, is that we socialist feminists had very little to do with bringing this about.

HABER: I think that much of the energy withdrawn from the socialist feminist movement has gone into individualistic pursuits: that is, nuclear families and careers. Most left entities have died or diminished because of that. Were the women in these Marxist-feminist groups upwardly mobile, nuclear-family-oriented academics and professionals, whose real priorities were individualistic things? Was socialist feminism a sideline which, as long as it didn't interfere with these priorities, could be part of their lives? And was the shape of those groups meant to be compatible with the lifestyle of the upwardly mobile professional? That's my own belief, but I'm asking it as a question because I'm not positive.

Second, I think that activists who were in socialist-feminist groups have been pulled into organizations outside the socialist-feminist camp, where people are acting on the world and where people are going through an ongoing process of examining their own lives and experiences in terms of acting on the world. I don't see any of that going on in the Marxist-feminist groups. What I see is relatively academic discussions, usually quite interesting, that reflect the academic nature of the group. I mean academic in two senses: one, that they are dominated by women who work in academia, and two, that there is no commitment to social change and no commitment to an ongoing process of consciousness raising.

We stopped raising our own consciousness years ago. I think that many of us long ago decided we had excessively raised consciousness. Meanwhile, we live ten years of our lives and don't really examine it; we don't look at our relationships with the men in our lives; we don't look at our relationships with women; we don't look at our economic situation; we don't look at our choices about career or family. Ten years later we have tenure, or we have a Ph.D. in psychology, or we have more money, or we own a home, but we have not examined these changes collectively. The only way to examine your life seriously is to have a serious commitment to change. Once you lose that commitment and in fact have an avoidance of that commitment, because it will shake up your comfortable lifestyle, then anything you discuss is academic.

EPSTEIN: I absolutely agree with you. My perspective is that socialist feminism has become part of academia and has been killed by it.

PHILIPSON: Why did that happen?

EPSTEIN: There was a moment in the 1960s and early 1970s

when it looked as if people were genuinely playing with the idea of shaping their lives differently, while keeping their options open. That moment passed. Options shriveled, and people scrambled for professions and family. That is the nature of mass movements; there are some people who are really dedicated to pursuing ideals, but a mass movement draws in very large numbers of people, most of whom may not have deep commitment to pursuing those ideals. If history had gone differently, if there had continued to be a left-liberal atmosphere in this country and a high level of prosperity, I think things might have been different. But there was a closing-up, and the way people responded to that closing-up was to head back to the lifestyles that the movement tried to transform or reject.

Since socialist feminism had always been an intellectual wing of the women's movement, and the women who were developing it often had the greatest ability to go back into academia because they were the ones who had graduate degrees, socialist feminism became ensconced in academia. Socialist-feminist theory in particular has been narrowed and hobbled by academic environs; it's been shaped to the demands of academia, and it's been cut off from any kind of movement. The fact that people put off career and family for so many years, and the fact that the movement was never able to offer a vision of a life that was structured differently, meant that when people did go back to career and family, they felt they had to catch up in ten years what other people had been doing all along.

HABER: I think one of the biggest tasks for our generation is to reexamine the choices we have made to sell out, and not to assume that those choices were automatic results, either of aging or of changed economic and social conditions.

MACLEAN: I was among the women who called themselves socialist feminists who were not in academia and who were activists. I think what pushed socialist feminism into academia had more to do with the fact that we were always trying to think of some project where we could organize people around socialist-feminist principles, where we could somehow set ourselves off from the liberal feminists and the radical feminists. And that was very hard to do. Either you were doing something that was essentially very similar to what those other feminists were doing, and then you engaged in these long exercises trying to tack Marxist theory onto the activity, or you couldn't think of anything to do. So you sat around in your group feeling very frustrated. It would have been a better tactic to jump into whatever was going on than just to sit back and think of what was the most perfect thing we could do that would showcase socialist-feminist theory. I think our failure was the inability to do that in the world.

ENGLISH: While the liberal feminist movement has remained

strong, its goals are so limited. I disagree with you, Judy, in feeling that so many socialist-feminist ideas have been incorporated into the mainstream feminist movement; I don't think that's true. I think that mainstream groups have gone way off, have really gone wrong, and I cannot identify with them very much. I was always comfortable just calling myself a feminist in any situation, but now I don't feel very comfortable calling myself a feminist anymore, because socialist feminism is dead, my version of radical feminism is dead, and the mainstream feminist movement is just barking up the wrong tree. I not only don't identify with it; I disagree with and abhor many things about mainstream feminism. I think it's missing all the major truths about women's predicament today and in fact perpetuating some of them. I think that many middle-class women can remain active in mainstream feminism, because it's very compatible with professional life and with the nuclear family, and it's not at all destabilizing to fight for a woman vice-president or the ERA or equality in insurance premiums or sports facilities for girls.

On the other hand, the lesbian parts of the radical feminist movement remain very active, so that women who really rejected men and the nuclear family and formed collectives are sustained and emotionally nurtured so they can be politically active. But that doesn't leave a place where women—or women and men—are working together to further a vision of profound, feminist social change. We have abandoned a lot of serious issues, such as what a feminist sexual revolution would look like, how men should relate to children, how the female electorate should be organized, how a women's labor movement could arise, what our ideas of masculinity and femininity are. There are changes in all these areas of society and only a weak and liberal feminism to address them.

HABER: There are two choices that you have to make ultimately: either you have to go into the mainstream life, liberal feminism, or you really have to create institutions outside the mainstream that will sustain you. I think radical feminists have done that. All those covens and collectives and songs make a lot of difference, and they sustain people.

Second, there are things in radical-feminist theory that have helped that movement go beyond the issues with which it was once narrowly concerned. Large segments of the radical-feminist community have become involved in the environmental movement and the peace movement. This is not accidental. Their theory helped them get there, because it is a theory that talks a lot about the earth and talks a lot about an ecological view that is close to some of American Indian culture. It talks about being stewards of the earth rather than dominators and really speaks to the issues of domination and subordination as major aspects of society. It asks, what is your relationship to other human beings, to other living beings, and to the earth itself?

This theory has led women into the environmentalist movement, to the nuclear energy issue, and to the movement against nuclear weapons. From there they are able to look at the fact that nuclear weapons are connected to U.S. interventionism, and U.S. interventionism interestingly is linked right back to a certain attitude of domination by which the male leadership of the United States thinks it owns the world, can consume all the world's goods and boss the world around. So the theory allows for steps of movement.

EPSTEIN: I think one of the things socialist feminism has gotten caught in is that its perspective and its issues were more appropriate for the 1960s than for the 1980s. As much as I identify myself with the socialist tradition, I don't know that socialism is the issue right now. Socialist feminism always tried to deal with the tension between insisting that there is a role for an autonomous women's movement around gender issues and wanting to infuse that movement with socialist goals. My feeling is that at the moment neither of those is a top priority. Those were issues of the 1960s and they partly had to do with the very rapid movement of women into the labor force and education after World War II and through the mid-1960s.

Issues change, and I think at this point that among the issues of greater priority is first the issue of nuclear war. Although there are special things that women can do around that, and there are special ways in which women's theory can address that problem, it's not a gender-linked problem. I think there's less of an argument for an autonomous women's movement being the main priority today than was the case when we first got involved. Second, challenging the traditional nuclear family and having the courage to step out of it was very important for a lot of people in the 1960s, especially for the white middle class. We have a very differently structured family now, and priorities simply are different. There are enormous numbers of women who are outside nuclear families, and the question is, how do you deal with that? The rebellion against the traditional nuclear family is passé, because the traditional nuclear family doesn't exist for most people.

ENGLISH: I really feel strongly that the need for a women's movement is greater than ever and that the potential for it is strong. There is more potential for bringing in working-class women now than there has ever been. Look at the progressive impact of nonwhite and working-class women in the gender gap. I also think that a revitalized women's movement needs a leftist perspective desperately, will flounder without it, will be misled by mainstream feminism without it, so that the need for some kind of left feminism is greater than ever. I feel that the energy and potential for left feminism is profound, and I think many men as well as women would subscribe to it.

We've got to understand what was wrong with socialist-feminist theory, because it led our movement into some dead ends. Too many of the issues that socialist feminists thought were important issues to analyze were dying issues. The problem of domination of women in the nuclear family just as the nuclear family was going out of style is a good example of this. The whole capitalism-plus-patriarchy model was a political and theoretical dead end, and that was the basic political model we came up with. Multinational, postindustrial capitalism turned out to be a lot less paternalistic and a lot harsher than we expected. The capitalism-plus-patriarchy model just misconstrues what happened in history: it completely fails to understand that the men who run this sytem are the sons who overthrew the patriarchal fathers and not the fathers themselves. It fails to understand the rise of multinational, corporate dominance, which doesn't see women as women at all—just as workers, and throwaway ones at that.

EPSTEIN: I wouldn't go that far. I think what happened was that feminism, especially socialist feminism, emerged in part in a period in which the traditional family was falling apart, women were being forced into different roles, and yet the culture had not changed. The culture still included a definition of femininity and personal life that rested on the old model, and feminism played a very important role in attacking that ideology and culture, which were no longer consonant with the way women were living their lives. So it's the problem of what you do when you have a society where things are changing sharply for lots of people, especially women, and yet a new culture really hasn't emerged. How do you have a movement that both attacks the old culture and tries to force it to come to terms with changing realities, and also understands that the changing realities are oppressive without being oppressive in the old ways?

HABER: Deirdre, I agree with what you said about what got us to the dead end theoretically, but I think there was something else going on too. We wanted to be part of the socialist movement with men, and therefore we wanted a feminist theory that fit with that. We wanted a feminist theory that was consonant with socialism, with Marxism, and that would make it comfortable to be in a mixed movement.

ENGLISH: But the motivation we had to fit feminism to Marxism was not just a terrible thing having to do with capitulating to men or not having our own ideas. It came out of something good. It came out of understanding that we had to have an economic analysis of society; we had to understand the entire structure of society, not just personal relations, not just things like male violence, the way that other feminists were doing.

We really were trying to get to the roots, like radicals, and Marxism seemed like the best set of tools available for doing that job. I think we were right to pick up those tools and use them, and I don't think the tools were wrong either; I think we sometimes misused them.

Is There a Future?

PHILIPSON: Given your various critiques of our past as a movement, what is your vision of the future?

MACLEAN: I try to look for the things I have in common with what other feminists are doing, instead of ways that I am different and therefore superior (which is the way we socialist feminists looked at things). I see a lot of hope in the ways that movements have had to come together over the Reagan years, and have had to look at what we hold in common. I see what the women's movement is doing today a lot more positively than Deirdre does. There's a whole different world out there for women than there was in the 1960s. It's not a perfect world; it's not the feminist world I envisioned. But there's no doubt that it's a better world, with more options, more opportunities, more chances to see yourself in a variety of ways, whether you are ten or fifty-five. And I think the women's movement has made a lot of those changes come about.

I think the concrete organizing that the women's movement is doing around issues like wife-beating, comparable worth, Social Security, pensions, and other issues affects the lives of millions of women. I also think the ideas of the women's movement have changed my own thinking and that of millions of other women in ways that are so pervasive we sometimes take them for granted. I'm glad the women's movement has so many different groups and approaches—it reaches more women that way. My hope for the future is that we can ride out this wave of reaction and get on to moving forward again, forward in the multiple directions that feminism tends to take.

HABER: My fantasy is that there will continue to be a lot of little single-issue groups that are a mixture of liberal feminists, infused perhaps by the presence of socialist feminists or left feminists, around issues like reproductive rights or equal pay for equal work. I see a more antiimperialist, anticapitalist kind of feminism emerging from women's participation in antiinterventionist and antinuclear movements. I think these will not be labeled socialist. I think the vision of the future that is emerging now is a conglomeration of anarchism, feminism, radical environmentalism, and antiimperialism.

EPSTEIN: I would like to see a vital movement that includes a feminist perspective and is infused with other kinds of radical critiques of society. I doubt that it will see socialism as an immediate goal. I would certainly like to see a movement come to be the center of whatever ideology emerges, rather than academia as the center of it.

ENGLISH: I guess I'd like to return to the idea that turned me on in the first place, which is the notion that feminism is big enough to include everything in its perspective. We need to get away from the place where we keep refighting battles of the past decades, like abortion or the ERA, or arguing endlessly about pornography. I deeply admire the women who have kept fighting to retain the necessary feminist reforms, but I also think we need to revitalize feminism at the core with fresh thought. I like what Patricia Robinson said in a letter to *Socialist Review* that appeared in the May–August 1984 issue: "Ideals are like the stars. You can never reach them but you need them to chart your course." We need a non-1960s politics that still can talk about the realities of class, that has an international view of women's fate, that can take on the really deep questions about the future of humanity.

I can think of two directions that might help us make this leap. First, there is the urgent need for feminists to extend their objective of analysis to include economies and even the world economy. We need to understand more about what's happening to the worldwide division of labor and therefore to women. A left approach may not provide all the answers, but it helps give us the confidence and the means to tackle economic problems.

Second, there is the need to take on the problem of what a human being is or should be from our point of view. Right now the dominant tendency of mainstream feminism is to say that women should become more like men, while the more separatist parts of radical feminism seem to argue that only women are human. We need a feminist psychology of aggression, of the relationship of masculinity to femininity, of the relationship of humans to nature. The big questions! But we have to articulate them, to have a position on aggression, war, nuclear weapons and the human future—if there is one. Women may not prove to be any less aggressive than men, but the last word has not been said on that, and in any case, it doesn't mean we can't have a feminist theory that calls for a radically new pacifism in our very model of human nature—a new morality. After all, we have never believed that human nature is biologically determined. Feminists of both sexes ought to be thinking about what kind of change is needed in both the male and the female—in the interests of common survival.

I think there is still a lot of intellectual excitement left to be experienced and a lot of leadership that still should be exercised by people—again, both men and women—who are in touch with the socialist and feminist traditions together. I'm still optimistic.

II. The Present

*Family Life in
Postindustrial America*

14   The Fading Dream
Economic Crisis and the New Inequality

Elliott Currie, Robert Dunn, and David Fogarty

In the 1980s no one any longer doubts that the United States is
in the midst of a deep crisis in expectations. In the 1950s and 1960s most
Americans were led to believe in a future of indefinite economic expansion. Rising living standards, it was said, had made most people feel part
of the "middle class." Real economic deprivation, to the extent that it was
acknowledged at all, was presumed to be confined to the margins of the
"affluent" society.

The combination of economic stagnation and high inflation—"stagflation"—in the 1970s replaced that rosy vision with the sense that the United
States was slipping rapidly into economic decline. Suddenly the celebrated
American standard of living seemed to be falling precipitously, and easy
optimism was quickly displaced by gloom and anxiety about the future.
Faith in the American Dream disintegrated with dizzying speed, bringing
fear, resentment, and a widespread demand to "turn the country around"

Source: This article is reprinted from *Socialist Review* No. 54 (November–December
1980), pp. 102–18, by permission of the authors. Copyright © 1980, Elliott Currie,
Robert Dunn, and David Fogarty.

at whatever cost. Today, some variant of a program for economic revitalization is on everyone's agenda, at all points on the political spectrum.

But beyond the sense of crisis and the urgent call for change, there is remarkably little agreement about the degree to which the era of "stagflation" has actually damaged American standards of living or clouded the prospects for the future. *Fortune* magazine described, with considerable accuracy, the national pessimism about the state of the economy at the close of the 1970s.

> Of all the changes in American society during the Seventies, none was more fundamental than the erosion of faith in the future. By the end of the decade, the conviction that the material aspects of life will get a little bit better each year had given way to the bleakness of spirit known as diminishing expectations. It seems that most people nowadays aspire to little more than holding on to what they've already got, and many become downright despondent when they contemplate the world their children will inherit.[1]

Fortune hastened to assure us, however, that such "dour resignation" was "out of phase" with the "upbeat outlook" for family income in the 1980s and also exaggerated what really happened during the 1970s. Many groups "did a lot better in the 1970s than is generally appreciated." The real problem, *Fortune* insisted, was psychological: people's expectations had been too high to begin with, so they "didn't *think* they were doing particularly well."

The disagreement has been sharpest over the impact of inflation. The business-oriented Committee for Economic Development, for example, describing inflation as a "pernicious addiction," declared that "the damage inflation does to the fabric of both our economic system and our society is so great that it must not be allowed to proceed unchecked." Others have argued, with the economist Robert Heilbroner, that whatever dangers inflation may hold for the future, its impact on current living standards has been "much less than we commonly believe." "Despite our sense of being impoverished by inflation," Heilbroner writes, inflation has not "substantially" affected the "national standard of well-being and comfort."[2]

Which of these views is accurate? As with so many social issues, the answers we get depend greatly on the kinds of questions we ask. In what follows, we want to delve beneath the conventional statistics on income and earnings to ask a different, broader, set of questions about how the economic crisis has affected social life and living standards in the United States.

In particular, we want to address two crucial problems in the usual statistics and the debates based on them: (1) they tell us nothing about the measures people have had to take in order to cope with recession and inflation, and (2) they are *averages* that tell us nothing about how *different groups* have fared under the impact of economic crisis.

The answers to these questions are crucial to an understanding of the social impact of the current economic crisis and, consequently, for evaluating policies that claim to confront it. We look at the way inflation and recession have affected work and family life, patterns of saving and debt, and the availability of housing and jobs, and we argue that neither the relatively optimistic view—that the crisis has had only a mild effect on living standards—nor the more drastic vision of a massive economic decline adequately conveys what has happened to American life under the impact of stagflation.

The real picture is more complicated. Developments in the economy have brought a complex sorting of the population into "winners" and "losers"—a recomposition, or reshuffling of the deck, rather than a uniform decline. On the one hand, many American families have maintained living standards, if at all, only by working harder, sacrificing leisure and family life, and/or mortgaging their futures and those of their children. Those hardest hit by the economic crisis, and with the least resources to cope with it, have suffered real decline; poverty-level styles of life have appeared among people who once thought of themselves as part of the middle class. Some of the basics of the American Dream—the home of one's own, the successful job as the reward for education and effort—have moved, for all practical purposes, beyond their reach. At the same time, at the other end of the scale there is a new affluence for the relative "winners" in the restructuring of social and economic life in America.

Increasingly, one's chances of affluence or poverty, comfort or insecurity, are crucially determined by a complex web of conditions that includes not only one's sex, color, and age but also family composition, position in the housing market, and much more. One implication of this complex trend—as we will see—is that policies of economic renewal, designed to stimulate the economy as a whole through such means as cuts in taxes and social spending, may only accelerate the re-sorting of the American population into affluent "winners" and impoverished "losers." And the destruction of the social programs that have traditionally cushioned the blows suffered by those "losers" can only hasten the process.

The Plight of the Three-Job Family

How we define the contours of a problem depends crucially on the way we choose to measure it. Measured in terms of overall family income, the rapid growth in living standards that fed rising expectations throughout postwar America came to an abrupt halt in the early 1970s. The median income for all American families approximately doubled (in constant dollars) between 1950 and 1973. But it fell—by over a thousand dollars—during the recession of the mid-1970s and by 1979 had inched back no further than its level of six years before.[3]

Some economists dispute the relevance of these figures, arguing that real living standards actually *rose* even at the height of the mid-1970s stagflation. This view is based on the argument that *per capita* income—total personal income divided by the number of people—is a much better measure, since it allows us to take account of the statistical impact of population changes. For example, since families are smaller, on the average, than they used to be, measures of overall family income give a misleading picture of trends in how well off families are; what we need to know is the income available per person, which may have increased even while total family income has stagnated. As Lester Thurow argues, "From 1972 to 1978, real per capita disposable income rose 16%. After accounting for inflation, taxes, and population growth, real incomes have gone up, not down. The average American is better off, not worse off."[4]

What this argument ignores is that behind the soothing figures on per capita income is the grinding reality that for many families that income has been achieved only by sending more people to work. The clearest evidence of this fact comes when we look not simply at income per family or per person, but per *worker*. Thus, discretionary income—basically, disposable income minus expenditures for necessities and transfer payments—declined by about 5 percent between 1973 and 1979. But this figure ignores one of the most striking features of the 1970s—the great increase in the number of people working. As *Business Week* points out, "Adjusting discretionary income for the huge recent increases in employment, to reflect the sweat that goes into producing that income, shows that discretionary income per worker over the past six years declined by 16%."[5] These figures show that families increasingly need two—or more—workers just to keep up, much less to get ahead. Statistics on the trend of family incomes in the 1970s bear this out: the incomes of families with only one earner fell about 7 percent behind the cost of living from 1969 to 1978; those of two- and three-earner families came out about 6 percent above it.[6]

This trend has given the family a crucial—and somewhat paradoxical—role in the contemporary economy. On the one hand, the material support of other family members is often all-important as a protection against the erosion of living standards. Such support is especially crucial for women, given the pervasive discrimination they face in the labor market. This difference is most apparent in what has been called the "feminization of poverty"; single women, especially those with young children, have become the most predictably impoverished group in America. But at the same time, increased labor places severe strains on many dual-earner families. The need for two incomes in such families means that three jobs are now being done for the price of one—two in the paid labor force, one unpaid: the household and child-rearing tasks done in the home. As the work time needed to keep up with living costs increases, something has to give. And there is considerable evidence that often what is "giving" is the quality of family life.

On the one hand, the tasks of child-rearing and housework are often being pushed out of the home—usually to the private sector—as working people, if they can afford to, consume more and more day care, fast food, and even paid housekeeping. (A result is the rapid growth of low-wage, quasi-domestic "service" occupations that both cater to the needs of the multi-earner household and often supply what passes for job opportunities for the second earner.) On the other hand, especially for those who cannot afford outside services, modern family life often means a decline in the possibility of real leisure—or, what amounts to the same thing, an increase in the pace of life, a kind of social speedup resembling the deliberately increased pace of an industrial assembly line. With an extra job to do and little public provision for domestic services, many people wind up routinely cutting corners, compressing their lives, and feeling "hassled" much of the time they are supposedly off the job. While this situation has always been the fate of many lower-income working families, it is now becoming a predictable aspect of the lives of many who once saw themselves as part of the middle class.

But—like other effects of the rising cost of living—the burden of this social speedup has not been evenly distributed among working people. Instead, it has served to widen the gap between men and women, and between income groups, in ways that are obscured by the conventional statistics on income and earnings.

Most of the extra work brought by the speedup has fallen on women, because they are most of the second earners in the paid labor force and because paid work has not freed most women from unpaid work at home. Instead, the extra job that women do has usually been coupled with continuing responsibility for running the household. As Willard Wirtz, head of the National Commission on Working Women, puts it,

> For a great many women, taking a job outside the home isn't a matter of substituting one kind of work for another; what it means is double duty. . . . If limited opportunities on the new job away from

home are part of the problem, the rest of it is the unchanging terms
and conditions of the job at home. When all the old duties still have
to be performed, body and mind sag under the double burden.[7]

Much of that burden involves child care. A 1978 study by the University of Michigan Survey Research Center found that nearly half of women
working in the paid labor force, versus only 13 percent of men, reported
spending three and a half hours or more—*on working days*—with their children; 44 percent reported spending an additional three and one-half hours
on household chores.[8]

It is remarkable, in fact, how closely the overall working time of typical
two-earner families matches the time requirements of three full-time jobs
—and what a large proportion of the third job falls to women. Another
recent study found that among working couples, the men spent an average of about nine hours a week on family care, the women an average of
about twenty-nine hours. At the same time, the men averaged forty-four,
to the women's forty, hours of paid work (because men were more often
in jobs with frequent overtime). Put together, this amounts to an average
of sixty-nine hours of work a week for women, fifty-three for men, or 122
altogether for a family—the equivalent of three full-time jobs.[9]

For many women, then, entering the labor force to keep the family
standard of living intact has meant more work, less leisure, and a more
harried family life. What one critic has called the "overwhelming poverty
of time" in these families is given abundant testimony in a national survey of women wage earners undertaken by the National Commission on
Working Women. An astonishing 55 percent of the women surveyed reported having *no* leisure time; 39 percent had no time to pursue education.
Only 14 percent were able to say that job and family life did not seriously
interfere with each other.[10]

There is, of course, another side to this increase in women's work. It
is doubtless true that moving into the paid labor force has provided many
women with wider options and may have helped undermine the traditional
subordination of women in many families. But because of the persistence
of the sexual division of labor in the home and the lack of adequate public
support services, it has also meant that women have shouldered a disproportionate—though often hidden—share of the burdens imposed by the
economic crisis. And the potential benefits in greater independence for
women have also been constrained by the rising cost of living—especially
in housing—which in some areas has made "coupling" almost an economic
requirement.

Obviously, the effects of entering the labor force are different for the grocery clerk's wife who gets a job as a telephone operator than for the lawyer's wife who becomes a stockbroker or psychotherapist. And this difference illustrates one of the most striking trends of the stagflation era. For women who have the resources to enter well-paying and rewarding jobs, and to afford the costs of the private-sector "industrialization" of domestic services, the two-paycheck family can represent an enviable and liberating way of life. At the other end of the scale, it can mean a virtually unrelieved round of dull rote work, in and out of the home. And the distance between these two ways of life is growing—in part because an increasing proportion of the wives entering the paid labor force comes from more affluent families, with the result that, as a Labor Department study puts it, "the gap between above-average income families and below-average income families will widen" in the coming years.[11]

As access to extra work becomes more and more important in maintaining or improving standards of living, we can expect this gap to widen for another reason as well. Not everyone has the *opportunity* to take on more work—even relatively unrewarding work—in response to threats to their living standards. In a survey of how different kinds of families coped with recession and inflation, David Caplovitz found that about two out of five tried to handle inflation by working more—either sending more family members to work or taking on overtime or an extra job. But poorer people, often lacking access to even *one* job, were less often able to exercise those options.[12]

The "new impoverishment"—of time as well as income—of many American families, then, is only one side of the coin; the other is the growing affluence of some families. Between 1970 and 1977, when average family incomes barely improved at all and many families' living standards fell sharply, the proportion of families with incomes above $25,000 (in constant dollars) jumped by about 23 percent. The rise in the number of relatively affluent families was even sharper for blacks, at the same time that many blacks suffered even greater stagnation or decline in living standards.[13]

At one end of the new scale of living standards is what *Fortune* has gushingly termed the "superclass": those two-income families with the additional "formidable advantages of connections, intelligence, and education" whose incomes may reach six figures.[14] At the other end is a broad stratum of the poor and nearly poor: single parents, one-earner families with low incomes, and people on fixed incomes. Somewhere in the middle are the broad ranks of two-earner families with middling incomes who must cope with the escalated costs of necessities and the increased need for domestic services, for whom even two paychecks barely cover expenses from one week to the next.

Mortgaging the Future

Conventional data on living standards, then, obscure the enormous increases in labor—and the resulting changes in family life—that have gone into keeping up with the rising cost of living. Something similar happens with the conventional picture of working people's consumption. The fact that levels of buying and spending have, on the whole, remained remarkably high in the stagflation era is often taken as evidence that things can't be as bad as we might think. Again, though, this conclusion ignores what working people have *done* in order to maintain consumption. For many families, stagflation has meant sacrificing the future to pay for the present, making the future a source of anxiety and dread—a situation most clearly visible in the changing patterns of savings and debt.

In the fourth quarter of 1975, the rate of personal saving—the proportion of people's income put away for the future—stood at 7.1 percent. By the fourth quarter of 1979 it had dropped to 3.3 percent, less than half its level only four years before. This general figure masks much lower rates of saving at the lower levels of the income ladder and among younger people, but the inability to save afflicts even many middle-class families that have otherwise been able to weather inflation's attack fairly well. As Caplovitz's survey discovered, "Even if they are able to maintain their standard of living within limits, many white-collar families find for the first time that they are unable to save money." [15]

Along with reduced saving has come rising consumer debt. The average American consumer now holds only about three dollars in assets for every dollar of debt owed, compared with about five dollars in the 1950s. Installment credit as a proportion of disposable income rose by about 42 percent between 1960 and 1978. Like the increase in labor, the growth of debt has struck some people much more severely than others—in this case, particularly lower-income and younger people. Debt repayments as a percentage of disposable income were 25 percent for the lowest income fifth in 1977, only 6 percent for the highest fifth. And that disparity has been increasing steadily; the proportion rose from 19 percent for the lowest-income fifth since 1970, while it dropped slightly for the most affluent. [16]

The result is that low- to moderate-income families have become ever more highly "leveraged," in financial jargon, and hence ever more precarious financially. As a leading student of debt patterns in the United States notes, "As measured by the ratio of debt payment commitments to income, vulnerability to recession has increased, especially among the lowest 20 percent of the income distribution."[17] Debt use is also most frequent among the young—especially younger families.

Why have debts grown and savings evaporated so rapidly while average family incomes have remained relatively stable? Part of the answer, as research by the National Center for Economic Alternatives has shown, is that costs for the necessities—food, energy, housing, health care—have risen much faster than the Consumer Price Index as a whole in the past few years.[18] This rise in the cost of necessities seriously undermines the value of income even when it is measured in "real" terms—that is, adjusted for rises in the overall cost of living: hence the sharp rise in the debt burden of families at the lower end of the income scale, where necessity costs already take a larger chunk of total income.

But there is a more subtle and less measurable reason for the growth of debt: more expenses become necessary as inflation creates its own set of escalated needs. Thus sharply rising housing prices may force a family out of easy commuting range to jobs and services, raising transportation and energy costs, perhaps requiring a second car. Paying for the extra car and the extra gas may require a second job. The second job in turn increases transportation costs still further; it may also create the need for more paid day care and probably changes eating habits in a vastly more expensive direction—more eating out, less careful food shopping, and less economical food preparation. Thus, the changes in family living patterns we noted above lead not only to increased labor but to escalating expenses as well. At the extreme, the new expenses may cancel out most of the benefits of increased work, in an inflationary "Catch 22."

Greater leveraging of family income to cope with these inflation-induced "needs," as well as the rising cost of necessities, is hard to avoid, given the insufficiency of public services that could cushion the need for ever-higher individual expenditures. But this leveraging means that some families—again, especially younger and poorer ones—may not be able to provide for a reasonably secure future. They won't be able to send their kids to college, cope with such emergencies as major illnesses or deaths, or add savings to their pensions to help ensure a decent retirement.

These issues have become especially keen because of the specter of disintegration of the traditional systems of support for old age. Although Social Security benefits have so far kept up with inflation, the entire system's funding is increasingly in jeopardy. Living on Social Security benefits alone, in any case, is a sure ticket to poverty; and private pensions, the most common alternative support, are rarely adjusted for increases in the cost of living.

The need to sacrifice security to keep up with essentials can only have a devastating psychological impact on the quality of life. It not only makes the present more frightening but is one reason why many can no longer look forward to the ideal of a decent old age as the reward for a lifetime of labor—and why opinion polls show that Americans, for the first time in memory, think that their children will live in conditions worse than the present. In 1979, according to a *Washington Post*/ABC News poll, 66 percent of respondents still believed that their children would be "better off" than they were; 18 percent thought their children would be worse off. By March 1981 only 47 percent thought their children would be better off, and 43 percent believed their children would lead worse lives than their own.

The Vanishing Prospect for Home Ownership

Coping with stagflation, then, has meant cutting deeply into savings and going further into debt, as well as greatly increasing labor—for some people much more than others. But even with these adaptations, there are aspects of the traditional American Dream that many working people—especially the young—may never achieve, given the peculiar contours of the economic crisis. One of them, as we'll see in a moment, is the good job with reasonable chances for achievement—or at least good pay. Another is a home of one's own.

What has happened to housing represents a drastic change from traditional expectations. Decent housing, even rental housing, is fast becoming an unrealistic goal for all but a dwindling fraction of young Americans. Between 1972 and 1978 the price of an average one-family new home increased 72 percent nationally, 86 percent in the West, and much more in some high-demand metropolitan areas, while median family income increased only 40 percent. The Department of Housing and Urban Development estimates that in 1970 half of the American people could have afforded a median-priced new house (then costing $23,400), using the standard rule of thumb that no more than a fourth of pretax income should be spent on mortgage costs. In 1979, by the same standard, only 13 percent could afford new-home ownership (the median price then being $62,000), and 38 percent of all actual new-home buyers were ignoring the prudent rule of thumb.[19]

The "affordability crisis" has hit renters as well, and both owners and renters overspend in order to put a roof over their heads. In 1979 American families are paying an average of almost 36 percent of disposable income for housing and housing-related expenses, double the average of 1969. For low-income households the situation is much worse; by 1977, some 5.8 million households—4.2 million renters and 1.6 million owners —were paying over half of their incomes for shelter, and the problem has worsened considerably since then.[20]

For many of these families, the cost of housing has meant stretching their budgets beyond the point where they can pay for other necessities and has made them terribly vulnerable to recession-caused disasters—either forced sale, default, or learning to live with poverty-level habits in all other realms of life.

Rising housing costs, moreover, have priced some groups out of the housing market altogether, notably low-income families, young couples, singles, and minorities. In 1975 a couple earning $16,650 could have bought a median-priced California home for $41,000. They would have made a 20 percent down payment of $8,000, and their monthly mortgage payment—including insurance, interest, and taxes—would have been $347. By the end of 1979 the same home cost $88,300. A buyer had to earn over $35,000 to qualify for a loan, put down $17,750 as a 20 percent down payment, and pay out $878.42 per month.[21]

At those rates a broad segment of American working people, especially those now coming of age and those who, for whatever reasons, have delayed entry into the housing market for too long, may never have a chance to own a home. The fading dream of home ownership represents a crucial change in living standards, not only because it condemns some people to inferior housing but, perhaps even more important, because it eliminates one of the only tangible assets traditionally available to people without high incomes. The fact that roughly two-thirds of American families own their own homes today suggests how far down the income scale home ownership has extended in postwar America. Without the home as asset, the material security of these people will drop precipitously, again suggesting that ordinary income and wealth data greatly underestimate the real losses that stagflation has caused for some groups.

Meanwhile, those who already have a strong foothold in the housing market have seen their homes appreciate wildly in value and their relative mortgage costs decline, often dramatically, because of inflation. The benefits of inflation for people who already own their homes should not be exaggerated, however, because other costs—maintenance and taxes particularly—have risen dramatically. For people with limited or fixed incomes these costs can tip the balance between being able to keep a home and being forced back into the rental market. Still, the crisis in housing has created one of the deepest and most powerful divisions between winners and losers in the stagflation era.

The Outlook for Jobs

The divisions between winners and losers multiply and deepen when we look at what recent changes in the American economy have meant in terms of the kinds of jobs that will be available in the future. Like housing, the job outlook is changing—in ways that will mean intensified competition for a shrinking proportion of good jobs. The losers in that competition may face a lifetime of poorly paid, dull, and unstable work.

Some point to the rapid growth of overall employment, even during the recessionary 1970s, as evidence of the fundamental health of the economy. Nearly thirteen million new jobs were created between 1973 and 1979. The American economy, in fact, produced new jobs at a rate much faster than its chief economic competitors, West Germany and Japan.[22] What is striking, however, is that the economy stagnated and living conditions flattened in *spite* of all those new jobs. Why, with so many people newly at work, did only a minority of families see their standard of living rise?

The answer lies partly in the nature of the new jobs themselves, and it bodes ill for the future: the new jobs have overwhelmingly been in those parts of the economy that offer the poorest pay, the fewest chances for advancement, and the least possibility of providing an adequate livelihood. And it is precisely these jobs that are expected to continue to grow, while those that have traditionally offered a ticket to higher living standards will correspondingly decline.

By the end of the 1970s well over two-fifths of all American workers in the private, nonagricultural economy were employed in just two sectors: retail trade and "services." More significantly, over 70 percent of all *new* jobs created in the private economy between 1973 and 1980 were in those two sectors. What kinds of jobs are these? Labor Department economists estimate that by 1990 there will be some four million new jobs in various private medical-care services: nursing homes, hospitals, blood banks, and laboratories. Another fast-growing sector is "miscellaneous business services," including janitorial, photocopying, and temporary office help. More than five million new jobs are expected in retail trade, mainly in fast food restaurants, department stores, and food stores.[23]

The jobs in these expanding fields are notoriously low paying. In 1979 workers in manufacturing industries averaged about $232 a week in spend-able earnings. Workers in service industries averaged $162; in wholesale and retail trade, $155. Part of the reason for these low average earnings is that these jobs are often part time, as is illustrated by the short, and declining, work weeks in service and retail trade. The average work week in retail trade was almost forty hours in 1959, had dropped to thirty-three hours by 1977, and is expected to drop to thirty hours by 1990. Workers in manufacturing, as Emma Rothschild points out, had an average work week (in 1979) of about forty hours, while workers in eating and drinking places, one of the fastest-growing sectors of the economy, averaged just twenty-six hours a week.[24]

In the 1950s and 1960s social critics often worried that technological changes in the economy were on the verge of eliminating work. A whole literature about the "postindustrial" society emerged, in which the problem of what to do with the predicted increase in leisure was a primary concern. But the reality today is not quite what these critics expected. Technological change has not so much eliminated jobs, in the aggregate, as it has changed the mix of jobs available—and with it, the relative chances that work will bring economic security. The prediction of a "postindustrial" or "service" economy has been partly realized, and will become even more so during the remainder of this century. But as we've already seen, the rise of the "service society" has brought not greater leisure but, in many cases, the opposite; not increased freedom from toil but, often, an ever faster race to stay in one place.

The impact of these changes is already ensuring that young people are among the greatest casualties of the economic crisis. Men and women under twenty-four are earning less today, in real terms, than their counterparts did in 1967. Even *Fortune* magazine, in its generally upbeat rendering of the income picture during the 1970s, notes that the combination of the "bulge" of baby-boom workers and a declining job market has played havoc with youth's life chances. Men aged fifty-five to sixty-four, the magazine points out, enjoyed a real income increase of nearly 18 percent between 1969 and 1977; those twenty-five to thirty-four saw their incomes rise less than 3 percent; men eighteen to twenty-four suffered a slight decline. The cumulative effect has been dramatic: "By the end of the Seventies," *Fortune* notes, "the baby boomers had effectively lost about ten years' income growth relative to the group just ahead of them. One of the biggest uncertainties about income in the Eighties is whether they will be able to make up that lost ground."[25] The division between those with a clear shot at the dwindling proportion of good jobs and those who may never rise out of the poorly paid, unstable workforce in the spreading retail and service sectors will become increasingly important in the coming years.

That division will probably be intensified by the wholesale destruction of many blue-collar jobs under the impact of the decline and restructuring of such key industries as autos, steel, and rubber. Traditionally, these industries provided high-wage jobs that often offered a path into relative affluence (though that affluence was always threatened by job instability). Until the late 1970s workers in these industries, and in certain others such as coal mining, fared best in terms of real income. By 1977 nearly a third of all American families making between $25,000 and $50,000 a year were officially classified as "blue collar." But these jobs, of course, are threatened with elimination as those industries either shut down, move away, or automate in response to intense competition. It has been estimated, for example, that by late 1980 the crisis in the American auto industry had cost the jobs of close to 300,000 workers in the industry itself and another 600,000 in related industries.[26] And it is clear that even if that industry does ever regain its past level of production, it will do so with a workforce that is considerably smaller, replaced as much as possible by new, superefficient "robots."

To the extent that these and other well-paying blue-collar jobs are obliterated, the result will be a still greater split between a relatively few high-level professional and technical jobs on the one hand and a growing array of poorly paid rote jobs on the other. This split will strike hardest at younger workers' expectations for a decent job in the future, especially young minority workers, for whom industrial blue-collar jobs have long been a main route to a decent standard of living.

The New Inequality and Economic Policy

Two themes stand out most strongly from the strands of evidence on changes in work and family life, expectations for jobs and housing, and patterns of spending, saving, and debt.

First, it is true that as *Business Week* magazine puts it, "the American credo that each generation can look forward to a better life than its predecessor has been shattered."[27] What's more, it has been shattered in particularly threatening ways, for what have been most powerfully assaulted by the changes in the economy are the most fundamental expectations and most basic sources of stability and security: the quality and character of home and family life, the security of one's future, and the fate of one's children.

At the same time, these burdens have been felt very differently by different groups. The lineup of winners and losers in this redistribution of life-chances is complicated and sometimes unexpected. The traditional differences of sex, race, and age have been widened and redefined, while newer ones based on family composition, position in the housing market, or —increasingly—participation in specific industries have arisen or become more important. The brunt of stagflation's impact on living standards, patterns of labor and family life, and job prospects has been borne by a few especially hard-hit groups. Others, better endowed with the appropriate resources, have coped more than adequately, carving out new kinds of affluence in the midst of economic "decline."

What do these trends tell us about the social and economic policies that could reverse the harshest effects of the new inequality? It would take another article to do justice to such a large, and freighted, question. But a few general points seem clear.

Most important, our analysis suggests that the kind of economic "revitalization" so fashionable among the legions of the "new right"—and given political momentum by the Reagan administration—is more likely to aggravate the trends we've outlined than to alter them. At the core of the conservative program is a set of incentives designed to fuel economic expansion by stimulating private investment. These incentives include across-the-board tax cuts, deregulation of industry, and drastic reductions in public spending on social programs (coupled, of course, with massively increased spending for defense). According to the conventional wisdom of supply-side economics, these policies would both fight high inflation and "get America moving again" by "unleashing" private enterprise.

At bottom, the supply-side vision is the most recent (and most drastic) variant of the long-standing argument that the way to increase jobs, income, and well-being throughout the society is to allow them to "trickle down" from an expanding private economy. By shifting the balance of social resources upward and improving the "business climate," society as a whole—including its poorest members—should benefit.

Whether such a program can, in fact, cause a spurt of economic growth —as measured by a rising Gross National Product or a higher rate of productivity—is a question we won't venture to answer. For our purposes, it is the wrong question. The more important one is not whether we can generate *some* kind of economic growth but whether the growth we produce will be translated into better lives and greater opportunities across all sectors of society. And this is where the supply-side program seems badly out of touch with the reality of modern society.

The supply-side program assumes, at least implicitly, that the problem we face is a general economic decline—a decline that can be reversed by providing sufficient lures to ever greater investment. But the notion of a *general* economic decline, as we've demonstrated, is misleading. Something far more complex has been taking place. Rather than a simple, overall stagnation, we are witnessing a complicated process of recomposition and restratification, bringing new sources of affluence along with new forms of poverty. Economic shifts have been translated into complex changes in work, family, and other social institutions. Policies of revitalization that fail to take account of those changes—of the institutional structure that necessarily forms the context of economic life—will only deepen present inequalities, worsening the situation of those "losing" and accelerating the advance of those already "winning" in the social and economic reshuffling we've described.

Illustrations are not hard to come by. How will an economic "boom," fueled by tax cuts for the wealthy, help an unskilled single mother find economic security, especially when the same policies are, with the other hand, taking away public funds for the child care that would enable her to take a job—if a job were there? How will growth in nursing homes and hamburger stands help a skilled blue-collar worker whose $20,000-a-year job has been lost to a more "productive" industrial robot? How will the expansion of defense industries in the Southwest help a young minority couple facing the runaway housing market in New York? Or an unemployed eighteen-year-old in Chicago's ghetto?

Dealing effectively with the new forms of impoverishment will require policies targeting directly those groups most at risk in the modern economy, and those sectors of the economy where inflation and recession have taken their worst toll. A program to confront the new inequality cannot simply bank on the "trickling down" of jobs and income from expanding private investment but must involve active intervention in economic life toward explicit social goals.

Addressing these problems will require *more* government intervention, not less; a larger (if more efficient) public sector, not a diminished one; more planning, not less. We know that these strategies go strongly against the stream. But we believe that without them the alternative scenario is clear: a sharper division between the newly affluent and the newly poor; for the young, fast-vanishing opportunities for good jobs and decent housing; and continued inflation with its devastating pressures on home and family. The choice is clear. We will either decide to engage in serious, democratic public planning to redress the social imbalances generated by economic development, or we will watch helplessly as an uncontrolled "revitalization" brings greater insecurity, desperation, and misery in its train.

Stagflation, Inequality, and the Political Culture

What are the prospects for that kind of democratic social planning? At first glance, the outlook seems less than hopeful. In the face of the injuries inflicted by the economic crisis, there have been some encouraging expressions of public mobilization and concern. But at least as often, the crisis has seemed to generate cynicism and political withdrawal, epitomized by the fact that the winner of the 1980 presidential election came into office on only 26 percent of the potential popular vote. Contemporary politics and contemporary American culture as a whole often seem mired in narrow interest-group concerns and a spirit of individual indulgence.

And these responses—negativism, cynicism, withdrawal from social concern—are themselves partly rooted in the changes we have already described. The heightened insecurity that economic crisis has brought to personal life in America—the receding prospects for decent jobs and housing, the looming threats of downward mobility and a pauperized old age— helps explain the resurgence of broader cultural themes of competition and individual survival. ("Tomorrow only the fit will survive," declares an ad for a new magazine for "entrepreneurs," "and only the *very* fit will flourish.")[28] And it also offers fertile soil for the desperate focus on the "self" that Barbara Ehrenreich has aptly called a "psychological version of the 'lifeboat ethic' "—the "me-first" character of life lived mainly in the present because the future seems less and less certain or worth building toward.[29] Given the particularly harsh effects of the economic crisis on family life, it isn't surprising that political campaigns narrowly focused on the "defense" of the traditional family—like the campaign against the Equal Rights Amendment—have enjoyed especially wide appeal in the era of stagflation.

All these tendencies have been reinforced by the increasing *fragmentation* we have described. When relative prosperity or impoverishment may hang on the timing of a house purchase or the fact of working in (say) the aerospace rather than the auto industry or having been born in 1940 rather than 1950, the sense of commonality of experience and needs disintegrates. Individual or, at best, familial solutions to social and economic problems can easily come to seem the only alternatives available, the only visible avenues to security and well-being.

This individualization is aggravated by the growing split between the newly affluent and other working people—what we might call the "Brazilianization" of the American class structure. Working people see some enjoying considerable success—"making it" in highly visible ways—while others sink; some are buying second homes in the mountains, speedboats, and Cuisinarts, while others descend into the ranks of the welfare poor. Those differences act both as a spur to individual striving and as a demonstration that the proper management of personal life can bring significant rewards—that it can put you, as *Fortune* pants, on "a fast track to the good life."[30] And for those at the upper reaches of the scale it provides a sharp and nagging incentive to hold on more tightly to what they have.

These trends—fragmentation, individualization, the narrowing of political concern to family and personal life—are not the only ones now evident in the United States. As Michael Harrington has pointed out, the American people seem to be moving in several different ideological directions at once.[31] There is a new theme of narrow self-seeking in American culture, but there is also—as public opinion polls reveal—a growing support for guaranteeing jobs through public programs and for accepting wage and price controls in response to runaway inflation. There is in some quarters a new reverence for private gain and the forces of the "market," but there is also evidence of a growing concern for what the psychologist Urie Bronfenbrenner has called the "human ecology"—a recognition of the connectedness of the fabric of social life and a rejection of the periodically fashionable idea that human life should be left to the not-so-tender mercies of the "free market."[32] Which trend will prevail depends crucially on the seriousness and energy with which we build a broad movement for democratic planning and control of economic life.

Notes

1. A. F. Ehrbar, "The Upbeat Outlook for Family Incomes," *Fortune*, 25 February 1980, pp. 120–24.

2. Robert Heilbroner, "The Inflation in Your Future," *New York Review of Books*, 1 May 1980, pp. 8–9.

3. *Economic Report of the President, 1981* (Washington, D.C.: U.S. Government Printing Office, 1981), 286.

4. Lester Thurow, *The Zero-Sum Society* (New York: Penguin Books, 1980), 48.

5. "The Shrinking Standard of Living," *Business Week*, 8 April 1980, p. 73.

6. Calculated from U.S. Bureau of the Census, *Current Population Reports, Series P-60, #120, Money Income and Poverty Status of Families and Persons in the United States (Advance Report)* (Washington, D.C.: U.S. Government Printing Office, 1980), table 1.

7. Willard Wirtz, Testimony in U.S. Senate, Committee on Labor and Human Resources, *The Coming Decade: American Women and Human Resources Policies and Programs*, January–February 1979, p. 214.

8. Robert P. Quinn and Graham L. Staines, *The 1977 Quality of Employment Survey* (Ann Arbor: University of Michigan Survey Research Center, 1978), 152, 251.

9. Janice Neipert Hedges and Earl F. Mellor, "Weekly and Hourly Earnings of U.S. Workers, 1967–78," *Monthly Labor Review*, June 1979, p. 42.

10. Nancy Barrett, Testimony in *The Coming Decade*, 1053: figures from Wirtz, Testimony in *The Coming Decade*, 214.

11. Paul N. Ryscavage, "More Wives in the Labor Force Have Husbands with Above-Average Incomes," *Monthly Labor Review*, June 1979, p. 42.

12. David Caplovitz, *Making Ends Meet: How Families Cope with Inflation and Recession* (Beverly Hills: Sage, 1979).

13. *Current Population Reports, Series P-60, #118*, 36.

14. Ehrbar, "The Upbeat Outlook for Family Incomes," 128.

15. Caplovitz, *Making Ends Meet*, 76.

16. William Dunkelberg, Testimony in U.S. House of Representatives, Budget Committee, *Hearings: Cures for Inflation*, April 1979, p. 195.

17. Ibid., 196.

18. Cf. National Advisory Commission on Economic Opportunity, *12th Annual Report* (Washington, D.C.: U.S. Government Printing Office, 1980), 83–102.

19. Data from U.S. Department of Housing and Urban Development, cited in *Time*, 23 July 1979, pp. 66–67.

20. Cushing Dolbeare, Statement in U.S. House of Representatives, Budget Committee, *Hearings: Economic Issues for Fiscal 1981*, 5 February 1980, p. 454.

21. Kathryn Eaker, "California's Housing Crisis," *California Journal*, April 1980.

22. *Economic Report of the President, 1981*, 259.

23. "Industry Output and Employment: BLS Projections to 1990," *Monthly Labor Review*, April 1979, pp. 3–14.

24. Emma Rothschild, "Reagan and the Real America," *New York Review of Books*, 5 February 1981.

25. Ehrbar, "The Upbeat Outlook for Family Incomes," 126–27.

26. "Detroit's Uphill Battle," *Time*, 8 September 1980, pp. 46–47.

27. "The Shrinking Standard of Living," 72.

28. Advertisement for *Venture* magazine in *Mother Jones*, September–October 1980, p. 54

29. Barbara Ehrenreich, "It's about Repression," *Moving On*, March 1979.

30. Gwen Kinkead, "On a Fast Track to the Good Life," *Fortune*, 7 April 1980, p. 74.

31. Michael Harrington, *Decade of Decision* (New York: Simon and Schuster, 1980), 286.

32. Urie Bronfenbrenner, *The Ecology of Human Development* (Cambridge: Harvard University Press, 1979).

15   Sexism by a Subtler Name?

Postindustrial Conditions and Postfeminist Consciousness in Silicon Valley

Judith Stacey

> When I moved here, there were orchards all around, and now there are integrated-circuit manufacturing plants all around. . . . That's been the thrill, because I've been part of it, and it's the most exciting time in the history of the world, I think. And the center of it is here in Silicon Valley.
>> Female engineer at Hewlett-Packard,
>> quoted in *San Jose Mercury News*,
>> February 19, 1985

During the past three decades profound changes in the organization of family, work, and gender have occurred in the United States, coincident with the rise of second-wave feminism.[1] Feminist scholars have demonstrated that an important relationship exists between the development of the earlier feminist movement and that of capitalist industrialization in the West. In the United States, for example, the disintegration of the agrarian family economy and the reorganization of family, work, and gender relationships that took place during the nineteenth century provided the major impetus for the birth of American feminism.[2] Although

Source: This article is reprinted from *Socialist Review* No. 96 (November–December 1987), pp. 7–28, by permission of the publisher, *Socialist Review*, 3202 Adeline, Berkeley, CA 94703.

the more recent history of feminism and social change is equally intimate, it has received far less attention.

This essay explores a number of connections between the recent transition to an emergent "postindustrial" stage of capitalist development and the simultaneous rise and decline of a militant and radical phase of feminism in the United States.[3] First I reflect on the ironic role second-wave feminism has played as an unwitting midwife to the massive social transformations of work and family life that have occurred in the post–World War II era. Second, I draw from my field research on family life in California's "Silicon Valley"—a veritable postindustrial hothouse—to illustrate some of the effects of this ironic collaboration in fostering emergent forms of "postfeminist" consciousness.

Let me begin, however, by explaining my use of the troubling term "postfeminist," a concept offensive to many feminists who believe that the media coined it simply "to give sexism a subtler name."[4] Whatever the media's motives, I find the concept useful in describing the gender consciousness and the family and work strategies of many contemporary women. I view the term as analogous to "postrevolutionary" and use it not to indicate the death of the women's movement but to describe the simultaneous incorporation, revision, and depoliticization of many of the central goals of second-wave feminism.[5] I believe "postfeminism" is distinct from "antifeminism" and "sexism," for it aptly describes the consciousness and strategies that increasing numbers of women have developed in response to the new difficulties and opportunities of postindustrial society. In this sense, the diffusion of postfeminist consciousness signifies both the achievements of, and challenges for, modern feminist politics.

Feminism as Midwife to Postindustrial Society

Hindsight allows us to see how feminist ideology helped legitimate the massive structural changes in American work and family that invisibly accompanied the transition to postindustrial society in the 1960s and early 1970s.[6] I believe this period of postindustrialization should be read as the unmaking of a gender order rooted in the modern nuclear family system: the family of male breadwinner, female homemaker, and dependent children that was grounded in the male family wage and stable marriage, at least for the majority of white working-class and middle-class families. Family and work relations in the emergent postindustrial order, by contrast, have been transformed by the staggering escalation of divorce rates and women's participation in paid work. As the United States changed from having an industrial to a service-dominated occupational structure,[7] unprecedented percentages of women entered the labor force and the halls of academe, while unprecedented percentages of marriages entered the divorce courts.[8] Unstable and often incompatible work and family conditions have become the postindustrial norm as working class occupations become increasingly "feminized."

This process has generated an extreme disjuncture between the dominant cultural ideology of domesticity—an ideology that became particularly strident in the 1950s—and the simultaneous decline in the significance placed on marriage and motherhood and the rise of women's employment.

The gap between the ideology of domesticity and the increasingly nondomestic character of women's lives helped generate feminist consciousness in the 1960s. As that consciousness developed, women launched an assault on traditional domesticity: an assault, that is, on a declining institution and culture.[9] Therefore, this feminist movement was backward looking in its critique and unwittingly forward looking (but not to the future of our fantasies) in its effects.

Feminism developed a devastating critique of the stultifying, infantilizing, and exploitative effects of female domesticity on women, especially of the sort available to classes that could afford an economically dependent housewife. Although the institutions of domesticity and its male beneficiaries were the intended targets of our critique, most housewives felt themselves on the defensive. Feminist criticism helped undermine and delegitimize the flagging but still celebrated nuclear family and helped promote the newly normative double-income (with shifting personnel) middle- and working-class families. We also provided ideological support for the sharp rise of single-mother families generated by the soaring divorce rates.[10] By 1986 fewer than 10 percent of U.S. families consisted of a male breadwinner, a female housewife, and their dependent children.[11]

Millions of women have derived enormous, tangible benefits from these changes in occupational patterns and family life and from the ways in which feminist ideology encouraged women to initiate and cope with these changes. Yet it is also true that since the mid-1970s, when the contours of the new postindustrial society began to be clear, economic and personal life has worsened for many groups of women, perhaps for the majority. The emerging shape of postindustrial society seems to have the following, rather disturbing characteristics: As unionized occupations and real wages decline throughout the economy, women are becoming the postindustrial "proletariat," performing the majority of "working-class," low-skilled, low-paying jobs.[12] Because the overall percentage of jobs that are secure and well-paying has declined rapidly, increasing numbers of men are unemployed or underemployed. Yet the majority of white, male workers still labor at jobs that are highly skilled and comparatively well paid.[13] Family instability is endemic with devastating economic effects on many women, as the "feminization of poverty" literature has made clear.[14] Increasing percentages of women are rearing children by themselves, generally with minimal economic contributions from former husbands and fathers.[15] Yet rising numbers of those single mothers who work full time, year round do not earn wages sufficient to lift their families above the official poverty line.[16]

In the emerging class structure, marriage is becoming a major axis of stratification because it structures access to a second income. The married female as "secondary" wage earner lifts a former working-class or middle-class family into comparative affluence, while the loss or lack of access to a male income can force women and their children into poverty.[17] In short, the drastic increase in female employment during the past several decades has meant more work for mother but with very unevenly distributed economic benefits and only a slight improvement in relative income differentials between women and men.[18]

This massive rise in female employment also produces a scarcely visible but portentous social effect through the drastic decline in the potential pool of female volunteers, typically from the middle class, who have sustained much of family and community life in the United States since the nineteenth century. The result of this decline may be a general deterioration of domesticity and social housekeeping that in turn is fueling reactionary nostalgia for traditional family life among leftists and feminists as well as among right-wing forces.[19]

In light of these developments, many women (and men) have been susceptible to the appeals of the antifeminist backlash and especially to profamily ideologies. Because of its powerful and highly visible critique of traditional domesticity, and because of the sensationalized way the media disseminated this critique, feminism has taken most of the heat for family and social crises that have attended the transition from an industrial to a postindustrial order. Despite efforts by feminists like Barbara Ehrenreich to portray men as the real family deserters, many continue to blame feminism for the general decline of domesticity and nurturance within families and communities.[20] Feminism serves as a symbolic lightning rod for the widespread nostalgia and longing for "lost" intimacy and security that presently pervades social and political culture in the United States.[21] Not by accident do 1950s fashions and symbols dominate popular culture in the 1980s.

It is in this context, I believe, that we can best understand why during the late 1970s and the 1980s even many feminists began to retreat from the radical critique of conventional family life of the early second wave.[22] The past decade, during which postindustrial social patterns became firmly established, has been marked instead by the emergence of various forms of postfeminist consciousness and family strategies.

Family and Work in the Silicon Valley

Material from my study of family and work experience in California's "Silicon Valley" highlights a number of features of postindustrial society and several of the diverse postfeminist strategies that contemporary women have devised to cope with them. After briefly describing the major postindustrial contours of the region, I will draw from my fieldwork to illustrate some of these strategies.

As the birthplace and international headquarters of the electronics industry, Silicon Valley—Santa Clara County, California—is popularly perceived as representing the vanguard of postindustrialism. Until the early 1950s the region was a sparsely populated agricultural area, one of the major fruit baskets in the United States. But in the three decades since the electronics industry developed there, its population has grown by 350 percent, and its economy, ecology, and social structure have been dramatically transformed.[23]

During this period electronics, the vanguard postindustrial industry, feminized (and "minoritized") its production workforce. In the 1950s and 1960s, when the industry was young, most of its production workers were men, for whom there were significant opportunities for advancement into technical and, at times, engineering ranks even for those with very limited schooling. But as the industry matured, it turned increasingly to female, ethnic minority, and recent migrant workers to fill production positions that offered fewer and fewer advancement opportunities.[24] By the late 1970s the industry's occupational structure was crudely stratified by gender, as well as by race and ethnicity. At the top was an unusually high proportion (25 percent) of the most highly educated and highly paid salaried employees in any industry—the engineers and professionals employed in research and design. As in traditional industries, the vast majority were white males (89 percent males, 89 percent non-Hispanic whites). At the bottom, were the women, three-fourths of the very poorly paid assembly workers and operatives who performed the tedious, often health-threatening work assigned to 45 percent of the employees. In between were the moderately well-paid technicians and craft workers, also primarily Anglo males but into whose ranks women and Asians were making gradual inroads.[25]

In the heady days of technological triumph and economic expansion, when Silicon Valley was widely portrayed as the mecca of the new intellectual entrepreneurs and as a land where factories resembled college campuses, its public officials also liked to describe it as a feminist capital. Indeed, San Jose, the county seat, had a feminist mayor in the late 1970s and was one of the first public employers in the nation to implement a comparable worth standard of pay for city employees.

What is less widely known is that the area is also the site of a significant degree of family turbulence. Much of the data on local family change represent an exaggeration of national and even California trends, which tend to be more extreme than the national averages. For example, whereas the national divorce rate has doubled since 1960, in Santa Clara County it has nearly tripled; by 1977 divorces exceeded marriages. Likewise the percentage of "nonfamily households" grew faster than in the nation, and abortion rates were one and a half times the national figures. And although the proportion of single-parent households was not quite as high as in the United States as a whole, the rate of increase has been far more rapid.[26] Thus the coincidence of pathbreaking changes in both economic and family patterns makes Silicon Valley an ideal site for examining women's responses to these transformations.

During the past three years I have conducted intermittent fieldwork in the valley, concentrating on an in-depth study of two kinship networks of people, which mainly consist of nonethnic Caucasians who have lived in the region during the period of postindustrialization. My key informant in each network is a white woman now in her late forties who married in the 1950s and became a homemaker for a white man who was to benefit from the unusual electronics industry opportunities of the 1960s. Both of these marriages and careers proved to be highly turbulent, however, and in response both of the women and several of their daughters have devised a variety of postfeminist survival strategies. At first glance their strategies appear to represent a simple retreat from feminism, but closer study has convinced me that these women are selectively blending and adapting certain feminist ideas to traditional and modern family and work strategies. Vignettes from their family histories suggest the texture and purpose of such strategies as well as important generational variations.

Paths to Postfeminism

Let me first introduce Pam, currently a staff analyst in a municipal agency.[27] We became friendly in 1984 when I was interviewing clients
at a feminist-inspired social service program where she was then an administrator. From various informal conversations, lunches, and observations of
her work goals and relations, I had pegged Pam as a slightly cynical di-
vorcee who came to feminist consciousness through divorce and a women's
reentry program at a local community college. I had learned that Pam's first
husband, Don, to whom she was married for twelve years and with whom
she had three children, was one of those white male electronics industry
success stories. A telephone repair worker with an interest in drafting when
they married, Don entered the electronics industry in the early 1960s and
proceeded to work and job-hop his way up to a career as a packaging
engineer, a position that currently earns him $50,000 annually.

I had heard too that Don's route to success had been arduous and
stormy, entailing numerous setbacks, failures, and layoffs and requiring
such extraordinary work hours that Don totally neglected Pam and their
children. This and other problems led to Pam's divorce, resulting in the
normative female impoverishment. Pam became a single mother on welfare, continued her schooling (eventually through the master's level), developed feminist consciousness, experimented with sexual freedom, cohabited with a couple of lovers, and began to develop an administrative career
in social services. Before the 1984 election Pam made many scornful remarks about Reagan, Reaganomics, and the military buildup. Therefore, I
was quite surprised when, four months after meeting her, I learned that she
was now married to Al, a construction worker with whom she had cohabited
earlier. I also learned that they were both recent converts to charismatic,
evangelical Christianity and that they were participating in Christian marriage counseling to improve their relationship. Pam had been separated
from but was on a friendly basis with her second husband, Al, when he
had an automobile accident followed by a dramatic conversion experience.
Al "accepted Jesus into his life," and Pam suddenly accepted Al and Jesus
back into hers.

Pam acknowledges the paradoxes and contradictions of her participation in "Christian marriage"[28] and Christian marriage counseling, based,
as they are, on patriarchal doctrines; however, she credits the conversion
experience and the counseling with helping her achieve a more intimate,
positive marital relationship than she had experienced before. The conversion, she claims, changed Al from a defensive, uncommunicative, with-
holding male into a less guarded, more trusting, loving, and committed

mate.[29] Although their marriage is not as communicative, nurturant, and intimate as Pam would like, she believes that their shared faith is leading them in this direction. And she believes that "if you can work out that kind of relationship, then who would care who's in charge, because it's such a total wonderful relationship?" Moreover, Pam cedes Al dominance only in the "spiritual realm"; financially, occupationally, interpersonally, and politically, she retains strong independence or even control.

Pam's selective adaptation and blending of feminist and fundamentalist ideologies first struck me as quite unique as well as extremely contradictory. I have gradually learned, however, that a significant tendency in contemporary fundamentalist thought incorporates some feminist criticisms of patriarchal men and marriage into its activism in support of patriarchal profamilialism. Quite a few evangelical ministers urge Christian wives to make strong emotional demands on their husbands for communication, commitment, and nurturance within the framework of patriarchal marriage, and they actively counsel Christian husbands to meet these demands.[30]

Feminism served Pam well as an aid for leaving her unsatisfactory first marriage and for building a career and sense of individual identity. But Pam failed to form successful, satisfying, intimate relationships to replace her marriage. Struggling alone with the emotional and social crises to which two of her three children were prone, Pam describes herself as having been desperately unhappy much of the time. Although she received support from several intense friendships with women, neither this nor feminism seemed to offer her sufficient solace or direction. Her retreat from feminism and her construction of an extreme form of postfeminist consciousness took place in this context.

Dotty Lewison, a key informant in the other kinship network I studied, has a more complex story. I first sought out Dotty because of her early experience in electronics assembly work and because of her intact thirty-year marriage to Lou Lewison, another white male electronics industry success story. Dotty had been a teenager in 1954 when she met and married Lou, a sailor who had dropped out of school in the ninth grade. Although Dotty primarily had been a homemaker for Lou and the five children she bore at two-year intervals during her first decade of marriage, she also had made occasional forays into the world of paid work, including one two-year stint assembling semiconductors in the late 1950s. But Dotty neither perceived nor desired significant opportunities for personal advancement in electronics or any occupation at that time. Instead, several years later she pushed Lou to enter the industry. This proved to be a successful strategy for *family* economic mobility, although one that was to have contradictory effects on their marital and family relationships as well as on Dotty's personal achievement goals. With his mechanical aptitude and naval background, Lou was able to receive on-the-job training and advance to the position of line maintenance engineer. Then, as he told me, "the companies didn't have many choices. No one even knew what a circuit looked like. . . . [But] you can't find many engineers starting out now who don't enter with degrees . . . because the companies have a lot more choices now."

When I first arrived at the Lewisons' modest, cluttered tract home, Dotty was opening a delivery from a local gadgets sale. A "knickknack junkie" by her own description, Dot unpacked various porcelain figures and a new, gilded Bible. My social prejudices cued me to expect her to hold somewhat conservative and antifeminist views, but I was wrong again. She reported a long history of community and feminist activism, including work in the antibattering movement. And she still expressed some support for feminism, "depending," she said, "on what you mean by feminism."

Later I learned that Dotty's intact marriage had been broken by numerous short-term separations and one of two years' duration that almost became permanent. During that separation Dot too was a welfare mother who hated being on welfare, and she had a serious live-in love affair. Dot does not repudiate very many of her former feminist ideas, but she has not been active since the late 1970s. She specifically distances herself from the "militant man-hating types."

Dotty is a feisty, assertive woman who had protofeminist views long before she (or most of us) had heard of the women's liberation movement. Yet for twenty years she tolerated a marriage in which she and her husband fought violently. Her children were battered, sometimes seriously, most often by Lou but occasionally by Dotty as well. Before I learned about the violence, Dotty and Lou both led me to believe that their near-divorce in the mid-1970s was caused by Lou's workaholism as an upwardly mobile employee in the electronics industry. They spoke of the twelve- to fourteen-hour days and the frequent three-day shifts that led Lou to neglect his family completely. Later I came to understand the dynamic relationships between that workaholism and their marital hostilities. Dotty had become a feminist and community activist by then, involved in antibattering work and many other community issues. Partly as a result of her involvement with feminism (again, some of it encountered in a college women's reentry program), Dotty was beginning to shift the balance of power in her marriage. In this situation, I suspect Lou's escape into work was experienced on all sides as relief more than as neglect. Although now Dotty blames the work demands of the electronics industry for Lou's heart disease and his early death at the age of fifty-two, at the time his absence from the family gave Dotty the "space" to develop her strength and the willingness to assume the serious economic and emotional risks of divorce and an impoverished life as a single parent.

Dotty kicked Lou out but did not file for divorce. Two years later she took him back, but only after his nearly fatal and permanently disabling heart attack, and after her live-in lover had left her. Even then she took Lou back on her own rather harsh terms. She was to have total independence with her time and relationships. Despite the economic inequality between them, Dotty now held the undeniable emotional balance of power in the relationship, but only because she had proved that she could survive impoverishment and live without Lou. And, of course, Lou's disability contributed to the restructuring of the division of labor and power in their household. Lou did most of the housework and gardening, while Dotty participated in the paid labor force. Nonetheless, Dotty remained economically dependent on Lou, and she regrets her limited career options. Indeed, this was one crucial factor in her decision to resume her marriage with Lou.

By the late 1970s Dotty was no longer active in feminist or community causes. She says she "got burned out" and "turned off by the 'all men are evil' kind of thinking." More important, I believe, Dotty's life stage and circumstances had changed so that she did not feel she needed or benefited from feminism any more. In the mid-1970s she "needed to have my stamp validated," to be reassured that her rebellious and assertive feelings and her struggles to reform her marriage were legitimate. But partly because of the feminist-assisted success of those struggles, Dotty came to feel less need for reassurance from feminists then and finds she has no room for feminism today. She is "too tired, there's too much other shit to deal with." She has been trying to maintain her precarious hold on her underpaid job at a cable television service while heroically struggling to cope with the truly staggering series of family tragedies that befell the Lewisons this year. Lou and two of the adult Lewison children died, and one son spent four months in prison. Under these circumstances Dotty too has found more comfort from organized religion than from feminism. After the death of their first son, Dotty and Lou left a spiritualist church they had been attending and returned to the neighborhood Methodist church in which Dotty once had been active. Since Lou's death, Dotty's oldest daughter, Lyn, and her mother have joined her in attending this church regularly.

Parallels and idiosyncracies in the life histories just described illustrate some of the complex, reciprocal effects of the family and work dynamics and gender consciousness that I have observed in Silicon Valley. Pam and Dotty both were young when they married. They both entered their marriages with conventional Parsonsian gender expectations about family and work responsibilities and "roles." For a significant period of time they and their husbands conformed to the then culturally prescribed pattern of "instrumental" male breadwinner and "expressive" female housewife/mother. Assuming primary responsibility for rearing the children they began to bear immediately after marriage, Pam and Dotty supported their husbands' successful efforts to develop middle- to upper-middle-class careers as electronics engineers. In the process, both men became workaholics, increasingly uninvolved with their families.

As their marriages deteriorated, both Pam and Dotty enrolled in a women's reentry program where they were affected profoundly by feminist courses. Both women eventually left their husbands and became welfare mothers, an experience each of them found to be both liberating and debilitating. Each experienced an initial "feminist high," a sense of enormous exhilaration and strength in her new independent circumstances. One divorced her husband, developed a viable career, experimented with the single life, and gradually became desperately unhappy. The other did not develop a career, lost her lover, and only then decided to take back her newly disabled husband (with his pension). Their rather different experiences with failed intimacy and their different occupational resources, I believe, help explain their diverse postfeminist strategies.

Postfeminist Daughters

Between them, Pam and Dotty had five daughters who, reckoning by the calendar, were members of the quintessential postfeminist generation.[31] (One died recently at the age of twenty-six; the surviving four range in age from twenty-three to thirty-one.) To varying degrees, all the daughters have distanced themselves from feminist identity and ideology, in some cases in conscious reaction against what they regard as the excesses of their mothers' earlier feminist views. At the same time, however, most of the daughters have semiconsciously incorporated feminist principles into their expectations and strategies for family and work. A brief description of the family and work histories and gender consciousness of Dotty's and Pam's oldest and most professionally successful daughters illustrates this depoliticized incorporation of feminist thought.

Pam's oldest daughter, Lanny, is twenty-three. Like Dotty's oldest daughter, Lyn, she is a designer-drafter who received her initial training in a feminist-inspired skills program. She is now in her second marriage, with one child from each marriage. Lanny dropped out of high school and at seventeen married a truck driver who moves electronics equipment, and whom she describes as addicted to drugs and totally uncommunicative.

Staying home with their baby, she found herself isolated and unbearably lonely. Pam encouraged Lanny's entry into a drafting course sponsored by a county agency, and Lanny soon found ready employment in electronics via various temporary agencies.[32] After she discovered her husband's narcotics addiction and convinced him to enter a residential detox program, Lanny spent a brief period as a welfare mother. Although she hated drafting, she job-shopped frequently to raise her income sufficiently to support herself and her daughter. She was earning fourteen dollars an hour, without benefits, in 1985 when she met her present husband, Ken, at one of these jobs, where he worked as an expediter in the purchasing department for eight dollars an hour until a recent layoff.

Lanny does not consider herself a feminist and has never been active or interested in politics. She also hates her work but has no desire to be a homemaker and is perfectly willing to support her husband if he wants to stay home and take care of the children or if, as they hope, she can afford to send him back to engineering school. She would like to become an interior designer.

Although Lanny started out in a rather traditional working-class marriage, she is an authentic postfeminist. She was not able to tolerate the isolation, boredom, and emotional deprivation of that traditional marriage. Lanny's goals are to combine marriage to a nurturant, communicative, coparenting man (the way she perceives Ken) with full-time work at a job she truly enjoys. There is an ease to Lanny's attitudes about the gender division of labor at home and at work, and about gender norms more generally, that is decidedly postfeminist. These are not political issues to Lanny nor even conscious points of personal struggle. She did actively reject her traditionally gendered first marriage but without conceptualizing it that way. Lanny takes for granted the right to be flexible about family and work priorities. Remarkably, Ken appears to be equally flexible and equally oblivious to feminist influences on his notably enlightened attitudes.

The postfeminism of Dotty's daughter Lyn, however, represents a somewhat more conscious and ambivalent response to feminism. Like Lanny, Lyn was a high school dropout who took a variety of low-wage service-sector jobs. But unlike Lanny's husband, the father of her child, with whom she cohabited, left during her pregnancy, making her an unwed welfare mother. Lyn got off welfare by moonlighting at an electronics security job while developing her successful career in drafting. She is now a hybrid designer at one of the world's major semiconductor companies. Unlike Lanny, Lyn loves her work in drafting, although she is constantly anxious, exhausted, and deeply frustrated by the extreme demands, stress, and unpredictability of her working conditions and by their incompatibility with her needs as a single mother. There have been long periods when Lyn hardly saw her son and depended upon her parents and friends to fill in as babysitters.

Lyn's desire for a father for her son was a major motive for her brief marriage to a man who quickly abused her. She has lived alone with her son since she divorced her husband five years ago. Although Lyn is proud and fiercely independent, during the past two years she has somewhat ambivalently pursued a marital commitment from her somewhat resistant boyfriend, Tom. Like Lanny's husband Ken, Tom appears both unthreatened by Lyn's greater career drive and income and quite flexible about gender norms generally. He, however, seems much less willing or able than Ken to commit himself to the long-term responsibilities of marriage and parenthood.

Lyn is aware of sex discrimination at work and of issues of gender injustice generally and will occasionally challenge these by herself. Yet more explicitly than Lanny, Lyn distances herself from a feminist identity, which she regards as an unnecessarily hostile and occasionally petty one: "I do not feel like a feminist, because to me my mother is a perfect feminist. . . . If someone asks her to make coffee, she first has to determine if it is because she is a woman." Upon reflection, Lyn acknowledges that it is the word "feminist" that she does not like, "because of the way I was brought up with it. It meant slapping people in the face with it. . . . I do what I think is right, and if I am asked, I tell them why. . . . Honestly, I guess I am a very strong feminist, but I don't have to beat people with it."

I consider Lyn a stronger postfeminist than feminist because of her thoroughly individual and depoliticized relationship to feminist issues. She cannot imagine being active politically on any issue, not even one like battering, which she experienced: "I leave them for people like my mother who can make issues out of that, because I don't see it that way. I'll help the neighbor next door whose husband is beating her to death . . . but I do it my way. My way is not in a public form. I am very different from my mother." Equally postfeminist are the ways Lyn fails both to credit feminist struggles for the career opportunities for women she has grown up taking for granted, or to blame sexism or corporations for the male-oriented work schedules and demands that jeopardize her family needs. For example, she would like to have a second child but accepts the "fact" that a second child does not fit with a successful career. Lyn shares Lanny's postfeminist expectations for family and work: that is, the desire to combine marriage to a communicative, egalitarian man with motherhood and a successful, engaging career. While Lanny has achieved more of the former, Lyn has more of the latter.

Conclusion

The emergent relationships between postindustrialism, family turbulence and postfeminism are nuanced and dynamic. Crisis in the family, as manifested in escalating rates of divorce and single-mother households, contributes both to the peculiar gender stratification of this postindustrial workforce and to a limited potential for feminist consciousness. Marital instability continually refuels a large, cheap female labor pool that underwrites the feminization both of the postindustrial proletariat and of poverty.[33] But this crudely gender-stratified and male-oriented occupational structure helps to further destabilize gender relationships and family life. Moreover, the skewed wages and salaries available to white men help to inflate housing costs for everyone, thereby contributing to the rapid erosion of the working-class breadwinner and the family wage.[34]

One consequence of family instability in such an environment seems to have been an initial openness on the part of many women, like Dotty and Pam, to feminist ideas. Feminism served many mothers of the postfeminist generation well as an ideology for easing the transition from an unhappy 1950s-style marriage and for providing support for efforts to develop independent career goals. Neither feminism nor other progressive movements, however, have been as successful in addressing either the structural inequalities of postindustrial occupational structure or the individualist, fast-track culture that makes all too difficult the formation of stable intimate relations on an egalitarian or, for that matter, any other basis. Organized religion, particularly evangelical groups, may offer more effective support to troubled family relationships in these circumstances.

I believe this explains the attractiveness of various kinds of postfeminist ideologies and strategies for achieving intimacy or for just surviving in a profoundly insecure milieu. Postfeminist strategies correspond to different generational and individual experiences of feminism as well as postindustrial family and work conditions. For many women of the "mother" generation, feminism has become as much a burden as a means of support. Where once it helped them to reform or leave unsatisfactory relationships, now it can intensify the pain and difficulty of the compromises most women must make in order to mediate the destructive effects of postindustrial society on family and personal relationships. Too seldom today can women find committed mates, let alone those who also would pass feminist muster.

Perhaps this helps to account for Pam's simultaneous turn to religion and her subtle adaptation of patriarchal, evangelical Christian forms to feminist ends, and for Dotty's return to but also reform of a previously unsatisfactory marriage coupled with her shift from political engagement to paid work and organized religion. In a general climate and a stage of their lives characterized by diminished expectations, both seek support for the compromises with and commitments to family and work they have chosen to make, rather than for greater achievement or independence. Without repudiating feminism, both Dotty and Pam have distanced themselves from feminist identity or activism. On the other hand, their postfeminist daughters take for granted the gains in female career opportunities and the male participation in child rearing and domestic work for which feminists of their mothers' generation struggled. Lanny and Lyn do not conceptualize their troubling postindustrial work and family problems in political terms. To them, feminism and politics appear either irrelevant or threatening.

These diverse forms of postfeminism, I believe, are semiconscious responses to feminism's unwitting role as midwife to the new family and work conditions in postindustrial America. Some versions are more reactionary and some more progressive, but all, I believe, differ from *anti*feminism. They represent women's attempts to both retain and depoliticize the egalitarian family and work ideals of the second wave. This is an inherently contradictory project, and one that presents feminists with an enigmatic dilemma. Is it possible to devise a personal politics that respects the political and personal anxieties and the exhaustion of women contending with the destabilized family and work conditions of the postindustrial era? To do so without succumbing to conservative nostalgia for patriarchal familial and religious forms is a central challenge to contemporary feminism.

Notes

Acknowledgments: I wish to thank Linda Gordon, Carole Joffe, David Plotke, Rayna Rapp, and Barrie Thorne for their challenging and supportive responses to earlier drafts of this article.

1. By "second-wave feminism" I refer to the resurgence of feminist politics and ideology that began in the mid-1960s, peaked in the early 1970s, and has been a major focus of social and political backlash since the late 1970s.

2. Historians have argued that the establishment of separate spheres for the sexes had as one of its paradoxical consequences the development of feminist consciousness and activity. See, e.g., Nancy Cott, *The Bonds of Womanhood: "Woman's Sphere" in New England, 1750–1835* (New Haven, Conn.: Yale University Press, 1976); Mary Ryan, *Womanhood in America* (New York: Franklin Watts, 1983). There were similar developments in Europe. By contrast, feminism has been weak in most preindustrial and "underdeveloped" societies, including even revolutionary societies with explicit commitments to gender equality.

3. Like "postfeminist," which I discuss below, I use the term "postindustrial" with trepidation, as it carries a great deal of ideological charge. I use it here exclusively in a descriptive sense to designate a form and period of capitalist social organization in

which traditional industrial occupations supply a small minority of jobs to the labor force, and the vast majority of workers labor in varieties of clerical, sales, and service positions. Daniel Bell claims to have formulated the theme in a 1962 essay, "The Post-Industrial Society"; see Bell, *The Coming of Post-Industrial Society: A Venture in Social Forecasting* (New York: Basic Books, 1973), 145.

4. Thus Geneva Overholser concludes a *New York Times* editorial opinion titled "What 'Post-Feminism' Really Means," 19 September 1986, p. 30.

5. My appreciation to Steven Buechler for first suggesting this analogy to me.

6. For an analogous argument about the relationship between feminism and de-industrialization in modern England, see Juliet Mitchell, "Reflections on Twenty Years of Feminism," in Mitchell and Ann Oakley, eds., *What Is Feminism?* (Oxford: Basil Blackwell, 1986), 34–48.

7. There is considerable debate among economists concerning the accuracy of labeling the United States as a service economy. See, e.g., Richard Walker's challenge to this characterization, "Is There a Service Economy? The Changing Capitalist Division of Labor," *Science & Society* 49, no. 1 (1985): 42–83. The debate involves the politics of semantics. Few disagree, however, that significant occupational changes have occurred in the past few decades, or that these involve the decline of unions and real wages and the rise of female employment. For a synthetic analysis of occupational trends, see Bennett Harrison and Barry Bluestone, "The Dark Side of Labor Market 'Flexibility': Falling Wages and Growing Income Inequality in America," International Labor Office, File ILo2 (June 1987).

8. Labor-force participation rates for women increased steadily but slowly between 1900 and 1940, from 20.5 percent to 25.4 percent. However, this pattern accelerated rapidly in the post-1940 period. In 1950, 29 percent of women fourteen years and older were in the labor force; in 1960, 34.5 percent; in 1984, 63 percent of all women ages eighteen to sixty-four were in the labor force. See Valerie Kincade Oppenheimer, *The Female Labor Force in the United States*, Population Monograph Series No. 5 (Berkeley: Institute of International Studies, University of California, 1970); and Barbara F. Reskin and Heidi I. Hartmann, eds., *Women's Work, Men's Work* (Washington, D.C.: National Academy Press, 1986). The dramatic rise in female enrollment in colleges occurred in the 1960s and 1970s, rising from 38 to 48 percent of enrollees between 1960 and 1979: Rosalind Petchesky, *Abortion and Woman's Choice* (Boston: Northeastern University Press, 1984). U.S. marriage rates peaked at 16.4 per 1,000 people in 1946, declined sharply to 9.9 in 1952, and have fluctuated around 10 ever since, while divorce rates increased steadily to 5.0 in 1985: National Center for Health Statistics, Annual Summary of Births, Marriages, Divorces, and Deaths, *Monthly Vital Statistics Reports*. More significantly, the age of women at their first marriage has risen and their rate of marriage has declined steadily since 1960. Fertility rates peaked at 3.6 per 1,000 women during the famous mid-1950s baby boom and declined steadily thereafter to 1.8 in 1976; see Petchesky, *Abortion*, 103–7. Even more striking are the rising proportions of women who never marry or bear children. The cohort of women born 1935–39 had the lowest rate of childlessness in the twentieth century—10 percent. The Census Bureau projects a childless rate of 20–25 percent, however, for women born in the 1960s and estimates that 40 percent of college-educated women born in that decade will never bear children: "The Birth Question," *USA Today*, 28 February 1986, p. 1.

9. Betty Friedan, *The Feminine Mystique* (1963) was one of the earliest, most successful polemical examples of this assault.

10. In 1960 one of every eleven children lived with only one parent, but by 1986 one of four children lived in a single-parent household, and 90 percent of these lived with their mothers: Tim Schreiner, "U.S. Family Eroding, Says Census Bureau," *San Francisco Chronicle*, 10 December 1986.

11. "A Mother's Choice," *Newsweek*, 31 March 1986, p. 47.

12. See Harrison and Bluestone, "Dark Side of Labor Market 'Flexibility.'"

13. These are among the findings of a study that attempted to operationalize Marxist criteria for assigning class categories to workers in the United States. Even though the study excluded housewives from its sample, it found that "the majority of the working class in the United States consists of women (53.6 percent)." See, Erik Olin Wright et al., "The American Class Structure," *American Sociological Review* 47 (December 1982): 22. For additional data on female occupational patterns and earnings and an astute analysis of the paradoxical relationship between female employment and poverty, see Joan Smith, "The Paradox of Women's Poverty: Wage-Earning Women and Economic Transformation," *Signs* 10, no. 2 (1984).

14. The concept "feminization of poverty" also misrepresents significant features of contemporary poverty, particularly the worsening conditions for minority men. See Pamela Sparr, "Reevaluating Feminist Economics: 'Feminization of Poverty' Ignores Key Issues," and Linda Burnham, "Has Poverty Been Feminized in Black America?" in Rochelle Lefkowitz and Ann Withorn, eds., *For Crying Out Loud: Women and Poverty in the United States* (New York: Pilgrim Press, 1986).

15. As the much publicized findings from Lenore Weitzman's study of no-fault divorce in California underscore: in the first year after divorce, women and minor children in their care suffer a 73 percent decline in their standard of living, while husbands enjoy a 42 percent gain (*The Divorce Revolution: The Unexpected Social and Economic Consequences for Women and Children in America*, Lenore J. Weitzman [New York: Free Press, 1985]). For a qualitative study that focuses on the plight of divorced single mothers, see Terry Arendell, *Mothers and Divorce: Legal, Economic, and Social Dilemmas* (Berkeley: University of California Press, 1986).

16. In 1980, households headed by fully employed women had a poverty rate almost three times greater than husband-wife households and twice that of households headed by unmarried men. The number of female-headed families doubled between 1970 and 1980. By 1981, women headed almost one fifth of all families with minor children (Smith, "Paradox of Women's Poverty," 291).

17. Households with working wives accounted for 60 percent of all family income in 1985, which made it possible for 65 percent of all families to earn more than $25,000 per year, compared with only 28 percent of families who achieved comparable incomes twenty years ago. In 1981 the median earnings of full-time year-round women workers was $12,001, 59 percent of the $20,260 that men earned. That year married women contributed a median of 26.7 percent of family income. The lower the family's annual income, the higher the proportion contributed by women; paradoxically, however, there is an inverse relationship between family income and the percentage of wives working. See *The Working Woman: A Progress Report* (Washington D.C.: Conference Board, 1985), and Reskin and Hartmann, *Women's Work, Men's Work*, 4. The combined effects of these trends are acute for black women, for whom astronomical divorce rates have overwhelmed the effects of their relative gains in earnings, forcing them increasingly into poverty. For data see U.S. Department of Labor, *Time of Change: 1983 Handbook on Women Workers* Women's Bureau Bulletin 298 (Washington D.C.: Department of Labor, 1983), 29; Paula Giddings, *When and*

Where I Enter: The Impact of Black Women on Race and Sex in America (Toronto: Bantam, 1985), 353.

18. For a more optimistic evaluation of the economic and social effects of these changes on women, see Heidi I. Hartmann, "Changes in Women's Economic and Family Roles in Post World War II United States," in Lourdes Beneria and Catherine Stimpson, eds., *Women, Households, and Structural Transformation* (New Brunswick, N.J.: Rutgers University Press, 1987).

19. It seems plausible that there has been a concomitant decline in political activism as well. Note, e.g., the stark contrast in the amount of time available for politics for women active on opposing sides of the abortion controversy. In a recent study of this conflict, most of the antiabortion activists were housewives who spent at least thirty hours per week on antichoice politics, whereas most of the prochoice activists were career women, few of whom spent more than five hours per week on this issue. See Kristin Luker, *Abortion and the Politics of Motherhood* (Berkeley: University of California Press, 1984). Although there are problems with Luker's prochoice sample that may exaggerate its career and income levels, it seems unlikely that the contrast is spurious.

20. Barbara Ehrenreich, *The Hearts of Men: American Dreams and the Flight from Commitment* (Garden City, N.Y.: Anchor Press/Doubleday, 1983).

21. Christopher Lasch has made a sideline industry out of this sort of attack on feminists. For some of his most recent polemics, see "What's Wrong with the Right?" *Tikkun* 1, no. 1 (1986); and "Why the Left Has No Future," *Tikkun* 1, no. 2 (1986). The latter was his response to critics of the former, including Lillian Rubin, "A Feminist Response to Lasch." The most comprehensive and popular recent book to scapegoat feminism in this way is probably Sylvia Ann Hewlett, *A Lesser Life: The Myth of Women's Liberation in America* (New York: Morrow, 1986). For a critical discussion of this book that does not deny the power of its approach, see Deborah Rosenfelt and Judith Stacey, "Second Thoughts on the Second Wave," *Feminist Studies* 13, no. 2 (1987); also Chapter 28 in this book.

22. The most conspicuous representatives of this backlash within feminist thought are Betty Friedan, Jean Bethke Elshtain, and Germaine Greer. For critical discussions of their writings, see my "Are Feminists Afraid to Leave Home? The Challenge of Conservative Pro-family Feminism," in Mitchell and Oakley, *What Is Feminism?* and Zillah Eisenstein, *Feminism and Sexual Equality: Crisis in Liberal America* (New York: Monthly Review Press, 1984).

23. The county population grew from 290,547 in 1950 to 1,295,071 in 1980. See U.S. Bureau of the Census, *Census of Population: 1950*, vol. 2, *Characteristics of the Population*, pt. 5, California, 1952; and *Census of Population: 1980*, vol. 1, *Characteristics of the Population, General Population Characteristics*, pt. 6, California, 1982.

24. For data and a superb ethnographic and analytical account of this transition, see John Frederick Keller, "The Production Worker in Electronics: Industrialization and Labor Development in California's Santa Clara Valley," (Ph.D. diss., University of Michigan, 1981).

25. For data on the occupational structure of the electronics industry, see ibid.; Marcie Axelrad, *Profile of the Electronics Workforce in the Santa Clara Valley* (San Jose, Calif.: Project on Health and Safety in Electronics, 1979); Lennie Siegel and Herb Borock, "Background Report on Silicon Valley," prepared for the U.S. Commission on Civil Rights (Mountain View, Calif.: Pacific Studies Center, 1982).

26. For the data on divorce rates and household composition for Santa Clara

County in comparison with California and the United States as a whole, see Bureau of the Census, *Census of Population*, for 1960, 1970, and 1980. During the 1970s Santa Clara County recorded 660 abortions for every 1000 births, compared with a statewide average of 489.5 and a ratio of less than 400 for the nation. See Bureau of the Census, *Statistical Abstract of the United States*, 1981.

27. I have given pseudonyms to all the individuals described here.

28. Like many evangelical and fundamentalist Christians, Pam uses the term "Christian" to designate only "born-again" Christians.

29. Al, as well as Pam's children, agree with this description.

30. The most influential representative of this tendency may be James Dobson, founder and president of Focus on the Family, "a nonprofit corporation dedicated to the preservation of the home." Focus produces a radio talk show on family issues aired as much as three times daily on hundreds of Christian stations throughout the United States and abroad. The organization also produces and distributes Christian films, tapes, and audiocassettes on family topics. Dobson, who served on the Meese Commission on Pornography, has also authored scores of advice books and pamphlets on family and personal relationships, most of which advocate the doctrine of "tough love." The uneasy fusion of patriarchal and feminist thought is marked in his advice book on marital crisis, *Love Must Be Tough* (Waco, Tex.: Word Books, 1983). For a discussion of the infusion of the female sexual revolution into fundamentalist culture, see Barbara Ehrenreich, Elizabeth Hess, and Gloria Jacobs, *Re-Making Love: The Feminization of Sex* (New York: Anchor Press, 1986), chap. 5.

31. Indeed the first media use of the term "postfeminist" to catch my attention was in the title of an essay about women in their late twenties: Susan Bolotin, "Voices from the Post-Feminist Generation," *New York Times Magazine*, 17 October 1982.

32. The very concept of "temporary" employment is being reshaped by postindustrial labor practices. High-tech industries in the Silicon Valley make increasing use of temporary agencies to provide "flexible staffing" and to cut employee benefits. In 1985 one of every 200 workers in the United States was a "temp"; in Silicon Valley, one of sixty. See David Beers, "'Temps': A High-Tech's Ace in The Hole," *San Bernadino Sun*, 28 May 1985.

33. Nor are the effects of the relationship between marital instability, female production work, and poverty confined to the United States. As many have noted, in the postindustrial economy women work on a "global assembly line." Maria Patricia Fernandez-Kelly discusses the effects of these international processes on Mexican women who work in electronics and garment factories on the Mexican-U.S. border in "Mexican Border Industrialization, Female Labor Force Participation, and Migration," in June Nash and Maria Patricia Fernandez-Kelly, eds., *Women, Men, and the International Division of Labor* (Albany: SUNY Press, 1983), 205–23.

34. More work needs to be done on ways in which the practice of one pattern of family life by some constrains options for others. The most obvious of the asymmetrical relationships among family patterns available to different social classes is that between affluent dual-career couples and the poorly paid women who provide the child care and domestic services upon which their egalitarian marriages depend. For a valuable study of the former, see Rosanna Hertz, *More Equal than Others: Women and Men in Dual-Career Marriages* (Berkeley: University of California Press, 1986). For a sensitive analysis of other kinds of unanticipated feedback effects of the electronics industry on the social ecology of Silicon Valley, see Anna Lee Saxenian, "Silicon Chips and Spatial Structure: The Industrial Basis of Urbanization in Santa Clara County, California" (master's thesis, University of California, Berkeley, 1980).

16   Is the Legacy of Second-Wave Feminism Postfeminism?

Rayna Rapp

Judith Stacey's "Sexism by a Subtler Name? Postindustrial Conditions and Postfeminist Consciousness in Silicon Valley" (see Chapter 15) challenges us to ask some hard questions: What is the relationship between women's experiences of domestic turbulence and abuse, and their ability to transform or escape those conditions? What is the role of feminist consciousness, or its lack, in those struggles? How does a period of economic turbulence both force and foster female initiative to escape marital violence? These are some of the issues toward which Stacey's ethnographic investigations into women's domestic networks in Silicon Valley point.

Family stress, fighting, battering, and addiction all play complex roles in the lives of the women of California's Silicon Valley. There, "the future is female," and the boom-and-bust economy already incorporates women as central actors. These women alternate between unstable marriages and time served as single heads of households, often and periodically on welfare. The legacy of family reform movements in Silicon Valley includes no-fault divorce and diminishing state entitlements as shock absorbers to domestic unrest. In the shadow of such social forces and household transformations, Pam and Dotty, the women Stacey came to know, strive to construct safety nets under their grown daughters and sons. Only time (and the case workers' records) will reveal the contours of their successes and failures.

Pam and Dotty's lives reflect the boomerang economy and marital pat-

Source: This article is reprinted from *Socialist Review* No. 97 (January–March 1988), pp. 31–37, by permission of the publisher, *Socialist Review*, 3202 Adeline, Berkeley, CA 94703.

terns of the region. Judith Stacey helps us understand the circumstances under which they came to think of themselves as feminists and then to distance themselves from organized feminism. Through her eyes, we see that Pam's and Dotty's daughters are recipients of feminism's strengths, although they are wary of its labels. The second generation adamantly rejects being called "feminist," as their mothers never did. Why? They are not unsympathetic toward the social transformations feminism demanded; they have benefited from the changes in education, jobs, and domestic services that feminist groups have helped to bring forth. But they are clearly concerned with questions of "personal choice" rather than politics.

Stacey labels their stance "postfeminist" and provides us with a provisional definition of that painful phenomenon: "The simultaneous incorporation, revision and depoliticization of many of the central goals of second-wave feminism." And, I would add, that depoliticization often takes the form of the reduction of feminist *social* goals to individual "lifestyle." It's a process as American as apple pie, in a culture where hegemonic claims are strongly influenced by a very Protestant notion of free and individual will. And Protestant evangelicalism in turn responds to aspects of women's family-based dilemmas, renaming them and offering guidance toward their individual, but not their social, resolution.

What are we to make of that vexatious term, "postfeminism"? A quick backward glance suggests that first-wave feminists debated analogous incorporations, revisions, and depoliticizations as their organized movement became disorganized. Running through the pages of the *Nation* in the late 1920s was a provocative series of essays in which aging and successful feminists commented on their individual, expanded choices. By turns triumphant, nostalgic, Freudian, and embittered, these feminists proclaimed their movement simultaneously over and transformed. After winning the vote, it was hard for many activists and former activists to imagine another creative, concerted mass movement on behalf of women's interests, although some remained committed to specific causes like the ERA and protective legislation. But would our foremothers have labeled their era "postfeminist" in the midst of a dormant period? Would such a label have helped or hindered the gathering forces of the second wave almost two generations later?

And what about today? As Stacey points out, "postfeminism" must be taken as more than media hype, for it describes the assumptions of entitlement to decent work and decent home lives of millions of American women who would be quick to distance themselves from our label of "feminist." They take our victories for granted! And well they should—as we took for granted the vote, the existence of widespread higher education for women, and the relative accessibility of divorce when we wandered, barely historically conscious, onto the stage of women's political history as new actors in a discontinuous, but continuing drama.

Paradoxically, the "taking for granted" in Lanny's and Lyn's lives constitutes our greatest victory and simultaneously poses a very large problem. It is a victory because it represents the fruition of the gains won by the feminist movement and feminist-inspired social services. Would Pam and Dotty or their daughters have their current options without programs for returning women at local community colleges, or training courses for women in the "nontraditional" skilled trades? Their consciousness is surely both transformed by and transformative of those myriad second-wave institutions, as the consciousness of the "former feminists" writing in the *Nation* was transformed by the temperance, child-saving, social purity, and social work institutions that dotted the landscape they increasingly proclaimed as barren.

But that "taking for granted" does not happen all at once, nor is it all of one piece or even inevitable. For diverse women separated by class, race, ethnic, sex-preferential, and other embodied divides live their history differently. To dignify an obvious point, we are here confronted with what Ernst Bloch labeled "non-synchronous fragments." We all share a chronology, but we do not live or make or experience the same history.

To make this point most dramatically, I want to shift my gaze from Silicon Valley back to my hometown, New York, where a group of "second wavers" has been privileged to participate in a series of women's studies conferences organized with and for trade-union women. In the "progressive" unions where organizing in female sectors is a do-or-die proposition, trade-union women by the thousands now struggle for goals that entail high feminist consciousness: comparable worth, child-care facilities, protection from sexual harassment, and contract language extending sick days to care for all dependents. And they struggle against male privilege and control in their unions while simultaneously confronting sexual inequalities in the labor market.

At meeting after meeting, our team of women's studies activists witnessed important conflicts among trade unionists, some of whom claimed the label of "feminism" while others rejected it. A group of rank-and-file retail workers, who had struggled for many months to have a women's history course offered as part of their trade union's education program, finally won their goal. They had no use for the word "feminist" until they actually sat in the course. Then they claimed it as their own, citing historical precedents.

A very successful organizer scorned *Ms.* magazine when we offered a reprinted article as part of an educational packet. In querying why, teeth clenched for an attack on feminism, we discovered it was the anti-union stance of some *Ms.* editors to which she objected; the magazine's definition of feminism posed no problem. Health-care workers on a women's conference planning committee made it clear that child care had to become a top union priority; otherwise, they threatened to withdraw their time and energy from crucial union projects. "This is a woman's union, and until they make our kids welcome here, it's no home to us. Doesn't matter if we have to turn the union world upside down to do it, it's got to be done," one member of the planning committee told us. None of them would ever identify with the label "postfeminist." They're too busy fighting over what the initial term can bring to or detract from their immediate concerns.

Nor do I think we can call the extraordinary phenomenon of the divided responses to *The Color Purple* in black communities "postfeminist." The struggles of black feminists to name themselves, organize themselves, and mobilize their sisters, in spite of the perceived whiteness of the label "feminist," must be understood in its own terms. It requires confrontation with issues like domestic violence, teen pregnancy, and lesbian-baiting, all of which may reveal divisions rather than solidarities within already embattled communities. These are not easy issues to discuss in a language formulated by a movement that has often taken the experiences of white women as its point of orientation. Such struggles are not reducible to the "postfeminism" expressed by young, predominantly white, highly privileged female doctors, lawyers, and business executives whose efforts to build integrated home and work lives are gleefully covered by the *New York Times Magazine.* Movements that may feel "dead" to second-wave feminists are actually just beginning or continuing for other groups of American women, depending on the social fault lines upon which their experiences are constructed.

But how can we locate ourselves in a political era that has no unified name we all can share? Without an obvious and defined national political feminist movement, many struggles for women's rights and agency continue to bubble in fragmented ways, under the surface of daily life. But the *lack* of a unified name also points to a problem: women dispersed among men and children (as blacks are not, for example, dispersed among whites in an intensely racially segregated society) are not likely to constitute a self-conscious social movement without a political name.

Individuals may work for personal transformation without naming collective problems. The "discovery" of male violence and marital rape, like the naming of sexual harassment, or even that controversy-laden term the "feminization of poverty," is an essential part of feminist process. And it is a process that has forever changed the ways we all think about women. While the victory of naming a problem through women's eyes is far from accomplishing the abolition of the conditions that caused the problem, it is a necessary step. If we want future generations to assume the gains that second-wave feminism has made, we must preserve and move forward those struggles in ways that are *social,* part of collective memory and consciousness, and not simply individual. Does a concept like "postfeminist" help or hinder that process?

How can we insist on the social at a time of great political reaction, when feminism is simultaneously everywhere and nowhere? How can we shape collective strategies in a culture whose hegemonic values and material constraints beckon us all to enact individual "lifestyle" solutions, sometimes providing our own upscale versions of Dotty's, Pam's, Lanny's and Lyn's less privileged choices? Surely we must take the sobering weight of cultural individualism in response to fragmenting political economic circumstances very seriously. But just as surely, we must never wallow in the mistaken and nostalgic view that if certain aspects of organized second-wave feminism are declining, *all* forms of activism that will enhance women's interests are dead. Not only are individual "postfeminists" asserting personal rights and agency, but other organized groups—trade-union women, black feminists —are mobilizing on other terrains. We must listen *very* attentively to what women across many divides can teach one another. And we must squarely confront the complex task of developing political strategies when we too are deeply influenced by organized second-wave feminism's decline. Women's historical agency neither began nor ended with second-wave feminism, and the individualistic incorporation of some but not all of our goals as "postfeminism" does not speak to the contradictions that most women still experience in juggling the pressures of their domestic and public lives.

Wearisome as it may be, that old Chinese curse bears repeating: "May you live in interesting times." We did, we do, and we shall and must continue to do so. In the central, critical task of avoiding outmoded rhetoric in favor of facing the really *difficult* questions that now confront us, the work of Judith Stacey offers some hardheaded and useful guidance. We can use her insights to open, rather than close, our understanding of feminism's influence and its limitations. She helps us to understand how social movements permeate the bedrock of American society, sedimenting, eroding, and occasionally exploding familiar turf. We need at least to begin to chart the diverse terrain in which American women have both constructed and are reconstructing their lives.

Note

Acknowledgments: This brief comment grows out of a session at the Seventh Berkshire Conference of Women Historians held at Wellesley College in June 1987. In addition to Judith Stacey's presentation, Linda Gordon read a chapter of her subsequently published book, *Heroes of Their Own Lives: The Politics and History of Family Violence* (New York: Viking, 1988), and Barri Brown presented a second comment on the meaning of feminism in "nonfeminist" times. Our ideas were developed jointly, and it is impossible to separate the "mine" from the "ours" in the themes that run through this comment.

Minority Families in Crisis

The Public Discussion

Maxine Baca Zinn

The Civil Rights movement of the 1960s brought hope to black people as legal segregation was broken, voting booths were opened, and new occupational opportunities beckoned. As long as improvement in the well-being of blacks was perceived, family structure and lifestyle were not defined as a problem. The promises of the 1960s were dashed, however, as the black underclass expanded rather than contracted in the 1970s and 1980s. Along with the reversal in black poverty rates, a reversal has occurred in the direction of thoughts and preoccupations about family structure.

Public discussions of urban poverty have made the "disintegrating" family the force most responsible for the growth of the underclass. This category, by definition poor, is overwhelmingly black and disproportionately composed of female-headed households. The members are perceived as different from striving, upwardly mobile whites. The rising numbers of persons in the underclass have provided the catalyst for the recent attention in the media and by scholars to this disadvantaged category. The typical interpretation given by those social commentators is that the underclass is permanent, being locked in by its own unique but maladaptive culture. This thinking, though flawed, provides the popular rationale for treating the poor as the problem.

Current formulations about poverty and family tend to emphasize either

Source: This article was part of the working paper series circulated by the Center for Research on Women, Memphis State University, 1987. A substantially revised version will appear in *Signs: Journal of Women in Culture and Society*, forthcoming.

black cultural conditions or conditions generated by the larger economic structure of U.S. society. Popular images of the underclass are couched in cultural themes and assumptions. Yet a wide variety of studies have presented evidence to show that poverty and family structure among racial ethnics are created more by economic conditions external to the family than by race-specific cultural patterns. Not only does this body of research challenge resurgent culture of poverty theories; it also draws our attention to the interrelationship of class, race, and gender in producing the urban underclass.

The Popular Resurgence of Cultural Deficiency Theories

Three different approaches to the problem of the underclass may be found in the public discussion of urban poverty. The first approach ascribes the cause of the swelling underclass to a value system characterized by low aspirations, excessive masculinity, and the acceptance of female-headed families as a way of life.

The second approach assigns the cause of the growing underclass to the structure of the family. Though it often addresses unemployment, this argument always returns to the causal connections between poverty and the disintegration of traditional family structure.

The third approach treats welfare and antipoverty programs as the cause of illegitimate births, female-headed families, and low motivation to work. It sees welfare transfer payments to the poor as creating disincentives to work and incentives to have children out of wedlock—a self-repeating trap of poverty.

Culture and Poverty

A revival of old ideas about disintegrating family patterns is occurring alongside the declining economic status of black Americans. The "culture of poverty" framework, developed by anthropologist Oscar Lewis, contended that the poor have a different way of life from the rest of society and that these cultural differences *explain* continued poverty. In this view, poverty is passed down from generation to generation, and this way of life represents an effort to cope with feelings of hopelessness and despair.[1] According to this theory, an array of psychological disabilities keeps the poor responsible for their poverty by virtue of values, attitudes, and behaviors that are different from those of the middle class. In this argument, poverty is a function of the thought processes more than of physical environment.[2] This reasoning may be found in current discussions of ghetto poverty, family structure, welfare, unemployment, and out-of-wedlock births.

The connections being made between culture and poverty today recall the 1965 Moynihan Report.[3] Because Moynihan assigned the "pathology" within black ghettos to deterioration of the Negro family, his report became the generative example of "blaming the victim" by naming a black "culture of poverty" instead of racism as the cause of poverty.[4] Lest we forget, Moynihan argued that the tangle of pathology was "capable of perpetuating itself without assistance from the white world."

The reaction of scholars to the deficiency model was swift and extensive, although not as well publicized as the model itself. Research by Andrew Billingsly, Herbert Gutman, Robert Hill, Joyce Ladner, Elliot Leibow, and Carol Stack, to name a few, documented the many strengths of black families, strengths that allowed them to survive slavery, the enclosures of the South, and the depression of the North.[5] Such work revealed that many patterns of family life were not created by a deficient culture but were instead "a rational adaptational response to conditions of deprivation."[6]

A rapidly growing literature documents the disproportionate representation of black female-headed families in the poverty population. The most recent studies of such families are largely unconcerned with questions about adaptation. Rather, as Wilson and Aponte point out, they give more attention to the strong association between female-headed families and poverty, to the effects of family disorganization on children, to demographic and socioeconomic factors that are correlated with single-parent status, and to the connection between the economic status of men and the rise in black female-headed families.[7] While most of these studies do not advance a social pathology explanation, they do signal a shift in analytic focus. Many academics who intend to call attention to the dangerously high level of poverty in black female-headed households have recently emphasized the family structure and the black ghetto way of life as causes for the underclass.

The popular press, on the other hand, has openly and enthusiastically embraced the Moynihan thesis both in its original version and in Moynihan's restatement in a newer book, *Family and Nation*.[8] Here Moynihan repeats his assertion that poverty and family structure are associated, but now he contends that the association holds for blacks and whites alike. Popular journalism, however, sees family structure and out-of-wedlock births as black problems. A profoundly disturbing example was a widely publicized television documentary in the January 1986 *CBS Reports* series, "The Van-

ishing Family: Crisis in America." According to this refurbished version of
the old Moynihan Report, a breakdown in family values has allowed black
men to renounce their traditional breadwinner role, leaving black women
to bear the economic responsibility for children.[9] The program generated
favorable response from television talk show hosts and syndicated newspaper columnists. The argument that the black community is devastating
itself fits neatly with the resurgent conservatism that is manifested among
black and white intellectuals and policymakers.

The most explicit adoption of the culture-of-poverty thesis has been
Nicholas Lemann's two-part *Atlantic* article about the black underclass in
Chicago.[10] According to Lemann, family structure is the most visible manifestation of black America's bifurcation into a middle class that has escaped
the ghetto and an underclass that is irrevocably bound within the walls of
the ghetto.

He explains the rapid growth of the underclass in the 1970s by pointing
to two mass migrations of black Americans. The first, from the rural South
to the urban North, numbered in the millions from the 1940s through
the 1960s before ending in the early 1970s. This migration is said to have
brought the black class system to the North virtually intact, although the
underclass became more pronounced in the cities. The second migration,
beginning in the late 1960s, was a migration out of the ghettos by members of the black working and middle classes who had been freed from
housing discrimination by the civil rights movement. As a result of the
exodus, the indices of disorganization in the ghettos (such as crime and
illegitimate births) have risen, and the underclass has flourished. Casual
attitudes toward marriage, high illegitimacy rates, and family disintegration are said to be a heritage of the rural South. In Lemann's words, they
represent the power of culture in producing poverty:

> The argument is anthropological, not economic; it emphasizes
> the power over people's behavior that culture, as opposed to eco-
> nomic incentives, can have. Ascribing a society's conditions in part
> to the culture that prevails there seems benign when the society
> under discussion is England or California. But as a way of thinking
> about black ghettos it has become unpopular. Twenty years ago,
> ghettos were often said to have a self-generating, destructive culture
> of poverty (the term has an impeccable source, the anthropologist
> Oscar Lewis). But then the left equated cultural discussions of the
> ghetto with accusing poor blacks of being in a bad situation that was
> of their own making. The left succeeded in limiting the terms of the
> debate to purely economic ones, and today the right also discusses

the ghetto in terms of economic "incentives to fail," provided by the welfare system. . . .

In the ghettos, though, it appears that the distinctive culture is now the greatest barrier to progress by the black underclass, rather than either unemployment or welfare.[11]

Lemann's photojournalistic essay provides no supportive evidence that might substantiate his thesis. His "misreading of left economic analysis and cultural anthropology itself[12] should render the two-part work nothing more than a defense of conservative economic policies. However, this revival of the old theory that blacks themselves are to blame for their worsening economic status provides ideological justification for the newly repressive racial order.[13]

Cultural explanations emphasize the low aspirations and the lack of achievement motivation that extend from one generation to the next and produce permanent states of poverty. Both permanence of poverty and low aspirations of the poor, however, have been called into question by the University of Michigan's Panel Study of Income Dynamics (PSID). This study has gathered annual information on five thousand families across the nation from 1969 through 1978. A growing body of findings from this study contradicts many stereotypes about poverty, especially the view that poverty results from a set of values and beliefs held by poor people. The most striking discovery has been the high turnover of individuals and families in poverty. Each year the number of people below the poverty line may remain the same, but the poor in one year are not necessarily the poor in the following year: "Blacks from welfare dependent families were no more likely to become welfare dependent than similar Blacks from families who had never received welfare. Further, measures of parental sense of efficacy, future orientation, and achievement motivation had no effects on welfare dependency for either group (Blacks or Whites)."[14] This research has found no good evidence that highly motivated people are more successful at escaping from poverty than those with lower scores on motivational tests.[15]

The racial expansion of the underclass provides yet another avenue for challenging the theory that the current crisis is traceable to a rural southern heritage. Popular discussions have remained blind to Hispanics, their growth, and their redistribution within American society. A complete understanding of poverty in this society requires recognition of its new face. By 1990 Hispanics are expected to replace blacks as the racial-ethnic group with the highest poverty rate in the United States. "The flow of Hispanics to urban America is among the most significant changes occurring in the 1980s."[16] By 2000, Hispanics will be the largest minority in the schools. By 2020, they will surpass blacks as the most populous minority.[17] Hispanics could show a steady increase in their rates of joblessness, crime, teenage pregnancy, female-headed homes, and welfare dependency.[18] Already, Hispanics constitute a majority in certain areas. They fall well behind the general population on all measures of social and economic well-being: jobs, income, educational attainment, housing, and health care. Hispanics have proportionately more female-headed families than whites. By 1985, women headed 44.1 percent of black families, 23.4 percent of Hispanic families, and 13.2 percent of white families.[19] The expansion of the underclass may be taken as evidence that urban conditions, not black culture, create distinctive forms of racial poverty.

Family Structure and the Underclass

A central notion within culture-of-poverty thought is that family disintegration is the source and sustaining feature of poverty. Today, nearly six of ten black children are born out of wedlock, compared to roughly three of ten in 1970. In the twenty-five to thirty-four age bracket the ratio for separation and divorce for black women is twice as high now as for white women. The result is a high probability that a black woman and her children will live alone. The "deviant" mother-only family, so common among blacks, is typically assumed to explain poverty. This is usually expressed in the phrase, "the feminization of poverty," a shorthand reference to the fact that women living alone are disproportionately represented among the poor. The publicity given to increased marital breakups, to unmarried women, and to the household patterns that accompany these changes implies that the bulk of contemporary poverty is a family structure phenomenon. Changes in family structure are seen to "cause" most poverty or to have led to current poverty rates that are much higher than they would have been if family composition had remained stable.[20]

Despite the growing concentration of poverty among black female-headed households in the past two decades, however, there is no hard evidence that family structure causes poverty. Common assumptions about "correlation" and "association" between poverty and family breakdown avoid harder questions about the character and direction of causal relations between the two phenomena.[21]

To what extent poverty *follows* changes in family structure, relative to its existence *before* those changes, is the question that guides Mary Jo Bane's longitudinal research on household composition and poverty. She finds that much poverty, especially among blacks, is the result of "reshuffling": that is, already poor, two-parent households break up, producing poor female-headed households. This differs from the *transition* to poverty that is more common for whites:

> Three-quarters of whites who were poor in the first year after moving into a female-headed or single-person household became poor simultaneously with the transition; in contrast, of the blacks who were poor after the transition, about two-thirds had also been poor before. Reshuffled poverty as opposed to event-caused poverty for Blacks challenges the assumption that changes in family structure have created ghetto poverty. This underscores the importance of considering the ways in which race produces different paths to poverty.[22]

A two-parent family is no guarantee against poverty for racial minorities. Analyzing data from the PSID, Martha Hill concludes that the long-term income of black children in two-parent families throughout the decade studied was even lower than the long-term income of non-black children who spent most of the decade in mother-only families:

> Thus, increasing the proportion of Black children growing up in two-parent families would not by itself eliminate very much of the racial gap in the economic well-being of children; changes in the economic circumstances of the parents are needed most to bring the economic status of Black children up to the higher status of non-Black children.[23]

Barbara Ehrenreich makes the same point about race-neutral explanations of poverty and family structure:

> It takes just a few calculations to reveal the [economic] inadequacy of the two-parent Black family. first, we observe that the median Black male income is $9,448, which is approximately $1,000 less than the official poverty level for a family of four. So adding one median-type Black male to a preformed family unit consisting of a mother and two children leaves us with a Black family that still has a problem, namely, poverty. Adding two Black males is still not much of an improvement; only by adding three can we hope to clear the

median U.S. family income, which is $26,433. If our hypothetical
Black family is to enter the middle-class mainstream, which means
home ownership, it will need at least $36,596 or four Black men.[24]

Welfare Dependence and Poverty

An important variant of the family structure explanation is the
argument that welfare causes poverty. Actually, this thinking combines elements of family disintegration with deficient culture in proposing that
welfare undermines incentives to work and causes families to break up by
allowing black women to have babies and encouraging black men to escape family responsibilities. This position has been widely publicized by
Charles Murray's influential book *Losing Ground*. According to Murray, the
war on poverty with its generous welfare benefits has increased dependency and altered family structure. AFDC benefits make it economically
attractive in the short run to forgo marriage and thus spur the growth of
poor female-headed households; such benefits are thus destructive in the
long run.[25]

Several studies challenge Murray's conclusion that increased welfare has
created more poverty instead of alleviating it. Research conducted at the
University of Wisconsin's Center for the Study on Poverty concluded that
poverty increased after the late 1960s because of a weakening economy.
No support was found for Murray's assertion that growth in spending did
more harm than good for blacks because it increased the percentage of
families headed by women. Welfare spending increased between 1960 and
1972 and declined between 1972 and 1984, yet there were no reversals in
the trends of family composition during this period. The percentage of
households headed by women increased steadily from 10.7 percent to 20.8
percent between 1968 and 1983.[26]

Further evidence against the notion of welfare dependency as the motivation for the dramatic rise in the proportion of black families headed by
females is provided by William Darity and Samuel Meyers. Using statistical causality tests, they find no short-term effects of variations in welfare
payments on female headship in black families.[27]

Other research draws similar conclusions about the impact of welfare
on family structure. Using a variety of tests, David Ellwood and Lawrence
Summers dispute the adverse affects of AFDC. They highlight two issues
that raise questions about the responsibility of welfare in producing female-
headed households. First, although the real value of welfare payments has
declined since the early 1970s, family dissolution has continued to rise;

family structure changes do not mirror benefit level changes. Second, variations in benefit levels across states do not lead to corresponding variations in divorce rates or percentages of children in single-parent families. A comparison of groups collecting AFDC with groups that were not showed small effects of welfare benefits on family structures.[28] In sum, the systematic research on welfare and family structure indicates that AFDC has far less effect on changes in family structure than has been alleged.

The current explanations of the underclass represented by Bill Moyers on television, Nicholas Lemann in the *Atlantic*, Charles Murray and Daniel Patrick Moynihan in their books all blame the victims—ghetto-dwelling blacks—for their sorry plight. Each argues in one form or another that these blacks have a flawed culture that causes them to maladapt. These interpretations provide an intellectual defense for the conservative economic theories currently in vogue. They make it necessary to resurrect the decades-old debate on the relative importance of culture and environment (or social situation). Wilson and Aponte contend that the culture/structure debate resulted in rigid either/or positions without producing definitive research on situational versus cultural views of poverty and social change.[29] They are undoubtedly correct in their claim that we lack adequate understanding of the relative significance of social structure and culture in social change. However, interpretations based on the assumption that certain cultural systems are responsible for ongoing poverty cannot be reconciled with growing bodies of empirical information.

The Role of the Economy in Black Family Structure and Poverty

Because family life is bound up with the social and economic circumstances of particular times and places, labor market restructuring has had far-reaching effects on family formation in urban settings.

The contemporary patterns of economic life and family structure for black workers began to crystallize during and after World War II. Blacks followed traditional channels of northern migration and moved to the older northeastern and midwestern cities where labor markets were segmented by race. The primary market contained jobs with high wages, good working conditions, fringe benefits, and opportunities for advancement. The secondary labor market contained jobs characterized by poor working conditions, low wages, few opportunities for advancement, and little job security. The distinction between labor markets was crucial for racial ethnics: although blacks entered many peripheral manufacturing industries, for the most part they remained locked in the secondary segment of the labor force. Yet despite the persistent pattern of labor segregation by race, some blacks and Chicanos did find better-paying work within manufacturing and use their blue-collar jobs as an avenue to mobility and security. Movement into higher-level blue-collar jobs was one of the most important components of black occupational advancement in the 1970s.[30]

A meaningful analysis of black families, however, must also consider the postwar marginalization of black males, especially young black men, in the U.S. labor force. The composition of black male employment has changed dramatically. The proportion of employed black men dropped from 80 percent in 1930 to 56 percent in 1983.[31]

The decline in black male job opportunities has long-term roots. Since the end of the Civil War, working primarily in agriculture and low-wage manufacturing occupations, black men have served as a pool of cheap labor for the U.S. economy. As the economy changed and the requirements for such labor declined, black men were left out of the labor force. The contraction of the manufacturing sector and the expansion of the service sector of the labor market has further narrowed job opportunities for semiskilled and unskilled workers. Coupled with this decline is the most crucial transformation of the U.S. economy affecting black Americans in the past three decades: the mechanization of southern agriculture. Thirty-five years ago, 50 percent of all black teenagers had agricultural jobs, and more than 90 percent of those workers lived in the South. As these jobs disappeared, the black unemployment problem in urban centers mushroomed. The recent deindustrialization of northeastern and midwestern cities has exacerbated the problem.[32]

Major sources for the rise of the underclass are the fundamental structural changes in the economy that are creating new forms of inequality throughout society. Blacks and other minorities are profoundly affected by (1) the decline of industrial manufacturing sectors and the growth of service sectors of the economy; (2) shifts in the geographical location of jobs from central cities to the suburbs and from the traditional manufacturing cities (the "rustbelt") to the sunbelt and to other countries.

In their classic work *The Deindustrialization of America*, Barry Bluestone and Bennett Harrison reveal that "minorities tend to be concentrated in industries that have borne the brunt of recent closing. This is particularly true in the automobile, steel, and rubber industries."[33] In a follow-up study Bluestone, Harrison, and Lucy Gorham show that people of color, particularly black men, are more likely than whites to lose their jobs as a result of the restructuring of the U.S. economy.[34] Further evidence of the consequences of economic transformation for minority males is provided by Richard C. Hill and Cynthia Negrey. In their examination of deindustrialization in the Great Lakes Region, they found that black male production workers were the race-gender group hardest hit by the industrial slump: fully 50 percent in the five Great Lake cities studied lost their jobs in durable goods manufacturing between 1979 and 1984.[35] Black male production workers also suffered the greatest rate of job loss in the region and in the nation as a whole.

The decline of manufacturing jobs has altered the most important role once played by the cities as opportunity ladders for the disadvantaged, reducing the potential for movement into higher-level blue-collar jobs that assisted black occupational advancement in the 1970s. The current restructuring of industries creates the threat of downward mobility for the minority middle class.[36] Rather than providing opportunity ladders for minorities, the cities have become centers of poverty for large concentrations of blacks and Hispanics caught in the transformation—in composition and size—of the urban employment base.

Today inner cities are shifting from centers of production and distribution of physical goods to centers of administration, information, exchange, trade, finance, and government service. Changes in local employment structures have been accompanied by changes in the demographic composition of large central cities—from European white to predominantly black and Hispanic populations—with rising unemployment. The shift of jobs away from central cities to the suburbs has created a residential job opportunity mismatch that literally leaves minorities behind in the inner city. Without adequate training or credentials they are relegated to low-paying, nonadvancing exploitative service work, or they are unemployed. Thus, blacks have for the most part become superfluous people in cities that once provided them opportunity. Even though most older, larger cities have experienced substantial job growth in occupations associated with knowledge-intensive service industries, selective job growth in these high-skill, predominantly white-collar industries has not compensated for employment decline in manufacturing, wholesale trade, and other predominantly blue-collar industries that once constituted the urban economic backbone.[37]

Although cities once sustained large numbers of less skilled persons, today the newer service industries typically have high educational requisites for entry. Knowledge and information jobs in the central cities are virtually closed to minorities, given the required technological education and skill level. Commuting between central cities and outlying areas is increasingly common: white-collar workers commute daily from their suburban residences to the central business districts, while streams of inner city residents are commuting to their blue-collar jobs in outlying areas.[38]

But for inner city minorities, their increased distance from current sources of blue-collar and other entry-level jobs is an additional structural impediment. As industries providing these jobs have relocated in the suburbs and nonmetropolitan peripheries, racial discrimination and inadequate incomes have prevented many members of inner city minorities from moving along with their traditional sources of employment. And the dispersed nature of the new job sites makes public transportation from inner city neighborhoods impractical, requiring virtually all city residents who work in peripheral areas to commute by personally owned automobiles. The severity of this problem is documented by John Kasarda: "More than one half of the minority households in Philadelphia and Boston are without a means of personal transportation. New York City's proportions are even higher with only three out of ten black or Hispanic households having a vehicle available."[39]

Economic restructuring is characterized by an overall pattern of uneven development. Traditional industries have declined in the North and Midwest as new growth industries locate in the southern and southwestern part of the nation. This regional shift has produced some gains for minorities. Black poverty rates in the South have begun to converge with poverty rates outside the South, though this is related to industrial decline in the North as much as to black employment in the South. Still, given the large minority populations in the sunbelt, it is conceivable that industrial restructuring could offset the economic threats to racial equality. But hope is clouded for several reasons. For one thing, the sunbelt expansion has been based largely on low-wage, labor-intensive enterprises that use large numbers of underpaid minority workers.

All these economic forces—the placement of racial minorities in the secondary labor market, the decline of agricultural jobs, the decline in industrial manufacturing, the shift of jobs from the central cities to the suburbs and away from the rustbelt—combine to exacerbate the plight of urban blacks. These forces have led to more unemployment, more female-headed households, and more poverty among blacks.

Several studies by William J. Wilson and his colleagues at the University of Chicago have documented the relationship between increased male joblessness and female-headed households. Wilson and Neckerman have devised an indicator they call the "index of marriageable males," which reveals a long-term decline in the proportion of black men and particularly young black men who are in a position to support a family. Their indicator, which includes mortality rates, incarceration rates, and labor force participation, reveals that the proportion of black men in unstable economic situations is even higher than that conveyed by current unemployment figures.[40]

These structural conditions make it necessary for many black women to leave a marriage or forgo marriage altogether. Adaptation to structural conditions leaves black women disproportionately separated, divorced, and solely responsible for their children. Family structure is thus the consequence, not the cause, of poverty.

How does black teenage pregnancy fit into the picture? In fact, the overall rate of childbearing by teenagers is declining; for black teenagers it was 40 percent lower in 1983 than in 1960. The problem is not the rate of pregnancies among teenagers; it is the fact that teens who get pregnant these days are not getting married. In 1960, 42 percent of black teenagers who had babies were unmarried; by 1970 the proportion had jumped to 63 percent, and by 1983 it was 89 percent.[41] According to Wilson, this increase is directly tied to the changing labor market status of young black males. He cites the well-established relationship between joblessness and marital instability in support of his argument that "pregnant teenagers are more likely to marry if their boyfriends are working."[42] Out-of-wedlock births are sometimes encouraged by families and absorbed into the kinship system because for the girl to marry the suspected father would simply bring an additional financial burden.[43]

Instead of blaming minorities by "using the language of the family to explain the status to which society consigns them,"[44] we must examine those macrostructural conditions that shape intimate relationships. The racial underclass is not destroying itself by a culturally deficient family structure, but millions of human lives are being destroyed by economic forces. Socioeconomic circumstances limit the range of choices people can make about their living arrangements. As poor urban residents struggle with the problems of everyday life, they may appear to be engaging in maladaptive coping tactics. Yet "what may seem like poor coping strategies are often the result of severely limited options."[45]

The current forms taken by families of the urban underclass are conditioned by economic restructuring that deprives racial-ethnic people of their share of society's resources.

Lessons for Feminist Scholarship

This critique of some popular images of family and poverty is not meant only to reiterate issues that were raised twenty years ago. Today, the social factors that generate and regenerate poverty are occurring within a web of structural change. The large increase in families headed by women is one of the most important developments of the recent past. But though

the association between female-headed households and poverty is indisputable, popular conceptions of "the feminization of poverty" assume a false
universality that ignores class and race. Women's poverty is not exclusively
a phenomenon of gender. Most discussions, however, neglect those sources
of women's poverty that are rooted in race and class. As Linda Burnham
put it, they incorrectly shift the "focal point of analysis from class and
race to gender."[46] This ignores the impoverishment of black men and obscures the fundamental class relations that are responsible for poverty in
this sociohistorical period.

The reconceptualization of poverty and family structure in macrostructural terms exposes the dynamics of class and race that interact with gender
to produce inequality. The formation of female-headed households is but
one example of the closely intertwined fate of racial-ethnic women and
men and of the racially divergent reasons for the growth of mother-only
families. As Wilson and Neckerman explain:

> The chief cause of the rise of separation and divorce rates among
> whites is the increased economic independence of white women as
> indicated by their increasing employment and improving occupa-
> tional status. It is not that this growing independence gives white
> women a financial incentive to separate from or to divorce their
> husbands; rather it makes dissolution of a bad marriage a more
> viable alternative than in the past. That the employment status of
> white males is not a major factor in white single motherhood or
> female-headed families can perhaps also be seen in the higher rate
> of remarriage among white women and the significantly earlier age
> of first marriage. By contrast, the increasing delay of first marriage
> and the low rate of remarriage among Black women seem to be
> directly tied to the increasing labor force problems of men.[47]

To underscore the economic marginalization of black men is not to subsume the inequality of black women within hierarchies of class and race but
to highlight the interrelationships of stratification systems. For racial-ethnic
people, class, race, and gender are not dichotomous frames of reference.
It is precisely their connections that we must analyze in order to understand distinctive ways of life. Careful attention to family patterns as they
are conditioned by race and class should allow us to examine the ways in
which structures of inequality create different sets of structural constraints
and require different forms of adaptation and survival.

Notes

1. Oscar Lewis, *La Vida: A Puerto Rican Family in the Culture of Poverty* (New York: Random House, 1966).

2. See Mary Corcoran, Greg J. Duncan, and Martha S. Hill, "The Economic Fortunes of Women and Children: Lessons from the Panel Study of Income Dynamics," *Signs* 10, no. 2 (1984): 232–48.

3. Daniel P. Moynihan, *The Negro Family: The Case for National Action* (Cambridge, Mass.: M.I.T. Press, 1965).

4. See Margaret Cerullo and Marla Erlien, "Beyond the 'Normal Family': A Cultural Critique of Women's Poverty," in *For Crying Out Loud*, ed. Rochelle Lefkowitz and Ann Withorn (New York: Pilgrim Press, 1986), 246–60.

5. Leith Mullings, "Anthropological Perspectives on the Afro-American Family," *American Journal of Social Psychiatry* 6, no. 1 (1986): 11–16. See the following revisionist works on the black Family: Andrew Billingsley, *Black Families in White America* (Englewood Cliffs, N.J.: Prentice-Hall, 1968); Robert Hill, *The Strengths of Black Families* (New York: Emerson-Hall, 1972); Herbert Gutman, *The Black Family in Slavery and Freedom* (New York: Pantheon, 1976); Joyce Ladner, *Tomorrow's Tomorrow: The Black Woman* (New York: Doubleday, 1971); Elliot Leibow, *Talley's Corner: A Study of Negro Street Corner Men* (Boston: Little, Brown, 1967); Carol Stack, *All Our Kin* (New York: Harper & Row, 1974).

6. William J. Wilson and Robert Aponte, "Urban Poverty," *Annual Review of Sociology* 11 (1985): 231–58.

7. Ibid.

8. Daniel Patrick Moynihan, *Family and Nation* (San Diego, Calif.: Harcourt Brace Jovanovich, 1986).

9. See "Hard Times for Black America," *Dollars and Sense* 115 (April 1986): 5–7.

10. Nicholas Lemann, "The Origins of the Underclass," pts. 1–2, *Atlantic*, June 1986, pp. 31–55, and July 1986, pp. 54–68.

11. Ibid., 35.

12. Jim Sleeper, "Overcoming 'Underclass': More Jobs Are Still the Key," *In These Times*, 11–24 June 1986, p. 16.

13. For a discussion of the reformulation of the racial order in the 1980s, see Michael Omi and Howard Winant, *Racial Formation in the United States* (New York: Routledge & Kegan Paul, 1986).

14. Martha S. Hill and Michael Ponza, "Poverty and Welfare Dependence across Generations," *Economic Outlook U.S.A.*, Summer 1983, pp. 61–64.

15. "Economic Mobility," *Institute for Social Research Newsletter*, Autumn 1985, p. 3.

16. Paul E. Peterson, "Introduction: Technology, Race, and Urban Policy," introduction to *The New Urban Reality*, ed. Paul E. Peterson (Washington, D.C.: Brookings Institution, 1985), 1–32.

17. Cary Davis, Carl Haub, and JoAnne Willette, "U.S. Hispanics, Changing the Face of America," *Population Bulletin*, June 1983.

18. William J. Wilson, "The Urban Underclass in Advanced Industrial Society," in Peterson, *New Urban Reality*, 129–60.

19. "Women Who Maintain Families," *Facts on U.S. Working Women*, U.S. Department of Labor, Women's Bureau Fact Sheet No. 86–2 (1986).

20. Mary Jo Bane, "Household Composition and Poverty," in *Fighting Poverty*,

ed. Sheldon H. Danziger and Daniel H. Weinberg (Cambridge, Mass.: Harvard University Press, 1986), 209–31.

21. Betsy Dworkin, "40% of the Poor Are Children," *New York Times Book Review*, 2 March 1986, p. 9.

22. Bane, "Household Composition and Poverty," p. 277.

23. Martha Hill, "Trends in the Economic Situation of U.S. Families and Children, 1970–1980," in *American Families and the Economy*, ed. Richard R. Nelson and Felicity Skidmore (Washington, D.C.: National Academy Press, 1983), 9–53.

24. Barbara Ehrenreich, "Two, Three, Many Husbands," *Mother Jones*, July to August 1986, p. 8.

25. Charles Murray, *Losing Ground* (New York: Basic Books, 1984).

26. Sheldon Danziger and Peter Gottschalk, "The Poverty of Losing Ground," *Challenge* 28 (May to June 1985), pp. 32–38.

27. William A. Darity and Samuel L. Meyers, "Does Welfare Dependency Cause Female Headship? The Case of the Black Family," *Journal of Marriage and the Family* 46 (November 1984): 765–79.

28. David T. Ellwood and Lawrence H. Summers, "Poverty in America: Is Welfare the Answer or the Problem?" in Danziger and Weinberg, *Fighting Poverty*, 78–105.

29. Wilson and Aponte, "Urban Poverty."

30. Joan W. Moore, "Minorities in the American Class System," *Daedalus* 110, no. 2 (1981): 275–99; Elliott Currie and Jerome H. Skolnick, *America's Problems: Social Issues and Public Policy* (Boston: Little, Brown, 1984).

31. William J. Wilson and Kathryn M. Neckerman, "Poverty and Family Structure: The Widening Gap between Evidence and Public Policy Issues," in Danziger and Weinberg, *Fighting Poverty*, 232–59.

32. Cornel West, "Unmasking the Black Conservatives," *Christian Century*, 16–23 July 1986, pp. 644–48.

33. Barry Bluestone and Bennett Harrison, *The Deindustrialization of America* (New York: Basic Books, 1982).

34. Cited in "Hard Times for Black America," 6.

35. Richard C. Hill and Cynthia Negrey, "Deindustrialization and Racial Minorities in the Great Lakes Region, U.S.A.," in *The Reshaping of America: Social Consequences of the Changing Economy*, ed. D. Stanley Eitzen and Maxine Baca Zinn (Englewood Cliffs, N.J.: Prentice Hall, 1989), 168–77.

36. Currie and Skolnick, *America's Problems*, 182.

37. John D. Kasarda, "Caught in a Web of Change," *Society* 21 (November to December 1983): 41–47.

38. Ibid., 45–47.

39. John D. Kasarda, "Urban Change and Minority Opportunities," in Peterson, *New Urban Reality*, 33–68.

40. Wilson and Neckerman, "Poverty and Family Structure," 23.

41. Jerelyn Eddings, "Children Having Children," *Baltimore Sun*, 2 March 1986, p. 71.

42. Cited in ibid.

43. Noel A. Cazenave, "Alternate Intimacy, Marriage, and Family Lifestyles among Low-Income Black Americans," *Alternative Lifestyles* 3, no. 4 (1980): 425–44.

44. Mullings, "Anthropological Perspectives," 15.

45. Diana Dill, Ellen Feld, Jacqueline Martin, Stephanie Beukema, and Deborah Belle, "The Impact of the Environment on the Coping Efforts of Low-Income Mothers," *Family Relations* 20 (October 1980): 507.

46. Linda Burnham, "Has Poverty Been Feminized in Black America?" *Black Scholar* 16 (March to April 1985): 15.

47. Wilson and Neckerman, "Poverty and Family Structure," 256.

18   Heterosexual Antagonisms and the Politics of Mothering

Ilene J. Philipson

The belief that there is at present a "crisis" in the family serves as the foundation for the new right's program and ideology and is a mainstay of the popular media. The use of the term "crisis" or "decline," however, frequently masks what people actually mean in expressing their fears, beliefs, or analysis of what is currently taking place in the family. Ingredient in the term "crisis" are typically one or more of the following: state intervention in the family; a soaring divorce rate; wife battering; the decline of paternal authority; the inability of people to find or sustain committed relationships; teenage sex and pregnancy; violence against children; single-parent families; a pervasive antagonism between women and men; homosexuality; women working outside the home; abortion on demand; the absence of affordable and quality child care. While in fact people on the right and on the left usually give quite different meaning to the "crisis," identifying very strongly with certain aspects of this list and condemning the others as *causes* of the problems, both sides of the political spectrum agree that there is something terribly wrong in family relations.

In looking at this list of what constitutes the crisis, we can discern two major axes along which problematic relations can be recognized: those between women and men, and those between parents and children. Many of these problems have implications for both sets of relations. State intervention into the family can be seen as both undermining parental authority

Source: This article is reprinted from *Socialist Review* No. 66 (November–December 1982), pp. 55–77, by permission of the publisher, *Socialist Review*, 3202 Adeline, Berkeley, CA 94703.

and causing strains in the husband-wife relationship; the lack of affordable child care affects the relations not only between mothers and children but also between parents. While most of what is seen as problematic within the family affects both axes, the right and the left tend to emphasize different axes in their respective descriptions of family crisis.

The new right seems to be most concerned with relations between parents and children. The constant condemnation of government intervention into the family, the attempt to require parental consent before teenagers may obtain contraceptives, and the fervent desire to control what children are and are not taught in school exemplify this concern. This is not to say that the new right is mute in regard to relations between women and men. Clearly, opposition to women's labor-force participation and to abortion on demand is evidence of deep-seated fear and antagonism. But the right does emphasize the problematic nature of parent-child relationships in a way that the left definitely does not.

The left, represented best by the socialist-feminist critique of the family, has traditionally directed its rancor toward the relations between women and men and the gender roles that foster these relations. Socialist feminists from Charlotte Perkins Gilman to Barbara Ehrenreich have focused on heterosexual relationships and the ways in which economic inequality has infused marriage with radically different appeal, meaning, and constraint for men and women.

Yet however we may define the current "crisis" in the family, it is critical to note that changes in the relations between women and men, mothers and fathers, inevitably affect the parent-child relationship, just as transformations in the relations between parents and children live on in daughters and sons who, in most cases, eventually enter into heterosexual unions. To focus exclusively on one axis of family dynamics provides only a partial picture of contemporary family life.

In what follows I attempt to show how both axes in the family—woman/man, parent/child—have interacted historically to make heterosexual relations more difficult in the last quarter of the twentieth century, and how these difficulties raise serious questions about the way we raise our children and structure our families. To be able to appreciate the interaction of these two axes, I believe it is necessary to incorporate a social-historical approach with a psychoanalytic one. For it is in the family that individuals internalize a system of historically defined familial relationships that in turn shape their relational needs and desires as adults. The family is the arena in which personality is developed and feelings of self-worth and relatedness to others are initially formed. The relationships a child has with her or his family members not only influence the assumption of roles and beliefs but, more important, color all future relationships with friends, lovers, and figures of authority. What originally transpires within the family remains ensconced in the unconscious—although in transformed and distorted ways —only to reemerge as attempts at repression, repair, or re-creation in adult relationships.

That these attempts can be conflictual both for the individual and for the functioning of the social order is clear to anyone studying real human beings in specific social and historical settings. And it is only through such study that we can begin to untangle the causes of the current difficulties within the family that revolve around the tensions between women and men. What follows, then, is an effort to locate the historical origins of those difficulties and to demonstrate how the new right's response to the crisis of the family can only serve to exacerbate family conflict and instability.

The Post–World War II Family

The generation of individuals that is now most likely to have difficulty in finding and maintaining relationships, experiencing the most divorce, filling the practices of couple's counselors and therapists, and facing the possibility of not having children because there is no one to have them with is the generation bred in post–World War II families. It is the baby-boom generation in general that most frequently bemoans the impasse in heterosexual relations.[1]

The middle-class, post–World War II family represents a culmination and intensification of certain historical trends that find their origins in the process of industrialization beginning in the eighteenth century.[2] Middle-class families of the late 1940s and 1950s were more nuclear and more isolated and were built around marriages that occurred at an earlier age than ever before.[3] At the same time, however, these families served as momentary reversals of trends begun in the late nineteenth century toward declining fertility and increasing labor-force participation of women outside the home.[4] The middle-class, newly married housewife of this period had more education and/or work experience prior to marriage on the average than any of her historical counterparts, yet she was told through virtually every ideological organ of the period that true feminine fulfillment could be achieved only through success as a wife, mother, and housekeeper, that a woman's place was most definitely in the home.[5] These contradictory circumstances of the middle-class family in the post–World War II era have left as their legacy not only fertile ground for inquiry into the ways in which the family mediates larger social forces and personal development but also actual personalities who find intimate, loving relationships extremely difficult.

Middle-class children of the baby boom were a historically unique generation. They were born into the most isolated *and* nuclear families that had come into existence. As a result of both suburbanization and the historical process of removing boarders, servants, and kin from the household, these children came into a relatively deserted environment.[6] They also had a rather awesome task ahead of them: they were to compensate their mothers for the job, career, or schooling these women had left behind in order to marry or have children. In other words, children of the post-war era were the vehicle through which women were supposed to fulfill the requirements of what Betty Friedan termed the "Feminine Mystique" and thus prove their femininity. What was not so obvious a task, yet equally important, was the need for children to compensate for the loss of adult companionship that most full-time mothers and housewives experienced during most of their waking hours. The effect of both suburbanization and the nuclearization of the middle-class family was to separate mothers from their husbands, relatives, and friends. Writing in 1970, Philip Slater summarized this situation quite well:

> The idea of imprisoning each woman alone in a small, separate, and self-contained dwelling is a modern invention. . . . In Moslem societies, for example, the wife may be a prisoner but at least she is not in solitary confinement. In our society the housewife may move about freely, but since she has nowhere to go and isn't a part of anything anyway, her prison needs no walls. . . . Most of her social and emotional needs must be satisfied by her children, who are hardly equal to the task. . . . Even if the American housewife were not a rather deprived person, it would be the height of vanity for anyone to assume that an unformed child could tolerate such massive inputs of one person's personality.[7]

From a study I conducted of middle-class family life in the 1950s, I found that children were in fact expected to tolerate massive inputs of one person's personality.[8] The history of the post–World War II period is a history of family life in which mothers were compelled through ideological, social, and economic forces to live for and through their children. Because their own needs for recognition, meaningful work, and relationship to other adults were so frequently denied, child rearing assumed a significance in the minds and activities of women that was historically unprecedented.

Among the families I looked at, 83 percent of the mothers were full-time housewives, and 99 percent of these women had worked, gone to college, or both before marriage.[9] Most of them lived in the suburbs, more than a half-hour car drive from their families of origin, and 91 percent of the intact families with children lived in a nuclear situation: that is, with only parents and children present. Most of the mothers found the adjustment from work or college to housecleaning and child rearing somewhat difficult, and many complained of their husbands' actual or emotional absence. Because men and women occupied such distinct and radically different spheres during the majority of their waking hours, their daily experiences were often unintelligible to each other. Husbands often evidenced a lack of empathy for their wives' needs for emotional sustenance and intimacy, which in part arose out of the women's confined and isolated daily environments. Consequently, a large number of women turned to their children for meaning and love. As one women stated: "I'm crazy about the youngsters—get my love that way. . . . [My husband's] not demonstrative or affectionate with me. He works at night . . . and part of the day. . . . It's not a satisfactory life except for the children."

Children therefore were used in a variety of ways. Their care replaced work outside the home and gave purpose and meaning to a woman's life. Their presence often acted as a substitute for that of other adults, who were more available in previous historical periods. Their love not infrequently was turned to as a replacement for the intimacy and affection that husbands did not provide. In short, children were often seen and experienced as being more, and fulfilling more emotional needs, than in any other period in history.

The Psychological Dimension

Women turned to their children to fulfill unmet needs in large part because of certain unconscious desires engendered in them as a result of their own upbringing. Because these mothers were primarily parented by women—as women have been throughout history—they possessed certain psychological requirements and potentialities that compelled them to overinvest in their children in response to the social circumstances surrounding their lives as mothers.

As Nancy Chodorow indicates in her book *The Reproduction of Mothering*, because it is women who have primary responsibility for the rearing of small children, female offspring develop with different conceptions of self and identity and different relational needs and capacities from those of their brothers. In order to become masculine—that which is other than female—a son erects well-defined ego boundaries that firmly set him apart psychologically from the human being he is originally bonded with. This process of rigid differentiation allows the boy to develop a distinct sense of self and a need for relationship to others that respects the autonomy of that self as prerequisite. Any close interpersonal relationship that begins to resemble the union or symbiotic character of the early mother-son bond carries within it the threat to masculinity, which is founded on opposition and distancing.

Girls, on the other hand, develop their sense of self in *relation* to the mother rather than in *opposition*. Because they are mothered by someone of the same gender, girls' process of separation from the mother retains a greater sense of connection and continuity than that which exists between mother and son. Daughters therefore develop more fluid or permeable ego boundaries than sons and a greater tendency to define themselves, to find their identity, in relationship to others. Their relational needs are more centered on maintaining feelings of closeness and contact with others, largely because they never had to deny the original bond with their mother in order to form their identities.

This need to define oneself in relation to others and to feel intensely connected with other human beings is satisfied in many ways by becoming a mother. It is through the bond with one's own child that a woman can re-create the primary identification and primary love that she experienced with *her* mother. A woman's relational capacities enable her to parent empathically an infant or child who is unable to express its needs and feelings verbally. But these same capacities cause women to overinvest and live through their children, given certain social circumstances.

> The preoccupation with issues of separation and primary identification, the ability to recall their early relationship to their mother— precisely those capacities which enable mothering—are also those which may lead to overidentification and pseudo-empathy based on maternal projection rather than any real perception or understanding of their infants' needs. Similarly, the need for primary relationships becomes more prominent and weighted as relationships to other women become less possible and as father/husband absence grows. . . . Capacities which enable mothering are also precisely those which can make mothering problematic.[10]

The post–World War II era represented for middle-class mothers an extreme form of isolation that made relationships with other adult women difficult to come by and the absence of husbands and fathers pronounced. Not only were young mothers largely prohibited from working outside the home for real material reasons such as the absence of child care, but because of the "Feminine Mystique" they were made to feel guilty if they were not completely fulfilled in their roles as full-time housewives and mothers.

Since these mothers had experienced themselves in arenas outside the home—the workplace and/or college campus—many of them had expectations and needs for intellectual stimulation, responsibility, and an active social life that were frustrated within the home. Because these mothers were also women who had been mothered by women, they had needs for intense emotional relationships that were largely unfulfilled by their husbands and unattainable from kin and close friends, given the mobility of middle-class families in the 1950s and the concomitant collapse of community. The responsibility for satisfying these unmet needs and expectations thereby often fell upon the children who physically and emotionally occupied most of these mothers' energies. It was through feeling needed, important, and loved by their children that mothers frequently attempted to find the answer to what Betty Friedan termed the "problem that has no name."

As a result, many of the mothers in the 1940s and 1950s had difficulty both in disentangling their own needs and feelings from those of their children and in accepting their children's autonomy. When involvement with children is substituted for meaningful work and satisfying emotional relationships with other adults, children's own needs can easily be ignored or misperceived. When the rearing of children justifies a woman's existence and constitutes her identity, the movement of those children toward autonomy logically can be seen as a threatening and frightening occurrence. When children are used to replace husbands for affection, physical closeness, and love, their growing physical and affective independence from the mother may be open to conscious or unconscious disapproval. As Jessica Benjamin notes: "There is considerable evidence to suggest that women, the primary caretakers of small children then and now, are more isolated in their mothering activity. We should assume that this would make the mother both more dependent on the child and loathe to allow it autonomy.[11]

Psychological Outcomes

Psychoanalytic observers report that when mothers are dependent on their children, loathe to grant them autonomy, and unable to disentangle their own needs from their children's, it is likely that a child will experience its mother as unempathic or erratically empathic. A mother may project "her own moods and tensions onto the child," "overrespond selectively to certain moods and tensions in the child which correspond to her own . . . tension states and preoccupations," and/or "be unresponsive to the moods and tensions expressed by the child when her own preoccupations are not in tune with the child's needs. The result is a traumatic alternation of faulty empathy, overempathy, and lack of empathy." [12] A mother might be feeling abandoned, frustrated, harried, or helpless and still her child may *experience* her as unempathic or rejecting and unavailable. A mother in fact may be feeling all these things because of factors unrelated to her child, and yet her child, because of its inability to see her as a human being with interests and needs emanating from outside the mother-child relationship, may tend to believe that its own needs or its wish to be independent or assertive has caused its mother's anger or withdrawal.

Because the child does not experience consistency in empathic response from the mother, it is frequently unable to internalize a consistent sense of maternal approval. As the child psychologically separates from the mother in the course of its development, it is unable to feel autonomous and whole without the continual reassurance of the mother. It does not build that component of internal psychic structure that esteems the self in the absence of external reinforcement. Therefore, the child does not internalize a fundamental sense of self-esteem or self-worth. This means not that the child grows up without internalized standards and values (a superego) but that it will obtain little or no intrinsic satisfaction from living up to these standards. As the child matures it will often find it difficult to derive any pleasure from accomplishing a goal or upholding a value without the external acknowledgment and approval of others. Any thought or act will be bereft of importance unless it is witnessed and acclaimed by someone else. Consequently, the child can never experience self-esteem or self-regard merely through living up to its own ambitions and standards, for valuation of the self must be continually extracted from outside sources.

Psychoanalysts believe that this developmental dilemma or deficit characterizes what takes place in the formation of what are termed narcissistic personalities. According to psychoanalytic clinicians and theorists, narcissists possess a fundamental lack of self-esteem and an inability to experience love or even to engage in mutually caring relations with others. [13] They in fact experience, on a primitive, unconscious level, terrifying loneliness and hunger for love, which they defend against by displaying an unusual degree of self-reference in their interactions with others. Because they failed to internalize a sufficiently consistent sense of self-worth as children, they remain extraordinarily dependent upon the tribute and attention of

others to give them feelings of self-esteem. Other people are valuable insofar as they supply the narcissistic individual with the esteem and approval
that he or she lacks within. Therefore, the relationships entered into by
narcissistic people are frequently exploitative and/or parasitic.

It is here, then, that we begin to see the legacy of the post–World War II
era in clearer relief. Mothers who turned to their children to compensate
them for the restrictiveness, barrenness, or boredom of their lives laid a
potential foundation for the development of personalities that would remain dependent upon external valuation and would use other people to
obtain their lacking esteem and sense of self-worth. Because there was
usually no other adult in the middle-class child's environment to offset a
mother's faulty empathy—no one else even actively engaged in child rearing—this intrapsychic deficit would be firmly rooted by the time many of
the children of the baby boom began entering into close or emotionally
evocative relationships with others. The psychological configuration has,
of course, different meaning for women than it has for men.

The Importance of Gender

Faulty empathy results from a parent's inability to tend to a child
on the basis of the child's needs as they are expressed through verbal and
nonverbal cues and signals. Such inability frequently results from unconsciously viewing the child as another person—as an extension of oneself,
or as embodying the salient characteristics of a significant other (brother,
mother, father, husband). When mothers view their children in such a manner, they do so in a *gender-specific* fashion; that is, sons are most likely to be
seen as husbands, fathers, and brothers, daughters as women's mothers or
as extensions of themselves.[14] What this means is that a son is more likely to
be seen as the *other* in his mother's unconscious projections, and a daughter
is more likely to be viewed as an extension of a self that is, to some degree,
an extension of her own mother's, given a woman's more fluid boundaries with the woman who was her primary caretaker. This dissimilarity is
confirmed in the "Guidance Study" sample.

When sons represent other figures in a mother's inner world, they are
viewed as significant male figures. This shows up even on a conscious level:

> The mother constantly complained about her son: he is "just like
> his father . . . his quietness, his shyness, his stubbornness and also
> perhaps his temper." (GI3I)[15]

> "I feel closer to him . . . Tommy looks like my father—in build. . . .
> It's Tommy's personality, too, that's outgoing like my father's." (C72)

And an interviewer reports:

> "She [the mother] speaks quite freely, perhaps too freely of her own emotional difficulties as she interacts with her second son. She not only does not have the same sense of empathy for Stuart that she does for Scott [oldest son], but her description of Stuart seems tinged by some dislike and disapproval. . . . She feels . . . Stuart [to be] more like her husband which leads one to wonder whether there are some problems and strains in the marital adjustment." And later the mother reveals that she feels Scott to be just like her father.
>
> (C100)

When daughters are represented, they are often viewed as being "just like" the mother or her own mother.

> "The reason she [oldest daughter] is so disturbing to me . . . is because she's a carbon copy of me."   (G102)

> "I'm more strained with her [daughter] and more strict with her. I lose patience with her more quickly. . . . He [son] can do things that she never even tried. . . . Actually she's better behaved than he is, but she has qualities that irritate me more than he does. . . . I can see myself in her sometimes and I know quite a bit of it's my fault."
>
> (C146)

> "I have been ignoring her [daughter]. I've been real nasty to her. After a while it dawns on me—that's exactly what my mother did to me. I feel terrible about it. I know how it must feel to Bonnie." According to the interviewer the mother "displayed quite a lot of uneasiness in talking about Bonnie, as though she could not get the line clear between Bonnie and herself." And the interviewer goes on to ask: "Have you any hunches as to why it is, in your relationship with Bonnie rather than Kent [son] that you feel this sense of uneasiness?" Mother: "Well, my mother took it out on me, and so I think I do on her. Because she's my first child, and then too, I think it's the fact that she's a girl."
>
> (C150)

While mothers thus may see and tend to their sons and daughters on the basis of feelings they have toward themselves and other significant figures, rather than on the basis of their children's own expressed needs, they are more likely to view sons as *others* or *objects* in their unconscious (and as indicated above, not so unconscious) mental life, and daughters as extensions of themselves.

Nancy Chodorow confirms this view. Drawing on the work of Enid Balint, Dorothy Burlingham, and Melitta Sperling, Chodorow describes how daughters who have experienced a mother's faulty empathy "act *as extensions of* their mothers . . . , act out the aggression which their mothers feel but do not allow themselves to recognize or act on," whereas sons "*react to* their mothers' feelings and wishes as if they were the *objects* of their mothers' fantasies rather than the subjects."[16]

Therefore, a mother's faulty empathy has different meaning for sons and daughters. As noted above, because it is women who have primary responsibility for the rearing of small children, a son erects well-defined ego boundaries that set him apart from his mother. This "otherness" from the mother allows or requires a son to play the part of the object in his mother's unconscious fantasies and their manifestations. He is the longed-for father, the resented husband, the erotic object that replaces the absent or inadequate mate.

A daughter, however, is rarely granted the psychic freedom and mobility of her brother. As Chodorow has shown, because they are mothered by someone of the same gender, girls maintain a greater sense of connection and continuity with the mother than do boys. A girl's "sameness" to her mother allows or requires her to serve as an extension of the mother's self or as a substitute for a woman's own mother to whom she is still attached. This asymmetrical situation therefore provides sons and daughters with different psychological and emotional resources with which to respond to a mother's faulty empathy.

A son may use his "otherness" to defend himself rigidly against his mother's erratic or unempathic behavior, while a girl may fail to develop the ego boundaries that permit her to be psychologically autonomous from the mother who remains emotionally unpredictable.

> That women turn to children to fulfill emotional and even erotic desires unmet by men or other women means that a mother expects from infants what only another adult should be expected to give.
>
> These tendencies take different forms with sons and daughters. Sons may become substitutes for husbands, and must engage in defensive assertion of ego boundaries and repression of emotional needs. Daughters may become substitutes for mothers, and develop insufficiently individuated senses of self.[17]

A mother's unpredictability and faulty responsiveness can impair a child's ability to identify with her and to internalize her affirming and esteeming of the child's worthiness. The child therefore can have difficulty in establishing a sense of self-worth and feelings of self-esteem. It will only feel valued when it is esteemed by and through external sources. The manner in which males and females go about extracting external valuation will differ according to their disparate developmental situation vis-à-vis the mother.

A daughter who has experienced faulty maternal empathy can gain self-worth through acting as an extension of her mother. She can feel esteemed not for herself but as part of one who is perceived as omnipotent. As an adult, this daughter can feel esteemed in a similar fashion. She can choose a love object whom she views as omnipotent, or whom others perceive as such, and achieve self-valuation through her identification or "fusion" with this person. Psychoanalyst Annie Reich describes two such groups of women:

> The first group is that of women who are in a particular relation of dependent subservience to the man, whom they consider great and admirable and without whom they cannot live. The second group consists of women who . . . "fall in love" with men whom they "deify" and without whom they consider life unbearable. They take over the man's personality, interests and values completely; it is as if they had no judgment of their own, no ego of their own. But suddenly, after a short time, the thus elevated object is dethroned again.[18]

Reich adds that the attempt to become "one with a grandiose love partner was related to the original homosexual object, the mother, primitive attachments to whom had never been relinquished."[19]

"Primitive attachments" to the mother may not be given up because the unpredictable quality of a mother's empathy prevents her daughter from establishing autonomy and causes her to remain dependent upon the mother for feelings of self-worth. Love objects are then chosen in adult life who permit this dependency to flourish by allowing a woman to feel esteemed, grandiose, or omnipotent through identification and fusion. Often a woman who uses this method of maintaining her self-esteem must change love objects frequently, as she discovers that the person whom she has come to "deify" is only human and not truly a substitute for the omnipotent mother of infancy and childhood. In limiting a discussion to heterosexual relations then, for a woman, male love partners can become part of the woman's self, can act as replacements for her mother, whose legacy to her daughter remains ill-defined ego boundaries and insufficient autonomy. As Chodorow indicates, a "woman who remains ambivalently dependent on her mother, or preoccupied internally with the question of whether she is separate or not, is likely to transfer this stance and sense of self to a relationship with her husband."[20]

For men, on the other hand, women partners do not become parts of the self; in fact, they are used to admire and esteem the defensively autonomous and tenuously maintained self. Women admire men's grandiosity, while male partners are constitutive of women's sense of self-worth. Women esteem men, while men are the vehicles through which women frequently attempt to find their self-esteem.[21]

Therefore, while both males and females may experience mothers' emotional inconsistency or faulty empathy, their characteristic ways of reacting are different. Certainly the low self-esteem, the deficiently developed psychic structures, and the deeply unconscious hunger for love that is at the root of what psychoanalysts term the narcissistic dilemma are shared by women and men. But because women are reared primarily by individuals of the same gender, they develop ego boundaries that allow or compel them to feel esteemed and loved through identification or "fusion" with others and that prompt them to deal with this psychological impoverishment through acting as an extension of another. Because men need to erect rigid ego boundaries in order to establish their gender identities in opposition to the women who rear them, their manner of managing such impoverishment is different.

It is men who are more likely to reveal extreme self-centeredness and the need to be admired by others. In this way the male reenacts the experience of being an *other* to his mother, dependent upon her for the praise and admiration that he cannot supply himself from internal sources. Self-centeredness and the need for external admiration imply separateness, even though that separateness may be defensive in nature. To have a self, to be admired, defines mother and child as discrete entities. Women, conversely, are more likely to deal with the same set of psychological problems through overinvesting and overidentifying with significant others. They attempt to repair their fragmented psychic structures by living through a love partner or child, reproducing the relationship to a mother whose self was unclearly differentiated from her daughter's.

In short, there are asymmetrical ways in which men and women come to deal with a particular situation, experienced in early childhood, that can result from women as mothers having sole responsibility for child rearing in isolated, unstimulating, and frequently emotionally barren nuclear families. In response to the erratic or faulty maternal empathy occasioned by such socially constructed circumstances, sons are more likely to develop a need to be admired, a fear of dependence, and an exploitative stance toward relationships with women. Daughters, on the other hand, are more likely to have a profound need to identify with and/or live through other people, to have markedly deficient ego boundaries, and to be capable of feeling good about themselves (to have self-esteem) only when they are attached or "fused" with some significant other. Both of these unconsciously based situations can make heterosexual relationships very difficult.

Men with this developmental background tend to need women to admire them, to provide them with the valuation they lack within. Therefore, a woman who is nonadmiring, assertive about her own needs and desires, or self-absorbed probably will not be a suitable object for such a man. A woman who is continually admiring, selfless, and easily controlled will be far more compatible. It is also not surprising for such men to be extremely fearful of women and to loathe developing any real dependency upon them. Such dependence would unconsciously recreate the early childhood experience of feeling misunderstood and exploited, of having one's sense of autonomy and separateness—which is so important to the male—manipulated according to the seemingly incomprehensible needs and fantasies of the mother. This "narcissistic" male uses women primarily to regard and adore his grandiose self. When a woman tires of doing this or when the male needs fresh supplies to prop up such a self, the woman partner can be abandoned so that he may find still another admiring and nonthreatening source of psychic nourishment.

The sadistic extreme of men's fear of women can also be understood in this light. In attempting to repair the early childhood experience of feeling emotionally exploited, out of control, and at the mercy of a stronger, more powerful woman, a man may attempt to reverse the situation by unconsciously declaring as an adult: "I am strong and powerful as evidenced by the fact that I can exploit and control women." While this sadistic urge may be acted out through actual acts of bondage and punishment, the far more "acceptable" forms of sadism through reading some forms of pornography, watching sexually violent films, and denigrating women in general is probably far more common. As Philip Slater has succinctly stated: "A society which derogates women produces envious mothers who produce narcissistic males who are prone to derogate women."[22] And as Jessica Benjamin has pointed out, sadistic violence is "a way of expressing or asserting control over another, of establishing one's own self-boundary and negating the other person's. . . . In other words, the relationship of erotic domination is a repetition or reliving of an earlier thwarting of the drive for differentiation."[23] It is an attempt to turn passive into active, to assert boundaries against a maternal response that was experienced as unempathic and unmindful of the tenuously and rigidly maintained ego boundaries with which the male establishes his gendered identity.

For women, on the other hand, the needs involved in heterosexual relations are not much better. Daughters who grow up with mothers who treat them unempathically and are unable to experience them as autonomous beings will often search for men in their adult lives with whom they can merge or identify in order to recapitulate the experience of childhood that permitted them feelings of esteem and self-worth. If we take Annie Reich's dichotomy seriously, such women look for men whom they can "deify" and live through to gain self-esteem. While some women are capable of finding and maintaining a long-term relationship with such a "deity," others eventually realize the man's faults and limitations, his inability to be a god, and thus must continually seek out fresh objects to idealize, fuse with, and eventually discard. Behaviorally, this latter situation parallels the male narcissist's heterosexual involvements. But while the *behavioral* manifestations are alike, the *motivational* circumstances that propel women and men into unstable or transient love relationships are quite different. Stated most generally, it is women's unconscious desire to reestablish relationship to the mother and men's wish to deny and/or dominate that relationship that color the landscape against which desperate and fleeting heterosexual relations are so frequently played out.

These psychological configurations represent *tendencies* in the ways sons and daughters might react to a particular kind of family life. While the sort of developmental scenario depicted here probably describes some actual individuals, the value of this analysis lies more in its location of different aspects of women's and men's unconscious needs in relationship to each other. Few individuals match these starkly drawn portraits exactly, but many women and men may find themselves mired in heterosexual relations where dependency, commitment, and issues regarding self-esteem are the most critical bones of contention.

With this in mind, I would argue that for sons and daughters who grow up in families where they constitute and justify their mothers' reason for being, substitute for absent or emotionally unavailable husbands, family, or friends, and are used to absorb all of their mothers' intellectual and emotional energies, heterosexual relations can be very problematic in any long-term, intimate, and mutually caring form. While many of these daughters may grow up to be overly dependent on their heterosexual partners and/or children, for at least some of them and probably for many more of the sons, the fundamental psychological prerequisites for maintaining sustained, loving, heterosexual relationships, which have traditionally formed the basis of family life and of parenting, will be lacking. Consequently, the more that women have the exclusive responsibility for mothering and are kept isolated within the home in the practice of that mothering, the greater the likelihood is that their children, and particularly their sons, will be reluctant or unable to form families of their own. Because women's faulty empathy, overinvestment in their children, and ambivalence over their autonomy is significantly determined by the social circumstances in which they mother, the program of the new right, which confines women exclusively to solitary homes while they raise their offspring, can produce narcissistic sons and, secondarily, overly dependent daughters who, in turn, are crippled in their ability to find and maintain love/sexual relationships.

The Politics of Mothering

In this sense, then, the call for a return to the "traditional family" contains a fundamental contradiction. The assertion that every child's birthright is a full-time, isolated mother, the refusal to provide affordable and quality child care, and the resistance to implementing employment practices that would improve mothers' access to jobs outside the home (job sharing, more part-time work, paid maternity leaves, and so on)—all in the name of children, motherhood, and the sanctity of the family—implicitly act to ensure the *instability* of the nuclear family and to threaten its continuity. By indirectly aiding in the production of individuals who are incapable of maintaining enduring relationships with others, the ideology and social policy that attempt to keep mothers at home through "expert" advice or assertion, the lack of child care, and restrictive employment practices undermine that which they explicitly try to sustain.

The United States is one of only a few industrialized Western nations with virtually no national policy that supports mothers in the parenting enterprise. Almost every European nation has public programs for children aged three to five, and increasingly for two-year-olds as well, while the United States has no federally sponsored child-care program.[24] Thus, middle-class mothers here are having to choose between working and never having children, and having children but raising them in circumstances quite similar to those of their mothers in the 1940s and 1950s.[25]

But it is not social policy alone that determines whether the experience of mothering eventually gives rise to narcissistic men and overly dependent women. If mothers are confronted with a pervasive ideology asserting that their first priority must always be their children—whether such children be in utero or in high school—and that the rearing of those children can be effectively accomplished only by the biological (or adoptive) mother on a full-time basis, if only for the preschool years, then it is not unreasonable to conclude that mothers will experience the same pull toward overinvolvement with their children as the mothers of the post–World War II era.[26] Given the political climate in this country, there is every reason to believe that such an ideology will once again become a driving force and that social policy will not only fail to support the working mother but attempt to penalize her for moving outside her traditional domain.

Because of this national political trend, the left should be defending mothers' labor-force participation, proposing and endorsing programs to enable co-parenting by fathers and mothers, and seeking means for establishing quality child care that is accessible to all people who need it. These goals would probably strengthen the family in the long run, since according to the analysis presented here, they take into account the potential effects of family life on the personalities of the next generation.

Current attempts to revitalize the "traditional family" are hollow if they do not consider the effects of family life on future generations. On the basis of the material I have presented I would suggest that the future of the family is not pinned to any such "revitalization," to bringing mothers home from the workforce, to denying their rights to abortion or contraception, or to reinforcing an ideology that offers a recycled version of the "Feminine Mystique." Rather, I believe that the future of the family—a family founded in emotional intimacy, reciprocity, and equality—is linked in the most ultimate sense to the production of personalities who are whole, nondefensively autonomous, capable of self-valuation and respect, and hence able to love and value others. Such personalities will be created only when and if the needs of the individuals who mold them in infancy and childhood are recognized and acted upon.

Notes

1. It may be that the left emphasizes this axis of family crisis, as opposed to that of parents and children, because the left is still largely populated by children of the baby boom.

2. While my discussion is limited to what occurred in middle-class families, the trends I describe certainly were experienced in all classes of society, but to differing degrees. It is also important to point out that what takes place in the middle class is considered normative for all of society. Thus, 1950s middle-class family life was not only a reality for a certain stratum of society but an ideal for the classes below it.

3. See Barbara Laslett, "The Family as a Public and Private Institution: An Historical Perspective," *Journal of Marriage and the Family*, August 1973; and William Goode, *World Revolution and Family Patterns* (New York: Free Press, 1970).

4. See Goode, *World Revolution*, and U.S. Department of Labor, *Manpower Report of the President* (Washington, D.C.: Department of Labor, 1975).

5. Betty Friedan, *The Feminine Mystique* (New York: Dell, 1974).

6. See Laslett, "The Family."

7. Philip Slater, *The Pursuit of Loneliness* (Boston: Beacon Press, 1976), 72–73.

8. This study was based on the "Guidance Study" of the longitudinal Intergenerational Studies of Development and Aging from the Institute of Human Development, University of California, Berkeley, which follows the life cycle of individuals randomly selected from all children born in Berkeley in 1928 and 1929. The 151 subjects were married and became parents in the late 1940s and 1950s. The vast majority and their families were white, and a plurality were middle and upper middle class. They and their families were interviewed extensively by research psychologists in their homes throughout the United States and at the Institute of Human Development between 1957 and 1960, and again in 1971. For a fuller discussion of my findings, see Ilene Philipson, "Narcissism and Mothering: The 1950s Reconsidered," *Women's Studies International Quarterly*, vol. 5, no. 1: and "Gender and Narcissism," *Psychology of Women Quarterly* 9 (1985): 213–28.

9. This is based on a sample of 69 women. *Ladies Home Journal* in November 1958 found that 90 percent of the full-time housewives and mothers responding to its survey had worked, gone to college, or both before marriage.

10. Nancy Chodorow, *The Reproduction of Mothering* (Berkeley: University of California Press, 1978), 205.

11. Jessica Benjamin, "Authority and the Family Revisited: or, A World Without Fathers?" *New German Critique* No. 13 (Winter 1978): 54.

12. Heinz Kohut, *The Analysis of the Self* (New York: International Universities Press, 1971), 65–66.

13. For extensive descriptions and explanations of narcissism as a clinical disorder, see Heinz Kohut, *Analysis of the Self*, and *The Restoration of the Self* (New York: International Universities Press, 1977); see also Otto Kernberg, *Borderline Conditions and Pathological Narcissism* (New York: Jason Aronson, 1975).

14. I have never come upon a case, either in clinical material or in the "Guidance Study" sample, of a daughter who was seen as a mother's sister. The reasons for this are unclear but may be linked simply to a limited reading.

15. Numbers in parentheses following quotations are the case numbers of individual families assigned by the Institute of Human Development staff.

16. Chodorow, *Reproduction of Mothering*, 103.

17. Ibid., p. 212.

18. Annie Reich, "Narcissistic Object-Choice in Women," *Journal of the American Psychoanalytic Association*, vol. I (1953), pp. 25, 31. While this analysis refers to heterosexual love objects, I see no reason why the same sort of analysis would not apply to homosexual love objects.

19. Ibid., pp. 27–28.

20. Chodorow, *Reproduction of Mothering*, p. 195.

21. Certainly sexual partners are not the only means by which women can gain self-worth through attaching themselves to or identifying with significant others. The work of Chodorow suggests how women's low self-esteem—structured in their own childhoods and exacerbated by the particular social-historical environment in which *they* mother—is the basis of their overidentification and fusion with their own children. In other words, children are used as the missing part of the self, allowing women to recapitulate the feeling of attachment or merger with a loved and valued other.

22. Philip Slater, *The Glory of Hera* (Boston: Beacon Press, 1968), 45.

23. Jessica Benjamin, "The Bonds of Love: Rational Violence and Erotic Domination," *Feminist Studies* 6, no. 1 (1980): 150, 165. While Benjamin correctly captures the psychodynamic causes of male sadism toward women, her understanding of women's experience in sado-masochistic relations is somewhat lacking. According to her argument, men establish "selfhood by controlling the other," while women lose "selfhood by being controlled" (p. 155). "The female posture disposes the woman to accept objectification and control in order to flee separation" (p. 167). This, I believe, defines women's experience only through the negation of selfhood, rather than through the attempt to realize the self through fusion with or submission to the idealized other. In this sense it can be seen that women's needs to "establish selfhood" are just as great as men's, but because it is women who mother, their method for realizing selfhood is different from that of men.

24. Kathleen Fury, "Getting Ahead," *Ladies Home Journal*, May 1980, p. 50.

25. Ruth Daniloff, "Matching Up Working with Motherhood," *San Francisco Chronicle*, 11 May 1980.

26. For a review and analysis of the resurgence in this type of ideology, see Nancy Chodorow and Susan Contratto, "The Fantasy of the Perfect Mother," in Barrie Thorne, ed., *Rethinking the Family: Some Feminist Questions* (New York: Longmans, 1982).

19   When Women and Men Mother

Diane Ehrensaft

In the late 1960s and early 1970s the women's movement put the traditional nuclear family on trial and declared it oppressive to women. Entrapment as housewives and mothers was targeted as key to female oppression. A prime focus, both theoretical and strategic, was to free women from their iron apron strings. Some women, particularly radical feminists, called for a boycott of women's involvement with marriage, men, or motherhood. Others demanded universal child care to free women from the home. Some opted for motherhood but no men. A minority of women within the movement, who were either already in nuclear families or still desired involvement with men and children, opted for a different solution in their own lives—the equal sharing of parenthood between mothers and fathers. Contrary to traditional heterosexual relationships in which men are reported to spend an average of twelve minutes a day on primary child care, this new model of parenting assumed that mothers and fathers would share the full weight of rearing their children.[1]

Ten years later, a combination of forces pressures those of us who chose this latter solution to talk about and assess our experience. Recognizing the confusion and turmoil experienced by people in this country around issues of personal life, astute new right organizers have responded with the rallying cry of "save our families, save our future" as the road to surviving contemporary crises. The emergence of the new right is marked very strongly by a bid for women to remain responsible for primary child care.

Source: This article is reprinted from *Socialist Review* No. 49 (January–February 1980), pp. 37–73, by permission of the publisher, *Socialist Review*, 3202 Adeline, Berkeley, CA 94703.

At the same time, more and more mothers are working outside the home to support themselves and their families. For many women, this means two full-time jobs. The popular press abounds with news reports, articles, and books attesting to the growing interest of men in family life, accompanied by a drop in male workaholism, while the women they live with no longer settle for being "just housewives."[2]

Simultaneously, feminist theory, particularly in such books as Dorothy Dinnerstein's *Mermaid and the Minotaur* (1976) and Nancy Chodorow's *Reproduction of Mothering* (1978), has stressed that gender differentiation and sex oppression will exist as long as women continue to be totally responsible for mothering. The call for shared parenting by men and women moves those of us already involved in attempting such a reorganization of family life to reflect and analyze its potential and actual effects on the reorganization of gender and child-rearing structures. We are further moved by pressures from the new right to develop this analysis within the larger project of a left counterprogram that more effectively addresses people's fears about crumbling family stability, lack of personal commitment, increased social violence, and dissolution of knowable social forms. This must come not as a romantic plea for a return to the good old days but as a step forward to new social structures that provide the emotional and social intimacy and sense of community for which people are legitimately searching.

Most of the small group of men and women whose experiences are examined here do not represent the mainstream of American society. We are, on the whole, white graduates of the new left of the 1960s, which puts most of us in our thirties at this writing. Often we hold professional, nontraditional, or "movement" jobs with greater opportunity for flex-time than most people have. We tend to congregate in liberal communities such as Boston, the San Francisco Bay Area, New York, and western Massachusetts. While most of us hold that ideally all mothers and fathers living together should share equally in the parenting process, this is indeed not the ultimate solution for all people. Parenting by women alone, by men alone, in extended families, in gay couples, in communal situations within neighborhood networks are all models to be explored and understood. Economic necessity and social context will influence different parenting solutions. But the experiences of our small group are important not only because they reveal the parameters and possibilities of gender reorganization within the family at this point in history; they also simultaneously reflect and speak to the concern of growing numbers of both women and men who find they no longer survive in or accept traditional family roles. Shared parenting exists not in isolation but as part of the larger struggle facing contemporary adults in redefining their position in (and out of) the family.

The political meaning of this analysis is twofold. On one hand, if feminist theory stands correct in pinpointing enforced motherhood as a major source of women's oppression through confirmation and reproduction of their domesticity, shared parenting challenges that situation. If, as Dinnerstein and Chodorow respectively argue, misogyny and gender-divided personality structures have their roots in female-dominated parenting, shared parenting sets the stage for a new generation of men and women and challenges a universal structure in the organization of gender.

On the other hand, an examination of actual shared parenting experiences confirms that "'production' and 'reproduction,' work and the family, far from being separate territories like the moon or sun or the kitchen and the shop, are really intimately related modes that reverberate upon one another and frequently occur in the same social, physical, and even psychic spaces."[3] Focusing on the experiences of men and women who have taken an equal share in parenting while also maintaining outside work identities, I argue that equalization of parenting between men and women is problematic within American capitalism. The interpenetration of work and family makes it very hard to alter power and psychological structures in the family without a concomitant restructuring of power and ideology in the public world of work and politics. By looking at the general nature of shared parenting, observing the division of labor and male-female relationships between shared parents, and speculating about the outcome for children in these families, we can explore the tension between the tremendous political potential and the actual limitations of shared parenting in the reorganization of gender.

Shared Parenting in a Capitalist Context

Who is engaged in shared parenting? Any two individuals both of whom see themselves as primary caretakers to a child or children. As defined by Nancy Press Hawley, elements of shared parenting include (1) intimacy, both between sharing adults and between adults and children; (2) care of the child in a regular, daily way; (3) awareness of being a primary caretaker or parent to the children; (4) ongoing commitment; and (5) attention paid to the adult relationship.[4] In addition to daily caretaking functions, we are talking about two individuals who fully share responsibility for the ongoing intellectual, emotional, and social development of the child.

In the late 1960s and early 1970s, some people coming out of new left lifestyles tried to establish a model in which both parents split their work time between part-time paid work and parenting responsibilities. Others had a vision of a "one year on, one year off" model, with mother and father alternating primary parenting responsibilities from one year or so to the next: "We had fantasies of each of us getting half-time jobs while we had babies so we could share in their care and taking turns working once the children were older."[5] But economic downturn smashed those visions for many. With part-time jobs hard to come by and the sum total of one income insufficient to support a family we are more likely to be talking about two parents absent for much of the day, using child-care facilities, and sharing parenting responsibilities.

We have no statistics on how many women and men in this country fit the criteria of shared parenting listed above. Those of us involved do know we are a rare phenomenon: in the left and in the women's movement because so few of our contemporaries (until recently) were parents at all; in the world at large because of economic, social, and ideological realities which dictate that *women* mother.

At the same time we find ourselves in a comparatively recent majority category: two-working-parent families.[6] Why should shared parenting therefore be so rare? Despite the trend of growing numbers of women in the work force, the lack of decent child care for very young children (particularly breastfed babies), inadequate maternity policies at the workplace, income and job inequalities between men and women, and lack of flexible job structures leave women moving cyclically between home and workplace, men more firmly planted as the primary breadwinners: "The sexual division of labor and society remains intact even with women in the paid economy. Ideology adjusts to this by defining women as working mothers and the two jobs get done for less than the price of one."[7]

Simultaneously, the ideology of motherhood remains strong. With even liberals and feminists such as Selma Fraiberg and Alice Rossi arguing for the primacy of women as mothers,[8] the pressures on women to maintain parenting responsibilities remain great. An article in the *Los Angeles Times* reports that women with both children and jobs see themselves as nearly twice as harassed as women with no children and no job. "The strange thing about the study," reports the investigator, "is that women don't seem to mind"; in fact, they often shooed away their husbands' attempts to help, not wanting encroachment on their defined territory by an inept assistant.[9] Years spent within female-dominated households and other social institutions lead many to believe it could not be otherwise: motherhood is women's "natural" calling and her obligation, or her sphere of power and expertise.

The traditional socialist belief was that entry into the sphere of production would be the ultimate road to women's liberation. Only through entering the socialized arena of paid work could women establish the collective political leverage to free them from their shackles of oppression. Instead, we find the reverse to be true. They now have a double workload—as paid worker and as housewife and primary parent. While many fathers have come forward to "help out" with kids and housework, doing more work in the family than in our parents' time, the full sharing of parenting between women and men remains a rare phenomenon. When we hear about mothers and fathers gone all day at work, and Dad coming home to plop in front of the TV while Mom puts in her extra day's labor as housewife and mother, we feel compelled to demand shared parenting as a mass phenomenon rather than the rare experience it is now. At the same time, we recognize the ideological and power dynamics that maintain the status quo. Mom will be reluctant to shoo Dad away from the television if the consequence is that he and his larger paycheck walk out the door, leaving her to support three kids on her own.

What have the women's movement and the left offered as guidance toward the solution of this parenting problem? Interestingly enough, left-feminist and left politics, which have argued against this dual oppression of women as paid and unpaid workers, have yet been vague about or blind to the demand for men's involvement in parenting. For example, in a document drawn up by the Mothers' Caucus at the National Socialist-Feminist Conference in Yellow Springs, Ohio, in 1975, the demand that men and women share equally in the responsibility for child care is not mentioned once. The closest statement is that "collective childrearing is an absolute necessity." The 1974 Principles of Unity of the Berkeley-Oakland Women's Union were also vague on this point, going only so far as to demand that unpaid work in the home be recognized as socially necessary and that all productive human activity become the collective responsibility of the whole society. This lack of an explicit call for fathers to come forth is again apparent in Juliet Mitchell's *Woman's Estate* (1966). Remaining vague, she calls for the diversification of socially acknowledged relationships now rigidly defined in the nuclear family. As for the rearing of children, the dominant demand has been for universally available child care to assist women, without an explicit concomitant demand that men and women also share equal responsibility for finding that child care or parenting those children.[10]

It is true that much of feminist writing and politics, with the exception of sex-role socialization and child-care projects, has been focused specifically on *woman* and her oppression, and only tangentially on men and the needed changes in their gender-related experience ("leave it to the men to figure that out"). Radical and socialist feminists, in particular, identified the nuclear family as a patriarchal underpinning of women's oppression and therefore often shied away from such solutions as shared parenting, which might ostensibly reinforce this abhorrent social institution. Some radical feminists have taken the extreme "matriarchal" position that men ought not to be involved in the rearing of children at all (men as sons but not as fathers). It has been liberal feminists who have spoken most directly to the issues of fathers who parent. While socialist feminists have remained abstract (dealing with the larger issues of sex, race, and class), and radical feminists have avoided male-female parenting issues, liberal feminists have tackled the structural reforms that speak most directly to the actual experiences of daily parenting life. Liberal feminism also claims among its ranks more mothers than any other feminist tendency. However, as more left feminists have children—in an atmosphere where it is no longer politically incorrect to do so—and recognize that, to be effective, socialist feminism must connect more directly to people's daily lives, we, too, begin looking for analyses of parenting and male-female relationships.

The lack of attention to men in parenting is not simply a feminist problem, but the left's as well. In an article on the baby boom written for the independent socialist newspaper *In These Times*, Sidney Blumenthal, pinpointing changes in parenting in the 1980s, never once mentions the willingness of or need for fathers to share child-care responsibilities.[11] Instead, he identifies *women's* desire and need to work and *women's* increased acceptance of day-care centers as critical differences between the new baby boom and that of the 1950s. No mention of men's increased involvement in family life. The lack of attention to men's involvement when addressing parenting issues, both by the left and by much of the women's movement (with the exception of a particular radical feminist counter-ideology that only *women should* mother), reflects a deeply entrenched ideology, not easily shed, that simply equates parenthood with mothers.

From a political point of view, then, shared parenting between men and women is a novel phenomenon. Most left approaches have called for the emancipation of women by freeing them from the house and providing entry into the public sphere of work and politics: "The emancipation of women will only be made possible when woman can take part in production in a large social scale and domestic work no longer claims anything but an insignificant amount of her time," said Engels.[12] Traditional left feminists such as Simone de Beauvoir have argued a similar approach. Alice Rossi, in her "Immodest Proposal," could only envision the freeing of (middle-class) women from their homes into the world of the professions by calling on other (working-class) women to enter these homes as paid substitute mothers.[13] In contrast, shared parenting among heterosexual couples demands that men enter the feminine sphere of baby powder and diapers. It is the practical embodiment of the socialist-feminist demand that women's traditional work be socially recognized and shared. But rather than turning to the state or to the public sphere—as in the demand for wages for house-work/mothering or for universal child care—shared parenting challenges the mystique of motherhood and the sexual division of labor at another critical point of reproduction: the home. As stated by a sharing father: "For me, the equal sharing of child care has meant bringing the feminist 'war' home—from the abstraction it would have remained in my mind, to those concrete day-to-day realities that transform us as few other situations I can think of."[14] It is a demand that accepts the viability of heterosexuality as one, though not the only, structure for personal life but insists on a radical transformation in male-female relationships.

At this moment, shared parenting has several social and political dimensions. We have already pinpointed the pressing need to relieve growing numbers of women from the dual oppression of paid worker and primary parent. In theory, shared parenting also (1) liberates women from full-time mothering; (2) affords opportunities for more equal relationships between women and men; (3) allows men more access to children; (4) allows children to be parented by two nurturing figures and frees them from the confines of an "overinvolved" parent who has no other outside identity; (5) provides new socialization experiences and possibly a breakdown in gender-differentiated character structures in children; (6) challenges the myth buttressed by sociobiology that women are better equipped biologically for parenting and that women *are* while men *do;* (7) puts pressure on political, economic, and social structures for changes such as paternity and maternity leaves, job sharing, and freely available child-care facilities.

What, though, do we know about the actual implementation of shared parenting today? We have few models from the past and few reports of present experiences. A woman writing about "Motherhood and the Liberated Woman" urges that "if women's liberation is to mean anything for people who have children or want to have them it must mean that fathers are in this, too. But in what ways it must change, my husband and I don't exactly know."[15] What can we conclude about the viability and political significance of shared parenting from the experience of those men and women who are trying to share "mothering"?

The Dialectics of Pampers and Paychecks: The Sexual Division of Labor in Shared Parenting
Can Men Mother?

In this argument, the word "mothering" is used specifically to mean the day-to-day *primary* care of a child; it involves the consciousness of being *directly* in charge of the child's upbringing. It is to be differentiated from the once-a-week baseball games or twenty-five minutes of play a day that characterize the direct parenting in which men have typically been involved. One mother put it aptly: "To a child Mommy is the person who takes care of me, who tends my daily needs, who nurtures me in an unconditional and present way. Manda has two mothers; one is a male, Mommy David, and the other a female, Mommy Alice."[16]

According to recent psychological studies, anyone can "mother" an infant who can provide frequent and sustained physical contact, soothe the child when distressed, be sensitive to the baby's signals, and respond to a baby's crying promptly. Beyond these immediate behavioral indices, psychoanalysts argue that anyone who has personally experienced a positive parent-child relationship that allowed the development of both trust and individuation in his or her own childhood has the emotional capabilities to parent. However much as sociobiologists would take issue there is no conclusive animal or human research indicating that female genitals, breasts, or hormonal structure provide women with any better equipment than men for parenting.[17] Yet years in female-dominated parenting situations and in gender-differentiated cultural institutions can and do differentially prepare boys and girls for the task of "mothering."[18] And in adulthood social forces in the labor market, schools, media, and so on, buttress these differential abilities. To understand what happens when two such differentially prepared individuals come together to parent, two issues have to be addressed: parenting and power, and the psychic division of labor in parenting.

Power and Parenting

I recently read four articles in the popular press acclaiming a shifting in family structure. Women, they said, have become more and more interested in and committed to extrafamilial lives, while men have fled from the heartless world to the haven of the family. Knowing that theirs is not the only paycheck coming in, more men walk off the job, come late to work, rebel against the work ethic. The articles speak optimistically of a new generation of "family men" and "career women" and a greater sharing among men and women in both family and work life.[19]

But we who know the behind-the-scenes story take a moment of pause. We women who have shared parenting with men know the tremendous support and comfort (and luxury) of not being the only one there for our children. We see opportunities to develop the many facets of ourselves not as easily afforded to our mothers or to other women who carried the primary load of parenting. We watch our children benefit from the full access to two rather than one primary nurturing figure, affording them intimacy with both women and men, a richer and more complex emotional milieu, role models that challenge gender stereotypes. We see men able to develop more fully the nurturant parts of themselves as fathers, an opportunity often historically denied them. And we develop close, open, and more equal relationships between men and women as we grapple with the daily ups and downs of parenting together. The quality of our lives no doubt has been improved immensely by the equalization of parenting responsibilities between men and women.

Yet we also know that shared parenting is easier said than done. Because it has remained so unspoken, it is this latter reality I speak to here, while urging the reader to keep in mind the larger context of the successes, the improvements in daily life, and the political import that accompany the shared parenting project.

> Men and women are brought up for a different position in the labor force: the man for the world of work, the woman for the family. This difference in the sexual division of labour in society means that the relationship of men as a group to production is different from that of women. For a man the social relations and values of commodity production predominate and home is a retreat into intimacy. For the woman the public world of work belongs to and is owned by men.[20]

While men hold fast to the domination of the "public sphere," it has been the world of home and family that is woman's domain. Particularly in the rearing of children, it is often her primary (or only) sphere of power. For all the oppressive and debilitating effects of the institution of motherhood, a woman *does* get social credit for being a "good" mother. She also accrues for herself some sense of control and authority in the growth and development of her children. As a mother she is afforded the opportunity for genuine human interaction, in contrast to the alienation and depersonalization of the workplace:

> A woman's desire to experience power and control is mixed with the desire to obtain joy in childrearing and cannot be separated from it. It is the position of women in society as a whole, their dependent position in the family, the cultural expectation that the maternal role should be the most important role for all women, that make the exaggerated wish to possess one's child an entirely reasonable

reaction. Deprived and oppressed, women see in motherhood their only source of pleasure, reward, and fulfillment.[21]

It is this power and control that she must partially give up in sharing parenting equally with a father.

What she gains in exchange is twofold: a freedom from the confines of twenty-four-hour-a-day motherhood and the same opportunity as her male partner to enter the public world of work and politics, with the additional power in the family that her paycheck brings with it. But that public world, as Rowbotham points out, is still controlled and dominated by men and does not easily make a place for women within it. The alteration in gender relations within the "shared parent" family is not met by a simultaneous gender reorganization outside the home. A certain loosening of societal gender hierarchies, the opening of new job opportunities for women, no doubt has prefigured and created the structural conditions that have allowed a small number of men and women to share parenting at this historical moment. But those structural changes are minor in contrast to the drastic alteration of gender relations and power necessary for shared parenting to succeed. So the world the sharing mother enters as she walks out her door will be far less "fifty-fifty" than the newly created world within those doors.

For men taking on parenting responsibilities, the gain is also twofold: he gains access to his children and is able to experience the pleasures and joys of child rearing. His life is not totally dominated by the alienated relations of commodity production. He is able to nurture, discover the child in himself. But he too loses something in the process. First, in a culture that dictates that a man "make something of himself," he will be hard pressed to compete in terms of time and energy with his male counterparts who have only minimal or no parenting responsibility. In short, parenting will cut into his opportunities for "transcendence." Second, the sharing father is now burdened with the daily headaches and hassles of child care which can (and do) drive many a woman to distraction: the indelible scribble on the walls, the search for a nonexistent good child-care center, the two-hour tantrums, and so on. He has now committed himself to a sphere of work that brings little social recognition—I'm *just* a housewife and a mother.

In *shared* parenting the gains and losses are not equal for men and women. Mom gives up some of her power only to find societally induced guilt feelings for not being a "real" mother and maybe even for being a "bad" mother. (Remember: she may have grown up believing that she should and would be a full-time mommy when she was big.) The myth of motherhood remains ideologically entrenched far beyond the point when its structural underpinnings have begun to crumble. She is giving up power in the domestic sphere, historically her domain, with little compensation from increased power in the public sphere. Discrimination against women in the labor force is still rampant. She will likely have less earning power, less job opportunity, less creative work, and less social recognition than her male partner. When push comes to shove, she is only a *"working mother."* There is as yet no parallel term "working father."

The power dynamic for Dad is quite different and more complicated. On one level he gains considerable authority in the daily domestic sphere of child rearing, a heretofore female domain. But by dirtying his hands with diapers he also removes himself from his patriarchal pedestal as the breadwinning but distant father, a position crucial to men's power in the traditional family. He now does the same "debasing" work as the mother, and she now has at least some control of the purse strings. Nonetheless, as the second "mother," the father has encroached on an arena of power that traditionally belongs to women, yet he most likely retains more economic and social power vis-à-vis Mom in the public world of work and politics.

The societal reaction is also double-edged for the sharing father. Given the subculture that most current sharing parents come from, in his immediate circles Dad often receives praise for being the "exceptional" father so devoted to his children or so committed to denying his male privileges. In challenging a myth so deeply embedded as motherhood, the man who marches with baby bottle and infant in arm can become quite an antisexist hero. But in the larger culture reactions are often adverse. A man who stays home to care for children is assumed by many to be either disabled, deranged, or demasculinized. One father, pushing his child in a stroller past a school on a weekday afternoon, was bemused by a preadolescent leaning out the school window yelling, "Faggot, Faggot." Some time ago my grandmother, in response to my mother's praise of my husband's involvement with our children, snapped, "Well, of course, he doesn't work." But as pressures of shifting family structures increase, popular response is rapidly swinging in the sharing father's favor, at least among the middle classes; and the response to his fathering from his most immediate and intimate circles is most likely a positive or even laudatory one.

When the results are tabulated, the gains and losses for men and women are not comparable: women come out behind. Where does this newly experienced power imbalance leave mothers and fathers vis-à-vis their commitment to shared parenting? Women can feel deprived of status both at home and at work. The experienced sexual inequalities in the world outside the family can create a tension in the "sharing" mother to reclaim dominance as primary parent in order to establish control and autonomy *somewhere:*

> I was angry and I was jealous. I was jealous because he not only had the rewards of parenthood, he was into work he could relate to. I think one reason I nursed as long as I did was to keep myself as Amanda's most special person. It was also difficult to share one area of competence I felt I had. . . . After all, if she prefers David, what else do I have. I am woman therefore mother. I held on to my ambivalent identity as student in order to have something of my own.[22]

Structural forces dictate that she'll be much more successful in claiming control in the family sphere than in the public sphere. For some women, particularly those who start as primary parents and then move to shared parenting, it is not a question of reclaiming but of giving up control of parenting in the first place. As expressed by one woman:

> Neither of us could find a satisfactory way to increase his involvement. The children would have nothing to do with him. This situation probably came about because he was home less often and also because for many years the children were my own arena and thus my main base of power. At some level I probably did not want Ernie to be equally important in the lives of the children.[23]

The reclaiming of or unwillingness to give up a more primary role in parenting is not easy. It often culminates in frustration or anger (self- or other-directed) when a woman sees herself as doing more or too much parenting in comparison with her male partner.

The man, on his part, can feel a number of things when his female partner claims more parenting responsibility for herself: resistant to being shut out, inadequate in his own seeming lack of parenting skills, relieved to relinquish 50 percent of control in a sphere that he was never meant or prepared to participate in anyway. This is not to say that father merely reacts to mother's power tactics. As I discuss more fully in the next section, he is often quite active in "granting" women increased power in the sphere of parenting to give him the time he wants, needs, or has been conditioned to devote to extrafamilial activities.

The underlying point is this: powerful tensions arise when the sexual divisions of labor and power in the family are altered without simultaneous sweeping restructuring of gender-related power relations outside the family. Women under advanced capitalism spend too much time feeling powerless to relish a situation where, under the auspices of liberation, they find themselves with less power. I have watched many a sharing mother —undervalued, sexually harassed, or discriminated against in the work-place—waffle on her outside work identity and refocus on the pleasure, reward, and fulfillment to be found in identity as a mother. This is not to say that she relinquishes her paid work but that indeed she becomes a *working mother*. Fathers, for their part, are not often prepared for the arduous, but undervalued task they take on in becoming the other mommy:

> I get an empty feeling when people ask me what I'm doing. Most of my energy in the last six months has focused on Dylan, on taking care of him and getting used to his being here. But I still have enough man-work expectations in me that I feel uncomfortable just saying that.[24]

Even if he, too, balks at the alienation of the workplace, the flight into parenthood is not a likely one.

The tension between men and women over this issue was illustrated by the marked female-male differences in response to the first draft of this article. Women, whether mothers or non-mothers, urged me to emphasize how *rare* it is for men to involve themselves in parenting or for shared parenting actually to work. Men, on the other hand, wanted me to put more emphasis on the growing involvement of men in family life and the actual fathering that men have done historically *and continue to do*. Both are true, and both reflect the unresolved dialectic between women and men regarding parenting responsibility.

Physical vs. Psychic Division of Labor in Parenting

The tensions in shared parenting cannot, however, be reduced to power politics in personal relationships. External expectations, attitudes, and ideology collide with deeply internalized self-concepts, skills, and per-sonality structures to make the breakdown of the sexual division of labor in parenting an exciting but difficult project. Often the sharing of *physical* tasks is easily implemented: you feed the baby in the morning, I'll do it in the afternoon; you give the kids a bath on Mondays, I'll do it on Thursdays. What is left at least partially intact is the sexual division of the *psychological* labor in parenting. There is the question "Who carries around in their heads knowledge of diapers needing to be laundered, fingernails needing to be cut, new clothes needing to be bought?" Answer: mothers, because of years of socialization to do so. Vis-à-vis fathers, sharing mothers often find themselves in the position of cataloguer and taskmaster—We really should change the kids' sheets today; I think it's time for the kids' teeth to be checked. It is probable that men carry less of the mental load of parenting, regardless of mutual agreements to share the responsibility; this leaves the women more caught up in the psychic aspects of parenting.

The more significant division of psychological labor, however, is the different intrapsychic conflict that men and women experience in integrating their parent and nonparent identities. We have already looked at the power imbalance that pulls mothers back into the home and fathers away from it. A tremendous ambivalence or guilt in relinquishing full-time mothering responsibilities is common among women who depart from full-time mothering, either by working outside the home or sharing parenting responsibility with other(s):

> The myth of motherhood takes its toll. Employed mothers often feel guilty. They feel inadequate, and they worry about whether they are doing the best for their children. They have internalized the myth that there is something their children need that only they can give them.

> To have children but turn over their rearing to someone else—even their father—brings social disapproval: a mother who does this must be "hard," "unloving," and of course, "unfeminine."[25]

Numerous studies negating any ill effects to children who are not totally mother-raised pale in the public light in contrast to sensationalist reports of the delinquency, psychopathology, and emotional deficiencies that befall children who are not provided with the proper "mother-love." And this love is "naturally" *woman's* duty and domain. Raised in this culture, even the most committed feminist "sharing" mother will experience doubt. Doubts and fears are profound because the stakes are so high. By sharing parenting, we are experimenting with the growth and development of our children, adopting new child-rearing structures in the face of reports from psychologists, pediatricians, and politicians that we will only bring ruin to our young.

These fears are fueled by pressures from individuals in the sharing mother's immediate life. *Her* mother is often appalled or threatened by her daughter's deviation from her own parenting model. Relatives are often resistant to the notion that a man should hang around the house taking care of a kid. People will inadvertently (or deliberately) turn to mother rather than father in asking information about the children. Letters from school come addressed to "Dear Mother." From the point of view of the outside world, even though men are being given more and more attention for their participation in family life, the father remains an invisible or minimal figure in the daily rearing of children. A feeling so deeply internalized as "mother guilt," constantly rekindled by these external pressures and messages, creates in the sharing mother a strong ambivalence. Our intellectual selves lash out at the Alice Rossis telling us that we as women are the best-made parents, but our emotional selves struggle hard to calm the fear that our feminist views on motherhood may be ill founded.

As if mother guilt were not enough, women confront two additional conflicts. First, the traditional structures of child rearing have produced in a woman a psychological capacity to mother. With personal observations and experience to back her up, she may have a hard time believing that a father, with no parallel long-term preparation, is really capable of fulfilling "mothering" responsibilities. As she watches her male partner stick the baby with a diaper pin (even though she as a new parent may have done the same thing the day before) or try unsuccessfully to calm a screaming child, her suspicions are confirmed. Thus, internal forces pressure the mother to reclaim control over parenting in order to be assured that her children will survive intact. Men are often accomplices in this process: "Some men act out unconscious resistance to shared parenting by accentuating their ignorance, asking a lot of questions they could figure out themselves."[26] Sometimes women are not willing to be teachers. In the short run, they find it easier to do it themselves.

The second conflict arises from a woman's establishment of an "extra-mother" identity. We've already mentioned that women do not accrue much social recognition at the workplace, that they are seen as mothers first and workers second, and that when they attempt shared parenting they sometimes retreat from the world of paid work back into the female sphere of family life. Within her own psyche the sharing mother has a hard time integrating a work identity with being a mother: "When you go out to work, the job is something you *do*. But the work of a housewife and mother is not just something you do, it's something you *are*."[27]

For men, however, the experience is quite different. Historically, since the advent of industrialization, fathers' daily involvement with the kids in the nuclear family has been peripheral—usually concentrated on evening, weekend, and holiday play or instructional activities. There is no doubt that fathers have always been important figures in their children's lives and socialization experiences, even if as a result of their absence. The traditional father is very actively involved in his child's life as breadwinner, as role model, as disciplinarian, but not in the day-to-day nurturant fashion that shared parenting dictates. The challenge for the man in shared parenting is to move from being a "father" to a "mother."

The growing participation of men in the birth experience of their children still often stops at the delivery room doors. Contrasted to mothers, the sharing father more likely enters the parenting experience with a notion that parenting is something you *do* rather than someone you are. In early preparation for this consciousness, preschool boys in a recent study not once reported "Daddy" as something they would be when they grew up, while a majority of girls named "Mommy" as a projected adult identity.[28] In popular writing today, involved fathering is often presented as a *choice:* "only if the man wants to."

Only this consciousness could yield an article in the *San Francisco Chronicle* about a football coach who "tossed in the towel" after a sixty-eight-day attempt at mothering: "Peters said yesterday he's convinced 'motherhood' is an impossible *task* [my emphasis] for a normal human being."[29] If parenting is something you *do*, then it is something you can stop doing. But it is much harder to stop being someone you are.[30]

The guilt that the sharing father experiences is markedly different from the mother guilt reported above. Often he feels caught up in his own inadequacies, his own lack of socially molded "intuition" in handling the everyday intrapsychic and interpersonal aspects of parent-child relationships. It was mentioned earlier that men often resist shared parenting by accentuating their ignorance. But often they feel genuinely ignorant, lacking the psychological skills to meet their children's emotional needs. Learning practical skills like changing diapers or administering nose drops is one thing. Developing the traits of "empathy," "nurturance," "taking the role of the other" necessary to good "mothering" is a far more challenging task. These are the very traits that often remain underdeveloped or atrophy in the man's life history and are not easily reinstated at a later developmental period. The shared father's male guilt parallels the guilt felt more generally by men who feel accountable for the oppression of women (or a woman) and for the perpetuation of sexism. But within a relational context it can become magnified in shared parenting because the object of the father's guilt is not just the women he lives with but also the children he loves and feels responsible for. This is not to say that father guilt is limited only to the *sharing* father. Given that all fathers are involved in some parenting functions, any man who feels he is shirking his responsibilities (not spending enough time with the kids, not providing enough of an income) can experience guilt.

But the guilt is felt in relationship to something he *does*, in contrast to a more central and deep-seated guilt in mothers for something she *is*. Because of this the "sharing" man is less likely to be consumed by father guilt than the woman by mother guilt. Instead, he feels caught between parenting responsibilities and extrafamilial identity. When people ask him what his paid work is, nobody asks him, as they do his female partner, who takes care of the kids while he works. No one is awestruck by his dual responsibilities as worker and father; on the contrary, people and institutions will put pressure on him to perform as if he had no child-care responsibilities. And as a child who grew up believing he should make something of himself, that aspiration can gnaw at him. In Beauvoir's sense of "transcendence," being a successful parent does not qualify. Being successful or fulfilled in one's paid work or in public life does. Even when a man repudiates the work or public success ethic, as some men in our generation have done, he seldom turns to parenting as the locus of fulfillment and positive identity. This is well illustrated in the *San Francisco Chronicle* account of a financial wizard on Wall Street, a father of three, who took a year off to find himself. He spent his time lying on the couch, talking on the phone, collecting tropical fish, setting himself a "schedule bristling with physical, intellectual, and cultural self-improvement projects," and "marveling" at his wife's frantic schedule as homemaker and mother. His only parenting activity during this year was watching his son from behind a tree when his class had sports in the park.[31] Does this represent, at least in part, the actual content of "men's growing involvement in the family," which is making such a media splash? Coming home to a haven where one's own psychological needs can be nurtured is a far cry from taking on new responsibilities for the nurturance of others.

Gender-differentiated intrapsychic conflicts of sharing parents do not necessarily remain quietly within the mother's and father's heads. They appear in subtle male-female differences in actual parenting. The obvious difference often cited is that because of years of dolls and playing house, women will continue in our generation to make better parents than men because of their preparation and social induction into parenting. The woman, grappling with the repudiation of socially induced guilt that to mother less than full time is to abandon one's intimate relationship with the child, often vacillates among three stances: (1) overinvolvement with her child, often to prove to the world, her child, and herself that she is "supermom";[32] (2) respectful human interaction with her children based on her ability to explore both her parent and nonparent self and not carry the whole weight of parenting on her shoulders; (3) tension, frustration, or underlying resentment directed at the child (or other parent), reflecting her own struggle, in the face of institutional and ideological obstacles, to integrate her identity as both a mother and a nonparenting adult.

The sharing father is less likely to experience such a tension-ridden relationship or overinvolvement with the children. He is not consumed by guilt for not parenting enough; more likely, he is being raised to the level of sainthood in certain of his immediate circles for parenting at all. He can maintain effective boundaries between himself and his child and provide unconflicted warmth and nurturance. But with doing rather than being as the basis of day-to-day fathering, and with pressures to do something loftier than change diapers all day, the pull on the man may manifest itself instead in a psychic (or physical) disappearing act vis-à-vis the children, a phenomenon reminiscent of men's general coping style in other emotional relations. Instead of an overtly conflict-ridden relationship, the father's relationship with the children may be somewhat diluted in contrast to the mother's, or it may periodically dissipate. A father may feel the same frustration as a mother in trying to integrate parenting with other parts of his life, but he has a safety valve not as easily accessible to women. With more power in the outside world than women have and less indoctrination in the inevitability of parenthood as his primary adult role, he is freer to pull back from his parenting and direct more energy elsewhere. One mother reports that she had to leave town to accomplish the same redirection of energy away from parenting. The gender-related differences in handling this conflict are further exemplified in the following account. A mother was responsible for arranging child care for her child one year; the father was responsible the next year. Because she didn't have a paid job and felt it would allow her time with her child, the mother had consciously limited the number of days her child would attend child care during her year. In handling child-care arrangements for the following year, with the option of three or five days of child care per week, the father responded, "Five days of child care, of course. It's my freedom we're talking about."

The foregoing mother-father differences are most representative of sharing couples who try to balance parenting and outside work. It is somewhat different for the "one year on, one year off" parenting pair. Here, when Dad is "on," he is more firmly planted in his parenting seat; Mom is out working and just isn't there to take over. And Mom, by periodically finding herself structurally in the traditional fathering role, can theoretically make a cleaner break from being a hovering mother in her "working" year.[33] But the advantages of this model must be weighed against its problems: (1) It is becoming increasingly difficult as more people discover that one parent's income is financially insufficient. (2) Often the mother's "year on" is during the child's infancy, when mother is recovering from pregnancy and breastfeeding. It is also when strong infant-parent bonding is developing, bonding that carries into later years and makes Mom more central than Dad in the child's psyche. (3) Even with the "on again, off again" parenting model, both parents are integrally involved in the child's life, and for all the reasons cited above Mom is still often more involved in her children during her "off" years than Dad in his "off" times.

In sum, both women and men in shared parenting relationships find themselves in a dialectical tension between breaking away from and retreating back into gender-differentiated parenting. The challenge and success in breaking away from traditional fathering and mothering is one of the most exciting social projects for our generation. The parents of those of us who come from second-generation left families look at our own shared parenting relationships with admiration and some sense of loss and frustration that their historical moment did not open up the same consciousness and opportunities for them. At the same time, the difficulties we encounter in actually implementing shared parenting bring home to us the long-term nature of our project and the necessity of working on all three fronts at once —production, social reproduction, and ideology—in the reorganization of personal life.

In this project we remind ourselves that shared parenting is necessary not just for the development of healthier relationships between mothers and fathers but also for the elimination of destructive engenderment and the provision of healthier socialization experiences along socialist-feminist principles for our children. What reflections can be made about the possible outcomes for the children of sharing parents?

What Happens to the Children?

JESSE: Daddy, Daddy, pick me up.
DADDY: No, Jesse, I'm cooking dinner.
MOMMY: Come on, Jesse, I can pick you up. I'm your mother.
JESSE: No, Daddy's my mother.
(*Unsolicited statement from a three-year-old son of shared parents*)

We do not know what the long-term gender outcomes for the children of shared-parenting families will be. Most of these children are still growing and have yet to unfold their own full history. But we can make some predictions and analytic reflections on the basis of observations and theories of parenting, socialization, and engenderment.

According to Chodorow, "The sexual and familial division of labor in which women mother and are more involved in interpersonal, affective relationships than men produces in daughters and sons a division of psychological capacities which leads them to reproduce this sexual and familial division of labor."[34] This is not simply a product of behavioral modeling and imitation. It is the result of a complex set of family structures and relationships between child and same- and opposite-sex parents that resolve themselves in gender-specific personality constructs. It begins early in life when mother and mother alone becomes unique in the infant's eyes as the provider of primary care, and unfolds as the child attempts to individuate him- or herself from the parents and develop a self- and sexual identity. The daughter, according to Chodorow's analysis, raised by a same-sex parent, grows up with a sense of self as connected to the world. She has developed relational capacities and needs, a psychological sense of self in relationship to others. Sons, raised by opposite-sex parents, will develop a basic sense of self as separate, not in relation to another. This construct is predicated on the notion that object relations between same-sex parent and child will vary markedly from opposite-sex parent and child and that the child's development of a sense of self as male or female is critical in the formation and organization of personality.

In shared parenting situations that begin at the child's birth, the mother and father become equal in the child's eyes as individuals who provide primary care.[35] In contrast to the female-raised infant, a mother and a father are equally internalized early in the child's life. The infant's sense of self is developed in relationship to two people, a man and a woman. This means that later individuation of self will also be from two people, both a mother and a father. In shared-parenting situations fathers are no longer abstractions or once-in-a-while idealized figures to the young child; they are as real and concrete as mothers. And both girls and boys will have parallel struggles of individuation from like- and opposite-sex parents, albeit in different combination. They will have a parental interpersonal environment that is not gender-linked: both men and women will be available for strong emotional attachments. If different interpersonal environments for girls and boys in the family create different "feminine" and "masculine" personalities and preoccupations, an elimination of the different interpersonal environment through equal parenting by men and women should eliminate those personality differences.

But this is predicated on two assumptions: (1) that women and men are really equally involved in the parenting process, and (2) that families rather than the larger culture are the primal force in gender development. Concentrating first on the former assumption, we identified in the last section a tension that occurs in both men and women who attempt shared parenting at this moment in history, a tension that still draws women closer to the home and men farther away from it. What might be the effects of these subtle (or sometimes not so subtle) tensions on the children's development of gender identity and concepts?

Because of ideological pressures, institutional barriers, and their own psychological preparation for motherhood, many women experience much more inner turmoil than men in sharing parenting with another person and in balancing parenting with a nonparenting identity. This turmoil can influence the relationship between mother and child. Children now understand that Mom does other things besides take care of them; she goes out in the world, can be an effective human being outside the family sphere: mommies can be anything (if the society and internalized norms will let them). Mommy can also have more "quality" interactions with the child because she is not suffocated or psychologically withered by twenty-four-hour imprisonment in child-care responsibilities. But she is also under the strain of a great deal of ambivalence. After a frustrating day at work, where she spent half her day worrying about her child's day at school and the other half ill-treated by colleagues, employers, or internalized lack of confidence, she comes home to find that her daughter did indeed have a terrible day at school. (Father may have had an equally rotten day at work, but remember that he is probably carrying around less of the mental baggage of parenting.) Mother vacillates between wanting her child to disappear and wanting to quit her job immediately to be the kind of mother she ought to be. The child may experience some very schizoid qualities in the mother, a dynamic in which the mother draws her child close but at the same time resents the child for the guilt the child induces in her. The child also experiences the mother's drift into "taking over," the competition with the father for the parenting role that is still the mother's most legitimate sphere of power, the "bossing" or directives to Daddy who is just not as attuned to "mothering" as Mommy. If the mother herself cannot resolve how much of a mother she is going to be, her children may concurrently experience the parallel ambivalence—how much of a mommy is she? And what exactly is a woman's primary identity in life?

Fathers, we have said, also feel a pull between their parenting and nonparenting identities. The child of the sharing father experiences intimacy and nurturance from a man. The child learns that Daddy, like Mommy, is a day-to-day real person in the family sphere. But if the child experiences resentment from the father for the sapping of an otherwise productive worklife, that child must integrate the male nurturance received with the negativity of experiencing her- or himself as a drain. Equally likely, the father, rather than expressing direct hostility, will at times slip off his fathering cape and do a psychological disappearing act. He simply makes himself less accessible to the child.

But relating to children involves more than the behavioral manifestations of conflicts and ambivalences around parenting. There is also the laundry list of things daddies do with the kids versus things mommies do with the kids. In my own observation this varies so enormously from one shared-parenting family to another that it is nearly impossible to generate a common profile. But some salient differences repeatedly appear: Sharing mothers get more involved in their children's peer relations, worry more if their children are well liked, spend more time talking to friends about their children, buy the children's clothes, wash dirty faces and comb hair more, and do more things *at home* with the kids. In contrast, sharing fathers take their kids on more outings, take more overnight (often work-related) trips away from home, spend more time reading in the same room as the child, put kids' clothes on backward, do not "fly off the handle" with the children as much, are able to distance themselves more from the children's squabbles and peer conflicts, and (sad but true) engage in more rough-and-tumble play with the kids. These differences accurately reflect the dynamics of a somewhat more involved mother and a more "balanced" but sometimes more distant father.

There is also the more complicated issue of whom Mom and Dad are modeling their parenting after. Shared parenting involves moving men away from the social definition of fathering into the sphere of socially defined mothering. Whereas a woman too moves away from traditional mothering in taking on a nonparenting adult role as well as sharing primary caretaking with another person, in her actual *parenting* behavior it is more likely that she thinks back, both consciously and unconsciously, to her own *mother* in developing parenting skills. But who does the man reflect back on, identify with, when he "mothers"? One sharing father reports that he thinks of both his mother and his father when he conceptualizes himself as a parent: more of his mother for everyday situations, more of his father for a global conception of himself as a parent. Sharing fathers may present to their children a more integrated identity of parent, resulting from a more complete merging of elements of both mother and father from their own childhood.

These patterns are not universals for either men or women in shared parenting situations, but they are commonly observed and reported patterns in my own experience and collection of accounts. Inasmuch as they do exist, the implication is that gender-differentiated interpersonal environments are not easily eliminated in shared-parenting families. Still, the children of the "fifty-fifty" generation will experience, the difference between a more involved mother and more distant father in a much reduced or subtle form. To what extent this will affect the children of these families or reproduce gender differences remains to be seen. There is no doubt that male children, given the models and relationship with their sharing father, will grow up more prepared to "mother" than their own fathers:

> Our child Blake is now in fourth grade. One of the most touch-
> ing things about him is that he "instinctively" loves to take care of
> younger children. This isn't for approval or even for show. It's be-
> cause his early memories include not solely his mother, but as far
> back and just as often, this grumpy lovable old shoe of a person who
> snored sometimes when cuddling his baby to sleep.[36]

But within the structural family context, their sisters may still have at least a slight edge over them. And both boys and girls may still retain a notion of mothering differentiated from fathering, as opposed to a global notion of parenting. In the dialogue introducing this section it is not insignifi-cant that three-year-old Jesse made daddy into a "mother" as the one who would pick him up and care for him.

We are not only concerned, however, about our children's ability to par-ent. We are also concerned about what kind of human beings they will grow up to be—their sense of competence, their empathy and capacity to love, their sexuality, their political and social consciousness. Here is where we must look at the second assumption. The child of sharing parents, like other children, does not grow up in a family vacuum. She or he is social-ized in day-care centers, schools, and other institutions in which women remain primary caretakers and sex-typing abounds. The media are also a constant and pervasive force in children's lives. It is probably true that out-side their own father, close friends, or relatives, and occasional successes in drawing men into day-care or early childhood settings, young children will meet up with very few men in their everyday lives.[37] Notes coming home from school addressed to mother or inviting *mother* to participate in class reinforce this tendency. And whereas definite gains have been made by the feminist movement in alleviating sexist practices and structures in social institutions, the fact remains that sexist divisions are still prevalent—in the job market, in the school curriculum, in most people's families, in media content, and elsewhere. Television, in particular, bombards the child with sex-role stereotypes and presents a world where shared parenting is vir-tually unknown. Extrafamilial institutions are strong forces in the child's life, not just in the behavioral shaping or reinforcement of actions but in the development of the child's cognitive and emotional constructs of "who

I am" in the world as a male or female. For the child of sharing parents, these influences are often in direct contradiction to the intent and effect of non-gender-divided socialization at home.

What effects do we see of these influences on the child of shared parenting? Superficially, in a day-care center or classroom you cannot easily pick out shared-parented children from a crowd. They know that girls can be doctors and boys play with dolls, but so do a lot of other kids exposed to nonsexist curricula. They know that mommies can go off to work in the morning, but so do children of single mothers or of working mothers in nonsharing two-parent households. Despite all conscious practices to the contrary at home, the girls may look as "fem" and the boys as "macho" as any of their classmates. Influenced in the cognitive organization of their experience by the normative structures of the world around them, at pre-school age they may look you straight in the eye and tell you only men can be lawyers (even though their own mother is a lawyer) or that mommies stay home and do all the cooking and daddies go off to work (even though Dad made meals all week while Mom was off at a conference). In a society where more and more of a child's socialization experiences occur outside the home, societal norms and standards are bound to affect a child's self-concept and organization of social experience.

The influence of gender-based ideological, productive, and reproductive forces does not wait to impinge on the child just as he or she leaves the sanctity of the home to face the outside world. The parents also become mediators of the culture, either intentionally or unintentionally, as it relates to gender development. For example, if the children are aware that Daddy's paid work receives more social recognition than Mommy's, this may well affect their self-identity and their concept of gender. If Mommy's work is more marginal or seasonal, the children may integrate that fact into their concept of who a mommy is and who a daddy is. If the sharing mother is in an ill temper, her child may accuse her of being a witch or a mean old stepmother. No similar social insult falls off the tongue for a mean male parent. Also, the parents' ongoing process of transcending their own gender-linked socialization is witnessed and possibly absorbed by the child. The child cannot help noticing that Daddy may be clumsier with the sewing machine and Mommy a bit more awkward with the tools.

But the children are not passive in all this. They bring to the situation a cognitive and social set largely determined by experiences in their most intimate environment. The child is an active participant in making sense of that situation. Scratching below the surface of appearances, we do discover some distinctive characteristics of shared-parenting children. For example, a six-year-old daughter is watching *The Brady Bunch* on TV. Alice, the maid in the show, is in her apron washing the dinner dishes.

> SHARING MOTHER: What do you think about Alice working for the Brady's, getting paid to do all their cooking and cleaning?
> DAUGHTER (in irritated voice): Mom, she doesn't get paid. She just lives there.
> MOTHER: Oh, well what do you think about her *not* getting paid and doing their work?
> DAUGHTER (in a tolerant voice): Mom, they all take turns. This is just Alice's night to do the dishes. And then the mommy takes a turn, and then the daddy. She just likes living with them.

In other words, Alice is just a collective member (who happens to wear an apron) in this sharing household of both parents and nonparents. While any child today exposed to "Free to Be You and Me" can spout a rhetoric of expanded options for women and men in the world, it is the children of sharing parents who deeply internalize these understandings from exposure to their own family experience. In their developmental progression they indeed may go through a preschool stage, as mentioned earlier, where normative societal features appear more salient than intimate family experience, but over the long term they reveal a clear and "taken for granted" conceptualization of both mothers and fathers as both parents and as nonparents. Whereas many children of single parents grow up with an internalized concept of *one* parent (usually the mother) as also an outside worker, it is in shared parenting that children are presented, within their family experience, with parenting reorganization for both men and women. They not only know that mothers can go out and work; they also know that fathers can nurture them, cuddle them, and run the house for days at a time.

In the great burst of studies supporting nonsexist education, numerous findings pointed to the greater cognitive competence and creativity in children who were not sex-typed.[38] This referred not only to children of shared parents but to any child who was not socialized into sex-stereotyped functioning. By extrapolation, however, it makes sense that a low degree of sex-typing within the family would occur where women and men actively merge socially defined aspects of "masculinity" and "femininity" into their own functioning. Inasmuch as sharing parents do this, their children ought to have high levels of competence and creativity. While the family's class, social position, and content of parental practices, not to mention school experience, are obviously also strong determinants of a child's competence and creativity, my observations do attest to the sense of assuredness, initiative, and innovativeness with which many children of shared parents move through the world. They not only receive messages of what men, women, and therefore any person *can* do; they actively watch and experience their own mothers and fathers doing it. In a society where gender is still so important, these internalized experiences become critical to an expanded notion of self.

One problem, however, is that we may be creating family structures where boys and girls both get to observe directly what was traditionally "feminine," albeit now done by women and men, while the traditionally "masculine" functions remain abstract. Few modern households necessitate a large number of heavy physical activities. Either outside experts are called in or mechanical devices do the work that was traditionally "masculine" and done in the home (carpentry, plumbing, heavy yard work). What is left for the children to observe and experience is mothers and fathers actively involved in traditionally "feminine" tasks—child rearing, housekeeping, and the like. Then Mom or Dad disappear each day into the abstract world of paid work, which is for the most part separate from the child's direct experience. What opportunity do the children have to *directly* observe Mom and Dad functioning in traditionally "masculine" tasks? Compared with direct observation of feminine tasks, very little. If we accept that gender reorganization should include a blending of the socially defined masculine and feminine, then parents must in addition not only bring children to their workplaces (which, unfortunately, often tends to be sex-segregated) but must also be conscious of infusing into the child's immediate experience a greater degree an awareness of Mom and Dad functioning in spheres stereotypically of male domain.[39]

We can speculate that children of shared parenting will develop a greater sense of trust in the world than children with only one primary parent. They grow up with a confidence that at least two persons, rather than just one, can offer them basic nurturance and security. One could also predict that monogamy would not be as deeply ingrained. If monogamy is in part shaped in the child's psyche by the original mother-infant possessive dyad, breaking up the dyad with basic nurturing from another person conceivably shapes in the child a concept of love beyond a *pas de deux*. We might even predict an expanded notion of sexuality, perhaps a greater incidence of bisexuality. With primary care coming equally from women and men, and with individuation from both a father and a mother, rapprochement will also be toward a man and a woman for children of either sex. If gender becomes a less central factor in who these children are, then sexuality may be more loosely tied to whether the object of love is male or female. But these are areas in which we must wait patiently for the children to grow to adulthood and unfold their own stories.

Both the new right and left-wing critics of feminism condemn the notion of children growing up in anything but traditional nuclear families; they see a life of narcissism, neurosis, or psychopathy stemming from the breakdown of authority in the family. What becomes confused in their argument is the differentiation between *authority* and *authoritarianism*. Children of sharing parents indeed understand a hierarchy of responsibility and the "leadership" position of their parents in the family. What they do not experience is the unilateral power base of a patriarchal father who offers conditional love in exchange for unconditional submission. Because these children continually observe two adults democratically negotiating decision-making and division of responsibility in the home, they are presented with a new model of authority based on collectivity and flexibility rather than unchallenged power. When two people fully share the parenting responsibility, one cannot simply criticize the other's parenting as a role foreign to him- or herself. The criticism comes within a joint endeavor in which they must mutually arrive at a parenting solution satisfying to both. Thus mutuality and consensus, rather than directives and compliance, further inform the child's internalization of democratic processes. In the actual parent-child interaction, the child learns quite early that authority does not lie in just one person's hands; there are always two, whom the child can equally approach or consult on matters requiring parental decisions or guidance. Neither parent unilaterally holds the purse strings, manages the household, or enforces disciplinary actions. With authority more diffused than centralized, the child has more room to move as a meaningful participant in family decisions and functioning.

Shared parenting alters authority relations not only between parent and child but between males and females. With all the qualifications noted above, shared-parenting families substitute "unisex" parenting for the "instrumental-emotional" gender division of traditional families. Girls and boys develop a new understanding of equal authority among males and females. Even though all children in our culture have no doubt been affected by the Wonder Woman mystique, girls and boys in shared-parenting families understand at a concrete level, not just in surreal fantasies, the strength and independence of women vis-à-vis men and the possibility of equality, rather than dominance-submission, in male-female relationships. This is often translated into peer relationships in which daughters are pugnacious, audacious, and stalwart in their interactions with boys, and sons have a healthy respect and acceptance of the social power of girls.

While trust, democratic impulses, and a balancing of social power between females and males may be outcomes for these children, a smothering from overparenting is also possible. An ostensible advantage of shared parenting is that with two (or more) primary caretakers, one of the caretakers can comfortably take "time off," have private space away from the children. The reality, however, is that shared parenting often leads to a consciousness of "on all the time" for both parents. From the point of view of the child, not just one parent but two parents are actively ego-involved in the child's development. Not just one but both parents tell the child to drag an umbrella to school on a rainy day. The potential for overprotectiveness, overinvolvement, or a stifling of autonomy is obvious. Also, the implication for *two* parents now totally absorbed in parenting consciousness is potential "parent burn-out" in not just one but two people, leaving the child with two strung-out parents.

There is no doubt that children growing up in a shared-parenting household are exposed to a different socialization experience than are children from other family structures. When Daddy can be mother, something crucial has changed. But we must wait to see what the *adult* personality outcomes of these children will be. In the reorganization of gender, the degree of reduction in the female-male division of psychological capacities can help us understand the significance of family structure and processes in producing gender. If female and male differences are indeed reduced in these people, compared with people who did not experience shared parenting, we will find validation for the primacy of family structure in gender development. If these children grow up with psychological capacities undifferentiated from families where parenting is more conventional, this will reflect either the greater primacy of extraparental forces or the ineffectiveness of shared parenting in successfully reorganizing gender-related parenting (or both). These experiences will help us understand the ways in which reproduction, production, and ideology interpenetrate and can thus inform our strategy for transforming gender relations.

Conclusion

I have analyzed the experiences of a very small group of people in this country. At the same time, all signs show a rapidly changing family structure in which parents do not live in nuclear families at all or, when they do, both continue in the labor market. Disequilibrium is great right now; the concurrent pressures of work and what is experienced as "family upheaval" overwhelm many. For these reasons a reorganization of parenting becomes for many not a "choice," as it has been for most who attempt shared parenting, but a necessity. It is this necessity that gives us on the left the leverage to introduce a new concept of family structure that challenges both the sex/gender system and capitalist modes of reproduction. The new right has developed partly by addressing people's fears about the rapidly deteriorating quality of life. Recognizing people's concern for the future, particularly the well-being of their children, the new right offers reactionary programs which, retreating to old patriarchal forms, claim to save unborn offspring from murder, shield families from untoward homosexual influence, and put the dollar back in the family's pocket where it belongs. The left and the women's movement have to address the concerns that underlie these issues. Many of us have begun to look more closely at issues of family or personal life. Some have taken the tack of defending or rebuilding the family in the face of capitalist attack. Others feel wary of an approach which, by uncritically "defending the family," tends to reproduce the romantic, antifeminist thrust of the new right. We need to demonstrate the ability of *new* social and family structures to provide the satisfactions that people legitimately long for: emotional and sexual intimacy, child rearing by caring people, a sense of community.

In the latter context, shared parenting is an important political effort. It challenges an oppressive feature of the family—the universality of motherhood. Shared parenting frees women from the dual burden of paid and unpaid work, affords men access to the growth and development of children and children access to the growth and development of men, and helps to eliminate gender-linked divisions between males and females that reproduce the sex/gender system.

But shared parenting must also be seen as only one aspect of the larger demand for new forms of personal life to replace the decaying traditional nuclear family and provide solutions to the problems of personal tension, violence, and loneliness experienced by so many. We need to restructure social responsibility for children so that not just mothers and fathers but also nonfamily members have access to and responsibility for the care of children. What is labeled by many as a crisis of the family should more aptly be approached as a historical shift in family structure. In this period of flux, we can try to create and sustain a new fluidity between family and nonfamily for the responsibility of children, a greater involvement of men in this process, new kinds of authority relations between parents and children, and forms other than the traditional nuclear family in which people can choose to live. These goals necessitate addressing the interpenetration of reproduction, production, and ideology. These goals will not be achieved overnight. Yet we know much *can* be accomplished, and such efforts will be an increasingly important part of political and social life in the coming years.

Notes

Acknowledgments: I want to thank Nancy Chodorow, Jim Hawley, Barry Kaufman, Gail Kaufman, Joanna Levine, Elli Meeropol, Robby Meeropol, David Plotke, Marcy Whitebook, and the Socialist Review West collective for their criticism and support in writing this paper.

1. Joseph Pleck, *Men's New Roles in the Family: Housework and Child Care* (Ann Arbor, Mich.: Institute for Social Research, 1976). This model is often linked to a broader demand for fuller involvement not just by both biological parents but by other "significant others" in the child's life, either housemates, relatives, or intimate friends. Here, however, I look specifically at the relationships of mother and father.

2. See, e.g., Betty Friedan, "Feminism Takes a New Turn," *New York Times Magazine*, 16 November 1979; Caroline Bird, *The Two-Paycheck Marriage* (New York: Rawson-Wade, 1979); Jane Geniesse, "On Wall Street: The Man Who Gave Up Working," *San Francisco Chronicle*, 13 November 1979; Lindsy Van Gelder, "An Unmarried Man," *Ms.*, November 1979.

3. Rosalind Petchesky, "Dissolving the Hyphen: A Report on Marxist-Feminist Groups 1–5," in Z. Eisenstein, ed. *Capitalist Patriarchy and the Case for Socialist Feminism* (New York: Monthly Review Press, 1978), 376.

4. Nancy Press Hawley, "Shared Parenthood," in Boston Women's Health Collective, *Ourselves and Our Children* (New York: Random House, 1978). This framework differentiates shared *parenting* from shared *custody*, in which children go back and forth between separated or divorced parents.

5. Alice Abarbenal, "Redefining Motherhood," in Louise Kapp Howe, ed., *The Future of the Family* (New York: Simon & Schuster, 1972), 349.

6. According to 1979 U.S. Department of Labor statistics 28 percent of American households consist of both a father and a mother who are wage earners, in contrast to 17 percent in which father is the sole wage earner and mother is a full-time homemaker.

7. Zillah Eisenstein, "Developing a Theory of Capitalist Patriarchy and Socialist Feminism," in Eisenstein, *Capitalist Patriarchy*, 29; also Chapter 4 in this book.

8. See Selma Fraiberg, *In Defense of Mothering: Every Child's Birthright* (New York: Basic Books, 1977); and Alice Rossi, "A Biosocial Perspective on Parenting," *Daedalus*, Spring 1977, pp. 1–31.

9. Susan Stewart, "Working Women Don't Get All the Breaks," *Los Angeles Times*, 31 August 1977.

10. The alteration of family relationships between men and women was most often translated into a direct demand for sharing of housework (see, e.g., Pat Mainardi, "The Politics of Housework," in Robin Morgan, ed., *Sisterhood Is Powerful* [New York: Vintage Books, 1970]). The lack of attention given to men as *fathers* in the family can likely be explained by the childlessness of most of the women involved in the feminist movement in the late 1960s to early 1970s. Parenting was an issue that did not hit home for the majority of the women in the movement. Those who were in fact parents were often afraid or ashamed to admit it. At that moment in history, motherhood became for many a politically incorrect act.

11. Sidney Blumenthal, "A Baby Boom in the 80's?" *In These Times*, 30 August–5 September 1978.

12. Frederick Engels, in *The Woman Question* (New York: International Publishers, 1951).

13. Alice Rossi, "Equality between the Sexes: An Immodest Proposal," *Daeda-

lus, Spring 1964; reprinted in Robert J. Lifton, ed., *The Woman in America* (Boston: Beacon Press, 1967).

14. Kenneth Pitchford, "The Manly Art of Child Care," *Ms.*, October 1978, p. 98.

15. D. Baldwin, "Motherhood and the Liberated Woman," *San Francisco Chronicle*, 12 October 1978.

16. Abarbenal, "Redefining Motherhood," 366.

17. Cf. Ann Oakley, *Women's Work* (New York: Vintage Books, 1974), chap. 8, "Myths of Woman's Place, 2: Motherhood"; Wini Breines, Margaret Cerullo, and Judith Stacey, "Social Biology, Family Studies, and Antifeminist Backlash," *Feminist Studies*, February 1978, pp. 43–68.

18. Nancy Chodorow, *The Reproduction of Mothering: Psychoanalysis and the Sociology of Gender* (Berkeley: University of California Press, 1978).

19. See n. 2 above.

20. Sheila Rowbotham, *Woman's Consciousness, Man's World* (Baltimore, Md.: Penguin, 1973), 61.

21. Oakley, *Woman's Work*, p. 220.

22. Abarbenal, "Redefining Motherhood," 360. This reaction is paralleled in the public sphere of work by the resistance of female child-care workers to allowing men in their field, as it is one area of paid work where women do have control (and can get jobs).

23. Quoted interview in Hawley, "Shared Parenthood," 134. This desire to maintain parenting within woman's sphere as a source of power may have had some influence, conscious or unconscious, on the feminist movement's tendency to avoid demands for fathers' involvement in parenting.

24. David Steinberg, "Redefining Fatherhood: Notes after Six Months," in Louise Kappe Howe, ed., *The Future of the Family* (New York: Simon and Schuster, 1972), 370.

25. Oakley, *Woman's Work*, 211, 189.

26. Hawley, "Shared Parenthood," 139.

27. Rowbotham, *Woman's Consciousness*, 76.

28. Barbara Chasen, "Sex Role Stereotyping and Pre-Kindergarten Teachers," *Elementary School Journal*, 1974, pp. 74, 225–35.

29. "A Father Who Failed as a Mother," *San Francisco Chronicle*, 6 September 1978.

30. In the general population, the large number of desertions or failures to pay alimony or child payments by fathers testifies to the male-female difference in "parenting permanence"; the number of women who similarly desert their parenting role is infinitesimal in comparison.

31. Jane Geniesse, "On Wall Street: The Man Who Gave Up Working," *San Francisco Chronicle*, 13 November 1979. *Ms.* magazine has reported similar situations.

32. This is parallel to the phenomenon that many lesbian mothers feel even more strongly. To answer society's accusations that they are unfit mothers, they are constantly under pressure to be even better than the best moms.

33. The importance of this structural position, often outweighing the saliency of gender, is highlighted in the account of a lesbian parent who holds a paid job while her partner, the actual biological mother of the child, stays home to care for the baby. She reports feeling just like a father when she arrives home, wanting to be cared for and attended to by her partner after a long day at work.

34. Chodorow, *Reproduction of Mothering*, 7.

35. The exception is in the provision of food, which in breastfed babies will obviously be done by women. While food and sucking certainly are core concerns of the newborn baby, substantial evidence from both humans and monkeys indicates that touch, warmth, softness, and responsiveness are equally if not more important to the infant. This allows for equal sharing of the provision of basic needs by both women and men, even when mother is the only source of food (see Oakley, *Women's Work*, chap. 8). This is not to deny the reality that mothers' lactation has often erupted as a point of tension between parents attempting to share equally their infant's caretaking—including jealousy in men and resentment or feelings of added importance in women.

36. Pitchford, "Manly Art," 89.

37. Despite ideological commitments or policy statements striving toward equal involvement by men and women, I have never been involved in a parent co-op daycare program where the men have been able or willing to participate as regularly as the women.

38. See Eleanor Maccoby and Carol Jacklin, *The Psychology of Sex Differences* (Stanford, Calif.: Stanford University Press, 1974).

39. My thanks to Nancy Chodorow for her thoughts on this aspect of shared parenting.

Sexuality and Pornography

20   I'm Black and Blue from the Rolling Stones and I'm Not Sure How I Feel about It:

Pornography and the Feminist Imagination

Kate Ellis

The Debate on Sexuality

In 1976 a group of angry southern California feminists organized a protest that forced Warner Brothers to remove a billboard of a woman in chains with bruises on her legs and face, and a caption reading, "I'm black and blue from the Rolling Stones and I love it." The billboard could not be called pornographic by traditional definitions; it was meant to sell records, not to arouse. Nevertheless, it contained a number of elements that over the next few years would be drawn together by feminists under the heading of pornography: the display of a woman's body for purposes of selling a product, the depiction of women as victims of violence, and the suggestion that women find this stance exciting. At the 1978 San Francisco conference on "Feminist Perspectives on Pornography," organized by

Source: This article is reprinted from *Socialist Review* Nos. 75–76 (May–August 1984), pp. 103–25, by permission of the publisher, *Socialist Review*, 3202 Adeline, Berkeley, CA 94703.

Women against Violence in Pornography and Media (WAVPM), a definition of pornography emerged that equated it with violence against women even when violence was not itself depicted. As similar (though not uniform) organizations sprang up in other cities—Women against Pornography (New York, 1979), Women against Violence against Women (Cincinnati, Philadelphia, and numerous other places), Women against Sexist Violence in Pornography and Media (Pittsburgh)—and several anthologies and books placed pornography at the center of women's oppression, it was the hope of the organizers and writers that this was one issue on which all women could unite.

Instead, the women's movement has been divided, with a degree of bitterness that shocks both sides. When a conference on sexuality was organized at Barnard College in 1982, the conference planners, of whom I was one, felt that there had been only one feminist perspective on pornography advanced by the movement up to that point. Having decided to address "women's sexual pleasure, choice, and autonomy, acknowledging that sexuality is simultaneously a domain of restriction, repression, and danger as well as a domain of exploration, pleasure, and agency,"[1] we were unprepared—perhaps naively—for the intensity of the counter-attack. A leaflet handed out to those attending the conference began thus: "We are a coalition of radical feminists and lesbian feminists who have joined together to protest this conference's promotion of one perspective on sexuality and its silencing of the views of a major portion of the feminist movement." The leaflet went on to focus on particular groups (No More Nice Girls, Samois, the Lesbian Sex Mafia) and individual members of those groups whose sexual politics it labeled reprehensible: "For all of their claims of radicalism all of the organizations and individuals listed above are advocating the same kind of patriarchal sexuality that flourishes in our culture's mainstream, that is channeled into crimes against women, and that is institutionalized in pornography." The key word here is "advocating," as if the mere discussion of certain sexual practices could not but slip into an advocacy so persuasive that it would overwhelm feminism's fragile gains.

Anyone who wants to get beyond the rumors should read the concept paper that Carole Vance delivered at the opening plenary of the conference and the descriptions of the workshops—also printed in the *Diary of a Conference on Sexuality*, which was put out by the planning committee, initially suppressed by Barnard, then finally released with all mention of the college deleted. The opposition of Barnard and of the Helena Rubenstein Foundation, which withdrew its funding from future conferences, is easy to understand. These are institutions that want to confine feminism within very narrow limits. What I attempt to explore here is what was at stake

among the opposing camps of feminists, what we who planned the conference saw and rejected in the antipornography vision, and why we believe it
is necessary to go beyond it.

At the simplest level, what was unforgivable in the eyes of the authors
of the leaflet was that the conference planners did not invite speakers who
espoused their perspective, while the speakers who were invited did not
single out certain sexual practices—in particular butch-femme role-playing
and sado-masochism (s/m)—and call them patriarchal. This might seem
like a minor semantic point, but it is not. When the conference diary was
impounded by the Barnard administration in order to prevent its distribution on the day of the conference, Andrea Dworkin got hold of a copy,
photocopied it, and sent it to a wide range of people with the following
warning:

> There is no feminist standard, I believe, by which this material and
> these arguments taken as a whole are not perniciously anti-woman
> and antifeminist. It is doubtful, in my view, if the feminist movement
> can maintain its political integrity or moral authority with this kind
> of attack on its fundamental and essential premises from within.

I would like to question the truth of that accusation, the assumptions on
which it rests, and the possible reasons for its appearance at this time in the
history of the women's movement and in this political climate. For many
feminists and people concerned with feminism, the passion spent in discussing pornography, s/m, and other sexual issues is passion that might be
better directed against the feminization of poverty or attacks on reproductive rights. But here I would agree with Dworkin: what is being fought out,
I believe, is the very nature and thus to some extent the future direction of
our movement.

At the core of the debate is the meaning of the word "pornography" itself. The antipornography movement is not always consistent, but there is a
tendency to extend the concept of pornography in such a way that it could
cover almost all representations of women. Asked if they objected to pornography when there was no violence, Laura Lederer and Diana Russell,
two of that movement's leaders, responded yes. "Not all pornography is violent," they said, "but even the most banal pornography objectifies women's
bodies." They went on to say that "an essential ingredient of much rape
and other forms of violence to women is the 'objectification' of women."[2]
Pornography depicts violence or causes violence or both. All pornography
is therefore violent.

Gloria Steinem is making a similar point when she distinguishes between two forms of representation: pornography and erotica. "'Erotica,'" she says, "is rooted in 'eros' or passionate love, and thus in the idea of positive choice, free will, the yearning for a particular person." Pornography, on the other hand, means "'writing about' or 'description of,' which puts still more distance between subject and object, and replaces a spontaneous yearning for closeness with objectification and voyeurism."[3] This distinction between responding to a person and responding to an image makes a very heavy value judgment on representation and "looking at," which are surely involved in sexual practices (masturbation, for instance) that none of us would want to avoid entirely. In Steinem's view, sexuality inspired by erotica is caring and tender, in contrast to pornographically inspired sex, which is alienated and emotionless. In her ideal world, nothing would stimulate either party except the physical presence of the other.

I want to argue for a feminist sexuality that is open to artifice as well as spontaneity, representation and fantasy as well as the much less controllable world around us that Susan Griffin (see below) might call "nature." To imagine such a sexuality means loosening the connections, which feminists in the consciousness-raising groups of the late 1960s and early 1970s discovered and insisted on, between fantasies, the artifacts that produce them, and sexist behavior. It means making a distinction, for instance, between violence in the world and the staged scenes of consensual aggression and role playing that certain feminists call s/m[4] but which the anti-porn movement labeled "violence" and (when depicted) "violent pornography." Some of these elements of artifice might not, in isolation, be feminist as any or all of us understand the term. But I would argue that in striving to create a sexual practice in which each component conforms to a public conception of pro-woman practice, anti-porn feminism has made our proposed revolution unappealing even to some of us who want such a revolution. And seeing violence against women everywhere makes it less, not more likely that we will have it.

What are these fundamental and essential premises that are being called into question by a refusal to label particular sexual practices and predilections patriarchal? To answer this, it is helpful to go back to the early days of the second wave of feminism, the late 1960s and early 1970s, when the realization that this is indeed a sexist society, one that *systematically* creates women unequal, was exhilarating and disturbing but above all new. One way of documenting the discovery was to point to the ways in which women were depicted in the mass media. "Objectification" became a key word in describing this depiction by and for (as we then insisted) male consumption. We were not physically controlled by a father or husband who had the literal power of life and death over us, but a more impersonal power was killing us softly with Clairol ads.

In the years since the women's movement made itself publicly visible, it has worked to revise public consciousness about the female of the species in industrialized countries. In many important respects, we insisted, we were not all that different from men. We could run large corporations as well as they could, perform operations, argue cases and judge them, work in mines or drive forklifts, put out fires or handle squad cars. Whether or not we wanted a world in which these were the jobs to divide up was a matter for debate, but there was no disagreement about capability. And of course men were just as good at typing, filing, answering phones, and running a sewing machine as we were.

One result of all this hard work is that the demand of women for equality is slowly becoming embedded in mainstream public consciousness; hence the public realm has been altered. A "gender gap" has emerged in voting patterns. Johnny Carson has been heard saying "his or her." The working woman has taken her place alongside the housewife as a norm, a market, a locus for glamour and fulfillment. But as women probed the roots of their inequality and of male power, they came into increasing contact with the ugliest manifestation of both: male violence (including, but not limited to sexual violence) against women and against children of both sexes. In looking for the source of this persistent horror, rather than simply seeking to bandage the resulting cuts and bruises, many feminists focused on the lucrative pornography industry. Sensing a dramatic rise in the incidence of violence against women despite the best efforts of their movement, or perhaps as a response to them, these feminists developed a dedicated following among women who shared their anger and frustration, and who came to share their view of the world.[5] They concluded, it would seem, that any woman who doesn't share that view is not angered at or frustrated by the persistence of male domination. How could such a woman be a feminist? What does feminism mean if not the public expression of that very anger and frustration?

These are the steps, then, by which the feminist opponents of particular sexual practices that they deem "male" or "patriarchal" have come to see their movement as an endangered species, threatened in its very core by women who engage in these practices or defend the right of others to do so. The outlines of their position are these: the oppression of women is valorized and maintained by a pornography industry that shows women acting out their own degradation because men find that arousing. If women find these postures arousing, it is because they have internalized the patriarchal culture that informs them. A truly feminist sexuality is not grounded in that culture and is not aroused by images of dominance and submission but only by images of tenderness and mutuality, or erotica. Therefore, the most radical task, the one that goes to the root of the oppression of women, lies in removing pornography and pornographic images from their central place in our culture. This cultural alteration is not censorship, its proponents insist. It is, rather, the radical task that feminists have set themselves from the inception of this second wave: changing the world and the way we are perceived in it. Could any but the fainthearted object?

A major stumbling block in this debate over sexuality is the assertion, made not only in the anti-Barnard-conference leaflet but also fairly widely in the feminist media, that one cannot be a feminist and disagree with the foregoing scenario.[6] By laying out what I believe to be the grounds for objection to this view by the Barnard conference planners and their sympathizers, my aim is to move the discussion beyond this unproductive and harmful phase. The potential value of that discussion, on the other hand, is that it forces feminists to look again at certain assumptions that we have taken to be axioms of our movement, to probe more deeply the process by which consciousness is formed and changed. The issue of pornography and its role in a feminist program for change brings up the conflicting assumptions upon which both sides of the debate rest, which is undoubtedly why it has become such a central issue.

Images of Pornography

The view of pornography put forward by WAVPM and its spin-off groups, by Susan Griffin and Andrea Dworkin in book-length studies of the subject, and by authors of the pieces in the two anthologies *Take Back the Night* and *Against Sadomasochism*, as well as several periodicals addressing themselves to feminist issues,[7] can be summed up in Robin Morgan's often quoted slogan "Pornography is the theory; rape is the practice." That is, pornography causes violence against women and is itself a form of violence against women. How one gets from the pornographic image to the violent, woman-abusing man involves a model for the formation of consciousness, and the antipornography movement relies on basically three: a stimulus-response model, a psychoanalytic model, and an essentialist model. Taking up each in turn, I point up where my disagreement with it lies.

When the President's Commission on Pornography and Obscenity published its findings in 1970, it concluded that a connection between the use of pornography and sexually violent behavior had not been proved by the data. Its members speculated that materials produced with the specific intent of arousing men functioned as a source of catharsis for their sexual frustrations, which might otherwise get acted out in the world. Rather than supporting a causal link between pornography and violent behavior, the logic of catharsis suggests that without pornography there would be more violence on the part of its male consumers. Since then, however, several researchers have conducted experiments whose results support the anti-pornography position. Edward Donnerstein of the University of Wisconsin is the principal source, along with Neil Malmuth and his associates at the University of Manitoba, of clinical studies that claim to prove a link between exposure to pornography and sexual violence.

These researchers follow a "learning theory" or "behavior modification" explanation for their findings. Donnerstein found that male students who had seen a four-minute film of a rape at gunpoint administered severer shocks to subjects than those who had seen a clip from a talk show or a nonviolent love scene.[8] Moreover, the shocks they delivered to women were more intense than those they inflicted on men. Donnerstein was measuring aggressive behavior, and he concluded that pornographic materials increased it. In one of Malmuth's studies, subjects were shown the films *Swept Away* and *The Getaway* while a control group watched feature-length films with no sexual aggression in them. A week later, they were given questionnaires testing the degree to which they accepted myths about rape: that women like it, want it, seek it. He found that the level of acceptance of these myths was higher among those who had seen the films with more male aggression in them. In another study he found that men were more aroused by a story of rape if they had read another story with violence in it beforehand.[9]

In all these studies a single stimulus and response is being made to stand in for a long conditioning process. It is assumed that repeated contacts with pornography will elicit the same response and thus "condition" it, so that it will come forth in the absence of the original stimulus, the pornographic image. Men will then respond to real women the way they have been "conditioned" to respond to them by that image. This is the logic behind the claim of the feminist antipornography movement that consumers of pornography "are conditioned by text and images to disavow their sentiments of caring and to abdicate their social responsibility for respect in female-male relationships and for nurturance in adult-child relationships." From there, Judith Bat-Ada goes on to claim that "men are using mass media to break apart values and create new cultural patterns" whose dictates women "have no choice but to follow."[10]

Suggestive and compelling as this conditioning analogy may be, it lacks real parallelism. Pavlov's dog, presented with a sound stimulus and an edible reward, learned to respond to the bell even in the absence of a dish of food, as if the food were there. But in a darkened theater there is only the bell, which triggers infantile memories of "good," if you will, through the exaggerations that are typical of pornography, with its huge breasts, its extremes of power and powerlessness, its fountains of ejaculate, its mono-maniacal focus. Susan Griffin is right when she observes that the male viewer of pornography is "chained and enslaved, not to a real woman, not to a body, but to a past and his image of the past, which he must recreate again and again." [11] But to equate the repeated use of pornography to an experimental setup in which certain responses are conditioned by being rewarded is not as helpful as it might appear to be at first look. Images that do not have a profound, even a lasting effect on a viewer have not achieved the purpose for which they were made. Generalization from a laboratory situation to the world beyond it is at best difficult, and there is simply no proof that repeated exposure to images of war, crime, or male abuse of women in itself destroys our capacity for loving concern.

Susan Griffin's book *Pornography and Silence: Culture's Revenge against Nature* makes the most extended and convincing case for a psychoanalytic connection between pornographic images and women's victimization. Griffin traces the origin of the pornographic mind to the male infant's memories of dependency vis-à-vis his mother. Common pornographic images of women driven to the point of frenzy by their need for sex, and for oral sex in particular, are seen by Griffin as projections and reversals: the man projects the helplessness his culture will not let him acknowledge onto a female over whom he then has the power his mother once had over him. [12] That these images might reverberate directly with a woman's infan-tile memories, and thus carry erotic charges for her as well, finds no place in Griffin's analysis. Here is a scheme in which the (male) self has been partitioned into an acceptable male part and a forbidden female part. The male side of this divided self is what Griffin means by "the pornographic mind," a universal category whose genesis she traces through time. Like that of the behaviorists, her villain is culture, but she is asking not only about its effects but also why culture offers men the kind of images it does, and why they find them so exciting.

The problem with Griffin's otherwise compelling insights is that they are entirely asymmetrical. Using Marilyn Monroe as a touching example, she intuits the process whereby women become alienated from their true sexual feelings as they become objects for male delectation. But like Freud in his early writings on psychosexual development, Griffin talks only about men: *their* infantile anger toward their mothers and the way that anger becomes inscribed in later erotic patterns. In her insistence that early female devel-opment does not simply follow that of the male with all the gender markers reversed, she concurs with other feminists exploring the bond between mothers and daughters. Nancy Chodorow, Jane Flax, Dorothy Dinnerstein,

Jean Baker Miller, and Adrienne Rich, though disagreeing among themselves, all emphasize the role of the mother as primary nurturer for both sexes and posit a process of female development that stresses continuity rather than separation, interrelatedness rather than individuation.[13]

Separating from a primary nurturer of the same sex calls forth, in this culture at least, different traits from those called forth by the male's separation from his mother. Conflicting conclusions can be drawn from this asymmetry, and the division between the planners of the Barnard conference and their opponents is simply the current expression of a division in the women's movement, going back into the nineteenth century, a division between sex radicals who want more freedom for women, and what we now call cultural feminists who want more protection for women.

The sex radicals tend to view the incomplete break between mother and daughter as a liability, a source of stress around the issue of the daughter's individuation and a constraint on her ability to get angry, assert her sexuality, and break the bonds of dependency.[14] Thus they stress similarities between male and female sexual needs and male and female eroticism. Cultural feminists, on the other hand, have used this same condition of greater connectedness between the mother and her female child to support their view that women are superior to men. By turning on its head the formula "woman is to nature as man is to culture," which is often invoked as an explanation for women's universal subordination, Mary Daly, Carolyn Merchant, and Griffin herself in her earlier *Woman and Nature: The Roaring inside Her*, argue that the scientific culture that men have created is an expression of male alienation from the female nature within and around them.[15] The women-against-pornography movement, with its stress on female purity and female victimization, is the activist component of this ideology.

Given the view of women as "naturally superior," it becomes inconceivable that they could have even the potential for a pornographic mind, one that images the object of desire and tries to possess, control, and deprive him/her of any vestige of a will. Yet infants of both sexes experience frustration born of their helplessness and dependence on their mothers, a frustration that is complicated in girls, but not necessarily canceled out, by their identification with the same-sex parent. Therefore, if men project, in fantasy, a culturally tabooed part of themselves onto women in order simultaneously to indulge and to control it, why should we assume that women do not project onto men the aggression that is as culturally taboo for women as is the feminine side of men? Women are supposed to love those distant, penis-bearing creatures rather than trying to join the baseball team. But perhaps men act *for* them as well as against them when they convert anger into domination. To acknowledge that women have experienced deep and perhaps unavoidable rage toward their first love-object destroys the basis of the feminist argument of female superiority on which the psychoanalytic case against pornography rests. The disloyal opposition, of which I count myself a part, is not so willing to deny this admittedly disturbing and difficult part of the female personality.

Griffin sees pornography as the mirror of the male mind whose female component has been placed off limits by "culture." "Culture" is synonymous with systematic male domination, or patriarchy, and is uniformly hostile to women across time and geographical space. All the horrors of history have flowed forth from the male desire to control and punish what is other to himself, beginning with what is other in himself. Male violence is not a response, then, to an external stimulus but emanates from a socially constructed internal condition that pornography reflects and supports. The psychoanalytic model is positioned between the model of learned aggression—in which pornography is the "teacher"—and an essentialist, or mythic, explanation for male violence and the role of pornography in precipitating that violence. It is behaviorist in that violence is learned. The male infant is a "naturally" whole creature in whose consciousness an alien culture has intervened. At the same time it is an essentialist model in that this explanation doesn't tell us why "culture" takes up the task of dividing men from the parts of themselves it deems female.

The essentialist or mythic connection between pornography and male violence says that men mistreat women not simply because they are conditioned by pornographic images, nor even because they want to control the powerful mothers who once controlled them, but because the essence of maleness is violent. Andrea Dworkin is the most articulate and widely published proponent of this model, and her popularity as a speaker would indicate that she is not a lone voice crying in the wilderness. Her book *Pornography: Men Possessing Women* begins like this:

> The power of men is first a metaphysical assertion of self, an *I am* that exists a priori, bedrock, absolute, no embellishment or apology required, indifferent to denial or challenge. It expresses intrinsic authority. It never ceases to exist no matter how or on what grounds it is attacked, and some assert that it survives physical death. This self is not merely subjectively felt. It is protected by laws and customs, proclaimed in art and literature, documented in history, upheld in the distribution of wealth. This self cannot be eradicated or reduced to nothing. It is. When the subjective sense of self falters, institutions devoted to its maintenance buoy it up.

Dworkin surrounds this self-in-assertion with other forms of male power: physical strength; the power of naming, of owning, of sexual dominance; the control of money; and the capacity to induce terror "*in* a whole class of persons *of* a whole class of persons." Terror "issues forth from the male," says Dworkin. "It illuminates his essential nature and his basic purpose." [16] In this scheme women have nowhere to run, nowhere to hide. In their absolute victimization, but only there, they are uncontaminated by the imperial, omnipotent male self.

This extreme view of gender differences is appealing in the same way that the extreme anti-abortion position is appealing. If a fetus is always a person, then abortion will always be murder: there is no room for the complexity and ambiguity of human negotiations if right and wrong are divinely laid out and invariable. Similarly, if women are invariably victims there is no possibility of complicity in their own oppressed condition. More than that: they are never villains and they are never victimizers. Our sexist culture has insisted that women always provoke violence. We have countered this by saying that we neither provoke it nor commit it. But the movement now needs to go beyond this initially necessary reaction formation. The assumptions underlying the feminist opposition to pornography are the logical development of ideas that laid the groundwork for a movement that went beyond liberal piece-by-piece reformism. Connecting the mechanisms of production and distribution to experiences of intimate life made it possible to imagine transforming intimate relations along with economic ones, making them both less susceptible to fears of scarcity and feelings of alienation. Making those connections was the jumping-off point of second-wave feminism, and the anti-porn movement is right to keep them before our eyes.

Politics and Sexuality

Nevertheless there are serious problems with the conclusions the theorists of the anti-porn movement draw from this premise of interconnectedness. By carrying it to an extreme they surround us with a monolithic world "out there," a patriarchal system of which all the parts are equally developed and fit perfectly together. When Andrea Dworkin observes that "pornography is not a genre of expression separate and different from the rest of life; it is a genre of expression fully in harmony with any culture in which it flourishes," [17] she is connecting up one expression of sexism with others and saying they are part of a system that oppresses women. But she misses the unevenness of the system. In order to stress the point that particulars are not isolated, she leaves them out altogether. Pornography images a world where you (if you're a man) can get what you want when you want it. Yet only for the very rich could it be at all in harmony with the world of work. And if pornography were fully in harmony with the family, there would probably be much less interest in it. Its connection to these institutions is the universality of male supremacy, but the gratification male supremacy offers varies widely from one concrete situation to the next.

Looking at the unevenness of patriarchal control means looking for places where potential or actual conflicts in the dominant ideology may be found. Fantasies of absolute powerlessness give rise to fantasies of absolute power, and though these may serve a healing function, they don't help individuals or social movements figure out their goals or the next step toward reaching them. As the women's movement was forming, it was crucial to see that sexism reverberated at every level of our culture. We do not need to replace these perceptions but to add others. For it is in the fissures and weak points in the armor of patriarchy that we can work to weaken it piecemeal. The antipornography feminists despair of this process. Refusing to take a historical look, they insist that violence against women is either a constant or is rising to unprecedented heights, and that women are the principal victims of violent crime. If men "love death," as Dworkin says they do, and if they "especially love murder," then we can punish them for abusing their absolute power, but we can never stop them.[18]

The second problem I find in the anti-porn analysis is a corollary to this overvaluation of male power. It is the devaluation of female subjectivity, a stance that negates the possibility of female choice and self-directed action no less than an image of an unbeatable male enemy. This is nowhere more clear than in the arguments against sadomasochism put forward by the antipornographers. "I think the issue of 'mutual consent' is utterly beside the point," declares Diane Rian in the collection *Against Sadomasochism*:

> I find this argument as irrelevant and unconvincing as the antifemi-
> nist argument from women who claim that their greatest satisfaction
> is in "consenting" to sexual subservience to men. Since our sexuality
> has been for the most part constructed through social structures
> over which we have had no control, we all "consent" to sexual desires
> which are alienating to at least some degree.[19]

John Stoltenberg, writing in the same volume, makes the same point:

> Between a man and a woman, the structure of sadomasochistic
> erotic encounters is predicated on the constraint of the woman's will

as well as her body. The woman's compliance in sadomasochism is therefore entirely delusional and utterly meaningless. In no sense does she share in the man's privileged capacity to act.[20]

Both writers view sexual desire and sexual behavior as socially constructed, an insight first introduced into feminist dialogue by Gayle Rubin.[21] But Rubin sees sexual desire as less malleable than do her opponents, who insist that sexuality can be reconstructed without reference to its infantile roots.

That heterosexual relationships are structurally unequal is an axiom of feminist thinking. But Karen Rian takes this insight to the point of denying that women actually consent to them. While it is true, as Adrienne Rich points out, that compulsory heterosexuality is so much the bedrock of our culture that most people don't even notice it, women have some degree of sexual autonomy.[22] Women may have fewer options than men, and older women fewer than younger women, and poor women fewer than rich women, but this does not mean that they have no control at all over their lives and their sexuality. Free will is a relative matter, even for white men. To set an ideal feminist sexuality that is totally free against a present reality that is totally controlled makes it impossible to distinguish between degrees of autonomy or consent.

Behind this political stance lies a profound pessimism about heterosexuality itself, a view that is shared not only by lesbian separatists but also by many feminists who continue to opt for heterosexuality. Part of the project of feminism has been to interrogate that institution, to expose its deficiencies in such a way as to allow women to free themselves from culturally instilled beliefs in its power to affect their salvation. This led in the mid-1970s to the creation of a network of shelters and counseling for battered women, a set of counterinstitutions which, however fragile their funding, have served as spaces from which the struggle against sexism in one of its ugliest forms could be waged. The workers in these shelters were exposed on a daily basis to the underside of heterosexuality and found it incomprehensible, many times, that women would continue their relationships with men who treated them so badly. Either they could accept the culture's sexist explanation that these women and women in general were masochists, or they could say that these women and women in general had been coerced, brainwashed, raped—by the culture if not by individual men. Wanting to break decisively with the prevailing sexist stance of blaming the victim, the battering movement, as it is called, adopted the latter position, for which they then found reinforcement in the difficult and sometimes frustrating work they were doing.

Diana Russell's book *Rape in Marriage* illustrates both the strengths and the weaknesses of this political choice. Russell defines rape in marriage as

444   *The Present: Sexuality and Pornography*

"forced sexual activity" that includes "forced oral, anal, digital and vaginal [with a penis] penetration."[23] But her concern is not limited to these clear instances of bodily violation. She is interested in the whole phenomenon of unwanted male-initiated sex in a situation where the two parties have made a contractual commitment to stay together and whose relationship has some history. She is talking, she estimates, about one of every seven married women. The dominant theme in her interviews is violence and the threat of violence, but there is another: many of the women she interviewed said they were less interested in sex than their husbands were. In some cases they married to achieve security, approval, or social standing. Russell is clear that this situation will persist until the option not to marry is as socially sanctioned as the option to marry. Her solution has the positive feature of making women potentially less available to men: if they want us, they will have to treat us better. But for her the problem is only with the husbands of her subjects. There would be less rape in marriage if men wanted the same amount of sex that women want: that is to say, less than they do now. In the meantime, they can only be avoided or submitted to.

A similarly bleak view of male sexuality animates Robin Morgan's definition of rape. Male desire, in her view, is always oppressive except when it is in response to, and thus controlled by, a woman's desire. Therefore "rape exists any time sexual intercourse occurs when it has not been initiated by the woman out of her own genuine affection and desire." This last qualifier is necessary, she adds, "because the pressure is there, and it need not be a knife blade against the throat."

> How many millions of times have women had sex "willingly" with
> men they didn't want to have sex with? Even men they loved? How
> many times have women wished just to sleep instead or read or
> watch "The Late Show"? It must be clear that, under this definition,
> most of the decently married bedrooms across America are settings
> for nightly rape.[24]

The only subjectivity Morgan can grant to a woman who is not in complete control of her sexual exchanges is "the humiliation felt by the woman whose husband hides *Penthouse* or some harder core version of it in the bathroom and then forces himself on her at night—or on other women when [not if, please note] she fends him off."[25] A situation in which male sexual arousal, however achieved, might elicit a complementary response in a woman and be a source of pleasure to her is to Morgan simply inconceivable.

This image of an alternative to patriarchal sex denies the possibility of mutuality. It puts the woman in the position of the mother with respect to her infant: she has the power to give or withhold. Aristophanes elaborated this strategy for getting men to behave in his play *Lysistrata*, and various versions of it informed discussions of heterosexuality in our early consciousness-raising groups. Our numerical superiority to men, combined with time limits on our fertility, led many feminists to look for a more mutual model than one of living with "the enemy." The motive for this was partly fear but also partly a recognition that subduing the male through sex, a traditional female stance, did not really give women freedom to become sexual persons in their own right.

In the closing chapter of *Pornography and Silence* Susan Griffin offers a less antagonistic vision of postpatriarchal sexuality. The bottom line of her opposition to pornography is that pornography claims to elicit eros, whereas in fact "pornography exists to silence eros." Eros springs from that part of us untouched by patriarchal culture, the preverbal child.

> To make love is to become like this infant again. We grope with our mouths toward the body of another being, whom we trust, who takes us in her arms. We rock together with this loved one. We move beyond speech. Our bodies move past all the controls we have learned. We cry out in ecstasy, in feeling. We are back in the natural world before culture tried to erase our experience of nature.[26]

Since Griffin traces the origins of the pornographic mind to the male experience of helplessness and humiliation at his mother's breast, we would have to conclude that Griffin's eros is an eros between women, harking back, in the words of Adrienne Rich, to "the flow of energy between two biologically alike bodies, one of which has lain in amniotic bliss inside the other, one of which has labored to give birth to the other."[27] Is there in women, and in the tabooed female part of men, this purity untouched by human hands called nature?

This question involves the concept of "social construction," an essential but troubling component of any feminist theory of gender.[28] The question is: does sexuality begin as an unmediated "it" that is later constructed by societal input, or is sexuality like language, only brought into being through the process of "learning" it? When Juliet Mitchell suggested this latter possibility in 1974 in *Psychoanalysis and Feminism*, many feminists were wary of her reclamation of Freud's Oedipus complex for the cause.[29] A social-construction model that left no part of the psyche untouched by patriarchal input simply ruled out the possibility of a feminist revolution. Griffin's child-as-eros needs to be seen as an expression of that concern. Nevertheless, her image of freedom from patriarchy, so similar to Rousseau's and Wordsworth's, has a disturbing tendency to fit in with the dominant culture's idealization of the prepubescent female as an erotic object. Presumably the incest-perpetrating father is seeking exactly the experience Griffin describes.

An alternative way to deal with the problem posed by social construction is to see conflict between different parts of the psyche as an inevitable part of mental life, one that may never be entirely overcome with the obliteration of sexism. This brings us to the third problematic area that I see in the antipornography analysis. The argument for a causal relationship between pornography and violence against women assumes a virtually seamless connection between behavior, fantasy, and the unconscious, as if each were simply a replication of the others in a different mode. I don't like the image of eros as a child any more than I like it imaged as a frowzy bleached blonde with unreal-looking breasts. But if Griffin images eros as the sort of mother-and-child reunion she describes but she does not molest little girls, if the child for her is a symbol that does not literally dictate the form of her sexual practice, then she must grant that freedom with metaphor to others. A complicated relationship between behavior and symbols, whether internally produced or coming from external sources, obviously exists. We must simply keep in mind that there are places of rupture as well as places of connection between these two.

The hypothesized link between pornography and abusive or degrading treatment of women is this: the pornographic image becomes a fantasy in the consciousness of the reader, or triggers a memory buried in the unconscious, whereupon the recipient of this stimulus attempts (or is driven) to actualize, in the world outside his (or her) mind, the scene depicted. Deirdre English was the first to criticize feminists for relying too much on a behaviorist explanation for the persistence of sexism, with its assumption that in order to accomplish our goal, "all we need to do is seize control of the programming mechanisms that form our consciousness and substitute a non-sexist input." [30] At the beginning of the movement in the late 1960s, when feminism had almost no visibility in the public realm, this seemed like a plausible aim. But in the mid-1980s, with feminism so widely acknowledged if so little implemented, such ideas seem like vanguardism— yet one more way of infusing an exclusionary moralism into the women's movement, implicitly criticizing women who cultivate "incorrect" fantasies, who wear "incorrect" clothing, or who are aroused by "incorrect" images or behaviors.

But what can feminism mean if it does not oppose these things? What would it mean, for instance, if some women acknowledged that "forced" sex was not always entirely unwanted or even uninvited, that it was part of fantasy life, that it could be a source of excitement as well as pain? The fear is that if we acknowledge that we have been complicitous in our oppression, that we have dressed seductively or fantasized rape, then we won't be taken seriously when we say we do not want to be raped, trivialized, or sexually harassed. Don't we risk losing the credibility and momentum we have worked so hard to build up if we open up the connections between pain, danger, sexual arousal, and power and acknowledge that women carry the same irrational traces from infancy that men do? In most cultures, excitement in the presence of danger, even at the prospect of annihilation, has always been part of heroism. The most intense feelings of power emerge in response to the most intense challenges to survival. When they happen in the immediate present, too much of the rush of adrenalin is directed toward warding off the danger itself. But contemplating them from a safe distance and in a totally different context is apparently highly erotic to consumers of what the anti-porn movement calls "violent pornography."

I would speculate that this "danger at a distance" is part of our socially constructed heritage as infants that we bring into the realm of sexuality. The "at a distance" factor puts erotic stimuli in a different category from stimuli that elicit violent behavior. There is an element of contemplation made possible by the very feature of those stimuli that the antipornography movement abhors: they are detached from life and made into *objects*. The danger to which we give an erotic response is thus not unlike the mishaps and humiliations that make up comedy and that elicit laughter precisely because we are relieved to be viewing them from a distance. The symbols that make danger erotic may in their usual context be quite repellent: the implements and insignia of war, repression, or torture. The wish to encounter these terrifying realities at as close a range as possible under highly controlled circumstances is the impulse behind many activities in which men engage with an abandon that is commonly seen to be sexual: any physical activity to which you "give it your all." In the seventeenth century the word "die" had the same double meaning that the word "come" has for us. "I die to rise again," said John Donne, referring to more than the resurrection of Christ.

What I am suggesting is that the fascination with metaphors for death may reach into the core of our erotic beings. I am not speaking here of some transhistorical essence but of concrete infant experiences that may differ in their meaning from culture to culture but are tied to infant helplessness and survival in the face of that (temporarily unalterable) condition. Sadomasochism might then play upon this strand of sexual stimulation, bringing out under controlled circumstances the erotic connections between enduring pain, taking risks, and triumphing over danger. Why should bondage, imagined or staged as part of a sexual scene, intensify desire? Some say it does so only in those who are "sick," just as it was assumed until not long ago that intense desire in the presence of a member of your own sex indicated "sickness." A revolutionary sexuality should surely explore what is irrational in us, not in order to let exploitation loose in the world but in order to deepen mutuality.

In 1817 Mary Shelley published a novel that deals with the danger of driving out, in the name of domestic harmony, the explosive aspects of the human psyche. Its hero, Victor Frankenstein, is brought up in a family whose members "were strangers to any species of disunion or dispute." His parents provided everything for him, including a future bride. Yet when he reaches college age, he is compelled to leave home and to create a monster who murders several members of this household from which all conflict, and thus all opportunities for passionate boundary-breaking and creativity, had been driven. The feminists who see pornography as a genre to explore, even while finding some of it repellent, experience the antipornography view of sexuality as confining in the same way that Victor Frankenstein found his household too confining.

Victor does not understand what drove him to leave this domestic paradise, but Shelley does. The Frankenstein household has become a perfect refuge from the violent outside world with all its monsters. But in becoming so it has made Elizabeth, left at home when her fiancé goes off to the university, unable either to communicate with Victor or to protect herself from the rage his monster embodies. The opponents of pornography and s/m want to make women's sexuality a similarly cordoned-off space into which nothing disharmonious, violent, or vulgar can enter. But by stressing the vulnerability of the "little women," they reinforce the ideology that requires and nourishes it. The demand for a safe space in which sex can be enjoyed without fear of harassment has been made by sexual minorities and young people. But as long as that safe space is demanded in the name of "women and children" only, as long as Elizabeth cannot go not only to college but to the graveyards and the lab where Victor defied all of "nature's laws," her sexuality will be killed by his monster, as it was in Mary Shelley's extraordinarily prophetic novel.

Notes

1. Carole Vance, "Concept Paper: Towards a Politics of Sexuality," in *Diary of a Conference on Sexuality* (New York: Faculty Press, 1982), 38–40.
2. Laura Lederer and Diana Russell, "Questions We Get Asked Most Often," WAVPM Newsletter, November 1977, reprinted in Laura Lederer, ed., *Take Back*

the Night (New York: Morrow, 1980), 24. I take this statement to be the working program of the antipornography movement.

3. Gloria Steinem, "Erotica and Pornography: A Clear and Present Difference," in Lederer, *Take Back the Night*, 37.

4. I use "s/m" to mean the controlled, consensual rituals described in Samois, ed., *Coming to Power* (Palo Alto: Up Press, 1981).

5. Jean Bethke Elshtain, "The Victim Syndrome: An Unfortunate Turn in Feminism," *Progressive*, June 1982, pp. 42–47. Elshtain cites FBI and Justice Department statistics to make the point that "the chief targets of male crime are other males—not women."

6. See articles on the conference by Carol Ann Douglas, Alice Henry, Tacie Dejanikus, Fran Moira, and Claudette Charbonneau in *Off Our Backs* 12, no. 6 (1982); letters in response by conference speakers Gayle Rubin, Shirley Walton, and Amber Hollibaugh, along with many other letters and the text of the postconference petition drawn up by the planning committee, *Off Our Backs* 12, no. 8 (1982); Dorchen Leinholdt, "Sexual Radicalism or Reaction," *Off Our Backs* 12, no. 7 (1982): 17–21; Cherrie Moraga, "Played between White Hands," ibid., 23; Lisa Orlando, "Lust at Last: or, Spandex Invades the Academy," *Gay Community News*, 15 May 1982; Marcia Palley, "Fireworks Invade the Sexuality Conference," *New York Native*, 24 May–6 June 1982, p. 4; Peg Byron, "Sex Spurs Censorship," *Womannews*, May 1982, p. 4; Laura Cottingham, "Pornography," *Win*, 15 July 1982, pp. 10–14; Lisa Orlando, "Bad Girls and 'Good' Politics," *Village Voice Literary Supplement* No. 13 (December 1982): 1, 16–17.

7. Representative books that embrace this view of feminist sexuality are Kathleen Barry, *Female Sexual Slavery* (Englewood Cliffs, N.J.: Prentice-Hall, 1979); Susan Brownmiller, *Against Our Will* (New York: Simon & Schuster, 1975); Diana Russell, *The Politics of Rape* (New York: Stein & Day, 1975). Periodicals sympathetic to the antipornography position include *Off Our Backs*, *Sinister Wisdom*, *Trivia*, and to a lesser extent *Ms.* and *New Women's Times*.

8. Edward Donnerstein, "Aggressive Erotica and Violence against Women," *Journal of Personality and Social Psychology* 39 (1980): 269–77.

9. Edward Donnerstein and J. Hallam, "The Facilitating Effects of Erotica on Aggression toward Females," *Journal of Personality and Social Psychology* 36 (1978): 1270–77.

10. "Playboy Isn't Playing," an interview with Judith Bat-Ada, in Lederer, *Take Back the Night*, 124, 127.

11. Susan Griffin, *Pornography and Silence: Culture's Revenge against Nature* (New York: Harper & Row, 1981), 60.

12. Ibid., 61ff.

13. Adrienne Rich, *Of Woman Born: Motherhood as Experience and Institution* (New York: Norton, 1976); Dorothy Dinnerstein, *The Mermaid and the Minotaur: Sexual Arrangements and Human Malaise* (New York: Harper & Row, 1976); Nancy Chodorow, *The Reproduction of Mothering* (Berkeley: University of California Press, 1978); Chodorow, "Family Structure and Feminine Personality," in Louise Lamphere and Michelle Zimbalist Rosaldo, eds., *Women, Culture, and Society* (Stanford, Calif.: Stanford University Press, 1974), 43–66; Chodorow, "Mothering, Object Relations, and the Female Oedipal Configuration," *Feminist Studies* 4, no. 1 (1978): 137–58; Chodorow, "Feminism and Difference: Gender Relation and Difference in Psychoanalytic Perspective," *Socialist Review* No. 46 (July–August 1979): 51–69; Jane Flax,

450 The Present: Sexuality and Pornography

"The Conflict between Nurturance and Autonomy in Mother/Daughter Relations and within Feminism," *Feminist Studies* 4, no. 2 (1978); Adrienne Rich, "Compulsory Heterosexuality and Lesbian Existence," in Catherine Stimpson and Ethel Spector Person, eds., *Women, Sex, and Sexuality* (Chicago: University of Chicago Press, 1980); Sara Ruddick, "Maternal Thinking," *Feminist Studies* 6, no. 2 (1980). For a review of this scholarship, see Marianne Hirsch, "Mothers and Daughters," *Signs* 7, no. 1 (1981).

14. See, e.g., Lucy Gilbert and Paula Webster, *Bound by Love: The Sweet Trap of Daughterhood* (Boston: Beacon Press, 1982).

15. Susan Griffin, *Women and Nature: The Roaring inside Her* (New York: Harper & Row, 1978); Mary Daly, *Gyn/Ecology* (Boston: Beacon Press, 1978); Carolyn Merchant, *The Death of Nature: Women, Ecology, and the Scientific Revolution* (San Francisco: Harper & Row, 1980).

16. Andrea Dworkin, *Pornography: Men Possessing Women* (New York: Perigree Books, 1981), 16.

17. Andrea Dworkin, "Pornography and Grief," in Lederer, *Take Back the Night*, 289.

18. Ibid., 148.

19. Diane Rian, "S/M and the Social Construction of Desire," in Leigh Starr, ed., *Against Sadomasochism* (East Palo Alto, Calif.: Frog in the Well Press, 1982), 49.

20. John Stoltenberg, "Eroticized Violence, Eroticized Powerlessness," in Starr, *Against Sadomasochism*, 128.

21. Gayle Rubin, "The Traffic in Women," in Rayna Rapp Reiter, ed., *Toward an Anthropology of Women* (New York: Monthly Review Press, 1975), 157–210; also Chapter 3 in this book.

22. See Rich, "Compulsory Heterosexuality," 62–91.

23. Diana E. H. Russell, *Rape in Marriage* (New York: Macmillan, 1982), 43.

24. Robin Morgan, "Theory and Practice: Pornography and Rape," in Lederer, *Take Back the Night*, 136 (originally published in Morgan, *Going Too Far: The Personal Chronicle of a Feminist* [New York: Random House, 1977]).

25. Ibid., 139.

26. Griffin, *Pornography and Silence*, 254.

27. Rich, *Of Woman Born*, 225–26.

28. See Carole Vance, "Radical Surgery: Taking Sex out of the Sex/Gender System," paper presented to the American Anthropological Association, Washington, D.C., 7 December 1982.

29. Juliet Mitchell, *Psychoanalysis and Feminism* (New York: Pantheon, 1974), esp. 370–98. Mitchell's conclusion is that capitalism has destroyed the basis for the incest taboo, the foundation of patriarchy. Therefore, insofar as there is feminist input into the struggle for a socialism to replace capitalism, the unconscious will eventually be reconstituted around a new nonpatriarchal law that will supersede the incest taboo.

30. Deirdre English, "The Politics of Porn," *Mother Jones* 5, no. 3 (1980): 44.

21 Beyond the Virgin
and the Whore

Ilene J. Philipson

In the 1980s many socialist feminists have become leaders of the
attack on the feminist antipornography movement. In newspapers, journals, forums, and now books, they attack the antipornography movement's
tactics as inflammatory and divisive, and its theory as deficient, simplistic,
and often moralistic at its core. Endless pages have been spent revealing
Susan Griffin's epistemological inadequacies, Andrea Dworkin's fanatical
hatred of men, and the unmitigated villainy of Women against Pornography.[1]

Today, both the antipornography movement and a growing number
of socialist-feminists see sexuality as the most critical feminist issue. Both
groups claim that a woman's stance toward sexuality reveals not only what
kind of feminist she is but shapes the direction of the entire feminist movement. As Ellen Willis has stated in uncompromising terms, "I believe that
as the sexuality debate goes, so goes feminism."[2] And in similar fashion
Kate Ellis declares:

> For many feminists and people concerned with feminism, the pas-
> sion spent discussing porn, s/m and other sexual issues is passion
> that might be better directed against the feminization of poverty or
> attacks on reproductive rights. But here I would agree with Andrea

Source: This article is reprinted from *Socialist Review* Nos. 75–76 (May–August 1984),
pp. 127–36, by permission of the publisher, *Socialist Review*, 3202 Adeline, Berkeley,
CA 94703.

Dworkin: what is being fought out, I believe, is the very nature, and thus to some extent the future direction, of our movement.[3]

The parameters of this debate are increasingly set in dichotomous terms. One is either "pro-sex" or "anti-sex", a "good girl" whose "view of sex is that it is something that good/nice women do not especially like," or a "bad girl" who accepts or endorses depersonalized sex and sadomasochism.[4] This categorization also applies to women's relationships with their mothers: women either believe "mother knew best" or maintain "mother didn't know shit."[5] Kate Ellis now elevates this starkly drawn dichotomy to a more abstract plane: there are sex radicals who believe that women's more continuous ego boundaries with their mothers are a "liability," and cultural feminists who claim that such boundaries are evidence of women's "superiority" to men. Many socialist feminists argue that these dichotomous categories find their historical antecedents in the nineteenth century.[6] Thus, Ellis argues, "The division between the planners of the Barnard conference ["bad girls"] and their opponents ["good girls"] is simply the current expression of a division in the women's movement, going back to the nineteenth century, between sex radicals who want more freedom for women, and what we now call cultural feminists who want more protection for women." This bifurcated understanding of feminism therefore transcends history and specific social arrangements.

As I have watched the sexuality debate develop, I increasingly have felt that none of these exclusionary categories fits my experience. I find the antipornography movement moralistic and its tactics fundamentally misguided, but I also have basic questions about pornography, sadomasochism, and depersonalized sex. I feel ambivalent about my mother and believe that continuous ego boundaries with her have had both positive and negative consequences. I do not feel comfortable with the label either of "sex radical" or of "cultural feminist" as Ellis defines them. In truth I feel transported back to junior high school, where the two alternatives for girls were often to be branded a "slut" or taunted as a "goody-goody." I certainly thought adulthood, not to mention the women's movement, had rescued me from such choices, but it appears I was wrong. The antipornography movement and a number of socialist feminists have resurrected the virgin and the whore.

Since the antipornography movement has been raked endlessly over the coals for being divisive, exclusionary, and moralistic, I think it is time to examine its critics' role in the sexuality debate. I believe the socialist-feminist participants in this debate have come to share a great deal of the responsibility for the very divisiveness they condemn "cultural feminists" for. While they are not responsible for the original acrimony, simplemind-edness, and dichotomous thinking that was brought to the feminist discussion of sexuality by members of the antipornography movement, they have increasingly responded in kind. They offer largely simplistic and extreme labels ("bad girls," "sex radicals," "pro-sex feminists") within the political discourse they are constructing along with the antipornography movement.

This is a binary discourse: it permits only two perspectives—polar opposites. Thus pornography is either discussed as though it is always violent *or* valorized as an emblem of sexual liberation for women and men, as when Ellen Willis describes it as "a form of resistance to a culture that would allow no sexual pleasure at all."[7] Some socialist-feminist authors view the material world as a reflection of this binary division: there are geographic "zones" of sexual freedom such as the gay community and the porn districts on the one hand, and there is the repressive suburban family on the other.[8]

This discussion lacks both an analysis that permits ambiguity, nuance, overdetermination—that is, the elements of lived reality—and any recourse to that reality. The argument over whether pornography is either all violent and therefore thoroughly reprehensible or liberatory and therefore defensible can be debated infinitely in the abstract if pornography itself is never examined; if its massive popularity, effects on men, and recent historical origins and growth are never evaluated in the concrete. A porn district can be seen purely as a zone of sexual freedom if the activities and materials within it are never alluded to. The contemporary antipornography movement can be understood as the "current expression" of nineteenth-century social-purity movements only if the actual social world in which both groups of women have acted is never explored.

Antipornography feminists have made some attempts to study pornography and its effects empirically and to analyze the sexual needs and gender differences that underlie pornography's appeal. Many of these attempts have been analytically misguided, as a number of socialist-feminist critics have invaluably revealed. But these critics increasingly seem to dismiss findings and analyses of pornography or sexuality *because* they emanate from the antipornography movement.[9] Thus the useful information and insights that the anti-porn proponents have to offer are scorned by critics whose participation in the sexuality debate is premised on there being only a right or wrong, liberated or repressed, position. This dismissive attitude acts to keep the debate at an abstract and simplistic level. If evidence is necessarily disregarded because it emanates from the "wrong" side, then the terrain of debate is limited to assertion. The complexity of the real world and its actors is vitiated.

Ellis's "Black and Blue"

"I'm black and blue from the Rolling Stones and I'm Not Sure How I Feel about It" is a good example of both the dismissal of anything tainted by the antipornography movement and the reluctance to support bold-faced assertions with any reference to lived reality.

Kate Ellis dismisses studies showing that exposure to violent pornography increases men's potential to rape or abuse women on the basis that (1) experimental tests *prove* nothing about real-world behavior, and (2) they rely on an inadequate stimulus-response perspective of human motivation. While both these criticisms are valid, they do not necessarily negate the import of the studies Ellis cites; they should merely caution us to view such studies with discretion, to be aware of the shortcomings ingredient in laboratory studies of human behavior. Donnerstein's work is some of the only empirical research that examines the relationship between violent pornography and violent behavior directed against women. Therefore it demands serious scrutiny. It certainly is as relevant—if not more so—than the assertions and musings of Ellis and other critics of the antipornography position, who seem to base their arguments on introspection and discussions with like-minded colleagues. While a critique of social-science experiments for their inability to "prove" anything may warm the hearts of antipositivists everywhere, such a critique should be taken with a grain of salt if it is not used to evaluate the critic's own work as well. And I don't believe Kate Ellis lives up to the rigors of her own requirements, as she does not *prove* or seek to prove any of her assertions.

Ellis then turns her critical eye to the "psychoanalytic" basis for understanding pornography. She states that the psychoanalytic case against porn is based on the notion of "female superiority," and that because "women have experienced deep and perhaps unavoidable rage toward their first love object," the belief in female superiority and thus the psychoanalytic stance against pornography is destroyed.

The logic and assumptions here are deeply misguided. While there is a significant psychoanalytic literature that views pornography negatively, *none* of it even broaches the topic of "female superiority." [10] Nancy Chodorow, Jane Flax, Dorothy Dinnerstein, and Jean Baker Miller draw on psychoanalysis, but none of them argues for female superiority either. Thus for Ellis the "psychoanalytic case" against pornography is no more or less than the work of Susan Griffin. Yet Griffin's "psychoanalytic" understanding parallels Ellis's. Because women "have experienced deep and perhaps unavoidable rage toward their first love object," Ellis asserts, Griffin's psychoanalytic case is destroyed. But in *Pornography and Silence*, Griffin herself proclaims: "To the cultural message that women are degraded and lesser beings is added a powerful childhood memory of rejection, and here is born a desire for revenge which colors *both male and female* feeling towards women." [11] Certainly we cannot dismiss a paradigm on the basis of one author's work. And such dismissal is particularly out of place here when the author's ideas are misrepresented. This is not to say that Ellis's fundamental critique of Griffin's belief in female superiority is wrong but that it has nothing to do with using a psychoanalytic paradigm to unravel the meaning of pornography and sexuality.

Ellis's most salient criticism, however, is directed toward the feminist movement as a whole. She reproaches feminism for (1) not acknowledging that women sometimes like "forced" sex, dress seductively, fantasize rape, and "carry the same irrational traces from infancy that men do"; and (2) failing to recognize that erotic excitement in the presence of danger occurs in most cultures and that sadomasochism is tied to universal though culturally distinct experiences of infant helplessness. Ellis thus suggests that women are not the innocent and passive victims that the antipornography movement postulates, and that violence and sexuality have some universal relationship.

First, the argument that women too have violent, erotic fantasies speaks to a specific problem within feminism: namely, the exclusionary moralism that indicts women for their "incorrect" sexuality. This undoubtedly important criticism speaks to a fundamental issue in the women's movement. It has no bearing, however, on the "hypothesized link between pornography and abusive or degrading treatment of women" that is the very object of Ellis's entire critique. That women fantasize rape is irrelevant to the questions of why women are the primary objects of sexual violence and how pornography influences the actual incidence of that violence. Women in general are not rapists, pornographers, or consumers of pornography. Therefore, asserting that they have violent, erotic fantasies may respond to the moralism of the feminist movement, but it does not begin to speak to what causes women to be the objects of men's sexual violence. While Ellis rejects the idea that pornography has any relationship whatsoever to this question, her only affirmative contribution is the suggestion that we "acknowledge that we have been complicitous in our oppression, that we have dressed seductively or fantasized rape." But what do women's fantasies have to do with men's behavior? Certainly Ellis is not suggesting that women's clothing or fantasies *cause* men to abuse them, for that too closely parallels the stimulus-response behaviorism she deplores.

Nor does the suggestion that some relationship between sex and violence is universal speak to the question of why *women* and not *men* are the objects of sexual violence, and why the depiction of sexual violence against women has increased historically. By tying sadomasochism to the universal experience of infant helplessness, and by asserting that "women carry the same irrational traces from infancy that men do," Ellis obliterates the significance of gender. As such authors as Nancy Chodorow and Dorothy Dinnerstein have demonstrated, gender fundamentally mediates the way infants experience their helplessness. Girls and boys develop asymmetrical, relational capacities and needs vis-à-vis the mother, and these needs in turn help shape our sexuality. Yet this asymmetrical development is not based in the biological fact of infant helplessness but rather in the social fact of women's universal responsibility for the rearing of infants and small children. Thus, as many psychoanalytically informed thinkers have suggested, there is a good possibility that eroticized rage against women is the result of social relations rather than a universally experienced "fascination with metaphors for death [that] may reach into the core of our erotic beings." [12]

Furthermore, the assertion of a historically constant interest in symbols of erotic danger obscures historical changes in the acceptance and availability of sexually violent images. Since World War II the United States has witnessed the sudden appearance and tremendous growth of a "mainstream" pornography industry (porn sold in neighborhood supermarkets, for example, rather than in "dirty" bookstores), and a simultaneous acceptance of violence against women in media that are not considered "pornographic" in any sense. As an example: when Alfred Hitchcock's *Psycho* appeared in 1960, Americans were shocked to see a major motion picture, directed by an esteemed Hollywood figure, show a woman being killed so realistically. Today, violence and the graphic murder, dismemberment, and rape of women have become mainstays of the motion picture industry, and *Psycho* seems restrained and discreet in comparison. Why has this change occurred? To posit infant helplessness is as inadequate an explanation as the antipornography argument that transhistorical, male domination simply assumes different forms in different places or periods. Both interpretations are reductionist and ahistoric.

Where Is Reality?

An ad in the *San Francisco Chronicle* for an R-rated film reads:

See bloodthirsty butchers, killer drillers, crazed cannibals, zonked zombies, hemoglobin horrors, plasmatic perverts and sadistic slayers slash, strangle, mangle, and mutilate bare breasted beauties in bondage.

This sort of advertising represents a common ingredient of our everyday reality, yet it is a reality that rarely appears in the socialist-feminist polemics on sexuality and pornography. To ask why such thinking and what it represents infuses our culture, why we have learned to accept it, or how it affects our identities and behavior is to ask tabooed questions. If we do ask them, many socialist feminists will charge that we are more concerned with women's sexual protection than with freedom, that we are repressed or prudish analogues of the nineteenth-century social-purity feminists. But I believe that not to ask these questions ensures that we will never move beyond the level of superficial and ultimately meaningless debate in which dichotomous categories exclude understanding and lived experience. We will have no basis to appreciate how sexuality and the social control/stimulation of it change historically; we will be unable to make informed choices about such topics as censorship or nontraditional sexual identities and practices. We must be able to speak about sexuality without being pigeonholed or stereotyped.

Perhaps what is so upsetting about the antipornography movement to many socialist feminists is that it has captured women's energies; it has channeled anger against male domination into a real movement; it has affected women emotionally and behaviorally in a way that socialist feminism never has. But socialist feminists should be able to offer far more than critique in the current sexuality debate.

Given the appreciation of history ingredient in a Marxist tradition, we shouldn't have to cling to ahistorical and anachronistic notions of sexual repression and liberation in order to argue for women's sexual freedom.[13] First, we should throw out the historically specific term "patriarchy" with the pre-twentieth-century values and social relations it connotes and strive to come to terms with describing, naming, and analyzing the form of male domination we live under today. Barbara Ehrenreich, Deirdre English, and Barbara Epstein have begun this process, but we need to debate their suggestions and examine the impact on sexuality of new forms of male domination.[14]

Second, because we supposedly acknowledge the complex—dare I say dialectical—relationships between ideology and behavior, values and social interaction, we should dispense with dichotomous ways of viewing the world and ourselves. Pornography is neither the "theory" of rape nor a form of cultural resistance. Feminists are not "good girls" or "bad girls." Women's more continuous ego boundaries with their mothers are neither a "liability" nor a source of "superiority." The construction and social control or stimulation of sexuality are exceptionally complicated topics to unravel and thereby demand the most sensitive and nuanced forms of analysis.

Because of this complex and overdetermined quality, the study of sexuality demands a plurality of methods. We need tools that can help us plumb the unconscious, analyze the relationship between personality and social structure, define and measure sexual behaviors, and evaluate history. Psychoanalysis, experimental tests, sociological surveys, cross-cultural comparisons, and serious historical research all have a necessary place in the study of sex.

But in all our discussions we need to keep in mind that sex is perhaps the most difficult subject to debate politically, because people of our age feel so passionate about it. It is not only an activity but an inextricable part of our identity and thus not open to facile or conventional political scrutiny and discussion. As long as the debate progresses along the lines of determining who engages in "vanilla sex" or is an enemy of the feminist movement; as long as we are confronted with a political discourse that alternatively valorizes lesbian sadomasochism and a disembodied eros, we can only expect to enrage and alienate more women. Now is the time to turn away from provocation for its own sake—in our criticism, titles of articles, labels for ourselves and other feminists—and work to understand sexuality and pornography in terms of women's needs for both protection and liberation, security and freedom.

Notes

Acknowledgments: I would like to thank Jeff Escoffier, Vicki Smith, Dick Bunce, and Karen Hansen for their comments and suggestions.

1. To cite just a few of the contributions I am referring to, see *Diary of a Conference on Sexuality* (New York: Faculty Press, 1982); Alice Echols, "The New Feminism of Yin and Yang," in Ann Snitow, Christine Stansell, and Sharon Thompson, eds., *Powers of Desire* (New York: Monthly Review Press, 1983), 439–54; Deirdre English, Amber Hollibaugh, and Gayle Rubin, "Talking Sex," *Socialist Review* No. 58 (1981): 43–62; Gayle Rubin, "The Leather Menace," in Samois, ed., *Coming to Power* (Palo Alto: Up Press, 1981), pp. 192–225; Ellen Willis, "Toward a Feminist Sexual Revolution," *Social Text* No. 6 (Fall 1982): 3–21, and "Who Is a Feminist?" *Village Voice Literary Supplement*, December 1982, p. 16.

2. Ellen Willis, quoted in *Diary*, 72.

3. Kate Ellis, "I'm Black and Blue from the Rolling Stones and I'm Not Sure How I Feel about It," *Socialist Review* Nos. 75–76 (1984): 105; also Chapter 20 in this book.

4. See Rubin, "Leather Menace," 215.

5. Lisa Orlando, "Bad Girls and 'Good' Politics," *Village Voice Literary Supplement* No. 13 (December 1982): 17.

6. E.g., see Echols, "New Feminism"; Judith Walkowitz, "Male Vice and Female Virtue: Feminism and the Politics of Prostitution in Nineteenth-Century Britain," in Snitow, Stansell, and Thompson, *Powers of Desire*, 419–38; and Linda Gordon

and Ellen DuBois, "Seeking Ecstasy on the Battlefield: Danger and Pleasure in Nineteenth-Century Feminist Thought," *Feminist Studies* 9, no. 1 (1983): 7–25.

7. Willis, "Who Is a Feminist?"

8. English, Hollibaugh, and Rubin, "Talking Sex," 53.

9. In this regard, a number of socialist feminists are mimicking the exclusionary and dismissive position that many anti-porn feminists have taken. Thus Women against Pornography can condemn the Barnard conference on sexuality on the basis of who spoke rather than what was said, and Robin Morgan can read women like Ellen Willis, Amber Hollibaugh, and Deirdre English out of the women's movement because of their positions on sexuality.

10. Excellent psychoanalytic approaches to the issue of pornography are contained in M. Masud R. Khan, *Alienation in Perversions* (London: Hogarth Press, 1979); and Robert Stoller, *Perversion: The Erotic Form of Hatred* (New York: Pantheon, 1975) and *Sexual Excitement* (New York: Pantheon, 1979).

11. Susan Griffin, *Pornography and Silence* (New York: Harper & Row, 1981), 143 (emphasis added).

12. See Dorothy Dinnerstein, *The Mermaid and the Minotaur* (New York: Harper & Row, 1976); and Jessica Benjamin, "The Bonds of Love: Rational Violence and Erotic Domination," *Feminist Studies* 6, no. 1 (1980): 144–74.

13. For a fuller discussion of the issue of repression in the current sexuality debate, see my "Repression of History and Gender: A Critical Perspective on the Feminist Sexuality Debate," in *Signs* 10, no. 1 (1984).

14. Barbara Ehrenreich and Deirdre English, *For Her Own Good* (Garden City, N.Y.: Anchor Press, 1978); and Barbara Epstein, "Feminism and the Contemporary Family," *Socialist Review* No. 39 (May–June 1978): 11–36.

22   Subverting Power in Sexuality

Lorna Weir and Leo Casey

Power and sexuality: the relationship between these two concepts raises a variety of difficult questions for socialists attempting to develop a progressive sexual politics. Years after the reemergent women's and
gay movements first insisted on a vital interconnection between power and
sexuality, their relationship remains mysterious, although not from want
of trying. Like a Dickensian street urchin who stumbles uninvited into the
most elaborate of banquets, feminism and gay liberation rudely disrupted
the decorum of the prevailing theoretical orthodoxies—including the "critique of political economy"—that positioned the categories of power and
sexuality in separate social discourses so that they did not enter into direct
relation with each other. Feminism and gay liberation challenged the assumption that analyses of society must presuppose two mutually exclusive
spheres of private sexuality (the family and personal relationships) and
public power (the economy and politics), thereby breaching the ideological barrier between the private and the public. Yet while there was and is
a nearly universal consensus within the women's and gay movements that
power and sexuality are connected, there is little agreement as to how this
connection is to be specified.

The journals and gatherings of the women's and gay movements are
increasingly consumed by debates over questions of power and sexuality:
the representations of power in sexual images (the problem of "objectification" in pornography/erotica), the manifestations of power in different

Source: This article is reprinted from *Socialist Review* Nos. 75–76 (May–August 1984),
pp. 127–36, by permission of the publisher, *Socialist Review*, 3202 Adeline, Berkeley,
CA 94703.

forms of sexual desire (the problem of "inequality," from romantic roles to sadomasochism), and the exercise of sexual power (the problem of "exploitation," and the boundaries of consent and force). If, as is generally acknowledged, these debates do not concern isolated issues but reflect important differences of analysis and principle, it is because this unanswered question of the relationship between power and sexuality remains central to the development of a progressive sexual politics.

In this analysis we outline some serious theoretical shortcomings present in the dominant tendencies of feminism and gay liberation with respect to their understanding of sexuality and power. We then suggest how to reconceptualize some of the most perplexing issues in contemporary sexual politics. We hope these suggestions will be helpful in moving feminist and gay liberation theories to a more sound analytical terrain and will thus provide a better foundation for political strategy.

At present, debates on the politics of sexuality have frequently focused on pornography, with debaters divided into two major camps: one revolves around a feminist critique of pornography as violence against women; the other, a sexual—primarily gay—liberationist perspective sees pornography as a form of sexual liberation. We reject both these positions for the reasons developed below and from a perspective that values a plurality of ethical sexualities, excluding only those practices that have been established through democratic discussion as coercive or violent.

The Problem of Naturalism

To begin, let us pose the problem of power in general and necessarily oversimplified terms. Every progressive movement that challenges some aspect of the existing relations of power invariably finds itself contending with the argument that those relations are *natural* and thus both immutable and just. This argument appears regularly, whether the issue at hand is class, race, gender, or sexual identity. The origin of this pattern can be traced to a fundamental mechanism of hegemonic ideologies in the West; that mechanism naturalizes, or represents as natural, social relations of power. The bearers of those relations live and experience them not as the evolving product of a social process of domination and subordination but as a fixed product of nature. And since they are both natural and fixed, these various relations are understood as parts of a given order of things—an order in which every power relation has a specific purpose and function that serves the general good. Within this framework, to deny this order of things is tantamount to advocating social chaos and nihilism. The dominant ideology poses social relations of power in such a way that an alternative order is seen as neither practically possible nor morally justifiable.[1]

On the terrain of sexual politics, the modern women's and gay movements have confronted a major ideological barrier in the commonsense view of sexual power as biologically determined. Within the dominant ideology, human reproduction has as its "natural" corollary a sex/gender system of male supremacy and heterosexual exclusivity. The biological given that women alone can bear and nurse children is understood as the *raison d'être* of sex/gender roles: it purportedly makes the "nurturing woman" dependent upon the physical protection and material goods supplied by the "aggressive male" and ensures that complementary passive-active roles are joined together in the natural whole of heterosexual union. Therefore, according to this reasoning, the development of an independent, self-supporting woman or a lesbian/gay identity is perverse: that is, opposed to nature.

Both feminist and gay liberation theories have engaged elements of this ideology in direct battle with some considerable success. Yet for the most part, the theories generated by both movements have not thoroughly rejected the primacy of the category of the natural, nor have they overcome the antinomy between the category of nature and the categories of culture and society. To the contrary, these theories have simply postulated an alternative vision of sexual naturalism that is then opposed to existing power relations.

While the differences between the dominant strains of feminist and gay liberation theory are many, there is an ideological level at which they are united. Their common vision starts from the premise of a primal/primordial sexuality characterized by conditions of complete autonomy and equality. This sexuality is implicitly theorized as an undivided whole, having no particular sexual objects (it is polymorphous in the most rigorous sense of the term) and no mediated forms (it does not objectify in any way the sexual other). While this natural sexuality exists in all women and (perhaps) men, the current sexual power structure thwarts its realization: it represses it, allowing only one culturally and socially acceptable form of sexuality—a phallus-centered heterosexuality—to be expressed. Therefore, the concept of sexual repression rests upon the assumption of sexual naturalism. The project of emancipation from sexual oppression is then formulated as a moment of liberation in the literal sense of the word—as a revolution that restores the state of natural, sexual liberty.

This "naturalist-repressive" theoretical framework is conceived as implacably and uncompromisingly opposed to the existing sexual power relations. In the grand millenarian tradition of dual power strategies that mark

Western revolutionary thought, its vision of sexuality is seen as the polar opposite of the existing order. A world of nurturance and cooperation, for example, is constructed as the complete adverse of a world of aggression and competition. Within this tradition, these two contrary principles wage constant battle until that apocalyptic point when unalienated, unmediated innocence—a world absolutely exterior to existing power and domination —completely destroys hierarchy.

Despite and, in a sense, because of this image of the last judgment, the prevailing theoretical model within feminist and gay liberation theories is but the inverse of the dominant ideology. The body of the ideology and its categories for understanding the world remain the same.

The use of such categories as natural sexuality places us on the very same ideological terrain as those who defend the traditional order against the women's and gay movements—a terrain on which they have a considerable advantage, since it is defined by the dominant relations of power. Moreover, by framing our concerns (whether they be violence against women or state campaigns against the institutions of gay culture) within the dominant ideological categories, we increasingly open ourselves to the subsumption of these concerns within the established discourses and politics of sexual power.

Feminist Sexual Naturalism and the Antipornography Movement

The founding manifestos of the contemporary women's movement, from Kate Millett's *Sexual Politics* to Shulamith Firestone's *Dialectic of Sex*, rooted their analyses in an antinomy between nature and culture; Juliet Mitchell's trenchant critique of their approaches to psychoanalysis revealed this point of commonality.[2] More recent theoretical works of the radical feminist current, such as Mary Daly's *Gyn/Ecology* and Susan Griffin's *Woman and Nature*, are even more explicit in their use of this opposition. Just like the dominant ideology, these works portray women as naturally nurturing and men as the bearers of an innately competitive and aggressive culture. The respective valorization of these two roles is simply inverted in order to provide the basis for seeking the overthrow of the violent male culture that currently dominates nature.

"The association of women with nature and men with culture is by no means new," British feminists Penelope Brown and L. J. Jordanova have noted. "[It] draws on assumptions and stereotypes which have been deeply embedded in our culture for several centuries."[3] Yet despite this transparent connection, an entire generation of radical feminist theorists have treated their formulations of the opposition as if they were original discoveries. That the alignment of men with culture and women with nature was the explicit foundation of the first modern theories of patriarchy from Rousseau to Hegel is not reflected in radical feminist thought.[4] Nor is the central role this formulation has played in the methodology of the modern social sciences—well known for their hostility to feminism—ever acknowledged.

As this theoretical convergence suggests, the use of the dichotomous framework of "immutable gender," as Susan Brownmiller approvingly calls it, has the potential of making important issues of women's oppression seem as though they are simply part of "natural" sexual divisions.[5] There is perhaps no more telling illustration of this possibility than the application of the polar divisions of sexual naturalism to the grave problem of violence against women. Analytical distinctions collapse left and right, as the problem is quickly reduced to pornography: "Pornography is the theory, and rape is the practice."[6]

The key concept in this reductionist thesis is the philosophical notion of "objectification." This term has various meanings, and the antipornography argument constantly switches from one to another seemingly without notice, playing on the resultant ambiguities in such a way that any representation of sexuality, as well as male sexuality itself, comes to be identified with violence.

We believe there is a sense in which sexuality is impossible without objectification: if there were no specific *objects* of desire—specifically desirable men and women with particular characteristics—then the conditions for sexual attraction would not be present. Our consciousness of the subjectivity of others in the social world is mediated by the materiality of their bodies. The rudimentary conditions of embodiment, which are indeed immutable (even for socialists), entail that "pure" subjectivity does not exist.

There is also another sense of the term "objectification" in which every representation—be it a photograph, a novel, or a film—is complicit. The material nature of representations necessitates their presentation as objects for other people. What is unacceptable, of course, is the violent exploitation identified by a third meaning of objectification, which has two variants: one individual, the other collective. The former concerns the use of the body of an unwilling, coerced subject for a sense of sexual power; the latter, the reinforcement of the oppression of dominated social groups.

In the most sophisticated of the antipornography texts, Susan Griffin's *Pornography and Silence: Culture's Revenge against Nature*, pornography is opposed to a natural "eros" which is immediate and universal; this eros literally knows no objects of any kind. Eros can be understood, Griffin approvingly quotes Carl Jung, only as "the unknown by the more known." It is a utopian state in which one loses oneself in perfect union with the natural world (one is tempted to say, fusion with the mother), free at last from corporeal limitations, and thus free from all sexuality—despite Griffin's protests to the contrary. The discussion of eros and the book end with a contemplation of the sacred and eternal soul. No profane bodies here.[7]

In fact, eros—good, bad, or indifferent—must pass through the "defiles of the signifier," to adopt Jacques Lacan's phrase, in order to be shared by others: intersubjectivity of any kind is contingent upon representation, which in its turn is a form of objectification. Sweeping critiques of objectification, well motivated as most of them may be, nonetheless backfire on their exponents, for perfection in nonobjectification rests in inaction and silence. Feminist analyses of sexist representations have in general tended to slide from an initial definition of objectification as denial of the will in another person to a criticism of any objectification of women's bodies per se.[8] This is more than a trivial debating point, since feminist artists on occasion have been accused of objectifying women's bodies, and their work has been condemned on this basis. Crudities in feminist usage of the concept of objectification may inadvertently lead from the praise of eros to the suppression of the conditions for its possibility.

Griffin's philosophical argument has unfortunate political consequences. By collapsing the various meanings of objectification and thus implicitly merging all sexuality and its representations with sexual violence, this line of reasoning submerges the vital issue of violence against women into a polemic which, despite the intentions of the author, can easily be read as antisexual. The traditional gender role of women as the asexual, spiritual guardians of moral order against unfettered "male lust" follows easily from this nurturance-aggression dichotomy.

The political dangers here are twofold. On the one hand, Griffin's analysis could lead the women's movement into forming alliances with other movements controlled by the most conservative forces in the social order, a process that had invidious effects on the first wave of feminism.[9] When an article printed in a respected antipornography anthology argues that feminists should accept the judgments of police authorities that pornography is the primary source of violence against women—despite everything that has been shown concerning police attitudes toward the victims of such violence—there is cause for serious worry.[10]

On the other hand, if one accepts as literal the claim that sexual objectification in general is the source of violence against women, then the problem of violence becomes inescapable, and an egalitarian sexuality can be little more than an apocalyptic utopia. Griffin's culture of objectification has no internal contradictions: it is absolute in its pervasiveness and homogeneity. A millenarian, dual-power strategy necessarily flows from this analysis; unless the culture of objectification is completely overthrown by unmediated and universal eros, there is little that can be done other than abstractly condemn it. When power is characterized as absolute, its victims have only the consolation of some utopia. Therefore, in either case, this antipornography analysis disarms the struggle against sexual violence.

Pornography: Toward an Alternative Analysis

We do not intend our critique of anti-porn theory to be taken as a dismissal of feminist concerns about pornography. As a whole, male heterosexual pornography is a "regime of representation of sex" constructed by men for the use of other men in which the meaning of the sexual is constituted by men and borne by women.[11] Male heterosexual pornography reproduces an ideology of sexism that is not inherent in the nature of objectification but pertains to the specific encoding procedures used to signify women's bodies.[12] Sexist representations of women are part of a general economy of visual pleasure that is bifurcated into active male and passive female, with women's bodies produced as the surveyed and men as the surveyors.[13] Heterosexual male pornography does not subvert the sexism; it in fact reinscribes women's position as a sight for the active male look and, as such, is socially and artistically regressive. Therefore, it is not surprising that many feminists should be hostile to sexual representation per se and find it difficult to imagine a nonsexist structure of visual pleasure.

Rosalind Coward has suggested that feminists should criticize sexist representations as a whole rather than concentrating on pornography as a single issue.[14] As she points out, such a critique would neither run the risk of subsuming feminist politics under right-wing ideology nor invite the Moral Majority or the police as potential allies in political campaigns. Further, a concentration on sexism would begin to allow feminists to differentiate the sexist from the sexual elements in pornography. While a nonsexist regime of representation of sex may be hard for women to conceive of, we need new forms of representation in which women can be subjects of the look, not a disavowal of sexual signifying altogether.

Given the long history of sexist representations of women, the temptation of contemporary feminist analysis has been to interpret pornography as essentially the same phenomenon, whether one is talking about Florence in the sixteenth century or New York in the latter part of the twentieth. While it is undoubtedly the case that the oppression of women cross-cuts

all historical epochs and modes of production, it does not hold that the oppression of women is specified everywhere in the same way.[15] Pornography
is not an eternal idea in the mind of man, expressed everywhere and always
in identical fashion, with quantitative variations. It is a material practice
organized by strategic and tactical mechanisms that differ considerably in
different times and places.

To locate pornography historically, one must begin by noting that the
pornography industry has grown exponentially since World War II. In
1953 no sexually explicit publications were available on newsstands in large
American cities; by 1977 such newsstands averaged forty sexually explicit
publications.[16] At this writing, six of the ten best-selling newsstand monthly
magazines are "men's entertainment monthlies."[17] While police estimates
that five billion dollars a year are spent on pornography in the United
States are undoubtedly overstated, there can be little argument that pornography is a major, multibillion-dollar trade. Given that pornography is
a growth industry and that videocassettes, clearly the major growth sector
in the distribution of pornography, were first mass-marketed in 1980, the
future seems to hold only prospects for further expansion. Interpretations
of pornography will continue to cause dispute, but this much cannot be denied: although prior to the twentieth century pornography seems to have
been for the most part a prerogative of the elite, the explosion in the availability of sexually explicit material since the 1940s has so democratized
pornography that it is now available for consumption by men of all social
classes.

What is the logic of this explosion in the production of pornography?
Michel Foucault's work on sexuality can provide us with insights in this
regard. The central claim of his *History of Sexuality* is that the West, far
from being reticent about matters sexual, has been the site of a proliferation of discourses on sexuality since the eighteenth century. According to
Foucault, the primary function of this discursive explosion has not been
to prohibit or censor sexuality but rather to implant, excite, optimize, and
regulate it. He chooses to speak of the *deployment* rather than the *repression*
of sexuality, emphasizing the fact that the discourses have had a paradoxical effect: "What is peculiar to modern societies, in fact, is not that they
consigned sex to a shadow existence, but that they dedicated themselves to
speaking of it *ad infinitum,* while exploiting it as *the* secret.[18] Foucault argues
that sexual repression can be best interpreted as a limited tactic within a
strategic model operating overall to intensify sexuality and incite sexual
discourse. His critique of the "repression hypothesis" is not intended to
deny the existence of sexual misery; he simply disputes the adequacy of
the hypothesis for explaining how such misery is socially produced.

Pornography, especially in its post–World War II expansionary phase, can be better understood against a backdrop of the intensification of sexuality than against one of prohibition and censorship. Pornography is a tactic by means of which power incorporates and intensifies sexuality, rather than a war in which sexuality resists power. In speaking of the particular forms of desire embodied in different "sexualities," Foucault has called attention to "the countless economic interests which, with the help of medicine, psychiatry, prostitution and pornography, have tapped into this analytical multiplication of pleasure, and this optimization of the power that controls it."[19] Asked in an interview whether advertising and pornography "recuperate" the body, Foucault replied:

> Sexuality, through thus becoming an object of analysis and concern, surveillance and control, engenders at the same time an intensification of each individual's desire for, in, and over his body. . . . The revolt of the sexual body is the reverse effect of this encroachment. What is the response on the side of power? An economic (and perhaps ideological) exploitation of eroticization, from suntan products to pornographic films. Responding to this revolt of the body, we find a new mode of investment which presents itself no longer in the form of control by repression but that of control by stimulation.[20]

The path to overcoming the tension between the heavy-handed methods of policing the intensification of sexuality characteristic of the eighteenth and nineteenth centuries on the one hand, and the collective desire for greater pleasure in the body on the other, has been understood in terms of the repression hypothesis. To date, all sex-positive politics have taken a sexual liberationist cast: that is, have been antirepressive. But the present political conjuncture requires a sex-positive politics that is not under the tutelage of the repression hypothesis.

Pornography is part of a larger ideology that reduces pleasure to sex and takes sex as the paradigm of truth. Our lives are perceived as but signifiers for our sexual habits; once our sexual practices are exposed, the truth of who we are will supposedly be revealed. But it would be a mistake to look to pornography for assistance in recovering from such reductionism. To resist the deployment of sexuality, one must resist a fundamental assumption underlying pornography: that the truth of pleasure is sex and that sex is truth.

Gay Liberation, Feminism, and Foucault

The work of Michel Foucault provides an alternative to the naturalist-repressive theory of sexuality, as we have seen, through its application to the problem of pornography. Foucault vociferously denounces resistance organized around the repression hypothesis, maintaining that resistance to the deployment of sexuality must not be fought on a ground entirely defined by this very deployment. The chief strategic implication of his book *The History of Sexuality* is that we must be prepared to recognize and fight local prohibitions and silences regarding sexuality without having recourse to the repression hypothesis as a world view that explains sexuality in modern society.

From this perspective, homosexuality is a transitional category absolutely necessary for sound political reasons and completely arbitrary for others. That homosexuality should be a defining characteristic of one's soul is simultaneously completely true and utterly absurd. It is extremely difficult, if not impossible, to imagine what a society of nonadministered sexual heterogeneity would look like. What we can say is that in the absence of a disciplinary apparatus for the deployment of sexuality, sex would no longer be constituted as a form of truth but as a species of pleasure; people would not suffer from an obsessive concern to confess and investigate their own or others' sexual tastes; sexual activity would lack the political significance it has today. Sexual pluralism would be the case, with sexuality no longer under surveillance to divide norm from anti-norm.

Gay liberation has proved successful with certain tactics. One of its chief victories has been the decline of mental health models of homosexuality. Yet while gay liberation has resisted various aspects of the sexual regime, it has left others untouched, because, as Foucault once remarked, its self-understanding has remained sexological.[21]

A dominant strain in gay liberation politics is increasingly identifying itself as a sexual liberation movement with a theory dominated by the repression hypothesis and strategic demands for more and better sexual services. The response of this current in the gay movement to anti-porn advocates is reflective of this shift. Joining the leading theorists of the anti-porn movement in obliterating all distinctions between gay male and heterosexual male porn, this current dismisses all feminist concerns with sexist representations as antisexual. In these accounts the feminist movement is seen as a repressive force seeking to stifle "natural" gay male desire. This is an apt illustration of how the repression hypothesis can lead to the unquestioning acceptance of some aspects of the sexual regime. To counter this tendency, gay men and lesbians need to develop a larger, nonsexological discourse and strategy of resistance: new social institutions, artistic practices, a broader concept of pleasure—in short, a sex-positive theory of gay liberation that cannot be reduced to a theory of sexual liberation.

One of the successes of the women's movement has been the constitution of a politics organized on a basis different from that dictated by the deployment of sexuality. Foucault has made the interesting observation that the course of the women's movement has been "a veritable movement of desexualization, a displacement effected in relation to the sexual centering of the problem, formulating the demand for forms of culture, discourse, language and so on, which are no longer part of that rigid assignation and pinning down to their sex."[22] It is evident that the repression hypothesis and the idea of sex as the ultimate truth have had much less influence in the women's movement than in the gay movement.

During the 1960s the disciplinary apparatus "discovered" women's sexual specificity. The dissemination in the mass media of findings on this subject has restructured women's sexual practices, creating in women greater desire for sexual pleasure in their own bodies. Consumer capital attempted to deploy and incorporate women's sexuality, but important elements of the women's movement tried simultaneously to claim sexually specific pleasure and to resist the terms of its inscription within the sexual regime. Control by stimulation thus poses the question of sexual difference within the patriarchal symbolic order, an order that presupposes for its stability the negation of sexual differences. Although the "discovery" of women's sexual specificity is a form of control by stimulation, its long-term political effects might have the potential for disrupting elements of male domination in the sexual regime.

Another accomplishment of the contemporary women's movement has been its critique of the "sexual revolution," that tactical shift in the deployment of sexuality which relaxed certain censorships. Sexual liberation presupposes a degree of power and autonomy over the use of one's body that most women simply do not possess. Therefore, the sexual politics of the women's movement has not generally taken a sexual liberationist form, tending rather to be articulated under the slogan "control of our bodies." Feminist resistance to the deployment of sexuality has had a much broader focus than that in the gay community: there have been critiques of compulsory heterosexuality, sexual harassment, rape, incest, and the medicalization of pregnancy. The critique of forced sterilization has attacked new forms of population control, while criticism of "expert" male authority has undercut the disciplinary apparatus. Control by stimulation has been restricted on many fronts, among them pornography and advertising.

While feminist opposition to the deployment of sexuality was and often is dismissed as necessarily antisexual by libertarians of meager historical sensibility, we nevertheless must beware of facile criticisms of sexual liberation. A critique of sexual liberationist ideology has the capacity to be dangerous if used in the service of a politics that attempts to prohibit or tightly control sexual expression. A progressive critique of sexual liberation that truly advances the "desexualization" of power must itself be sex-positive. As Foucault has pointed out, one must begin with the sexological categories in order to surmount them in political practice.[23] The sexological must be contained as an element in a larger nonsexological politics, not abolished by theoretical fiat for fear of co-optation.

Lesbianism is particularly relevant in this regard. The challenge lesbians represent to the women's and gay movements is inversely proportional: to many heterosexual feminists, lesbians are uncomfortably sexual; to gay liberationists, lesbians are antisexual. It is one thing for lesbian feminists to counter the dominant tendency in gay liberation and refuse to have their interests subsumed within a sexual liberationist ideology; it is quite another to resist the deployment of sexuality by desexualizing lesbianism, as does the well-meaning but misguided concept of the "political lesbian." Lesbians are in a position in some sense analogous to the position of women as a whole in the nineteenth century: they are seen as beings determined in every way by their sexual "nature." In an attempt to cast off this image, many feminists, including some lesbian feminists, have taken as their target this reductionist mentality. In their concern to construct a nonsexological lesbian politics, which is needed to resist the sexual regime effectively, they have paradoxically tended to desexualize lesbianism. Because lesbians as homosexuals are oppressed on the basis of their sexuality, their political resistance, at least in part, must have a sexological base. But like other women, lesbians must also refuse to confine their politics to the sexological. Access to nontraditional jobs, equal pay, day care, new forms of community and artistic practices are an integral, nonsexological part of lesbian politics. Because the contemporary social organization of lesbianism is in part a creation of the deployment of sexuality, resistance to the sexual regime must include critiques of compulsory heterosexuality, the sex/gender system, restrictions on reproductive rights, and so on.

A refusal by feminists to discuss women's sexuality on the grounds of contributing to the deployment of sexuality would be fundamentally mistaken. The sexual oppression of women and the oppression of women's sexuality do not historically originate in the deployment of sexuality, but aspects of this deployment offer footholds suitable for contesting the male control of women's bodies.[24] The new forms of disciplinary control over women's bodies, from abortion clinics to the pill to the "discovery" of the clitoral orgasm, are changing the organization of women's sexual practices. We cannot avoid talking about these forms of power that are reorganizing women's lives. To articulate a language of women's desire in the midst of a massive nonfeminist proliferation of sexual discourses gives rise to constant problems, but because resistance to the sexual regime can never be complete or absolute, the discussion of women's pleasure by the women's movement falls neither fully within nor without the deployment of sexuality. Realizing that one must be able to talk about sex/sexuality in order to oppose the sexual regime leaves us with the general political guideline that our discussions of sex should not be bound by the repression hypothesis and the logic of sex as truth.

Freed of assumptions, we can begin to ask new questions. The relation between the intensification of sexuality and new forms of reproductive control, and the relation between the implantation of heterosexuality and the construction of heterosexism, are obvious topics for investigation. The resistance of women and the women's movement to the deployment of sexuality and the tension in heterosexuality between nonreproductive and reproductive sexual practices also need systematic treatment. Our inquiries must reflect an awareness that sex is not a domain in which power is automatically subverted but simply one of the many forms of pleasure.

Toward a Pluralist Ethics

In all its forms, even the inverted feminist and gay liberation variants, sexual naturalism contains an implicit moral ethos. By postulating a natural order of sexuality that serves the general good, sexual naturalism sets an absolute ethical standard by which all sexual activity will be judged. The state of natural sexuality is, by definition, a given norm of what is ethically proper or, in the more common parlance of contemporary feminism and gay liberation, what is politically correct.

Whatever the intention of its advocates, the morality of sexual naturalism inevitably turns to a moral authoritarianism. Insofar as the feminist and gay liberation variants of naturalism also necessarily adopt a given norm as the basis for their ethical stance, they unwittingly become one with the dominant morality. To cite one example of this problem: there has been a notable reluctance on the part of many feminists to accept as valid anything other than what they consider to be monogamous, mutually nurturing sex. To cite another: many gay liberationists hold that the open sexuality of the gay male ghetto is the only "natural" form sexual desire assumes once it is freed from repressive and puritanical social barriers.

In rejecting the naturalist-repressive theoretical framework, Foucault's alternative concept of power brings into question the analytical underpinnings of this system of sexual morality. Some critics, however, argue that Foucault's theorizing leads to moral relativism and nihilism; that it is better to retain some notion, however flawed, of what is "natural" and "good" than to throw out all such notions. There is a grain of truth in this, since thus far no one has been able to devise a system of ethics that does not rest on either a naturalist or an arbitrary religious foundation. While the concept of personal politics has indeed broken with the long-standing split inaugurated by Machiavelli between morality and politics and has provided us with some guidance in our lives, feminists and gay liberationists applying this concept have unfortunately often ended by acting as a new moral and political police. Naturalism still lurks in our personal discussions and in our community values. On the other hand, those who have questioned the naturalist foundations of "politically correct" sexuality have often fallen into a vapid liberalism to justify their vision of sexual libertarianism. Using an individualistic and ahistorical framework, they claim that any consensual sexual activity is just fine, without critically examining the material basis of consent, the power relations involved in sex, and the complex relations between desire and the deployment of sexuality.

It is our firm belief that a position that respects sexual diversity and examines the social construction of various sexual discourses and practices without given norms and hierarchies does not necessarily lead to moral nihilism and political liberalism. Rather, the approach we advocate is one of moral pluralism, rooted in open and democratic decision-making. Such a morality does not constitute itself around one moral norm but assumes a multiplicity of ethical sexualities. It does not posit one path to the subversion of the dominant power relations but investigates the numerous terrains on which power can be subverted. Insisting upon a multiplicity of ethical sexualities, such morality allows for genuine cultural and sexual diversity in which individuality can be realized. Most important, it removes sexual morality from the category of the naturally given, thus opening ethical judgment to the possibility of meaningful community consensus.

Certain ideas generated by feminists and gay liberationists—the critique of the private/public split, the emphasis on collective and egalitarian decision-making, the critique of "natural" gender roles—are important examples of the subversion of a power that has come to seem "natural." But without a thorough understanding of the pervasiveness of sexual naturalism and of its nefarious influence on otherwise radical thought, it will not be possible to move beyond the false debate between a naturalist moralism on the one hand and a superficial sexual-liberationism on the other.

In rejecting the one absolute norm in sexuality, we do not assume the contrary position that "anything goes" but merely remove sexual ethics from the realm of the natural and place it in the world of politics. Only when this is accomplished can the question of the relation between power and sexuality be posed; only then can we begin to subvert, and not reinforce or maintain, power in sexuality.

Notes

Acknowledgments: We would like to thank Joanne Barkan, Bert Hansen, Jo-Anna Isaak, Mariana Valverde, Liz Weston, and Eve Zaremba for their critical comments and helpful suggestions. Because this text was completed in July 1982, few references appear to literature produced after that date, but the general shape of our argument has not changed.

1. Which is not to say that dominated groups are not represented, albeit subordinately, within the dominant ideology, or that competing ideologies cannot be formulated. But it is clear that the dominant ideology places definite limits on the representation of dominated groups and that these limits exclude the possibility of a clear alternative.

2. Juliet Mitchell, *Psychoanalysis and Feminism: Freud, Reich, Laing, and Women* (New York: Random House, 1975), pt. 2, sec. 2, "Feminism and Freud." Firestone and Millett read Freud incorrectly, in Mitchell's view, as a biological reductionist: i.e., as a thinker who reduces the culture and society of male supremacy to biology, and who thereby fails to locate the true divide between nature and culture.

3. Penelope Brown and L. J. Jordanova, "Oppressive Dichotomies: The Nature/Culture Debate," in *Women in Society* (London: Virago Press, 1981), 225.

4. See Jean-Jacques Rousseau, *Emile* (New York: Basic Books, 1979), bk. 5; and G. W. F. Hegel, *The Philosophy of Right* (New York: Oxford University Press, 1976), pt. 3: "The Ethical Life," sec. 1, "The Family."

5. Susan Brownmiller, *Against Our Will: Men, Women, and Rape* (New York: Bantam, 1976), 2.

6. Robin Morgan, "Theory and Practice: Pornography and Rape," in Laura Lederer, ed., *Take Back the Night: Women on Pornography* (New York: Morrow, 1980), 139.

7. Susan Griffin, *Pornography and Silence* (New York, Harper & Row, 1980); quoted phrase, p. 262.

8. *Vide* Griffin's remarks on objectification (ibid., 47): "To be made a thing is to become a being without a will. But it is not the nature of a living being to have no will. Objectification of another is in itself a sadistic act, for to be made an object is to experience a pain of a loss of a part of the self: the soul."

9. See Judith Walkowitz, "The Politics of Prostitution," *Signs* 6, no. 1 (1980).

10. Ann Jones, "A Little Knowledge," in Lederer, *Take Back the Night*, 181.

11. The quoted phrase was coined by Rosaline Coward, "Sexual Violence and Sexuality," *Feminist Review* 11 (Summer 1982): 11.

12. The analysis in our text deals solely with male heterosexual pornography. Both gay porn/erotica, the production of sexually explicit texts/images of men for consumption of other men, and the recent attempts at a "soft-core" female hetero-

sexual porn in magazines such as *Playgirl* must be analyzed separately, because they do not fall within the dominant scopic economy. One of the major analytic deficiencies of the anti-porn movement is its reductionist treatment of these disparate forms. While it is not desirable to have mutually exclusive theories of heterosexual and homosexual, male and female porn/erotica—any more than there should be parallel theories of sex and sexuality divided by gender or sexual orientation—the literature is not yet anywhere near being able to produce a unitary explanation. For some suggestions as to how the rift might be overcome, see Claire Pajaczkowska, "The Heterosexual Presumption: A Contribution to the Debate on Pornography," *Screen* 27, no. 1: 90.

13. The classic source on the role of woman in the economy of visual pleasure is the third essay in *Ways of Seeing* by John Berger, Sven Blomberg, Chris Fox, Michael Dibb, and Richard Hollis (London: BBC/Penguin, 1972). Feminist analysis of representational systems has advanced considerably since its publication, moving in the direction of semiotic and post-Lacanian theory. This has especially been the case in England and France, much less so in North America. The language of this theory is not immediately accessible, a fact of great difficulty to feminists, since it is the only vocabulary available for a nonnaturalistic, feminist critique of pornography. Due to the opacity of semiotics and the length of our essay, we have merely scratched the surface of an alternative analysis of the present regime of sexual representations.

14. Coward, "Sexual Violence," 21.

15. We are predictably in complete disagreement with the following remarks made by Andrea Dworkin in an interview with Elizabeth Wilson: "I think that the situation of women is basically ahistorical. . . . I think that men's history has changed in a way that women's history has not because of the specific nature of sex-class labour" (in Elizabeth Wilson, "Interview with Andrea Dworkin," *Feminist Review* 11 [Summer 1982]: 27).

16. Cf. Laura Lederer, "Playboy Isn't Playing: An Interview with Judith Bat-Ada," in Lederer, *Take Back the Night*, 121.

17. Cf. Valerie Miner, "Fantasies and Nightmares: The Red-Blooded Media," *Jump Cut* No. 26: 48.

18. Michel Foucault, *The History of Sexuality*, vol. 1, trans. Robert Hurley (New York: Pantheon, 1978), 35.

19. Ibid., 48.

20. Michel Foucault, "Body/Power," in Foucault, *Power/Knowledge: Selected Interviews and Other Writings, 1972–1977*, ed. Colin Gordon, trans. Colin Gordon, Lee Marshall, John Mepham, and Kate Soper (New York: Pantheon, 1980), 56–57.

21. Michel Foucault, "The Confession of the Flesh," in *Power/Knowledge*, 191.

22. Ibid., 220.

23. Michel Foucault, "Power and Sex: An Interview with Michel Foucault," *Telos* No. 32 (Summer 1977): 155.

24. Foucault nowhere discusses the relation between the present sexual regime and preexistent forms of power, especially reproductive control, over the bodies/sex of women. Nor does he remark on the impact of the sexual regime on gender. These, together with his lack of awareness that the disciplinary apparatus is administered by men (a not insignificant fact in gender-divided, male-dominant social systems), give his writings a marked androcentricity.

Women, Work, and the Labor Movement

23   The Just Price, the Free Market, and the Value of Women

Alice Kessler-Harris

For feminist historians, the 1980s might be described in the words with which Charles Dickens introduced his famous novel, *A Tale of Two Cities*: they are the best of times; they are the worst of times. On the one hand the creative outpouring of historical scholarship on women is a source of energy and of continuing pressure for change. In the absence of a mass political movement, the enormous extension of historical knowledge of which women's history is the center, if it does nothing else, should ensure that women's orientations are permanently imprinted in the vocabulary of the past. But there is another hand: our sense of purpose seems to have wavered, our direction to have become unclear. The feminist community no longer looks to history as the leading edge of scholarly research. Esoteric forms of literary criticism seem to have moved into that exalted rank. And even within the profession, women's history has lost some of its shine as accusations of partisanship and fears of politicization limit our courage and restrict our vision.

And yet this is a moment when the voices of historians of women are

Source: This article is reprinted from *Feminist Studies* 14, no. 2 (1988), pp. 235–50, by permission of the publisher, Feminist Studies, Inc., c/o Women's Studies Program, University of Maryland, College Park, MD 20742.

needed more than ever. Some of the most significant social issues on the political agenda—family life, abortion, reproduction, and a range of issues having to do with economic equality—have a special meaning for women. As these become grist for legislative committees and judicial decisions, lawyers and policymakers increasingly invoke the past. In their hands the history of women emerges as something other than the product of historians. Women appear historically as well as philosophically "other," as a single unified whole instead of an amalgam of diverse experience.

A few examples will illuminate the issue. Feminist lawyers have disagreed sharply about whether to struggle for special treatment for women in the work force or to opt for equal treatment with men. In 1986 and 1987 the argument focused on pregnancy disability leaves. In the case of *California Federal Savings and Loan Association* v. *Mark Guerra et al.* (commonly known as the CalFed case), the U.S. Supreme Court upheld a state law that provided such leaves for women without providing comparable time off for disabled men. Feminists, who came down on both sides, agreed in repudiating protective labor legislation that "classified men and women based on stereotypical notions of their sex roles." But they differed dramatically on the message of the past. One side drew a parallel between pregnancy disability legislation and the discredited protective laws, arguing that special treatment for women had distorted the contours of the labor force, encouraging employers to discriminate against women and contributing to occupational segregation in the labor market. Opposing lawyers insisted that a law providing pregnancy leaves differed from earlier legislation in that it focused on "how women's unique reproductive role affects them in the workplace." Pregnancy disability laws would not repeat the history of discrimination, this group suggested, but would instead enhance the possibility of achieving equality for women.[1]

In a second 1987 decision the Supreme Court sustained the affirmative action plan of Santa Clara County, California. The plan included gender among the qualifications an employer could consider in assessing candidates for promotion and hiring. The majority affirmation of this moderate plan evoked a blistering dissent from Justice Antonin Scalia, who called attention to the central issue underlying such cases: "It is a traditionally segregated job category," he noted of the road dispatcher's job in question, "*not* in the Weber sense, but in the sense that, because of long-standing social attitudes, it has not been regarded *by women themselves* as desirable work."[2] Scalia followed this up with his own historical commentary: "There are, of course, those who believe that the social attitudes which cause women themselves to avoid certain jobs and to favor others are as nefarious as conscious, exclusionary discrimination. Whether or not that is so . . . the two phenomena are certainly distinct." With all due respect to Justice Scalia, his description of these "two phenomena" reflects a historical consciousness to which many of us might object. Are conscious discrimination and social attitudes so easily separated? We once called this the difference between long-range and immediate causes.

A third example comes from an interview on comparable worth that appeared recently in *New Perspectives*, a magazine published by the U.S. Civil Rights Commission. In the last several years the commission has been an outspoken opponent of most forms of affirmative action and of all forms of comparable worth. "We do not have massive evidence that there was wage discrimination against women over the past one hundred years," commented the interviewer, an editor of the magazine. "So why should we now pass legislation or have a court make a ruling that assumes that the difference between men and women is due to discrimination?"[3] Does anyone dispute the fact that invidious distinctions between women and men are deeply rooted in the history of women's work? What "massive evidence" would satisfy this interviewer?

These examples illustrate how popular conceptions of the past can construct the future. They remind us that we have a responsibility as scholars to speak to public issues, to shape the visible perception of a past whose contours we have so fundamentally altered. They suggest that history, as a way of thinking, speaks to contemporary issues—whether we, as individuals, will it or not—and therefore plays a crucial role in forming consciousness. A concern with contemporary issues enhances our capacity to think about the theoretical implications of the concrete empirical data in which we are immersed. Attention to historical reality encourages public policymakers to consider context, particularity, and diversity in the formulation of issues. A reciprocal relationship between history and public policy thus strengthens both areas, each on its own terms. And it offers us as historians of women a way of enhancing women's understanding of our womanly traditions.

Comparable Worth

I want to illustrate how this dialogue might work by looking at one of the burning issues of the day: pay equity, or comparable worth. A major tenet of the feminist demand for equality is equity or fairness or justice. The demand underlines affirmative action programs and equal pay slogans. But what is equity in the job market? Like surrogate motherhood, homework, and pregnancy disability leaves, the pay equity strategy evokes contrary responses among feminists as well as antifeminists. Antifeminists suggest that it could increase labor conflict, worsen America's international competitive posture, and encourage a destructive female independence that would finally destroy the patriarchal family. Feminists who dismiss these arguments worry that it might nevertheless produce a host of evils including ghettoization in segregated occupations, economic inflation, expanded female unemployment, and increased female welfare dependency.

But comparable worth is clearly on the nation's political agenda. More than twenty states have some legislation that favors it; the 1984 Democratic party platform supported it; and the AFL-CIO and several of its constituent unions have made it a priority issue. Minnesota has already implemented it for state jobs. The state of Washington is well on the way to doing so. Yet proponents and opponents of comparable worth differ sharply as to its justice or fairness.

Proponents suggest that the need for equity is self-evident. As one study observed, "The work women do is paid less, and the more an occupation is dominated by women, the less it pays." That, they say, is manifestly unfair. But they disagree as to the basis for paying women more. Some argue that "jobs that are equal in value to the organization ought to be equally compensated whether or not the work content is similar."[4] Others suggest that the inequity resides in the market's failure to pay women a fair return on the human capital they have invested in the job.[5] Each calls on a different perception of history to solve two seemingly intractable historical problems facing women who earn wages: persistent occupational segregation, and the stubborn wage gap between female and male workers. On the theory that low wages inhere in the job, which is itself sex-typed, advocates of comparable worth posit two central assumptions: first, that the free market has not worked for women; second, that every job has an inherent value which can be compared with that of other jobs. Value, according to proponents of comparable worth, can be measured by such factors as the skill, effort, responsibility, training, and working conditions that are its requisites.

Critics ridicule the notion that value inheres in jobs. The market, they suggest—the demand for labor and the available supply—determines the wage paid. If women are not paid well, it is because they have made bad choices. And if these choices are historically conditioned, why should employers be held responsible? The language they use indicates something of the fear the idea evokes. Phrases like "the looniest idea since loony tunes" and "the feminist road to socialism" are the catchwords of the day.[6]

Subjectivity and the Free Market

The historian hears these arguments impatiently, for whatever the abstract models proffered by economists, the historical record introduces the balm of experience. The market, as it functions in the daily lives of people, is not independent of the values and customs of those who participate in it. Justice, equity, and fairness have not been its natural outcomes. Rather, market outcomes have been tempered by customary notions of justice or fairness. The specific forms these take have been the object of struggle. And just as ideas of fairness influence our response to the market, so too do they influence how the market works.

Such notions go back to the earliest days of commerce. In the eleventh century, church authorities developed widely accepted notions of "just price" to resist an incipient market. Trying to avoid the inevitable disruption of traditional relationships that would occur if scarce labor were able (by means of restricting supply) to raise wages above those appropriate for its station, church authorities and educators who interpreted doctrine argued for an objective assessment of value. Measured by fair exchange or an equivalence of labor, value—and therefore price—inhered in every article of commerce and in the wage of every worker. Trade, in the minds of Thomas Aquinas and Albertus Magnus, might be a necessary evil, but it should be engaged in within the "customary estimate." Departure from that norm infringed on both religious and moral codes.

From the beginning, the notion of just price embodied a subjective judgment. Because an important component of the wage and the price of the commodity to be sold was determined by the extent of the laborer's needs, just price rested on medieval conceptions of social hierarchy. "It corresponded," in the words of one economic historian" to a reasonable charge that would enable the producer to support his family on a scale suitable to his station in life."[7] Economic historians still debate the extent to which that correspondence emerged from the "common estimate" or market value of an object. But everyone agrees that a complex array of exchange factors mingled with a sense of propriety to form the final price. Thus, in one sense, just price was a subterfuge that enabled public authority to regulate an emerging market.

Whatever the weaknesses of just-price theory and its rootedness in the moral concerns of the church, it passed down a continuing notion that non-market considerations have a place in the valuation of objects or wage rates. In a period of labor shortages, notions of just price restricted the wages of labor and prevented skilled workers from banding together in what were labeled "conspiracies." When labor shortages gave way to surpluses and the consensual wage that had been used to keep wages down began to decline, artisans and laborers (sometimes organized in guilds) resorted to just-price theory to maintain a floor under wages. And as just price began to break down in the fifteenth century when the market expanded, notions that the wage ought to reflect some sense of need, rather than merely supply, persisted. Its components are visible in the market system that emerged in the fifteenth century and reached full flower by the nineteenth. The customary wage, the wage demanded by the craftsperson or laborer, reflected a social sense of how a worker should live, as well as of the amount of labor that entered into the product for sale. We have not yet abandoned these notions. Changing ideas of fairness are implicit in our evaluation of the market and influence the way we impose taxes and otherwise regulate its outcomes.

In the free market, theoretically, demand and supply determine price. But in practice, wage theorists recognize a variety of what Harvard professor and former Secretary of Labor John Dunlop has called "exterior" factors in determining the wage.[8] These exterior factors are influences on the labor market that emerge from such non-market factors as union contracts, seniority systems, and a sense of equity. Contemporary wage theorists have elaborate ways of describing how the market is restricted by these historical tendencies. Arthur M. Ross argues that wages move in what he calls "orbits of coercive comparison." This is simply another way of saying that traditional market forces do not have "compelling significance" in the determination of wages.[9] Rather, wages are influenced by the force of ideas about justice and equity and the power of organizations and individuals to sustain them. In this widely accepted model workers compare their wages to those of other workers; pride and dignity prevent them from settling for less than what their peers are getting. Other economists talk about "job clusters": firefighters insist on parity with police; steelworkers strike to maintain equivalent wages nationwide, although in fact the market could easily pay less in some areas of the country. All these ideas and the social sensibilities that sustain them limit or modify market wages.

According to Ross, workers use comparisons to establish the dividing line between a "square deal and a raw deal." In a competitive market where most workers do not leave jobs for wages but are promoted from within and rely on the job for security, a worker might not earn what he would like but, as Ross put it, "he wants what is coming to him. . . . [It is] . . . an affront to his dignity and a threat to his prestige when he receives less than another worker with whom he can *legitimately* be compared."[10] I leave hanging for the moment the gendered content of "legitimately."

If wages reflect the relationship between some workers and others, they also tell us something about the relation between the craftsperson and the object produced, between the laborer and the employer, and among employers as well. Autoworkers, for example, agree that productivity and profits are appropriate factors to consider when determining the wage. They demand a share in the distribution of profits in good years and may reluctantly accept cutbacks in bad ones. Similarly, employers refuse wage increases that would raise the standard in an industry, even when profits make such raises possible. "Wage rates," as economist Michael J. Piore suggests, "perform certain basic social and institutional functions. They define relationships between labor and management, between one group of workers and another," and they define "the place of individuals relative to one another in the work community, in the neighborhood, and in the family." [11]

Because wages function, like the labor market itself, to structure relationships, comparable worth provides a parallel rather than a substitute strategy for achieving equity. Some feminists criticize comparable worth on the grounds that it will ghettoize women. The wage, they suggest, is a function of jobs held, and the proper remedy for women who want equal wages is to seek access to the traditionally male jobs where the pay is better. After all, the argument goes, affirmative action legislation, now in place, will open up the market to women's labor and eliminate the main cause of the wage gap—occupational segregation. The Equal Pay Act of 1963 will then ensure that women are treated equally. Fighting for affirmative action increases women's admission to male bastions and, by encouraging women to act on male conceptions of the market, will secure for them permanent access to the best jobs.

But like the wage the labor market is itself a regulating device, the product of a long history of social relationships heavily influenced by traditional conceptions of gender roles. Although abstract market models indicate that people *choose* jobs, the historical record suggests that occupational segregation has been the product of deeply ingrained attitudes. What appears to be a "natural" consequence of women's social roles has to be measured against the specific shape of occupational segregation at a given historical moment. Ideas about women "following" jobs into the marketplace, or choosing jobs that fill nurturing roles, or preferring to satisfy some abstract social ethic rather than to make money—all these are ways of rationalizing nonmarket behavior by means of some other notion of equity. These and other specific social customs help legitimate the continuing and changing shape of the labor market. But they are and have been the frequent subject of negotiation and challenge by women. The historian who explores the workings of the labor market and reads complaints about its rigidities in particular times and places learns how segmentation functioned at certain moments and can contribute to understanding the way in which gender roles have helped to construct the market as well.

Defining Justice

Notions of craft and brotherhood, of masculinity and femininity, are embedded in and confirmed by the labor market, raising questions as to the definition of justice embodied in a "free labor market" in which inclusion and exclusion are a function of many things—including sex. Even a cursory glance at the rationalizations that employers and managers have used to regulate women's participation leaves no doubt that the labor market has been socially, not abstractly, constructed. Thus, particular notions of equity were expressed by the London guilds that declared in the fourteenth century: "No man of the trade should set any woman to work other than his wife and daughter."[12] Medieval injunctions are echoed by those of many trade unions and male workplaces in our own time. As late as the 1960s and 1970s, employers explained why they had no women in certain jobs by calling upon customary ideas. "The nature of the work [did] not lend itself to employment in production of either women or the handicapped," said one wire manufacturer in 1973. And a pharmaceutical manufacturer told an interviewer in 1968 that the company would hire women in clerical occupations and elsewhere where the physical requirements of the task involved did not preclude it.[13] Such social attitudes continue down to this moment to serve as guides to what is equitable in the labor market. A 1987 cover story in *Business Week* notes that women "are being promoted because they bring new management styles to the corporation." According to the article, experts report that "female personality traits such as an ability to build consensus and encourage participation are in demand today. . . . Women typically show more warmth and concern about human relationships and human sensitivities."[14] And when such qualities go out of fashion, will women be demoted?

We begin now to see why the idea of comparable worth is so threatening. Just-price theory imbued the market with a sense of equity that serves as a compelling (if sometimes unpredictable) influence on it. But whose sense of equity? An important element of equity, itself historically rooted, is a subjective evaluation of gender roles. A customary wage—a wage that reflects a social sense of how women and men should and do live—is partially an effort to preserve the status quo. Because the customary wage was built on a sense of the family as economic unit, it incorporated and passed down prevailing conceptions of gender. Because it was tied to continuing social hierarchy and women's restricted place, it affirmed women's secondary position. Thus, "a woman's wage" has long been a term of opprobrium among men. A male worker could not legitimately be compared with a female worker without violating his sense of dignity and justice. Nor did the sense of justice of most female workers historically require such comparisons.

But times have changed, and along with them, our conceptions of justice are altering. As Edward H. Carr put it, abstractions "are indispensable categories of thought but they are devoid of meaning or application till specific content is put into them." Like checks drawn on a bank, "the printed part consists of abstract words like liberty and equality, justice and democracy . . . valueless until we fill in the other part, which states how much liberty we propose to allocate to whom, whom we recognize as our equals and up to what amount. The way we fill in the cheque from time to time is a matter of history." [15] Many (but never all) women in the past accepted a model of equity in the labor market based on the ideology of the patriarchal family. Most arguments for female equality derived from male conceptions of justice and were debates about access, not about new rules. New material conditions have shifted the content of equity from a demand for equality with men to a challenge to male structures. The altered terms of the debate no longer ask how women can achieve equality in a predominantly male work world so much as how to revalue the world of work and workers in a way that incorporates female self-interest. Rooted not in the moral economy of the male but in the traditions, customs, and practices of women, the idea of comparable worth evokes a history that assesses the changing sense of right or dignity on which people will act.

That sense emerges from a historical context that alters definitions of what people are willing to accept. The disruptive conditions of early industrialization framed nineteenth-century arguments for a male wage sufficient to keep wives out of the work force. Early twentieth-century battles for a wage adequate to sustain women who were not secondary earners reflected a mature industrial economy in which women had essential but apparently temporary roles as wage laborers. In the 1920s the U.S. Women's Bureau fought bitterly to defend protective labor legislation—a battle rooted in a historically conditioned understanding of women's primary task as the bearers and rearers of children. By the mid-twentieth century campaigns for equal pay for equal work reflected a shift to notions of equity rooted in the job to be performed rather than in an abstract conception of women's roles. Within the last ten years the increasing pauperization of women and children in the United States has become a major incentive to redistribute income and thus an important argument for comparable worth. The campaign for pay equity reflects this new historical stage; because both women and men are recognized providers, the search for equity now includes a demand that jobs be evaluated on their own terms. Changing family structures have clearly played a political part in encouraging a revaluation of women's economic roles. The emergence of the argument is itself an indication that the conception of justice that underlined the legitimacy of a woman's wage is now called into question.

Like other redefinitions of equity, the consequences of this one are not self-evident. Thus, we argue over whether struggles for the family wage in the nineteenth century reflected women's interests in stable family life or men's desire to push women out of the labor market, over whether the capacity of women to earn wages yielded independence and autonomy or served to extend family obligations. Each stage reflects a social transformation that delegitimized certain customary roles and replaced them with others, and from which some women benefited while others did not. And so it is with the struggle for pay equity for women. We can and must debate the way it will affect particular groups of women within a context that observes the social transformation of which the demand is a part.

A Challenge to Gender Differences

Comparable worth now appears as part of a long political process within which women have tried to achieve some sense of equity and justice as it is defined in their historical period. It is so strongly resisted in part, I suggest, because a large and potentially powerful group of wage earners, in questioning the conception of the free market, challenges its ideological roots as well. And because it raises to consciousness the issue of equity on which the market rests, comparable worth challenges the legitimacy of gender lines. It purports to delegitimize one element of the market pattern—namely, sex. The end result would be to equate female and male workers; to threaten a male worker's sense of self, pride, and masculinity; and to challenge the authority of basic institutions that touch all aspects of social and political life. The federal district court that rejected the request of Denver nurses that they be paid as much as the city's tree trimmers caught the problem exactly. Such a change, the court commented, in a much-quoted decision, "was pregnant with the possibility of disrupting the entire economic system of the United States."[16]

The point is that it might be true. In refusing to sanction gender distinctions, comparable worth raises a long line of earlier challenges to a new level. The historical context reveals pay equity to be an issue both of the gendered definition of justice and of the way justice manifests itself in the market. Seen from that perspective, comparable worth calls for nothing less than the revaluation of women. Its strength lies in its potential for acting upon female traditions, for it assumes that women have a right to pursue traditional roles and to achieve equity in that pursuit. Thus, it sustains those presumed qualities of womanhood—nurturance, community, and relational abilities—that are likely to have been products of women's cultural and social roles and that have, as a result, been traditionally devalued by the job market.

But comparable worth poses one other crucial challenge to historians. Because it rests on a redefinition of equity, which is historically specific, it confronts us with definitions of difference that are rooted in historical experience. The debate over comparable worth thus opens the question of what difference has meant to various groups of women and how it has manifested itself. The task is crucial to understanding changing forms of justice. If we allow abstract descriptions of "woman" and abstract notions of "woman's culture" to govern our interpretations of the past, we provide what Carr called a blank check. We offer empty categories that invite ideological uses of the past. We have seen in the Sears case [17] the consequences that this blank check can have in arguments that the nurturing and biological roles of all women preclude working women and needy women from seeking rewards in the work force, discourage them from investing in human capital, and lead them to devote more time and attention to families. These arguments, which are partly sustained by appeals to recent philosophy and psychology of sex differences and which rest on conceptions of the universal female, are negated by historical experience. It is not that most women have not performed traditional tasks but that the history of women's actual work force roles demonstrates a far more complex set of struggles by which different women at different times and places have tried to find their own directions in their own ways. In the United States immigrant women, educated women, black women, poor women, and married and unmarried women have each in their own ways come to locate their places within the shifting bounds of historical possibility.

Notions of universal womanhood blind us to the reciprocally confirming relationship of the work force and gendered ideas of social role. Judith Long Laws talks about how the labor market provides information that conditions aspiration and channels people's expectations along realistic paths. [18] The historical record, however, reveals how readily information changes in wars and depressions, how selectively it is presented to poor women as opposed to those who are well off, how much more limited it is for women of color than for white women. It demonstrates that difference is not a universal category but a social specific. And it reveals that how women handle differences can vary dramatically with historical circumstance. Carole Turbin and Mary Blewett, among other scholars, offer evidence of "nondichotomous" differences.[19] They suggest that women can be different in terms of life patterns and family commitments and yet struggle in the work force like men and with them.

Rooting Theory in Historical Experience

We are led to two conclusions. First, although social and cultural differences between women and men surely exist, their abstract expression is less instructive than a clear-eyed analysis in historical context. Second, such analysis should not be allowed to obscure differences among women and the historically specific ways in which they manifest themselves and serve as sources of tension and change. Poet Audre Lorde put it this way: difference, she argued, "must not be merely tolerated, but seen as a fund of necessary polarities between which our creativity can spark like a dialectic."[20]

In the labor market, difference provides the core of struggle. It is entrenched in the cultural symbolism of jobs. Outdoor, heavy, and skilled work are associated with pay/provider roles, and dexterity and compassion are tied to poor pay and secondary jobs. Difference is reflected as well in the struggle of women and men to maintain dependent as well as independent relationships. The working-class husband tells an interviewer that his wife "doesn't know how to be a real wife, you know, feminine and really womanly. . . . She doesn't know how to give respect because she's too independent. She feels that she's a working woman and she puts in almost as many hours as I do and brings home a pay check, so there's no one person above the other. She doesn't want there to be a king in this household."[21] He is revealing something about his expectations of traditional roles that we need to hear. The women who opposed the Equal Rights Amendment because they feared giving up alimony are reluctant to abandon their conceptions of equity for new and unknown forms. But these are not universal statements. They are pieces of a historical struggle we need to understand. They tell us something about the distribution of rewards in a society and about the role that sexual constraints play in it, about the structures of power and about their gendered meanings. They therefore tell us something about the reciprocal relationship between sexuality and social power.

In negating individual and particular experience, abstract arguments from difference ride roughshod over the aspirations and motivations of most women. The undifferentiated "woman" becomes a reified object instead of a social category subject to analysis, an abstraction rather than an actor in the historical enterprise. This is not an argument against theory or against conceptualizing. Rather, it is a plea that our theories be conditioned by the experiences of real actors—an expression of concern that the "universal female" not become a device to negate the possibility of equity and inadvertently open the door to perpetual inequality.

We are brought full circle. History offers a picture of wage relations that are not systemic but constructed and processual—a picture from which most women were once excluded and into which they are now drawn. Like the labor market itself, the wage relation is constructed out of subjective experience and rests ultimately on the legitimacy of historically specific notions of gender "difference." The historical record puts teeth into arguments for pay equity. As part of a changing battle for a changing definition of justice, its political parameters become comprehensible, and the meaning of the argument becomes more apparent.

Comparable worth illustrates how we construct consciousness out of historical experience. And it illustrates as well how the historian who explores the past in dialogue with the present can develop a richer understanding of the past. The struggle of women to redefine such concepts as justice, liberty, and power, which reflect a vision of the future, pushes us to explore the past from which such ideas emerged. Because ideas don't come from thin air, our attempts to discover how they took shape—how diverse groups appropriated, shaped, and rejected them—enriches our understanding of the historical process and places content into what is otherwise a blank check or an empty box.

The reverse is also true. Without a history, public policy follows the paths of social myth. By entering the debate, we, historians of women, have in our hands the possibility of shaping the future. Without a history, our argument that women have a right to paid work can be turned into an excuse to push women with small children to take poorly paid, meaningless jobs. Without a history, our search for safe and accessible methods of birth control can be (and has been) translated into forced sterilization for the most vulnerable among us. Without a history, it is plausible for policymakers, legislatures, new right groups, and ordinary women to interpret the problems women encounter in doing paid jobs as products of personal "choices" rather than as social issues. Without a history, employed women are asked to find solutions to what are called their own personal problems in their own ways.

An influential pair of sociologists demonstrated the consequences of

an obligingly absent historical consciousness this way: when "family obligations come to be perceived as obstacles to self-realization in [women's]
careers, individual women will have to decide on their priorities. Our own
hope is that many will come to understand that life is more than a career
and that this 'more' is above all to be found in the family. But, however
individual women decide, they should not expect public policy to underwrite and subsidize their life plans."[22] To which the historian of women,
politely eschewing the temptation to tackle the false historical assumptions
contained in the statement, responds that as long as policymakers can invent a history that ignores the rich diversity of women's experiences, our
task will not be completed.

Notes

Acknowledgments: This is a slightly revised version of the keynote address given
at the Seventh Berkshire Conference on the History of Women, Wellesley College,
19 June 1987. The author wishes to thank Susan Reverby, Dorothy Helly, and the
program committee of the Berks for inviting her to deliver the address and Bert
Silverman for sharing ideas and information.

1. Brief of the American Civil Liberties Union et al., amici curiae, in California Federal Savings and Loan Association v. Mark Guerra et al., 85-494 U.S. 12-14
(1986); and Brief of Equal Rights Advocates et al., amici curiae, in California Federal
Savings and Loan Association v. Mark Guerra, 85-494 U.S. 7-9 (1986).

2. In U.S. Steelworkers v. Weber, 443 U.S. 193 (1979), the court sustained a voluntary and temporary affirmative action plan to redress past grievances suffered by
a specific group. Quotations are from the decision as it appeared in the *Daily Labor
Report,* 20 March 1987, p. D16 (emphasis added).

3. "Comparable Worth: An Interview with Heidi Hartmann and June O'Neill,"
New Perspectives 17 (September 1985): 29.

4. Donald J. Treiman and Heidi Hartmann, eds., *Women, Work, and Wages: Equal
Pay for Jobs of Equal Value* (Washington, D.C.: National Academy Press, 1981), 28, ix.

5. Barbara R. Bergmann, "Pay Equity—Surprising Answers to Hard Questions,"
Challenge 30 (May–June 1987): 47. See also Helen Remick, ed., *Comparable Worth and
Wage Discrimination: Technical Possibilities and Political Realities* (Philadelphia: Temple
University Press, 1984), for essays generally favorable to comparable worth.

6. Michael Levin, "Comparable Worth: The Feminist Road to Socialism," *Commentary* 79 (September 1984): 13–19. See also E. Robert Livernash, ed., *Comparable
Worth: Issues and Alternatives* (Washington, D.C.: Equal Employment Advisory Council, 1984), for essays generally opposed to comparable worth.

7. Raymond de Roover, "The Concept of the Just Price: Theory and Economic
Policy," in *Economic Thought: A Historical Anthology,* ed. James Gherity (New York:
Random House, 1969), 23.

8. John Dunlop, "Wage Contours," in *Unemployment and Inflation: Institutional and
Structural Views,* ed. Michael Piore (White Plains, N.Y.: M.E. Sharpe, 1979), 66.

9. Arthur M. Ross, *Trade Union Wage Policy* (Berkeley: University of California
Press, 1948), 49.

10. Ibid., 50–51 (emphasis added).

11. Michael J. Piore, "Unemployment and Inflation: An Alternative View," in Piore, *Unemployment and Inflation*, 6.

12. Eileen Power, *Medieval Women* (London: Cambridge University Press, 1975), 60.

13. William Bielby and James Baron, "Undoing Discrimination: Job Integration and Comparable Worth," in *Ingredients for Women's Employment Policy*, ed. Christine Bose and Glenna Spitz (Albany: SUNY Press, 1987), 218.

14. "Corporate Women: They're About to Break Through to the Top," *Business Week*, 22 June 1987, p. 74.

15. Edward Hallett Carr, *What Is History?* (New York: Knopf, 1962), 105–6.

16. Quoted in Mary Heen, "A Review of Federal Court Decisions under Title VII of the Civil Rights Act of 1964," in Remick, *Comparable Worth*, 217.

17. See Ruth Milkman, "Women's History and the Sears Case," *Feminist Studies* 12 (Summer 1986): 375–400; and Alice Kessler-Harris, "Equal Employment Opportunity Commission v. Sears Roebuck and Company: A Personal Account," *Radical History Review* 35 (April 1986): 57–79.

18. Judith Long Laws, "Work Aspiration of Women: False Leads and New Starts," in *Women and the Workplace: The Implications of Occupational Segregation*, ed. Martha Blaxall and Barbara Reagan (Chicago: University of Chicago Press, 1976), 33–49.

19. Carole Turbin, "Reconceptualizing Family, Work, and Labor Organizing: Working Women in Troy, 1860–90," *Review of Radical Political Economy* 16 (Spring 1984): 1–16; Mary Blewett, *Men, Women, Work, and Gender* (Champaign: University of Illinois Press, 1988).

20. Audre Lorde, "The Master's Tools Will Never Dismantle the Master's House," in *This Bridge Called My Back: Writings by Radical Women of Color*, ed. Cherrie Moraga and Gloria Anzaldua (New York: Kitchen Table/Women of Color Press, 1983), 99.

21. Lillian Breslow Rubin, *Worlds of Pain: Life in the Working-Class Family* (New York: Basic Books, 1976), 176.

22. Brigitte Berger and Peter L. Berger, *The War over the Family: Capturing the Middle Ground* (Garden City, N.Y.: Anchor Press/Doubleday, 1983), 205.

24   Feminist Political Discourses

Radical versus Liberal Approaches to the Feminization of Poverty and Comparable Worth

Johanna Brenner

The "feminization of poverty" and "comparable worth" have become feminist issues in part so that feminist politics might include the
central concerns of working-class women and women of color. Women
social scientists have played an important part as scholars producing data
to attest to the social reality of gendered inequality and as technical ad-
visers to organizations and governments concerned with remedying economic inequities.[1] Because of the role feminist social scientists play in both
campaigns, we need to consider carefully the broader politics within which
these issues are inserted.

I contend that situated within a liberal political discourse, both the
"feminization of poverty" and "comparable worth" campaigns, in practice
and often in rhetoric, fail to bridge class and race divisions among women
and instead reinforce the separation of feminism from the movements of
other subordinated groups. While appearing to speak to problems that
women share, they have tended to unite only through a denial of race
and class differences. My point is not that these campaigns and the issues
they raise are mistaken. Rather, it is that the current organization of these
campaigns, in particular the policy demands and their accompanying justifications, may not constructively address differences in the situation and

Source: This article by Johanna Brenner is reprinted from *Gender and Society* 1, no. 4
(1987), pp. 447–65, copyright © 1987 by Sage Publications, Inc. Reprinted by permission of Sage Publications, Inc., 2111 West Hillcrest Drive, Newbury Park, CA
91320.

needs of all classes of women. I suggest here an alternative framework that does not court the danger of strengthening the ideological and social underpinnings of women's subordination.

The Liberal Discourse and the Radical Alternative

A liberal discourse on equality operates with two interrelated assumptions. The first assumption involves issues of organization and allocation: that is, how necessary social functions—governance; education; the production of goods, services, and knowledge—should be organized (hierarchy) and how resources and labor time should be allocated (differential rewards). The second assumption involves the issue of dependence and the related separation of the public and private spheres: liberal thought assumes that social relationships of economy and polity are created by autonomous, independently contracting individuals.

A liberal discourse on equality centers on the ideal of meritocracy. The first assumption of liberal political thought accepts the notion of inequality and hierarchy: some will have more, some less; some will command, others follow; some will create, others only implement. Equality is defined as equal opportunity; thus, from a liberal perspective, fairness exists when the distribution of individuals within unequal positions reflects their individual qualities—their differential motivation, talent, intelligence, and effort—and not their gender, race, religion, or family background. Liberal demands have changed over time. In the eighteenth century they were tied to the free market and unregulated competition; in the twentieth century they are compatible with state intervention in the economy. But there is a continuity in liberal goals and argument. The free market was rejected when it became clear that the market alone would not distribute people in a meritocratic way. Inequalities in family economic and social status and historic prejudices led to unfair outcomes for meritorious individuals. State intervention was required to ensure equality of opportunity. The goal of twentieth-century policy is still a just distribution of individuals within a hierarchy of rewards and power.

The compelling character of this view is not surprising, since its crucial premises about social organization and human nature are widely accepted in advanced capitalist society: that there are large and significant differences between individuals in talent and potential; that a complex industrial society requires hierarchies; that competition and differential rewards for various positions within the hierarchies will motivate the most talented people to fill the most central and important positions.[2] A radical critique challenges these premises, claiming that most individuals are capable of making valuable contributions to society and, collectively, of governing it. Socialists (and many radical and socialist feminists) have contended that hierarchy brings out the worst, not the best, in individuals and that while those at the bottom suffer particularly, everyone is distorted and narrowed by competitive striving. They also contend that collective decision-making and responsibility are workable alternative forms of social organization even in an advanced industrial society, and that such forms promote the full development of individual talents and offer the greatest individual freedom.[3]

The second fundamental assumption of liberal political thought is that dependence belongs in the private sphere; there is no place for dependent individuals either in the notion of economic contract or in the concept of the citizen. Indeed, political citizenship is defined by independence, by the capacity to make choices based on individual self-interest, free from control by others on whom one is dependent. Similarly, wage laborers own their own persons and can sell their labor power as independent contractors. As Daniel Bell so nicely puts it:

> The liberal theory of society was framed by the twin axes of individualism and rationality. The unencumbered individual would seek to realize his own satisfactions on the basis of his work—he was to be rewarded for effort, pluck, and risk—and the exchange of products with others was calculated by each so as to maximize his own satisfactions. Society was to make no judgements between men— only to set the procedural rules—and the most efficient distribution of resources was the one that produced the greatest net balance of satisfactions.[4]

The contribution of women within the family in reproducing the male breadwinner and replacing his labor over a generation is of course hidden in liberal economic theory. The dependence of the whole society, the economy, and the political system on the family and women's work within the family is ignored. As Linda Gordon argues, "Liberal political and economic theory rests on assumptions about the sexual division of labor and on notions of citizens as heads of families."[5] A society of "freely contracting" male citizens relies on the prior existence of the noncontractual relationships of the family. Women and children (and other non-earners) are regarded as dependents of men. How they fare depends on the "effort" and "pluck" of their male protector. Michèle Barrett and Mary McIntosh argue that "in order to elevate the morality of the market into an entire social ethic it is necessary to ignore all those members of society who do not themselves enter the market. . . . Those who cannot earn a living are subsumed under those who can." [6] Women's dependence within the family makes them non-citizens, and their family commitments make them politically suspect. [7]

Welfare-state intervention is justified within a political framework that retains the notion of the independent citizen. Just as the society has an obligation to promote the conditions for a free and fair exchange between competing individuals but no obligation to secure their livelihood, the society has a collective obligation to care only for those individuals who cannot legitimately be asked to care for themselves and who, through no fault of their own, cannot be cared for within the family system. Welfare policy has generally been constructed so as to restore the male-breadwinner family, not to substitute for it. [8] Thus, men and women have had a very different relationship to the welfare state and different ways of legitimating their claims to state support. Women have had to prove that they are morally deserving (their dependence is assumed); men have to prove they are legitimately dependent (their independence is assumed). For example, the rules and regulations of workers' compensation, disability programs, and unemployment insurance—developed primarily in response to the demands and needs of male workers—require that workers prove in the first two instances that they are no longer "able-bodied"; in the third, that they are without work through no fault of their own. [9]

The radical alternative to the liberal framework has argued for interdependence and the legitimate claim of each individual on the community to meet her or his needs for good and productive work, physical sustenance, emotional support, and social recognition. Radical and socialist feminists have further argued that men are as dependent on women's unpaid labor (including women's emotional work) as women are on men's income and that parenthood is a social contribution and should be recognized as such. Socialist feminists have envisioned a society in which the right to contribute and the right to be cared for are equally shared by men and women. This depends on a reformulation of individual and collective responsibilities and the redistribution of material resources such that the care of dependent individuals is no longer primarily a private responsibility of the family. [10]

Feminists have of course been divided on how to approach the state: whether to demand "a fair field and no favor" or "protection." [11] The comparable worth campaign is organized around the first approach: it is essentially a campaign to rectify distortions of the market, which has failed to reward women according to the value of their work. It therefore appeals directly to the liberal principle of meritocracy. The feminization of poverty campaign is organized around the second approach: it aims to rectify men's failure to provide for their wives through refusing child support and spousal support (in the case of divorced women) or through life insurance (in the case of widows). Women's claims on the state for support are justified by their lack of a male breadwinner. In what follows I discuss the ways in which both campaigns reflect a liberal political discourse, outline the likely consequences, and suggest an alternative approach.

The Feminization of Poverty

Two central assertions of the concept of the feminization of poverty—"Divorce produces a single man and a single mother"; "Forty percent of ex-husbands contribute nothing to their children's support"—link women's poverty primarily to men's failure to support their families. They also picture women's poverty as something that happens even to good middle-class people. In this regard the campaign to alleviate such poverty shares with earlier feminist campaigns, such as those for women's legal right of separation and for mothers' pensions, an imagery of female victimization. While attempting to provide women with an alternative to marriage, these campaigns operated within ideological terms and political limits that assumed rather than undermined the male-breadwinner family.[12]

Like those campaigns, too, the feminization of poverty campaign responds to a real problem facing women and has a potentially radical side. Yet in all three instances, in seeking to legitimize their demands and to be most effective in gathering political support, feminists have appealed to broadly held liberal political values and assumptions. As Nancy Folbre argues, the increasing pauperization of motherhood reflects a consensus that AFDC mothers are not among the "deserving" poor.[13] The feminization of poverty campaign attempts to change this perception. But while portraying poor women as innocent victims of men's irresponsibility may win more sympathy for the plight of poor women, it does so at the cost of failing to challenge deeply held notions about feminine dependence on a male breadwinner and distinctions between the deserving and the nondeserving poor—in particular between the "good" woman who is poor because her husband refuses support and the "bad" woman who is poor because she has had a child outside of marriage or has married a poor man who cannot provide.

The feminization of poverty literature often assumes that women of all races and classes have a common destiny as poor, single heads of families following divorce or widowhood. It is true that women's standard of living generally declines after divorce, while their ex-husbands' standard of living rises.[14] But relative deprivation is not impoverishment. Some women—for example, those with the more affluent ex-husbands, those employed during marriage, those with marketable job skills—are less likely to end up poor.[15] Moreover, race and ethnic differences are quite striking in this regard. The 1983 median income for black and Hispanic women maintaining families was only 60 percent of the median income of white women maintaining families: $7,999 and $7,797 compared to $13,761. The unemployment rate for black and Hispanic women maintaining families is double that of white women: 18.7 percent and 16.7 percent compared to 8.6 percent.[16] And while many white women are "only a husband away from poverty," many minority women with husbands are poor: 13.8 percent of all black married-couple families were below the poverty level compared to 6.3 percent of all white married-couple families.[17]

A study comparing separated and divorced women with children whose family income when married had been in the upper, middle, or lower thirds of the income distribution showed that although divorce and separation had a leveling effect, significant differences in women's income after divorce or separation remained even after five years. Women who when married had a family income in the top third lost the most proportionately (50 percent of family income); women in the poorest third experienced the least drop (22 percent of family income). But women from the highest third had post-divorce or -separation incomes twice that of women from the lowest third and 131 percent of that of women from the middle third, because women from more affluent marriages were more likely to receive alimony and child support.[18] Women from the lowest income brackets were most likely to be eligible for welfare and food stamps (71 percent in the first year), whereas in the first year only one-fourth of the women from marriages in the middle third income bracket received welfare or food stamps, and that had dropped to one-eighth by the fifth year.

In addition to ignoring class and race differences among women, the feminization of poverty campaign denies the poverty of men, especially minority men. Women make up an increasing proportion of the poor because more women are falling into poverty, not because more men are getting out. As Julianne Malvaux argues, the slogan that "by the year 2000 all the poor will be women and children" is true only if genocide (or full employment) is planned for minority men.[19]

One reason poor women outnumber poor men is that men have a shorter life span: after age sixty-five there are 1.5 women for every man. However, older black men are twice as likely to be poor as older white women and three times more likely than older white men. Hispanic men

over sixty-five are also more impoverished than white women—20.7 percent compared to 7.2 percent.[20] In 1984 white widows had a mean family
income of $23,469 and an average income per family member of $8,331,
compared to a mean income of $13,464 and $3,663 per family member
for widowed black women, and $15,503 and $4,515 per family member for
widowed Hispanic women.[21]

The astonishing growth in families headed by a woman between 1970
and 1984 (from 11.5 percent to 22.9 percent overall and from 33 percent to 56 percent among blacks) and the consequent increasing poverty of
women may be the result, at least in part, of the economic structure rather
than of men's neglect of their familial responsibilities. Many black men
do not have access to steady employment and well-paid work. Carol Stack
describes the cross-household survival networks that organize family life
among poor blacks: black fathers may contribute to their children's support even while living in a different female-headed household.[22] In 1979,
15 percent of black men aged twenty-five to sixty were living in households
in which they were not the head, compared with 6 percent of white men
in the same age group.[23] For the underclass, minority or white, poverty is
not simply a problem of women without men; it includes sons, husbands,
ex-husbands, and fathers.

When the feminization of poverty campaign focuses on the increased
standard of living of divorced men compared with that of their ex-wives
and looks to legislation to enforce child support as a solution to women's
poverty, it fails to address this reality. By 1984, in the United States, never-
married women constituted one-half of the household heads among black
women-headed families. Sixty percent of these women were under thirty.
Black men between the ages of fifteen and twenty-nine (those most likely to
be the fathers of these women's children) were not making enough money
to support them: a substantial proportion had no income, and a majority
were earning less than $10,000 a year.[24] A California study found that half
of the ex-husbands of women in the welfare system had incomes less than
$15,000 a year.[25]

There is surely a fine but very important line between the feminist demand that men take responsibility for their children and the antifeminist
demand that men have the obligation to be the family breadwinner. The
new right recognizes the poverty of abandoned women. Its solution is to
force men to support women and children by making divorce more difficult (in order to tie men to their families), demanding that welfare women
name the child's father and tell how to find him, and so forth.[26] The claim
that women's poverty is caused by deadbeat fathers—like the claim that
black poverty is caused by teenage mothers—is not only factually incorrect

but looks to the restoration of the nuclear family as the solution to the problem of dependent care.[27]

The point is not to let men escape their obligations but rather to address women's poverty in a more comprehensive way. In the face of political opposition and constricted government budgets, expanded public services for single mothers—increased eligibility for means-tested benefits, inexpensive quality child care for the working poor and near poor, and so on —will not be easy to win. The desperate need of poor women may seem to justify the use of whatever arguments appear politically effective. However, we ought to be alerted to the dangers of this temptation by the way that previous reform campaigns (protective legislation for women workers, for example) appealed to prevailing gender ideals and thereby contributed to perpetuating a gender ideology that justified women's exclusion from public life.[28]

The alleviation of women's poverty ought to be incorporated into a broader program of social and economic change. The familistic ideology and state policy that deny collective responsibility for dependent individuals, force women to take on the burdens of caring, and assume that only men have a claim to economic independence and citizenship must be transformed. For instance, a comprehensive system of supplements to low-income households, regardless of their composition, would benefit all the poor and near poor but would benefit female-headed families most. Paid parental leave (for meeting the needs of older children as well as infants) would benefit single mothers as well as help men and married women to combine wage work and care-giving.

In the longer run a living wage, quality child care, and good work are necessary for everyone but especially for women who choose not to share child care with a man. A program that incorporates short-term reforms into the larger goal of expanded social responsibility for caring would counteract both the stereotypical dependence of women as care-givers and the stereotypical independence of men as citizen-workers. This approach would frame the feminization of poverty issue in a way that connects it to the movements of working-class people and people of color.[29]

Comparable Worth

As its proponents have argued, the concept of comparable worth focuses attention on the systematic devaluation of women's work and the roots of that devaluation in a general cultural denigration of women and womanly activities. Unlike equal pay and affirmative action programs, comparable worth offers the possibility of raising the wages of the vast majority of women working in jobs that have traditionally been held mostly by women. Trade unions, especially in the public sector, have embraced comparable worth as a strategy for raising their members' wages, and many working women have been brought into union activity around the issue.

Because it is taken up by trade unions and because it has met resistance from employers, employer organizations, and political conservatives, advocates of comparable worth have tended to assume that it is a radical or potentially radical campaign. Heidi Hartmann and Donald Treiman argue: "Claims of comparable worth force explicit discussion about relative pay rates. As such, they politicize wagesetting in a new, possibly even revolutionary, way."[30] Similarly, Roslyn Feldberg argues that comparable worth "has radical implications because it initiates an end to women's economic dependency and questions the market basis of wages."[31]

Comparable worth has often been referred to as the civil rights issue of the 1980s. Yet its significance as a remedy for women's low pay and occupational segregation is limited. Its application has been most effective among workers in public settings because these workers are often unionized and because these unions can bring pressure through legislatures or elected officials. The state of Washington finally bargained a comparable worth settlement with the American Federation of State, County, and Municipal Employees, even after the union's comparable worth lawsuit lost on appeal. The city of San Francisco was forced to give comparable worth raises to women and members of minority groups—a step Mayor Diane Feinstein had resisted—after voters approved a ballot measure directing city officials to resolve the pay inequities.[32] Lacking such political pressure, the chances for imposing comparable worth on the private sector through the courts are slim, at least in the near future: such suits are rarely won, and only a small proportion of women employees in the private sector are unionized.[33]

While a demand for recognition of the value of their work and higher pay is a possible strategy for all women workers, raising wages by comparing women's and men's wages in comparable jobs will not work in such industries as insurance, where men are employed mostly at the top and middle levels and women at the bottom.[34] Affirmative action remains crucial to encouraging women's employment in nontraditional occupations and management. Further, as even its supporters point out, comparable worth will not improve the access of women of color to jobs and education.[35]

As a political discourse, comparable worth's fundamental claim to legitimacy reinforces an existing ideology: the necessity and validity of meritocratic hierarchy. Rather than questioning the market as an arbiter of wages, comparable worth attempts, as two of its most prominent advocates say, to

pay a fair market wage to jobs historically done by women. This
means that the wage rate should be based on the productivity-
based job content characteristics of the jobs and not on the sex of
the typical job incumbent . . . comparable worth advocates seek to
disentangle and remove discrimination from the market.[36]

Job evaluations use wage surveys to fix a dollar value to the factor points
for "benchmark" jobs, which are then used to establish a salary scale. Job
evaluations measure only the traits of jobs; the money value of the traits
is determined by the wages prevailing in the labor market.[37] Thus, comparable worth aims primarily to rationalize the sorting and selecting of
individuals into unequal places and does *not* eliminate market criteria from
job evaluation.

From this point of view, comparable worth is a relatively conservative
approach to women's low pay in that it situates its rationale firmly within
the hegemonic liberal political discourse. A radical approach to women's
low pay would not only challenge the existing inequities between women's
and men's pay for comparable jobs but would also contest the notion that
people's income should be determined primarily by where they fit in an
occupational hierarchy. If jobs are assessed in terms of their necessity to
an integrated labor process, it is equally important that all jobs be done
consistently and well. Anyone who contributes his or her best efforts in a
particular job is as deserving as any other individual.

Western contemporary society will not accept "from each according to
his/her ability, to each according to his/her need" as a standard of fairness.
Nonetheless, the claim that everyone who labors deserves to live decently
has been, particularly in periods of working-class mobilization, a central
value. Historically, of course, trade unions have appealed to the right of
the working *man* to make a family wage. Perhaps because that strategy has
served to institutionalize women's marginalization in wage labor, feminists
have preferred to address the problem of women's low pay in terms other
than their life needs as individuals and as mothers. Perhaps also because
it relies on broadly shared meritocratic values, comparable worth may appear to be the more practical approach to raising women's pay. But so long
as comparable worth efforts remain within that liberal discourse, they risk
increasing racial and occupational divisions among working women in the
long run.

The heart of the comparable worth strategy is the job evaluation. Certain dimensions of every job are measured and given a numerical rating:
knowledge and skill, effort, responsibility, and working conditions are the
major dimensions used. These dimensions are then weighted. Typically,

skill and responsibility are given higher weights than working conditions. In the Hay study on which a comparable worth adjustment for Idaho state employees was based, the weight given the dimension of responsibility was forty-two times the weight given to working conditions.[38] Supervision of other people and responsibility for money or expensive equipment are measures that may not reflect responsibilities typical of women's jobs.

Leslie McArthur argues that important dimensions of jobs are left out of most job evaluations. Low opportunity for advancement, questionable job security, and how boring the work is might also be considered as compensable factors; jobs might deserve higher compensation not only for poor physical working conditions but for poor psychological conditions. Yet of course, as McArthur also reports, the more desirable a job is, the higher its monetary worth is judged—not the other way around.[39] Therefore, the impact of a given job evaluation scheme on a given work force will depend on how the evaluations are constructed. Donald Treiman demonstrates that those evaluation methods which put a low value on working conditions and physical strength will tend to assign higher scores to jobs typically done by whites. He concludes:

> The choice of factors and factor weights in job evaluation schemes should not be regarded as a technical issue beyond the purview of affected parties but rather as an expression of the values underlying notions of equity and hence as a matter to be negotiated as part of the wage-setting process.[40]

To evaluate the probable impact of comparable worth, then, we need to consider who will participate in the negotiations over the factors and factor weights and with what sorts of assumptions. Since less than one-fifth of the U.S. work force and only 13 percent of all women workers are unionized,[41] we can expect that in most cases technical experts and management will formulate the evaluation policies. We can further expect that existing cultural biases will be replicated in factors and factor weights. Joan Acker demonstrates how difficult it is to overcome experts' and managers' resistance to altering evaluation systems even in a unionized and public setting, especially when alterations might change the rank order of jobs or undermine pay differentials between management and nonmanagement employees.[42]

Malvaux contends that black men and women will benefit from comparable worth adjustments because the jobs they hold tend to be even more underpaid, relative to comparable white men's jobs, than are white women's jobs.[43] However, the implementation of a job evaluation scheme that all parties agree is "equitable" may also help to legitimize large differences in pay by race and occupation. Even after the implementation of comparable worth among Washington state employees, one of the highest nonmanagement women's jobs will pay 149 percent of one of the lowest women's jobs.[44] Estimating the impact of comparable worth adjustments under different conditions, Aldrich and Buchele found the earnings gap between women by quintiles would be reduced by at most 6.5 percent. Since women are not distributed proportionately by race within job categories, large inequities by race will remain, appearing to be reflections of differential merit and thus more difficult to challenge.[45]

Comparable worth may also exacerbate hierarchies in women's jobs. For example, hospital administrations do not award differential salaries among nursing specialties, although there is a clear hierarchy of rewards to medical specialties. Remick predicts that job evaluation systems may expose "internal squabbles that will have to be dealt with by the nursing profession."[46] At hearings conducted by the U.S. Equal Employment Opportunities Commission in 1980, the American Nurses Association testified to the similarities between intensive-care-unit nurses and doctors.[47] Comparable worth adjustments may encourage nurses with such specialties to claim higher pay.

Comparable worth may very well open up discussion of how society values work, but that discussion must be framed by a broader challenge to the prevailing culture. The superior value of mental over manual skills and the greater importance of supervisory over other kinds of responsibility should be not assumed but questioned. Otherwise, we can expect comparable worth to readjust women's and men's pay but to make very little change in—perhaps even to solidify—the existing divisions in the work force: divisions between whites and minority workers, between designated professionals and nonprofessionals, between white-collar and blue-collar workers. These divisions cut across gender and have been an important source of trade-union disunity. Yet any radical potential for politicizing the wage-setting process depends on the strength of worker organization.

Gender divisions within the work force have played an important part in perpetuating women's low pay. Male-dominated trade unions have been willing to take up the issue only as women workers have become organized. The kinds of strategies used for raising the pay of women workers can aggravate or undermine men's resistance, increase or decrease the possibility of overcoming employer opposition, and create a more unified or a more divided work force.

Job evaluation studies often find men's job classes "overpaid" for the content of their jobs, especially the craft jobs that tend to be held by white men.[48] Since it may be felt that market realities require relatively higher wages in order to recruit and hold those workers, and it may be illegal to equalize pay scales by lowering men's wages, most plans attempt to achieve equity over the long run by gradually increasing women's wages. Some plans freeze men's wages; others simply raise men's wages more slowly by, for example, giving all workers a cost-of-living raise and women workers an equity bonus. The plan selected influences the impact of a comparable worth settlement on relationships between the men's and women's sections of a work force. Freezing men's wages is divisive, but because it is cheaper, comparable worth adjustments will probably take that route except where worker organization and union leadership mount effective opposition.

A less divisive strategy is to adjust women's wages to a level commensurate with the intrinsic value of their work. In the strike by women clericals at Yale, the union demanded higher pay on the grounds that the women make an important contribution to the university, a contribution historically undervalued because they were women. The union did not center its strategy on a direct comparison with men's wages or claims about the comparative value of men's and women's work. The women were well organized; the unionized, predominantly blue-collar men had nothing to lose and much to gain from a united work force. Hence, the men were willing to honor the women's picket line for the entire ten weeks of the strike. The women reciprocated and supported the men when their contract came up, which allowed the men to make gains that they had unsuccessfully struck for in the past.[49] In short, although the women's and men's pay scales were adjusted separately rather than in relation to each other, the gender gap was narrowed.

In sum, comparable worth seems to offer an immediate remedy to a pressing problem, but it may institutionalize divisions among women that will make future collective campaigns difficult. While some supporters of comparable worth themselves signal the dangers—such as the dominance of technocrats and managers in wage-setting, and divisions among women workers[50]—they tend to minimize the risks and overestimate the campaign's radical potential. It seems to me that unless a very different kind of organizing is done around the issue, this potential is not likely to be realized.

Comparable worth has been presented as a demand for removing discrimination and improving women's position within an existing system. The demand for equity could, however, be put forward as part of a broader set of longer-range goals that challenge the terms of the system itself. A radical strategy would argue for raising the pay of the lowest-paid workers, most of whom are women and minorities, on the grounds that everyone who contributes her or his labor deserves a comfortable and secure existence. This strategy would not only protest the undervaluation of women's work but would also argue that existing salary differentials among jobs, especially between management and nonmanagement jobs, are unnecessarily large. And it would argue that if we are looking at the work people do, then we should ask whether that work is productive and safe, and whether it allows people to use their talents and skills and to develop new ones.

Conclusion

Feminist historians have written at length about the ways that the dual-spheres ideology of the nineteenth and early twentieth centuries shaped feminist politics and blunted the radical potential of the women's movement.[51] Liberal political discourse has similarly shaped contemporary feminist thinking. The feminization of poverty and comparable worth campaigns argue their case in terms of claims that reflect and in turn reinforce the assumptions of a liberal political framework.

A radical framework contests these assumptions, challenges the hierarchical organization of work and the privatization of care-giving, and generates a more inclusive set of claims. A language of rights does not have to be limited to a narrowly defined meritocratic standard but can be expanded to include the rights to contribute one's best efforts, to do work that enriches, and to receive in return a decent standard of living. It can also include the right of children to care from their community and the right of parents to economic and social support in carrying out their responsibilities to their children.

Neither the feminization of poverty nor comparable worth are inherently radical concepts. Their impact will depend on how solutions are conceptualized, how they are implemented, and how they are used politically.

Notes

1. Pamela S. Cain, "The Role of the Sciences in the Comparable Worth Movement," in *Social Science and Social Policy*, ed. R. Lance Shotland and Melvin. M. Mark (Beverly Hills, Calif.: Sage, 1985), 156–70; Diana M. Pearce and Harriet McAdoo, *Women and Children: Alone and in Poverty* (Washington, D.C.: National Advisory Council on Economic Opportunity); Donald J. Treiman and Heidi I. Hartmann, eds., *Women, Work, and Wages: Equal Pay for Jobs of Equal Value* (Washington, D.C.: National Academy Press, 1981).

2. Kingsley Davis and Wilbert E. Moore, "Some Principles of Stratification." *American Sociological Review* 10 (1945): 242–49.

3. Kathy Ferguson, *The Feminist Case against Bureaucracy* (Philadelphia: Temple University Press, 1984); Ronald M. Mason, *Participatory and Workplace Democracy: A Theoretical Development in Critique of Liberalism* (New York: Basic Books, 1982); Joyce Rothschild-Whitt, "The Collectivist Organization: An Alternative to Rational Bureaucratic Models," *American Sociological Review* 44 (1979): 509–27.

4. Daniel Bell, "On Meritocracy and Equality," *Public Interest* 29 (1972): 58.

5. Linda Gordon, "Feminism and Social Control: The Case of Child Abuse and Neglect," in *What Is Feminism? A Re-examination*, ed. Juliet Mitchell and Ann Oakley (New York: Pantheon, 1986), 81.

6. Michèle Barrett and Mary McIntosh, *The Anti-social Family* (London: Verso, 1982), 48–49.

7. Susan Okin, *Women in Western Political Thought* (Princeton, N.J.: Princeton University Press, 1979); Carole Pateman, "'The Disorder of Women': Women, Love, and the Sense of Justice," *Ethics* 91 (1980): 20–34.

8. Jane Lewis, ed., *Women's Welfare/Women's Rights* (London: Croom Helm, 1983); Eli Zaretsky, "The Place of the Family in the Origins of the Welfare State," in *Rethinking the Family: Some Feminist Questions*, ed. Barrie Thorne, with Marilyn Yalom (New York: Longman, 1982), 188–220.

9. Barbara J. Nelson, "Women's Poverty and Women's Citizenship: Some Political Consequences of Economic Marginality," *Signs* 10 (1984): 209–31.

10. Barrett and McIntosh, *Anti-social Family*.

11. Jane Lewis, "Feminism and Welfare," in Mitchell and Oakley, *What Is Feminism?* 85–100; Alice Kessler-Harris, *Out to Work: A History of Wage-Earning Women in the United States* (New York: Oxford University Press, 1982), chap. 7.

12. Eileen Boris and Peter Bardaglio, "The Transformation of Patriarchy: The Historic Role of the State," in *Families, Politics, and Public Policy*, ed. Irene Diamond (New York: Longman, 1983), 70–93; Elizabeth Pleck, "Feminist Responses to 'Crimes against Women,' 1868–1896," *Signs* 8 (1983): 451–70.

13. Nancy Folbre, "The Pauperization of Motherhood: Patriarchy and Public Policy in the United States," *Review of Radical Political Economics* 16, no. 4 (1984): 72–88.

14. Lenore J. Weitzman, *The Divorce Revolution: The Unexpected Social and Economic Consequences for Women and Children in America* (New York: Free Press, 1985).

15. Ibid.; Robert S. Weiss, "The Impact of Marital Dissolution on Income and Consumption in Single-Parent Households," *Journal of Marriage and the Family* 46 (February 1984): 115–27.

16. Alliance against Women's Oppression, *Poverty: Not for Women Only* (San Francisco: Alliance against Women's Oppression, 1983).

17. U.S. Bureau of the Census, *Characteristics of the Population below the Poverty Level: 1984*, Current Population Reports, Consumer Income, ser. P-60, no. 152 (Washington, D.C.: Government Printing Office, 1984).

18. Weiss, "Impact of Marital Dissolution," tables 1, 3.

19. Julianne Malvaux, "The Economic Interests of Black and White Women: Are They Similar?" *Review of Black Political Economy* 14, no. 1 (1985): 4–27.

20. Bureau of the Census, *Characteristics of the Population below the Poverty Level: 1984*.

21. U.S. Bureau of the Census, *Money Income of Households, Families, and Persons*

in the U.S.: 1984, Current Population Reports, Consumer Income, ser. P-60, no. 151 (Washington, D.C.: Government Printing Office, 1984).

22. Carol B. Stack, *All Our Kin: Strategies for Survival in a Black Community* (New York: Harper & Row, 1975).

23. U.S. Bureau of the Census, *Census of the Population, 1980: Detailed Population Characteristics, U.S. Summary* (Washington, D.C.: Government Printing Office, 1980).

24. Margaret C. Simms, "Black Women Who Head Families: An Economic Struggle," *Review of Black Political Economy* 14, nos. 2–3 (1985–86): 140–51.

25. Women's Economic Agenda Project, *Women's Economic Agenda* (Oakland, Calif., n.d.).

26. Barbara Ehrenreich and Karen Stallard, "The Nouveau Poor," *Ms.*, July–August 1982, pp. 217–24.

27. William A. Darity, Jr., and Samuel L. Myers, Jr., "Changes in Black-White Income Inequality, 1968–1978: A Decade of Progress," *Review of Black Political Economy* 10, no. 4 (1980): 167–77; Wendy Sarvasy and Judith Van Allen, "Fighting the Feminization of Poverty: Socialist-Feminist Analysis and Strategy," *Review of Radical Political Economics* 16, no. 4 (1984): 89–110.

28. Johanna Brenner and Maria Ramas, "Rethinking Women's Oppression." *New Left Review* 144 (May–June 1984): 33–71; Kessler-Harris, *Out to Work*.

29. For a more detailed presentation of a socialist-feminist politics on the "feminization of poverty," see Sarvasy and Van Allen, "Fighting the Feminization of Poverty."

30. Heidi I. Hartmann and Donald J. Treiman, "Notes on the NAS Study of Equal Pay for Jobs of Equal Value," *Public Personnel Management* 12 (1983): 416.

31. Roslyn L. Feldberg, "Comparable Worth: Toward Theory and Practice in the United States," *Signs* 10 (1984): 313.

32. "San Francisco Agrees to Pay Rise for Women," *New York Times*, 20 March 1987, p. 11.

33. Frances C. Hutner, *Equal Pay for Comparable Worth: The Working Woman's Issue of the Eighties* (New York: Praeger, 1986); "Union Membership of Employed Wage and Salary Workers, 1985," *Monthly Labor Review* (May 1986): 44–46.

34. Helen Remick, "Major Issues in *a priori* Applications," in *Comparable Worth and Wage Discrimination*, ed. Helen Remick (Philadelphia: Temple University Press, 1984), 99–117.

35. Feldberg, "Comparable Worth"; and Julianne Malvaux, "Comparable Worth and Its Impact on Black Women," *Review of Black Political Economy* 14, nos. 2–3 (1985–86): 47–62.

36. Helen Remick and Ronnie J. Steinberg, "Technical Possibilities and Political Realities: Concluding Remarks," in Remick, *Comparable Worth*, 289.

37. Mark Aldrich and Robert Buchele, *The Economics of Comparable Worth* (Cambridge, Mass.: Ballinger, 1986).

38. Donald J. Treiman, "Effect of Choice of Factors and Factor Weights in Job Evaluation," in Remick, *Comparable Worth*, 79–89.

39. Leslie Zebrowitz McArthur, "Social Judgment Biases in Comparable Worth Analysis," in *Comparable Worth: New Directions for Research*, ed. Heidi I. Hartmann (Washington, D.C.: National Academy Press, 1985), 53–70.

40. Treiman, "Effect of Choice of Factors," 89.

41. "Union Membership."

42. Joan Acker, "Sex Bias in Job Evaluation: A Comparable Worth Issue," in *In-*

gredients for Women's Employment Policy, ed. Christine Bose and Glenna Spitze (Albany: SUNY Press, 1986), 183–96.

43. Malvaux, "Comparable Worth," p. 54.

44. Calculated from Remick, "Major Issues."

45. Aldrich and Buchele, *Economics of Comparable Worth*, p. 147.

46. Helen Remick, "Dilemmas of Implementation: The Case of Nursing," in Remick, *Comparable Worth*, 97.

47. Lorraine D. Eyde, "Evaluating Job Evaluation: Emerging Research Issues for Comparable Worth Analysis," *Public Personnel Management* 10 (1983): 425–44.

48. Robert L. Farnquist, "Pandora's Worth: The San Jose Experience," *Public Personnel Management* 12 (1983): 358–68.

49. Molly Ladd-Taylor, "Women Workers and the Yale Strike," *Feminist Studies* 11 (1985): 465–91.

50. Feldberg, "Comparable Worth"; Remick, "Dilemmas of Implementation."

51. See, e.g., Linda Gordon and Ellen DuBois, "Seeking Ecstacy on the Battlefield: Danger and Pleasure in 19th Century Feminist Sexual Thought," *Feminist Studies* 8 (1983): 451–70.

25 Radical Challenges in a Liberal World
The Mixed Success of Comparable Worth

Ronnie J. Steinberg

The emergence of the contemporary women's movement has ushered in a profound change in consciousness about the position of women. Accompanying these changing expectations in American society has been a quiet, unsubtle revolution in women's role in politics. Women have become an institutionalized force in American politics, with dramatic results: in the 1970s Congress passed 71 laws that were part of the feminist political agenda.[1] Gains have been greatest in the extension of legal entitlements in employment and education, among them equal pay for work of comparable worth.[2] Nonetheless, although women's rights are fuller than they were twenty years ago, specific changes for women that have thus far come about have been minimalist.[3] As feminist advocates are fully aware, comparable worth is no exception to this pattern.

Academic social scientists are finally catching up with pay equity activists in their understanding that comparable worth is a limited remedy for occupational segregation and the wage gap.[4] Johanna Brenner's well-reasoned, sympathetic critique of the reform locates these limitations in a reliance on meritocratic values and a failure to challenge the market as the arbiter of wages.[5] Comparable worth, according to Brenner, relies too heavily on liberal feminist discourse: proponents demand "a fair field and

Source: This article by Ronnie J. Steinberg is reprinted from *Gender and Society* 1, no. 4 (1987), pp. 466–75, copyright © 1987 by Sage Publications, Inc. Reprinted by permission of Sage Publications, Inc., 2111 West Hillcrest Drive, Newbury Park, CA 91320.

no favor" as the standard for correcting market distortions on wages. This, she contends, rationalizes the sorting of individuals into unequal places and justifies a wage structure based on occupational hierarchy.

Job evaluation is the tool that proponents offer to correct inequities, but the very structure of job evaluation, as Brenner points out and Joan Acker has also noted, reproduces class relations in compensation systems.[6] Mental work continues to be valued over manual work; supervision over nonsupervision. By using male wages as a standard of comparison, proponents pit nonmanagerial workers against one another, driving a wedge between men and women. Pay equity carries the risk of creating even deeper divisions among women in such lower-paying positions as nurse, secretary, and waitress, because it legitimates the basis of compensable differences among jobs.

I agree with much of what Brenner is saying. Comparable worth is compatible with meritocratic values. Above all else, it requires consistency in wage-setting practices: if jobs historically performed by women and male minorities require equivalent amounts of education or levels of supervision, these jobs should be paid at the same rate as white male jobs that have these prerequisites and responsibilities. Comparable worth examines the wage structure as it applies to compensation for jobs, not individuals; therefore, it does not sort individuals into positions, as Brenner suggests, but sorts positions on the basis of a more consistent and less biased application of existing policy. At its essence, it takes a structural as opposed to an individualistic approach to setting wages.

We proponents consciously argue for the reform using terms borrowed from conventional labor-market ideology, adopting the National Research Council framework that wages can be partially based on the market.[7] We defend the use of job evaluation, even though we are highly critical of the practical application of the technique.[8] And although comparable worth may exacerbate tensions among men and women workers in the short run—because continued worker solidarity would bring with it continued gender stratification—to the extent that comparable worth eliminates inequality based on gender, it creates an internally more egalitarian basis for solidarity.

The Complicated Trajectory of Reform

Brenner's analysis develops only one side of a far more complicated story about the logic and trajectory of the reform. This alternative story examines political discourse in relation to a specific political agenda and to the historical and political context out of which the struggle over the control of the discourse emerged. It thus locates the use of a discourse within a particular power constellation. It suggests, for pay equity, that the discourse adopted was less a reflection of the political agenda of proponents than it was a strategic and at times even desperate attempt to keep their agenda alive.

We did keep the issue alive, and we even achieved some results. Comparable worth has broadened public thinking on what discrimination is and has redefined standards of fairness. It has stimulated women to compare their wages with those of their male counterparts, an unthinkable comparison three decades ago. Large numbers of men and women express collectively their anger at the wages they receive. And we have improved the wages paid for female and minority work, even if the adjustments were more modest than we had hoped. In some initiatives including Florida and New York City, the results of pay equity study point to much higher adjustments on the basis of race than of gender, contrary to Brenner's fears.

This strategy has been both a success and a failure. Liberal political discourse is a symptom of the failure, but the cause lies in the severe power imbalance between proponents and opponents. Early on, proponents were forced to defend comparable worth as not inconsistent with the market *because* powerful, vocal, and conservative opponents of pay equity threatened to discredit the reform before it was even attempted. In fact, they succeeded in defeating large numbers of pay equity claims in the courts. The *Lemons* v. *City and County of Denver* decision regarded comparable worth as "pregnant with the possibility of disrupting the entire economic system." Not surprisingly, the decision dismissed pay equity claims, even in the face of employer collusion in wage setting. From *Christensen* v. *Iowa* to *Spaulding* v. *State of Washington*, the courts have allowed a reliance on the market and prevailing wage practices as grounds for perpetuating a two-tiered wage structure by gender and race.[9] We were reactive for tactical reasons, but we also put some dents in a favorite conservative power resource.

Proponents have chosen to deny not that there is a market in which wages are set but that the free market is an accurate or even an adequate basis for determining wages. Contrary to the neoclassical market myth, proponents describe a market driven by bureaucratic wage-setting practices, by custom, prejudices, and ideologies that have been mediated by struggles between employers and employees.[10] Even the National Research Council has entered the debate, concluding that wage differentials between men and women are better explained by institutional approaches than by neoclassical analysis.[11] Ray Marshall and Beth Paulin, testifying before the unsympathetic U.S. Commission on Civil Rights, went so far as to characterize the debate over comparable worth as a debate over competing models of the market.[12]

Proponents were thus engaged in a struggle over the *meaning* of the market. We influenced some people and kept the reform on the political agenda. Comparable worth, which does violate the *ideology* of an unconstrained market, was redefined in terms somewhat consistent with the market. At best, the two now coexist in uneasy tension, awaiting more favorable political times.

Meritocracy Reexamined

Analogously, proponents have done significant work to expose the ideological basis of meritocracy even as we relegitimated it. We asked, for example, why people who work with money earn substantially more than people who work with people. We asked other questions that revealed the association of skills and gender.[13] We also asked questions about unacknowledged responsibilities: why, for example, secretaries of university deans, public school superintendents, and personnel directors are not compensated for working with confidential information while their bosses are. All these issues treat women as a class. If compensation systems revalue caretaking, for example, all nurses and health aides will benefit equally, regardless of where they fall on the hierarchy.[14]

We questioned why managers received so many job evaluation points for supervising work while nonmanagers received so few points for actually *doing* it. By questioning which characteristics are worthy of compensation and the relative value of different job characteristics, proponents initiated "a discussion of how value is assigned to jobs," which stimulated a debate "about social values and priorities underlying the wage hierarchy."[15] Not only did we raise questions about the meritocracy; we also raised questions about its objective foundations.

This strategic approach is shaped by an alternative view of how change happens. It would require *both* "improving women's position within an existing system" *and* "changing the terms of the system itself," to borrow from and transcend Brenner's dichotomy. Because the free market and the meritocracy are largely myths perpetuating existing institutional arrangements to the benefit of those in power, a strategy of exposing how far actual wage-setting practices deviate from these standards can simultaneously legitimate the reform initiative (to be sure, in terms of the existing state) and require those in power to abide by their own ideology. It is exactly the point made by E. P. Thompson in his analysis of eighteenth-century class struggles over the meaning of property rights: "What was often at issue was not property, supported by law, against no property; it was alternative definitions of property rights. . . . And, it is often from within that very rhetoric that a radical critique of the practice of society is developed." [16]

Granted, this approach to change represents a messy route through the existing institutions in which the conventional discourse is used as the basis to redefine the existing discourse. At times, proponents appeared to be defending institutions and ideologies that were antithetical to the goal of pay equity as we originally envisaged it. [17] But, I would argue, this messy route was the only route open to travel.

To be sure, comparable worth flows from a different and less inherently radical agenda than the one proposed by Brenner. It will not usher in a society premised on a guarantee that each person, regardless of work status, is entitled to a livable income or to democratic decision-making in the workplace. Nonetheless, were we to realize the meritocracy, women's wages would increase, on average, 10 to 30 percent—which, according to Heidi Hartmann, would have radical consequences for the economic independence of women. [18] If implemented fully, it would go a long way toward eliminating gender stratification in compensation. Moreover, comparable worth calls for more open and informed scrutiny of wage-setting decisions and thereby intrudes on the guarded rights of management. It radically undermines the substructure of highly skewed employer-employee relations. Some have concluded that maintaining control is even more important to employers than saving money, suggesting that the exposure of compensation practices is highly subversive. [19]

Unfortunately, we are not even ushering in the meritocracy. Male manual labor continues to be valued more highly than female mental skills. Actual pay equity adjustments have fallen far short of those projected by Hartmann, ranging from 5 to 15 percent of salaries. Compensation systems are not being cleansed of sex bias. In New York state, for example, the recently announced pay equity plan is based on a compensation model that *negatively* values work performed in historically female and minority jobs: if you work with difficult clients, your salary is less than it would be without this job component. (The unions, by the way, have not been explicitly informed by management of this feature of the compensation policy.) [20] Compensation systems are not even being made consistent in their application to jobs by gender and race. In Washington state, to cite one of several instances, undervalued female-dominated jobs are being adjusted as much as 5 percent *below* the average male salary line. [21] In Massachusetts, management continues to bargain *separate* salary plans across highly sex-segregated bargaining units. This means that male- and female-dominated jobs with the same number of evaluated points receive different wages. Not surprisingly, male-dominated bargaining units do better; worker solidarity aside, these male-dominated unions have generally supported management preferences.

Power Struggles in Implementation

Pay equity proponents have been able to pass the critical first hurdle: legislation has been enacted, studies have been begun, court cases filed, union contracts negotiated, and task forces established with at least some feminist representation. However, even when pay equity has apparently been won and monies appropriated, feminists have never controlled its implementation. Brenner seems well aware of the importance of implementation when she abandons her analysis of discourse to point to "the need to consider who will participate in the negotiations over factors and factor weights." But she fails to develop this political line of reasoning.

Personnel departments in Vermont, West Virginia, and North Carolina, for example, used monies appropriated for pay equity to do what they had always wanted to do but could not get the political leverage—update classification procedures.[22] In New York, after the apparent success of a feminist-controlled study, the whole question was restudied by a staff of seventeen from Civil Service, without a full-time feminist or trade-union proponent monitoring their efforts.[23] Here was an initiative funded jointly by labor and management, in which labor was able to bargain only "meet and confer" rights over management deliberations, because public employees in the state were legally prohibited from bargaining matters of compensation. To add insult to injury, in announcing its implementation plan the state legitimated its policy by associating its more limited results with those of the proponents' early study.

Typically, bureaucrats, though not ideological opponents of the reform, have found it necessary to "manage" comparable worth, cleansing it of its radical features. Largely male trade-union leadership, too, has paid lip service to the reform but often drifts back to solutions that encompass all workers, which perpetuates gender stratification. This union strategy has backfired on occasion, as management insists that it downgrade all employees above the line if labor wants to upgrade all employees below the line.

Proponents were thus either pushed out of the decision-making process entirely, placed in a minority position, or constrained. Political debates were turned into technical decisions, which were made inaccessible to those who would benefit from the reform. Information was withheld, making it impossible for proponents to come up with proactive counterproposals. And other political agendas were put on the table and treated as being of greater importance than comparable worth.

Suppose we were to start with an even more radical discourse, like Brenner's goal of a decent, livable income for all who work. All too easily, such radical discourse gets co-opted and transformed into less than radical agendas. For example, the demand for a livable income turned into a minimum wage law with industry and firm size restrictions, excluding virtually all minority workers. As the law was amended to increase the scope of coverage, the wage standards declined. Since 1968, when the standards reached their peak, the purchasing power of the minimum wage has deteriorated, and it has fallen as a share of average wages.[24]

Democratic decision-making, another of Brenner's goals, has been taken up by management with a vengeance but not in its radical form. Instead, we have quality circles: management-formed committees that problem-solve around a set of workplace issues narrowly defined by management. These not only give employees the false impression that they have a say in how things are run but also filter up to management information that it might otherwise not receive. Workplace democracy has also been used to sidestep unions where they exist and to avoid them where they are not yet found.

We need to look beyond discourse to examine power and tactics. We need a radical politics to accompany our radical principles. We can no longer leave our goals to liberals and then criticize them when they're insufficiently powerful or don't understand the contradictions of the situations in which they find themselves. Alternative strategies will grow out of mobilization efforts and electoral strategies. But they need to go beyond them to consider ways for feminist insiders to gain control of the terms of debate, greater access to information, and greater control over policy decisions. If we succeed in carving out new strategies, we will be more likely to achieve our agendas—not because policymakers see the intrinsic validity of the arguments we are making but because the costs of opposing our agenda prove greater than the costs of doing it our way.

Notes

Acknowledgements: Joan Acker, Michael Ames, Ralf Dahrendorf, Lois Haignere, and Jerry Jacobs offered extremely insightful comments on earlier drafts and in discussion of key ideas for this paper.

1. Ethel Klein, *Gender Politics* (Cambridge, Mass.: Harvard University Press, 1984), 30. See also Janet Flammang, ed., *Political Women: Current Roles in State and Local Government* (Beverly Hills: Sage, 1984).

2. Ellen Boneparth, "A Framework for Policy Analysis," in Ellen Boneparth, ed., *Women, Power, and Policy* (New York: Pergamon, 1982), 2–3.

3. Ronnie Steinberg, "The Unsubtle Revolution: Women, the State and Equal Employment," in Jane Jensen et al., ed., *Work and Politics: The Feminization of the Labor Force* (London: Oxford University Press, 1988).

4. See Barbara Reskin, "Sex Differences and the Devaluation of Women's Work: Implications for Women's Occupational Progress and Comparable Worth," working paper, Department of Sociology, University of Illinois, Urbana 1987.

5. Johanna Brenner, "Feminist Political Discourses: Radical versus Liberal Approaches to the Feminization of Poverty and Comparable Worth," *Gender and Society* 1, no. 4 (1987); also Chapter 24 in this book.

6. Joan Acker, "Sex Bias in Job Evaluation: A Comparable Worth Issue," in Christine Bose and Glenna Spitze, ed., *Ingredients for Women's Employment Policy* (Albany, N.Y.: SUNY Press, 1987), 183–96.

7. Donald Treiman and Heidi I. Hartmann, *Women, Work, and Wages: Equal Pay for Jobs of Equal Value* (Washington, D.C.: National Academy Press, 1981).

8. Helen Remick, "Dilemmas of Implementation: The Case of Nursing," in Helen Remick, ed., *Comparable Worth and Wage Discrimination* (Philadelphia: Temple University Press, 1984); Ronnie Steinberg and Lois Haignere, "Equitable Compensation: Methodological Criteria for Comparable Worth," in Bose and Spitze, *Ingredients for Women's Employment Policy*, 157–82.

9. Mary Heen, "A Review of Federal Court Decisions under Title VII of the Civil Rights Act of 1984," in Remick, *Comparable Worth*; Paula England and Dorothea Weir, "Comparable Worth: Recent Developments in the Federal Courts," Working Paper No. 8703, Center for Applied Research, University of Texas, Dallas.

10. Roslyn Feldberg, "Comparable Worth: Toward Theory and Practice in the United States," *Signs* 10, no. 2 (1984): 319, 324–25.

11. Treiman and Hartmann, *Women, Work and Wages*, 45.

12. Ray Marshall and Beth Paulin, "The Employment and Earnings of Women: The Comparable Worth Debate," in *Comparable Worth: Issue for the 80s* (Washington, D.C.: Government Printing Office, 1984), 1:204.

13. Anne Phillips and Barbara Taylor, "Sex and Skills: Notes Towards a Feminist Economics," *Feminist Review* 6 (1980): 79–88.

14. To be sure, comparable worth *may* exacerbate existing tensions among women workers. Whether or not it *will* do so is an empirical question. The answer will depend on such factors as the history of working relationships among groups of women, the educational strategies developed by union leadership, and the strategy for containing the reform adopted by management. In Wisconsin, e.g., the legislative task force proposed an implementation plan in which *all* female-dominated jobs were upgraded two salary grades, or approximately 10 percent, to adjust for pay equity.

15. Feldberg, "Comparable Worth," 324.

16. E. P. Thompson, *Whigs and Hunters: The Origins of the Black Act* (New York: Pantheon, 1975), 261, 265.

17. Ronnie Steinberg, "Feminist Critiques and Feminist Politics: The Case of Comparable Worth," paper presented at the Eastern Sociological Association meeting, 1987.

18. Heidi Hartmann, "Comparable Worth and Women's Economic Independence," in Bose and Spitze, *Ingredients for Women's Employment Policy*, 251–58.

19. Richard Edwards, *Contested Terrain: The Transformation of the Workplace in the Twentieth Century* (New York: Basic Books, 1979); Ronnie Steinberg, *Wages and Hours: Labor and Reform in Twentieth Century America* (New Brunswick, N.J.: Rutgers University Press, 1982).

20. Ronnie Steinberg, "From Radical Vision to Minimalist Reform: The Politics of Pay Equity," paper presented at the Russell Sage Foundation, 1987.

21. Helen Remick, "Long-Run Technical Implications of Comparable Worth," in Ronnie J. Steinberg, ed., *The Politics and Practice of Pay Equity* (Philadelphia: Temple University Press, forthcoming).

22. Elaine Johansen, *Comparable Worth: The Myth and the Movement* (Boulder, Colo.: Westview Press, 1984).

23. The Civil Service commissioner under whom the Implementation Task Force worked was a feminist pay equity proponent. The task force was housed in a department headed by a prominent pro–pay equity feminist. For reasons discussed at length elsewhere (Steinberg, "From Radical Vision to Minimalist Reform"), including the fact that there was no strong external base of support, she was unable to obtain her agenda in the face of overwhelming constraints from other segments of management. In addition, the day-to-day manager of the task force was the assistant director of classification, who admittedly regarded pay equity as secondary to achieving a rational classification system.

24. Ralph Smith and Bruce Vavrichek, "The Minimum Wage: Its Relation to Incomes and Poverty," *Monthly Labor Review*, June 1987, pp. 24–30.

26   The New Economy
Female Labor and the Office of the Future

Barbara Baran

Advanced industrial economies are clearly in the throes of a fundamental economic transition, as new technologies and new forms of competition restructure the productive base and transform the relationships among economic actors. Within this context, it is commonplace to note the growing role of female labor. But what really is this new role? What is the relationship, for example, between the much heralded technological revolution and the feminization of the work force that analysts have observed across a range of industries—but most particularly in the white-collar industries where women are concentrated?

The constructs at our disposal for analyzing periods of change are limited and tend initially to be borrowed from earlier historical epochs. Thus, when socialist feminists first began addressing this question, they relied heavily on the pioneering work of Harry Braverman.[1] Braverman argues that despite the differences between old and new technologies, the dynamic of transformation is a familiar one. Just as the Industrial Revolution robbed skilled artisans of their trade, automation of the office will deskill and degrade white-collar labor. As in the factory, office work is being divided into hundreds of minute fragments parceled out among thousands of "detail" workers who thereby lose control over the product of their labor and any

Source: This article is a substantially revised version of "Office Automation and Women's Work: The Technological Transformation of the Insurance Industry," an essay that appeared in Manuel Castells, ed., *High Technology, Space, and Society* (Beverly Hills, Calif.: Sage Publications, 1985), pp. 143–71, copyright © 1985 by Sage Publications, Inc. Reprinted by permission of Sage Publications, Inc., 2111 West Hillcrest Drive, Newbury Park, CA 91320.

variety in their daily activity. Most, or perhaps all, of each day is spent operating a machine. As middle-level jobs are deskilled, the work force is polarizing into a mass of unskilled workers on the one hand and a tiny coterie of managers and professionals on the other. The only difference between the factory and the office is the gender of those at the bottom.

Extending this line of argument, socialist-feminist writers suggested that it would be women rather than men who would suffer skill degradation as computers moved into the new white-collar settings.[2] This process, they pointed out, is not a new one. The entrance of women into the formerly all-male domain of office employment at the turn of the century coincided with a dramatic decline in the status, pay, and working conditions of the clerk. The creation of a relatively cheap, abundant labor force was in fact a pre-condition for the dramatic expansion of administrative activity after World War I. The introduction of a new, sex-neutral technology—the typewriter —paved the way for the transition from male to female labor. Historically, these analysts suggest, women and machinery have been introduced into a labor process simultaneously, women being used to break the resistance of skilled workers to the reorganization and deskilling of their work. In the present period, women are again being forced to assume this role; feminization is therefore likely to accompany computerization.

Finally, the feminist literature also warned that women will likely be excluded from whatever new *skilled* jobs are created by automation. In reply to those who point to an explosion of managerial and computer-related technical occupations as evidence of likely skill upgrading, the feminists argued that women have always been disproportionately underrepresented in such work.

The findings of the study reported here, based on a three-year investigation of the insurance industry, challenge many of these hypotheses.[3] First, my findings suggest that the Bravermanist analysis misses much of what is radically new about the new technologies insofar as it elevates the factory—with its assembly line and detail workers—to an essential aspect of the capitalist organization of production. Second, I conclude that it is the more highly skilled jobs and functions that are, on balance, being retained or created. As automation eliminates lower-level clerical positions, the remaining work force either is more highly skilled than in the past or requires new kinds of skills. Finally, I argue that the peculiar nature of female labor is indeed playing a central role in shaping the trajectory of the transformation now under way in the insurance industry. The salient characteristic of this labor force is not, however, that it is unskilled but rather that it is both *skilled* and *cheap*.

Critical to this argument is the fact that the process of office automation is an evolving one. The first wave of computerization did largely correspond to the expectations of the Bravermanists. Nevertheless, in the last few years it has been possible to discern the outlines of a fundamentally new dynamic that I attempt to describe here.

The First Wave

The first applications of computer-based technology in the insurance industry involved simple mechanization of extremely structured, high-volume operations. The early mainframes were used primarily as numbers-crunching machines. The automated tasks were fairly discrete so that the shift from manual to computerized performance had little effect on the organization as a whole; task fragmentation, or Taylorization, had already isolated these routinized functions.

Both the cost and technical requirements of the early machines and the tendency to automate in conformity with the rationalized structure of traditional administrative bureaucracies resulted in intensification of the long-term trend toward task fragmentation and functional centralization. Routine keyboarding was separated more sharply from other clerical functions and was often spatially isolated from the rest of the firm. Work in these processing centers (both data processing and word processing) was machine-linked, machine-paced, and often machine-supervised.

Task fragmentation was not limited to processing functions. Overall, the labor process in insurance companies was centralized by narrow function. For example, in a number of companies even the main professional occupation, underwriting, was rationalized: At the bottom end, low-level underwriting functions were transferred to a newly created clerical position; at the top end, more specialty underwriting categories were created. Workers were grouped into sections of underwriters, raters, typists; paper flowed from one section to another, mimicking the assembly line. This spatial segregation by occupation was tantamount to spatial segregation by gender. The professional and managerial categories were overwhelmingly male; the growing clerical work force solidly and increasingly female.

In line with the Bravermanist model, then, the first stage of automation tended to increase job fragmentation, centralize production by narrow function, heighten occupational sex segregation, and make many routine keyboarding functions spatially "footloose." More recently, however, the greater sophistication of the technologies and transformed market conditions are dictating a new organizational logic that promises to reverse many of these early trends.

The Office of the Future
The New Environment

During the 1970s the implementation of advanced office systems proceeded much more slowly than expected. The barriers to rapid diffusion were both technological and organizational. First, at the level of the technology itself, the task of representing the more complex white-collar activities in computer algorithms proved to be exceedingly difficult. Competition within the vendor community also slowed the development of the effective communications networks that are critical to the implementation of sophisticated, integrated office systems.

Second, resistance to automation within the user community proved to be an equally serious barrier to diffusion. Professionals, managers, and even secretaries balked at the introduction of machinery that threatened to transform the character of their work and the relations of power in their workplaces. It has taken a dramatic change in the competitive dynamics of the industry to begin to erode this resistance.

Falling interest rates and the slow but steady deregulation of the financial services sector have brought new competitors into the game and cut sharply into insurers' profit margins. Whereas formerly, as a regulated industry, insurance carriers were virtually assured a reasonable rate of return, today even some giants in the field are struggling for survival. Companies in which paternalism protected job security even through the Great Depression have recently been rocked to their foundation by layoffs of up to 1,500 employees virtually overnight.

At the same time, three technical developments in particular have improved the cost-effectiveness of systems implementation and widened the possible range of applications. First, the increasing miniaturization of electronic circuits has produced quantum leaps in the computing power of ever smaller and cheaper machines. Second, significant improvements in telecommunications technology and the merging of communications and computer technologies have allowed insurers to link their data processing equipment to numerous other office machines (word processers, facsimile transmitters, microfilmers, optical character recognition devices) both within buildings and across continents. Third, the simplification of computer language and greater sophistication of computer software have made possible a whole new range of applications.

A New Approach to Automation

Beginning in the late 1970s, as the range of possible computer implementations widened and systems analysts began winning their battle against middle-level knowledge workers, approaches to the problem of automation changed as dramatically as the machines. This evolution can be characterized as the movement from functional approaches to systems approaches: that is, from automating discrete tasks (typing, calculating) to rationalizing an entire procedure (new business issuance, claims processing) to restructuring and integrating all the procedures involved in a particular division, product line, or group of product lines.

New business issuance provides a good example. The trend in new business processing has been toward on-line, single-source entry. In a great many of these applications, rating, billing, and printing functions are performed entirely by the computer. The underwriting function is computer-assisted; that is, the computer provides actuarial guidelines, performs calculations, facilitates rapid access to policyholder files, and so on. Increasingly the policy moves electronically through the various steps in this process, producing daily reports on policy status at each work station. In the case of highly standarized policies, the computer may even perform the underwriting function.

On the basis of these integrated, on-line systems insurance companies have recently begun a serious redesign of the labor process. Although Taylorist logic continues to inform their efforts, the emerging organization of work bears little resemblance to the assembly line.

The Redesign of Work

The ideal operative on Ford's assembly line turned one bolt. The ideal production worker in the insurance company of the future, with the aid of a sophisticated computerized work station, will rate, underwrite, and issue all new policies for some subset of the company's customers, handle the updates and renewals on those policies, and, as a by-product, enter the information necessary for the automatic generation of management reports, actuarial decisions, and so on.

In many of the companies studied, two closely related processes are occurring. The first is the emergence of highly computer-linked, multi-activity jobs that combine tasks formerly performed by data entry clerks, other clerical workers, and professionals. Typically, data entry, rating, routine underwriting, and sometimes policy preparation have been transferred to a skilled clerical worker; a similar change has occurred in the claims handling process.

In these cases, unskilled clerical work has been largely eliminated; workers in the new clerical jobs, although closely circumscribed in their decision-making, are a long way from the typing pool. Judgment calls do have to be made by these clerks. Often they are required to interact directly with the agents, a level of responsibility formerly reserved for professional underwriters. Perhaps most important, because these workers are accepting risk and directly issuing policies, they are almost solely responsible for "quality control." Some kinds of quality checks are built into the computer systems, of course, but at this stage, at least, such monitoring functions only to catch gross errors and inconsistencies. Basically, in increasing numbers of insurance lines, clerks are responsible for the soundness and accuracy of the millions of routine risks their companies write and claims they settle.

Professionals are also having their work redefined, as clerks take over their lower-level functions. First, they have become "exceptions" handlers; that is, they are responsible only for the policies or claims that fail to fit into the "pigeonholes" of the computerized system, so their work is therefore become more interesting and complex. Second, in the case of underwriters at least, there has been a reorientation of the job function away from churning out policies and toward planning and marketing. In this way the job has been enlarged to combine tasks formerly divided among managerial, professional, and sales personnel. "Mental" and "manual" labor are also to some extent being recombined as higher-level employees are required to enter data directly into the machines, eliminating numerous clerical intermediaries.

The second major reintegrative process that is occurring is the elimination of single-activity units in favor of multi-activity teams. Whereas typists, raters, and underwriters were formerly divided into separate units, each with its own supervisor, now a small team consisting of one or two of each kind of worker will service some subset (often geographical) of the company's customers. In some cases this form of organization probably simply presages and prepares the organization for the more complete electronic reintegration of work just described; however, where the products are more specialized, complex, low volume, or changing rapidly, the team structure is likely to be a long-term arrangement.

Significantly, even the physical environment reflects this new approach. The walls of private offices have been torn down, and managers, professionals, and clericals work side by side in shoulder-high cubicles. Open office plans not only reduce overhead costs and permit flexible response to changing technologies; they work to erode outmoded social relations.

As the focus of automation shifts from the simplest to more complex functions, integrated systems begin to reverse the decades-long legacy of work fragmentation and to blur the distinctions between "front" office activities (dealing with customers) and "back" office activities (primarily paper processing). Workers who formerly served as appendages to a machine system are increasingly peripheralized from the direct activity of production into either "border" (public contact) functions or what Larry Hirschhorn has called "controlling the controls": that is, overseeing the operations of a largely automatic system.[4] At the same time, cost pressures are dictating that labor be moved out of clerical or other kinds of routine production work into higher value-added activities. A new emphasis on marketing is drawing the work force into service and sales. A new emphasis on product innovation is creating pressure for flexible machine systems and flexible work systems capable of adapting to rapid and ongoing change.

The New Efficiency in Production

What is most significant about the new systems is the extent to which they have restructured the organization as a whole, both internally and in its relationships to its customers. In many instances the new systems have not only transformed the logic of production but have also made it considerably more efficient. A comparison showing the leap in efficiency achieved by the shift from a partially automated to a more fully automated claims system gives a sense of the magnitude of the labor savings.

With the older system, the following work experience was typical:

> When the report of loss came into the office, a claims adjustor spent a couple of days verifying the loss and the identity of the insured. After determining the type of claim, the adjustor manually filled out an instruction sheet, received approval from a supervisor, and then sent the instruction form to a typist who used it to produce a coded encurl [an insurance form]. These documents were then shipped in batch form to the company's data processing center, which had to pull a Xeroxed copy of the policy to check the premium levels. If the policy was missing from the file—which was often the case— the clerk had to send a duplicate copy of the original rating sheets; claims coders then had to recode the premium in order to code the

claim. If the policy was in the file, coders simply copied the original codes and then sent the claim to the keypunch department, where it was entered into the system. Processing occurred on a batch basis at night; the system was updated only once a month. Claims payments were not only recorded automatically, but were also hand-logged onto a file folder and then reconciled with the computer file once a year.[5]

With the new system, although clerks still screen and sort the incoming claims, the adjustors (professional workers) themselves—using highly automated work stations—then investigate and encur the claims and authorize the checks, which are printed automatically. All the other steps in the process have been eliminated. Because this system is linked to the company's integrated master file, policyholder data is instantaneously available and does not have to be reentered; records are updated immediately and automatically.

A New Occupational Structure

Predictably, these changes in the organization of work are reflected in a new occupational structure. But in contrast to analysts who argue that automation tends to eliminate higher- and middle-level clerical occupations, this study suggests that narrow routine clerical jobs are the ones disappearing most rapidly. While most traditional clerical categories are declining, computers are best able to perform the highly structured functions associated with routine work.

Between 1970 and 1978, clerical employment as a percentage of total employment in the industry fell from 50 percent to 45 percent; in effect, 73,000 clerical jobs were eliminated by the shift in the occupational structure. Keyboarding and filing occupations were particularly seriously affected; the number of keypunch operations dropped by 22 percent, the number of file clerks by 20 percent, and the number of typists by 12 percent.[6] Whereas the first round of automation did, indeed, deskill and "proletarianize" much clerical work, the second round is totally eliminating many of those degraded functions.

The activities now being deskilled are those formerly performed by professional labor. Both users and vendors of office automation equipment have largely shifted their attention away from the task of automating routine activities and are struggling with the problems of how to translate the functions performed by knowledge-workers into computer software. As they are successful, these functions are turned over to cheaper labor.

In net, however, the rolling process of deskilling and redundancy is probably raising average skill levels within the industry. Large numbers of low-skilled clerks who formerly made up the bulk of the work force are being expelled; skilled clericals are taking over low-level professional functions; and the (smaller) professional staff is having its work upgraded. In all categories, then, there are relatively fewer jobs, but the remaining work is, overall, more skilled. In this case, therefore, it is critical conceptually to separate the individual workers from their functions. Elements of the work process are being degraded, but the specific agents now performing those functions are being either upgraded or rendered redundant.

New Job Requirements

As this discussion has begun to suggest, the newly emerging occupations require a different skill set from those associated with comparable positions in the past. Even the most task-specific of all job categories, routine data entry, is objectively being assigned new levels of responsibility: the most important of these is responsibility for the quality of the data. In the context of integrated databases, errors can be more significant, more costly, and most difficult to detect and correct, because data entered anywhere throughout the system is immediately recorded in all relevant files. There is also evidence that even routine data entry positions involve greater levels of mental concentration than traditional text entry because of the extent to which the work is mediated by a multiplicity of codes. Finally, the fact that systems are continually changing means that the work force must be unusually flexible and adaptable, sufficiently polyvalent to easily learn new routines, new codes, new procedures.[7] As machines assume narrow, detailed clerical functions, measurable skills like typing become much less important, and there is a new emphasis on intangible skills and personal qualities.

The broadening of job requirements is not simply the result of automation; it also represents a conscious management strategy designed to push certain aspects of decision-making downward from professional workers and from middle management. This strategy of what might be called "responsibilization" has several goals. The first and most important is simply to improve efficiency and reduce costs. Highly Taylorized, authoritarian work settings are inefficient on several counts: error rates are often intolerably high; turnover can be a problem; and most important, the costs of supervision are considerable. On the other side of the occupational hierarchy, expensive human capital can be wasted making relatively minor decisions. In the face of these inefficiencies, employers have been ready to exploit the capacity of the new technologies to circumscribe the scope and impact of decisions, allowing them to be turned over to workers at lower levels.

There is also, of course, a dark side to these trends. In some cases work is being deskilled in almost classic fashion. In many more cases, while computers electronically reintegrate job functions, the actual daily activity of the worker may be monotonous. Multifunction jobs are not necessarily multi-activity work, even when the worker's scope of knowledge and responsibility have widened. The combination of responsibility and monotony, in fact, constitutes a new source of occupational stress. Even more onerous are the cases in which the new technologies are being used to monitor worker performance and/or speed up the pace of work. Finally, despite rising skill levels, career paths may be structurally truncated.

In the past the barrier to mobility between clerical and professional occupations was primarily sex discrimination. Women were raters; men were underwriters. Theoretically, a rater could be prepared by her job and on-the-job training for an underwriting position, although in practice this rarely happened because of the gender-identification of job categories.

Affirmative action victories have created new opportunities for women to move up. Perhaps a third of the female underwriters and managers interviewed in one company had entered the firm ten to twelve years before in clerical positions. Now, however, as lower-level professional functions are automated, the "bridge" jobs between clerical and professional occupations are being eliminated. In the words of one personnel manager, there will be a "quantum jump" between the new machine-linked clerical or paraprofessional categories and the remaining more highly skilled professional, managerial, or sales work.

Overall, firms are moving away from an internal mobility system based on single or limited ports of entry to one in which the number of entry points has been expanded and career ladders have been much more sharply segmented. Although the personnel managers I interviewed expressed a continued commitment to internal promotion—and often even a preference for its effect on employee loyalty and the corporate culture—they also admitted to its decline.

The turn to external labor markets places an increasing emphasis on formal education and training as a prerequisite for career advancement. Workers already in the system who want to move into a more lucrative career path may have to exit entirely and return to school, or else acquire the necessary new skills (and even degrees) after work, on their own time. Workers not in the system can no longer look to on-the-job training as an alternative to formal education.[8]

The Growing Importance of Female Labor

As new technologies and new forms of competition transform the character of work in the insurance industry, the work force itself is undergoing an equally radical process of feminization. Almost overnight, whole occupational categories are shifting from predominantly male to predominantly female. Between 1970 and 1980 women claimed approximately 307,000 of the 352,000 new jobs created; and over the next two years women gained 8,900 jobs, whereas men lost 5,500. In total during this period female employment rose by 46 percent, compared to a meager 7 percent rise in male employment. In contrast to the economy as a whole, where the ratio of women to men increased by 4.7 percentage points, in the insurance industry the ratio climbed by 7.2 percentage points.

In this same period, however, clerical workers declined as a percentage of the work force. In other words, the increase in female employment cannot be explained by the disproportionate growth of traditionally female-typed jobs. On the contrary, in fact, what seems to be occurring is a major movement of women into traditional male occupations—professional, managerial, technical, and even clerical.

Between 1970 and 1979 the number of female managers and officers grew from 11 percent to 24 percent of the insurance work force, professionals from 17 percent to 38 percent, and technicians from 38 percent to 65 percent.[9] The percentage of women insurance examiners and investigators (formerly male clerical occupations) grew from 9 percent in 1962 to 26 percent in 1971 and 58 percent in 1981.[10]

Overall, the ratio of women to men in professional and technical occupations in the insurance industry rose by 19 and 27 percentage points respectively, as opposed to a 4.3-point gain for women throughout the economy in professional and technical occupations combined. Although the disaggregated comparative statistics are not extremely reliable, during this period women seem to have increased their share of professional employment in the insurance industry more rapidly than in any other major sector of the economy.[11]

There are a number of plausible explanations for this rapid transition from male to female labor. The first is simply affirmative action victories. Successful affirmative action suits have been waged against insurance companies, and as a result companies throughout the industry have developed more egalitarian hiring and promotion policies. For example, because of affirmative action litigation between 1977 and 1983, one company studied increased its percentage of female managers from 4 to 33 percent; professionals from 27 to 46 percent; and technicians from 29 to 67 percent.

There is also, however, reason to believe that cheaper female labor is being substituted for more expensive male labor throughout the occupational hierarchy and that women are being used to smooth the process of job redesign and introduction of the new machinery. The professional staffs in the new highly automated personal lines centers of the company where I conducted my intensive case study are so overwhelmingly female that the chief administrator of one joked about being under pressure to develop affirmative action goals for men. She explained that the reason they chose to hire women was that women are more "flexible" than men in adjusting to the computer-mediated labor process.

In another company the introduction of computer-assisted underwriting has shifted the bulk of policy processing from a department that is over 60 percent male to one that is entirely female. In still another the change to a computerized claims process not only brought protests from the older male adjustors but was accompanied by an increase in the percentage of female employees from approximately 25 percent of the claims force to over 60 percent.

Significantly also, although women are moving up in the occupational hierarchy, female wage rates in the industry remain extremely low. In one case study company, female professionals earn only 16 percent more than male clericals (whereas male professionals earn 50 percent more), and the majority of white female managers (57 percent) earn on the average four dollars *less* per week than white male clericals. Between 1970 and 1979 in the finance, insurance, and real estate (FIRE) sector as a whole, wages for nonsupervisory personnel fell more dramatically than in any other sector of the economy: whereas total real wages increased by 2 percent, in the FIRE sector real wages fell by 8 percent.[12]

Although it is possible that these kinds of data simply reflect the differences in the tenure of male and female workers in the better paid professional, managerial, and sales jobs, the evidence of gender segregation by occupation or, within broad occupations, by line of business is disturbing. The percentage of female professional and technical workers in the insurance industry varies widely by product line. In the more highly automated life and medical/health segments, women's share of employment is considerably higher.

Drawing together these statistics with the earlier description of changes occurring in the labor process, automation in the insurance industry seems to be creating precisely the kinds of jobs for which women always have been preferred—semiskilled, low-paid, and dead-end. In the face of growing competitive pressures, the substitution of women for men across a range of occupations serves to depress wage levels without sacrifices in the quality of labor.[13]

The Shift to the Suburbs

One critical indicator of the growing importance to the insurance industry of a literate but cheap female labor force is the extent to which insurers are following their workers to the suburbs. In the central cities, feminism and affirmative action gains have made it increasingly difficult to attract educated women into dead-end, low-wage work. White surburban housewives offer companies a partial solution to this dilemma. Because of their household and child-care responsibilities, these women are less career oriented and therefore more willing to accept jobs with limited occupational mobility; they may trade higher wages for flexible or shorter hours, and benefits may be less important to them if they and their children are covered by their husbands' plans. These women also, according to clerical organizers, are considerably less likely to be responsive to union initiatives than are minority women in the central cities, many of whom are the sole supporters of their households.

Kristin Nelson's study of where companies locate automated office activities (including insurance) concluded that, holding land costs constant, companies have chosen to site these portions of their operations in areas with a disproportionately high percentage of white, married suburban housewives.[14] My own case work tends to corroborate these observations. Executives in one company explained in great detail the analysis of census data that preceded the siting of their new automated centers; the chosen workers for the first of these to open in a small town in the Northeast were "white housewives of Germanic descent." Similarly, four companies studied have recently moved parts of their operations from major cities to adjacent suburban areas reportedly in search of a higher-quality clerical work force. Companies experimenting with homework consciously see this program as a way to take advantage of the labor pool of educated women with small children.

Female Labor as the Solution to a Managerial Dilemma

Women are being hired over men and firms are relocating operations because female labor provides a solution to an irksome emerging managerial dilemma: how to enhance the flexibility of the organization and increase the responsibility and performance capacity of the work force without relinquishing control or raising salaries.

First, married women workers of the kind the insurance industry is seeking to employ are a uniquely flexible work force. Their relative docility and cooperativeness lower the cost to the firm of job redesign and work reorganization, thus removing barriers to the diffusion of new technologies, the introduction of new products, and the transformation of the structure of the industry. Their relatively low career aspirations and limited alternative employment opportunities offer firms many of the advantages associated with bureaucratic control structures—that is, a responsible, stable work force—without the associated price tag in the form of developed avenues of mobility, rising salaries, and increasing labor "fixedness." [15] Employers are considerably more free to expand and contract labor demand: on the one hand, the latent supply of such workers is almost always readily available; on the other, married women tend to melt without complaining back into the family. [16]

The role of patrimonial relationships in all of this is ironic. Patrimony in the office, insofar as it encompasses both the male and female roles, rigidifies the organization and strengthens its ability to resist change; the mini-fiefdoms of middle managers, based on personal loyalties and buttressed by the private relationships between bosses and their secretaries, are the best example. The "social office" as such has been a prime target of top management, and gender relations within the workplace are moving toward greater equality. At the same time, however, the preferred female work force is fundamentally defined by the traditional relations of gender domination within the family which govern its outlook and behavior, and the kinds of jobs it is being offered by industry assume continued female dependence on the male wage and on the identity provided by marriage and motherhood. Exploiting the full rewards of this work force therefore entails some careful tightrope-walking.

Second, in addition to enhancing the flexibility of the organization, educated, married housewives offer a solution to an emerging skill dilemma. If skill is understood as both substantive complexity and autonomy/control, [17] one problem now facing managers in the insurance industry is how to separate these two components and raise the performance requirements of jobs—including the responsibility of the work force for outcomes (as opposed simply to work effort)—without substantially loosening their control over the organization, or in fact perhaps with the possibility of tightening it. Again, secondary wage earners in traditional family structures are often willing to accept work situations in which their scope of responsibility is fairly delimited so that they are free to meet their primary commitment, which is to the family.

Finally, as I have argued throughout, an educated female work force comes at a bargain rate: the discount in the industry is still almost 40 percent.

Opportunities for Women Will Vary by Class and Race

For all these reasons, although we can expect to see continued feminization of the work force in the insurance industry, employment opportunities for minority and less well-educated white women may decline. According to 1979 statistics from the Equal Employment Opportunity Commission, insurance carriers over the last decade have employed a relatively high percentage of minority clericals—22 percent of their clerical work force as compared to the industrywide average of 17 percent.[18] Undoubtedly, this is because insurance has unusually large numbers of routine, back-office jobs, the categories of clerical labor in which minority workers tend to be overrepresented.[19]

As the data processing centers begin to close and routine clerical categories shrink, minority clericals are in real danger of losing their jobs. Sally L. Hacker's study of technological change at AT&T concluded that the single best indicator of a job slated for elimination by automation was the disproportionate presence of minority women.[20]

The threat to minority workers is especially great insofar as the new offices are sited outside the central cities in white suburbs and small towns. For example, the three new personal lines centers of one company studied were set up in towns where minorities represented 3.1 percent, 3.3 percent, and 14.3 percent of the population. Finally, also, as Nelson has argued, the move to teams that involve close working relations among higher- and lower-level employees may well favor the hiring of "socially compatible" white women.[21]

Conclusion

Overall, although the new technologies may be freeing women from the pink-collar assembly lines and even raising skill levels of the female work force, there may be in the end little cause for good cheer.

For women at the bottom of the clerical hierarchy, jobs are simply disappearing. For skilled and particularly white clericals, there may be jobs but not opportunities; in this sense, their situation may actually worsen, relative to the possibilities for advancement that appeared to be opening up over the last two decades. Similarly, numbers of college-educated women may make their way into professional and managerial ranks only to find their talents undervalued. One high-ranking woman manager pointed to the emergence of what she called "velvet ghettos," industries dominated by women where the pay and prestige of top positions erode as a result.

At the same time, however, because of the significantly greater opportunities available to college-educated women than to their working-class sisters, the female occupational structure is apt to bifurcate more sharply than in the past, diminishing even further the egalitarian thrust of feminist strategies such as affirmative action. In general, in fact, the new technologies will likely make it more difficult for women to organize on their own behalf as work is increasingly isolated and companies are increasingly footloose.

The early feminist analyses of the impact of white-collar automation argued that the new technologies would degrade and deskill female workers. This study cautions against confusing the skill level of a job with other positive job attributes. Despite repeated assertions in the academic, popular, and even feminist press that women's work is unskilled work, female-dominated occupations across the economy are in fact associated with higher levels of skill on average than male-dominated occupations.[22] What they lack are the social rewards that neoclassical economic theory would have us believe are associated with skill. The new technologies may be radically transforming the organization of work, but they are doing so within the context of a division of labor that continues to devalue female labor.

Notes

1. Harry Braverman, *Labor and Monopoly Capital* (New York: Monthly Review Press, 1974).

2. See, e.g., Jane Barker and Hazel Downing, "Word Processing and the Transformation of the Patriarchal Relations of Control in the Office," *Capital and Class* 10 (Spring 1980): 64–99; Rosemary Crompton and Gareth Jones, *White Collar Proletariat: Deskilling and Gender in Clerical Work* (Philadelphia: Temple University Press, 1984); Rosemary Crompton and Stephen Reid, "The Deskilling of Clerical Work," in Stephen Wood, ed., *The Degradation of Work: Skill, Deskilling, and the Labour Process* (London: Hutchinson, 1982); Margery Davies, "Women's Place Is at the Typewriter: The Feminization of the Clerical Labor Force," in Richard C. Edwards et al., eds.,

Labor Market Segmentation (Lexington, Mass: Heath, 1975); Martin DeKadt, "Insurance: A Clerical Work Factory," in Andrew Zimbalist, ed., *Case Studies in the Labor Process* (New York: Monthly Review Press, 1979); Evelyn N. Glenn and Roslyn L. Feldberg, "Technology and Work Degradation: Effects of Office Automation on Women Clerical Workers," in Joyce Rothschild, ed., *Machina Ex Dea* (New York: Pergamon, 1983); Evelyn N. Glenn and Roslyn L. Feldberg, "Degraded and Deskilled: The Proletarianization of Clerical Work," in *Social Problems* 25 (October 1977): 52–64; Karen Nussbaum and Judith Gregory, *Race against Time: Automation of the Office* (Cleveland, Ohio: Working Women Education Fund, 1980); Jackie West, "New Technology and Women's Office Work," in Jackie West, ed., *Work, Women, and the Labor Market* (London: Routledge & Kegan Paul, 1982).

3. This study was conducted while I was a fellow at the Berkeley Roundtable on the International Economy; the study was funded by the U.S. Congress Office of Technology Assessment. For a complete version, see Barbara E. Baran, "The Technological Transformation of White Collar Work: A Case Study of the Insurance Industry" (Ph.D. diss., University of California, Berkeley, 1986). For other discussions of automation in the insurance industry, see Paul Adler, "Rethinking the Skill Requirements of the New Technologies," Harvard Business School working paper (October 1983); Eileen Appelbaum, "The Impact of Technology on Skill Requirements and Occupation Structure in the Insurance Industry, 1960–1990," unpublished paper, Temple University, 1984; Olivier Bertrand and Thierry Noyelle, "Changing Technology, Skills, and Skill Formation in French, German, Japanese, Swedish, and U.S. Financial Services Firms: Preliminary Findings," report to the Center for Educational Research and Innovation of the Organization for Economic Cooperation and Development, 1987; Matthew Drennan, *Implications of Computer and Communications Technology for Less Skilled Service Employment Opportunities*, final report to the U.S. Department of Labor under Grant No. USDL 21-36-80-31 (New York: Columbia University, 1983); International Labour Organization, Advisory Committee on Salaried and Professional Workers, *The Effects of Technological and Structural Changes on the Employment and Working Conditions of Non-Manual Workers*, 8th Session, Report II (Geneva, 1981); Jon Shepard, *Automation and Alienation: A Study of Office and Factory Workers* (Cambridge, Mass: MIT Press, 1971).

4. Larry Hirschhorn, *Beyond Mechanization: Work and Technology in a Post-industrial Age* (Cambridge, Mass: MIT Press, 1984).

5. Personal interview.

6. U.S. Department of Labor, Bureau of Labor Statistics, *The National Industry-Occupation Employment Matrix, 1970, 1978, and Projected 1990*, Bulletin 2086, 1981.

7. For a fuller discussion of these trends, see Adler, "Rethinking the Skill Requirements."

8. For more on the changing nature of internal labor markets, see Bertrand and Noyelle, "Changing Technology," and Thierry J. Noyelle, "Beyond Industrial Dualism: Market and Job Segmentation in the New Economy," unpublished paper, Conservation of Human Resources, Columbia University, December 1985.

9. Bureau of Labor Statistics, *Industry-Occupation Matrix*, and U.S. Department of Labor, Employment and Training Commission, *Selected Characteristics of Occupations Defined in the Dictionary of Occupational Titles*, 1981.

10. Appelbaum, "Impact of Technology."

11. U.S. Department of Labor, Bureau of Labor Statistics, *Employment and Unemployment: A Report on 1980*, Special Labor Force Report 244, April 1981; U.S.

Department of Labor, Bureau of Labor Statistics, *Handbook of Labor Statistics*, Bulletin 2070, December 1980; and unpublished data from Insurance Information Institute.

12. U.S. Department of Labor, Bureau of Labor Statistics, *Employment and Earnings*, 1980.

13. The classic study arguing the position that women are hired because they are a cheap, skilled labor force is Valerie Oppenheimer, *The Female Labor Force in the United States* (Berkeley: Institute of International Studies, University of California, 1970).

14. Kristin Nelson, "Back Offices and Female Labor Markets: Office Suburbanization in the San Francisco Bay Area, 1965–1980" (Ph.D. diss., University of California, Berkeley, 1984).

15. For an analysis of bureaucratic control structures, see Richard Edwards, *Contested Terrain: The Transformation of the Workplace in the Twentieth Century* (London: Heinemann, 1979).

16. Nelson, "Back Offices."

17. For a discussion of these two aspects of the definition of skill, see Kenneth T. Spenner, "Deciphering Prometheus: Temporal Change in the Skill Level of Work," *American Sociological Review* 48 (December 1983).

18. U.S. Equal Employment Opportunity Commission, *Minorities and Women in Private Industry*, 1979.

19. Bureau of Labor Statistics, *Employment and Unemployment*. In 1980, for example, blacks constituted 11.2 percent of the work force but 21.6 percent of all file clerks, 17.5 percent of office machine operators (including 22 percent of all keypunch operators), and 15.5 percent of all typists. In contrast, only 5 percent of all secretaries and 7 percent of all receptionists were black.

20. Sally L. Hacker, "Sex Stratification, Technology, and Organizational Change: A Longitudinal Case Study of AT&T," *Social Problems*, 1979.

21. Nelson, "Back Offices."

22. Oppenheimer, *Female Labor Force.*

III. The Future

27 The Future of Motherhood
Some Unfashionably Visionary Thoughts

Elayne Rapping

The brave new world of reproductive technology—contraceptive techniques, labor and childbirth "management," fetal monitoring, artificial insemination and surrogacy—more than any other social or scientific phenomenon I can think of forces feminists to confront central issues that have plagued us for twenty years. What is motherhood? What is a family? What is the relationship between sexuality and reproduction? What is the relationship of women to the scientific establishment and the capitalist economic order? And perhaps most difficult of all, what does it mean—really mean—to be a woman?

In the late 1960s and early 1970s, heady days for feminists and leftists, radical approaches to these matters were the order of the day. The very questioning of established thinking about motherhood and femininity was a radical and exhilarating act. For a generation raised on *Leave It to Beaver* and Freudian biological determinism, the realization that biology need not be destiny was liberating.

Things have changed since then, for reasons that are in some ways understandable and in others—to me at least—mysterious. In the heat and passion of feminist debate about reproductive technology one hears the rumblings of retreat from radical political visions to an at times alarmingly conservative view of the personal and political future of women, and of the relationships among women, men, children, and the larger community.

Before getting down to the nuts and bolts of the technical and political issues facing us today, it seems important to retrace the history of radical- and socialist-feminist thinking on these matters. It is in the imaginative literature that these feminist movements spawned—the novels we read and discuss with passion—that the convergence of the feelings and ideas that fuel our politics is often most clearly revealed. This seems particularly true in matters of motherhood.

In the groundbreaking 1970 political study *The Dialectics of Sex*, Shulamith Firestone, a radical feminist in those innocent days when left and radical feminists shared some crucial political visions, presented a theoretical and programmatic response to those who argued that women are biologically determined to be mothers: "the freeing of women from the tyranny of their reproductive biology . . . and the diffusion of the childbearing and childrearing role to the society as a whole" through the development of the very reproductive technologies that now seem, to many, anything but liberating.[1]

Some of Firestone's ideas were given imaginative life in left feminist Marge Piercy's 1976 futuristic novel *Woman on the Edge of Time*. In it Piercy describes in fascinating detail a future world in which all resources—technological and natural—are used to further such democratic, life-affirming values as pleasure, beauty, and individual development and expression in the context of full personal choice. Part of this vision, the most radical part, includes a fully delineated program for childbirth and parenting wholly separate from biological imperative and from the nuclear family. Each child, artificially produced in special reproductive nurseries, has three biological parents, none of whom are lovers. Men are as capable of nursing as women, and the choice to be or not be a parent is as accepted as the choice to be celibate or nonmonogamous.[2]

Such feminist political utopias, whether fictional or theoretical, seem a quirky, aberrant glitch in today's dominant, and gloomier, approach to sexual and family matters. As early as 1979, British feminist Zoe Fairbairns's *Benefits* presented a very dystopian futuristic response to Piercy's idyllic vision. Fairbairns's future is one in which genetic engineering, in the hands of a mysoginist government, is the greatest weapon against feminism and the ultimate force for the enslavement of women. Socially and racially "fit" women are given rewards for returning to the traditional wife/mother role, while poor, black, and otherwise "unfit" women are deprived of their reproductive rights and forced to fill demeaning roles. Margaret Atwood's more recent *Handmaid's Tale* envisions a similarly bleak and terrifying future for women at the hands of an all-powerful reactionary government.[3]

Sue Miller's 1985 book *The Good Mother*, about a single mother who loses custody of her daughter when her ex-husband charges her and her unconventional lover with "sexual irregularities," brings home—depressingly—

how little progress women have actually made in our quest for sexual and political freedom. Divorced, impoverished, but happy for the first time in a fulfilling relationship with a man who loves her and her child, Anna Dunlap capitulates immediately to the obvious power of the male-dominated state once her lifestyle is challenged. Losing her beloved Molly, she embarks, like some latter-day Hester Prynne, on an apparent future of penance and personal misery. She breaks with her lover and moves to another city in order to have the few hours a week granted to her with her child.[4]

Anna's plight is heartbreaking and tragic. The sensitive reader cannot judge her too harshly; after all, mother love is real, as is male power and sexual guilt. What's troubling about this novel is the way it poses its heroine's problems. While the first half of the book presents Anna's new and hopeful life from a perspective of optimism and spiritual growth, the second half—devoted to the custody case—switches perspectives in a way that is literarily brilliant but politically disturbing. The male power structure—represented by almost every man in the book—speaks, and Anna crumbles in total defeat. Sexual fulfillment and motherhood are seen—once more—as mutually exclusive, not because of Anna's own nature but because of the immovable force of patriarchal ideology. And when forced to choose, it is motherhood—even the disfigured form in which it is offered her—that she chooses. In the end, this one child is Anna's reason for being. She imagines no future life, no future children. More distressing, from my own perspective as a mother, she chooses to present herself to her growing daughter as a fallen woman, a loser, a victim. The real needs of a child must surely include the need to see one's mother as a model, a woman whose life is meaningful and dignified.

This novel (discussed in greater depth by Deborah Rosenfelt and Judith Stacey in the next chapter) is emblematic of the state of much feminist (or postfeminist) thought in the 1980s. In its sense of women's powerlessness against masculinist institutions, and in its reversion to an image of motherhood as the sole arena of female power, it mirrors the dominant feminist responses to the issues raised by the new reproductive technologies. Male power, in the realms of science, law, economics, and politics, is seen as absolute. Challenging that power is implicitly brushed aside by feminists in favor of a feverish focus on individual control of one's body and its offspring. Outside the context of a broader social vision, this narrow, single-minded focus too often leads not only to contradictory, even dangerous, political positions and alliances but to unconscious reversion to an essentialist view of femininity as defined by biology, by the ability to bear children.

With rare exceptions, feminist responses to the reproductive sciences have been grounded in totalizing visions of male power and female victim-ization.[5] Andrea Dworkin, in a 1980s version of radical feminism as dour as Firestone's was hopeful, sets the tone for this discourse in *Right-Wing Women*. "Motherhood is becoming a new branch of female prostitution with the help of scientists who want access to the womb for experimentation and for power," she states in a chapter called "The Coming Gynocide."[6]

Gena Corea, another radical feminist who works with members of FINNRET, the Feminist International Network on the New Reproductive Technologies, paints a similarly harrowing and far more technically de-tailed picture in *The Mother Machine*. In chapters with titles such as "Clon-ing: The Patriarchal Urge to Recreate" and "Reproductive Control: The War against the Womb," she depicts a social and scientific world in which these techniques are used solely to exploit and oppress us. Jan Zimmer-man's *Once upon a Future* is a similar but broader study of the science and technology, including the reproductive technologies, wholly controlled by men who intend, and successfully manage, to exploit and destroy women. *Test Tube Women*, an anthology of scholarly and personal essays, does include a few articles defending the use of reproductive technologies in individual cases. But like the others, it is primarily a critique of reproductive science as wholly oppressive. Most recently, *Made to Order: The Myth of Reproductive and Genetic Progress* echoes this common refrain.[7]

I do not for a moment question the vital political truths these books present. Certainly women are being exploited by the scientific/medical profession. Certainly there are fascistic overtones to the current techno-logically based regimes that rate some women fit for motherhood on the basis of class, race, and marital status, while channeling others into "sur-rogacy" for their more fortunate sisters and depriving them of the right to reproduce and mother for themselves. A feminist would have to be a fool not to understand the class, race, and sex biases of capitalism. She or he would have to be worse than a fool not to see the importance of a feminist response to the situation. But what is the correct response? "Discourses of totalizing morality," says Rayna Rapp, astutely, in a review of some of these books, "persuade at a high price. When we accept them, we give up pre-cious ground so recently won: on that ground science as well as nurturance, culture, not just nature, could be women's turf."[8]

It is that precious ground that I am concerned to reclaim, because once we give it up, we easily fall into thought and behavior that feeds into the worst right-wing agendas. As German writers Juliette Zipper and Selma Sevenhuisjen remind us, "the opponents of surrogacy in the Social Demo-cratic Party in West Germany" fell into a program that "the right would ap-plaud: the ties between marriage, love, sexuality and reproduction may not be loosened; surrogacy must be prohibited and reproductive technology may not be applied outside of marriage."[9]

The Socialist-Feminist Response

While the books referred to above primarily express radical-feminist thinking, socialist and other left feminists have more often than not concurred. The case of Baby M—in which the birth mother, Mary Beth Whitehead, reneged after being inseminated by William Stern and legally committed to giving him the child—brought the issues raised by reproductive technologies into the mainstream media in a most dramatic and sensational way. In the process it also forced feminists of all stripes to take positions. Many of these were particularly revealing of the widespread postfeminist sense of political pessimism about social change.

For example, 125 prominent feminists signed a statement supporting Whitehead's claim to her birth child. For the left feminists who took this position the primary issue was one of class. If Whitehead, a working-class housewife, was seen as less fit than the Sterns, who were both educated, wealthy professionals, then theoretically, millions of women could be deemed unfit and lose our children on the basis of our class standing.

On this level the argument is irrefutable. Poor women, black women, lesbians, and sexually unconventional women do in fact lose children all the time to those rare fathers who choose to sue for custody. But the Baby M case raised deeper issues for feminists. It demonstrated how socialist analysis of class and race bias can lead to a retreat from an equally crucial socialist-feminist tenet: that motherhood is socially, not biologically, constructed. Sympathy for Whitehead, the class underdog, led socialist feminists to not so logically agree with Whitehead's own political argument: that the child "belonged" to her as the birth mother. As a result, a number of feminists—liberal, radical, and socialist—were suddenly arguing as vehemently for the rights of the biological mother and the sanctity of the biological bond between mother and child as they had once argued for the right *not* to mother and the need for fathers to share equally in child rearing.

The May 1988 issue of *Ms.* magazine, devoted entirely to the matter of reproductive technologies, is telling. After presenting an overview of "the dilemmas posed by the new reproductive technologies," the bulk of the issue, the really hot articles, are almost uniformly "pronatal." Phyllis Chesler, in an excerpt from her book on the Baby M case, asks—as though no sane person could disagree—"How can we deny that women have a profound and everlasting bond with the children they've birthed; that this bond begins in utero?" A few pages later the mother of physician/novelist Perri Klass describes helping her liberated daughter deliver her first-born as "a transcendent moment" shared with her daughter and son-in-law (white professionals with the time and money to "choose" the most intimate, natural setting for the occasion, one that was also safe, comfortable, and efficient). And Barbara Ehrenreich worries—as have so many feminists recently—that legitimizing "surrogacy," which defines the birth mother as something less than a "real" mother, "flagrantly trivializes the process of childbirth," reducing it to "womb rental." [10]

What all these pieces seem to me to have in common—and they are simply a representative sampling of feminist opinion on the matter—is an implicit and largely emotional sense that in a post-Reagan world where so much has been taken from us and so much that we dreamed of twenty years ago has not materialized, we must at all costs hang on to the two things we can still hope to own and control, our bodies and our biological offspring. And yet these articles are fraught with political blind spots and contradictions. Motherhood, after all, is not experienced by all women as an unmixed blessing. Nor do all women have the material advantages of many white feminists, which allow childbirth and parenting to be experienced in such neoromantic terms.

Motherhood Demystified

The truth is that most women today live lives characterized by emotional and material deprivation, compromise, and a healthy dose of spiritual and/or physical suffering. Among my own friends the issue of motherhood is often painful and usually at least difficult. Among those fortunate enough to have financial security and supportive mates—and, often, to have been lucky enough to conceive later in life than biology prefers—there are still the problems of child care, curtailment of social and political activity, and coping with a dangerous social environment. But more distressing are the problems of single women: those whose personal and economic positions prohibit them from having longed-for children; those who struggle to raise children alone, on inadequate incomes and with no help from ex-partners; and those who use reproductive technologies to become single mothers by choice at enormous economic and emotional sacrifice.

Among my own children's friends and acquaintances I see even greater misery and trouble looming. Teen pregnancy, especially among poor, black women, is widely known to be epidemic. What may be less well known is that many of these young women are among the brightest in their classes. Yet their futures—their potential for self-fulfillment, much less material security—are cut short because they believe, as do the writers in *Ms.* and Anna in *The Good Mother*, that biological mother love is at any cost the greatest, most meaningful fulfillment for a woman.

Finally, there are the women, whom I do not know personally, who do in fact choose to "rent their wombs" and their bodies to men because, in fact, it is the best option they see for surviving in this cruel, sexist society. What of their right to control their bodies? What of the realities of their situations? I am not suggesting that prostitution or surrogacy, as now practiced, are good things. I am suggesting that any socialist-feminist discussion of these matters must take into account the realities of capitalism for most women and the choices that exist.

From a broader, less personal perspective, the issues surrounding motherhood and reproduction appear even more politically difficult and confusing. Women's needs, desires, and situations do differ, after all. To assume that the fight for the "maternal rights" of the biological mother and against technical or commercial intrusion into this "natural" realm is the obviously correct feminist position is more than theoretically regressive. It is simplistic in its failure to confront political reality in its entirety. Looking more closely at the specific reproductive techniques available, we see a maze of political contradiction more mind-boggling than any survey of one's personal circle of friends could reveal.

The categories of reproductive technologies are varied, but each is fraught with its own apparently irreconcilable contradictions. Birth control itself is the most common and accepted of these techniques, yet its promise of sexual freedom to women has always been compromised by the social and economic context in which it was developed and distributed. Health risks, unequal access by poor and Third World women, and sterilization abuse of women who want to have more children than society wants them to have are well-known facts. Moreover, the possibility of fertility control is balanced by a strong ideological belief—widely held in the medical professions and society at large—that "motherhood is the natural, desired, and ultimate goal of all 'normal' women." Those who "deny their maternal instincts are selfish, peculiar and otherwise disturbed."[11] This thinking clearly influences political decisions to invest more in fertility research than in contraception. Still, who would do away with contraception because it is badly used by those in power?

The management of labor and childbirth and the monitoring of fetal development by the scientific community are also fraught with contradiction. Financially secure women have access to the best care and are in a position to make choices about continuing a pregnancy when the fetus is less than "perfect." On the one hand, such techniques can be a boon to the individual woman fortunate enough to have access to them. On the other, control of the birthing process, once in the hands of female midwives, is now taken from us. Moreover, the fascistic implications of a set of techniques and policies that allow for the production of "perfect" babies and the possibility of aborting the less than perfect is obvious. But again, what pregnant woman would wish away these methods?

In the realm of conceptive technologies—artificial insemination, *in vitro* fertilization and surrogacy—the political contradictions are most extreme. Poor women, single women who are not economically privileged, Third World women, lesbians and other sexual nonconformists do not have equal access to this technology. Surrogacy today is certainly an economically exploitative practice. Yet for individual lesbian, single, or infertile women, this technology can be a godsend.

In even so sketchy a survey, two things become obvious. First, single-issue fights for "maternal rights" or an end to the commercialization of sex and childbirth are inadequate, often wrongheaded and at cross-purposes with other feminist values. And second, the real issues we need to be addressing are the big ones that we started with: What is a mother? What is a family? What is the responsibility of the community to women and children? And how does technology fit into this picture? I believe these questions demand a return to visionary thinking and to a view of technology that sees it—despite what we know of the male power structure—as potentially progressive, liberatory, and positive in its promise of a better world, a better human family.

To begin rethinking our relationship to technology, we might reread Piercy's *Woman on the Edge of the Time* from the less idealistic perspective of late 1980s realities. While reading this we might want to remind ourselves how we have trapped ourselves, as Zipper and Sevenhuisjen suggest, "in an opposition between [views that stress total] oppression or liberation." Technology inherently serves neither; "it is not technology itself that complicates theory and strategy" but "the *terms* in which technology and its social consequences are spoken about."[12] Free in her imagination, Marge Piercy envisioned a world—albeit a fantastic one—in which people do control technology and make it work for them. We may be far from the power to do so, but that is all the more reason to remind ourselves, in these hard times, of what we are ultimately fighting for, what kind of world we want our grandchildren and great-grandchildren to inhabit.

A Feminist Future

This brings me to the first matter, the questions about mother-hood, family, and community as socialist feminists would like them to exist. As feminists, we began by challenging patriarchal notions of family and sexuality. In place of paternal ownership and control of women and children, we demanded individual freedom, shared child care, and social responsibility for the human family. In place of blood ties and inherited property as the basis of the distribution of wealth, we demanded social ownership, control, and sharing of our common resources. In place of hierarchical structures, we demanded democratic institutions in which each of us had some power and importance. In place of a single norm for "proper womanhood," we demanded choice and a recognition of the vast differences not only in women's natures and desires but in the material and emotional situations of women of different backgrounds and lifestyles. And in place of the good girl/bad girl dichotomy, we demanded the right to be fully integrated persons, capable of experiencing sexual freedom and intellectual fulfillment without losing our right to be—or not be—mothers.

As grandiose and unrealistic as all this may now seem, the fact is that we were right to make these demands. While some of us are shoring up our little havens in this heartless world and counting our blessings, most of us are in worse shape than we imagined twenty years ago. The feminization of poverty, rising divorce rates, sexual and physical abuse of women and children, illiteracy and alienation among youth, loneliness and isolation among the old and not-so-old—these are the realities of life today. We don't have the choice of returning to the family structure of the 1950s except in isolated, lucky cases. In fact, to be politically realistic is to face the fact that terms such as "family" and "mother" have lost their traditional meanings for most of us, and no amount of romanticizing the mysteries of pregnancy will change that. In the face of these truths, the need for imaginative, even visionary speculation seems obvious, if difficult to manage.

Difficult, but not impossible. If Marge Piercy seems bizarre and fantastic to today's young women, there is another literary tradition, that of black women novelists, which is easier for young readers to relate to and in its own way often as visionary in its view of family, motherhood, and community as the work of earlier white feminist writers. *The Color Purple* is Alice Walker's marvelous example.[13] In it, we see the most oppressed woman imaginable grow into a heroine of mythic proportions in the context of a radically progressive, supportive community. The novel, as fantastic in its way as *Woman on the Edge of Time*, pictures a community of black women that creates the kind of family and lives out the kind of sexual and emotional relationships earlier feminists envisioned. In a world in which white and male power can at any moment separate families, destroy people, and leave children motherless, Walker shows what family—certainly for blacks and increasingly for all of us—must become if love and community are to survive.

In *The Color Purple* children are raised by friends and relatives when parents disappear. Sexual relationships end abruptly, if not because of forced separation then because of the enormous strain under which relationships exist in a world of pain, trouble, and powerlessness. Sexual jealousy is overcome in the interest of sisterhood and community survival. Most marvelously, sex roles and heterosexual norms are turned on their head. Love between any two people is a blessing, albeit one that will almost inevitably be short-lived. Even men—those emotional laggards—are allowed to grow and change under the influence of these magical, majestic women.

This vision is very close to what 1960s feminists believed in. It's not surprising, however, that it is now black women who are the feminist visionaries of family and sexual matters, given the breakdown of the black community under the stress of capitalism. The role of women in preserving it —in lovingly raising whatever children need care, in constructing a new definition of family much more realistic than the one white society has tried to impose upon it—stands as a model to white socialist feminists. It is a model that is accepting of difference, accepting of the fragility of the biological "maternal bond," accepting of the need for radical alternatives in these nasty times.

To be sure, *The Color Purple* is economically and technologically anachronistic in its portrayal of a small family-based craft industry as the material basis for the extended family's survival. Which brings us back to the matter at hand—reproductive technologies. Rather than hanging on to our little bit of biological power to reproduce, we might consider the issues raised by reproductive technologies in the context of creating a truly loving, democratic, nonsexist, nonrepressive environment in which technologies are widely and inexpensively available and used in the interest of women and children themselves. It is only in that context that the contradictions raised by these technologies, as they affect different kinds of women, can be resolved. The idea of social responsibility for "family policy" is discussed ad nauseam, and to little effect, these days. A socialist-feminist agenda that transcends immediate special interests to raise larger questions of what a decent society would look like, and how it would distribute its economic and technical resources, is not unrealistic. It is the only realistic approach I can conceive of to the increasing impoverishment and deprivation of our lives and our political imaginations.

I am particularly concerned with the return of the visionary in political discourse because I have a grown daughter of my own and teach young women of her age every day. These daughters of the second wave are remarkable and irritating. They have a vast sense of their own personal potential, their own right to "have it all": meaningful love, important work, children, pleasure, and joy. But their sense of how to achieve these things is as narrow and socially constrained as their self-confidence and energy are vast. They understand Anna in *The Good Mother* perfectly. They accept the limits and contradictions of her choices as given, and in their own lives they plan to avoid her tragedy by being smarter, more careful about their life choices. Implicitly, they have opted for less than sexual freedom, less than real freedom of any kind, less than what we, their biological and spiritual mothers, hoped to be able to offer them—although they cannot possibly know that that is what they are doing.

They can't know because they can't understand *Woman on the Edge of Time* any more than they could understand Shulamith Firestone, should I be foolhardy enough to assign it. Yet they will be inheriting the world we leave them and the values for which we fought. Most alarmingly, they will be inheriting a world in which technology is an ever greater part of their lives, while their control over that technology is virtually nonexistent. Surely they need to know that their biological and spiritual mothers thought, wrote, and even tried to do something about that state of affairs and that it is therefore possible, necessary, even imperative that they do the same.

Notes

1. Shulamith Firestone, *The Dialectic of Sex* (New York: Bantam, 1971), 206.
2. Marge Piercy, *Woman on the Edge of Time* (New York: Fawcett, 1976).
3. Zoe Fairbairns, *Benefits* (New York: Avon, 1979); Margaret Atwood, *The Handmaid's Tale* (New York, Fawcett Crest, 1985).
4. Sue Miller, *The Good Mother* (New York: Dell, 1986).
5. The one thoughtful and politically balanced work is Michelle Stanworth, ed., *Reproductive Technologies: Gender, Motherhood, and Medicine* (Minneapolis: University of Minnesota Press, 1987).
6. Andrea Dworkin, *Right-Wing Women* (New York: Perigree, 1983), 180.
7. Gena Corea, *The Mother Machine: Reproductive Technologies from Artificial Insemination to Artificial Wombs* (New York: Harper & Row, 1985); Jan Zimmerman, *Once upon a Future: The Woman's Guide to Tomorrow's Technology* (New York: Pandora, 1986); Rita Arditti, Renate Duelli Klein, Shelley Minden, eds., *Test-Tube Women: What Future for Motherhood?* (New York: Pandora, 1984); Patricia Spallone and Deborah Steinberg, eds., *Made to Order: The Myth of Reproductive Progress* (New York: Pergamon, 1987).

8. Rayna Rapp, "A Womb of One's Own," *Women's Review of Books*, April 1988, p. 10.

9. Juliette Zipper and Selma Sevenhuisjen, "Surrogacy: Feminist Notions of Motherhood Reconsidered," in Stanworth, *Reproductive Technologies*, 135.

10. Mary Thom, "Dilemmas of the New Birth Technologies"; Phyllis Chesler, "What Is a Mother?"; Sheila Solomon Klass, "A Transcendent Moment"; and Barbara Ehrenreich, "The Heart of the Matter," all in *Ms.*, May 1988, pp. 70–76, 38, 41, 20.

11. Barbara Stanworth, "Reproductive Technologies and the Deconstruction of Motherhood," in Stanworth, *Reproductive Technologies*, 15.

12. Zipper and Sevenhuisjen, "Surrogacy," 120.

13. Alice Walker, *The Color Purple* (New York: Pocket Books, 1985).

28   Second Thoughts on the Second Wave

Deborah Rosenfelt and Judith Stacey

A rapidly growing body of literature that documents, reacts, and sometimes overreacts to the circumstances of women in the contemporary United States has generated the awkward concept of "postfeminism."[1] Most frequently, journalists use this term to describe views expressed by relatively affluent and ambitious women in their late twenties and early thirties about the difficulties they face in attempting to combine satisfying careers and family lives under present social and economic conditions. More broadly, postfeminism demarcates an emerging culture and ideology that simultaneously incorporates, revises, and depoliticizes many of the fundamental issues advanced by second-wave feminism.

Because it seems to imply the death of the women's movement, and because of the revisionist and depoliticizing aspects of the ideology it promotes, the term "postfeminism" itself troubles many feminists. Many would agree with the author of a *New York Times* op-ed piece that adherents of the new ideology use the term "only to give sexism a subtler name."[2] Although we share the concerns of those who recoil from its use, we believe that there are important distinctions between the ideologies and constituencies of postfeminism and those of antifeminism, distinctions that make it worthwhile to grapple with rather than simply dismiss the literature and issues of the former.

From a panoply of postfeminist texts we have selected three to discuss in some detail: the *Newsweek* cover story of June 2, 1986, "Too Late for Prince

Source: This article is reprinted from *Feminist Studies* 13, no. 2 (1987), pp. 341–61, by permission of the publisher, Feminist Studies, Inc., c/o Women's Studies Program, University of Maryland, College Park, MD 20742.

Charming"; Sylvia Hewlett's *A Lesser Life: The Myth of Women's Liberation in America*; and *The Good Mother*, a novel by Sue Miller.[3] We selected these because they have commanded so much media attention and because we believe they exemplify both what is so disturbing about and what is worth engaging within postfeminism. Many feminists have reacted with hostility to these works and to their popularity with the media establishment; they read the texts as antifeminist and the media acclaim as further evidence of the backlash of this period.[4] We too find much that is offensive in these texts, and we agree with most of the substantive criticisms of them voiced by feminist critics. But to overreact to these texts obscures their complexities as well as those of postfeminism generally.

The overreaction stems, we believe, from the difficulty of this moment for feminism as a social movement and for many feminists in our personal lives. In an era when the term "liberal" is an epithet, left feminists in particular often find ourselves struggling against a sense of political paralysis. Defeats in the political arena coincide with significant shifts in the personal needs and priorities of many who were in the vanguard of second-wave feminism, and together the public defeats and the personal changes have taken their toll on the confidence, vision, and solidarity of the left-feminist community in the United States. Questions of intimacy and loneliness absorb and divide left feminists today, generating between the single and coupled and the mothers and "childfree" among us tensions rooted in feelings of competition, betrayal, envy, resentment, and guilt. These often unacknowledged tensions undergird and complicate political differences over how to respond to the profamily ideology of the present period, a conflict that overlaps with a debate over the issue of equality and difference, particularly as it impinges on the development of legislation to reform U.S. family and work policies.

This essay emerges from our own struggles with these issues. One of our hopes in coauthoring it is to bridge the gulf between single and coupled feminists by bringing our perspectives as a single, new (adoptive) mother and a married, coparenting mother to bear on problems confronting and dividing left feminists today. More important, it is our attempt to find a constructive forum for our own struggles against political despair, for our efforts to identify a political ideology and program that seem viable in this period. As new left feminists, we find it sobering to recognize that social democracy and even old-fashioned liberalism currently look good to us— perhaps the best we can hope for in the foreseeable future as a soil for regenerating more utopian visions.

From this admittedly somber perspective we hope to provide an alternative reading of selected postfeminist texts in order to provoke constructive discussion of the issues we think they raise for left feminists and of our relationship to the emerging contours of mainstream feminist ideology and politics. For however problematic these texts can be, we believe they address important issues and constituencies for a new wave of feminism, a feminism already taking shape. Left feminists who hope to influence the emerging directions of a renewed movement need to give serious second thoughts to texts like these and to the texts' criticisms of the second wave.

Cumulatively, the *Newsweek* cover story, *A Lesser Life*, and *The Good Mother* transcend their generic diversity—popular journalism, social science, and fiction—to express a profound uneasiness with the quality of contemporary life for working women in this country, an uneasiness that may be the dominant mood of postfeminism. Respectively, these texts address the experiences in the United States today of single women without children, of working mothers (usually, for Hewlett, married ones), and of single mothers. They feature the loneliness of women without families, the frustration and exhaustion of mothers who also must or wish to work, and the anxiety of single mothers trying to reconcile heterosexual adult relationships with maternal responsibilities, although they do so with scant regard to variations in class or race or sexual identification. Both their media popularity and their notoriety in feminist circles suggest that these texts touch sensitive social nerves.

The *Newsweek* cover story was perhaps the best known of the myriad of media scare stories about an ostensible "male shortage" for college-educated women born in the mid-1950s. Based on an unpublished demographic study by social scientists at Yale and Harvard, the story forecasts a drastic decrease in the odds of marriage among college-educated women of the baby boom. Members of that cohort who are still single at age thirty reportedly have only a 20 percent chance of marrying; by age thirty-five, the odds are 5 percent; and (in the most notorious line from the *Newsweek* story), "forty-year-olds are more likely to be killed by a terrorist: they have a minuscule 2.6 probability of tying the knot" (p. 55). These statistics result partly from the discrepancy between the huge baby-boom cohort and the smaller pool of the slightly older men whom women typically have married. Yet the article also pushes its interpretation of these demographics toward a cautionary moral: women who choose education and career may never marry. This moral is graphically illustrated by vignettes of single women reacting with dismay and panic to news of the original study. The authors blame women of the yuppie generation, and implicitly feminism itself, for contributing to the dilemma by setting unrealistically high standards for men. "For many economically independent women," the writers conclude, "the consequences of their actions have begun to set in; even though they say they want to marry, they may not want it enough. . . . Chastened by the news that delaying equals foregoing, they [younger women] just may want to give thought to the question sooner than later" (p. 61).

While the *Newsweek* article features the loneliness of single career women, *A Lesser Life* by Sylvia Hewlett emphasizes the frustrations of women attempting to combine motherhood and work. The core of the book is an unremitting critique of the incompatibility of paid work and motherhood in the United States today. Hewlett documents the bleak economic conditions and lack of family support policies American working women encounter, in contrast to those in advanced industrial European societies. She argues that despite two decades of activist feminism, American working women have made virtually no progress in closing the income gap with men, which now is wider here than in any other advanced industrial society. (Women earn approximately 64 percent of men's wages in the United States, compared with 81 percent in Sweden, 86 percent in Italy, 73 percent in West Germany, 78 percent in France, and 86 percent in Denmark.) And many women who work full time year round do not earn enough to support families above the official poverty level. For example, Hewlett points out that in 1984, one out of four such women earned less than $10,000 annually (p. 71).

Even greater is the contrast between the family support policies in effect here and in Europe. Although mothers of young children are the fastest-growing portion of the U.S. labor force (by 1984, 48 percent of children under one year old had mothers in the labor force), they labor against all odds. Sixty percent of mothers have no maternity leave rights at all; 40 percent of working mothers have no maternity insurance coverage; and child-care subsidies, always meager, have been cut by 21 percent since 1980. In fact, the United States is the only industrial country without a statutory maternity leave policy, and it is the stingiest with maternity and child-care benefits.

Mothers in the United States are working much more yet earning less because of insufficient wages, inadequate maternity benefits, and escalating divorce rates (which are much higher in the United States than in Europe). Indeed, single working mothers and their children are the fastest-growing poverty population in the United States; the average income of single mothers is $9,000 a year. Yet 60 percent of divorced fathers contribute no financial support to their children, even though many can afford child support. Hewlett borrows heavily from Lenore Weitzman's startling study of the "unanticipated consequences" of no-fault divorce in California to paint a bleak portrait of how divorce generally impoverishes women and their children while benefiting men.[5] More broadly, *A Lesser Life* accuses feminism of many negative, if unanticipated, consequences for women in the United States.

As its dust jacket indicates, our third text, Sue Miller's *The Good Mother*, inscribes a different kind of conflict for contemporary women, especially for the growing numbers of single mothers: "a tragic conflict . . . between two powerful sets of feelings, the erotic and the maternal." This compelling novel begins shortly after the negotiation of an unusually amicable divorce between Anna, a rather passive and repressed woman, a "good mother" of four-year-old Molly and a part-time piano teacher, and Brian, also repressed and orderly, an upwardly mobile young lawyer. Anna takes custody of Molly, refusing alimony and accepting only minimal child support. Scarcely have the burdens of single motherhood begun to register when Anna's encounter with Leo, an artist, interrupts the quiet rhythms of Anna's and Molly's new life together. Anna and Leo become lovers, passionate, joyous, enmeshed lovers. Leo is attracted by Anna's reserve, Anna by Leo's wildness, "because I became with him, finally, a passionate person" (p. 116). Briefly, Anna reduces her maternal involvement with Molly, but gradually she includes Molly and Leo in a circle of love, a "new world . . . where I was beautiful, sex together was beautiful, and Molly was part of our love, our life" (p. 236). Soon, however, social reality intrudes: Brian accuses Leo of sexual misconduct with Molly and sues Anna for custody of Molly. With erotic and maternal needs now in conflict, Anna sacrifices her love for Leo in the struggle to keep Molly—but to no avail. The court awards custody to Brian and his new wife, Brenda, and Anna painfully reorganizes her life around the effort to maintain her now limited relationship with her daughter.

The Feminization of Loneliness

All three of these texts have provoked strong criticism from feminists who view them as exemplars of an antifeminist backlash. Although we do not read these texts as antifeminist, they do seem to us to represent the disturbing postfeminist retreat from sexual politics to a more conservative profamily vision, one that simply assumes the inevitability or superiority of heterosexual marriage and motherhood. However, we also hear other, less conservative voices in these texts, voices that intimate some potentially fruitful inconsistencies in postfeminism itself.

Feminist reactions to the *Newsweek* article have been especially uniform and vehement, and for good reason. The language and imagery of the essay irresponsibly sensationalize a deeply problematic set of statistics to paint a picture of desperate women doomed to perpetual singlehood. As one of the coauthors of the original study himself points out, *Newsweek* and other journalistic stories distorted "various subtleties" of their research.[6] *Newsweek* does point out that the study pertains to one specific cohort of women, the mid-1950s baby boomers, and to a highly select group of that cohort, college-educated women; that eight out of ten college graduates probably *will* marry; and that the data presented are demographic predictions that could change if, for example, women started marrying younger men or began to marry much later than the current mean age of twenty-four. But as the demographers themselves have complained, *Newsweek* does not point out that they could not estimate what percentage of the women over thirty were unmarried by choice nor that other studies predict far lower rates of nonmarriage.[7]

Much of the *Newsweek* story does seem to regard the specter of singlehood for women as conservatives view the advent of AIDS among male homosexuals: as a fitting curse brought on by the transgressions of the "victims." In this case, the sins consist of getting a college education, seriously pursuing a career, and raising one's expectations of an acceptable spouse. Although the essay foregrounds the "dire" demographic statistics, it implicitly blames feminism for giving women such unrealistic expectations.

The essay is not consistently committed, however, to the notion that single, career-oriented women inevitably face unhappy or lesser lives. Its authors, the majority of whom appear to be women, observe that many women prefer to be single, that many view their friendships with women as the more permanent of their relationships, that many are bearing or adopting children on their own, and that women in this group are benefiting from both an economic and a sexual independence that makes them far less dependent on marriage than were their predecessors. If feminism and its legacy in heightened career expectations for women are blamed implicitly for the dilemma of singleness, so too do we find evidence that, thanks to feminism, being single no longer carries the stigma and humiliation once reserved for the old maid.

The essay as a whole, then, is oddly uneven, as though it cannot decide finally between pity, admiration, and horror (identification, perhaps, as well) as an appropriate attitude toward this highly educated and potentially unmated cohort of women (all of whom it presumes to be heterosexual). The impulse to mock and minimize the problem has been remarkably consistent among both mainstream and left feminists. Some, like Susan Faludi and Katha Pollitt, have raised serious questions about the validity of the statistics featured by *Newsweek*; some, like Pollitt and Catherine Johnson, have suggested that only a conservative social construction of female singlehood makes it seem undesirable; and some, like Barbara Ehrenreich, have laughed off the "male shortage" as a red herring distracting women from the economic issues we ought to be confronting.[8] Almost all have argued that the "male shortage" is a crisis manufactured by the media to police women's behavior.

Although we too are outraged by the article and grateful for both the rebuttals and the ripostes, we are also troubled by what seems to us a denial of a genuine problem, the problem of women's loneliness. True, the *Newsweek* demographics paint a grimmer picture for younger women than seems likely. True, if heterosexual women could turn in larger numbers to younger men or even to men their own age, if lesbianism were a less stigmatized option, and if work in America were structured to accommodate instead of ignore the demands of nonpatriarchal family life, the demographics of the baby boom would have less gender-biased consequences. Still, it does seem likely that large numbers of educated women now in their thirties will not marry, even if they want to do so. In addition, the rates of remarriage after a divorce are far higher for men than for women, some of whom would like to marry again. In this age of historically unprecedented marital instability, any of us can become single at any time. And of course, as women move into later life, the proportion of single women increases dramatically. It seems futile to deny the pain of the many women, whether lesbian or heterosexual, who are single and who would prefer not to be, as though we could cure the pain by pretending that it does not exist.

In the early days of the women's movement, we felt ourselves part of a supportive feminist community whose bonds and beliefs made finding a mate seem far less imperative than it does for many women now. Lesbian or heterosexual, many of us now find ourselves aging in a period in which our old communities have become fragile and fragmented. This loss deepens the desire for committed partnerships to meet our needs for intimacy, for continuity, for reliable interdependence.

Ninety percent of all Americans try at least once to fulfill such needs through marriage, in spite of its problems and its rising rate of failure. Feminist criticism of the injustices of marriage helped to deconstruct this ailing institution without adequately foreseeing how difficult it would be to forge alternatives that would provide even comparable levels of stability. This is one major reason so many young women sympathetic to feminist aims today hold their distance from a feminist identity. They seem to fear that men will find them guilty by association with the antimarriage aura of the women's liberation movement. A text like that in *Newsweek* fans the flames of this anxiety, but denying the existence of a problem some have designated as the feminization of loneliness will only privatize the pain.

Feminism Distorted

Although it would be difficult for the most militant feminist to present a more scathing critique than Hewlett's of the social conditions afflicting working women in the United States today, *A Lesser Life*, like the *Newsweek* essay, has provoked considerable feminist wrath. This is no paradox, because much of the text serves as an outlet for Hewlett's own unresolved and generally misdirected anger toward second-wave feminism. Indeed, she places much of the blame for the sorry state of working mothers in the United States today at second-wave feminism's doorstep, a charge she levels in an infuriatingly superior tone, with swipes at "shrieking sisters," "strident feminists," and "Yuppies on the fast track—the constituency of NOW." The gist of her criticism seems to be that U.S. feminists misunderstood and failed contemporary women by pursuing a misguided equal-rights strategy that attempted "to clone the male competitive model" (p. 33) while overlooking and denigrating the primacy of motherhood in women's lives. "The feminists of the modern women's movement made one gigantic mistake: They assumed that modern women wanted nothing to do with children. As a result, they have consistently failed to incorporate the bearing and rearing of children into their vision of a liberated life" (pp. 179–80).

Like most postfeminist literature, *A Lesser Life* retreats from sexual politics and completely fails to analyze male power or to hold men accountable for sustaining the unjust economic and social conditions for women that Hewlett deplores. Thus, despite a rather devastating discussion of the "male rebellion" against the traditional responsibilities of marriage and breadwinning (a discussion that recapitulates but mysteriously fails to credit Barbara Ehrenreich's *Hearts of Men*),[9] Hewlett often seems more willing to blame feminists for the dilemma of contemporary women than men or the new right or capitalist employment policies. And she treats Phyllis Schlafly and her ideology with greater respect and sympathy than she accords American feminists.

Left feminists have further reason to be troubled by Hewlett's elitist reform strategy for family policy. As director of the Economic Policy Council (EPC) of the United Nations Association of the U.S.A., Hewlett selected some of this country's most powerful male business, labor, and political leaders to serve on an EPC policy panel called Parents and Work. Hewlett "never thought it appropriate to involve a large contingent from the women's movement" but she did handpick two feminists whose views and actions later disappointed and "confirmed [her in her] view that family policy hardly figures on the feminist agenda" (p. 371).

So deep is Hewlett's fear of radicalism that she retreats from the implications of her own better observations and insights. The policy changes concerning income disparities and family support measures she advocates would require a radical restructuring of economic and political power relations, including, of course, those between women and men. Yet when, by Hewlett's own embittered account, her elite reform strategy for implementing family support policies failed, an experience she found "profoundly disturbing, even radicalizing," she could envision no structural alternatives. Shunning a feminist analysis of power, Hewlett finds it "truly hard to explain why these powerful people were much less interested in family policy than in immigration reform or the International Monetary Fund" (p. 381).

Clearly, then, *A Lesser Life* is a text deeply offensive to most feminists. Particularly galling is the way it exaggerates the power of the U.S. women's movement and denigrates its achievements. Had the movement ever achieved even a fraction of the power to determine the social conditions of women's lives that Hewlett's analysis presumes, she would have had much less to write about. The power of second-wave feminism lay as much in its grassroots appeal and activism as in its impact in corporate boardrooms and legislative chambers. And this grassroots legacy remains considerable, reflected in continuing popular and public concern with such women's movement issues as health care, rape, battering, pay equity, poverty, and— contra Hewlett—even child care.

Although *A Lesser Life* is an appropriate target for feminist criticism, we think it a mistake simply to dismiss it as antifeminist. If we can move past the defensive hostility the book seems designed to incite, there are challenges in even some of the more controversial aspects of Hewlett's analysis that might contribute to a constructive reevaluation of the historic role and ideology of second-wave feminism.

Hewlett is correct, we believe, to portray the ultradomestic 1950s as an aberrant decade in the history of U.S. family and gender relations and one that has set the unfortunate terms for waves of personal and political reaction to family issues ever since. Viewed in this perspective, the attack on the breadwinner/homemaker nuclear family by the women's liberation movement may have been an overreaction to an aberrant and highly fragile cultural form, a family system that for other reasons was already passing from the scene. Our devastating critiques of the vulnerability and cultural devaluation of dependent wives and mothers helped millions of women to leave or avoid these domestic traps, and this is to our everlasting credit. But, with hindsight, it seems to us that these critiques had some negative consequences as well. In particular, we agree with Hewlett that part of feminism's overreaction to the 1950s was an antinatalist, antimaternalist moment, much briefer and less monolithic than she portrays but with enduring consequences.

The reaction to the cloying cult of motherhood freed millions of women like us to consider motherhood a choice rather than an unavoidable obligation, but it also may have encouraged many to deny, or to defer dangerously long, our own desires for domesticity and maternity. One of the ironic effects of this history is the current obsession with maternity and children that seems to pervade aging feminist circles, a romanticization of motherhood that occasionally rivals that of the 1950s. More serious, our assault on conventional domesticity helped to set up feminism to take the major blame for the disastrous effects on women of the rising rates of divorce and female employment that were well under way before the women's movement. Both the *Newsweek* article and *A Lesser Life* suggest how easily this implication can be drawn.

A second feminist issue that *A Lesser Life* prompted us to reconsider is the increasingly divisive one of equality versus difference. For good historical causes, modern feminism stressed an equal rights strategy over special protection for the "differences" of women. The recent debacle involving the use of the latter argument in the Sears sex discrimination case highlights the essential wisdom of this choice.[10] But the equal rights strategy also has difficulties that are cause for second thoughts. Without a radical restructuring of economic and social institutions, particularly the male-centered structures and schedules of work, an unnuanced equal rights strategy can disadvantage many women, particularly working mothers.

Although socialist feminists have long been sensitive to this irony, Hewlett is correct that few of us have made the needs of working *mothers* a central focus of our theory or politics. We suspect this relative neglect may have followed unwittingly from another overreaction: the determination to avoid all biological determinist theories of gender, particularly of women's maternal responsibilities, and thus to avoid policies that presume or enshrine these. This may be why maternity leave policies have provoked more dissension than activism among feminists.

Hewlett exploits the conflict between equal rights and the needs of working mothers in her deeply distorted discussion of the Garland case, the battle over maternity leave rights that was decided by the Supreme Court this year. Lillian Garland lost her receptionist job in a California bank when she tried to return to work after childbirth. Her appeal to the state's Fair Employment Department prompted the bank to challenge a state law protecting women's jobs for four months of maternity leave. The bank argued that pregnancy leave is a form of sex discrimination, and a federal district judge found in its favor. The case was appealed, and the

Ninth Circuit Court, reversing the lower court, found in Garland's favor. The National Organization for Women and the American Civil Liberties Union filed briefs supporting but modifying the arguments used to deny Garland's maternity leave. They wished to preserve the principle of equal rights by extending disability leave to all workers but to avoid special protection for the specifically female conditions of pregnancy and childbirth. When the Supreme Court heard the bank's appeal, NOW and the ACLU filed briefs that, by arguing against female maternity leave and in favor of equal rights to parental leave, sought to overturn the California law. Yet when the Supreme Court found in Garland's favor early in 1987, NOW publicly applauded the decision as a victory for working women.

Hewlett misrepresents NOW and the ACLU as opposed to Garland's leave and uses this distortion to recant her own former support for the ERA: "Garland desperately needed job protection in the wake of a difficult birth, and feminists lined up against her (and her child) because they did not want to discriminate against men. I cannot think that Garland will be voting for the ERA" (pp. 217–18). Although Hewlett's presentation distorts the goals and complexities of NOW's opposition to maternity leave, for both strategic and theoretical reasons it provoked us to reconsider part of our own equal rights ideology. First, it does seem likely that Garland and millions of working mothers will interpret NOW's intervention in terms similar to Hewlett's, thereby diminishing the appeal of feminism to one of its most important potential constituencies in this period. And second, such women would not be wrong in believing that an unmodified equal rights position denies biological sex differences they have little wish or cause to deny. Instead, there are instances in which sex-differentiated policies are necessary to achieve gender justice,[11] and it seems to us now that a women's movement whose commitment to equal legal rights prevents it from seeing this could be making a costly strategic error. On these grounds we question NOW's strategy in this case.

The Maternal versus the Erotic

The Good Mother has also generated anger and dismay from some feminists who read it as a morality play, as another cautionary tale to modern women.[12] If *Newsweek* seems to warn against too earnest a quest for professional autonomy, Miller's novel has been read as a warning against the quest for autonomy in the realm of sexual pleasure.

To us, *The Good Mother*'s inscription of conflict in a contemporary woman's life seems too nuanced and ambiguous to accommodate such a monolithic reading, but the text does contain much that can trouble feminist sensibilities. Most disturbing, perhaps, is Anna's acceptance of an enormous burden of guilt, an apparent willingness to take responsibility for losing Molly and to internalize the moralistic social judgments that her staid family, Brian and Brenda, and the court levy on her lapse from maternal grace. Rather than expressing feminist rage at the injustice of the sexual double standard, the economic disadvantages of women, and the patriarchal morality that contribute to her court defeat, Anna seems willing to accept most of the blame: "There was no one I blamed as much as myself. . . . It was a chain of events set in motion by me, by my euphoric forgetfulness of all the rules" (p. 280). Anna's rage turns inward, directed toward the self who sinned, because during her passion for Leo there was a sense in which she "*forgot* Molly." And Anna seems to atone ceaselessly for this "sin" of passion. Denied primary custody of Molly, she organizes her new penitent life around her painfully limited role as secondary parent. Maternalism regains primacy, despite its truncated form, and the novel offers no hint that Anna will seek adult erotic love ever again.

Anna's guilt and despair lead her at times to forget how competent and nurturant a single mother she has in fact proved to be. In her loss, she yields at moments to a profoundly conservative vision of the superiority of conventional family life:

> Brenda is pregnant again, and Molly is part of a family there. She loves being a big sister, she loves them—Brian and Brenda and Elizabeth, the baby. And sometimes when I imagine how it must be —the order, the deep pleasure in what happens predictably, each day, the healing beauty of everything that is commonplace—I yearn again myself to be in a family. [P. 308]

The expression of this yearning for a more conventional life does suggest the troubling postfeminist recuperation of some of the profamily values that feminism most systematically interrogated and must continue to interrogate. Anna's conservative inclinations arise from her fear and pain; she lapses at these moments into what Doris Lessing would call the danger of nostalgia. Indeed, it is the apparent timidity of the novel's "message" that is most troubling.

The broadest question the book raises for contemporary women concerns the nature of "fulfillment." Second-wave feminism, as critics from the right and the left have noted, emphasized self-realization for women, an emphasis that can be attacked as individualistic but that also proved an important counter to the prior cult of female self-sacrifice. The emphasis on female selfhood initially may have carried an antimaternalist and anti-male flavor, but that tendency quickly gave way in most circles to the well-publicized superwoman syndrome, an expectation that women can and should do everything and do it well—work (and work out), mother, make love. *The Good Mother* questions these expectations of women. Anna is a protagonist who declines to be heroic. She has no career but takes a series of jobs, doing all of them competently but dispassionately. She is a pianist but, by her judgment, not a gifted one. Leo, a successful artist, criticizes Anna for not having a "commitment to something outside herself." She says, "I have a commitment like that." "To music?" he asks. "To Molly. And to doing carefully and well what I do" (p. 118).

Anna, then, has consciously chosen to make motherhood her priority and an unambitious competence her mode. Although she returns to her music at the book's conclusion, she maintains a detachment from it that precludes us from reading into the novel a theme of self-discovery or self-expression. In this regard, this postfeminist novel is distinctly different from most of its feminist predecessors. Anna is no feminist hero, nor does Miller intend her to be. Rather, her story insists that women reexamine the relationships between achievement and fulfillment.

The daring and expansive rhetoric of feminism yields here to a bleaker, more troubled vision. Yet although the text does suggest a retreat from visions of a liberated artistry or of a liberated eroticism, we do not read it as a didactic morality play, a warning to mothers to behave or pay the price. If any voice in the novel is close to Miller's, it is probably that of Dr. Payne, the court-appointed psychiatrist, who vainly recommends that Anna keep custody of Molly:

> What I'm really suggesting is that for Molly the resonant emotional issue is feeling that you were pulling away from her. . . . I think you were distracted, withdrawn in a way she could feel. . . . But I see you also as very hard on yourself. You say I blame you, but I don't feel I have to say very much before you supply the blame, the guilt. [P. 238]

We cannot assume, then, that Anna's feelings of guilt represent Miller's final judgment of Anna. The novel contains competing voices.

Although Anna herself engages in little social analysis of the conditions of single motherhood, *The Good Mother* renders a significant, if quiet, critique of the attitudes and institutions that constrain the personal lives of women like her. The narrative exposes the double standard applied when the state intervenes to assess the relative merits of the home Anna offers

Molly and the home her remarried ex-husband can offer. Although Brian has been sleeping with Brenda before his divorce from Anna, wedlock has legitimated their relationship in a way that Anna as a single woman cannot match. The presence of a lover makes things worse for her, not better. The judge ignores the quality of the relationship, assuming the superiority of the conventional family.

Miller also reveals in Anna's postmarital life the reduced economic means of the divorced woman. Anna watches Brian "move buoyantly forward into his new life while I made arrangements for our more marginal existence" (p. 63). She takes pride in her chosen "shabbiness"; reversing the "upward purchasing spiral" that characterized her married life with Brian becomes a means of asserting her independence against the expectations of her achievement-oriented family, until the courts begin to scrutinize the details of her personal life, to assess what she can and cannot give her daughter. One thing she cannot afford to give is all her time, and the fact that Molly is in child care outside the home becomes part of the case against Anna. Although both Brenda and Brian work full time, they can afford a nanny. The novel, then, invites us to consider the social and economic contexts that marginalize single mothers regardless of the subjective experiences of their "condition." It suggests that Anna's real mistake may have been forgetting not Molly—although she accuses herself of that—but her own vulnerability. Thus, while Anna sifts through the past—a reflection that constitutes the textual fabric of the novel—for the failures in her character or judgment that might make the court's decision somehow tolerable, the reader simultaneously shares her search and situates it in a larger social context. *The Good Mother*, then, like much postfeminism, valorizes motherhood, but its literary treatment of the social dangers threatening those who mother outside the conventional nuclear family partakes of rather than rejects feminist analysis.

In fact, the ambivalent texture of the novel raises difficult questions for feminists. One question concerns the ethics of erotic expression in a context both more common and less commonly debated than the arena of pornography: the context of the home itself, particularly the home with young children. Such questions become particularly poignant in an era in which adults change sexual partners so frequently. Is it possible for single working mothers to integrate successfully their erotic, maternal, and working lives? Are there occasions when physical expressions of desire and intimacy between adults implicate a child too soon and too problematically in the puzzling world of sexuality? Where is the line between openness and ease of affection between adults and children and an inappropriate eroticism that exploits children's sexual curiosity?

Feminists have made the sexual abuse of children, particularly of female children by adult men, a major target of attack. This novel inscribes a whole shadow area where the issues are not so clear-cut, a territory that lies between our assertions about the rights of all women to seek erotic fulfillment, our sense that an openness about the body and eroticism itself is positive, and our rage at the frequency and consequences of child sexual abuse. In Anna's case, it is Leo's ostensible "abuse" of Molly that leads to the custody case, but it is Anna's responsibility for and guilt about another episode, an instance in which she allows her frightened daughter to come into her bed while Leo is still inside her, that proves more disturbing. The incident at the time fills her with a "sense of completion, as though I had everything I wanted held close, held inside me; as though I had finally found a way to have everything. We seemed fused, the three of us, all the boundaries between us dissolved" (p. 124).

Anna returns to this incident again and again in her efforts to make sense out of what has happened, and the incident becomes crucial in the court hearings. What are we to make of this episode? How can we judge Anna, especially when we must have assented to, envied even, the depth of her awakening passion? How can we fail to understand the urge toward the joyful sense of fusion with those one loves most in the world? Yet can we assent fully to including a child of four in this moment of intimacy between her mother and her mother's lover? It is the ambiguity of this moment and others like it in the novel that give the book much of its power, a power to disturb, to interrogate. The questions this novel raises have no easy answers. Having read it, we cannot say with Anna, as she says, in agony, in court, "I didn't think. I didn't think about it" (p. 264). Only in that sense is this a didactic novel.

A Call for the Third Wave of Feminism

Cumulatively, these texts, in both their inclusions and omissions, their insights and distortions, call attention to some of the major issues we must consider as we shape a feminist agenda appropriate to this moment in history. The socially conservative, depoliticized climate of postfeminism is all too readily and distressingly apparent in these texts, as in these times. That all three texts ignore the possibility of changing male behavior underlines the "post" of "postfeminism." Hewlett, for example, with rare exceptions, speaks repeatedly not of parental leave but of maternity leave, as though the discussions of the importance of involving men in early nurturing and infant care had never taken place. When Brian and Brenda, the "good parents" of *The Good Mother*, have a second child, Brenda works part time; Brian never considers altering his career pattern to accommodate his children's needs, nor, it seems, does the thought of serious male parenting occur to Miller. *Newsweek* presents the selfishness of men as a kind of bedrock psychological reality.

Feminists have often been less cynical about the possibility for a fundamental restructuring of gender behavior, of changing men as well as women, than have our "pro-male" opponents. Engaging men systematically in this process of change has proved maddeningly difficult, but we cannot afford to abandon the posture that holds men accountable for their conduct in personal and domestic life, although we must proceed with the awareness that many women wish to minimize the sexual antagonism such struggles often incite.

Certainly changes in gender organization and relations of power have proved harder to effect than we once anticipated, and the reasons for that difficulty are more complex than we once acknowledged. No doubt the conservatism of the current political context has affected both the production of texts like these and our reading of them, just as it will affect the nature of the agenda we construct and are able to implement. Like Anna, we must figure out how to get along in reduced circumstances.

Yet we believe these texts and times indicate also the potentially fruitful inconsistencies in postfeminist culture that suggest grounds for modest optimism. The subtexts of feminist social criticism discernible in even the most reactionary of these texts indicate how widely many pivotal elements of feminist ideology have been absorbed, how enormous and irrevocable the shift in popular consciousness and political discourse about gender inequity and women's potential the women's movement has achieved.[13] They give evidence as well of the fundamental shift in women's relationship to paid work that accompanied, indeed helped to generate, the modern women's movement. Irreversible changes in the U.S. occupational structure and family patterns reinforce the fact that most women today presume accurately that they will be employed for a significant portion of their adult lives. Hewlett appropriately takes for granted that women want and need to combine employment with motherhood. More revealing, maternalistic Anna and the court-approved mother, Brenda, also work at least part time even while married to a man able to support "his" family. And although *Newsweek*, the most reactionary on this score, challenges women's career ambitions and priorities, it too presumes that female employment, rather than marriage, is "here to stay."[14] Ironically, the integration of women into the U.S. labor force is so much more extensive and entrenched in the 1980s than it was when feminism was at its most militant, optimistic height that there may now be a stronger social and cultural basis for serious reform of work and family policies, as well as stronger incentives for alliances between feminism and the labor movement.[15] Many such policy initiatives and coalitions are emerging to brighten these otherwise sobering times.[16]

An economic agenda alone is not sufficient to address the emotional needs we have considered here. As we develop policies more supportive of the efforts of contemporary parents to reconcile parenting and work, left feminists must also renew our efforts to develop cultural forms that fill some of the same longings for intimacy, interdependency, and emotional security that most heterosexuals try to satisfy in marriage, however oppressive to women its unequal relations of power. In the women's movement and in the new left we did build a political culture that for a time considerably eased the sense of alienation, of aloneness, many of us now confront. We need to rebuild and renovate that culture. Such efforts might include planning for living cooperatives to anticipate and preclude some of the isolation of old age, working to secure the same benefits and social sanctions for unions of lesbians and gay men as marriage now provides to heterosexuals, and encouraging varying forms of cooperative child-care and babysitting arrangements that cross lines of age and family role. We envisage a pluralist culture, one that consciously nurtures many forms to gratify the need for support, intimacy, community, and one that acknowledges and tries to transcend the painful divide between single feminists and those in couples, between parents and those without children. For if we need to develop family support policies that will make women's and children's lives more tolerable and dignified, we also need to resist the tendency to privatism, to reconstruct the relations of power within families themselves, and to evolve other forms of committed human relations that will help us to survive emotionally in this fragmented and often mean-spirited postindustrial world.

The specific agendas of what some are calling a third wave of feminism are already taking shape, and they focus on the kinds of recommendations for pay equity, maternity and parental leaves, maternal and child health needs, child-care provisions, and revised work schedules with which Hewlett concludes her book. Many of the specific recommendations are desirable and worth supporting. Left feminists can work to frame such proposals in a broader and more progressive context, criticizing their privatistic, racist, and heterosexist limitations and drawing out their more radical implications.[17] In this way we can foster the revitalization of a feminism neither afraid to exercise its capacity for self-criticism nor forgetful of its liberating vision.

Notes

Acknowledgments: This paper and its authors have benefited far more than is customary from challenging and thoughtful responses to an early draft. We are grateful to Emily Abel, Wini Breines, Anne Farrar, Linda Gordon, Carole Joffe, Lillian Rubin, Herb Schreier, Margaret Strobel, and Judith Walkowitz.

1. So far as we know, the first media use of the term occurred in Susan Bolotin, "Voices from the Postfeminist Generation," *New York Times Magazine,* 17 October 1982, pp. 28–31, 103ff.

2. Geneva Overholser, "What 'Post-Feminism' Really Means," *New York Times,* 19 September 1986, p. 30.

3. "Too Late for Prince Charming," *Newsweek,* 2 June 1986; Sylvia Hewlett, *A Lesser Life: The Myth of Women's Liberation in America* (New York: Morrow, 1986); and Sue Miller, *The Good Mother* (New York: Harper & Row, 1986). Page numbers appear in parentheses in the text.

4. Among the critical responses to these texts are Judith Barnard, Letter to the Editor, *New York Times Book Review,* 22 June 1986; Alexander Cockburn, "Beat the Devil," *Nation,* 21 June 1986, p. 846; "Child Care: Feminists Get Bad Rap," *New Directions for Women* 16 (November–December 1986): 2; Catherine Johnson, "Exploding the Male-Shortage Myth," *New Woman,* September 1986, pp. 46–50; Robin Morgan, "A Maddening Take on Our Movement," *Ms.,* March 1986, pp. 74–76. See also note 8.

5. Lenore Weitzman's study claims that immediately following a divorce, a former wife and her children suffer a 73 percent decline in their standard of living, and her former husband enjoys a 42 percent rise in his. See *The Divorce Revolution: The Unexpected Social and Economic Consequences for Women and Children in America* (New York: Free Press, 1985).

6. In their op-ed article "Why Fewer American Women Marry," Neil G. Bennett and David E. Bloom deplore distortions of their study by the media (*New York Times,* 13 December 1986).

7. Susan Faludi, "Marry, Marry? On the Contrary!" *West,* 10 August 1986, pp. 6–10, 20–24. In 1987 a battle between Bennett et al. and U.S. Census Bureau demographic statistician Jeanne Moorman was featured in the media. Moorman conducted a study of her own in response to the Bennett/Bloom data. She found a much higher probability for rates of remarriage. See, e.g., Geraldine Baum, "Trendy Tussle over the Middle-Aged 'Spinster,' " *San Francisco Chronicle,* 19 January 1987, p. 17.

8. Faludi, "Marry, Marry?"; Katha Pollitt, "Being Wedded Is Not Always Bliss," *Nation,* 20 September 1986, pp. 239–42; Johnson, "Exploding the Male-Shortage Myth"; and Barbara Ehrenreich, "Where the Boys Are," *Mother Jones,* November 1986, p. 6.

9. Barbara Ehrenreich, *The Hearts of Men: American Dreams and the Flight from Commitment* (New York: Doubleday, 1983).

10. In successfully defeating a major sex discrimination suit by the Equal Employment Opportunities Commission, Sears, Roebuck & Company made use of testimony by Rosalind Rosenberg, a women's history scholar, that argued that women employees at Sears had lower pay then men not because of discrimination but because women have different priorities from men and thus chose less-pressured work assignments. For an analysis of the Sears case, see Ruth Milkman, "Women's His-

tory and the Sears Case," *Feminist Studies* 12 (Summer 1986): 375–400; for selections from Rosenberg's testimony and from testimony for the EEOC by feminist labor historian Alice Kessler-Harris, see "Women's History Goes to Trial: EEOC v. Sears, Roebuck and Company," *Signs* 11 (Summer 1986): 751–79.

11. Herma Kay Hill, a feminist legal scholar, has attempted to devise a legal framework for reconciling gender equality and difference. She suggests that a principle of "episodic analysis of biological reproductive sex differences" would allow for the episodic, brief, but still real need of many pregnant and postpartum women for legal protections different from those needed by male parents. See her "Equality and Difference: The Case of Pregnancy," *Berkeley Women's Law Journal* 1 (Fall 1985): 1–38.

12. See, e.g., Barnard, Letter. We have also encountered this reaction in discussions of the novel with colleagues and friends.

13. Although social survey data are problematic, they too suggest the depth of the feminist impact on popular behavior and thought. For example, a comprehensive study of the changing attitudes and goals of first-year college students from 1966 to 1985 concluded: "Perhaps the most dramatic finding is the extent to which the women's movement of the late 1960s has affected American higher education in the 1980s. It has had a profound impact on American college youth. . . . And there seems to have been no diminishing of that impact. In that sense, the changes seem irreversible. Women will surely never go back to where they were two decades ago." The study by Alexander W. Astin and Kenneth C. Green analyzed data involving almost six million students (quoted in "College Freshmen Still Reveal Liberal Streak," *San Francisco Chronicle*, 31 October 1986, pp. 1, 9).

14. This was the title of a rather myopic defense of the resilience of contemporary marital and family life in the United States. See Mary Jo Bane, *Here to Stay* (New York: Basic Books, 1976).

15. We are grateful to Peg Strobel for reminding us of the political implications of the precipitous rise of female employment. And labor analysts project that women's labor force participation rates will continue to grow through the end of this century. In fact, Labor Department and Census Bureau data project that women will account for 64 percent of the growth in the labor force between 1985 and 2000. See Tim Schreiner, "Demographic Change Is Reshaping Workforce," *San Francisco Chronicle*, 28 October 1986, p. 12.

16. Betty Friedan proposed family and work reforms in her call for a revitalized feminism, "How to Get the Women's Movement Moving Again," *New York Times Magazine*, 3 November 1985, p. 26. Inspired by Friedan, the National Association of Young Professional Women produced a position paper, "Continuing the Women's Movement: The Third Wave." See the op-ed piece "Feminism Lures Young Allies," *New York Times*, 2 June 1986. There are numerous initiatives in both the public and private sectors to address the need for child care. Weitzman's *Divorce Revolution* has helped to inspire a spate of legislative proposals for divorce reforms. In June 1986, NOW joined a broad range of civil rights and minority rights organizations in backing the Los Angeles local of the Service Employees International Union in a suit against Los Angeles County for discriminating against its 30,000 female black and Latina workers, the first suit addressing both gender and race discrimination to be filed in a state court.

17. One example of such a left-feminist discussion is Ellen Willis, "Handle with Care: We Need a Child-Rearing Movement," *Village Voice*, 15 July 1986, pp. 29–32.

29   The Race for Theory

Barbara Christian

I have seized this occasion to break the silence among those of us—critics, as we are now called—who have been intimidated, devalued by what I call the race for theory. I have become convinced that there has been a takeover in the literary world by Western philosophers from the old literary elite, the neutral humanists. Philosophers have been able to effect such a takeover because so much of the literature of the West has become pallid, laden with despair, self-indulgent, and disconnected. The New Philosophers, eager to understand a world that is today fast escaping their political control, have redefined literature so that the distinctions implied by that term—that is, the distinctions between everything written and those things written to evoke feeling as well as to express thought—have been blurred. They have changed literary critical language to suit their own purposes as philosophers, and they have reinvented the meaning of theory.

My first response to this realization was to ignore it. Perhaps, in spite of the egocentrism of this trend, some good might come of it. I had, I felt, more pressing and interesting things to do, such as reading and studying the history and literature of black women, a history that had been almost totally ignored and a contemporary literature bursting with originality, passion, insight, and beauty. But unfortunately, it is difficult to ignore this new takeover, since theory has become a commodity that helps determine whether we are hired or promoted in academic institutions—worse, whether we are heard at all. As a result of this new orientation, "works"

Source: This article is reprinted from *Cultural Critique* 6 (Spring 1987), pp. 51–63, by permission of the publisher, *Cultural Critique*, 2815 Claremont, Berkeley, CA 94705.

(a word that evokes labor) have become "texts." Critics are no longer concerned with literature but with other critics' texts, for the critic yearning for attention has displaced the writer and has conceived of him- or herself as the center. Interestingly, in the first part of this century, at least in England and America, the critic was usually also a writer of poetry, plays, or novels. But today, as a new generation of professionals develops, he or she is increasingly an academic. Activities such as teaching or writing one's response to specific works of literature have, among this group, become subordinated to one primary thrust: that moment when one creates a theory, thus fixing a constellation of ideas for a time at least, a fixing that no doubt will be replaced in another month or so by somebody else's competing theory as the race accelerates. Perhaps because those who have effected the takeover have the power (although they deny it) first of all to be published and thereby to determine the ideas that are deemed valuable, some of our most daring and potentially radical critics (and by *our* I mean black, female, Third World) have been influenced, even co-opted, into speaking a language and defining their discussion in terms alien to and opposed to our needs and orientation. At least so far, the creative writers I study have resisted this language.

In fact, people of color have always theorized—though in forms quite different from the Western form of abstract logic. And I am inclined to say that our theorizing (and I intentionally use the verb form rather than the noun) is often in narrative forms, in the stories we create, in riddles and proverbs, in the play with language, since dynamic rather than fixed ideas seem more to our liking. How else have we managed to survive with such spiritedness the assault on our bodies, social institutions, countries, our very humanity? And women, at least the women I grew up around, continuously speculated about the nature of life through pithy language that unmasked the power relations of their world. It is this language, and the grace and pleasure with which they played with it, that I find celebrated, refined, critiqued in the works of writers like Toni Morrison and Alice Walker. My folk, in other words, have always been a race for theory —though most often in the form of the hieroglyph, a written figure both sensual and abstract, both beautiful and communicative. In my own work I try to illuminate and explain these hieroglyphs, which is, I think, an activity quite different from the creating of the hieroglyphs themselves. As the Buddhists would say, the finger pointing at the moon is not the moon.

In this discussion, however, I am more concerned with the issue raised by my first use of the term *the race for theory* in relation to its academic hegemony, and possibly of its inappropriateness to the energetic emerging literatures in the world today. The pervasiveness of this academic hegemony is an issue continually spoken about—but usually in hidden groups, lest we who are disturbed by it appear ignorant to the reigning academic elite. Among the folk who speak in muted tones are people of color, feminists, radical critics, creative writers, who have struggled for much longer than a decade to make their voices—their various voices—heard and for whom literature is not an occasion for discourse among critics but necessary nourishment for their people and one way by which they come to understand their lives better. Clichéd though this may be, it bears, I think, repeating here.

The Tyranny of Academic Hegemony

The race for theory—with its linguistic jargon; its emphasis on quoting its prophets; its tendency toward "biblical" exegesis; its refusal even to mention specific works of creative writers, far less contemporary ones; its preoccupation with mechanical analyses of language, graphs, algebraic equations; its gross generalizations about culture—has silenced many of us to the extent that some of us feel we can no longer discuss our own literature, while others have developed intense writing blocks and are puzzled by the incomprehensibility of the language set adrift in literary circles. On any number of recent occasions I have had to convince literary critics who have pioneered entire new areas of critical inquiry that they did have something to say. Some of us are continually harassed to invent wholesale theories, regardless of the complexity of the literature we study. I, for one, am tired of being asked to produce a black feminist literary theory as if I were a mechanical man. For I believe such theory is prescriptive—it ought to have some relationship to practice. Since I can count on one hand the number of people attempting to be black feminist literary critics in the world today, I consider it presumptuous of me to invent a theory of how we *ought* to read. Instead, I think we need to read the works of our writers in our various ways and remain open to the intricacies of the intersection of language, class, race, and gender in the literature. And it would help if we were to share our process—that is, our practice—as much as possible, since, finally, our work *is* a collective endeavor.

The insidious quality of this race for theory is symbolized for me by the term "minority discourse"—a label which is borrowed from the reigning theory of the day and is untrue to the literatures being produced by our writers, for many of our literatures (certainly Afro-American literature) are central, not minor—and by many articles written under this label, which illuminate language as an assault on the other, rather than as possible communication and play with or even affirmation of another. I have used the passive voice in my last sentence construction (contrary to the rules of Black English, which like all languages has a particular value system), since I have not placed responsibility on any particular person or group. But that is precisely because this new ideology so prevalent among us behaves like so many of the other ideologies with which we have had to contend: it appears to have neither head nor center. At the least, though, we can say that the terms "minority" and "discourse" are located firmly in a Western dualistic or "binary" frame that sees the rest of the world as minor and tries to convince the rest of the world that *it* is major, usually through force and then through language, even as it claims many of the ideas that we, its "historical" other, have known and spoken about for so long. For many of us have never conceived of ourselves only as somebody's *other*.

Let me not give the impression that by objecting to the race for theory I ally myself with or agree with the neutral humanists who see literature as pure expression and will not admit to the obvious control of its pro-duction, value, and distribution by those who have power—who deny, in other words, that literature is of necessity political. I am studying an entire body of literature that has been denigrated for centuries by such terms as *political*. For an entire century Afro-American writers, from Charles Ches-nutt in the nineteenth century to Richard Wright in the 1930s, Imamu Baraka in the 1960s, Alice Walker in the 1970s, have protested the liter-ary hierarchy of dominance that declares when literature is literature and when literature is great, depending on what it thinks is to its advantage. The Black Arts Movement of the 1960s, out of which black studies, the feminist literary movement of the 1970s, and women's studies grew, articu-lated precisely those issues, which came *not* from the declarations of the New Western Philosphers but from these groups' reflections on their own lives. That Western scholars have long believed their ideas to be universal has been strongly opposed by many such groups. Some of my colleagues do not see black critical writers of previous decades as eloquent enough. Clearly, they have not read Richard Wright's "Blueprint for Negro Writ-ing," Ralph Ellison's *Shadow and Act*, Charles Chesnutt's resignation from being a writer, or Alice Walker's "Search for Zora Neale Hurston." There are two reasons for this general ignorance of what our writer-critics have said. One is that black writing has been generally ignored in this country. Since we, as Toni Morrison has put it, are seen as a discredited people, it is no surprise that our creations are also discredited. But this is also due to the fact that until recently dominant critics in the Western world have also been creative writers who have had access to the upper-middle-class institutions of education, and until recently our writers have decidedly been excluded from these institutions and in fact have often been opposed to them. Because of the academic world's general ignorance about the literature of black people and of women, whose work too has been discredited, it is not surprising that so many of our critics think the position arguing that literature is political begins with these New Philosophers. Unfortunately, many of our young critics do not investigate the reasons *why* that statement—literature is political—is now acceptable when before it was not; nor do we look to our own antecedents for the sophisticated arguments upon which we can build in order to change the tendency of any established Western idea to become hegemonic.

For I feel that the new emphasis on literary critical theory is as hegemonic as the world that it attacks. I see the language it creates as one that mystifies rather than clarifies our condition, making it possible for a few people who know that particular language to control the critical scene. And that language surfaced, interestingly enough, just when the literature of peoples of color, of black women, of Latin Americans, of Africans began to move to "the center." Such words as *center* and *periphery* are themselves instructive. *Discourse, canon, texts,* words as latinate as the tradition from which they come, are quite familiar to me. Because I went to a Catholic Mission school in the West Indies, I must confess that I cannot hear the word "canon" without smelling incense, that the word "text" immediately brings back agonizing memories of biblical exegesis, that "discourse" reeks for me of metaphysics forced down my throat in those courses that traced *world* philosophy from Aristotle through Thomas Aquinas to Heidegger. "Periphery" too is a word I heard throughout my childhood, for if anything was seen as being at the periphery, it was those small Caribbean islands that had neither land mass nor military power. Still, I noted how intensely important this periphery was, for U.S. troops were continually invading one island or another if any change in political control even seemed to be occurring. As I lived among folk for whom language was an absolutely necessary way of validating their existence, I was told that the minds of the world lived only in the small continent of Europe. The metaphysical language of the New Philosophy, then, I must admit, is repulsive to me and is one reason why I raced from philosophy to literature, since the latter seemed to me to have the possibilities of rendering the world as large and as complicated as I experienced it, as sensual as I knew it was. In literature I sensed the possibility of the integration of feeling and knowledge, rather than the split between the abstract and the emotional in which Western philosophy inevitably indulged.

Mystifying Language and Politics

Now I am being told that philosophers are the ones who write literature; that authors are dead, irrelevant, mere vessels through which their narratives ooze; that they do not work or have the faintest idea what they are doing but rather produce texts as disembodied as the angels. I am frankly astonished that scholars who call themselves Marxists or post-Marxists could seriously use such metaphysical language even as they attempt to deconstruct the philosophical tradition from which their language comes. And as a student of literature I am appalled by the sheer ugliness of the language, its lack of clarity, its unnecessarily complicated sentence constructions, its lack of pleasurableness, its alienating quality. It is the kind of writing for which composition teachers would give a freshman a resounding F.

Because I am a curious person, however, I postponed readings of black women writers I was working on and read some of the prophets of this new literary orientation. These writers did announce their dissatisfaction with some of the cornerstone ideas of their own tradition, a dissatisfaction with which I was born. But in their attempt to change the orientation of Western scholarship, they concentrated as usual on themselves and were not in the slightest interested in the worlds they had ignored or controlled. Again, I was supposed to know *them,* while they were not at all interested in knowing *me.* Instead they sought to "deconstruct" the tradition to which they belonged even as they used the same forms, style, language of that tradition, forms that necessarily embody its values. And increasingly as I read them and saw them substituting their philosophical writings for literary ones, I began to have the uneasy feeling that their folk were not producing any literature worth mentioning. For they always harked back to the masterpieces of the past, again reifying the very texts they said they were deconstructing. Increasingly, as *their* way, *their* terms, *their* approaches remained central and became the means by which one defined literary critics, many of my own peers who had previously been concentrating on dealing with the other side of the equation—the reclamation and discussion of past and *present* Third World literatures—were diverted into continually discussing the new literary theory.

From my point of view as a critic of contemporary Afro-American women's writing, this orientation is extremely problematic. In attempting to find the deep structures in the literary tradition, a major preoccupation of the new New Criticism, many of us have become obsessed with the nature of reading itself to the extent that we have stopped writing about the literature being written today. Since I am slightly paranoid, it has begun to occur to me that the literature being produced *is* precisely one of the reasons why this new philosophical-literary-critical theory of relativity is so prominent. In other words, the literature of blacks, women of South America and Africa, and so on, as overtly "political" literature was being preempted by a new Western concept proclaiming that reality does not exist, that everything is relative, and that every text is silent about something—which indeed it must necessarily be.

There is, of course, much to be learned from exploring how we know what we know, how we read what we read, an exploration which of necessity can have no end. But there also has to be a "what," and that "what," when it is even mentioned by the New Philosophers, are texts of the past, primarily Western male texts, whose norms are again being transferred to Third World, female texts as theories of reading proliferate. Inevitably, a hierarchy has now developed between what is called theoretical criticism and practical criticism, as mind is deemed superior to matter. I have no quarrel with those who wish to philosophize about how we know what we know. But I do resent the fact that this particular orientation is so privileged and has diverted so many of us from doing the first readings of the literature being written today as well as of past works about which nothing has been written. I note, for example, that there is little work done on Gloria Naylor, that most of Alice Walker's works have not been commented on (despite the rage around *The Color Purple*), that there has yet to be an in-depth study of Frances Harper, the nineteenth-century abolitionist poet and novelist. If our emphasis on theoretical criticism continues, critics of the future may have to reclaim the writers we are now ignoring—that is, if they are even aware such artists existed.

Theory as Prescription

I am particularly perturbed by the movement to exalt theory, because of my own adult history. I was an active member of the Black Arts Movement of the 1960s and know how dangerous theory can become. Many today may not be aware of this, but the Black Arts Movement tried to create Black Literary Theory and in doing so became prescriptive. My fear is that when Theory is not rooted in practice, it becomes prescriptive, exclusive, elitist.

An example of this prescriptiveness is the approach the Black Arts Movement took toward language. For its leaders blackness resided in the use of black talk, which they defined as hip urban language. So when Nikki Giovanni reviewed Paule Marshall's *Chosen Place, Timeless People*, she criticized the novel on the grounds that it was not black: the language was too elegant, too white; blacks, she said, did not speak that way. Having come from the West Indies where we do, some of the time, speak that way, I was amazed by the narrowness of her vision. The emphasis on *one way* to be black resulted in the works of southern writers being seen as non-black because the black talk of Georgia does not sound like the black talk of Philadelphia. Because the ideologues, like Baraka, come from the urban centers they tended to privilege their way of speaking, thinking, writing, and to condemn other kinds of writing as not being black enough. Whole areas of the canon were assessed according to the dictum of the Black Arts Nationalist point of view, as in Addison Gayle's *The Way of the New World*, while other works were ignored because they did not fit the scheme of cultural nationalism. Older writers like Ellison and Baldwin were condemned because they saw that the intersection of Western and African influences resulted in a new Afro-American culture, a position with which many of the Black Nationalist ideologues disagreed. Writers were told that writing love poems was not being black. Further examples abound.

It is true that the Black Arts Movement resulted in a necessary and important critique both of previous Afro-American literature and of the white-established literary world. But in attempting to take over power, it became, as Ishmael Reed satirizes so well in *Mumbo Jumbo*, much like its opponent, monolithic and downright repressive.

It is this tendency toward the monolithic, the monotheistic, that worries me about the race for theory. Constructs like the *center* and the *periphery* reveal a tendency to want to make the world less complex by organizing it according to one principle, to fix it through an idea that is really an ideal. Many of us are particularly sensitive to monolithism, since one major element of such ideologies of dominance as sexism and racism is to dehumanize people by stereotyping them, by denying them their variousness and complexity. Inevitably, monolithism becomes a metasystem in which there is a controlling ideal, especially in relation to pleasure. Language as one form of pleasure is immediately restricted and becomes heavy, abstract, prescriptive, monotonous.

Variety, multiplicity, eroticism are difficult to control. And it may very well be that these are the reasons why the writer is often *persona non grata* in political states, whatever form they take: writers/artists have a tendency to refuse to give up their way of seeing the world and of playing with possibilities; in fact, their very expression relies on that insistence. Perhaps that is why creative literature, even when written by politically reactionary people, can be so freeing, for in having to embody ideas and recreate the world, writers cannot produce merely "one way."

Authoritative Discourse in Feminism

The characteristics of the Black Arts Movement are, I am afraid, being repeated again today, certainly in the other area to which I am especially attuned. In the race for theory, feminists, eager to enter the halls of power, have attempted their own prescriptions. So often I have read books on feminist literary theory that restrict the definition of what *feminist* means and overgeneralize about so much of the world that most women as well as men are excluded. And seldom do feminist theorists take into account the complexity of life—that women are of many races and ethnic backgrounds with different histories and cultures and that as a rule women belong to different classes with different concerns. Seldom do they note these distinctions, because if they did, they could not articulate a theory. Often as a way of clearing themselves they do acknowledge that women of color, for example, exist, then go on to do what they were going to do anyway, which is to invent a theory that has little relevance for us.

That tendency toward monolithism is precisely how I see the French feminist theorists. They concentrate on the female body as the means to creating a female language, since language, they say, is male and necessarily conceives of woman as other. Clearly, many of them have been irritated by the theories of Lacan, for whom language is phallic. But suppose there are peoples in the world whose language was invented primarily in relation to women, who after all are the ones who relate to children and teach language. Some Native American languages, for example, use female pronouns when speaking about non-gender-specific activity. Who knows who, according to gender, created languages? Further, by positing the body as the source of everything, French feminists return to the old myth that biology determines everything and ignore the fact that gender is a social rather than a biological construct.

I could go on critiquing the positions of French feminists—who are themselves more various in their points of view than the label used to describe them—but that is not my point. What I am concerned about is the authority this school now has in feminist scholarship—the way it has become *authoritative discourse*, monologic, which occurs precisely because it does have access to the means of promulgating its ideas. The Black Arts Movement was able to do this for a time because of the political movements of the 1960s; so too with the French feminists, who could not be inventing "theory" if a space had not been created by the women's movement. In both cases, the group posited a theory that excluded many of the people who made that space possible. Hence, one of the reasons for the surge of Afro-American women's writing during the 1970s and its emphasis on sexism in the black community is precisely that when the ideologues of the 1960s said *black*, they meant *black male*.

I and many of my sisters do not see the world as being so simple. And perhaps that is why we have not rushed to create abstract theories. We know there are countless women of color, both in America and in the rest of the world, to whom our singular ideas would be applied; therefore, we feel a caution about pronouncing black feminist theory that might be seen as a decisive statement about Third World women. This is not to say we are not theorizing. Certainly our literature is an indication of the ways in which our theorizing is of necessity based on our multiplicity of experiences.

Empowerment versus Desire for Power

There is at least one other lesson I learned from the Black Arts Movement. One reason for its monolithic approach had to do with its desire to destroy the power that controlled black people, but it was a power that many of its ideologues wished to achieve. The nature of our context today is such that an approach which desires power single-mindedly must become like that which it wishes to destroy. Rather than wanting to change the whole model, many of us want to be at the center. It is this point of view that writers like June Jordan and Audre Lorde continually critique, even as they call for empowerment and emphasize the fear of difference among us and our need for leaders rather than a reliance on ourselves.

For one must distinguish the desire for power from the need to become empowered: that is, seeing oneself as capable of and having the right to determine one's life. Such empowerment is partially derived from a knowledge of history. The Black Arts Movement did result in the creation of Afro-American studies as a concept, thus giving it a place in the university where one might engage in the reclamation of Afro-American history and culture and pass them on to others. I am particularly concerned that institutions such as black studies and women's studies, fought for with such vigor and at some sacrifice, are not often seen as important by many of our black or women scholars precisely because the old hierarchy of traditional departments is seen as superior to these "marginal" groups. Yet it is in this context that many others of us are discovering the extent of our complexity, the interrelationships of different areas of knowledge in relation to a distinctly Afro-American or female experience. Rather than having to view our world as subordinate to others, or rather than having to work as if we were hybrids, we can pursue ourselves as subjects.

My major objection to the race for theory, as some readers have probably guessed by now, really hinges on the question "For whom are we doing what we are doing when we do literary criticism?" It is, I think, the central question today especially for the few of us who have infiltrated the academy enough to be wooed by it. The answer to that question determines what orientation we take in our work, the language we use, the purposes for which it is intended.

I can speak only for myself. But what I write and how I write is done in order to save my own life. And I mean that literally. For me, literature is a way of knowing that I am not hallucinating, that whatever I feel/know *is*. It is an affirmation that sensuality is intelligence, that sensual language is language that makes sense. My response, then, is directed to those who write what I read and to those who read what I read: put concretely, to Toni Morrison and to people who read Toni Morrison (among whom I would count few academics). That number is increasing, as is the readership of Walker and Marshall. But in no way is the literature that Morrison, Marshall, and Walker create supported by the academic world. Nor, given the political context of our society, do I expect that to change soon. For there is no reason for those who control these institutions to be anything other than threatened by these writers.

My readings do presuppose a need, a desire among folk who, like me, also want to save their own lives. My concern, then, is a passionate one, for the literature of people who are not in power has always been in danger of extinction or of co-optation, not because we do not theorize but because what we can even imagine—far less whom we can reach—is constantly limited by societal structures. For me, literary criticism is promotion as well as understanding, a response to the writer to whom there is often no response, to folk who need the writing as much as they need anything. I know, from literary history, that writing disappears unless there is a response to it. Because I write about writers who are now writing, I hope to help ensure that their tradition has continuity and survives.

So my "method," to use a new "lit. crit." word, is not fixed but relates to what I read and to the historical context of the writers I read *and* to the many critical activities in which I am engaged, which may or may not involve writing. It is a learning from the language of creative writers, which is one of surprise, so that I might discover what language I might use. For my language is very much based on what I read and how it affects me: that is, on the surprise that comes from reading something that compels you to read differently, as I believe literature does. I therefore have no set method—another prerequisite of the new theory—since for me every work suggests a new approach. As risky as that might seem, it is, I believe, what intelligence means—a tuned sensitivity to that which is alive and therefore cannot be known until it is known. Audre Lorde puts it in a far more succinct and sensual way in her essay "Poetry Is Not a Luxury":

> As they become known to and accepted by us, our feelings and the honest exploration of them become sanctuaries and spawning grounds for the most radical and daring of ideas. They become a safe-house for that difference so necessary to change and the conceptualization of any meaningful action. Right now, I could name at least ten ideas I would have found intolerable or incomprehensible and frightening, except as they came after dreams and poems. This is not idle fantasy, but a disciplined attention to the true meaning of "it feels right to me." We can train ourselves to respect our feelings and to transpose them into a language so they can be shared. And where that language does not yet exist, it is our poetry which helps to fashion it. Poetry is not only dream and vision; it is the skeleton architecture of our lives. It lays the foundations for a future of change, a bridge across our fears of what has never been before.[1]

Note

1. Audre Lorde, *Sister Outsider* (Trumansburg, N.Y.: Crossing Press, 1984), 37.

30 A Manifesto for Cyborgs:
Science, Technology, and Socialist Feminism in the Last Quarter

Donna Haraway

An Ironic Dream of a Common Language

This essay is an effort to build an ironic political myth faithful to feminism, socialism, and materialism. Perhaps more faithful as blasphemy is faithful than as reverent worship and identification are. Blasphemy has always seemed to require taking things very seriously. I know no better stance to adopt from within the secular-religious, evangelical traditions of U.S. politics, including the politics of socialist feminism. Blasphemy protects one from the moral majority within, while still insisting on the need for community. Blasphemy is not apostasy. Irony is about contradictions that do not resolve into larger wholes, even dialectically; about the tension of holding incompatible things together because both or all are necessary and true. Irony is about humor and serious play. It is also a rhetorical strategy and a political method, one I would like to see more honored within socialist feminism. At the center of my ironic faith, my blasphemy, is the image of the cyborg.

A cyborg is a cybernetic organism, a hybrid of machine and organism, a creature of social reality as well as a creature of fiction. Social reality is lived social relations, our most important political construction, a world-changing fiction. The international women's movements have constructed

Source: This article is reprinted from *Socialist Review* No. 80 (March–April 1985), pp. 65–107, by permission of the publisher, *Socialist Review*, 3202 Adeline, Berkeley, CA 94703.

"women's experience," as well as uncovered or discovered this crucial collective object. This experience is a fiction and fact of the most crucial, political kind. Liberation rests on the construction of the consciousness, the imaginative apprehension, of oppression, and so of possibility. The cyborg is a matter of fiction and lived experience that changes what counts as women's experience in the late twentieth century. This is a struggle over life and death, but the boundary between science fiction and social reality is an optical illusion.

Contemporary science fiction is full of cyborgs—creatures simultaneously animal and machine, who populate worlds ambiguously natural and crafted. Modern medicine is also full of cyborgs, of couplings between organism and machine, each conceived as coded devices, in an intimacy and with a power not generated in the history of sexuality. Cyborg "sex" restores some of the lovely replicative baroque of ferns and invertebrates (such nice organic prophylactics against heterosexism). Cyborg replication is uncoupled from organic reproduction. Modern production seems like a dream of cyborg colonization of work, a dream that makes the nightmare of Taylorism seem idyllic. And modern war is a cyborg orgy, coded by C^3I, command-control-communication-intelligence, an $84 billion item in 1984's U.S. defense budget. I am making an argument for the cyborg as a fiction mapping our social and bodily reality and as an imaginative resource suggesting some very fruitful couplings. Foucault's biopolitics is a flaccid premonition of cyborg politics, a very open field.

By the late twentieth century, our time, a mythic time, we are all chimeras, theorized and fabricated hybrids of machine and organism; in short, we are cyborgs. The cyborg is our ontology; it gives us our politics. The cyborg is a condensed image of both imagination and material reality, the two joined centers structuring any possibility of historical transformation. In the traditions of "Western" science and politics—the tradition of racist, male-dominant capitalism; the tradition of progress; the tradition of the appropriation of nature as resource for the productions of culture; the tradition of reproduction of the self from the reflections of the other—the relation between organism and machine has been a border war. The stakes in the border war have been the territories of production, reproduction, and imagination. This essay is an argument for *pleasure* in the confusion of boundaries and for *responsibility* in their construction. It is also an effort to contribute to socialist-feminist culture and theory in a postmodernist, non-naturalist mode and in the utopian tradition of imagining a world without gender, which is perhaps a world without genesis, but maybe also a world without end. The cyborg incarnation is outside salvation history.

The cyborg is a creature in a postgender world; it has no truck with bisexuality, pre-Oedipal symbiosis, unalienated labor, or other seductions to organic wholeness through a final appropriation of all the powers of the parts into a higher unity. In a sense, the cyborg has no origin story in the Western sense: a "final" irony, since the cyborg is also the awful apocalyptic *telos* of the "West's" escalating dominations of abstract individuation, an ultimate self untied at last from all dependency, a man in space. An origin story in the "Western," humanist sense depends on the myth of original unity, fullness, bliss, and terror, represented by the phallic mother from whom all humans must separate, the task of individual development and of history, the twin potent myths inscribed most powerfully for us in psychoanalysis and Marxism. Hilary Klein has argued that both Marxism and psychoanalysis, in their concepts of labor and of individuation and gender formation, depend on the plot of original unity out of which difference must be produced and enlisted in a drama of escalating domination of woman/nature. The cyborg skips the step of original unity, of identification with nature in the Western sense. This is its illegitimate promise, which might lead to subversion of its teleology as star wars.

The cyborg is resolutely committed to partiality, irony, intimacy, and perversity. It is oppositional, utopian, and completely without innocence. No longer structured by the polarity of public and private, the cyborg defines a technological polis based partly on a revolution of social relations in the *oikos*, the household. Nature and culture are reworked; the one can no longer be the resource for appropriation or incorporation by the other. The relationships for forming wholes from parts, including those of polarity and hierarchical domination, are at issue in the cyborg world. Unlike Frankenstein's monster, the cyborg does not expect its father to save it through a restoration of the garden: that is, through the fabrication of a heterosexual mate, through its completion in a finished whole, a city and cosmos. The cyborg does not dream of community on the model of the organic family, this time without the Oedipal project. The cyborg would not recognize the Garden of Eden; it is not made of mud and cannot dream of returning to dust. Perhaps that is why I want to see whether cyborgs can subvert the apocalypse of returning to nuclear dust in the manic compulsion to name the Enemy. Cyborgs are not reverent; they do not re-member the cosmos. They are wary of holism but needy for connection—they seem to have a natural feel for united front politics but without the vanguard party. The main trouble with cyborgs, of course, is that they are the illegitimate offspring of militarism and patriarchal capitalism, not to mention state socialism. But illegitimate offspring are often exceedingly unfaithful to their origins. Their fathers, after all, are inessential.

I return to the science fiction of cyborgs at the end of this essay, but now I want to signal three crucial boundary breakdowns that make the following political fictional (political scientific) analysis possible. By the late twentieth century in U.S. scientific culture, the boundary between human and animal is thoroughly breached. The last beachheads of uniqueness have been polluted if not turned into amusement parks; language, tool use, social behavior, mental events—nothing really convincingly settles the separation of human and animal. And many people no longer feel the need of such a separation; indeed, many branches of feminist culture affirm the pleasure of connection of human and other living creatures. Movements for animal rights are not irrational denials of human uniqueness; they are clear-sighted recognition of connection across the discredited breach of nature and culture. Biology and evolutionary theory over the last two centuries have simultaneously produced modern organisms as objects of knowledge and reduced the line between humans and animals to a faint trace re-etched in ideological struggle or professional disputes between life and social sciences. Within this framework, teaching modern Christian creationism should be fought as a form of child abuse.

Biological-determinist ideology is only one position opened up in scientific culture for arguing the meanings of human animality. There is much room for radical political people to contest the meanings of the breached boundary.[1] The cyborg appears in myth precisely where the boundary between human and animal is transgressed. Far from signaling a walling-off of people from other living beings, cyborgs signal disturbingly and pleasurably tight coupling. Bestiality has a new status in this cycle of marriage exchange.

The second leaky distinction is between animal-human (organism) and machine. Precybernetic machines could be haunted; there was always the specter of the ghost in the machine. This dualism structured the dialogue between materialism and idealism that was settled by a dialectical progeny, called spirit or history, according to taste. But basically, machines were not self-moving, self-designing, autonomous. They could not achieve man's dream, only mock it. They were not man, an author to himself, but only a caricature of that masculinist reproductive dream. To think they were otherwise was paranoid. Now we are not so sure. Late twentieth-century machines have made thoroughly ambiguous the difference between natural and artificial, mind and body, self-developing and externally designed, and many other distinctions that used to apply to organisms and machines. Our machines are disturbingly lively and we ourselves are frighteningly inert.

Technological determinism is only one ideological space opened up by the reconceptions of machine and organism as coded texts through which we engage in the play of writing and reading the world.[2] "Textualization" of everything in poststructuralist, postmodernist theory has been damned by Marxists and socialist feminists for its utopian disregard for lived relations of domination that ground the "play" of arbitrary reading.[3] It is certainly true that postmodernist strategies, like my cyborg myth, subvert myriad organic wholes (the poem, the primitive culture, the biological organism). In short, the certainty of what counts as nature—a source of insight and a promise of innocence—is undermined, probably fatally. The transcendent authorization of interpretation is lost and with it the ontology grounding "Western" epistemology. But the alternative is not cynicism or faithlessness: that is, some version of abstract existence, like the accounts of technological determinism destroying "man" by the "machine" or "meaningful political action" by the "text." Who cyborgs will be is a radical question; the answers are a matter of survival. Both chimpanzees and artifacts have politics, so why shouldn't we?[4]

The third distinction is a subset of the second: the boundary between physical and nonphysical is very imprecise for us. Pop physics books on the consequences of quantum theory and the indeterminacy principle are a kind of popular scientific equivalent to the Harlequin romances as a marker of radical change in American white heterosexuality: they get it wrong, but they are on the right subject. Modern machines are quintessentially microelectronic devices; they are everywhere and they are invisible. Modern machinery is an irreverent upstart god, mocking the Father's ubiquity and spirituality. The silicon chip is a surface for writing; it is etched in molecular scales disturbed only by atomic noise, the ultimate interference for nuclear scores. Writing, power, and technology are old partners in Western stories of the origin of civilization, but miniaturization has changed our experience of mechanism. Miniaturization has turned out to be about power: small is not so much beautiful as preeminently dangerous, as in cruise missiles. Contrast the TV sets of the 1950s or the news cameras of the 1970s with the TV wrist bands or hand-sized video cameras now advertised. Our best machines are made of sunshine; they are all light and clean because they are nothing but signals, electromagnetic waves, a section of a spectrum. And these machines are eminently portable, mobile—a matter of immense human pain in Detroit and Singapore. People are nowhere near so fluid, being both material and opaque. Cyborgs are ether, quintessence.

The ubiquity and invisibility of cyborgs is precisely why these sunshine-belt machines are so deadly. They are as hard to see politically as materially. They are about consciousness—or its simulation.[5] They are floating signifiers moving in pickup trucks across Europe, blocked more effectively by the witch-weavings of the displaced and so unnatural Greenham women, who read the cyborg webs of power very well, than by the militant labor of older masculinist politics, whose natural constituency needs defense jobs. Ultimately the "hardest" science is about the realm of greatest boundary confusion, the realm of pure number, pure spirit, C^3I, cryptography, and the preservation of potent secrets. The new machines are so clean and light. Their engineers are sun worshipers mediating a new scientific revolution associated with the night dream of postindustrial society. The diseases evoked by these clean machines are "no more" than the miniscule coding changes of an antigen in the immune system, "no more" than the experience of stress. The nimble little fingers of "oriental" women, the old fascination of little Anglo-Saxon Victorian girls with doll-houses, women's enforced attention to the small all take on quite new dimensions in this world. There might be a cyborg Alice taking account of these new dimensions. Ironically, it might be the unnatural cyborg women making chips in Asia and spiral dancing in Santa Rita whose constructed unities will guide effective oppositional strategies.

So my cyborg myth is about transgressed boundaries, potent fusions, and dangerous possibilities that progressive people might explore as one part of needed political work. One of my premises is that most American socialists and feminists see deepened dualisms of mind and body, animal and machine, idealism and materialism in the social practices, symbolic formulations, and physical artifacts associated with "high technology" and scientific culture. From *One-Dimensional Man* to *The Death of Nature*,[6] the analytic resources developed by progressives have insisted on the necessary domination of technics and recalled us to an imagined organic body to integrate our resistance. Another of my premises is that the need for unity of people trying to resist worldwide intensification of domination has never been more acute. But a slightly perverse shift of perspective might better enable us to contest for meanings, as well as for other forms of power and pleasure in technologically mediated societies.

From one perspective, a cyborg world is about the final imposition of a grid of control on the planet, about the final abstraction embodied in a star wars apocalypse waged in the name of defense, about the final appropriation of women's bodies in a masculinist orgy of war.[7] From another perspective, a cyborg world might be about lived social and bodily realities in which people are not afraid of their joint kinship with animals and machines, not afraid of permanently partial identities and contradictory standpoints. The political struggle is to see from both perspectives at once because each reveals both dominations and possibilities unimaginable from the other vantage point. Single vision produces worse illusions than double vision or many-headed monsters. Cyborg unities are monstrous and illegitimate; in our present political circumstances we could hardly hope for more potent myths for resistance and recoupling. I like to imagine LAG, the Livermore Action Group, as a kind of cyborg society, dedicated to realistically converting the laboratories that most fiercely embody and spew out the tools of technological apocalypse, and committed to building a political form that actually manages to hold together witches, engineers, elders, perverts, Christians, mothers, and Leninists long enough to disarm the state. Fission Impossible is the name of the affinity group in my town. (Affinity: related not by blood but by choice, the appeal of one chemical nuclear group for another, avidity.)

Fractured Identities

It has become difficult to name one's feminism by a single adjective—or even to insist in every circumstance upon the noun. Consciousness of exclusion through naming is acute. Identities seem contradictory, partial, and strategic. With the hard-won recognition of their social and historical constitution, gender, race, and class cannot provide the basis for belief in "essential" unity. There is nothing about being "female" that naturally binds women. There is not even such a state as "being" female, itself a highly complex category constructed in contested sexual scientific discourses and other social practices. Gender, race, or class consciousness is an achievement forced on us by the terrible historical experience of the contradictory social realities of patriarchy, colonialism, and capitalism. And who counts as "us" in my own rhetoric? Which identities are available to ground a potent political myth called "us," and what could motivate enlistment in such a collectivity? Painful fragmentation among feminists (not to mention among women) along every possible fault line has made the concept of *woman* elusive, an excuse for the matrix of women's dominations of each other. For me—and for many who share a similar historical location in white, professional, middle-class, female, radical, North American, mid-adult bodies—the sources of a crisis in political identity are legion. The recent history for much of the U.S. left and U.S. feminism has been a response to this kind of crisis by endless splitting and searches for a new essential unity. But there has also been a growing recognition of another response through coalition—affinity, not identity.[8]

Chela Sandoval, from a consideration of specific historical moments in the formation of the new political voice called women of color, has theorized a hopeful model of political identity called "oppositional consciousness," born of the skills for reading webs of power by those refused stable membership in the social categories of race, sex, or class.[9] "Women of color," a name contested at its origins by those whom it would incorporate, as well as a historical consciousness marking systematic breakdown of all the signs of Man in "Western" traditions, constructs a kind of post-modernist identity out of otherness and difference. This post-modernist identity is fully political, whatever might be said about other possible post-modernisms.

Sandoval emphasizes the lack of any essential criterion for identifying who is a woman of color. She notes that the definition of the group has been by conscious appropriation of negation. For example, a Chicana or U.S. black woman has not been able to speak as a woman or as a black person or as a Chicano. Thus, she was at the bottom of a cascade of negative identities, left out of even the privileged oppressed authorial categories called "women and blacks," who claimed to make the important revolutions. The category "woman" negated all nonwhite women; "black" negated all non-black people as well as all black women. But there was also no "she," no singularity, but a sea of differences among U.S. women who have affirmed their historical identity as U.S. women of color. This identity marks out a self-consciously constructed space that can affirm the capacity to act not on the basis of natural identification but only on the basis of conscious coalition, of affinity, of political kinship.[10] Unlike the "woman" of some streams of the white women's movement in the United States, there is no naturalization of the matrix, or at least this is what Sandoval argues is uniquely available through the power of oppositional consciousness.

Sandoval's argument has to be seen as one potent formulation for feminists out of the worldwide development of anticolonialist discourse, discourse dissolving the "West" and its highest product—the one who is not animal, barbarian, or woman: that is, man, the author of a cosmos called history. As orientalism is deconstructed politically and semiotically, the identities of the occident destabilize, including those of feminists.[11] Sandoval argues that "women of color" have a chance to build an effective unity that does not replicate the imperializing, totalizing revolutionary subjects of previous Marxisms and feminisms that had not faced the consequences of the disorderly polyphony emerging from decolonization.

Katie King has emphasized the limits of identification and the political/poetic mechanics of identification built into reading "the poem," that generative core of cultural feminism. King criticizes the persistent tendency among contemporary feminists from different "moments" or "conversations" in feminist practice to taxonomize the women's movement to make individual political tendencies appear to be the *telos* of the whole. These taxonomies tend to remake feminist history to appear to be an ideological struggle among coherent types persisting over time, especially those typical units called radical, liberal, and socialist feminism. All other feminisms are either incorporated or marginalized, usually by building an explicit ontology and epistemology.[12] Taxonomies of feminism produce epistemologies to police deviation from official women's experience. And of course, "women's culture," like women of color, is consciously created by mechanisms inducing affinity. The rituals of poetry, music, and certain forms of academic practice have been preeminent. The politics of race and culture in the U.S. women's movements are intimately interwoven. The common achievement of King and Sandoval is learning how to craft a poetic/political unity without relying on a logic of appropriation, incorporation, and taxonomic identification.

The theoretical and practical struggle against unity-through-domination or unity-through-incorporation ironically not only undermines the justifications for patriarchy, colonialism, humanism, positivism, essentialism, scientism, and other unlamented isms but *all* claims for an organic or natural standpoint. I think that radical and socialist/Marxist feminisms have also undermined their/our own epistemological strategies and that this is a crucially valuable step in imagining possible unities. It remains to be seen whether all "epistemologies" as Western political people have known them fail us in the task to build effective affinities.

It is important to note that the effort to construct revolutionary standpoints, epistemologies as achievements of people committed to changing the world, has been part of the process showing the limits of identification. The acid tools of postmodernist theory and the constructive tools of ontological discourse about revolutionary subjects might be seen as ironic allies in dissolving Western selves in the interests of survival. We are excruciatingly conscious of what it means to have a historically constituted body. But with the loss of innocence in our origin, there is no expulsion from the Garden either. Our politics lose the indulgence of guilt with the naiveté of innocence. But what would another political myth for socialist feminism look like? What kind of politics could embrace partial, contradictory, permanently unclosed constructions of personal and collective selves and still be faithful, effective—and, ironically, socialist feminist?

I do not know of any other time in history when there was greater need for political unity to confront effectively the dominations of "race," "gender," "sexuality," and "class." I also do not know of any other time when the kind of unity we might help build could have been possible. None of "us" have any longer the symbolic or material capability of dictating the shape of reality to any of "them." Or at least "we" cannot claim innocence from practicing such dominations. White women, including socialist feminists, discovered (that is, were forced kicking and screaming to notice) the noninnocence of the category "woman." That consciousness changes the geography of all previous categories; it denatures them as heat denatures a fragile protein. Cyborg feminists have to argue that "we" do not want any more natural matrix of unity and that no construction is whole. Innocence, and the corollary insistence on victimhood as the only ground for insight, has done enough damage. But the constructed revolutionary subject must give late twentieth-century people pause as well. In the fraying of identities and in the reflexive strategies for constructing them, the possibility opens up for weaving something other than a shroud for the day after the apocalypse that so prophetically ends salvation history.

Both Marxist/socialist feminisms and radical feminisms have simultaneously naturalized and denatured the category "woman" and consciousness of the social lives of "women." Perhaps a schematic caricature can highlight both kinds of moves. Marxian socialism is rooted in an analysis of wage labor which reveals class structure. The consequence of the wage relationship is systematic alienation, as the worker is dissociated from his [*sic*] product. Abstraction and illusion rule in knowledge, domination rules in practice. Labor is the preeminently privileged category enabling the Marxist to overcome illusion and find that point of view which is necessary for changing the world. Labor is the humanizing activity that makes man; labor is an ontological category permitting the knowledge of a subject and so the knowledge of subjugation and alienation.

In faithful filiation, socialist feminism advanced by allying itself with the basic analytic strategies of Marxism. The main achievement of both Marxist feminists and socialist feminists was to expand the category of labor to accommodate what (some) women did, even when the wage relation was subordinated to a more comprehensive view of labor under capitalist patriarchy. In particular, women's labor in the household and women's activity as mothers generally—that is, reproduction in the socialist feminist sense—entered theory on the authority of analogy to the Marxian concept of labor. The unity of women here rests on an epistemology based on the ontological structure of "labor." Marxist/socialist feminism does not "naturalize" unity; it is a possible achievement based on a possible standpoint rooted in social relations. The essentializing move is in the ontological structure of labor or of its analogue, women's activity.[13] The inheritance of Marxian humanism, with its preeminently Western self, is the difficulty for me. The contribution from these formulations has been the emphasis on the daily responsibility of real women to build unities rather than naturalize them.

Catherine MacKinnon's version of radical feminism is itself a caricature of the appropriating, incorporating, totalizing tendencies of Western theories of identity grounding action.[14] It is factually and politically wrong to assimilate all the diverse "moments" or "conversations" in the recent women's politics named radical feminism to MacKinnon's version. But the teleological logic of her theory shows how an epistemology and ontology —including their negations—erase or police difference. Only one of the effects of MacKinnon's theory is the rewriting of the history of the polymorphous field called radical feminism. The major effect is the production of a theory of experience, of women's identity, that is a kind of apocalypse for all revolutionary standpoints. That is, the totalization built into this tale of radical feminism achieves its end—the unity of women—by enforcing the experience of and testimony to radical nonbeing. As for the Marxist/ socialist feminist, consciousness is an achievement, not a natural fact. And MacKinnon's theory eliminates some of the difficulties built into humanist revolutionary subjects, but at the cost of radical reductionism.

MacKinnon argues that radical feminism necessarily adopted a different analytical strategy from Marxism, looking first not at the structure of class but at the structure of sex/gender and its generative relationship, men's constitution and appropriation of women sexually. Ironically, MacKinnon's "ontology" constructs a nonsubject, a nonbeing. Another's desire, not the self's labor, is the origin of "woman." She therefore develops a theory of consciousness that enforces what can count as "women's" experience: anything that names sexual violation—indeed, sex itself as far as "women" can be concerned. Feminist practice is the construction of this form of consciousness; that is, the self-knowledge of a self-who-is-not.

Perversely, sexual appropriation in this radical feminism still has the epistemological status of labor, the point from which analysis able to contribute to changing the world must flow. But sexual objectification, not alienation, is the consequence of the structure of sex/gender. In the realm of knowledge the result of sexual objectification is illusion and abstraction. However, a woman is not simply alienated from her product but in a deep sense does not exist as a subject, or even potential subject, since she owes her existence as a woman to sexual appropriation. To be constituted by another's desire is not the same thing as to be alienated in the violent separation of the laborer from his product.

MacKinnon's radical theory of experience is totalizing in the extreme; it does not so much marginalize as obliterate the authority of any other women's political speech and action. It is a totalization producing what Western patriarchy itself never succeeded in doing—feminists' consciousness of the nonexistence of women except as products of men's desire. I think MacKinnon correctly argues that no Marxian version of identity can firmly ground women's unity. But in solving the problem of the contradictions of any Western revolutionary subject for feminist purposes, she develops an even more authoritarian doctrine of experience. If my complaint about socialist/Marxian standpoints is their unintended erasure of polyvocal, unassimilable, radical difference made visible in anticolonial discourse and practice, MacKinnon's intentional erasure of all difference through the device of the "essential" nonexistence of women is not reassuring.

In my taxonomy, which like any other taxonomy is a reinscription of history, radical feminism can accommodate all the activities of women named by socialist feminists as forms of labor only if the activity can somehow be sexualized. Reproduction had different tones of meanings for the two tendencies, one rooted in labor, one in sex, both calling the consequences of domination and ignorance of social and personal reality "false consciousness."

Beyond either the difficulties or the contributions in the argument of any one author, neither Marxist- nor radical-feminist points of view have tended to embrace the status of a partial explanation; both were regularly constituted as totalities. Western explanation has demanded as much; how else could the "Western" author incorporate its others? Each tried to annex other forms of domination by expanding its basic categories through analogy, simple listing, or addition. Embarrassed silence about race among white radical and socialist feminists was one major, devastating political consequence. History and polyvocality disappear into political taxonomies that try to establish genealogies. There was no structural room for race (or for much else) in theory claiming to reveal the construction of the category woman and social group women as a unified or totalizable whole. The structure of my caricature looks like this:

Socialist Feminism—
    structure of class//wage labor//alienation
    labor, by analogy reproduction, by extension sex, by addition race
Radical Feminism—
    structure of gender//sexual appropriation//objectification
    sex, by analogy labor, by extension reproduction, by addition race

In another context, the French theorist Julia Kristeva claimed that women appeared as a historical group after World War II, along with groups like youth. Her dates are doubtful, but we are now accustomed to remembering that as objects of knowledge and as historical actors, "race" did not always exist; "class" has a historical genesis; and "homosexuals" are quite junior. It is no accident that the symbolic system of the family of man—and so the essence of woman—breaks up at the same moment that networks of connection among people on the planet are unprecedentedly multiple, pregnant, and complex. "Advanced capitalism" is inadequate to convey the structure of this historical moment. In the "Western" sense, the end of man is at stake. It is no accident that woman disintegrates into women in our time. Perhaps socialist feminists were not substantially guilty of producing essentialist theory that suppressed women's particularity and contradictory interests. I think we have been, at least through unreflective participation in the logics, languages, and practices of white humanism and through searching for a single ground of domination to secure our revolutionary voice. Now we have less excuse. But in the consciousness of our failures, we risk lapsing into boundless difference and giving up on the confusing task of making partial, real connection. Some differences are playful; some are poles of world historical systems of domination. "Epistemology" is about knowing the difference.

The Informatics of Domination

In this attempt at an epistemological and political position, I would like to sketch a picture of possible unity, a picture indebted to socialist and feminist principles of design. The frame for my sketch is set by the extent and importance of rearrangements in worldwide social relations tied to science and technology. I argue for a politics rooted in claims about fundamental changes in the nature of class, race, and gender in an emerging system of world order analogous in its novelty and scope to that created by industrial capitalism; we are living through a movement from an organic, industrial society to a polymorphous, information system—from all work to all play, a deadly game. Simultaneously material and ideological, the dichotomies may be expressed in the following chart of transitions from the comfortable old hierarchical dominations to the scary new networks I have called the informatics of domination:

Representation	Simulation
Bourgeois novel, realism	Science fiction, postmodernism
Organism	Biotic component
Depth, integrity	Surface, boundary
Heat	Noise
Biology as clinical practice	Biology as inscription
Physiology	Communications engineering
Small group	Subsystem
Perfection	Optimization

Eugenics	Population control
Decadence, *Magic Mountain*	Obsolescence, *Future Shock*
Hygiene	Stress management
Microbiology, tuberculosis	Immunology, AIDS
Organic division of labor	Ergonomics/cybernetics of labor
Functional specialization	Modular construction
Reproduction	Replication
Organic sex role specialization	Optimal genetic strategies
Biological determinism	Evolutionary inertia, constraints
Community ecology	Ecosystem
Racial chain of being	Neo-imperialism, United Nations humanism
Scientific management in home/factory	Global factory/electronic cottage
Family/market/factory	Women in the integrated circuit
Family wage	Comparable worth
Public/private	Cyborg citizenship
Nature/culture	Fields of difference
Cooperation	Communications enhancement
Freud	Lacan
Sex	Genetic engineering
Labor	Robotics
Mind	Artificial intelligence
World War II	Star Wars
White capitalist patriarchy	Informatics of domination

This list suggests several interesting things.[15] First, the objects on the right-hand side cannot be coded as "natural," a realization that subverts naturalistic coding for the left-hand side as well. We cannot go back ideologically or materially. It's not just that "god" is dead; so is the "goddess." In relation to objects like biotic components, one must think not in terms of essential properties but in terms of strategies of design, boundary constraints, rates of flows, systems logics, costs of lowering constraints. Sexual reproduction is one kind of reproductive strategy among many, with costs and benefits as a function of the system environment. Ideologies of sexual reproduction can no longer reasonably call on the notions of sex and sex role as organic aspects in natural objects like organisms and families. Such reasoning will be unmasked as irrational, and ironically, corporate executives reading *Playboy* and anti-porn radical feminists will make strange bedfellows in jointly unmasking the irrationalism.

Likewise for race, ideologies about human diversity have to be formulated in terms of frequencies of parameters, like blood groups or intelligence scores. It is "irrational" to invoke such concepts as "primitive" and "civilized." For liberals and radicals, the search for integrated social systems gives way to a new practice called "experimental ethnography" in which an organic object dissipates in attention to the play of writing. At the level of ideology we see translations of racism and colonialism into languages of development and underdevelopment, rates and constraints of modernization. Any objects or persons can be reasonably thought of in terms of disassembly and reassembly; no "natural" architectures constrain system design. The financial districts in all the world's cities, as well as the export-processing and free-trade zones, proclaim this elementary fact of "late capitalism." The entire universe of objects that can be known scientifically must be formulated as problems in communications engineering (for the managers) or theories of the text (for those who would resist). Both are cyborg semiologies.

One should expect control strategies to concentrate on boundary conditions and interfaces, on rates of flow across boundaries—and not on the integrity of natural objects. "Integrity" or "sincerity" of the Western self gives way to decision procedures and expert systems. For example, control strategies applied to women's capacities to give birth to new human beings will be developed in the languages of population control and maximization of goal achievement for individual decision-makers. Control strategies will be formulated in terms of rates, costs of constraints, degrees of freedom. Human beings, like any other component or subsystem, must be localized in a system architecture whose basic modes of operation are probabilistic, statistical. No objects, spaces, or bodies are sacred in themselves; any component can be interfaced with any other if the proper standard, the proper code, can be constructed for processing signals in a common language. Exchange in this world transcends the universal translation effected by the capitalist markets that Marx analyzed so well. The privileged pathology affecting all kinds of components in this universe is stress—communications breakdown.[16] The cyborg is not subject to Foucault's biopolitics; the cyborg simulates politics, a much more potent field of operations.

This kind of analysis of the scientific and cultural objects of knowledge that have appeared historically since World War II prepares us to notice some important inadequacies in feminist analysis, which has proceeded as if the organic, hierarchical dualisms ordering discourse in "the West" since Aristotle still ruled. They have been cannibalized, or as Zoe Sofia (Sofoulis) might put it, they have been "techno-digested." The dichotomies between mind and body, animal and human, organism and machine, public and private, nature and culture, men and women, primitive and civilized are all in question ideologically. The actual situation of women is their integration/ exploitation into a world system of production/reproduction and communication called the informatics of domination. The home, workplace, market, public arena, and the body itself can all be dispersed and interfaced in nearly infinite, polymorphous ways, with large consequences for women and others—consequences that are themselves very different for different people and make potent oppositional international movements difficult to imagine and essential for survival. One important route for reconstructing socialist-feminist politics is through theory and practice addressed to the social relations of science and technology, including crucially the systems of myth and meanings structuring our imaginations. The cyborg is a kind of disassembled and reassembled postmodern collective and personal self. This is the self feminists must code.

Communications technologies and biotechnologies are the crucial tools recrafting our bodies. These tools embody and enforce new social relations for women worldwide. Technologies and scientific discourses can be partially understood as formalizations—that is, as frozen moments—of the fluid social interactions constituting them, but they should also be viewed as instruments for enforcing meanings. The boundary is permeable between tool and myth, instrument and concept, historical systems of social relations and historical anatomies of possible bodies, including objects of knowledge. Indeed, myth and tool mutually constitute each other.

Furthermore, communications sciences and modern biologies are constructed by a common move—*the translation of the world into a problem of coding,* a search for a common language in which all resistance to instrumental control disappears and all heterogeneity can be submitted to disassembly, reassembly, investment, and exchange.

In communications sciences the translation of the world into a problem in coding can be illustrated by looking at cybernetic (feedback-controlled) systems theories applied to telephone technology, computer design, weapons deployment, or database construction and maintenance. In each case, solution to the key questions rests on a theory of language and control; the key operation is determining the rates, directions, and probabilities of flow of a quantity called information. The world is subdivided by boundaries differentially permeable to information. Information is just that kind of quantifiable element (unit, basis of unity) that allows universal translation, and so unhindered instrumental power (called effective communication). The biggest threat to such power is interruption of communication. Any system breakdown is a function of stress. The fundamentals of this technology can be condensed into the metaphor C^3I, command-control-communication-intelligence, the military's symbol for its operations theory.

In modern biologies, the translation of the world into a problem in coding can be illustrated by molecular genetics, ecology, sociobiological evolutionary theory, and immunobiology. The organism has been translated into problems of genetic coding and readout. Biotechnology, a writing technology, informs research broadly.[17] In a sense, organisms have ceased to exist as objects of knowledge, giving way to biotic components: that is, special kinds of information processing devices. The analogous moves in ecology could be examined by probing the history and utility of the concept of the ecosystem. Immunobiology and associated medical practices are rich exemplars of the privilege of coding and recognition systems as objects of knowledge, as constructions of bodily reality for us. Biology is here a kind of cryptography. Research is necessarily a kind of intelligence activity. Ironies abound. A stressed system goes awry; its communication processes break down; it fails to recognize the difference between self and other. Human babies with baboon hearts evoke national ethical perplexity—for animal rights activists at least as much as for guardians of human purity. Gay men, Haitian immigrants, and intravenous drug users are the "privileged" victims of an awful immune-system disease that marks (inscribes on the body) confusion of boundaries and moral pollution.

But these excursions into communications sciences and biology have been at a rarefied level; there is a mundane, largely economic reality to support my claim that these sciences and technologies indicate fundamental transformations in the structure of the world for us. Communications technologies depend on electronics. Modern states, multinational corporations, military power, welfare state apparatuses, satellite systems, political processes, fabrication of our imaginations, labor control systems, medical constructions of our bodies, commercial pornography, the international division of labor, and religious evangelism depend intimately upon electronics. Microelectronics is the technical basis of simulacra: that is, of copies without originals.

Microelectronics mediates the translations of *labor* into robotics and word processing; *sex* into genetic engineering and reproductive technologies; and *mind* into artificial intelligence and decision procedures. The new biotechnologies concern more than human reproduction. Biology as a powerful engineering science for redesigning materials and processes has revolutionary implications for industry, perhaps most obvious today in areas of fermentation, agriculture, and energy. Communications sciences and biology are constructions of natural-technical objects of knowledge in which the difference between machine and organism is thoroughly blurred; mind, body, and tool are on very intimate terms. The "multinational" material organization of the production and reproduction of daily life and the symbolic organization of the production and reproduction of culture and imagination seem equally implicated. The boundary-maintaining images of base and superstructure, public and private, or material and ideal never seemed more feeble.

I have used Rachel Grossman's image of women in the integrated circuit to name the situation of women in a world so intimately restructured through the social relations of science and technology.[18] I use the odd circumlocution "the social relations of science and technology" to indicate that we are dealing not with a technological determinism but with a historical system depending upon structured relations among people. But the phrase should also indicate that science and technology provide fresh sources of power, that we need fresh sources of analysis and political action.[19] Some of the rearrangements of race, sex, and class rooted in high-tech-facilitated social relations can make socialist feminism more relevant to effective progressive politics.

The Homework Economy

The "new industrial revolution" is producing a new worldwide working class. The extreme mobility of capital and the emerging international division of labor are intertwined with the emergence of new collectivities and the weakening of familiar groupings. These developments are neither gender- nor race-neutral. White men in advanced industrial societies have become newly vulnerable to permanent job loss, and women are not disappearing from the job rolls at the same rates as men. It is not simply that women in Third World countries are the preferred labor force for the science-based multinationals in the export-processing sectors, particularly in electronics. The picture is more systematic and involves reproduction, sexuality, culture, consumption, and production. In the prototypical Silicon Valley, many women's lives have been structured around employment in electronics-dependent jobs, and their intimate realities include serial heterosexual monogamy, negotiating child-care, distance from extended kin or most other forms of traditional community, a high likelihood of loneliness and extreme economic vulnerability as they age. The ethnic and racial diversity of women in Silicon Valley structures a microcosm of conflicting differences in culture, family, religion, education, language.

Richard Gordon has called this new situation the homework economy.[20] Although he includes the phenomenon of literal homework, emerging in connection with electronics assembly, Gordon intends "homework economy" to name a restructuring of work that broadly has the characteristics formerly ascribed to female jobs, jobs literally done only by women. Work is being redefined as both literally female and feminized, whether performed by men or women. To be feminized means to be made extremely vulnerable; able to be disassembled, reassembled, exploited as a reserve labor force; seen less as workers than as servers; subjected to time arrangements on and off the paid job that make a mockery of a limited work day; leading an existence that always borders on being obscene, out of place, and reducible to sex. Deskilling is an old strategy newly applicable to formerly privileged workers. However, the homework economy does not refer only to large-scale deskilling, nor does it deny that new areas of high skill are emerging, even for women and men previously excluded from skilled employment. Rather, the concept indicates that factory, home, and market are integrated on a new scale and that the places of women are crucial—and need to be analyzed for differences among women and for meanings of relations between men and women in various situations.

The homework economy as a world capitalist organizational structure is made possible by (not caused by) the new technologies. The success of the attack on relatively privileged, mostly white, men's unionized jobs is tied to the power of the new communications technologies to integrate and control labor despite extensive dispersion and decentralization. The consequences of the new technologies are felt by women both in the loss of the family (male) wage (if they ever had access to this white privilege) and in the character of their own jobs—office work and nursing, for example—which are becoming capital-intensive.

The new economic and technological arrangements are also related to the collapsing welfare state and the ensuing intensification of demands on women to sustain daily life for themselves as well as for men, children, and old people. The feminization of poverty—generated by dismantling the welfare state and by the homework economy where stable jobs become the exception, and sustained by the expectation that women's wage will not be matched by a male income for the support of children—has become an urgent focus. The causes of various female-headed households are a function of race, class, or sexuality, but their increasing generality is a ground for coalitions of women on many issues. That women regularly sustain daily life partly as a function of their enforced status as mothers is hardly new; the kind of integration with the overall capitalist and progressively war-based economy is new. The particular pressure, for example, on U.S. black women, who have achieved an escape from (barely) paid domestic service and who now hold clerical and similar jobs in large numbers, has large implications for continued enforced black poverty *with* employment. Teenage women in industrializing areas of the Third World increasingly find themselves the sole or major source of a cash wage for their families, while access to land is every more problematic. These developments must have major consequences in the psychodynamics and politics of gender and race.

Within the framework of three major stages of capitalism (commercial/ early industrial; monopoly; multinational)—tied to nationalism, imperialism, and multinationalism and related to Jameson's three dominant aesthetic periods of realism, modernism, and postmodernism—I would argue that specific forms of families dialectically relate to forms of capital and to its political and cultural concomitants. Although lived problematically and unequally, ideal forms of these families might be schematized as (1) the patriarchal nuclear family, structured by the dichotomy between public and private and accompanied by the white bourgeois ideology of separate spheres and nineteenth-century Anglo-American bourgeois feminism; (2) the modern family mediated (or enforced) by the welfare state and institutions like the family wage, with a flowering of afeminist heterosexual ideologies, including their radical versions represented in Greenwich Village around World War I; and (3) the "family" of the homework economy with its oxymoronic structure of female-headed households and its explosion of feminisms and the paradoxical intensification and erosion of gender itself.

This is the context in which the projections for worldwide structural unemployment stemming from the new technologies are part of the picture of the homework economy. As robotics and related technologies put men out of work in "developed" countries and exacerbate failure to generate male jobs in Third World "development," and as the automated office becomes the rule even in labor-surplus countries, the feminization of work intensifies. Black women in the United States have long known what it looks like to face the structural underemployment ("feminization") of black men, as well as their own highly vulnerable position in the wage economy. It is no longer a secret that sexuality, reproduction, family, and community life are interwoven with this economic structure in myriad ways that have also differentiated the situations of white and black women. Many more women and men will contend with similar situations, which will make cross-gender and race alliances on issues of basic life support (with or without jobs) necessary, not just nice.

The new technologies also have a profound effect on hunger and on food production for subsistence worldwide. Rae Lessor Blumberg estimates that women produce about 50 percent of the world's subsistence food.[21] Women are excluded generally from benefiting from the increased high-tech commodification of food and energy crops, their days are made more arduous because their responsibilities to provide food do not diminish, and their reproductive situations are made more complex. Green Revolution technologies interact with other high-tech industrial production to alter gender divisions of labor and differential gender migration patterns.

The new technologies seem deeply involved in the forms of "privatization" that Rosalind Petchesky has analyzed, in which militarization, right-wing family ideologies and policies, and intensified definitions of corporate property as private synergistically interact.[22] The new communications technologies are fundamental to the eradication of "public life" for everyone. This facilitates the mushrooming of a permanent high-tech military establishment at the cultural and economic expense of most people, but especially of women. Technologies like video games and highly miniaturized television seem crucial to the production of modern forms of "private life." The culture of video games is heavily oriented to individual competition and extraterrestrial warfare. High-tech, gendered imaginations are produced here, imaginations that can contemplate destruction of the planet and a science fiction escape from its consequences. More than our imagination is militarized; and the other realities of electronic and nuclear warfare are inescapable.

The new technologies affect the social relations of both sexuality and reproduction, and not always in the same ways. The close ties of sexuality and instrumentality, of views of the body as a kind of private satisfaction- and utility-maximizing machine, are described nicely in sociobiological origin stories that stress a genetic calculus and explain the inevitable dialectic of domination of male and female gender roles.[23] These sociobiological stories depend on a high-tech view of the body as a biotic component or cybernetic communications system. Among the many transformations of reproductive situations is the medical one, where women's bodies have boundaries newly permeable to both "visualization" and "intervention." Of course, who should control the interpretation of bodily boundaries in medical hermeneutics is a major feminist issue. The speculum served as an icon of women's claiming their bodies in the 1970s; that handcraft tool is inadequate to express our needed body politics in the negotiation of reality in the practices of cyborg reproduction. Self-help is not enough. The technologies of visualization recall the important cultural practice of hunting with the camera and the deeply predatory nature of a photographic consciousness.[24] Sex, sexuality, and reproduction are central actors in high-tech myth systems structuring our imaginations of personal and social possibility.

Another critical aspect of the social relations of the new technologies is the reformulation of expectations, culture, work, and reproduction for the large scientific and technical work force. A major social and political danger is the formation of a strongly bimodal social structure, with the masses of women and men of all ethnic groups, but especially people of color, confined to a homework economy, illiteracy of several varieties, and general redundancy and impotence, controlled by high-tech repressive apparatuses ranging from entertainment to surveillance and disappearance. An adequate socialist-feminist politics should address women in the privileged occupational categories, and particularly in the production of science and technology that constructs scientific-technical discourses, processes, and objects.[25]

This issue is only one aspect of inquiry into the possibility of a feminist science, but it is important. What kind of constitutive role in the production of knowledge, imagination, and practice can new groups doing science have? How can these groups be allied with progressive social and political movements? What kind of political accountability can be constructed to tie women together across the scientific-technical hierarchies separating us? Might there be ways of developing feminist science/technology politics in alliance with antimilitary science facility conversion action groups? Many scientific and technical workers in Silicon Valley, the high-tech cowboys included, do not want to work on military science.[26] Can these personal preferences and cultural tendencies be welded into progressive politics among this professional middle class in which women, including women of color, are coming to be fairly numerous?

Women in the Integrated Circuit

Let me summarize the picture of women's historical locations in advanced industrial societies, as these positions have been restructured partly through the social relations of science and technology. If it was ever possible ideologically to characterize women's lives by the distinction of public and private domains—suggested by images of the division of working-class life into factory and home, of bourgeois life into market and home, and of gender existence into personal and political realms— it is now a totally misleading ideology, even to show how both terms of these dichotomies construct each other in practice and in theory. I prefer a network ideological image, suggesting the profusion of spaces and identities and the permeability of boundaries in the personal body and in the body politic. "Networking" is both a feminist practice and a multinational corporate strategy—weaving is for oppositional cyborgs.

The only way to characterize the informatics of domination is as a massive intensification of insecurity and cultural impoverishment, with common failure of subsistence networks for the most vulnerable. Since much of this picture interweaves with the social relations of science and technology, the urgency of a socialist-feminist politics addressed to science and technology is plain. There is much now being done, and the grounds for political work are rich. For example, the efforts to develop forms of collective struggle for women in paid work, like SEIU's (Service Employees International Union) District 925, should be a high priority for all of us. These efforts are profoundly tied to the technical restructuring of labor processes and reformations of working classes. These efforts also are providing understanding of a more comprehensive kind of labor organization, involving community, sexuality, and family issues never privileged in the largely white male industrial unions.

The structural rearrangements related to the social relations of science and technology evoke strong ambivalence. But it is not necessary to be ultimately depressed by the implications of late twentieth-century women's relation to all aspects of work, culture, production of knowledge, sexuality, and reproduction. For excellent reasons, most Marxisms see domination best and have trouble understanding what can only look like false consciousness and people's complicity in their own domination in late capitalism. It is crucial to remember that what is lost, perhaps especially from women's points of view, is often virulent forms of oppression, nostalgically naturalized in the face of current violation. Ambivalence toward the disrupted unities mediated by high-tech culture requires not the sorting of consciousness into categories of "clear-sighted critique grounding a solid political epistemology" versus "manipulated false consciousness" but a subtle understanding of emerging pleasures, experiences, and powers with serious potential for changing the rules of the game.

There are grounds for hope in the emerging bases for new kinds of unity across race, gender, and class, as these elementary units of socialist-feminist analysis themselves suffer protean transformations. Intensifications of hardship experienced worldwide in connection with the social relations of science and technology are severe. But what people are experiencing is not transparently clear, and we lack sufficiently subtle connections for collectively building effective theories of experience. Present efforts— Marxist, psychoanalytic, feminist, anthropological—to clarify even "our" experience are rudimentary.

I am conscious of the odd perspective provided by my historical position: a Ph.D. in biology for an Irish Catholic girl was made possible by Sputnik's impact on U.S. national science-education policy. I have a body and mind as much constructed by the post–World War II arms race and Cold War as by the women's movements. There are more grounds for hope in focusing on the contradictory effects of politics designed to produce loyal

American technocrats, which produced as well large numbers of dissidents, than in focusing on the present defeats.

The permanent partiality of feminist points of view has consequences for our expectations of forms of political organization and participation. We do not need a totality in order to work well. The feminist dream of a common language—like all dreams of perfectly true language, of perfectly faithful naming of experience—is a totalizing and imperialist one. In that sense, dialectics too is a dream language, longing to resolve contradiction. Perhaps, ironically, we can learn from our fusions with animals and machines how not to be Man, the embodiment of Western logos. From the point of view of pleasure in these potent and taboo fusions, made inevitable by the social relations of science and technology, there might indeed be a feminist science.

Cyborgs: A Myth of Political Identity

I conclude with a myth about identity and boundaries which might inform late twentieth-century political imaginations. I am indebted in this story to such writers as Joanna Russ, Samuel Delaney, John Varley, James Tiptree, Jr., Octavia Butler, Monique Wittig, and Vonda McIntyre.[27] These are our storytellers exploring what it means to be embodied in high-tech worlds. They are theorists for cyborgs. Exploring conceptions of bodily boundaries and social order, the anthropologist Mary Douglas should be credited with helping us to consciousness about how fundamental body imagery is to world view, and so to political language.[28] French feminists such as Luce Irigaray and Monique Wittig, for all their differences, know how to write the body, how to weave eroticism, cosmology, and politics from imagery of embodiment and, especially for Wittig, from imagery of fragmentation and reconstitution of bodies.[29]

American radical feminists such as Susan Griffin, Audre Lorde, and Adrienne Rich have profoundly affected our political imaginations—and perhaps restricted too much what we allow as a friendly body and political language.[30] They insist on the organic, opposing it to the technological. But their symbolic systems and the related positions of ecofeminism and feminist paganism, replete with organicisms, can only be understood in Sandoval's terms as oppositional ideologies fitting the late twentieth century. They would simply bewilder anyone not preoccupied with the machines and consciousness of late capitalism. In that sense they are part of the cyborg world. But there are also great riches for feminists in explicitly embracing the possibilities inherent in the breakdown of clean distinctions between organism and machine and similar distinctions structuring the Western self. It is the simultaneity of breakdowns that cracks the matrices of domination and opens geometric possibilities. What might be learned from personal and political "technological" pollution? I will look briefly at two overlapping groups of texts for their insight into the construction of a potentially helpful cyborg myth: constructions of women of color, and monstrous selves in feminist science fiction.

Earlier I suggested that the category "women of color" might be understood as a cyborg identity, a potent subjectivity synthesized from fusions of outsider identities. There are material and cultural grids mapping this potential. Audre Lorde captures the tone in the title of her *Sister Outsider*. In my political myth, Sister Outsider is the offshore woman whom U.S. workers, female and feminized, are supposed to regard as the enemy preventing their solidarity, threatening their security. Onshore, inside the boundary of the United States, Sister Outsider is a potential amid the races and ethnic identities of women manipulated for division, competition, and exploitation in the same industries. "Women of color" are the preferred labor force for the science-based industries, the real women for whom the worldwide sexual market, labor market, and politics of reproduction kaleidoscope into daily life. Young Korean women hired in the sex industry and in electronics assembly are recruited from high schools, educated for the integrated circuit. Literacy, especially in English, distinguishes the "cheap" female labor so attractive to the multinationals.

Contrary to orientalist stereotypes of the "oral primitive," literacy is a special mark of women of color, acquired by U.S. black women as well as men through a history of risking death to learn and to teach reading and writing. Writing has a special significance for all colonized groups. Writing has been crucial to the Western myth of the distinction of oral and written cultures, primitive and civilized mentalities, and more recently to the erosion of that distinction in "postmodernist" theories attacking the phallogocentrism of the West with its worship of the monotheistic, phallic, authoritative, and singular word, the unique and perfect name.[31] Contests for the meanings of writing are a major form of contemporary political struggle. Releasing the play of writing is deadly serious. The poetry and stories of U.S. women of color are repeatedly about writing, about access to the power to signify, but this time that power must be neither phallic nor innocent. Cyborg writing must not be about the Fall, the imagination of a once-upon-a-time wholeness before language, before writing, before Man. Cyborg writing is about the power to survive, not on the basis of original innocence but on the basis of seizing the tools to mark the world that marked women of color as other.

The tools are often stories, retold stories, versions that reverse and displace the hierarchical dualisms of naturalized identities. In retelling origin stories, cyborg authors subvert the central myths of origin of Western culture. We have all been colonized by those origin myths, with their longing for fulfillment in apocalypse. The phallogocentric origin stories most crucial for feminist cyborgs are built into the literal technologies—technologies that write the world, biotechnology and microelectronics—that have recently textualized our bodies as code problems on the grid of C³I. Feminist cyborg stories have the task of recoding communication and intelligence to subvert command and control.

Figuratively and literally, language politics pervade the struggles of women of color; and stories about language have a special power in the rich contemporary writing by U.S. women of color. For example, retellings of the story of the indigenous woman Malinche, mother of the mestizo "bastard" race of the new world, master of languages, and mistress of Cortés, carry special meaning for Chicana constructions of identity. Cherríe Moraga in *Loving in the War Years* explores the themes of identity when one never possessed the original language, never told the original story, never resided in the harmony of legitimate heterosexuality in the garden of culture, and so cannot base identity on a myth or a fall from innocence and right to natural names, mother's or father's.³² Moraga's writing, her superb literacy, is presented in her poetry as the same kind of violation as Malinche's mastery of the conquerer's language—a violation, an illegitimate production, that allows survival. Moraga's language is not "whole"; it is self-consciously spliced, a chimera of English and Spanish, both conquerors' languages. But it is this chimeric monster, without claim to an original language before violation, that crafts the erotic, competent, potent identities of women of color. Sister Outsider hints at the possibility of world survival not because of her innocence but because of her ability to live on the boundaries, to write without the founding myth of original wholeness with its inescapable apocalypse of final return to a deathly oneness that Man has imagined to be the innocent and all-powerful Mother, freed at the End from another spiral of appropriation by her son. Writing marks Moraga's body, affirms it as the body of a woman of color, against the possibility of passing into the unmarked category of the Anglo father or into the orientalist myth of the "original illiteracy" of a mother that never was. Malinche was mother here, not Eve before eating the forbidden fruit. Writing affirms Sister Outsider, not the Woman-before-the-Fall-into-Writing needed by the phallogocentric Family of Man.

Writing is preeminently the technology of cyborgs, etched surfaces of the late twentieth century. Cyborg politics is the struggle for language and the struggle against perfect communication, against the one code that translates all meaning perfectly, the central dogma of phallogocentrism. That is why cyborg politics insists on noise and advocates pollution, rejoicing in the illegitimate fusions of animal and machine. These are the couplings that make Man and Woman so problematic, subverting the structure of desire, the force imagined to generate language and gender, and so subverting the structure and modes of reproduction of "Western" identity, of nature and culture, of mirror and eye, slave and master, body and mind. "We" did not originally choose to be cyborgs, but choice grounds a liberal politics and epistemology that imagine the reproduction of individuals before the wider replications of "texts."

From the perspective of cyborgs, freed of the need to ground politics in "our" privileged position of the oppression that incorporates all other dominations, the innocence of the merely violated, the ground of those closer to nature, we can see powerful possibilities. Feminisms and Marxisms have run aground on Western epistemological imperatives to construct a revolutionary subject from the perspective of a hierarchy of oppressions and/or a latent position of moral superiority, innocence, and greater closeness to nature. With no available original dream of a common language or original symbiosis promising protection from hostile "masculine" separation, but written into the play of a text that has no finally privileged reading or salvation history, to recognize "oneself" as fully implicated in the world frees us of the need to root politics in identification, vanguard parties, purity, and mothering. Stripped of identity, the bastard race teaches about the power of the margins and the importance of a mother like Malinche. Women of color have transformed her from the evil mother of masculinist fear into the originally literate mother who teaches survival.

This is not just literary deconstruction but liminal transformation. Every story that begins with original innocence and privileges the return to wholeness imagines the drama of life to be individuation, separation, the birth of the self, the tragedy of autonomy, the fall into writing, alienation (that is, war), tempered by imaginary respite in the bosom of the Other. These plots are ruled by a reproductive politics—rebirth without flaw, perfection, abstraction. In this plot women are imagined either better or worse off, but all agree they have less selfhood, weaker individuation, more fusion to the oral, to Mother, less at stake in masculine autonomy. But there is another route to having less at stake in masculine autonomy, a route that does not pass through Woman, Primitive, Zero, the Mirror Stage and its imaginary. It passes through women and other present-tense, illegitimate cyborgs, not of Woman born, who refuse the ideological resources of victimization so as to have a real life. These cyborgs are the people who refuse to disappear on cue, no matter how many times a "Western" commentator remarks on the sad passing of another primitive, another organic group done in by "Western" technology, by writing.[33] These real-life cyborgs—for example, the southeast Asian village women workers in Japanese and U.S. electronics firms described by Aiwa Ong—are actively rewriting the texts of their bodies and societies. Survival is the stake in this play of readings.

To recapitulate, certain dualisms have been persistent in Western traditions; they have all been systemic to the logics and practices of domination of women, people of color, nature, workers, animals—in short, domination of all constituted as *others*, whose task is to mirror the self. Chief among these troubling dualisms are self/other, mind/body, culture/nature, male/female, civilized/primitive, reality/appearance, whole/part, agent/resource, maker/made, active/passive, right/wrong, truth/illusion, total/partial, God/man. The self is the One who is not dominated, who knows that by the service of the other; the other is the one who holds the future, who knows that by the experience of domination, which gives the lie to the autonomy of the self. To be One is to be autonomous, to be powerful, to be God; but to be One is to be an illusion and so to be involved in a dialectic of apocalypse with the other. Yet to be other is to be multiple, without clear boundary, frayed, insubstantial. One is too few, but two are too many.

High-tech culture challenges these dualisms in intriguing ways. It is not clear who makes and who is made in the relation between human and machine. It is not clear what is mind and what body in machines that resolve into coding practices. Insofar as we know ourselves in both formal discourse (such as biology) and in daily practice (such as the homework economy in the integrated circuit), we find ourselves to be cyborgs, hybrids, mosaics, chimeras. Biological organisms have become biotic systems, communications devices like others. There is no fundamental, ontological separation in our formal knowledge of machine and organism, of technical and organic.

One consequence is that our sense of connection to our tools is heightened. The trance state experienced by many computer users has become a staple of science fiction film and cultural jokes. Perhaps paraplegics and other severely handicapped people can (and sometimes do) have the most intense experiences of complex hybridization with other communication devices. In *The Ship Who Sang*, Anne McCaffrey explored the consciousness of a cyborg, hybrid of girl's brain and complex machinery, formed after the birth of a severely handicapped child. Gender, sexuality, embodiment, skill: all were reconstituted in the story. Why should our bodies end at the skin, or include at best other beings encapsulated by skin? From the seventeenth century till now, machines could be animated—given ghostly souls to make them speak or move or to account for their orderly development and mental capacities. Or organisms could be mechanized—reduced to body understood as resource of mind. These machine/organism relationships are obsolete, unnecessary. For us, in imagination and in other practice, machines can be prosthetic devices, intimate components, friendly selves. We don't need organic holism to give impermeable wholeness, the total woman and her feminist variants (mutants?). Let me conclude this point by a very partial reading of the logic of the cyborg monsters of my second group of texts, feminist science fiction.

The cyborgs populating feminist science fiction make very problematic the statuses of man or woman, human, artifact, member of a race, individual identity, or body. Katie King clarifies how pleasure in reading these fictions is not largely based on identification. Students facing Joanna Russ for the first time, students who have learned to take such modernist writers as James Joyce or Virginia Woolf without flinching, do not know what to make of *The Adventures of Alyx* or *The Female Man*, where characters refuse the reader's search for innocent wholeness while granting the wish for heroic quests, exuberant eroticism, and serious politics. *The Female Man* is the story of four versions of one genotype, all of whom meet but, even taken together, do not make a whole, or resolve the dilemmas of violent moral action, or remove the growing scandal of gender. The feminist science fiction of Samuel Delaney, especially *Tales of Neveryon*, mocks stories of origin by redoing the neolithic revolution, replaying the founding moves of Western civilization to subvert their plausibility. James Tiptree, Jr., an author whose fiction was regarded as particularly manly until her "true" gender was revealed, tells tales of reproduction based on nonmammalian technologies: alternation of generations, male brood pouches, male nurturing. John Varley constructs a supreme cyborg in his arch-feminist exploration of Gaea, a mad goddess/planet/trickster/old woman/technological device, on whose surface an extraordinary array of postcyborg symbioses are spawned. Octavia Butler writes of an African sorceress pitting her powers of transformation against the genetic manipulations of her rival (*Wild Seed*), of time warps that bring a modern U.S. black woman into slavery where her actions in relation to her white master-ancestor determine the possibility of her own birth (*Kindred*), and of the illegitimate insights into identity and community of an adopted cross-species child who came to know the enemy as self (*Survivor*).

Because it is particularly rich in boundary transgressions, Vonda McIntyre's *Superluminal* can close this truncated catalogue of promising monsters who help redefine the pleasures and politics of embodiment and feminist writing. In a fiction where no character is "simply" human, human status is highly problematic. Orca, a genetically altered diver, can speak with killer whales and survive deep ocean conditions, but she longs to explore space as a pilot, necessitating bionic implants jeopardizing her kinship with the divers and cetaceans. Transformations are effected by virus vectors carrying a new developmental code, by transplant surgery, by implants of microelectronic devices, by analogue doubles, and other means. Laenea becomes a pilot by accepting a heart implant and a host of other alterations allowing survival in transit at speeds exceeding that of light. Radu Dracul survives a virus-caused plague on his outerworld planet to find himself with a time sense that changes the boundaries of spatial perception for the whole species. All the characters explore the limits of language, the dream of communicating experience, and the necessity of limitation, partiality, and intimacy even in this world of protean transformation and connection.

Monsters have always defined the limits of community in Western imaginations. The Centaurs and Amazons of ancient Greece established the limits of the centered polis of the Greek male human by their disruption of marriage and boundary pollutions of the warrior with animality and woman. Unseparated twins and hermaphrodites were the confused human material in early modern France who grounded discourse on the natural and supernatural, medical and legal, portents and diseases—all crucial to establishing modern identity.[34] The evolutionary and behavioral sciences of monkeys and apes have marked the multiple boundaries of late twentieth-century industrial identities. Cyborg monsters in feminist science fiction define quite different political possibilities and limits from those proposed by the mundane fiction of Man and Woman.

There are several consequences to taking seriously the imagery of cyborgs as other than our enemies. Our bodies, ourselves: bodies are maps of power and identity. Cyborgs are no exceptions. A cyborg body is not innocent; it was not born in a garden; it does not seek unitary identity and so generate antagonistic dualisms without end (or until the world ends); it takes irony for granted. One is too few, and two is only one possibility. Intense pleasure in skill, machine skill, ceases to be a sin and becomes an aspect of embodiment. The machine is not an *it* to be animated, worshipped, and dominated. The machine is us, our processes, an aspect of our embodiment. We can be responsible for machines; *they* do not dominate or threaten us. We are responsible for boundaries; we are they. Up till now (once upon a time) female embodiment seemed to be given, organic, necessary, and female embodiment seemed to mean skill in mothering and its metaphoric extensions. Only by being out of place could we take intense pleasure in machines, and then with excuses that this was organic activity after all, appropriate to females. Cyborgs might consider more seriously the partial, fluid, sometimes aspect of sex and sexual embodiment. Gender might not be global identity after all.

The ideologically charged question of what counts as daily activity, as experience, can be approached by exploiting the cyborg image. Feminists have recently claimed that women are given to dailiness, that women more than men somehow sustain daily life and so have a privileged epistemological position potentially. There is a compelling aspect to this claim, one that makes visible unvalued female activity and names it as the ground of life. But *the* ground of life? What about all the ignorance of women, all the exclusions and failures of knowledge and skill? What about men's access to daily competence, to knowing how to build things, to take them apart, to play? What about other embodiments? Cyborg gender is a local possibility taking a global vengeance. Race, gender, and capital require a cyborg theory of wholes and parts. There is no drive in cyborgs to produce total theory, but there is an intimate experience of boundaries, their construction and deconstruction. There is a myth system waiting to become a political language to ground one way of looking at science and technology and challenging the informatics of domination.

One last image: organisms and organismic, holistic politics depend on metaphors of rebirth and invariably call on the resources of reproductive sex. I would suggest that cyborgs have more to do with regeneration and are suspicious of the reproductive matrix and of most birthing. For salamanders, regeneration after such an injury as the loss of a limb involves regrowth of structure and restoration of function with the constant possibility of twinning or other odd topographical productions at the site of former injury. The regrown limb can be monstrous, duplicated, potent. We have all been injured, profoundly. We require regeneration, not rebirth, and the possibilities for our reconstitution include the utopian dream of the hope for a monstrous world without gender.

Cyborg imagery can help express two crucial arguments in this essay: (1) the production of universal, totalizing theory is a major mistake that misses most of reality, probably always, but certainly now; (2) taking responsibility for the social relations of science and technology means refusing an antiscience metaphysics, a demonology of technology, and so means embracing the skillful task of reconstructing the boundaries of daily life, in partial connection with others, in communication with all our parts. It is not just that science and technology are possible means of great human satisfaction, as well as a matrix of complex dominations. Cyborg imagery can suggest a way out of the maze of dualisms in which we have explained our bodies and our tools to ourselves. This is a dream not of a common language, but of a powerful infidel heteroglossia. It is an imagination of a feminist speaking in tongues to strike fear into the circuits of the super-savers of the new right. It means both building and destroying machines, identities, categories, relationships, spaces, stories. Though both are bound in the spiral dance, I would rather be a cyborg than a goddess.

Notes

Acknowledgments: Research was funded by an Academic Senate Faculty Research Grant from the University of California, Santa Cruz. An earlier version of the paper on genetic engineering appeared as "Lieber Kyborg als Gottin: Für eine sozialistisch-feministische Unterwanderung der Gentechnologie," in Bernd-Peter Lange and Anna Marie Stuby, eds., *1984* (Berlin: Argument-Sonderband 105, 1984), 66–84.

The people associated with the History of Consciousness Board of UCSC have had an enormous influence on this paper, so that it feels collectively authored more than most, although those I cite may not recognize their ideas. In particular, members of graduate and undergraduate feminist theory, science and politics, and theory and methods courses have contributed to the cyborg manifesto. Particular debts here are due Hilary Klein ("Marxism, Psychoanalysis, and Mother Nature"); Paul Edwards ("Border Wars: The Science and Politics of Artificial Intelligence"); Lisa Lowe ("Julia Kristeva's *Des Chinoises:* Representing Cultural and Sexual Others"); Jim Clifford ("On Ethnographic Allegory: Essays").

Parts of the paper were my contribution to a collectively developed session, Poetic Tools and Political Bodies: Feminist Approaches to High Technology Culture, 1984 California American Studies Association, with History of Consciousness graduate students Zoe Sofoulis, "Jupiter Space"; Katie King, "The Pleasures of Repetition and the Limits of Identification in Feminist Science Fiction: Reimaginations of the Body after the Cyborg"; and Chela Sandoval, "The Construction of Subjectivity and Oppositional Consciousness in Feminist Film and Video." Sandoval's theory of oppositional consciousness was published as *Women Respond to Racism: A Report on the National Women's Studies Association Conference* (Oakland, Calif.: Center for Third World Organizing, 1982). For Sofoulis's semiotic-psychoanalytic readings of nuclear culture, see Z. Sofia, "Exterminating Fetuses: Abortion, Disarmament and the Sexo-Semiotics of Extraterrestrialism," Nuclear Criticism issue, *Diacritics* 14, no. 2 (1984): 47–59. King's manuscripts ("Questioning Tradition: Canon Formation and the Veiling of Power"; "Gender and Genre: Reading the Science Fiction of Joanna Russ"; "Varley's *Titan* and *Wizard*: Feminist Parodies of Nature, Culture, and Hardware") deeply inform the cyborg manifesto.

Barbara Epstein, Jeff Escoffier, Rusten Hogness, and Jaye Miller gave extensive discussion and editorial help. Members of the Silicon Valley Research Project of UCSC and participants in SVRP conferences and workshops have been very important, especially Rick Gordon, Linda Kimball, Nancy Snyder, Langdon Winner, Judith Stacey, Linda Lim, Patricia Fernandez-Kelly, and Judith Gregory. Finally, I want to thank Nancy Hartsock for years of friendship and discussion on feminist theory and feminist science fiction.

1. Useful references to left and/or feminist radical science movements and theory

and to biological/biotechnological issues include Ruth Bleier, *Science and Gender: A Critique of Biology and Its Themes on Women* (New York: Pergamon, 1984); Ruth Bleier, ed., *Feminist Approaches to Science* (New York: Pergamon, 1986); Stephen J. Gould, *Mismeasure of Man* (New York: Norton, 1981); Ruth Hubbard, Mary Sue Henifin, and Barbara Fried, eds., *Biological Woman, the Convenient Myth* (Cambridge, Mass.: Schenkman, 1982); Evelyn Fox Keller, *Reflections on Gender and Science* (New Haven, Conn.: Yale University Press, 1985); R. C. Lewontin, Steve Rose, and Leon Kamin, *Not in Our Genes* (New York: Pantheon, 1984): *Radical Science Journal* (London); *Science for the People* (Cambridge, Mass.).

2. Starting points for left and/or feminist approaches to technology and politics include Ruth Schwartz Cowan, *More Work for Mother: The Ironies of Household Technology from the Open Hearth to the Microwave* (New York: Basic Books, 1983); Joan Rothschild, *Machina ex Dea: Feminist Perspectives on Technology* (New York: Pergamon, 1983); Sharon Traweek, "Uptime, Downtime, Spacetime, and Power: An Ethnography of U.S. and Japanese Particle Physics" (Ph.D. diss., University of California, Santa Cruz, 1982); R. M. Young and Les Levidov, eds., *Science, Technology, and the Labour Process*, vols. 1–3 (London: CSE Books); Joseph Weizenbaum, *Computer Power and Human Reason* (San Francisco: Freeman, 1976); Langdon Winner, *Autonomous Technology: Technics Out of Control as a Theme in Political Thought* (Cambridge, Mass.: MIT Press, 1977); Langdon Winner, "Paths in Technopolis," esp. "Mythinformation in the High Tech Era" (manuscript); Jan Zimmerman, ed., *The Technological Woman: Interfacing with Tomorrow* (New York: Praeger, 1983); *Global Electronics Newsletter* (Mountain View, Calif.); *Processed World* (San Francisco, Calif.); *ISIS* (Women's International Information and Communication Service, Geneva and Rome). Fundamental approaches to modern social studies of science that do not continue the liberal mystification that it all started with Thomas Kuhn include Karin Knorr-Cetina, *The Manufacture of Knowledge* (Oxford: Pergamon, 1981); K. D. Knorr-Cetina and Michael Mulkay, eds., *Science Observed: Perspectives on the Social Study of Science* (Beverly Hills, Calif.: Sage, 1983); Bruno Latour and Steve Woolgar, *Laboratory Life: The Social Construction of Scientific Facts* (Beverly Hills, Calif.: Sage, 1979); Robert M. Young, "Interpreting the Production of Science," *New Scientist* 29 (March 1979): 1026–28. More is claimed than is known about room for contesting productions of science in the mythic/material space of "the laboratory"; the 1984 Directory of the Network for the Ethnographic Study of Science, Technology, and Organizations (Stanford, Calif.) lists a wide range of people and projects crucial to better radical analysis.

3. Fredric Jameson, "Post Modernism, or the Cultural Logic of Late Capitalism," *New Left Review* July–August 1984, pp. 53–94. See Marjorie Perloff, " 'Dirty' Language and Scramble Systems," *Sulfur* II (1984): 178–83; Kathleen Fraser, *Something (Even Human Voices) in the Foreground, a Lake* (Berkeley, Calif.: Kelsey St. Press, 1984). A provocative, comprehensive argument about the politics and theories of "postmodernism" is made by Fredric Jameson, who argues that it is not an option, a style among others, but a cultural dominant requiring radical reinvention of left politics from within; there is no longer any place from without that gives meaning to the comforting fiction of critical distance. Jameson also makes clear why one cannot be for or against postmodernism, an essentially moralist move. My position is that feminists (and others) need continuous cultural reinvention, postmodernist critique, and historical materialism; only a cyborg would have a chance. The old dominations of white capitalist patriarchy seem nostalgically innocent now:

they normalized heterogeneity, e.g., into man and woman, white and black. "Advanced capitalism" and postmodernism release heterogeneity without a norm, and we are flattened, without subjectivity, which requires depth, even unfriendly and drowning depths. It is time to write "The Death of the Clinic." The clinic's methods required bodies and works; we have texts and surfaces. Our dominations don't work by medicalization and normalization anymore; they work by networking, communications redesign, stress management. Normalization gives way to automation, utter redundancy. Michel Foucault's *Birth of the Clinic, History of Sexuality,* and *Discipline and Punish* name a form of power at its moment of implosion. The discourse of biopolitics gives way to technobabble, the language of the spliced substantive; no noun is left whole by the multinationals. These are their names, listed from one issue of *Science*: Tech-Knowledge, Genentech, Allergen, Hybritech, Compupro, Genen-cor, Syntex, Allelix, Agrigenetics Corp., Syntro, Codon, Repligen, Micro-Angelo from Scion Corp., Percom Data, Inter Systems, Cyborg Corp., Statcom Corp., Intertec. If we are imprisoned by language, then escape from that prison house requires language poets, a kind of cultural restriction enzyme to cut the code; cyborg heteroglossia is one form of radical culture politics.

4. Frans de Waal, *Chimpanzee Politics: Power and Sex among the Apes* (New York: Harper & Row, 1982); Langdon Winner, "Do Artifacts Have Politics?" *Daedalus,* Winter 1980.

5. Jean Baudrillard, *Simulations,* trans. P. Foss, P. Patton, P. Beitchman (New York: Semiotext[e], 1983). Jameson ("Post Modernism," 66) points out that Plato's definition of the simulacrum is the copy for which there is no original: i.e., the world of advanced capitalism, of pure exchange.

6. Herbert Marcuse, *One-Dimensional Man* (Boston: Beacon Press, 1964); Carolyn Merchant, *Death of Nature* (San Francisco: Harper & Row, 1980).

7. Zoe Sofia, "Exterminating Fetuses," *Diacritics* 14, no. 2 (Summer 1984): pp. 47–59, and *Jupiter Space* (Pomona, Calif.: American Studies Association, 1984).

8. Powerful developments of coalition politics emerge from "third world" speakers, speaking from nowhere, the displaced center of the universe, earth: "We live on the third planet from the sun"—*Sun Poem* by Jamaican writer Edward Kamau Braithwaite, review by Nathaniel Mackey, *Sulfur,* II (1984): 200–205. *Home Girls,* ed. Barbara Smith (New York: Kitchen Table, Women of Color Press, 1983), ironically subverts naturalized identities precisely while constructing a place from which to speak called home; see esp. Bernice Reagan, "Coalition Politics, Turning the Century," 356–68.

9. Chela Sandoval, "Dis-Illusionment and the Poetry of the Future: The Making of Oppositional Consciousness" (Ph.D. qualifying essay, UCSC, 1984).

10. bell hooks, *Ain't I a Woman?* (Boston: South End Press, 1981); Gloria Hull, Patricia Bell Scott, and Barbara Smith, eds., *All the Women Are White, All the Blacks Are Men, but Some of Us Are Brave: Black Women's Studies* (Old Westbury, N.Y.: Feminist Press, 1982). Toni Cade Bambara, in *The Salt Eaters* (New York: Vintage/Random House, 1981), writes an extraordinary postmodernist novel, in which the women-of-color theater group The Seven Sisters explores a form of unity. Thanks to Elliott Evans's readings of Bambara, Ph.D. qualifying essay, UCSC, 1984.

11. On orientalism in feminist works and elsewhere, see Lisa Lowe, "Orientation: Representations of Cultural and Sexual 'Others,'" (Ph.D. diss., UCSC, 1986); Edward Said, *Orientalism* (New York: Pantheon, 1978).

12. Katie King has developed a theoretically sensitive treatment of the workings

of feminist taxonomies as genealogies of power in feminist ideology and polemic: "Prospectus," in *Gender and Genre: Academic Practice and the Making of Criticism* (Santa Cruz, Calif.: University of California, 1984). King examines an intelligent, problematic example of taxonomizing feminisms to make a little machine producing the desired final position: Alison Jaggar, *Feminist Politics and Human Nature* (Totowa, N.J.: Rowman & Allanheld, 1983). My caricature here of socialist and radical feminism is also an example.

13. The feminist standpoint argument is being developed by Jane Flax, "Political Philosophy and the Patriarchal Unconsciousness," in Sandra Harding and Merill Hintikka, eds., *Discovering Reality* (Dordrecht: Reidel, 1983); Sandra Harding, "The Contradictions and Ambivalence of a Feminist Science" (manuscript); Harding and Hintikka, *Discovering Reality*; Nancy Hartsock, *Money, Sex, and Power* (New York: Longman, 1983), and "The Feminist Standpoint: Developing the Ground for a Specifically Feminist Historical Materialism," in Harding and Hintikka, *Discovering Reality*; Mary O'Brien, *The Politics of Reproduction* (New York: Routledge & Kegan Paul, 1981); Hilary Rose, "Hand, Brain, and Heart: A Feminist Epistemology for the Natural Sciences," *Signs* 9, no. 1 (1983): 73–90; Dorothy Smith, "Women's Perspective as a Radical Critique of Sociology," *Sociological Inquiry* 44 (1974), and "A Sociology of Women," in J. Sherman and E. T. Beck, eds., *The Prism of Sex* (Madison: University of Wisconsin Press, 1979).

The central role of object-relations versions of psychoanalysis and related strong universalizing moves in discussing reproduction, caring work, and mothering in many approaches to epistemology underline their authors' resistance to what I am calling postmodernism. For me, both the universalizing moves and the versions of psychoanalysis make analysis of "women's place in the integrated circuit" difficult and lead to systematic difficulties in accounting for or even seeing major aspects of the construction of gender and gendered social life.

14. Catherine MacKinnon, "Feminism, Marxism, Method, and the State: An Agenda for Theory," *Signs* 7, no. 3 (1982): 515–44. A critique indebted to MacKinnon, but without the reductionism and with an elegant feminist account of Foucault's paradoxical conservatism on sexual violence (rape), is Teresa de Lauretis, "Violence Engendered," *Semiotica*, special issue on "The Rhetoric of Violence," ed. Nancy Armstrong (1985). A theoretically elegant feminist social-historical examination of family violence that insists on women's, men's, children's complex agency without losing sight of the material structures of male domination, race, and class is Linda Gordon, *Heroes of Their Own Lives: The Politics and History of Family Violence* (New York: Viking, 1988).

15. My previous efforts to understand biology as a cybernetic command-control discourse and organisms as "natural-technical objects of knowledge" are "The High Cost of Information in Post–World War II Evolutionary Biology," *Philosophical Forum* 13, nos. 2–3 (1979): 206–37; "Signs of Dominance: From a Physiology to a Cybernetics of Primate Society," *Studies in History of Biology* 6 (1983): 129–219; "Class, Race, Sex, Scientific Objects of Knowledge: A Socialist-Feminist Perspective on the Social Construction of Productive Knowledge and Some Political Consequences," in Violet Haas and Carolyn Perucci, eds., *Women in Scientific and Engineering Professions* (Ann Arbor: University of Michigan Press, 1984), 212–29.

16. E. Rusten Hogness, "Why Stress? A Look at the Making of Stress, 1936–56" (Healdsburg, Calif.).

17. A left entry to the biotechnology debate is *GeneWatch*, a Bulletin of the Com-

mittee for Responsible Genetics (Boston, Mass.); Susan Wright, "Recombinant DNA: The Status of Hazards and Controls," *Environment*, July–August 1982; Edward Yoxen, *The Gene Business* (New York: Harper & Row, 1983).

18. Starting references for "women in the integrated circuit": Pamela D'Onofrio-Flores and Sheila M. Pfafflin, eds., *Scientific-Technological Change and the Role of Women in Development* (Boulder, Colo.: Westview Press, 1982); Maria Patricia Fernandez-Kelly, *For We Are Sold, I and My People* (Albany, N.Y.: SUNY Press, 1983); Annette Fuentes and Barbara Ehrenreich, *Women in the Global Factory* (Boston: South End Press, 1983), with an especially useful list of resources and organizations; Rachael Grossman, "Women's Place in the Integrated Circuit," *Radical America* 14, no. 1 (1980): 29–50; June Nash and Maria Patricia Fernandez-Kelly, eds., *Women and Men and the International Division of Labor* (Albany, N.Y.: SUNY Press, 1983); Aihwa Ong, "Japanese Factories, Malay Workers: Industrialization and the Cultural Construction of Gender in West Malaysia" (manuscript); Science Policy Research Unity, *Microelectronics and Women's Employment in Britain* (University of Sussex, 1982).

19. The best example is Bruno Latour, *Les microbes: Guerre et paix, suivi de irreductions* (Paris: Métailié, 1984).

20. For the homework economy and some supporting arguments: Richard Gordon, "The Computerization of Daily Life, the Sexual Division of Labor, and the Homework Economy," in R. Gordon, ed., *Microelectronics in Transition* (Norwood, N.J.: Ablex, 1985); Patricia Hill Collins, "Third World Women in America," and Sara G. Burr, "Women and Work," in Barbara K. Haber, ed., *The Women's Annual, 1981* (Boston: G. K. Hall, 1982); Judith Gregory and Karen Nussbaum, "Race against Time: Automation of the Office," *Office: Technology and People* 1 (1982): 197–236; Frances Fox Piven and Richard Cloward, *The New Class War: Reagan's Attack on the Welfare State and Its Consequences* (New York: Pantheon, 1982); Microelectronics Group, *Microelectronics: Capitalist Technology and the Working Class* (London: CSE, 1980); Karin Stallard, Barbara Ehrenreich, and Holly Sklar, *Poverty in the American Dream* (Boston: South End Press, 1983), including a useful organization and resource list.

21. Rae Lessor Blumberg, "A General Theory of Sex Stratification and Its Application to the Position of Women in Today's World Economy," paper delivered to Sociology Board, UCSC, February 1983. Also Blumberg, *Stratification: Socioeconomic and Sexual Inequality* (Boston: Brown, 1981). See also Sally Hacker, "Doing It the Hard Way: Ethnographic Studies in the Agribusiness and Engineering Classroom," California American Studies Association, Pomona, 1984; S. Hacker and Lisa Bovit, "Agriculture to Agribusiness: Technical Imperatives and Changing Roles," *Proceedings of the Society for the History of Technology* (Milwaukee, Wis., 1981); Lawrence Busch and William Lacy, *Science, Agriculture, and the Politics of Research* (Boulder, Colo.: Westview Press, 1983); Denis Wilfred, "Capital and Agriculture, a Review of Marxian Problematics," *Studies in Political Economy* No. 7 (1982): 127–54; Carolyn Sachs, *The Invisible Farmers: Women in Agricultural Production* (Totowa, N.J.: Rowman & Allanheld, 1983). Thanks to Elizabeth Bird, "Green Revolution Imperialism," pts. 1–2 (manuscript, UCSC, 1984).

The conjunction of the Green Revolution's social relations with biotechnologies like plant genetic engineering makes the pressures on land in the Third World increasingly intense. USAID's estimates (*New York Times*, 14 October 1984) used at the 1984 World Food Day are that in Africa, women produce about 90 percent of rural food supplies, about 60–80 percent in Asia, and provide 40 percent of agricultural labor in the Near East and Latin America. Blumberg charges that world organizations' agricultural politics, as well as those of multinationals and national governments in the Third World, generally ignore fundamental issues in the sexual division of labor. The tragedy of famine in Africa may owe as much to male supremacy as to capitalism, colonialism, and rain patterns. More accurately, capitalism and racism are usually structurally male dominant.

22. Cynthia Enloe, "Women Textile Workers in the Militarization of Southeast Asia," in Nash and Fernandez-Kelly, *Women and Men*; Rosalind Petchesky, "Abortion, Anti-Feminism, and the Rise of the New Right," *Feminist Studies* 7, no. 2 (1981).

23. For a feminist version of this logic, see Sarah Blaffer Hardy, *The Woman That Never Evolved* (Cambridge, Mass.: Harvard University Press, 1981). For an analysis of scientific women's storytelling practices, esp. in relation to sociobiology, in evolutionary debates around child abuse and infanticide, see Donna Haraway, "The Contest for Primate Nature: Daughters of Man the Hunter in the Field, 1960–80," in Mark Kann, ed., *The Future of American Democracy* (Philadelphia: Temple University Press, 1983), 175–208.

24. For the moment of transition of hunting with guns to hunting with cameras in the construction of popular meanings of nature for an American urban immigrant public, see Donna Haraway, "Teddy Bear Patriarchy," *Social Text*, No. 11 (1985): 19–64; Roderick Nash, "The Exporting and Importing of Nature: Nature-Appreciation as a Commodity, 1850–1980," *Perspectives in American History* 3 (1979): 517–60; Susan Sontag, *On Photography* (New York: Dell, 1977); and Douglas Preston, "Shooting in Paradise," *Natural History* 93, no. 12 (December 1984): 14–19.

25. For crucial guidance for thinking about the political/cultural implications of the history of women doing science in the United States, see Haas and Perucci, *Women in Scientific and Engineering Professions*; Sally Hacker, "The Culture of Engineering: Women, Workplace, and Machine," *Women's Studies International Quarterly* 4, no. 3 (1981): 341–53; Evelyn Fox Keller, *A Feeling for the Organism* (San Francisco: Freeman, 1983); National Science Foundation, *Women and Minorities in Science and Engineering* (Washington, D.C.: NSF, 1982); Margaret Rossiter, *Women Scientists in America* (Baltimore, Md.: Johns Hopkins University Press, 1982).

26. John Markoff and Lenny Siegel, "Military Micros," UCSC Silicon Valley Research Project conference, 1983. High Technology Professionals for Peace and Computer Professionals for Social Responsibility are promising organizations.

27. Katie King, "The Pleasure of Repetition and the Limits of Identification in Feminist Science Fiction: Reimaginations of the Body after the Cyborg," California American Studies Association, Pomona, 1984. An abbreviated list of feminist science fiction underlying themes of this essay: Octavia Butler, *Wild Seed, Mind of My Mind, Kindred, Survivor*; Suzy McKee Charnas, *Motherliness*; Samuel Delaney, *Tales of Neveryon*; Anne McCaffrey, *The Ship Who Sang, Dinosaur Planet*; Vonda McIntyre, *Superluminal, Dreamsnake*; Joanna Russ, *Adventures of Alyx, The Female Man*; James Tiptree, Jr., *Star Songs of an Old Primate, Up the Walls of the World*; John Varley, *Titan, Wizard, Demon*.

28. Mary Douglas, *Purity and Danger* (London: Routledge & Kegan Paul, 1966), and *Natural Symbols* (London: Cresset Press, 1970).

29. French feminisms contribute to cyborg heteroglossia. Carolyn Burke, "Irigaray through the Looking Glass," *Feminist Studies* 7, no. 2 (1981): 288–306; Luce Irigaray, *Ce sexe qui n'en est pas un* (Paris: Minuit, 1977); Luce Irigaray, *Et l'une ne bouge pas sans l'autre* (Paris: Minuit, 1979); Elaine Marks and Isabelle de Courtivron, eds.,

New French Feminisms (Amherst: University of Massachusetts Press, 1980); *Signs* 7, no. 1 (1981), special issue on French feminism; Monique Wittig, *The Lesbian Body* (*Le corps lesbien*, 1973), trans. David LeVay (New York: Avon, 1975).

30. But all these poets are very complex, not least in treatment of themes of lying and erotic, decentered collective and personal identities. See Susan Griffin, *Women and Nature: The Roaring Inside Her* (New York: Harper & Row, 1978); Audre Lorde, *Sister Outsider* (New York: Crossing Press, 1984); Adrienne Rich, *The Dream of a Common Language* (New York: Norton, 1978).

31. Jacques Derrida, *Of Grammatology*, trans. and intro. G. C. Spivak (Baltimore, Md.: Johns Hopkins University Press, 1976), esp. "Nature, Culture, Writing"; Claude Lévi-Strauss, *Tristes Tropiques*, trans. John Russell (New York, 1961), esp. "The Writing Lesson."

32. Cherrie Moraga, *Loving in the War Years* (Boston: South End Press, 1983). The sharp relation of women of color to writing as theme and politics can be approached through "The Black Woman and the Diaspora: Hidden Connections and Extended Acknowledgments," An International Literary Conference, Michigan State University, October 1985; Mari Evans, ed., *Black Women Writers: A Critical Evaluation* (Garden City, N.Y.: Doubleday/Anchor, 1984); Dexter Fisher, ed., *The Third Woman: Minority Women Writers of the United States* (Boston: Houghton Mifflin, 1980); several issues of *Frontiers*, esp. vol. 5 (1980), "Chicanas en el Ambiente Nacional," and vol. 7 (1983), "Feminisms in the Non-Western World"; Maxine Hong Kingston, *China Men* (New York: Knopf, 1977); Gerda Lerner, ed., *Black Women in White America: A Documentary History* (New York: Vintage Books, 1973); Cherrie Moraga and Gloria Anzaldua, eds., *This Bridge Called My Back: Writings by Radical Women of Color* (Watertown, Mass.: Persephone, 1981); Robin Morgan, ed., *Sisterhood Is Global* (Garden City, N.Y.: Anchor/Doubleday, 1984). The writing of white women has had similar meanings: Sandra Gilbert and Susan Gubar, *The Madwoman in the Attic* (New Haven, Conn.: Yale University Press, 1979); Joanna Russ, *How to Suppress Women's Writing* (Austin: University of Texas Press, 1983).

33. James Clifford argues persuasively for recognition of continuous cultural reinvention, the stubborn nondisappearance of those "marked" by Western imperializing practices; see *Predicaments of Culture* (Cambridge, Mass.: Harvard University Press, 1988), and "On Ethnographic Authority," *Representations* 1, no. 2 (1983): 118–46.

34. Page DuBois, *Centaurs and Amazons* (Ann Arbor: University of Michigan Press, 1982); Lorraine Daston and Katharine Park, "Hermaphrodites in Renaissance France" (manuscript, n.d.); Katharine Park and Lorraine Daston, "Unnatural Conceptions: The Study of Monsters in 16th and 17th Century France and England," *Past and Present* No. 92 (August 1981): 20–54.

Notes on the Contributors

Maxine Baca Zinn is professor of sociology at the University of Michigan, Flint. She is the coauthor of *Diversity in American Families* (Harper & Row, 1987) and *The Reshaping of America: Social Consequences of the Changing Economy* (Prentice-Hall, 1989) and has published numerous articles on family and gender among racial-ethnics. Baca Zinn is now working with Bonnie Dill on a volume of readings about women of color, forthcoming from Temple University Press.

Barbara Baran has spent a decade as an organizer and administrator in community-based and feminist organizations. She received both her master's degree and Ph.D. in City and Regional Planning from the University of California, Berkeley. She is currently a regional program manager of the Massachusetts Industrial Services Program.

Johanna Brenner is coordinator of women's studies and associate professor of sociology at Portland State University. She is also an editor of *Against the Current*, a journal for socialist regroupment. Her analysis here draws on her experience as shop steward and union activist in a traditionally male blue-collar job and as a reproductive rights organizer.

Leo Casey has just completed a doctoral dissertation on the problem of the authoritarian state in democratic and socialist theory. He has recently been involved in a legal and political battle to force the New York City Board of Education to clean up an asbestos contamination of the inner city high school in which he works, and is active in the teachers' union.

Barbara Christian is professor of Afro-American studies at the University of California, Berkeley. She is the author of *Black Women Novelists: The Development of a Tradition, 1892–1976* (Greenwood Press, 1980), *Teaching Guide to Black Foremothers* (Feminist Press, 1980), and *Black Feminist Criticism: Perspectives on Black Women Writers* (Pergamon Press, 1985) and is an editor at *Feminist Studies*. *Black Women Novelists*, the first book on this subject, won the Before Columbus American Book Award in 1983.

Adele Clarke is a postdoctoral fellow at Stanford University and codirector of the Women, Health, and Healing Program at the University of California, San Francisco. Her recent research is in the sociology of science, focusing on the rise of reproductive science in the United States, 1910–40, the development of the life sciences at the turn of the century, and the industrialization of human reproduction since 1890.

Elliott Currie is the author of *Confronting Crime* (Pantheon, 1985). He is a research associate at the Institute for the Study of Social Change at the University of California, Berkeley, and chairs the program committee at the Eisenhower Foundation.

Robert Dunn teaches in the department of sociology at California State University, Hayward, focusing on social inequality, social theory, and popular culture. He has published theoretical articles on television and mass culture and is writing on the social foundations of postmodern culture.

Barbara Ehrenreich is a columnist for *Mother Jones* and *Ms.* magazines and is working on a book about American perceptions of class, tentatively titled "The Discovery of Class." She spends part of her time in Washington, D.C., as a fellow at the Institute for Policy Studies. Since 1983 she has served as co-chair of Democratic Socialists of America.

Diane Ehrensaft is professor of psychology at the Wright Institute in Berkeley, California. She is also a practicing therapist in Oakland and a clinical consultant to Children's Hospital, Oakland, and Children's Hospital, San Francisco. Her book *Parenting Together: Men and Women Sharing the Care of Their Children* (Free Press), was published in 1987, and she is working on a book about the changing concept of childhood and child-rearing dilemmas in the late twentieth century.

Zillah Eisenstein is professor and chair of the department of politics, Ithaca College. She edited *Capitalist Patriarchy and the Case for Socialist Feminism* (Monthly Review Press, 1979) and is the author of *The Radical Future of Liberal Feminism* (Northeastern University Press, 1981), *Feminism and Sexual Equality: Crisis in Liberal America* (Monthly Review Press, 1984), and *The Female Body in the Law* (University of California Press, 1988).

Kate Ellis teaches courses in creative writing, women writers, and feminist theory at Rutgers University. She is a founding member of the Feminist Anti-Censorship Taskforce and an editor of its collection *Caught Looking: Feminism, Pornography, and Censorship*. She is the author of *The Contested Castle*, a study of the early Gothic novel, and is at work on a novel about the 1960s.

Deirdre English is the executive series writer for a PBS series on the history of American women. Former executive editor of *Mother Jones* magazine, she is coauthor, with Barbara Ehrenreich, of *For Her Own Good: 150 Years of the Experts' Advice to Women* (Anchor/Doubleday, 1978). Earlier collaborations include the widely anthologized and translated booklets *Witches, Midwives, and Nurses: A History of Women Healers* (1971) and *Complaints and Disorders: The Sexual Politics of Sickness* (1973).

Barbara Epstein teaches in the History of Consciousness Board at the University of California, Santa Cruz. She is currently working on a book that will probably be called "Nonviolent Direct Action in the Seventies and Eighties: Postmodern Politics and Utopian Democracy." She was a member of the *Socialist Review* collective for many years.

David Fogarty received a master's degree in urban planning from the University of California, Berkeley. He works in the office of Economic Development for the city of Berkeley and is on the steering committee for Berkeley Citizens Action.

Barbara Haber, a feminist and activist since the 1960s, is a therapist in private practice in the San Francisco Bay Area. She is also an occasional social commentator and an editor of *Propaganda Review.*

Karen V. Hansen is an assistant professor of sociology at Brandeis University. As a long-time member of the *Socialist Review* collective, she was an editor of the journal's series assessing socialist feminism in the 1980s.

Donna Haraway is a professor in the History of Consciousness Board at the University of California, Santa Cruz, where she also participates in the women's studies program. She has two new books, *Primate Visions: Gender, Race, and Nature in the World of Modern Science* (Routledge & Kegan Paul, 1989) and *Simians, Cyborgs, and Women: The Reinvention of Nature in Late Capitalism* (Free Association Books, 1989).

Heidi I. Hartmann is director of the Washington-based Institute for Women's Policy Research, a think tank on policy issues of importance to women. For eight years she was a staff member of the National Research Council/National Academy of Sciences, where she contributed to many reports on women's employment issues, including the 1981 report on pay equity *Women, Work, and Wages: Equal Pay for Jobs of Equal Value.* She lectures and writes on the economics of gender relations.

Alice Kessler-Harris is professor of history at Temple University. She is the author of *Out to Work: A History of Wage-Earning Women in the U.S.* (Oxford, 1983) and of other books and articles. She is currently working on a history of the ideology of gender difference in twentieth-century America.

Judy MacLean, a freelance writer and editor, recently collaborated with Tish Sommers, Laurie Shields, and the Older Women's League Caregiver Task Force on *Women Take Care* (Triad Press, 1987).

Juliet Mitchell is a writer, lecturer, and psychoanalyst currently in full-time clinical practice in London, where she lives with her husband and daughter.

Sandra Morgen is assistant professor of women's studies at the University of Massachusetts, Amherst. She also directs the gender and curriculum projects for the American Anthropological Association and is an associate editor of *Signs*. In addition to publishing articles in *Women's Studies* and *Social Science and Medicine*, she has edited (with Ann Bookman) the anthology *Women and the Politics of Empowerment* (Temple University Press, 1988).

Ilene J. Philipson, a sociologist on the faculty of the graduate program in psychology at New College of California in San Francisco, is the author of *Ethel Rosenberg: Beyond the Myths* (Franklin Watts, 1988). She was associate editor of *Socialist Review* from 1981 to 1987.

Annie Popkin has taught women's studies and ethnic studies at California state universities for the last ten years. In addition, she has led "unlearning racism" workshops, has been a photographer and political activist, and set up a high school career center in a small, rural northeastern California town. She is currently acting director of women's studies at the University of Oregon, Eugene.

Rayna Rapp teaches in the anthropology department, Graduate Faculty, New School for Social Research, and helps edit *Feminist Studies*. She has been active for twenty years in the movement for reproductive freedom and is writing a book on the social impact and cultural meaning of prenatal diagnosis.

Elayne Rapping teaches film and television studies at Adelphi University, Garden City, New York, and contributes regularly to a variety of feminist, left, and media publications.

Deborah Rosenfelt is professor of women's studies and coordinator of the women's studies program at San Francisco State University. She has published widely on women's issues in literature and culture and is working on a collection of women's fiction from the 1930s.

Gayle Rubin is an anthropologist and feminist scholar in San Francisco. She is currently studying the interrelationships between sexually defined populations, neighborhood change, redevelopment policy, state intervention, and the ways in which sexual behaviors are coded and understood.

Judith Sealander, associate professor of history at Wright State University, Dayton, Ohio, is a specialist in the areas of American economic and social history. Her publications include *As Minority Becomes Majority: Federal Reaction to the Phenomenon of Women in the Work Force, 1920–1963* (Greenwood Press, 1983); and *"Grand Plans": Business Progressivism and Social Change in the Ohio Miami Valley, 1890–1929* (University Press of Kentucky, forthcoming).

Dorothy Smith is an archivist at Wright State University in Dayton, Ohio. It was her interest in the history of contemporary feminism that led to Wright State's acquisition of the records and papers of women's movement organizations in the Dayton area. Smith is currently editing the letters of an Ohio-born public health nurse who worked in the Near East and Greece between the world wars.

Judith Stacey teaches sociology and women's studies at the University of California, Davis. She is the author of *Patriarchy and Socialist Revolution in China*, various essays on feminist theory and politics, and an ethnography, *The Postmodern Family: Stories of Gender and Kinship in the Silicon Valley* (to be published by Basic Books in 1990).

Ronnie J. Steinberg is assistant professor of sociology at Temple University. She is the author of *Wages and Hours: Labor and Reform in Twentieth Century America* (Rutgers University Press, 1982), editor of *Equal Employment Policy for Women: Strategies for Implementation in the United States, Canada, and Western Europe* (Temple University Press, 1980), and editor (with Sharon L. Harlan) of *Job Training for Women: The Promise and Limits of Public Policies* (Temple University Press, 1989). She also edits the book series Women in the Political Economy for Temple University Press. She is writing a book on how such reforms as comparable worth happen.

Judith Van Allen has spent the past two years in southern Africa studying the emergence of women's issues within African capitalism in Botswana and in the mass democratic movement in South Africa. She has taught political theory, African politics, and women's studies, most recently at Ithaca College, and has been active in Democratic Socialists of America, particularly in the formulation of the organization's economic program. She is currently working as an anti-apartheid organizer.

Lorna Weir teaches in the department of sociology and anthropology at Carleton University in Ottawa, Canada. She has been active in feminist, lesbian, and gay politics. She is at work on a book of case studies dealing with the regulatory discourses and the administration of sexuality.

Alice Wolfson, a long-time activist in reproductive rights, has served as executive director of the Committee to Defend Reproductive Rights and was a founder and director of the National Women's Health Network. In addition to being a nationally recognized activist in women's health-care issues, she has just received her law degree from Hastings College of Law in San Francisco.